THE LIBRARY OF CONGRESS

The Library of Congress in the US Capitol Building, circa 1853. After renovation following the 1851 fire, it was dubbed "the Iron Room."

The Library of Congress

FROM JEFFERSON'S VISION TO THE DIGITAL AGE

JANE AIKIN

Foreword by Carla Hayden, Fourteenth Librarian of Congress

GEORGETOWN UNIVERSITY PRESS, IN ASSOCIATION WITH
THE LIBRARY OF CONGRESS / WASHINGTON, DC

LIBRARY LIBRARY OF CONGRESS

Library of Congress Cataloging-in-Publication Data

Names: Aikin, Jane, author. | Hayden, Carla Diane, 1952– writer of foreword.
Title: The Library of Congress : from Jefferson's vision to the digital age / Jane Aikin ; foreword by Carla Hayden, 14th Librarian of Congress.
Description: Washington, DC : Georgetown University Press, [2025] | Includes bibliographical references and index.
Identifiers: LCCN 2024025634 (print) | LCCN 2024025635 (ebook) | ISBN 9781647125714 (hardcover) | ISBN 9781647125721 (ebook)
Subjects: LCSH: Library of Congress—History. | National libraries—Washington (D.C.)—History.
Classification: LCC Z733.U6 A38 2025 (print) | LCC Z733.U6 (ebook) | DDC 027.373—dc23/eng/20240625
LC record available at https://lccn.loc.gov/2024025634
LC ebook record available at https://lccn.loc.gov/2024025635

♾ This paper meets the requirements of ANSI/NISO Z39.48-1992 (Permanence of Paper).

EU GPSR Authorized Representative
LOGOS EUROPE, 9 rue Nicolas Poussin, 17000, LA ROCHELLE, France
Email: Contact@logoseurope.eu

26 25 9 8 7 6 5 4 3 2 First printing

Printed in the United States of America

Cover design by Erin Kirk
Interior design by Classic City Composition, Athens, GA

CONTENTS

FOREWORD

The Library of Congress's progression from a small legal library to a grand national library, and one of the world's greatest intellectual and cultural resources, is a story shaped by extraordinary individuals and hardworking civil servants. Above all, it is a story of an institution constantly evolving to face the mutable and ever-expanding sources of knowledge. What started in 1800 with only 740 books and 3 maps rapidly expanded to include sheet music, prints, newspapers, and new technologies like photographs, recorded sound, and motion pictures.

Jane Aikin's new book, *The Library of Congress: From Jefferson's Vision to the Digital Age*, documents an esteemed history of preserving, recording, and making accessible our shared cultural heritage. She traces the story of the men and women who—through war, social upheaval, industrial expansion, population growth, and shifting political winds—diligently worked to keep the Library growing stronger, while continually adapting to serve the public and Congress. In the words of former Librarian Ainsworth Rand Spofford, the Library truly is "the book palace of the American people in which you all have equal rights with me, . . . in which the works of all of you will be welcomed and forever preserved."

I invite you to visit the Library in person or online, at www.loc.gov, to discover more about the oldest federal cultural institution in the United States and to explore the rich, diverse, and enduring sources of knowledge that continue to inform, inspire, and engage us in our intellectual and creative endeavors.

—Carla Hayden, Fourteenth Librarian of Congress

PREFACE

The Library of Congress (LC) is an institution unique not only in size, as the world's largest library, but also in diversity. From 4,000-year-old clay tablets, to fifteenth-century hand-press books, to seventeenth-century holograph music scores and scientific treatises, to eighteenth-century fine prints, to nineteenth-century photographs, and to twentieth- and twenty-first-century comic books, motion pictures, television programs, microforms, and electronic resources, the Library contains materials in more than 460 languages. Among the great libraries, it is the only one that collects worldwide.

The Library's 1897 Thomas Jefferson Building, opposite the US Capitol, is a treasure of Beaux Arts style and spectacular interior artistry. The John Adams Building (1939), across the street to the east, is dissimilar in every way, its classic simplicity conveying the sober mood of the 1930s. Newest of the LC's three buildings, the 1980 James Madison Memorial Building is a massive modernist structure. But these buildings house only part of the Library. There are also the Packard Campus of the National Audio-Visual Conservation Center, in Culpeper, Virginia; six overseas offices; and numerous facilities that store the collections. The Library's website (www.loc.gov) extends access to its collections and services worldwide.

The Library's history dates from 1800, when members of Congress needed books, especially law books, in a brand-new city that lacked libraries. When Thomas Jefferson sold his private library to Congress in 1815, after the loss of Congress's books during the War of 1812, his collection included many more fields of knowledge, turning the Library into a general collection. Over the years, the Congressional Library added materials and services and eventually opened to the public. Major themes of its history are first and foremost providing service to Congress; leadership in the national and international library communities; an important presence in the scholarly world; responsibility for national and international copyright activities; and a forum for folk, artistic, and literary cultures. Though it was never legally designated the national library of the United States, it occupies this space in the national imagination.

The Library has many constituencies—Congress, federal agencies, other libraries, musicians, poets, authors, artists, scholars, educators, publishers, benefactors, and the public. Library staff members and users often observe that each area of the LC's activity deserves its own history. Some have been written, and more surely will appear. This single-volume account necessarily limits the scope to the Library as a whole, centering on the origins, organization, and development of the institution, with mention of only a few major acquisitions (tempting though it is to include more). Likewise, the many officials, staff members, donors, and others who have contributed to its institutional growth appear only briefly.

Some previous accounts have defined the Library mostly by its chief executives. Thirteen men have held the office of Librarian of Congress. Carla Hayden, the fourteenth, is the first woman, and the first Black, Librarian of Congress. A change in Librarians has always brought different emphases, some originating with the executives themselves but others as responses to internal or external conditions or events. These other influences include, most importantly, Congress, but also national and international events; research libraries and the library community generally; donors and philanthropic institutions; and the activities of American and foreign scholars and other library users.

What focusing on the Librarians tends to obscure is the strong tradition of continuity: the long-term development of the LC's collections and services. Central to the history of libraries are the ceaseless, systematic acquisitions of materials and the design of systems to make them accessible. And central to the success of those efforts is the LC's expert staff. As L. Quincy Mumford once declared in an annual report, "Implicit in the chronicle that follows is the record of the effort of a group of human beings of exceptional skills and competences who have unsparingly given their time, their effort, and their devotion to the Library's program." This "devotion" has endured over the years in the Library of Congress, as it has in other libraries.[1]

A recurring issue in the Library's history is its designation and role as the national library of the United States. The national library as a type of institution has a large literature, much of which describes their varying functions and ambitions country by country. As Verner Clapp once commented, "The minimum requirements for a national library are that it should be a national institution and that it should attempt to form a comprehensive collection of the national publications; beyond that each national library will create its own personality." All of them have done so, and the Library of Congress is, perforce, both like and unlike other national libraries.[2]

A long tug-of-war between advocates of renaming the Library to reflect its national role and Congress, which has preferred to retain the Library as its own, is an important part of this history. Several Librarians have publicly opposed such a change. But ever since Ainsworth Rand Spofford expanded the Library to acquire national collections, every Librarian has devoted resources to this end. To the Librarians, the name has mattered less than the LC's advantageous position in the legislative branch and its direct relationship with Congress. The Library's top priority began as, and remains, congressional service.

A second issue in the Library's history is its leadership in the library community. Ainsworth Rand Spofford's conception of the LC as an independent institution was decisively overturned by Herbert Putnam, who inaugurated services to other libraries, beginning with a card service and interlibrary loans. He and his successors added international acquisitions and cataloging programs that built US research collections and, later, a nationally and internationally influential preservation program. With its 1960s development of machine-readable cataloging (MARC), the Library provided the means to share libraries' holdings electronically. Librarian James Billington inaugurated efforts to digitize the LC's materials and other collections, extending access beyond the Library's walls.

A third issue is the Library's role as a scholarly institution and its presence in the scholarly world, initially as an organizer of that world. In 1900, there were almost no indexing, abstracting, or copying services to assist scholars. Locating materials was a scattershot process, usually through contacts with librarians and archivists. Then came the Library of Congress card service, its depository catalogs, and ultimately the Union Catalog; printed bibliographies and guides to the collections; contracts with federal agencies for services such as specialized indexing and abstracting; and the formal enlistment of scholars as advisers. Today, scholars benefit from an electronically facilitated infrastructure of federal, state, and local institutions while also depending on commercial and nonprofit information providers. The foundations of this infrastructure were built by librarians and, prominently, by the Library of Congress.

ACKNOWLEDGMENTS

Many friends and colleagues helped to shape this book. Over many years, I have been fortunate to collaborate with John Y. Cole, the Library of Congress's first official historian and an unfailing source of encouragement and assistance. John read the manuscript and provided comments, insights, and invaluable background. I am immensely grateful to him and to Wayne A. Wiegand, who generously shared his knowledge of the library community. I also thank friends and former National Endowment for the Humanities colleagues—in particular, Catherine Whitaker, Russell Wyland, Stefanie Walker, Joel Wurl, Adam Wolfson, Claudia Kinkela, John Cox, Joseph Neville, and Helen Agüera—for their interest, encouragement, and helpful comments through the many years I have been researching the Library of Congress's history. There are more debts to the excellent LC staff members than I can count. In particular, I thank Cheryl Fox, curator of the Library of Congress Archives; expert advisers and editors Becky Clark and Peter Devereaux of the Publishing Office; and the Kluge Center's staff, especially John Haskell, Kevin Butterfield, Dan Turello, Travis Hensley, Michael Stratmoen, and David Konteh. For support from Georgetown University Press, I am indebted to Senior Acquisitions Editor Hilary Claggett.

ABBREVIATIONS

Standard postal abbreviations are used for US states. Year designations generally refer to federal fiscal years, which ran from July 1 through June 30 until 1976, when the fiscal year changed to October 1 through September 30.

AC	*Annals of Congress*
AL	*American Libraries*
ALA	American Library Association
ASP	*American State Papers*
ARL	Association of Research Libraries
ARLC	*Annual Report of the Librarian of Congress*
BALA	*Bulletin of the American Library Association*
C&RL	*College & Research Libraries*
CG	*Congressional Globe*
CCQ	*Cataloging & Classification Quarterly*
CLIR	Council on Library and Information Resources (1997–)
CLR	Council on Library Resources, Inc. (1956–97)
CR	*Congressional Record*
D	Democrat
DALB	*Dictionary of American Library Biography*, ed. Bohdan S. Wynar (Littleton, CO: Libraries Unlimited, 1978)
DALB-S	*Supplement to the Dictionary of American Library Biography*, ed. Wayne A. Wiegand (Englewood, CO: Libraries Unlimited, 1990)
DALB-S2	*Dictionary of American Library Biography, Second Supplement*, ed. Donald G. Davis Jr. (Westport, CT: Libraries Unlimited, 2003)
D-R	Democratic-Republican
Essays	William Warner Bishop and Andrew Keogh, eds., *Essays Offered to Herbert Putnam by His Colleagues and Friends on His Thirtieth Anniversary as Librarian of Congress 5 April 1929* (Freeport, NY: Books for Libraries Press, 1967)
Encyclopedia	John Y. Cole and Jane Aikin, eds., *Encyclopedia of the Library of Congress: For Congress, the Nation, & the World* (Lanham, MD: LC, in association with Bernan Press, 2004)
F	Federalist
GPO	US Government Printing Office; name changed in 2014 to US Government Publishing Office

IFLA	International Federation of Library Associations and Institutions
JCC	*Journal of Cataloging & Classification*
JLH	*Journal of Library History* (1966–72); *Journal of Library History, Philosophy, and Comparative Librarianship* (1973–87)
Johnston, *History*	William Dawson Johnston, *History of the Library of Congress, Volume 1, 1800–1864* (Washington, DC: GPO, 1904)
L&C	*Libraries & Culture* (1988–2006) *Libraries & The Cultural Record* (2006–11)
LC	Library of Congress
LCA	Library of Congress Archives, Manuscript Division, LC
LCACF	Library of Congress Archives, Central File, Manuscript Division, LC
LCIB	*Library of Congress Information Bulletin*
LCM	*Library of Congress Magazine*
Librarians	*Librarians of Congress, 1802–1974* (Washington, DC: LC, 1977).
LJ	*Library Journal*
LQ	*Library Quarterly*
LRTS	*Library Resources & Technical Services*
LT	*Library Trends*
Mearns, *Story*	David C. Mearns, *The Story Up to Now: The Library of Congress, 1800–1946*; reprinted from the *Annual Report of the Librarian of Congress for the Fiscal Year Ending June 30, 1946* (Washington, DC: LC, 1947)
NAL	National Agricultural Library
NEA	National Endowment for the Arts
NEH	National Endowment for the Humanities
NLM	National Library of Medicine
NSF	National Science Foundation
OCLC	Ohio College Library Center; later the Online Computer Library Center
PL	Public Law
QJLC	*Quarterly Journal of the Library of Congress; Library of Congress Quarterly Journal of Current Acquisitions*
R	Republican
RCHS	*Records of the Columbia Historical Society of Washington, DC*
RLG	Research Libraries Group
RLIN	Research Libraries Information Network
SLA	Special Libraries Association
SR	*Saturday Review of Literature*
SSRC	Social Science Research Council
Stat	US Statutes at Large

CHAPTER 1

Establishing a Library for Congress

THE SECOND SESSION of the first US Congress (1789–91) produced the Residence Act, establishing the location of the capital city on the Potomac River. During the many and heated discussions over possible locations, members of Congress often referred to the prestige and power attached to the national capital and to its potential to fuel economic growth but said less about the amenities they enjoyed while meeting in New York City and Philadelphia. Nevertheless, at the Potomac River site not only federal buildings but also residences, shops, services, and streets would need to rise from farmlands and woods.[1]

Among the services that Congress would lack was a library. Some members of the Continental Congress, the Confederation Congress, and the First Federal Congress had brought books from home, but as early as mid-1782 Theodoric Bland Jr. (VA) had proposed that Congress import books for the members' use,[2] and in early 1783 a committee consisting of James Madison (VA, chair), Thomas Mifflin (PA), and Hugh Williamson (NC) recommended purchasing "authors on the law of Nations, treaties, Negotiations, etc." They urged, too, collecting "every book & tract which related to American antiquities & the affairs of the US," partly because of the potential need to refute European claims to American territory.[3] The committee's report appears to have been prepared by Madison: a list of 307 mostly legal, historical, political, and geographical works in English, French, and Latin. Headed by Denis Diderot's *Encyclopédie Méthodologique* (Paris, 1751–72), the list included authorities such as Hugo Grotius and Samuel Freiherr von Pufendorf on international law; Edward Coke and William Blackstone on English law; Edward Gibbon on the Roman Empire and Plutarch on Greek and Roman biography; David Hume on English history; John Locke, Charles-Louis de Secondat Montesquieu, and Algernon Sidney on political philosophy; and Adam Smith on economics. Maps of America, Indian treaties, and travel narratives were also prominent. Clearly, Madison, who read for self-improvement (chiefly in the classics, history, politics, philosophy, and the law), intended to have a basic collection of the books that had shaped his contemporaries' political, legal, and economic thought and established precedents—works that they had used to support the colonies' legal and political claims against England and to buttress their arguments for self-governance.[4]

There were no objections to the list; but by a large majority, the members voted against the purchase. Their reasons were practical: They had their own books and good private libraries at hand, and they objected to the expense, especially during wartime.[5] They also observed that import costs (necessary because the American publishing output was small) would be lower after normal trade relations resumed.[6]

While meeting in New York's City Hall (renamed Federal Hall) in 1789–90, the members could use the New-York Society Library, comprising several thousand volumes and conveniently housed on the third floor of that building.[7] On August 6, 1789, nevertheless, Representative Elbridge Gerry (MA) moved that a committee be named "to report a catalogue of books necessary for the use of Congress, with an estimate of the expense, and the best mode of procuring them."[8] The motion was tabled, but it was called up during the second session, on April 30, 1790; Gerry became the chair, with Aedanus Burke (SC) and Alexander White (VA) as members.[9] On June 23, the committee reported, recommending an initial appropriation of $1,000 and $500 annually thereafter for volumes that would be useful to the legislative and executive departments, citing the inconvenience of transporting members' own books to congressional sessions.[10] Gerry's list included the statutes of various countries, legal treatises, works on political economy and economics, and legislative journals. But he proposed only a small collection, omitting the histories and Americana that Madison had recommended. In his history of the Library, David Mearns contends that the report embraced the idea of a library for the entire federal establishment and therefore reached toward the formation of a national library. The historian Carl Ostrowski, however, argues (and, given the context, more convincingly) that Gerry's list was not only designed to avoid opposition but also deliberately minimal and utilitarian to meet the needs of a small, elite group—a conception that would guide Library acquisitions during the early nineteenth century.[11]

The report drew sharp debate both in Congress and in the press, with some opposing members citing economic considerations (echoed by some newspapers, since the Confederation government was heavily in debt), while supporters emphasized the need for books essential to the governing process. In the end, Gerry's effort was unsuccessful: the report was tabled and never revived.[12]

After moving to Philadelphia in 1790, Congress was invited to use the Library Company of Philadelphia (just as the Continental Congress had that courtesy, beginning August 31, 1774, and delegates to the Constitutional Convention in 1787).[13] However, that arrangement, as with the New-York Society Library, eventually proved inadequate, despite the Library Company's larger 7,000-volume collection.[14] Late eighteenth-century social and circulating libraries were private ventures, serving the recreational, educational, and professional needs of their patrons rather than the more specialized demands of a national legislature. But many members of Congress were constant readers with catholic tastes, who were as much in touch with the classics as with more modern authors; and references to Blackstone, Hume, Locke, Montesquieu, and other philosophical and political writings were common in their debates.[15] Thus, in the fall of 1794, the members ordered copies of Blackstone's *Commentaries* and Emer de Vattel's *Law of Nations,* and both houses of Congress continued to add books as well as a few periodicals. By 1802, 243 volumes had been purchased.[16]

The Congressional Library

The suggestions to acquire books for Congress did not intend establishing a national library, or even a collection referred to as a library. Perhaps if an annual appropriation had been approved, Congress eventually would have faced the need to establish order among the volumes, but it was in fact the removal of the federal government to the new capital city that forced (or perhaps permitted) action: Representative Harrison Gray Otis (F-MA) called on his colleagues to make arrangements for the federal establishment on March 20, 1800, and the next day the matter was referred to the Committee on Ways and Means. The committee's chairman, Robert Goodloe Harper (F-SC), reported on March 24 "a bill making further provision for the removal and accommodation of the Government of the United States," which came up for discussion on April 2. Legislation that contained provisions as diverse as furnishings for the President's house and paving the streets raised long debate, extending to April 22, when the two houses came to agreement.[17] President John Adams signed the bill two days later.

The fifth section of the law stipulated:

> That for the purchase of such books as may be necessary for the use of Congress at the said city of Washington, and for fitting up a suitable apartment for containing them, and for placing them therein the sum of five thousand dollars shall be, and hereby is appropriated; and that the said purchase shall be made by the Secretary of the Senate and the Clerk of the House of Representatives, pursuant to such directions as shall be given, and such catalogue as shall be furnished, by a joint committee of both Houses of Congress to be appointed for that purpose; and that the said books shall be placed in one suitable apartment in the capitol in the said city, for the use of both Houses of Congress and the Members thereof, according to such regulations as the Committee aforesaid shall devise and establish.[18]

This provision is generally recognized as founding the Library of Congress. During debate, the proposal to purchase books drew no criticism—or even discussion—in either the House or Senate. By all indications, the intent was strictly utilitarian: the language "necessary for the use of Congress" is exactly the same as Gerry's 1789 proposal. The members, Mearns observes, seem to have envisioned something akin to the subscription libraries they were accustomed to use—but with a strictly limited clientele, a congressional oversight committee, and funded from the public purse.[19]

That President John Adams favored establishing a book collection would have been no surprise to those who remembered his work as the drafter of the 1780 Massachusetts Constitution. David McCullough and Richard Alan Ryerson called attention to Section II of Chapter 6, "The Encouragement of Literature, Etc.," as Adams's "original contribution" and "like no other declaration to be found in any constitution ever written until then." Adams wrote that it should be

> the duty of legislators and magistrates in all future periods of the commonwealth to cherish the interests of literature and the sciences, and all seminaries of them, especially the university at Cambridge, public schools, and grammar schools in the towns; to encourage private societies and public institutions, rewards and immunities, for the promotion of agriculture, arts, sciences, commerce, trades, manufactures.

Adams's passion for learning was long-standing: "I must judge for myself, but how can I judge, how can any man judge, unless his mind has been opened and enlarged by reading," he had written in his diary when he was only twenty-five.[20]

The establishment of the Library was, according to David McCullough, one of the few events that pleased Adams in the last year of his presidency, and it was also one of the measures on which he and Vice President Thomas Jefferson well agreed. Adams himself had a collection of 3,200 volumes, many of them carrying his marginal notes, though it never came close to Jefferson's, which eventually numbered more than twice as many.[21]

On April 25, 1800, the House appointed Robert Waln (F-PA), Thomas Evans (F-VA), and Leven Powell (F-VA) to the Joint Committee on the Library, and three days later the Senate designated Samuel Dexter (F-MA and chair), William Bingham (F-PA), and Wilson Cary Nicholas (D-R-VA). The committee moved promptly, placing an order on June 20 with the London booksellers and publishers Cadell and Davies.[22]

Assembling the books took time, delaying until December 11 the completion of the order, with shipment on the *American* to Baltimore two days later. "Several of the books sent were only to be procured second-handed, and some of them, from their extreme scarcity, at very advanced prices," the booksellers wrote, and the firm failed to supply ten of the requested titles. But they stated that they had procured the "best copies" available and "charged the lowest prices possible." The final bill included 152 titles in 740 volumes at a cost of £475/4s with a 5 percent discount for prompt payment, lowering the total to £451/9s.[23] The books included the classics and standard works of the day: history, economics, biography, geography, legal treatises, chronologies, parliamentary manuals, treaties, and works on international law. All but "possibly one" were in English, though there were forty-seven translations of European titles. In comparison with Madison's original list, there was much less Americana and more history and law, and for the first time a few literary works appeared on a congressional list—perhaps a concession to the lack of print resources in the new capital.[24] Packed in eleven hair trunks, which cost £17/12s (because "boxes . . . after their arrival would have been of little or no value"), the shipment also included a case containing "Arrowsmith's Two Maps of America," "Priestly's Charts of Chronology and Biography," and "Faden's Map of South America."[25]

The shipment arrived at the Baltimore Custom House on February 25, 1801, remaining there until April 1, when, consigned to Samuel A. Otis, Secretary of the Senate, it traveled to the port of Georgetown. Otis announced its arrival to President Jefferson on May 2, and he placed the containers in the Senate Clerk's office. But he did not open them, for Congress was not in session, and "whenever they are opened some person should be made answerable for them or in my opinion the volumes will be immediately dispersed and lost."[26]

The Capital and the Library

When the government moved to the site of the new federal city in 1800, there was little to see. On Capitol Hill, there were the half-finished Capitol Building's two wings, some houses, taverns, and shops; a mile west was the completed Treasury Building, next to the President's House and near the State and War Building, both still under construction. Most congressmen came to town only for the congressional sessions, staying in crowded boarding houses. Scattered houses and shacks, tree stumps. and muddy roads marked the site. According to Senator Gouverneur Morris (F-NY), "This is the best city in the world to live in—in the future." Yet rivers and streams framed the new city, drawing favorable comment from President Adams, and Representative Manasseh Cutler (F-MA) declared the site to be "much more delightful than I expected to find it." Secretary of the Treasury Oliver Wolcott, however, though he thought the Capitol and President's House "magnificent," was surprised at how much work both sites needed, as was Abigail Adams, though she and her daughter-in-law to be, Louisa Catherine Johnson, were as pleased with the landscape as Cutler. As just over 100 federal employees moved in, so did shopkeepers, lawyers, doctors, printers, newspapermen, clergymen, and their families.[27]

When Congress convened in December 1801, both houses appointed members "to make a report of their opinion respecting the future arrangement of said books and maps": Senators Uriah Tracy (F-CT) and Wilson Cary Nicholas (chair), and Representatives Joseph Hopper Nicholson (F-MD), Joseph Asheton Bayard Sr. (F-DE), and John Randolph (D-R-VA).[28] It was Randolph—a voracious reader, book collector, and author of the phrase "a good library is a statesman's workshop"—who drafted the report. And to at least some extent, the early character of the Library as a strictly utilitarian collection with restricted access reflected Randolph's preference for limited, economical government.[29]

A long discussion ensued on extending borrowing privileges to federal officials, the location of a room for the collection, the appointment of a librarian, the salary to be offered, an appropriation for book purchases, and the hours of opening. On December 31, the House approved a bill allowing the unexpended balance of the previous appropriation to be used to support the collection (for Randolph and other Democratic-Republicans opposed an annual appropriation), specifying that the librarian be appointed by the Speaker of the House and the President of the Senate.[30] Meanwhile, the Senate had passed its own bill on December 21 providing for an annual appropriation, the appointment of a Librarian by the President, and limiting the Library's use to members of Congress.[31] The main disagreements were therefore on the executive appointment, extending privileges to outsiders, and the appropriation. After debate, the Senate abandoned the appropriation, while the House agreed to a presidential appointment. On January 26, 1802, the "Act Concerning the Library for the Use of Both Houses of Congress" passed, and President Jefferson promptly signed it. Its six sections specified placing the books in a room in the Capitol; designating the President of the Senate and the Speaker of the House to establish rules and regulations "for the time being"; reserving the nomination of a librarian to the President; securing the librarian's bond; limiting borrowing privileges to members of Congress, the Vice President, and the President "for the time being"; fixing the librarian's remuneration at $2 a day; using the unexpended balance of the previous $5,000 appropriation, "together with such sums as may hereafter be appropriated," for purchases; and appointing the six-member Joint Committee to direct purchasing additional books.[32]

Jefferson appointed an ally, political operative, and public official—forty-four-year-old John James Beckley—as Librarian on January 29.[33] Beckley, a former clerk of the Virginia House of Delegates and the Virginia Senate, and also of the US House of Representatives (1789–97), was again elected Clerk of the House in December 1801. He was in penurious circumstances, and he proposed to James Madison that he also become Librarian, and Jefferson made the appointment, at least partly as acknowledgment of Beckley's political support.[34] According to Ainsworth Rand Spofford, a later Librarian, the Library "involved but little time or trouble" since "there was little occasion for official work with a view to its wider usefulness."[35] Beckley, in fact, delegated the Library's daily operations to assistants.[36] On March 5, the Senate appointed Abraham Baldwin (D-R-GA), DeWitt Clinton (D-R-NY), and George Logan (D-R-PA) to the Joint Committee, and the House named Nicholson, Bayard, and Randolph on March 11. Baldwin, a Yale graduate and former president of the University of Georgia, served as chair.[37]

The original design for the Capitol had no designated space for a library. First placed in the office of the Senate Clerk, the books were later moved to the room on the west side of the North Wing that had previously served as the House Chamber. It was large, measuring 86 by 35 feet, with a 36-foot ceiling, and it was lighted by two rows of windows.[38] Randolph's report specified that the books be numbered and labeled and placed in cases with handles and locking doors, to facilitate removal in case of fire. It also directed the Senate Secretary and Clerk to order furniture and book withdrawal slips and to prepare a catalog. The Library would be open every day except Sunday from 11 a.m. to 3 p.m., and members could borrow two books at a time, with folios to be returned within eight days and octavos and duodecimos in six. For members' families and guests, the Library soon became a popular place to visit—particularly because the city lacked churches, schools, and amusements.[39] In June 1804, for example, the American painter and naturalist Charles Willson Peale accompanied the visiting Prussian scientist and explorer Baron Alexander von Humboldt on a tour of the Capitol; and Peale later described the Library as "a spacious and handsome Room, and although lately organized, already contained a number of valuable books in the best taste of binding."[40] Two years later, Senator William Plumer (F-NH), noting that the collection contained nearly 2,000 volumes, described the Library as a "great boon in this desert-city," though admitting that the Speaker of the House, Nathaniel Macon (D-R-NC), thought it "a useless expense."[41]

Jefferson's List

President Jefferson, himself an avid book collector, was very interested in the Library. Invited by Senator Baldwin to provide advice on purchases, on April 14, 1802, the President sent a list

> in conformity with your ideas that books of entertainment are not within the scope of it, and that books in other languages, where there are not translations of them, are to be admitted freely. I have confined the catalogue to those branches of science which belong to the deliberations of the members as statesmen, and in these have omitted those desir-

> able books, antient and modern, which gentlemen generally have in their private libraries, but which cannot properly claim a place in a collection made merely for the purposes of reference.

In particular: "Under the law of Nature & Nations I have put down everything I know of worth possessing, because this is a branch of science often under the discussion of Congress, & the books written on it not to be found in private libraries." And Jefferson recommended a "compleat" parliamentary section because "it is only by having a law of proceeding and by every member having the means of understanding it for himself, and appealing to it that he can be protected against caprice & despotism in the chair." For general reference, there were two encyclopedias and various language dictionaries, and he hoped that his catalog "will enable you to form your general plan, and to select from it every year to the amount of the annual fund of those most wanting." He later asked Treasury Secretary Albert Gallatin to arrange for buying books in London and Paris and sent lists of books for such purchases.[42]

With $2,480.83 of the original appropriation remaining, the Joint Committee bought more books: on July 16 Jefferson notified Beckley that 700 volumes had been ordered—though not from Cadell and Davies, because the President considered that firm too expensive. Entrusting the task to his appointee George William Ewing, US Consul and Agent in London, the President urged Ewing to look for books "with neat bindings, not splendid ones," and "good editions, not pompous ones." Another order went to Robert R. Livingston, Minister to France.[43]

Beckley suggested to Jefferson the acquisition of works by the naturalists Georges-Louis Buffon and Mark Catesby, and he began urging authors to donate their books. In February 1803, he wrote his friend Samuel Harrison Smith, editor of the *National Intelligencer*, that authors were beginning to view donations as a means of advertising their books; and on February 13, 1803, and again on April 11, 1806, Smith advised his readers that authors and publishers ought to send copies of all their books, because "the fame and emolument of the writers and proprietors of printed books can perhaps be promoted in no manner more effectually." Donations in the early years amounted to only a dozen or two volumes annually but ranged widely—from James Madison's gift of copies of the Leyden *Gazette*, to the legislative acts of the Kentucky and Michigan territories, and to Mercy Warren's history of the Revolution (presented by the author). But when one William Tatham tried in 1806 to interest Congress in acquiring his collection of "scientific and useful" books and maps, the members failed to act.[44]

Expanding the Collection

The *Catalogue of the Books, Maps, and Charts Belonging to the Library of the Two Houses of Congress* appeared in April 1802, with a supplement in October 1803 and a revised catalog issued in 1804. Arranged by book sizes, a common practice at that time, the catalogs provided the number given each book, the number of physical volumes, and the value "as near as can be estimated" of each title—essential because borrowers who lost volumes must pay for replacements.[45] Since, in 1802, the Library possessed only

964 volumes and 9 maps, the first catalog had only seven pages. Sixty of the titles had appeared on Madison's list, but more recent purchases emphasized the classical writers who influenced eighteenth- and nineteenth-century political thought. The catalog of 1804 listed nearly 1,500 volumes, again by size, in thirteen pages.[46]

While the Library included statutes and legislative proceedings from various countries, Congress did not establish a collection of its own proceedings until January 1805, when President Jefferson signed an act stipulating that 300 copies of the laws and the journals of Congress (out of the 1,000 reserved for congressional use) be placed in the Library when they were printed after each session. Four years later, the House directed its Clerk to also provide the Library with all the documents and reports received by the two houses.[47]

In December 1805, the Senate appointed a committee to consider more purchases. Its chair, Samuel Latham Mitchill (D-R-NY), a graduate of the University of Edinburgh, had taught chemistry, natural history, and botany at Columbia College, and he founded the nation's first medical journal, the *Medical Repository*. Jefferson called Mitchill "the congressional dictionary"; John Randolph dubbed him "the Congressional Library"; and others weighed in with such nicknames as the "Stalking Library," the "living encyclopedia," and the "Chaos of knowledge."[48] Thus, it was no surprise that Mitchill's January 20, 1806, report proposed expanding the Library. "Every week of the session causes additional regret that the volumes of literature and science within the reach of the national legislature are not more rich and ample. The want of geographical illustration is truly distressing; and the deficiency of historical and political works is scarcely less severely felt," he wrote, urging that "steps should seasonably be taken to furnish the Library with such materials as will enable statesmen to be correct in their investigations and, by a becoming display of erudition and research, give a higher dignity and a brighter luster to truth."[49] An act of February 21, 1806, provided $1,000 a year for five years for acquisitions—the first authorization of an annual appropriation. The act also approved, for the first time, domestic book purchases, and the House bill provided the secretaries of State, War, Navy, and Treasury, and the Attorney General, access to the Library—though the Senate rejected the latter proposal.[50] The next summer, Joint Committee members Mitchill, John Quincy Adams (F-MA), and Joseph Clay (R-PA) patronized booksellers in New York, Philadelphia, and Boston to such good effect that Mitchill eventually reported receiving all except one box of books (lost when the ship sank), and he invited members of both houses to "furnish lists of good and proper books, and to suggest hints for the improvement of the library."[51]

A New Librarian

Thanks to Mitchill's vigorous support (and his donations of books), when John Beckley died in office on April 8, 1807, the Library was a small but going concern. Although the House had repossessed its former chamber in December 1805 while the South Wing of the Capitol was under construction—relegating the books to a small committee room in poor repair—the Joint Committee continued to add books, with finances handled by its agent.[52] When the Tenth Congress convened in October 1807, eight men applied for

Beckley's position as House Clerk. One of them, Assistant Clerk Nicholas Van Zandt, was rejected when John Randolph disclosed that Van Zandt had violated the secrecy of a closed session. The members turned instead to Patrick Magruder, a thirty-nine-year-old lawyer and Democratic-Republican representative from Maryland, who had been defeated for reelection in 1806. After he was elected Clerk on October 26, 1807, Democratic-Republicans Willis Alston Jr. (NC), Thomas Kenan (NC), and John Smilie (PA) recommended to President Jefferson that he select Magruder as Librarian.[53]

Jefferson, however, had a long list of candidates and was not sure he wanted to make a dual appointment. He delayed for several days, but on November 6 he informed Magruder that he would sign his commission as Librarian. Political considerations seemingly influenced the President, who cited the propriety of following congressional preferences regarding the selection of congressional officers.[54]

The Joint Committee met on November 20 to consider writing the Annual Report, preparing a new catalog, and calling on the President to discuss Library facilities. Magruder was not present. But the committee worked efficiently, delivering a forty-page catalog in 1808. The arrangement was again by book size, but with added sections for Plans, State Laws, Journals of the House of Representatives of the United States, Reports of Committees of the House, Executive Reports and Papers, Receipts and Expenditures, Bill Books of the House, and Gazettes. As Clerk, it was Magruder's responsibility to oversee the catalog's printing, but he does not seem to have had any other role in its preparation, which was supervised by committee member Representative Samuel W. Dana (F-CT).

The 1808 catalog also included rules regarding loan periods and fines for overdue materials and the use of congressional journals and laws. In general, the Librarian's responsibilities were defined as custodial, but the committee did not assume that the Librarian would also serve as Clerk, as demonstrated by a clause specifying that the Librarian would receive from the Senate Secretary and the House Clerk complete sets of laws and journals for deposit. Perhaps this was because the Library's hours had been extended; during congressional recesses, it would be open Tuesdays, Thursdays, and Saturdays, and the six-day schedule for regular sessions (from 9 a.m. to 3 p.m. and from 5 p.m. to 7 p.m.) would begin the week before Congress convened and end a week after Congress recessed.[55]

"Mitchill and I walk'd up to the Capitol, and passed an hour or two in the congressional library," Mrs. Catharine Mitchill recorded in February 1809. In her telling, it was a comfortable place: "A warm room & good fire, plenty of candle light and books of every description to amuse you." Moreover, the "handsome additions" to the collection over the past two years (resulting partly from her husband's urging), provided "a valuable & respectable collection of books."[56] While there is little information about how the members used the collection during the early years, Superintendent of the Reading Room Martin Roberts later noted that John Randolph, despite his own excellent personal library, was "surprisingly conversant with its contents," while Chief Justice John Marshall "derived pleasure and benefit from the large folios in the alcove devoted to legal works," and Baldwin, Mitchill, and Dana "were constant readers and rendered constructive aid."[57]

Users, Space, and the Collection

Over the years, Library privileges were extended to the Joint Committee's agent, Joseph Nourse (1810), and to the Supreme Court Justices (1812).[58] In 1811 Congress authorized the $1,000 annual appropriation for another five years and provided for the permanent Joint Committee on the Library.[59] There were also efforts to improve the Library's quarters: on January 5, 1811, the House appointed Adam Seybert (R-PA), Josiah Quincy (F-MA), and Nathaniel Macon to plan better accommodations. Reporting that roof leaks jeopardized the collection, they recommended moving the books into one of the Senate committee rooms; the matter was referred to the Joint Committee, and an appropriations act of February 20, 1811, provided for outfitting a room on the west side of the Capitol's North Wing.[60]

The 1812 catalog featured a new arrangement: it included 3,076 volumes in eighteen subject classes (with the books listed by size within classes), and fifty-three maps, charts, and plans.[61] The classification came from the Library Company of Philadelphia's 1789 catalog, which in turn was based on Diderot's *Encyclopédie*—and that in turn relied on Francis Bacon's division of knowledge into history, philosophy, and the fine arts, based on the three faculties of the mind: memory, reason, and imagination. Memory included sacred history, ecclesiastical history, civil history (chronology, biography, antiquities), geography and topography, and voyages and travels. Reason encompassed law, ethics, theology and mythology, logic, rhetoric and criticism, dictionaries, grammars and education, general and local politics and political economy, trade and commerce, military and naval tactics, agriculture, rural economy, natural history, natural and experimental philosophy, and medicine, surgery, and chemistry. Imagination included poetry and drama, fiction, wit, arts and sciences, and miscellaneous literature. After the classes came two other categories: gazettes and maps, and charts and plans. Counting by titles, history, law, and geography and topography were the largest categories, followed by general and local politics and political economy, totaling about 69 percent of the collection.

Heavily devoted to the practical and the secular, the Library contained little of the literature that social libraries of the period emphasized—for example, belles lettres, and sermons, theological tracts, and devotional works. It included more on contemporary politics, events such as the Santo Domingo slave rebellion and the Napoleonic Wars, and on geography, as shown by books and maps on the Louisiana Purchase and the western territories. The most expensive title in the collection, at $216, was the *Encyclopédie*, in thirty-five volumes. Over the years, the Joint Committee yielded a little to members who wanted more in the way of entertainment, but fiction, poetry, and drama were limited to forty-three titles, including works by Aeschylus, Cicero, Virgil, Cervantes, Shakespeare, and other British authors; and the *Gentleman's Magazine*, the *Spectator*, and the *Tattler* were among the periodicals.[62]

The 1812 catalog included the 1808 rules and added several more, emphasizing the authority of the President of the Senate and Speaker of the House for purchases of supplies, dealing with delinquent borrowers, and controlling materials accessible only within the Library. Members of Congress were not charged fines; but the members of the general public, who were admitted as borrowers for the first time in 1812 if approved by the Librarian, had to provide a receipt or note "of double the value" of the book, and they were fined $1 a day for folios, $.50 for quartos, and $.25 for octavos.[63] The Librarian's role remained restricted to labeling, shelving, and loaning books; maintaining lists and the catalog; and keeping accounts. Like Beckley, Magruder delegated daily operations to assistants.

By 1812, Washington also had grown. Grandly laid out by Major Pierre Charles L'Enfant as a landscape of sweeping vistas and radiating avenues, the built city would not live up to its ambitious design for a century. While the population had swelled to nearly three times the 1800 total, commercial and cultural establishments lagged behind,[64] and visitors and residents alike continued to deride the barren landscape.[65] "It was the common property of all the nation, and everybody had an opinion about it; . . . it is doubtful if any other city in the world was ever so peppered with epigrams," the historian Gaillard Hunt wrote. "Congress arrived for the sessions, promoting a flourishing social life, but the members mostly returned home when they ended. In all, the federal establishment comprised fewer than four hundred people, half of them Congressionals."[66]

Patrick Magruder won re-election as Clerk in 1809, 1811, and 1813, and he continued to serve as Librarian. Like Beckley, he did little to develop the collection or publicize the Congressional Library. But Magruder was not a well man, and he was sometimes absent from his duties. One particular absence would lead to his downfall.

CHAPTER 2

Jefferson's Collection and Its Legacy

PRESIDENT JEFFERSON and President Madison adopted policies restricting trade: the Non-Importation Acts of 1806 and 1811, the Embargo Acts prohibiting American exports (1807–9, 1813), and the Non-Intercourse Act of 1809. None of these laws induced the warring European nations to respect US shipping: the British continued to impress seamen from American vessels into His Majesty's service, and both the British and the French blockaded ports, confiscated cargoes, and generally ignored neutral rights. Between 1803 and 1812, nearly 1,500 American ships were seized.[1]

The restrictions decreased federal revenue and depressed the economy but affected the British relatively little. Hard-pressed shippers, farmers, and merchants, from New England maritime interests to southern cotton and tobacco planters, resorted to illicit commerce—sometimes with the collusion, willing or unwilling, of customs officials and courts.[2] As pressure mounted to repeal the embargo, Congress replaced it with nonintercourse, allowing trade with nations other than France and England. But while the French claimed to retreat from their antineutral policy, the British, suspecting deceit, did not relent. Meanwhile congressional prowar sentiment increased, fostered by Henry Clay (D-R-KY) and a group of "War Hawk" congressmen, among them westerners who wanted to rid the frontier of British outposts and hostile Indians. In response to Madison's November 1811 request for preparedness, Congress voted early in 1812 to increase the military establishment, and on June 1 the President sent a war message to the Capitol. He signed the Declaration of War on June 18.[3]

American forces met defeat in 1812 and the spring of 1813, when they again invaded Canada. However, on April 27 they captured York (now Toronto), the capital of Upper Canada, and during the brief occupation the Parliament buildings, including the Legislative Assembly's Library, were burned.[4] Meanwhile, Rear Admiral Sir George Cockburn's ships blocked Chesapeake Bay, raiding towns and plantations and encouraging slaves to run away and join the British forces.[5] In July 1814 Cockburn planned an attack on Washington, while some administration officials (including Secretary of War John Armstrong) continued to doubt that the capital was in danger.[6]

The British Burn Washington

Patrick Magruder was in such poor health that at the beginning of the congressional session on December 9, 1813, the House named his brother, George Magruder, Acting Clerk.[7] Patrick Magruder departed the city in late July 1814, traveling to the mineral springs in Virginia to recuperate. He was still there on August 24 when the British routed the American forces and entered Washington. Being too old for the militia, Assistant Clerk J. T. Frost was not affected when the District force was called up on August 19; and Colonel George Magruder ordered him not to leave unless the War Office began to evacuate. Though most federal departments began evacuating that same day, that news reached Frost only on Monday, August 22. Well before then, residents were fleeing the city, loading all available wagons with their belongings. Frost and another assistant clerk, Samuel Burch (released from militia duty at Magruder's request), searched for transportation, finally locating one cart and sending several loads of congressional records to "a safe and secret place in the country" 9 miles away.[8] Two days later, the British forces set fire to government buildings, including the Capitol.

The destruction in Washington was deliberate, intended to demoralize the residents, punish American intransigence, humiliate the federal government, and perhaps force the Americans to sue for peace.[9] But the city remained small, at just over 8,000 residents; there were no strategic targets except the arsenal at Greenleaf Point and the Navy Yard shipbuilding works. Naval officers destroyed the Yard just as the British arrived at about 8:30 p.m. on August 24.

George Gleig, a British soldier, was impressed only with the Capitol itself, which then consisted of House and Senate wings connected by a wooden shed. Gleig described it as "light, airy, and elegant," with "two spacious apartments" serving as the House and Senate chambers. He also saw "smaller rooms . . . furnished as a public library, the two larger being well stocked with valuable books, principally in the modern languages, whilst the others, filled with archives, national statutes, acts of legislature &c, were used as the private rooms of the librarians."[10] Lieutenant James Scott, RN, however, recalled the Capitol more sarcastically, as "an unfinished but beautifully arranged building; the interior accommodations were upon a scale of grandeur and magnificence little suited to pure Republican simplicity."[11]

British soldiers roamed the building, piling up flammable material and setting it ablaze. The Capitol was severely damaged: the interior of the west side was nearly destroyed, including the Senate Chamber, the Library, and the Supreme Court Chamber. Elias Caldwell, the Court clerk, had moved some volumes from the Court to his home.[12] But the Congressional Library seems to have been entirely consumed.[13]

When Congress met in special session on September 19, the issue of moving the government had already been raised, perhaps encouraged by an August 27 invitation from the Common Council of Philadelphia. Although Madison stated his opposition in a September 20 message to Congress, the members did consider, and at some length, moving to a more secure location.[14] Patriotic sentiment (largely voiced by southerners, who feared a permanent relocation) favored defying the British threat, and Washington businessmen understandably opposed the move. Northerners who disliked the capital's Potomac River location advocated moving the capital, but opponents countered that removal would undermine the 1790 compromise and could endanger national unity. While, on October 6, pro-removal congressmen won a nonbinding House vote, later that month a resolution to remain in Washington passed the House 83–74. The Senate delayed a decision for over three months, ultimately concurring after leading citizens offered assistance: in just six months, they erected a three-story building called the "Brick Capitol" to provide space for Congress.[15]

Congressional Investigation

On September 20, Patrick Magruder formally notified Speaker of the House Langdon Cheves (R-SC) of the destruction of the Library and his office records. He requested an investigation, and Cheves appointed a Select Committee, naming Joseph Pearson (F-NC) as chair.[16]

Frost and Burch told the committee that they learned of the War Department's evacuation at noon on August 22 and immediately prepared to move, but they had only one cart and four oxen. They halted their efforts on the morning of August 24 as the British approached, but Frost stated that he moved some material to a nearby house, which unfortunately also burned. They were most concerned to save the Clerk's records, not the Library, which as a result suffered perhaps the most of any federal office.[17]

The committee reported on December 12 that other agencies began evacuating well before Frost and Burch. "Due precaution and diligence were not exercised to prevent the destruction and loss which has been sustained," the report concluded. There were also other charges: the committee found discrepancies, omissions, and unaccounted-for expenditures in the Magruder brothers' accounts, including a shortage of nearly $20,000. It appeared that government and personal expenditures were mixed together.[18]

Patrick Magruder responded five days later, citing his doctor's advice as the reason for his absence; protesting that the staff was called up for militia service and therefore could not begin early to move materials; and stating that the executive departments were both better informed and better staffed, most of their clerks being too old for military service. He also declared that his accounts adhered to the prescribed procedures and that the House Committee on Accounts had approved his expenditures; if the records had not been lost, he could have accounted for all of them.[19]

In its January 16, 1815, report, the committee disagreed with the Magruder brothers' assertion that the city was not in danger, and it specified that the dereliction of duty lay in failing to provide transportation, a task for which Frost might have employed laborers. The bulk of the document addressed the misuse of funds: the accounts contained errors, George Magruder had not accounted for some funds advanced from the Treasury to pay outstanding bills, and some bills appeared to include excessive charges, with the funds diverted to private expenditures.[20] The committee reported a resolution to remove Magruder from the clerkship. On January 19, after an unrecorded debate, the House accepted the report; and two days later, Representative James Clark (R-KY) introduced the resolution to remove Patrick Magruder from office. In another unrecorded debate, some congressmen charged Magruder with allowing deputies to draw funds without notifying him, while supporters referred only to his "general good conduct." The House postponed action for a week.[21]

Patrick Magruder considered himself a scapegoat and decided that no defense he could mount would result in vindication. He perhaps also realized that the loss of the records might not be completely accidental.[22] On January 28, 1815, he resigned the office of Clerk (and by inference, the office of Librarian). The House tabled his resignation, but two days later it elected Thomas Dougherty as Clerk.[23]

Jefferson's Offer

Debate raged over the destruction in Washington. Though some British journalists insisted that the United States deserved a demonstration of British power, a Nottingham newspaper condemned it as "an act without example in modern wars or in any other wars since the inroads of the barbarians who conflagrated Rome and overthrew the Roman Empire." The *Niles' Register* pointed out that not even Napoleon had burned a capital city, while *Harper's Monthly Magazine* published an apocryphal drawing of British soldiers using the Library's books as kindling.[24]

When the news reached Thomas Jefferson at Monticello, he wrote angrily to his friend Samuel Harrison Smith, publisher of the *National Intelligencer*:

> I learn from the Newspapers that the Vandalism of our enemy has triumphed at Washington over science as well as the Arts, by the destruction of the public library with the noble edifice in which it was deposited. . . . The world will entertain but one sentiment. they will see a nation suddenly withdrawn from a great war, full armed and full handed, taking advantage of another whom they had recently forced into it, unarmed and unprepared, to indulge themselves in acts of barbarism which do not belong to a civilised age.

A lifelong collector, Jefferson possessed a library of over 6,000 volumes. "I presume it will be among the early objects of Congress to recommence their collection. this will be difficult while the war continues, and intercourse with Europe is attended with so much risk," he observed. Furthermore,

> You know my collection, its condition and extent. I have been 50 years making it and have spared no pains, opportunity or expense to make it what it is. while residing in Paris, I devoted every afternoon I was disengaged, for a summer or two, in examining all the principal bookstores, turning over every book with my own hand, and putting by everything which related to America, and indeed whatever was rare & valuable in every science. besides this, I had standing orders, during the whole time I was in Europe, in it's principal book-marts, particularly Amsterdam, Frankfort, Madrid and London, for such works relating to America as could not be found in Paris.

Jefferson continued to order books after returning home; his collection, while it included "what is chiefly valuable in science and literature generally, extends more particularly to whatever belongs to the American statesman." Doubting that there ever would be another opportunity to assemble such a collection, he disclosed that he had provided for it to be offered to Congress after his death, but the destruction of the Congressional Library made this "the proper moment."[25]

Jefferson had large debts, and selling his books would allow him to meet pressing obligations. But he perhaps anticipated congressional opposition, for he set generous terms. Requesting Smith to communicate the offer, he suggested that the members themselves determine the value and that payment be made "convenient to the public," perhaps as annual installments "so as to spare the present calls of our country, and await it's days of peace and prosperity." Congress could, however, have the books immediately so long as the entire library was accepted: he would sell it intact or not at all. "I do not know," he wrote, "that it contains any branch of science which Congress would wish to exclude from their collection. there is in fact no subject to which a member of Congress may not have occasion to refer." Enclosing an incomplete catalog, he left it to Smith to arrange an agreement.[26]

Jefferson informed President Madison and Secretary of State James Monroe of the offer, and he also discussed it with the Georgetown bookseller Joseph Milligan, who thought the proposal "will be very acceptable" and commented, "If Congress should purchase it, to literary men it would be a great privilege to be permitted at all times of the year to have free access, not to take away the books, but to read in the Library and make extracts. Therefore the place of the Librarian would be well to be a distinct office from the Clerk of the House of Representatives."[27]

Meanwhile, Congress considered replacing the books: Senator Robert Henry Goldsborough (F-MD) proposed on September 26 that the Joint Committee on the Library be charged to purchase a new collection. Smith presented Jefferson's proposal early in October, and Goldsborough submitted a resolution on October 7 to authorize the Joint Committee to contract for the purchase, which the Senate approved. After some House discussion that foreshadowed future disagreement, the Senate concurred in the House's stipulation that "the committee lay the terms of said contract before Congress, for their ratification." The Joint Committee then moved to secure an appraisal, and on November 28, Goldsborough reported a bill to authorize the purchase. The Senate passed it on December 3, but the House postponed consideration until January 26.[28]

The Debate

The House debate was bitter; as Representative Charles Ingersoll (R-PA) recalled, it betrayed "the English prepossessions of some, the narrow parsimony of others, the party prejudices of nearly all."[29] Federalists objected to both the cost and the collection itself, in which they discerned evidence of "atheism, immorality, effete intellectualism, and infatuation with France." Cyrus King (F-MA), for example, called the books, "good, bad, and indifferent, old, new, and worthless, in languages which many can not read and most ought not; which is true Jeffersonian-Madisonian philosophy, to bankrupt the Treasury, beggar the people and disgrace the nation." He proposed removing "all books of an atheistical, irreligious, and immoral tendency."[30] Some Republicans joined the Federalist opposition, arguing that the funds should be used for more pressing needs.

As the *Annals of Congress* reported,

> The objections to the purchase were generally its extent, the cost of the purchase, the nature of the selection, embracing too many works in foreign languages, some of too philosophical a character, and some otherwise objectionable. Of the first description, excep-

> tion was taken to Voltaire's works, &c, and of the other to Callender's Prospect Before Us. [However:] On the other hand, those who advocated the purchase proposed to be made, contended that so valuable a library, one so admirably calculated for the substratum of a great national library, was not to be obtained in the United States; and that, although there might be some works to which gentlemen might take exception, there were others of very opposite character; that this, besides, was no reason against the purchase, because in every library of value might be found some books to which exceptions would be taken, according to the feelings or prejudices of those who examined them.[31]

The press also weighed in: the Petersburg, Virginia, *Courier* complained that the objections to Voltaire and Locke "reflect the greatest discredit upon the national character of this country. What can be a greater stigma upon the members of our National Legislature than to assert that books of a philosophical description are improper for their perusal?" The *American Register* agreed: "The next generation will, we confidently predict, blush at the objections made in Congress to the purchase of Mr. Jefferson's library."[32] An anonymous correspondent wrote the *Intelligencer*:

> The library is such as to render all valuation absurd and impossible, if valuation were admitted into literature. It is such a library as cannot be bought in the ordinary mode in which books are purchased, because many of the books that are inestimable are wholly out of print, and many in manuscript that, of course, could not be procured. I have had an opportunity, from the privilege of frequent examination, imperfectly to discover that it is unique—a library which, for its selection, rarity, and intrinsic value, is beyond all price. For the satisfaction of calculators, I will barely mention the value marked in English catalogues, of a few books which this library contains: *DeBry's Collection of Voyages*, 3 volumes, £400 sterling; *Purchas' Pilgrimes*, 1 volume, £56 sterling; *Smith's History of Virginia*, 1 volume folio, £42 sterling, etc.; while the Government paid but $3 per volume.[33]

On the eve of the bill's passage, supporters Robert Wright (D-R-MD), James Fisk (D-R-VT), and John Rhea (D-R-TN) contended "that so valuable a library, one so admirably calculated for the substratum of a national library, was not to be obtained in the United States."[34]

Finally, supported by the Republican majority, the bill passed the House by ten votes on January 26, 1815, and President Madison signed it on January 30.[35] This was hardly a victory, for, as David Mearns put it, "cultural recognition"; it was an administration and party issue, lost in Federalist New England, divided in the mid-Atlantic, won in the South, and with an eight-vote majority in the West—all while the country was still at war.[36]

Jefferson's Collection and a New Librarian

Congress paid $23,950 for the 6,487 books, based on Joseph Milligan's recommendation to price them by size: $10 for a folio, $6 for a quarto, $3 for an octavo, and $1 for a duodecimo.[37] Jefferson had not purchased costly books but sought less expensive volumes, whenever possible octavos or smaller, but he also required clear print and high-quality bindings.[38] A visitor to Monticello, Francis Calley Gray, observed, for example, that the collection of classics was "complete as to the authors but very careless in the editions," but he and his companion, George Ticknor, were impressed with the English literature selections and also noted some rarities. There were no incunabula, though Jefferson had some sixteenth-century imprints.[39]

Not all Jefferson's books were purchased; George Wythe bequeathed books to Jefferson in 1806, and books likewise came to him on the deaths of his father-in-law, John Wayles, and his brother-in-law, Dabney Carr. There were volumes that Jefferson bought when the impressive library of William Byrd of Westover was sold, and he purchased the collections of other prominent Virginians, for example, Richard Bland and Peyton Randolph (who inherited the libraries of his father, Sir John Randolph, and his cousin, the historian William Stith). From the estate of the Reverend James Horrocks, president of the College of William and Mary, came additional volumes and also from the collections of two faculty members, Samuel Henley and Thomas Gwatkin, as well as books that had belonged to the Royal Governor of Virginia, Lord Dunmore, before he fled the Colonies. Jefferson also had books from Benjamin Franklin's library, some with Franklin's autograph notes. There were presentation copies from authors such as Joseph Cheetham, Pierre S. Dupont de Nemours, Joseph Priestley, Dr. Benjamin Rush, Sir John Sinclair, Joel Barlow, Thomas Paine, Abiel Holmes, Benjamin Waterhouse, and Mercy Warren.[40] Jefferson's books might not command high prices, but the total represented a large expenditure for the federal government.

On March 3, the members approved an appropriation for transporting the books and preparing space on the third floor of the building at Seventh and E streets (this was before the city was divided into quadrants) that temporarily housed Congress.[41] And pending the books' arrival, President Madison appointed a new librarian on March 21: George Watterston, the thirty-four-year-old editor of the Democratic-Republican organ, the *Washington City Gazette.* Watterston was the first librarian who did not also serve as Clerk of the House. Trained in the law—but best known as a writer, poet, novelist, and since 1813 editor of the *Gazette*—he was something of a local celebrity who had artfully addressed his 1810 poem, "The Wanderer in Jamaica," to Dolley Madison.[42]

As Watterston advertised for the return of any loaned-out books that might have escaped the fire,[43] Joseph Milligan traveled to Monticello to supervise packing ten wagons for the six-day journey to Washington. On May 8, 1815, Jefferson wrote Smith that the last wagon would depart that day:

> When I first proposed to you to make the overture to the library committee, I thought that the only trouble you would have had, that they would have said yea or nay directly, have appointed valuers, and spared you all further intermediation: and I saw with great regret this agency afterwards added to the heavy labors of your office. it is done, however, and an interesting treasure is added to your city, now become the depository of unquestionably the choicest collection of books in the US and I hope it will not be without some general effect on the literature of our country.[44]

Watterston, quite in agreement, sent a notice to the *Intelligencer* asking writers, artists, and engravers to donate their works. That both local and out-of-town newspapers and periodicals commented on the purchase perhaps encouraged his ambitions, particularly the *Intelligencer*'s prediction that "the Congressional or National Library of the United States [would] become the great repository of the literature of the world."[45]

Jefferson's library nearly doubled the size of the Congressional Library's collection and added books on many more subjects, including technology, architecture, gardening, painting, sculpture, and music.[46] But fully one-fourth of the collection was devoted to politics, ranging from Aristotle, Plato, Machiavelli, Montesquieu, and Locke to contemporary pamphlet literature. The next-largest subjects represented were the law and history, also in impressive depth, but emphasizing works pertinent to America—a collection well suited to the needs of American statesmen.[47]

Jefferson arranged his books by subject, drawing on Francis Bacon's "Table of Knowledge" classification and Jean le Rond d'Alembert's "Preliminary Discourse" in the *Encyclopédie* to construct a system embodying his conception of the relationships among branches of knowledge. He wrote Watterston that the books would arrive in the same order that he arranged them, explaining that he classified them "because of the peculiar satisfaction, when we wish to consider a particular one [subject] of seeing at a glance the books which have been written on it, and selecting those from which we expect most readily the information we seek."[48]

By 1815 Jefferson's plan had evolved to three "Faculties of the Mind": Memory, or History; Reason, or Philosophy; and Imagination, or Fine Arts. These were further divided into forty-four "chapters," or subdivisions: fifteen devoted to history, fourteen to philosophy, and fourteen to the fine arts, with a final chapter for encyclopedias, general works, and periodicals. Jefferson's manuscript catalog, sent with the books, listed them in chapter order.[49]

Pleased though he was that his library would remain intact, just as he had built it, and accessible to the nation, as he intended, Jefferson felt the loss. "I cannot live without books," he wrote John Adams, "but fewer will suffice where amusement, and not use, is the only future object." He continued to acquire books, engaging George Ticknor as his agent abroad.[50]

The 1815 *Catalogue* and Congressional Ambitions

Although the books arrived in Washington a week after leaving Monticello, they were not completely unpacked and arranged until mid-July. Watterston used Jefferson's classification in a new catalog. However, he eliminated some subdivisions, and within each of the forty-four chapters, he alphabetized the books—thus destroying Jefferson's conceptual order. Thanking the Librarian for sending him a copy, Jefferson noted that there were some errors in it, "but such a number of titles in so many different languages could not be expected to be otherwise. You ask how I like the arrangement within chapters? Of course, you know, not so well as my own; yet I think it possible the alphabetical arrangement may be more convenient to readers generally, than mine which was sometimes analytical sometimes chronological & sometimes a combination of both."[51] Nevertheless, Jefferson wrote his friend Joseph C. Cabell that "the form of the catalogue has been much injured in the publication."[52]

Neither did Congress care much for Watterston's initiatives. When his *Catalogue of the Library of the United States* appeared in the late fall of 1815 (having been completed during the congressional recess and without informing the Joint Committee), some members thought it less useful than the old system, though no one remarked on the title, a change from the earlier catalogs that called it "the library for . . . the two houses of Congress."[53] The Joint Committee also criticized the cost for 600 copies at $2.25 each, or $1,360.50, one-third more than the Library's appropriation, "and more than one twentieth of the actual cost of our whole library."[54] "The Library Committee are dissatisfied with me," Watterston wrote Jefferson, "for having the catalogue printed without having waited to consult their *superior judgement*, but the members generally speak very highly of your arrangement and the disposition of the books."[55]

The purchase seemed to awaken ambitions. Led by its new chairman, Senator Eligius Fromentin (D-R-LA), the Joint Committee proposed to "place within the reach of every member of Congress all the most valuable books in every department of arts and sciences, of which there is now such a lamentable deficiency." Committee members recommended a special $10,000 appropriation and increasing the Librarian's salary to $1,000 annually. Their report also stated that the Librarian should be appointed by the Joint Committee rather than the President, commenting, "It is difficult to conceive why an officer of both Houses of Congress . . . should not be appointed by the authority to which he ought to be amendable." Fromentin, a French refugee from the Reign of Terror, may have urged the special appropriation to take advantage of the wartime bargains available on the European book market—an opportunity mentioned in the report.[56] Congress did not approve the $10,000 or the suggestion for a Joint Committee appointment; but a few months later, President Madison signed a bill raising the Librarian's salary and extending Library privileges to the Attorney General and members of the diplomatic corps.[57]

The committee's next report, in January 1817, described recent purchases and proposed an appropriation of $3,000 for law books, and also for acquiring files of literary and political periodicals and the transactions of scholarly societies. There was again a suggestion to purchase foreign books and a proposal to renew the $1,000 annual appropriation for five years, with an increase to $1,500. The committee invited the chairmen of other congressional committees to suggest book titles and maps pertinent to their work, directed placing a suggestion box in the Library, and recommended allowing the "heads of departments" to use the books "on the same terms on which members of Congress are permitted to use them."[58]

At the same time, the Senate considered selecting books from those deposited for copyright with the Secretary of State. The bill ultimately failed, but its Senate passage revealed interest in a copyright deposit collection.[59] And on February 18, 1817, Fromentin introduced a resolution proposing a separate building for the Library "on Delaware Avenue, north of the Capitol,"[60] prompting the *American Register* to tout the "absolute obligation" to provide "a great reservoir of instruction in all the departments of human knowledge for the use of the public." When the House defeated the resolution, Watterston (signing himself "W") wrote the *Intelligencer* regretting the failure and grandiosely suggesting that an appropriate model would be the "elegant and splendid design for a national library at Paris."[61] At the time, the Bibliothèque de France held over 1 million volumes, while the Congressional Library had about 10,000.[62]

Congress, still meeting in the Brick Capitol, on the site where the Supreme Court building now stands, instead provided funding on December 3, 1818, to move the books to temporary quarters in the Senate wing of the Capitol, plus $2,000 for acquisitions. Over the next several years, the appropriation fluctuated, but in 1824 it increased to $5,000.[63] Interested in the collection as always, on September 1, 1820, Jefferson sent Watterston "a very full catalogue of books relating to America," presuming that "it is a primary object to obtain everything of that description."[64] Nevertheless, a proposal by Representative Enoch Lincoln (R-ME) to require the deposit of all manuscript records of the government was tabled in 1822.[65]

The interest in expansion perhaps also reflected new demands on the collection. Postwar prosperity fueled a building boom, and Washington drew travelers as well as foreign dignitaries, politicians, and bureaucrats—such that by 1817, Harrison Gray Otis (F-MA), returning to serve in the Senate, observed that Washington was much improved. But the city remained small, with few amusements other than the social life that politics fostered, and the Library was a popular gathering place.[66] Congressmen and senators' families, notables and dignitaries, and other visitors assembled at the Capitol: "the lounging place of both sexes, where acquaintance is as easily made as at a public amusement."[67]

Among the postwar efforts to expand the Library, the most important was increasing its annual appropriation. If there had been even modest additions from that time on, building the collections could have begun at an auspicious time for acquiring both American printers' small output and important titles from abroad. With Jefferson's books, the character of the Library changed, from a specialized to a general collection—"a most admirable substratum for a National Library."[68] As John Cole emphasized, Jefferson's books "provided the base for the expansion of the Library's functions. . . . Jefferson's belief in the power of knowledge and the direct link between knowledge and democracy shaped the Library's philosophy of sharing its collections and services as widely as possible."[69]

But Congress refused to seize the opportunities that its more ambitious members presented. Noting that appropriations for books averaged only $1,000 a year between 1815 and 1824, William Dawson Johnston called those years "the garret period in the history of the Library."[70] For many years, there would be little congressional support for making the Library a national institution.

CHAPTER 3

The Antebellum Library

"THE CONGRESS HAVE met this session in the Capitol for the first time since the conflagration," wrote Frances Wright, who visited Washington in April 1820. Wright found the capital city undeveloped, though with "the advantage of very choice society, . . . with peculiar courtesy and easy politeness." The House and Senate wings, she observed, were "restored to more than their original grandeur." And construction of the center section was "proceeding rapidly," though "the national library, which a native of England now feels awkward at finding bestowed in a few small apartments; at present it comprises little more than the collection supplied by Mr. Jefferson, but a stated sum being appropriated annually to its enlargement, the spoliations of the war will soon, I trust, be effaced. These volumes, however, marked with the name of America's President and philosopher, will always constitute the most interesting portion of the national library."[1]

The Library occupied crowded quarters in the attic of the Capitol's North Wing. The Joint Committee's 1820 report, presented on December 19 by Senator Mahlon Dickerson (D-R-NJ), explained that the members had intended purchasing books during the recess but had not, since there were no empty shelves to receive them.[2] George Watterston continued to preside over the collection. Not only the first full-time Librarian, he was also, a biographer wrote, "controversial throughout his tenure—critical (even of the congressmen he served), thin-skinned, outspoken and strongly partisan."[3] Acerbic commentary on the city, its inhabitants, visitors, and Congress entered his unsigned work, *A Wanderer in Washington*, and his earlier novel, *The L... Family at Washington*. In the novel, on entering the Library one character sees "honourable members and their ladies, more intent, I thought, on gazing at pictures, than on feasting their reason"; the young man then encounters "a man that I thought looked devilish sour at me: this was the librarian, but I passed on, determined not to regard any thing or any body, and to pick up a little diplomatick knowledge, if I could, among such a host of politicians."[4]

Watterston advocated a national role for the Library, supported by the *National Intelligencer*, which stated in 1823 that Congress ought to open its Library "to every citizen who may wish to avail himself of the use of such treasures of wisdom as may be collected there for the public benefit." The *Intelligencer* acknowledged that enlarging the collection required expenditures but insisted that "if the nation felt interested in accumulating and maintaining such a monument of its literary taste, it would not begrudge the small appropriation necessary to render it a constantly increasing source of pleasure and profit" for "all our countrymen and even foreigners who pass through, or who occasionally reside in, the Metropolis."[5]

The New Library

On August 17, 1824, the 14,000-volume collection moved to new quarters in the center of the Capitol's West Front, which had been designed by Charles Bulfinch. The *Intelligencer* described the new Library as the most beautiful room in the building, and *The National Journal* called it "decidedly the most beautiful, and in the best taste of any in this country." The large room—90 feet long, 30 feet wide, and 35 feet high—featured twelve arched alcoves "ornamented with fluted pilasters, copied from the pillars in the celebrated Octagon Tower at Athens. . . . Its decorations are remarkably chaste and elegant, and the architecture of the whole displays a great deal of taste."[6] Frances Trollope, a visitor to Washington, described it as a "very handsome room, . . . elegantly furnished; rich Brussels carpet; library tables, with portfolios of engravings; abundance of sofas, and so on. The view from it is glorious, and it looks like the abode of luxury and taste."[7] The new room attracted not only Washington society but also requests to extend access, for example, to "distinguished men of letters":[8] Watterston called it "the resort of the literary, as well as the fashionable lounger."[9] While not open to the local citizenry—who by the 1820s could patronize the Georgetown Library, the Davis and Force Washington Circulating Library, and the Washington Library—the Congressional Library remained popular, both as a refuge for the members and for liberally admitting visitors.[10]

Perhaps in anticipation of the new quarters, the House Committee on Ways and Means, at the behest of Representative Joel Poinsett (R-SC, a member of the Joint Committee on the Library) had reported on February 24, 1824, that an inquiry revealed the collection was "defective in all the principal branches of literature" and proposed increasing the annual appropriation to $5,000. The main argument was the need for material on subjects important to Congress: law, politics, commerce, history, and geography. But the committee also endorsed acquiring English translations of foreign publications and acknowledged the need for more culturally and intellectually significant works and works intended for amusement. The bill passed; moreover, the report perhaps supplied the background for Dickerson to secure passage of a bill directing the Secretary of the Treasury to waive import duties for Library materials.[11] The members also approved a resolution directing that the portrait of Christopher Columbus, presented as a gift from C. G. Burrell, the US Consul in Malaga, "be placed in the library of Congress." The original text read "be placed in the national library."[12]

The handsome new surroundings advertised Congress's pride in the Library, and borrowers' ledgers show that use increased—recording, for example, President Monroe's interest in the writings of Polybius; Representative James K. Polk's (D-OH) request for Voltaire; and Representative James Buchanan's (D-PA), Chief Justice John Marshall's, and Justice Joseph Story's use of legal tomes. But "few were more original and none more picturesque," noted Superintendent Martin Roberts, "than that old frontiersman David Crockett" of Tennessee, whose borrower's record included Voltaire's autobiography and the works of Eugène Vidocq.[13]

Fire and Dismissal

The Capitol Building and the Library were almost destroyed when a fire broke out on December 22, 1825, caused by a candle left burning in one of the galleries. Fortunately, because that area housed mostly duplicate sets of public documents, the Library's losses were minor, but there was considerable physical damage. Firemen fighting the blaze were reinforced by several congressmen "who vied with one another in their exertions to save the library," among them Dickerson, Daniel Webster (Anti-Jacksonian, MA), and especially Edward Everett (Whig-MA), who was the first to notice the glow in a window of the Capitol at about 11 p.m. and called the guards to investigate.[14]

An inquiry was immediately launched, and Watterston, who was annoyed at a second request that specified a sworn statement, replied, "I feel a little hurt that the committee should think I would deliberately state any thing on an occasion like this, that I would not feel myself justified in swearing to." And "I regret that it is not in my power to designate the individual from whose inattention I conceive the fire to have originated on the night of 22d ult."[15] The committee reported that it could not identify the culprit, and its report was tabled; Congress considered methods of fireproofing the building but concluded that the expense was too great and decided simply to take more precautions with lighting.[16]

Just before the fire, Everett had become chairman of the Joint Committee. "An inveterate reader," he had edited the influential literary periodical the *North American Review*, and he served as a professor of Greek at Harvard University. He was an active chairman, pressing Watterston for information, compiling lists of acquisitions, visiting bookstores, and attending auctions.[17] His brother, Alexander Hill Everett, served as Minister to Spain during John Quincy Adams's administration, and it was perhaps through Alexander that Edward Everett contacted Obadiah Rich, the US consul in Valencia, a collector of books and manuscripts and later a London bookseller specializing in Americana. Rich sent Everett a list of available titles, and a diary entry of May 17, 1828, indicates that the Joint Committee agreed to $5,000 for the purchase, but it was never concluded. Neither did Everett's February 24, 1827, resolution to obtain from England copies of all documents relating to US history win congressional approval, but he did succeed in acquiring a rare file of *The London Gazette*.[18]

Everett directed Watterston to prepare lists of needed titles and to collect state laws and law reports. Congress had provided $1,000 for assembling such a collection as early as 1821, but progress was so slow that Everett reminded the Librarian of his duty, suggesting at the same time that he "make a little interest with the Senators for an appropriation bill."[19] There is no indication that Watterston complied. Instead, he complained that he was overworked and requested an assistant, saying "the increase of the Liby—the extent of the room—the constant demand for books renders the duties of librarian almost too arduous to be discharged by one individual." When Everett suggested removing worn volumes, Watterston countered that that "may be leaving too much to the taste & discretion of the Librarian to select such books as he may deem imperfect or defective from any cause, for the purpose of excluding them from the Library." He did show an interest in collecting literary works, once suggesting purchasing Charles Brockden Brown's and James Fenimore Cooper's books, and, on another occasion, translations of Spanish fiction. He also guarded his turf: when the Senate took over the Library's document room for committee work, he asked the Joint Committee for more space.[20]

But the 1825 fire seemed to leave him vulnerable, and in mid-1826 he poured out his grievances to Representative William Czar Bradley (R-VT):

> I believe, until last winter, no murmur of complaint was ever heard. But there are so many greedy & hungry expectants of office who flock to the seat of gov't, during the sess. or who at a distance, pester & harass the members for situations, that, upon the occurrence of the slightest accident, & indeed, where no cause exists, they rush forward open mouthed & in full cry to fill the vacant place by any means whether just or unjust or whether fitted for it or not.[21]

There were occasional complaints that the Library should be better kept: a British visitor, the novelist Frederick Marryat, for example, observed that "the books are certainly not very well treated."[22] And Watterston, seemingly unable to stay out of politics—or at least political journalism—in 1827, in addition to publishing *A Wanderer in Washington* (which included praise for Representative Henry Clay, the well-known Kentucky Democratic-Republican), Watterston began earning $500 annually for contributing to *The National Journal.* While Congress did approve hiring an assistant in 1828, the Librarian might have perceived a hint when that same year the Committee on Ways and Means failed to include his salary in the appropriation bill.[23] He was furious when, on May 28, 1829, he learned that the new President, Andrew Jackson, had appointed John Silva Meehan as Librarian.[24]

As Washington newspapers publicized his dismissal, Watterston's *National Journal* connection gave him a forum for answering the pro-Jackson *United States' Telegraph*'s allegation that his conduct toward library users was "crude and supercilious." He replied that if his manners were "supercilious, it was found necessary to assume them to get rid of such impertinent and vulgar intruders." To the charge that books were missing and the Library was "in confusion," he replied that because of "the free ingress of strangers of classes, it must be a matter of surprise that more books were not purloined than appear to have been." The *Journal* complained, "This is one of the most extraordinary removals as well as appointments which the weak and tyrannical heads of the present administration have yet made. We regard this act as a gross outrage on the rights of Congress and an open violation of law."[25] Congressman John Holmes (Adams Republican–ME) rose in the House to complain: "The President has invaded our dominions" by removing "an officer of the two Houses of Congress."[26] And Henry Clay called it "a step in keeping with the open despotism which now rules at Washington," and regretted "that friendship for me may have been one of the causes which led to the exercise of vengeance upon you."[27]

Charging that Meehan was unfit for the position, Watterston wrote the *Washington City Chronicle,* "Custom has rendered it necessary for the Librarian, when called upon by members, to furnish such information as they may require, and which may be obtained in the Library." Merely knowing how to locate books was not sufficient; the Librarian must be able to supply "facts, dates, passages, acts, official communications, and even lines of poetry. The Librarian, too, must have a knowledge of bibliography and be able to point out the best and rarest editions, as well as to furnish lists of books to the committee."[28] But a biographer observed that Watterston was no bookman;[29] and moreover, in President Jackson's opinion, government officials' duties "are, or at least admit of being made, so plain and simple that men of intelligence may readily qualify themselves for their performance."[30] When Watterston left, he took with him Library records and Jefferson's manuscript catalog, and he began a lengthy but futile campaign to regain his position.[31]

A New Librarian

In 1829, the Library held 16,000 volumes. Acquisitions were small, and coverage was uneven, but issues such as whether to buy current or retrospective titles and whether it might become a library of record for the United States or a universal collection were discussed from time to time. It served both as a library and as keeper of congressional documents; in 1828, President John Quincy Adams had signed a joint resolution directing the Library to distribute copies of documents to congressmen, state legislative libraries, and universities and colleges—and authorizing the disposal of materials that were no longer needed.[32]

The new Librarian, thirty-nine-year-old John Silva Meehan, was a printer by trade, and, for several months in 1826, the editor of the *United States' Telegraph*. Amid the controversy over his appointment, he remained silent. By all accounts a mild-mannered man who was careful about his official position, the new Librarian deferred to his congressional employers and pursued cordial relations with all parties.[33]

On January 13, 1830, President Jackson approved a joint resolution extending Library privileges to the secretaries of State, Treasury, War, and Navy; the Postmaster General; the Senate Secretary and the House Clerk; congressional chaplains; and ex-presidents (when in the District of Columbia).[34] Otherwise, existing policies remained in force; Meehan was asked, for example, to enforce the rule that Library visitors must be introduced by a member of Congress; and Joint Committee members retained the authority to purchase books during recesses "up to an amount not exceeding $50." The committee employed dealers to handle large orders, but there were few; acquisitions were generally confined to subjects of legislative interest plus the illustrated volumes and lighter reading that visitors enjoyed. Though some Joint Committee members—such as Everett, Levi Woodbury (D-NH), Gulian Verplanck (D-NY), and Dickerson—argued for a more active acquisitions policy and once, in 1835, stirred the committee to request an appropriation of $10,000, double the usual amount, Congress was not receptive.[35]

However, perhaps acknowledging a need for better management, the committee sent Librarian Meehan to tour libraries in Baltimore, Philadelphia, New York, West Point, and Boston in 1832. Meehan wrote that the visits were useful, but he apparently did not much alter his administration of the Library.[36] Over the years, Congress also approved more staff, and Meehan hired his son, Charles Henry Wharton Meehan, along with Edward Barnes Stelle, who had been removed with Watterston.[37]

Meehan's arrangement of the books followed the chapters of Jefferson's classification. But the Librarian favored neatness and fixed shelves; as a biographer noted, "he was a precise man, as he thought all librarians should be." Thus, within subjects, the books were shelved by size, so that the smallest (duodecimos) filled the upper shelves, with octavos and quartos below them; folios and larger volumes occupied the lowest shelves. The printed catalogs that appeared in 1830, 1840, 1849, and 1861 reflected this arrangement. As the catalogs grew during that period from 258 to 1,022 pages, the use of several alphabets within subjects became confusing, particularly with the appearance of annual supplements and the lack of author indexes to the 1849 and 1861 catalogs.[38] Nevertheless, perhaps reflecting congressional pride in the growing collection, an 1843 resolution approved distributing the catalog not only to authorized users but also to US colleges, universities, and historical societies.[39]

The Law Library

The most important change was a separate department for the law. In 1826, 1828, and 1830, Representative Charles Wickliffe (Jacksonian-KY) had introduced resolutions to place the Library's law books under the Supreme Court's supervision, but without success. Even earlier, in 1816 and 1817, there had been efforts to provide special appropriations for the law, and Robert Goodloe Harper's 1816 bill included creating a law library. The 1821 appropriation legislation provided for collecting statutes and reports of the state courts, as did Joint Committee resolutions of 1830 and 1832. But it was not until July 14, 1832, that President Jackson signed Senator William Marcy's (Jacksonian-NY) bill establishing a separate room for law books and empowered the Supreme Court Justices to make rules and regulations for the collection—provided that the rules not restrict access by Congress, the President, and the Vice President. The act included a $5,000 appropriation for books and $1,000 annually for five years thereafter and described the Law Library as "part of the Library of Congress"; the Librarian would purchase books selected by the Chief Justice. The staff accordingly transferred 2,011 books, including 639 of Jefferson's books. Appointed in 1833, the first law librarian, Wharton Meehan, had the title "Assistant in Law."[40]

While the law books remained part of the Library, with the collection formally tied to another branch of government, the Library was no longer serving only Congress.[41] Further, the Justices were authorized to grant access to "attorneys and counselors" and to extend borrowing privileges to members of the bar arguing cases before the Court, thus admitting users outside the federal government. In 1837, Congress appropriated another $5,000 for law books and directed the Chief Justice to furnish a separate catalog;[42] in 1842, the law collection was moved to the floor below the Library, near the Court's chamber; and it was moved again in 1860, this time into the Court's chamber after the Court moved to the old Senate chamber.[43]

Congress Refuses Expansion

Even as ambitions for a larger library appeared again in the mid-1830s, Congress refused to act. An anonymous article in the January 8, 1834, *National Intelligencer* called the annual $5,000 appropriation "hardly sufficient to obtain the new works of merit" and advocated building a comprehensive collection. Some newspapermen and literary critics called for enlarging the collection and for increased access, as one anonymous correspondent put it, for men "of letters and science."[44] In an 1836 address to the American Historical Society, Secretary of War Lewis Cass proposed expanding the Library "in *all* the departments of human learning, as will render it worthy of the age and country, and elevate it to an equality with those great repositories of knowledge which are among the proudest ornaments of modern Europe."[45]

Congress did not agree. On March 15, 1836, the Joint Committee recommended purchasing the 25,000-volume library of the "late Count Bourtoulin of Florence," which was rich in early Italian, Greek, and Latin works, manuscripts, and incunabula. Senator William Campbell Preston (Nullifier-SC), the chair and also a devoted book collector, noted that the collection was strong in literature, literary history, the fine arts, and French and Italian books, which the Library generally lacked, and he invoked Jefferson's statement that there was "no subject to which a member of Congress may not have occasion to refer." Senator Daniel Webster (Anti-Jacksonian-MA) emphasized that while the Count's library had cost him nearly $250,000, the price was much less—between $50,000 and $60,000. The Joint Committee's report noted the difficulty of predicting what books might be needed because of the many subjects brought before Congress, discussed the lack of American resources compared with European libraries, and reminded the members that books purchased volume by volume cost much more than purchasing entire collections. And although about half the volumes were in foreign languages, that "might not be an undue proportion when it was considered that not a fourth of the literature of the world was in our own language."[46]

Acquiring the Bourtoulin Library would double the collection and greatly enhance its value, and the *National Gazette* and the *North American Review* supported the purchase; the historian George W. Greene wrote in the *Review* that the collection would provide "the nucleus of a great library" that might grow to rival European collections and supersede American scholars' need for foreign libraries. The publisher Charles Bowen stated in *The American Almanac* that Congress should not stop short of a library that would "rival the greatest establishments of this kind in Europe." Their statements advertised American intellectuals' ambitions for the United States to develop its own learned institutions. But on June 4, 1836, the Senate voted 16–17 against the purchase.[47] On Henry Clay's motion, the resolution was tabled; the written record does not state why Congress refused the purchase.[48] Acquiring a collection full of foreign-language works and rarities apparently seemed unsuitable to many congressmen. And so "a singular opportunity was lost, an opportunity which might have advanced incalculably the intellectual resources of the Nation."[49]

Eight years later, not even the Joint Committee approved a suggestion to purchase the 10,000-volume library of the Durazzo family of Genoa, one of the most valuable

European private libraries. Representative George Perkins Marsh (Whig-VT) argued that the Durazzo library, mostly foreign-language works, was better suited to a private institution. Though he considered the Library's collection deficient, March opposed the purchase because he thought that the members would reject spending a large amount for any collection, no matter how excellent. He was right; when George Washington's library was sold, not even reverence for the first President prompted congressional action. Nonetheless, public-spirited citizens bought Washington's books for the Boston Athenaeum.[50]

Congress Pursues Exchanges

Congressional interest in adding to the Library's collection centered instead on government publications and exchanges. A June 1834 resolution provided that twenty-five copies of US government publications be provided to the Joint Committee, to be sent in return for donations to the Library; and in January 1837, the committee authorized Librarian Meehan to use Gales and Seaton's *State Papers* and other public documents for exchanges with the French government. A joint resolution authorizing exchanges for foreign government publications passed July 20, 1840, after congressmen met Alexandre Vattemare, a French ventriloquist and promoter who came to the United States in 1839 to tout his plan for international exchanges. The Joint Committee's report on Vattemare's proposal emphasized the importance of "as minute a knowledge as authentic records can furnish in regard to foreign governments," and it argued that exchanges would also exhibit "the new and great experiments we are making" in public affairs. Probably because the plan involved no expenditures and because it would be limited to official publications (and not the general exchange that Vattemare envisioned), it drew a favorable response. The resolution authorized the Librarian to exchange duplicates and federal documents, with fifty copies to be printed for exchange purposes.[51]

In early 1848, Vattemare again visited Washington, this time seeking to be recognized as Congress's official exchange agent; and on June 26, President James Polk approved an act authorizing the Joint Committee to appoint agents to establish exchanges, with duty-free admission of materials.[52] The committee appointed Vattemare as its agent, but limited the venture to public documents because "the great fields of literature, science, and art belong almost exclusively to private individuals and associations, and the governments of the states." However, dissatisfaction arose on both sides: Vattemare complained that the Library had failed to implement the provisions of the 1840 resolution; and Meehan told the Joint Committee that the Library had few duplicates and no room to store exchange publications, and he found the quality of the receipts disappointing.[53] Others—including Charles Coffin Jewett, Assistant Secretary and Librarian of the Smithsonian Institution—echoed Meehan's criticism, leading to the repeal of the 1840 act. The committee directed Meehan to inform Vattemare that his services were terminated.[54]

The members were again reminded of the need for the laws of the states and territories when, in 1839, Senator William Allen (D-Ohio) told his colleagues that though he could consult British parliamentary proceedings in the Library, the state legislative and executive journal files were quite incomplete. The members approved Allen's resolution requiring Librarian Meehan to prepare a catalog of state and territorial documents, and they later acted to complete the collection of congressional documents.[55] Collection lacunae also troubled Senator Preston, who in 1842 invited the historian George Bancroft to recommend purchases because "we have a very scant bibliographical store of knowledge on the committee."[56]

Yet the Library had not only grown but also changed over the years. Carl Ostrowski compared the catalog of 1839 (recording 30,000 volumes) with that of 1815, confirming that while the Joint Committee had mostly added books needed for public business, current events also influenced purchases. In 1839, books on geography constituted 15 percent of the collections, testifying both to the allure of travel and the importance of westward migration. History and politics accounted for 11 percent and 17 percent, respectively, and the law for 15 percent. But in history, titles in modern history had an 1839 ratio of seven to one, whereas in 1815 it had been three to one. Another area of growing interest was science and technology, which increased to 15 percent of the collection, reflecting the appearance of canals, railroads, and the steam engine. The fine arts changed little, remaining at just over 2 percent of the collection; but literature and religion lost ground: Jefferson's collection was 17 percent literature; but by 1839, poetry, drama, and fiction accounted for only 7.8 percent, while religion, at 4.7 percent, was somewhat less than in 1815. Nevertheless, the Library had acquired European and American authors in general, and in March 1840 Meehan was even authorized to purchase the works of certain authors without specific approval. Over the next decade, the shape of the collection would change relatively little.[57]

The Smithsonian, Secretary Henry, and Senator Pearce

On April 20, 1846, Senator Stephen A. Douglas (D-IL) introduced an amendment to the Smithsonian Institution bill to require copyright deposit.[58] The principal European nations had long since mandated that copies of publications produced domestically be sent to their national or academic libraries; and the US Constitution, article one, section eight, secured "for limited Times to Authors and Inventors the Exclusive Right to their respective Writings and Discoveries." The first federal copyright law (1790) specified that one copy of each book, map, or chart be registered with the clerks of the district courts, and an 1831 statute stipulated that copyrighted items be sent to the Department of State, but it lacked a penalty for failure to deposit.[59] Douglas's proposal specified the deposit of three copies of each "book, map, chart, musical composition, print, cut, or engraving": one at the Congressional Library, one at the Smithsonian Institution, and one at the State Department: the latter as the collection of record.[60] Interest in copyright deposit reflected authors' and scholars' calls to encourage American writers, and Edward Everett and George Ticknor linked the development of a national literature to the development of large library collections. Such prominent periodicals as the *North American Review* and *The American Almanac and Repository of Useful Knowledge* adopted their views.[61] But Douglas's amendment also lacked a penalty for failure to deposit, and it would be repealed in 1859.[62]

Douglas's initiative succeeded, even amid the members' disagreements over the Smithsonian's mission, a conflict that highlighted the role of the Joint Committee's chairman: Senator James Alfred Pearce (MD). Pearce, who became chair in December 1845, was a graduate of the College of New Jersey (now Princeton University) and a lawyer who entered the House as a Whig in 1835 but won election to the Senate in 1843, joining the Democratic Party after the Whigs' demise.[63]

Described as a "gentleman of the old school" by a contemporary, Pearce was a strong advocate of the Congressional Library: he maintained cordial relations with Meehan while making all decisions on Library matters himself. He took a conservative view of the Library's role.[64] At a time when public libraries were beginning to be established in the United States, free and open to the populace at large, he strictly guarded access to the Congressional Library.[65] But he was interested in learning and in science, and he might have agreed with Senator Asher Robbins (Whig-RI), who cited Smithson's intention to provide for the "increase and diffusion of knowledge among men" in suggesting that the Smithsonian Institution focus on science and literature. When Senator Rufus Choate (Whig-MA) proposed in 1845 that the Smithsonian house a national library, Pearce supported the idea.[66]

Choate's proposal may have influenced the decision not to purchase the Durazzo Library; on June 6, 1844, Senator Benjamin Tappan (D-OH), a Joint Committee member, introduced his first bill to establish the Smithsonian, and a day later Marsh filed his negative recommendation on the Durazzo purchase.[67] Tappan's two bills failed in the 28th Congress, but Choate had offered an amendment (January 8, 1845) specifying that $20,000 of the bequest income be directed for twenty-five years to purchasing books for a national library. Choate argued that establishing a library followed the spirit of Smithson's bequest: it would further the republican ambition to diffuse knowledge, it would be a visible national asset, and the United States deserved as rich an intellectual life as the Old World. He also suggested that "someone has said that a great library molds all minds into one republic. It might, in a sense of which he little dreamed, help to keep ours together."[68] Responding to a suggestion that the Congressional Library might serve the same function, Choate stated, "I answer that I think it already quite good and improving; but that its existence constitutes no sort of argument against the formation of such a one as I recommend. In the theory of it that library is collected merely to furnish Congress and the Government with the means of doing their official business."[69]

The House debate continued for a year and a half, pitting members with intellectual interests against supporters of more utilitarian projects. Representative Robert Dale Owen (D-IN) opposed the library because he considered it elitist and thus unsuitable for a republican state. He and Tappan favored agricultural education, a normal school, scientific experiments, and popular lectures and publications. John Quincy Adams (Whig-MA), Choate, and Marsh proposed a research institution that might include an observatory, library, museum, or art gallery: Marsh argued that the Smithsonian could satisfy both intellectual tastes and the needs of American citizens generally.[70] On

August 10, 1846, President James Polk signed the bill establishing the Smithsonian Institution, to be governed by a Board of Regents and a Secretary. The act included Douglas's provision for copyright deposit and specified using part of the funds for "the gradual formation of a library, composed of valuable works pertaining to all departments of human knowledge."[71]

But the Board's December 1846 selection of Princeton University physics professor Joseph Henry as Secretary signaled opposition. Henry's plans for the Smithsonian emphasized the pursuit of scientific research and publication of the results, a program he thought better fulfilled the provisions of Smithson's will. Established in 1849, his International Exchange Service used federal documents for exchanges that prioritized foreign science publications. Henry supported establishing a national library, but he opposed placing it in the Smithsonian, stating that the limited income could never suffice to meet the needs of American scholars.[72]

The Regents' Decision

The Board of Regents included both proponents and opponents of a Smithsonian library (Pearce, Choate, and Owen), and when the board decided to appoint an Assistant Secretary in January 1847, library supporters proposed Charles Coffin Jewett for the post. The compiler of the much-praised 1843 "Catalogue of the Brown University Library," Jewett was a leader in the nascent American library profession. Aware of Henry's opposition to a comprehensive collection, he proposed making the Smithsonian's library a bibliographical center by collecting other libraries' printed catalogs and combining the entries in an alphabetical file.[73]

The prospect of a major library at the Smithsonian generated enthusiasm in literary and publishing circles: the *North American Review* proclaimed that the Smithsonian provided "one of the most favorable opportunities that was ever offered in any country for the establishment of such a library"; and *Norton's Literary Gazette* hoped for "that great want of American scholarship, a National Library for reference and research."[74] And Jewett's 1849 annual report explained the need for a collection based on copyright deposit to "form a documentary history of American letters, science, and art"; it was essential that the collection be complete, for "who can tell what may be important in future centuries?"[75]

At a national conference of American librarians—the first—held in September 1853, Jewett was elected conference president; and his colleagues enthusiastically resolved that "in no way can the government better promote the progress of learning through the whole country than by placing a central national library under the administration of the Smithsonian Institution."[76] But Jewett's plan to create a national catalog by manufacturing stereotype plates of the catalog entries he collected—though endorsed by the Board of Regents on February 12, 1853, and accepted by the Joint Committee on March 3 for the Congressional Library—proved expensive, and the technology was flawed.[77] Certainly, it was not approved by Librarian Meehan, who called it "altogether visionary" and "useless as a Catalogue in the Library of Congress."[78] Continually at odds with Jewett, Henry dismissed him in July 1854.[79]

Senator Pearce reversed his position on a Smithsonian library, declaring that neither the increase nor diffusion of knowledge could be accomplished by a library that would simply gather in material; he went so far as to call the idea "palpably absurd" and "a preposterous use of terms." James Meacham (Whig-VT) disagreed, but his attempt to make the case—even quoting Pearce's original words of support—went unheeded. The board's Special Committee on Distribution of the Bequest Income voted six to one with Chairman Pearce, and the Regents later voted six to four affirming Secretary Henry's power to remove Jewett.[80] Charging that the Regents had ignored Congress's original judgment on use of the funds, ex-Senator Choate resigned from the board, which was a great shock to his colleagues. But the Senate Judiciary Committee's investigation also vindicated Henry, and its report even asserted that if funding was appropriated for an "immense library at Washington," it would be better to place it in the Congressional Library. A House inquiry ended with a divided verdict.[81]

Carl Ostrowski attributed Pearce's reversal in part to his friendship with Henry and their mutual dislike of Jewett. Pearce favored federal support for scientific exploration and publications and supported Henry's emphasis on research. He also perhaps noted, as Henry certainly did, that the provision for sending copyright deposits to both the Congressional Library and the Smithsonian brought in much material of little value but rapidly filled up space. And since Pearce thought that library collections should avoid partisanship and remained wary of acquiring material likely to inflame sectional differences, he might well mistrust Jewett's plan for a library of record where "those who in 1950 may consult this library would view a complete collection of all the works printed in America in 1850."[82]

Pearce's attitude paralleled the general caution about upsetting the precarious sectional balance: it was "a tacit rule of conduct" in 1850s Washington, like "the stillness at the eye of a hurricane."[83] *Uncle Tom's Cabin*, Harriet Beecher Stowe's exposé of slave life, appeared in 1852, following close on the Compromise of 1850 and the enactment of the Fugitive Slave Law, all contributing to abolitionist ferment and southern opposition. Stowe's publisher, John P. Jewett, was Charles Coffin Jewett's brother, and the book arrived as a copyright deposit, a potent symbol of the explosion of printed materials—cheap books, periodicals, and newspapers—that was reaching an expanding reading public and fueling debate. While national library proponents like Jewett welcomed the expansion of print culture, and Marsh argued that the country should have an institution where "the poorest and humblest aspirant may slake his thirst for knowledge, without money and without price," Pearce barred inflammatory literature.[84]

The controversy drew extensive comment. While the *North American Review* deplored the decision to abandon a Smithsonian library, the *Southern Literary Messenger* supported Henry; and *Norton's Literary Gazette*, though advocating a national collection, decided that Smithson's bequest could only "lay the foundation of the library that our country should have."[85] The debate revealed rifts between scientific knowledge and humanistic scholarship: the collection of knowledge for its own sake versus the utility of scientific discoveries, and the importance of intellectual resources for national advancement versus the financial realities.[86] But the Congressional Library did not figure in this debate; it suffered a catastrophic fire on December 24, 1851.

The Christmas Fire

Before the fire, the Library contained over 50,000 volumes, maps and charts, and works of art. It was among the four largest libraries in the country, according to Jewett's 1849 survey, adding about 1,000 volumes a year; it was open daily during congressional sessions and three days a week during recesses; and the list of approved borrowers grew steadily. For its users, the library was an increasingly valuable resource—so valuable that its loss was a great shock.[87]

The fire started, according to Architect of the Capitol Thomas Ustick Walter, when a chimney flue caught fire and the blaze spread to the timber walls.[88] Because it was a structural fault, Walter concluded, "no human thought or vigilance could, under the circumstances, have prevented the catastrophe." It was only "at length subdued" at about noon the next day—a challenge to extinguish since there was no municipal water system. The fire did not reach the Law Library, which consequently remains the Library's oldest continuously developed collection. But an estimated 35,000 volumes were destroyed. Nearly two-thirds of Jefferson's books perished, as did Gilbert Stuart's portraits of the first five Presidents and busts of Washington, Jefferson, and Lafayette.[89]

Informed of the fire before 8 a.m. on Christmas Day, Librarian Meehan hurried to the Capitol:

> I found the principal room of the Library on fire throughout, the flames having spread with great rapidity. . . . The loss is very severe. Many of the books are very rare, and it will be difficult if not impossible to replace them. . . . This being Christmas Even, those who feel merry are celebrating the occasion by firing guns, pistols, etc., and the steady noise shows that the merry host is very numerous. The perpetual jingling of numerous sleigh bells add greatly to the jolly celebration. I feel sad![90]

On December 26, the House of Representatives approved a joint resolution for an investigation (but only after changing the wording from "National Library" to "the Library of Congress"). Perhaps harking back to the criticism of Watterston, Meehan assured the members that no fires and no candles or lamps were ever permitted in the Library; and ultimately, despite some suspicions of arson, Walter's account seems to have been accepted.[91] Former House Clerk Benjamin Brown French, who also blamed a faulty chimney, concluded firmly, "No public building should be erected in these enlightened days which is not made fireproof."[92]

Meehan immediately advised Senator Pearce, who was out of town, of the disaster, and Pearce replied:

> I heard with absolute grief and dismay of the loss of our Library. . . . The destruction of so noble a collection any where would be a subject of much regret; but to lose our own valuable and admirable Library, of which you and I have thought so much, which has been so long our pride, and has yielded us so much pleasure, . . . which is so necessary to Congress and to me was more attractive than any political honors is really a deep affliction. I thought of you, and knew how distressing it would be. I rejoice that the mode of its origin is so well ascertained. Had that remained in mystery, there are many who would, however unreasonably, have censured you.[93]

Pearce returned on January 4, conferred immediately with Meehan about replacing the Library, and requested funding. On January 13 President Millard Fillmore approved appropriations of $5,000 for fighting the fire and $10,000 for replacing volumes. Much beset not only by offers of "old thrice-read books" but also by "hyenas (booksellers) that are now striving to prey on us in our own country," Meehan received a letter from Rich Brothers, the Joint Committee's London agent, offering assistance "at the lowest possible terms." He sent off a list of titles, explaining that "it was decided to commence operations, without delay, for restoring the Library to its great usefulness, and for extending it in every department of literature." He expected, he wrote, that the firm would live up to its previous standards of "promptness, accuracy, cheapness, and fidelity," and he was pleased when Rich promised a reduced commission of 5 percent and "almost exclusive attention" to the Library's needs.[94]

On January 27, Walter presented a plan for repairing and enlarging the Library. He estimated a cost of $72,500, stating that only incombustible materials would be used and that the library would "embrace the entire western projection" of the Capitol. He would "build the bookshelves of thick glass or enameled iron, frame the roof in wrought iron, and set the floor in stone." [95] President Franklin Pierce signed the bill on March 19.[96] Congress later appropriated an additional $75,000 for books, furniture, and other expenses and authorized the sale of damaged materials, with the proceeds to be spent for new books.[97]

Some thought that more should be done. An anonymous letter to the *Intelligencer*, perhaps written by Jewett, stated that the $10,000 appropriation was not nearly enough and that there had been no attempt to systematically list the Library's needs. If Congress had sent an agent abroad, the letter continued, it might have been possible to purchase some fine private European libraries. The new library, in the writer's view, "should be a systematic collection of books chosen with competent bibliographical learning for a specified and well defined purpose," so that it might become a truly national library.[98] Noting the letter, Meehan wrote Pearce that he doubted the proposal to hire an agent would find favor with Congress or that the members would admit they could not select their own books. Meehan and Pearce did not call for bids, as suggested by Joint Committee member Horace Mann (Whig-MA); Pearce seems to have ignored the committee's wish that literary men and scientists be consulted; and when Meehan listed needed titles, he relied chiefly on the Library's catalog and thus mainly sought replacements. With a total of $85,000 eventually available, the two men moved rapidly, but using the agents they had always employed; and critics complained that they simply responded to offers from eager booksellers rather than seeking expert advice. Gifts and offers poured in, keeping Meehan constantly busy, and he warned Rich Brothers that future orders would be more limited. In fact, the appropriation for books remained at $5,000 a year (plus $2,000 for law books) through the mid-1860s.[99]

The Iron Room

The new fireproof Congressional Library on the Capitol's West Front and adjacent to the Rotunda opened on August 23, 1853, none too soon for Meehan, who, working in crowded quarters, received ceaseless inquiries about "how the room would be fitted up and about the purchase of new books." He described the new Library as "the largest room made of iron in the world," and "truly beautiful," measuring 91 feet long, 34 feet wide, and 38 feet high. Galleries circled the room, large windows and skylights provided illumination, and the new furniture harmonized with the neutral color of the paneling and pilasters "tinged with pale green and burnished with gold leaf."[100] The Librarian found himself "very much pressed by visitors," including President Pierce, who was accompanied by the British geologist Sir Charles Lyell.[101]

Critics of the new room were few, though one, writing in the New York art journal *The Crayon*, complained that the old library had been "far pleasanter," with its artworks and arched recesses rather than the forbidding cast iron. When Meehan heard former Virginia congressman Henry Wise complain that the room was "all gammon, frippery, tinsel," he said he was glad to hear it because "if everyone liked it, something was surely wrong." Something was: The summer sun, shining on the iron ceiling, made the room miserably hot. The solution was to install a louvered door and paint the underside of the skylights to absorb the heat. "Please attend to it as soon as possible," Architect Walter pleaded, "as Mr. Meehan is being roasted alive."[102]

In the wake of the fire, the Joint Committee seemed ready to broaden the Library's acquisitions policy, naming Hector Bossange, a Paris book dealer, as the Library's first purchasing agent on the continent in 1854 and, three years later, designating Edward G. Allen of Covent Garden as London agent.[103] Yet, on January 28, 1857, President Pierce signed a congressional joint resolution that transferred international exchanges to the State Department and the distribution of public documents to the Department of the Interior, thus removing two responsibilities common in national libraries. The Library would instead receive just two copies of congressional documents, and the Joint Committee would direct the purchase of foreign publications.[104] Furthermore, in February 1859, at Secretary Henry's behest (and likely with Meehan's and Pearce's consent), President James Buchanan approved repeal of the copyright law that specified deposit at the Library and the Smithsonian; thereafter, single copies would be sent to the Patent Office for the official record but not for public use. The 12,000-volume State Department collection containing deposits received from 1790 to 1846 was also transferred.[105]

By the mid-1850s Meehan had a staff of five, and by early 1856 the collection returned to its former size with the purchase of 36,000 volumes. The Library, William Dawson Johnston wrote, "was a good reference library for the average legislator, though it was little more, and aimed to be little more." A new 1,400-page catalog would appear in 1861, covering the accessions through 1859. Still largely made up of books, the collection also contained maps and newspaper files. While some manuscripts had been acquired, and occasionally Congress had opportunities to add to that collection, such opportunities were usually refused.[106]

The divisive politics of the 1850s, perhaps thanks to Pearce, seemed to have little effect on the Library. Among the borrowers were Senator Jefferson Davis (D-MS), who wanted the works of the Romano-Jewish historian Josephus and Bishop Reginald Heber's sermons; Representative Alexander Stephens (D-GA), who borrowed Plato's *Republic* and de Tocqueville's *Democracy in America*; Secretary of State Daniel Webster, who requested The Delphin Latin Classics; and Chief Justice Roger Taney, who, in addition to Vattel's *Law of Nations*, needed J. F. W. Herschel's *Astronomy*. Senator Charles Sumner (R-MA) borrowed James Russell Lowell's poems and Bancroft's *History of the United States*—the latter volume also read by Representative Stephen Douglas.[107]

A New Librarian

None of the presidents who followed Jackson replaced Meehan. Nevertheless, the Librarian's association with Senator Pearce (a Democrat and Buchanan supporter) might have raised doubts for the new Republican administration. Or perhaps it was simply, as the future Librarian Ainsworth Rand Spofford later put it, that he was "a very ancient fossil."[108] In a March 1860 letter to the new President, Abraham Lincoln, that was endorsed by Joint Committee members Senators William Pitt Fessenden (R-ME) and Jacob Collamer (Opposition-VT), Pearce attested to the abilities and nonpartisanship of the Library's staff. He added that during his service on the Joint Committee, presidents had always deferred to congressional preferences regarding the staff. There is no record of a reply. When Lincoln appointed John G. Stephenson as Librarian on May 24, 1861, Meehan, characteristically, made no public comment.[109]

Most historians of the Library have characterized the antebellum period as a time of missed opportunities: years when an active acquisitions policy would have addressed the collecting goals of a national library. But as Johnston observed,

> Only a few members of the committee—only a few members of Congress—took a bibliographical interest in the Library—cared to see there the books which had interested their predecessors, would interest their successors, and were of interest to legislators in other lands. Few in or out of Congress, indeed, had dreamed the dream of a national library, and fewer had attempted to define the functions of a national library.[110]

Although, by 1850, Congress had many new members and the average age fell from fifty-one to forty-seven, the federal establishment was not the primary concern.[111] The issues of slavery and states' rights, the Mexican War, and westward expansion occupied members' attention. The Joint Committee turned to other work: it was given the tasks of publishing Lieutenant Charles Wilkes's exploring expedition reports and the papers of Thomas Jefferson, John Adams, James Madison, and Alexander Hamilton; establishing a greenhouse and botanical garden; and purchasing art works for the Capitol.[112] The committee sometimes ventured into new collecting areas, approving the purchase of works on Hungary and Germany, and Spanish and Mexican legal works. But its most important task under Pearce's leadership was to replace the library after the 1851 fire. The collection grew slowly, reaching 70,000 volumes by 1861; the Librarian's annual salary increased, first to $1,800 and then to $2,160.[113] Nevertheless, the congressional conception of the Library's role remained static. The Civil War years would bring to the Library a more ambitious Librarian.

CHAPTER 4

The Idea of a National Library

DR. JOHN GOULD STEPHENSON, of Terre Haute, Indiana, President Lincoln's appointee as Librarian of Congress, was an early supporter of the Republican Party and of Lincoln. The thirty-three-year-old physician "spent much more of his time practicing politics than medicine" and, with Lincoln's election, sought national office. Writing to the President on May 7, 1861, he proposed that a new Librarian, with the "energy of his administration of its affairs, he may bring credit to himself . . . and convince protesting Senators that they erred in their protest against a change in that office." Stephenson asked prominent Republicans for support, and fellow Hoosiers Senator Henry Smith Lane and Caleb B. Smith (who would become Secretary of the Interior) recommended him to the President. Lincoln appointed him on May 21, 1861.[1]

To Senator Pearce's dismay, Stephenson removed all the staff except Wharton Meehan, instead employing men recommended by congressmen and other administration officials. "The Librarian complains of disorder & neglect in the Library which I think he fancies. If there has been anything wrong it has been because the officers have been unable to compel members to return all the books they have taken out," Pearce wrote on September 25, 1861, to Senator William Pitt Fessenden (R-ME). Moreover, "he is disposed to take too much authority on hand in the purchase of books. He has no right to purchase any book without the order of the committee or chairman, which I learn he has sometimes done."[2] Stephenson, however, maintained that he was convinced of the staff's "incapacity for their several posts."[3] Nevertheless, after Pearce died on December 20, 1862, Stephenson paid him an eloquent tribute as the Library's "friend and guardian. . . . He has left his mark on the Library ineffaceably."[4]

One of Stephenson's first problems resulted from the hard-pressed accommodations of wartime Washington, which was overrun with soldiers, wagons, horses, and ordnance. War Department kitchens in the Capitol basement spread smoke and soot throughout the building, harming furniture and books, and the Librarian protested to Commissioner of Public Buildings B. B. French, and to Congress, but the ovens were only removed a year later.[5]

Among Stephenson's new staff members was Ainsworth Rand Spofford, who was a friend of Stephenson's brother, Reuben Henry Stephenson. Thirty-six-year-old Spofford—who was the Washington correspondent for the Cincinnati Republican newspaper, the *Daily Commercial*—was a Lincoln supporter and a bookman; as a former partner in the Cincinnati bookstore Truman & Spofford, he had the book trade expertise that Stephenson lacked.[6] Though initially hesitant, Spofford finally accepted a job with Stephenson, escaping the evening work of a correspondent for "the appeal of a 'congenial intellectual occupation'" and enjoying the "largely increased opportunities of acquaintance, especially with public men, editors, & scholars."[7]

First Assistant Librarian Spofford described the Library in an early letter:

> The Library of Congress is a collection of 72,000 vols. embracing all departments of literature & science, & is the only national Library at the Capitol. The public uses it precisely as the Astor in N.Y. & members of Congress & of the gov't only draw out books. The Librarian (who is appointed directly by the President) receives $2160 salary. There are three asst. Librarians, . . . a messenger, . . . and two laborers. . . . The Law Library (which is kept in the old Supreme Court Room) is under the charge of one of the asst. librarians—who has been many years in that department. The two remaining assistants—whose position is equal in every particular—have charge of the administration of the miscellaneous Library, under the general direction of the Librarian. . . . Now for the duties of the place. They are exceedingly light—consisting of attendance daily from 9 am to 4 or 5 during the sittings of Congress—& 9 to 3 in the vacations which are usually more than half the year. Under no circumstances is the Library open after dark—the room being iron-cased and fire-proof, without gas fixtures. The labor consists of becoming familiar with the contents & location of the various chapters into which books are arranged—supplying the calls of readers, occasionally aiding Members of Congress—writing an occasional letter—keeping a few simple a/c's & cataloguing the new purchases as they come in. All this divided among three persons—besides the Librarian & the porters. The annual increase in the collection is about 3,000 vols.—& Congress appropriates every year $5,000 & $2,000 for miscellaneous Books.

Spofford also noted that the Librarian "leaves pretty much all to my management, and I have actually been doing the work of both assistant Librarians ever since I have been here (6 months)—keeping the other assistants in the Catalogue."[8] In fact, Stephenson departed for an extended absence for military service on September 23, 1861, the day Spofford arrived—forcing (or allowing) the new Assistant Librarian to take charge.

The Wartime Library

Senator Pearce soon found that the Library had not only a knowledgeable but also an aggressive bookman: Spofford changed the orders for binding the new catalog without consulting him. Pearce challenged him on the matter, but Spofford justified the decision. Other congressmen, too, found Spofford's initiatives well grounded. He began to select books for the collection, mostly taking over that task from the Joint Committee, and when Senator Edwin D. Morgan (R-NY) questioned some purchases, Spofford firmly replied, "I bought 'The Lover's Dictionary'—lately published by Harper & Brothers, because it is the largest dictionary of quotations of poetry, alphabetically arranged, ever published, and as such, indispensable to answer the questions continually arising in every library as to the authorship of particular sentences. . . . The other work to which your inquiry extends, Dr. Miller's 'Abuses of the Sexual Function,' I bought because it is a new treatise, by an eminent physician, on a subject in which the Library of Congress has every important work issued in English and French."[9]

Finding the library in poor condition, Spofford blamed (by implication) Meehan, Pearce, and Congress. Ralph Waldo Emerson, who visited early in 1862, quoted the Assistant Librarian as saying that the Library had "been under Southern domination, and as under dead men," with an abundance of medical and theological works, while the modern literature collection remained meager.[10] The unsigned December 16, 1861, report titled *Annual Report of the Librarian* contains details—the lack of up-to-date reference works, incomplete newspaper files, missing volumes, and excessive duplication—that reveal his systematic collection analysis.[11] Spofford's knowledge of both the book trade and the contents of books quickly established him as an expert.

During the war years, the *Indianapolis Journal* ran several articles on Indiana inhabitants of the capital, and an 1863 piece described the Congressional Library:

> The Library contains now 82,875 volumes, exclusive of duplicates, public documents, and everything but those works which are usually meant in speaking of a library, and the Law Library contains over 18,000 volumes, arranged as conveniently as the confined quarters assigned them in the building will admit, in a number of small rooms and passages adjacent to the main hall, and in the main hall of the library. . . . Mr. Stephenson is working his way as rapidly as possible to complete a convenient arrangement of all the unplaced books, and a general re-arrangement and enlargement of the Library, and when he succeeds, as he surely will, there will be few better in the country.

The *Journal* also praised Spofford, "who knows the size, dress, appearance, and contents of more books than any twenty of the usual class of erudite men."[12]

"In the dark days of the Civil War," Superintendent Martin Roberts later wrote, "there were few visitors to the Library of Congress, and these were, for the most part, members of Congress; but the Librarian and his aides were actively engaged in supplying the numerous demands of public men." Citing Senator David Wilmot (R-PA, and author of the Wilmot Proviso), Secretary of State William H. Seward, Senator Andrew Johnson (D-TN), and Attorney General Edward Bates as examples, Roberts also noted that President Lincoln was a frequent borrower:

> The records indicate that he retained books only long enough to admit of careful reading, and then would return them in exchange for others. The only exception to this rule was in the case of Halleck's *Science of War*, which was delivered to him on January 7, 1862, and was not brought back until March 24, 1864. Those who have marveled at his knowledge of tactics would do well to examine this work. Volume by volume, he read Hume's *History of England*, and when this doubtless pleasurable task was completed, he turned to Bancroft's monumental *History of the United States*. It would be interesting to know what crises in the affairs of the Union lie behind the fact that thrice he consulted "US Constitutions, 1783" and "US Constitutions, 1856." Lincoln's love of poetry is well known. Longfellow's "Hiawatha" he twice requisitioned. The writings of Sir Walter Scott, his beloved Shakespeare, and Alfred Tennyson proved undoubtedly a source of pleasure for him.[13]

Librarian Stephenson did not remain long in his position. In September 1861, one of Spofford's last articles for the *Commercial* had noted the scarcity of army physicians and cited Stephenson's volunteer service at Washington's Patent Office Hospital. By 1863 Stephenson was a volunteer aide de camp with the Army of the Potomac, serving in the battles of Fitzhugh Crossing, Chancellorsville, and Gettysburg. On December 22, 1864, the Librarian submitted his resignation, effective December 31.[14]

Spofford obtained the support of Senator Jacob Collamer (R-VT), Pearce's successor as chairman of the Joint Committee, and solicited the members, posting a petition in the Library to collect signatures. He forwarded sixteen letters to the President on November 11, 1864, explaining that he had "no special (recent) political claims," because he had to "attend to the duties of my position the engrossment even of my leisure time." Eight more letters and the petition arrived by December 22, representing endorsements from twenty-two senators and eighty-seven representatives. Lincoln made the appointment on December 31.[15]

Spofford, Congress, and the National Library

John Y. Cole, who has written extensively about Spofford's administration, called his leadership both unprecedented and decisive:

> The transformation of the Library of Congress from a legislative library into an institution of national significance was, in large measure, the achievement of one individual: Ainsworth Rand Spofford, Librarian of Congress from 1864 to 1897. From the day he started work at the library, Spofford assumed that it *was* the national library, and he spent the rest of his life making that conviction a reality. In the process, he provided his successors at the Library of Congress with the beginnings of comprehensive Americana collections and the spacious building necessary for the development of a truly modern American national library.[16]

A principal organizer of the Literary Club of Cincinnati in 1849, Spofford met there several men whose acquaintance would prove important: Reuben Stephenson, librarian of the Young Men's Mercantile Library Association; Murat Halstead, later the editor of the *Commercial*; Representative James A. Garfield (R-OH); and Representative Rutherford B. Hayes (R-OH), who in 1865–67 would serve as chair of the Joint Committee on the Library. Thus, he began his Washington career well connected, and he remained so. A firm believer in the accumulation of knowledge for its own sake, the Librarian compiled multivolume sets, such as the *American Almanac and Treasury of Facts, Statistical, Financial, and Political* (12 volumes, 1878–89), and *The Library of Choice Literature* (10 volumes, 1888).[17]

Spofford's *A Book for All Readers: Designed as an Aid to the Collection, Use, and Preservation of Books, and the Formation of Public and Private Libraries*, summed up views that he developed early in his career. In a sidelight, the perpetually busy Librarian offered a method for dealing with "The bore": someone who "inflicts himself upon the ones whom he credits with knowing the most—the librarians." Spofford advised listening

> courteously, but keep on steadily at the work you are doing when he enters; . . . revise title-cards, or mark a catalogue, or collate a book, or look up a quotation, or write a letter. . . . Never lose your good humor, never say that your time is valuable, or that you are

> very busy; never hint at his going away; but never quit your work, answer questions cheerfully, and keep on, allowing nothing to take your eyes off your business. By and by he will take the hint, if not wholly pachydermatous, and go away of his own accord. By pursuing this course I have saved infinite time, and got rid of infinite bores, by one and the same process.[18]

Spofford's knowledge was soon legendary: "The extent of his miscellaneous reading was remarkable, but even more so was the retentiveness of his memory, both for facts and for the sources in which facts might be found."[19] When General Lew Wallace asked for help locating material for his novel, *Ben Hur*, the Librarian referred him to a volume in the Harvard University Library, complete with shelf number.[20] For several members of the Ohio delegation, he began selecting books for their personal libraries, purchased with their own funds but at the Library's discount; and senators John Sherman (R) and Salmon P. Chase (R), and representatives Garfield and Hayes generally supported Spofford's initiatives, including a request for franking privileges for the Library.[21]

Although the Library's claims to a national role drew little congressional interest, Spofford viewed it as a unique and independent institution: a comprehensive collection of the national literature.[22] His assertion that the Library of Congress was in fact the national library rested as well on its chronological existence as "almost co-eval with the existence of the government in permanent form," and he cited the acquisition of Jefferson's library as a crucial step toward establishing the Library's national character. An able politician and communicator, the Librarian repeatedly emphasized these points to Congress.[23]

When Spofford became Assistant Librarian, the Congressional Library was the fifth-largest in the country, behind the Harvard University Library, New York City's Astor Library, the Boston Public Library, the Boston Athenaeum, and the Yale University Library. Under his energetic leadership, it would surpass them all.[24] The 1861 report included eight appendixes that reveal his talents as an organizer: a statement of expenditures, a list of institutions and individuals that should receive the Library's new catalog, a list of publications needed for international exchanges, an analysis of book prices, a proposed set of rules and regulations, a status report on the US Exploring Expedition publication project administered by the Library, a list of urgently needed titles, and a list of essential US government publications. The concerns with official publications and outreach to other institutions and individuals represented steps toward assuming national library responsibilities. The next report (dated January 7, 1863), signed by Stephenson, but likely written by Spofford, noted that Spofford had visited New York, Boston, and Philadelphia book dealers and negotiated an average price of \$1.70 per volume—much less than the \$3.27 paid by the Joint Committee's agent since December 1, 1860. He also had decreased binding costs by 15 percent and, with the 79,214-volume collection increasing annually by 6,000 to 7,000 volumes, he requested more space.[25]

The report was circumspect in tone but clearly politic: Spofford presented the Library's needs as practical and relatively inexpensive initiatives to assist Congress, he appealed to congressional and national pride, and he unabashedly employed flattery.

But he never presented a definition of the term "national library" or a formal program for its development.[26]

Mainly through his efforts, in September 1864, the "Alphabetical Catalogue of the Library of Congress: Authors," the Library's first complete author catalog, appeared. The classified arrangement of earlier catalogs, the preface announced, was abandoned to ensure "facility of reference." And, further,

> all former general catalogues of the Library have been arranged upon a system of classification prepared by Thomas Jefferson, and based upon Lord Bacon's division of knowledge. This classification, however well adapted, in some respects, to a small library like that of Mr. Jefferson . . . is wholly unsuited to the necessities of readers consulting a large library. It was never designed by its author as a bibliographical system, but rather as a scientific arrangement of the various branches of human knowledge. No further illustration of its defects need be given than the fact that in the last catalogue of the Library of Congress the titles are distributed through a series of 179 distinct alphabets, arranged in an arbitrary sequence and without an index. Few readers have the leisure and fewer still the inclination to study the intricacies of such a system of classification. In abandoning it for a more simple method, the officers of the Library are assured that they have consulted the convenience as well as the wishes of Congress and of other frequenters of the Library.

Five years later, the two-volume "Catalogue of the Library of Congress: Index of Subjects" appeared.[27]

Space, Copyright, and the Smithsonian

Spofford's most pressing need was space. With 2,000 volumes awaiting new shelving, the Commissioner of Public Buildings and Grounds recommended expansion, and after consulting the Architect of the Capitol, Spofford requested a $160,000 appropriation. To Treasury Secretary William Pitt Fessenden, the Librarian pointed out that although it was a large sum, the new British Museum Reading Room had cost $500,000 and the Boston Public Library's building had cost $240,000; much essential material was almost inaccessible; and gifts and exchanges were rapidly expanding the collection. Moreover, the new funding would simply carry out a plan approved in 1852 but never implemented.[28] On March 2, 1865, President Lincoln signed the appropriation bill, which included $160,000 for two fireproof wings, each 95 feet long by 35 feet wide; during construction, Spofford was able to install steam heat—thus ridding the Library of the hot-air furnace that transmitted soot and warped books.[29]

Like Jewett, Spofford recognized copyright deposit as the optimum means of acquiring a comprehensive collection of American imprints, and he deplored Librarian Meehan's consent to the 1859 law that ended the deposits. An effort to alter the practice of sending deposits to the Interior Department failed in 1862 but was revived in 1865, when Spofford enlisted the support of the Joint Committee member Representative Thomas A. Jenckes (R-RI), chairman of the Committee on Patents. The resulting legislation, approved March 3, 1865, required copyright registration and two deposit copies of every book, pamphlet, map, chart, musical composition, print, engraving, and photograph published.[30] The law included a $25 penalty for failure to deposit; however, the Librarian would have to request items that did not arrive.[31]

Secretary Henry saw an opportunity. In his 1864 annual report (completed after a January 1865 fire damaged the Smithsonian building), he broached the idea of transferring the Smithsonian's nearly 40,000-volume collection to the Library of Congress, stipulating that it be "received and arranged as one of its departments, while the free use and general control of the same shall still be retained by the Institution." Henry hoped to be relieved of a collection that usurped funding that he wanted to spend on research (at the same time, he sent the Smithsonian's art collection to the Corcoran Gallery and its herbarium to the Department of Agriculture).[32] When the Smithsonian Regents consented, Spofford presented the proposal to the Joint Committee (chaired by Hayes) on February 21, 1866: he was keen to acquire the Smithsonian's important scientific materials, a collection that continually increased through its international exchange system.[33] "The union of the two libraries will prove doubly advantageous to those heretofore resorting to either," he wrote, "and will insure the rapid growth of a great and truly national library, with far greater economy of means than would attend the duplication, so to speak, of two large libraries at the seat of government of the United States."[34] On April 5, 1866, President Andrew Johnson signed the bill. It provided, as Henry stipulated, that the Smithsonian would have the same access to the collection as Congress, and "the public shall have access thereto for the purposes of consultation."[35]

With Henry's support, Spofford next proposed to the Joint Committee improvements in the exchange system, and given the long-standing congressional interest in foreign official documents, his proposal succeeded. A resolution of March 2, 1867, directed that fifty copies of each printed public document be provided for exchange, with the publications received added to the Library's collections; and Henry asked State Department representatives abroad to invite more foreign governments to establish exchange relations.[36] Eighteen governments accepted, and the Emperor of China sent more than 900 volumes. That gift inaugurated the Library's Chinese collection, and a similar 1875 invitation established the Japanese collection. Jointly funded by the Smithsonian and the Library, an agent traveled abroad in 1884–85, contacting fourteen governments and gathering 7,000 volumes; Spofford recommended an annual appropriation for such visits.[37]

Acquiring Collections

Also on March 2, 1867, President Johnson approved an act providing a $100,000 appropriation to purchase the library of Peter Force, a Washington printer, historian, and former mayor.[38] Force had assembled his library in part to document Colonial and Revolutionary America for his multivolume *American Archives* series (1837–53). With congressional authorization, the State Department had sponsored the series, but Secretary William L. Marcy withdrew support in 1855, and Force's heavy debts forced the sale of his collections. Consisting of about 150,000 items—including books, incunabula, pamphlets, newspapers, manuscripts, and maps—the library was well known among historians, archivists, and librarians.[39] Spofford was familiar with the collection, and in 1866 he asked the historian George Bancroft for an expert opinion on its value. Bancroft, calling the price "liberal" but not extravagant, urged the purchase, because "such a collection can never again be made."[40] In July 1866 Spofford recommended the purchase to the Joint Committee, which authorized an inventory.

Spending several hours daily with the collection, the Librarian described its strengths: printed books; American newspapers; 40,000 pamphlets (the Library had only 6,000); maps; incunabula; manuscripts and autographs (the Library had no autograph collections); and other early, rare, and unpublished materials. He wrote Bancroft again on January 12, 1867, urging him to contact the Joint Committee, and Bancroft wrote directly to the chairman, Senator John A. J. Creswell (R-MD), expressing his hope that Congress would approve the purchase. Representative Hayes, an enthusiastic supporter, also secured a favorable opinion from the collector and bibliographer Henry Stevens. On January 25, 1867, Spofford presented a petition from the State Historical Society of Wisconsin urging the purchase, and he reminded the committee that the collection "represents the nationality of the American people, it is plainly of the utmost consequence to render it complete in all that can illustrate our history and progress as a nation." Noting that the Library did not possess a single original manuscript of any Revolutionary general or statesman, he asserted cannily: "Congress may safely be asked to do once in a century what the British government does every year of its existence. It is not creditable to our national spirit to have to admit the fact—which nevertheless is true—that the largest and most complete collection of books relating to America in the world is that now gathered on the shelves of the British Museum." The Joint Committee unanimously recommended the purchase,[41] and with more testimonials arriving almost daily, Hayes approached Representative Thaddeus Stevens (R-PA), chair of the House Appropriations Committee, to request that funding be included in the current bill. By April 6, the collection arrived at the Capitol.[42]

The Force Library was the Library of Congress's first large research collection acquired since the acquisition of Jefferson's library.[43] In this case, the collection held particular appeal: the rare Americana and founding documents of the Republic obviously should reside with the federal government. The importance of acquiring early manuscripts, in particular, seemed to increase through the years: in 1875 Spofford requested funding for a curator for the manuscripts collection, a position that was not approved for another twenty years.[44]

The Librarian's 1867 report stated that the collections had doubled in two years due to the acquisition of the Smithsonian and Force collections plus copyright deposits. The 165,000-volume Congressional Library was suddenly the largest in the country. In 1865, Spofford had increased weekday hours, and four years later he asked the Joint Committee to install lighting to allow evening hours. "The government would perhaps find itself better and more intelligently served were this means of improvement and education made free to the clerks in its departments," he argued, adding, "the question becomes one of national significance, since this library is built up and sustained by the contributions of the American people."[45]

The Copyright Act

Yet the copyright deposits remained incomplete, despite Spofford's trips to New York, Philadelphia, and Boston to examine court records and his requests for records from the other district courts. By late 1868, the Librarian estimated a 75 percent receipt rate, well short of a comprehensive collection.[46]

Samuel S. Fisher, who was appointed Commissioner of Patents on April 26, 1869, found the patent deposit system unwieldy and, with Representative Jenckes, developed a bill proposing changes in the patent law. Spofford had a cordial relationship with Jenckes and also knew Fisher, who was also a member of the Cincinnati Literary Club. The Librarian proposed to the Joint Committee and to Fisher that the bill include a provision to centralize copyright registration and deposit at the Library. After they approved it, Spofford wrote Jenckes, emphasizing that centralization would promote compliance but also stating his ultimate goal: "We should have one comprehensive Library in the country, and that belonging to the nation, whose aim it should be to preserve the books which other libraries have not the room nor the means to procure." And, he continued, "when it is considered that the Library of Congress is freely open to the public throughout the year, and is rapidly becoming the great reference library of the country." Jenckes used Spofford's arguments in a floor speech, stating that more efficient administration would ensure better access to copyrighted materials. Meanwhile, Spofford sent publishers and editors a circular explaining the copyright provisions, which drew favorable comments. The bill passed, and President Ulysses S. Grant signed it into law on July 8, 1870.[47]

The act required depositing two copies of each copyrighted book, pamphlet, map, chart, photograph, print, engraving, and dramatic or musical composition. One copy would serve as the deposit copy, the other would be added to the Library's collections, and the Librarian would administer the registration process. Copyright records from the courts and the Patent Office's copyright collection of 23,070 volumes also would be transferred to the Library. Spofford called the law "by far the most important step forward in the annals of the Library," assuring the development of comprehensive collections and the inclusion of both print and nonprint materials. He declared that copyright deposit would both benefit the public and protect authors; that the Library, as a public institution, "had an irrefutable claim to the deposit copy intended for public use"; that deposit was the best method of amassing a comprehensive Americana collection; that such a collection would form the optimum basis for an American national library; and that comprehensiveness could be achieved only by strong enforcement. The 1870 law provided the Library the right to the nation's publishing output and a unique role in preserving "the complete product of the American mind."[48]

Consequences soon appeared: from over 11,000 deposits in 1870, copyright receipts swelled to nearly 20,000 in 1871. The deposits, plus the Smithsonian, Force, and Patent Office collections, plus regular acquisitions nearly filled the new rooms, which held about 210,000 volumes. Spofford first suggested either a separate building or an extension of the Capitol's West Front. By late 1872, however, with copyright business rapidly increasing, he asked Congress for a building.[49] In the meantime, the Librarian wrote, he presided over "the greatest chaos in America," fretting that "masses of books, pamphlets, newspapers, engravings, &c., in the course of collation, cataloguing, labeling, and stamping, in preparation for their proper location in the Library, are necessarily always under the eye and almost under the feet of members of Congress and other visitors."[50] Moreover, the constant activity violated "that rule of silence which should be the law of all great libraries of reference," and storing materials outside the iron room risked fire. Noting the addition of fifty members to the House of Representatives, he commented that Congress also needed more room: "The dilemma plainly before us will be that the legislature will crowd out the Library, with the alternative that the Library will crowd out the legislative body."[51] Having established the means of acquiring national library collections, he had to wait for the building that would symbolize that status.

Library Users and Librarians

The crowded conditions seemed to escape James Dabney McCabe, whose *Behind the Scenes in Washington* called the Library "one of the pleasantest places in the Capitol, and one of the most interesting." McCabe dwelled on the "treasures of the Force collection" and other rarities, mentioning as well "the illustrated works and collections of engravings, which always attract visitors, who can sit at the tables there provided for their accommodation and enjoy the reproductions of the choicest art treasures of the Old World." Moreover, with "liberal appropriations" from Congress, the Library

> is thus beginning to assume national proportions, and is rapidly gaining on the Government libraries at Paris and at London, while it is made more practically useful by the annual issue of a printed catalogue of its accessions. . . . Fifteen years ago not more than three out of five congressmen used the Library; now nine out of ten take out books, some having over a hundred volumes during a session. Nor can any one visit the Library at any time without finding from ten to fifty citizens at the reading-tables.[52]

As the Congressional Library grew, so too had the library profession. In 1876, librarians founded the American Library Association (ALA), and soon after, Melvil Dewey (Amherst College) and the publishers Frederick Leypoldt and Richard Rogers Bowker established the first professional periodical, *Library Journal.* But while Spofford joined the ALA as a charter member, he did not consider himself—or the Library—a leader, and he attended few meetings. He did contribute articles to the Bureau of Education's compilation, *Public Libraries in the United States*, including one titled "The Library of Congress, or National Library." But rather than allying the Library with the library community, he emphasized its independence: unique in its copyright and exchange functions and in its responsibility to build national collections. When in 1876 Melvil Dewey provocatively inquired, "Is it practicable for the Library of Congress to catalogue for the whole country?" Spofford's silence conveyed opposition.[53]

Congress Expands the Library

The copyright law seemed to encourage expanding the collections. Congress approved special purchases—for example, Andrew Boyd's 1,500 books and pamphlets on Abraham Lincoln's life and work (1873); subscriptions to two newspapers (reflecting differing political views) from each state (1874); the collection of the first US Minister to China, Caleb Cushing (1879); a collection of Benjamin Franklin's manuscripts, pamphlets, and books (1882); Supreme Court records from the estate of Senator Matthew H. Carpenter (R-WI) and the papers of the Comte de Rochambeau (1883); and copies of European archives related to the 1783 Paris Peace Treaty (1884).[54] Through Representative Abram S. Hewitt (D-NY), in 1884, the Library received 375 volumes from Sultan Abdul-Hamid II of Turkey, establishing its Turkish collection.[55]

The Library's lack of space never discouraged Spofford from welcoming gifts. He was eager to accept when a Washington physician, Joseph Meredith Toner, offered his private library of about 40,000 items, with the promise of further gifts. When the Librarian informed his Ohio friend, Joint Committee chairman Senator John Sherman (R), of the offer, Sherman was cautious. Spofford told Toner that while Sherman had agreed that the committee had the authority to receive donations, he suggested that legislation be passed to accept the gift, including provisions for further acquisitions and collection care.[56] Congress accepted Toner's books (including medical works, biographies, periodicals, portraits, early imprints, local history, and materials by and about George Washington) by joint resolution on May 16, 1882, and President Chester A. Arthur approved it three days later.[57] Though storage space could be found only in the crypt under the Capitol Rotunda, Spofford predicted that "this first example of the gift of a large private library to the nation will be an incentive to other similar donations or bequests."[58]

"So long as our country prospers and maintains its place among civilized and enlightened nations, its national library will grow under laws of accretion which it would scarce be possible, even were it desirable, to control," declared an 1875 House appropriations report.[59] Nine years later, the members refused to consider limiting the Library's growth because "the Government of the United States is too far committed by the legislation of Congress to the encouragement of literature and fine arts through a system of copyright; because any supposed limitation which should fix the wants of the national legislature for books and information by any arbitrary standard is fallacious and impossible; and because to arrest the progress of this great repository of learning (more than half of which has been gathered without expense to the taxpayers) would be a step backward."[60] In 1885, a visitor found the Library

> almost always full of readers, and on Saturdays the crowd is so great that many do their reading while standing. . . . During my visit I saw two judges of the Supreme Court, Harlan and Bradley, working away at one table, while Senator Hoar of Massachusetts sat at another, and between them a school boy was busy reading a story. In another corner George Ticknor Curtis, the biographer, was grinding away with a lot of historical books before him, and near by a young Washington lawyer was looking over the great bound files of *The*

> *National Intelligencer* of the year AD 1800. A cabinet minister's wife stood at the table in the center of the room, behind which Mr. Spofford gives out the books, and beside her was a plainly dressed girl, who looked as though she might make shirts for a living. A half-dozen librarians were rushing here and there carrying great armfuls of volumes, and the stout man in charge of the newspaper-room was bringing in file after file of heavy newspapers.[61]

Library use increased as the city grew. The presence of the Smithsonian and four higher education institutions, and the growth of the federal government's scientific establishment, built the capital's reputation as a center of learning and research. Founded in 1871, the Washington Philosophical Society attracted scientists and intellectuals, followed in 1878 by the Cosmos Club and six more learned societies by 1894. Simultaneously, local businesspeople and citizens urged infrastructure improvements, a campaign supported by President Grant, who once described the city as "disagreeable to pass through in Summer in consequence of the dust arising from unpaved streets, and almost impassable in the winter from the Mud."[62] In 1871, Congress approved a new governance structure for the District of Columbia, making it a federal territory, but three years later mandated oversight by a congressionally appointed commission. The board of public works, led by the real estate developer Alexander "Boss" Shepherd, began an expensive, often disruptive construction program that nevertheless turned Washington into a more functional city, with sewers, gas lines, water mains, straightened roads, sidewalks, and streetlights.[63] Simultaneously, Congress authorized construction of a building for the State, War, and Navy departments (1871); approved funding to complete the Washington Monument (1876); expanded the Government Printing Office (1872–79); funded construction of the Smithsonian's Arts and Industries Building (1879); and of the Pension Building (1882–87, now the National Building Museum).[64]

New Projects and Copyright Expansion

The members proposed new projects for the Library, from reprinting and indexing the papers of the Continental Congress and the Congress of the Confederation (1876) to the continued preparation of Force's *American Archives* (1887).[65] Meanwhile, Spofford planned an index to congressional documents and debates in 1874 but had to abandon it several years later. Work on a new book catalog bogged down in 1880, after the first two volumes appeared.[66] The Joint Committee in 1888 suggested establishing a department of manuscripts, and two years later it discussed the need for an index of public documents, though Spofford protested that he had no time to supervise its preparation.[67]

On March 3, 1891, President Benjamin Harrison signed legislation that provided US copyright protection for foreign authors and publishers and also required the Library to prepare a weekly catalog of copyright entries. Receipts of foreign works were not large.[68] Nevertheless, the Library's collections occupied sixteen different Capitol locations by 1892. A visitor that year found Spofford in the center of the room standing at his desk, and observed that "its overloaded condition . . . shows what a heavy pressure of work he must be under. . . . The condition of the room, as regards the piles of books, magazines, papers, etc. lying around in apparent disorder, was dreadful. The whole place is overcrowded and the clerical force seems entirely inadequate."[69] The Library had grown to well over 700,000 volumes, plus pamphlets, maps, music, prints, and photographs—mostly received through copyright deposit, since between 1865 and 1897 annual appropriations for purchases averaged only $9,000, and exchanges added only a small number of items.[70]

The growing collections brought wider recognition, especially among librarians, publishers, scholars, and writers. In particular, the maps, music, and graphic arts collections—including, by the early 1890s, Thomas Edison's motion pictures—were unique. George Bancroft wrote to compliment Spofford on the collections, Samuel Clemens sent a nephew to "burrow a little" in the "grand literary storehouse," and the Washington journalist Kate Field lent support to the Librarian's efforts to secure a new building.[71] On April 12, 1892, President Harrison signed a congressional joint resolution providing that the collections of government departments would be open to "the scientific investigators and to students of any institution of higher education now incorporated or hereafter to be incorporated under the laws of Congress or of the District of Columbia."[72] While Spofford was keen to expand Library use, he had not extended much beyond official Washington. This legislation was another step toward a national role.

As the copyright business grew, the Librarian pleaded for more staff, citing as examples the Boston Public Library, which "with half the number of books has eighty-nine assistants, and the British Museum Library, with twice as many books, but no copyright business, has 95 assistants."[73] Congress responded only grudgingly to these requests, he complained, despite the fact that copyright income exceeded the cost of staff salaries and registrations increased every year. By 1897 the Library had forty-two employees, but twenty-four worked full time on copyrights, and Spofford admitted that copyrights absorbed three-fourths of his own time.[74] Well before then, beginning in 1891, he had to report "serious delays" in issuing copyright certificates. In 1895 the Treasury Department opened an investigation of a $30,000 shortage in the copyright accounts, which exposed the Librarian's habit of tucking cash, checks, and money orders into the books rather than depositing them immediately.[75] Then, in August 1896, two Library employees stole manuscripts from the valuable Force collection materials kept in Spofford's office, including George Washington's 1787 diary. This theft went undiscovered until a New York dealer approached by the two became suspicious and contacted the Secret Service.[76] Spofford was exonerated of wrongdoing but was very embarrassed.

The Library Building

Presidential approval of the commission to select a plan and a site for the new Library building had come on March 3, 1873,[77] swiftly following Spofford's 1872 appeal:

> In every country where civilization has attained a high rank, there should be at least one great library, not only universal in range, but whose plan it should be to reverse the rule of the smaller and more select libraries, which is exclusiveness, for one of inclusiveness. Unless this is done, unless the minor literature and the failures of our authors are preserved, as

> well as the successes, American writers will be without the means of surveying the whole field trodden by their predecessors. . . . In every great nation this comprehensive library should be obviously the library of the government, which enjoys the benefit of the copy tax, and has thus supplied without cost a complete representation of the intellectual product of the country in every field of science and literature.[78]

Senator Timothy O. Howe (R-WI, chairman of the Joint Committee), Senator Justin S. Morrill (R-VT, chairman of the Committee on Public Buildings and Grounds), and Spofford were the commission members. The Librarian's specifications called for a fireproof building with a marble exterior; a circular interior reading room (patterned on the British Museum's Reading Room), with alcoves and book stacks radiating from the readers' desks; and separate areas for copyright, maps, fine arts, and periodicals, plus a "packing room" for "mechanical operations." The capacity would be 3 million volumes, and the height of the structure, he noted, must be limited "on account of the proximity of the projected building to the Capitol." Spofford predicted that by 1975 the Library would hold 2.5 million volumes. Actually, it would possess more than 17 million by that date.[79]

From the twenty-eight applications submitted, the commission awarded the $1,500 first prize to the design by the Washington firm Smithmeyer & Pelz. John L. Smithmeyer, who had come to the United States from Vienna as a young man, had suggested the idea of a competition to Spofford. Paul J. Pelz, a German immigrant, was an architect and construction engineer at the US Lighthouse Board. Their design apparently appealed because it blended harmoniously with the architecture of the Capitol.[80]

But as Congress weighed in, the result was a long postponement, even as Spofford annually renewed his pleas, lamenting that "books are now, from sheer force of necessity, being piled on the floor in all directions," and other materials were "stored away in inaccessible and constantly accumulating piles."[81] After considering European national libraries, Senator Howe decided that the winning design was too plain and small; he preferred a larger structure in Victorian Gothic. Other members made similar proposals or called for expanding the Capitol Building instead—the latter advocated by senators Roscoe Conkling (R-NY), Henry L. Dawes (R-MA), and George F. Edmunds (R-VT). Prominent architects and librarians also commented, most of them strongly recommending a separate building. Neither was there agreement on location; while Senator Morrill favored a site across from the Capitol's East Plaza, Senator Howe and the Joint Committee suggested building on the grounds of the Botanic Garden, and others favored a location at Judiciary Square.[82]

While Spofford appealed successively to presidents Hayes, Arthur, and eventually Grover Cleveland, and to the ALA to press Congress to act, between 1874 and 1886 Smithmeyer and Pelz prepared plans for buildings in various styles: Italian and French Renaissance for Capitol Hill, Modern Renaissance and Romanesque for a location southwest of the Capitol, and Gothic and German Renaissance for Judiciary Square—and other architects also submitted new designs.[83] Pleas from Spofford's supporters, Senators Morrill and Daniel Voorhees (D-IN), failed to secure an agreement.[84]

Finally, an act of June 8, 1880, established the Joint Select Committee on Additional Accommodations for the Library of Congress, consisting of Spofford, Morrill, and

Voorhees as chair. They called on three architects—Smithmeyer, Architect of the Capitol Edward Clark, and Alexander Rice Esty of Framingham and Boston—for advice on expanding the Capitol versus a separate building. Reporting that within a few years the entire Capitol would be needed to house the growing collections, the architects recommended a building, and all three were invited to submit new designs and consult with Spofford on interior arrangements.[85]

The ALA and Other Objections

At the ALA's February 1881 conference in Washington, Spofford announced that the committee had selected Smithmeyer and Pelz's exterior design, and a plan submitted by Esty, with Spofford's modifications, for the interior. The basic design of a rectangular exterior with a circular interior reading room was unchanged, but Smithmeyer reported that the building would also have exhibit halls: to omit public space from the national library would, he stated, "not only be antagonistic to our free institutions, but directly in discord with the spirit of the age."[86] Spofford had arranged the Washington meeting to obtain the ALA's endorsement, but the plan drew criticism from William Frederick Poole, director of the Chicago Public Library. Poole maintained that librarians, not architects, were the rightful designers of functional library buildings, and he called for separate departments rather than a lofty reading room and broad corridors. Having books apportioned among departments, he insisted, was far more practical for librarians and readers. Some of his colleagues—including Charles Ammi Cutter (Boston Athenaeum)—agreed, perhaps unaware that the architects based their designs on Spofford's plan for a monumental edifice—a building that would embody congressional visions of a national library.[87] The *American Architect and Building News*, however, acknowledged that the functional designs of other libraries were not appropriate for the national library.[88]

Spofford would not jeopardize his congressional support, nor would he allow the Library of Congress to be modeled on other libraries. He temporized, assuring his library colleagues that he would supervise the plans for the building and expressing general agreement with Poole. Meanwhile, the Joint Committee sent Smithmeyer on a European tour in October 1882, charged by Spofford to examine alcove and stack arrangements, ventilation systems, and facilities for readers at the British Museum and the national libraries in Paris, Berlin, Munich, Vienna, and Rome. Smithmeyer subsequently prepared a pamphlet, "Suggestions on Library Architecture, American and Foreign," which repudiated Poole's ideas, and at the 1882 ALA convention, Poole renewed his criticism of impractical architectural monuments. He succeeded both in influencing the ALA against Smithmeyer's design and in bringing his complaints to Voorhees. In response, Spofford informed the 1883 ALA convention that Smithmeyer's plan was provisional, but he also expressed disagreement with Poole. In fact, with unusual candor, the Librarian declared that he would not have the interior "of a library building of national importance dwarfed to the dimensions of a prolonged series of packing boxes."[89] This time, however, most librarians, and the *Library Journal*, endorsed Spofford's plans.[90]

Opposition came from other quarters. In October 1882, John Shaw Billings, librarian of the Surgeon-General's Library, wrote anonymously to the *Nation* to oppose Spofford's proposal that all federal libraries move into the national library building. A few months later, the Joint Committee considered consolidating the Army Medical Museum and Surgeon-General's Library with the Library of Congress, but it made no decision.[91] Meanwhile, someone proposed lifting the Capitol dome by 50 feet to accommodate the growing collections, raising more controversy until General Montgomery Meigs, the former engineer of the Capitol, called the plan unfeasible.[92] Criticism also came from Representative William Holman (D-IN), a fiscal conservative, who called the plans an "attempt to create a national library in imitation of European monarchies." Holman declared that if there was to be a new building, it should also house the Supreme Court.[93]

On April 15, 1886, President Cleveland signed the bill authorizing the Library building across from the Capitol's East Plaza, to be constructed by the firm of Smithmeyer and Pelz according to an 1885 plan that also included an interior design.[94] As Morrill's biographer told the story, when the bill passed, Voorhees, Morrill, and Spofford joyfully embraced on the Senate floor.[95]

But this still was not quite the end. On August 5, Spofford wrote of

> a hard day's work, and at times a hurried and anxious one. It grew out of this being the last day of Congress and the great importance to the Library Commission of getting through the $35,000 appropriation to make certain the immediate progress of the building. I was on the floor of the House three hours, and Secretary Lamar was there about two hours, watching its chances, removing objections, taking care of Holman, McMillan, Blount, and others—for a single member's objection would have killed it at any stage. . . . At last, after running the gauntlet for the better part of the session, a favorable moment was seized, and the bill got through by unanimous consent! Speaker Carlisle was favorable or it would not have got a chance. At once I hurried it back to the Senate to be enrolled—got the signatures of Sherman and Carlisle, and was made special messenger to carry the bill to the White House for the President's signature. This goal was reached at 3:10 p.m. and both Houses had resolved to adjourn *sine die* at 4. Mr. Cleveland was at lunch, but I sent the bill down to him by Mr. Pruden the Secretary, and it came back in fifteen minutes with Grover Cleveland's name "approved." This saved the day—and I am the happiest man in Washington—the last obstacle to the way of the Library Building being removed.[96]

Constructing the Building

With Smithmeyer appointed architect and Pelz assistant architect, the project finally began, with appropriations of $500,000 in 1888 and $6 million in 1889. But none of the work proceeded without controversy—there were arguments between Smithmeyer, Pelz, and the three-man commission charged to supervise site clearing and construction: Spofford, Clark, and Secretary of the Interior Lucius Q. C. Lamar (chairman). There were also congressional complaints about Smithmeyer's relations with contractors. "I really had hoped to see the building completed within my lifetime," said Senator Morrill, "but I fear now I shall never see it done."[97]

On February 16, 1888, the House appointed a five-member special investigating committee, and when Lamar became a Supreme Court Justice, the new Interior Secretary, William F. Vilas, replaced him.[98] Protesting the $7 million estimated cost, the House Appropriations Committee voted to suspend funding, but Vilas ultimately succeeded in defusing controversies over the quality of building materials, hiring practices, and costs. With doubts persisting about Smithmeyer's conduct, on October 2, 1888, Congress abolished the commission and placed General Thomas Lincoln Casey, chief of the US Army Corps of Engineers, in charge of the project, with Smithmeyer removed and compensated for his services and Pelz retained as architect. Casey, with the engineer Bernard Richardson Green as superintendent of construction, had completed the Washington Monument and the State, War, and Navy Building (now the Eisenhower Executive Office Building); he had a reputation for controlling costs, and he obtained tacit agreement from congressional supporters to provide funding and refrain from interfering.[99]

Casey produced two designs adapted from the Smithmeyer and Pelz plan: one for $4 million, as Congress requested; and one for $6 million. He predicted that the capacity of the first would be exceeded in thirteen years, but the second would serve for ninety; and as a builder of monumental structures, he preferred the larger. With strong advocacy from Library supporters and Spofford's detailed space allocations before them, Congress approved the larger plan; President Cleveland signed the appropriation bill on March 2, 1889; and, without ceremony, the cornerstone was laid at the northeast corner of the building on August 28, 1890.[100]

With construction under way, Green addressed Spofford's request for rapid book delivery: he designed the first efficient pneumatic tube and conveyor system in an American library. Built by the Snead and Company Iron Works of Louisville, the system sent books via tunnel to the Capitol in 10 minutes. It won a medal at the 1893 World's Columbian Exposition in Chicago and, as John Russell Young later wrote, "may be said to have exhausted the resources of engineering science." With Green's expertise also applied to ventilation, heating, and lighting, the building soon became known as a model of technological achievement.[101]

Casey replaced Pelz in 1892 with his son, Edward Pearce Casey, who prepared the plans for the interior, and the superstructure rose over First Street, SE, by 1894.[102] In consultation with Spofford and the American Sculpture Society committee that selected the 1893 Chicago Exposition sculptors, the Caseys planned elaborate interior decoration, including sculptures and murals executed by forty-two American artists. Including the three massive bronze doors (representing Tradition, Writing, and Printing) at the main entrance, the cost of decoration reached $364,000; the outdoor fountain depicting the Court of Neptune added $22,000, and the gold leaf on the dome, $3,800. It was a protracted process, for the artworks were not all completed until 1902, long after Casey had died on March 25, 1896.[103] Congress appointed Green to complete the building.[104]

The 1896 Hearings

On March 2, 1895, President Cleveland approved the Legislative, Executive, and Judicial Appropriations Act for 1896, which included an order to Spofford to make "a full report touching a complete reorganization of the Library of Congress, and whether a separation of the law library is desirable, in view of the completion of the new Library building."[105] Spofford's report arrived on December 3, essentially elaborating ideas he had expressed in 1872 and presenting his view of the Librarian's role: to act "as the custodian, the protector, the enlarger, and, to a considerable extent, the interpreter of the great collection confided to his charge." He recommended departments for copyrights, printed books, periodicals, manuscripts, maps and charts, music, works of art, cataloging, binding, and superintendent of buildings and grounds. He also proposed a new position, Register of Copyrights, separate from the Librarian's duties, and recommended that the Law Library remain in the Capitol since the Supreme Court met there. The Librarian also urged expanding the staff, again, with comparisons to the Boston Public Library (140 staff members, but only two-thirds as many books and no copyright responsibility) and the British Museum (220 staff).[106] On February 6, 1896, the Librarian presented to the House Appropriations Committee an 1897 budget request incorporating his recommendations, including ninety-seven staff, of which thirty-nine were for copyright administration.[107]

However, in May 1896, the Joint Committee on the Library received authorization for its own investigation "for the purpose of inquiring into the condition of the Library of Congress, and to report upon the same at the next session of Congress, with such recommendations as may be deemed advisable; also to report a plan for the organization, custody, and management of the new Library building and the Library of Congress."[108] The library community took note: in the August issue of *Library Journal,* Richard Rogers Bowker's article, "The American National Library," stated that "it is time to recognize, in name, the fact that the Library of Congress, so called, is now the library of the nation as well as of Congress; and as part of the plan of reorganization it should undoubtedly be designated as the National Library." At the September ALA conference, Bowker and other colleagues presented a resolution enabling the ALA president to name a committee to assist the inquiry, provided that Congress invited their participation. The ALA was not officially invited, but as a result of communications between Bowker and Representative Lemuel Quigg (R-NY), several librarians were invited to testify.[109]

The Joint Committee scheduled hearings between November 16 and December 7, 1896, with Spofford and Green as witnesses and guides for a tour of the new building. The other witnesses were Samuel Langley (Smithsonian Institution), W. T. Harris (US Commissioner of Education), ALA president William Howard Brett (Cleveland Public Library), George H. Baker (Columbia University Library), Melvil Dewey (New York State Library), William I. Fletcher (Amherst College Library), Rutherford B. Hayes (ALA Secretary, Ohio State Library Commissioner, and the son of the former president), Herbert Putnam (Boston Public Library), and Charles C. Soule (Trustee, Brookline, Massachusetts, Public Library). Putnam and Dewey presented the most detailed testimony. Without directly criticizing Spofford, they made it clear that the Library of Congress did not match the efficiency of other American libraries and that its chief executive should be an expert administrator. Dewey's view of the Library's role directly opposed Spofford's: he advocated for "a center to which the libraries of the whole country can turn for inspiration, guidance, and practical help, which can be rendered so economically and efficiently in no other possible way."[110]

Herbert Putnam agreed, and after the hearings, he wrote the committee:

> On one point in particular we were strongly in unison: . . . an endeavor should now be made to introduce into the Library the mechanical aids which will render the Library more independent of the physical limitations of any one man or set of men; in other words, that the time has come when Mr. Spofford's amazing knowledge of the Library shall be embodied in some form which shall be capable of rendering a service which Mr. Spofford as one man and mortal can not be expected to render.[111]

Spofford discussed the Library's operations and his recommendations. He wondered aloud whether "something in the nature of a joint commission of trustees, acting with the congressional committee . . . might tend to a closer and more constant supervision of this growing institution."[112] But Baker and Hayes suggested that the Library should be an independent federal department, while Dewey asserted that a "national educational department" should be established, uniting the Library, the Bureau of Education, and the National Museum.[113] Putnam urged that the national library should be "foremost as a model and example of assisting forward the work of scholarship in the United States," and Harris suggested employing experts to respond to congressional and researchers' requests, while Dewey pressed for a new classification, centralized cataloging and card distribution, interlibrary loans, and a national reference system.[114] The librarians also emphasized the need for a well-trained, professional staff, though Quigg responded that congressional employees were named by Congress, a tradition that the Joint Committee was likely to respect.[115]

Organizing the Library

After the Joint Committee's hearings, the Appropriations Committee asked Spofford and Green to appear, and also Representative Quigg. In debate on December 19, it became clear that the two committees were taking very different approaches to administering the Library: while the Appropriations Committee's bill gave the Librarian sole authority to establish rules and to hire and dismiss employees, the Joint Committee proposed to retain its control. A key issue was patronage, which the Joint Committee's plan reserved to its members. But Appropriations Committee member Senator Alexander M. Dockery (D-MO) insisted that it would be a "grave mistake" to approve "a scramble for 187 offices to be disposed of under the direction and control of the joint committee of the two Houses of Congress, to the detriment of public service." And he emphasized to his colleagues that "the time has come when the national library should be in charge of a management fully abreast of the progress of the times."[116] Continuing the pressure from the profession, *Library Journal* editorialized that "the future of the national library in its new home is really *the* library question of the year," and it did not spare criticism of Spofford; an unsigned article in the same issue called on Congress "to renounce the right, now 96 years old, which it holds in the Library of Congress" and to establish a board of regents similar to that of the Smithsonian Institution.[117]

The Legislative, Executive, and Judicial Appropriations Act for Fiscal 1898—which was approved February 19, 1897, and became effective July 1—directed the President to nominate a Librarian, subject to Senate confirmation; gave the Librarian the authority to establish rules and regulations; and increased the staff from 42 to 108. Library governance therefore passed from the Joint Committee to the Librarian, and Spofford's organization plan was incorporated, including the separate Register of Copyrights. The act directed the Librarian to select the staff "by reason of special aptitude for the work of the Library," thereby somewhat diminishing the influence of patronage, and it provided for a reference library in the Capitol, for reading rooms for the House and the Senate, and for the Superintendent of Building and Grounds with a separate staff. Bernard Green was named to that post.[118] The Joint Committee's March 3 report acknowledged that the committee would no longer govern the Library; its only recommendation was for funding to keep the Library open at night.[119]

With the building completed in February, nothing delayed the move except a congressional special session on tariff revision, called by the new President, William McKinley. When the old Library closed on July 31, moving had already begun on April 10, with the shift of the Toner Collection from storage. At the same time, Casey reported to Congress that the net cost of the building was $6,032,124.54, amounting to $200,000 less than the appropriation.[120]

In an address before the Literary Club, Spofford said,

> While I take no personal pride in it, I am delighted to have lived to see its completion and to enjoy its many utilities, freed from the grinding cares which so long vexed my weary soul amid the frightful congestion of the nation's books in the narrow and overcrowded Capitol building. The remove to that airy and spacious edifice was like being suddenly translated from purgatory into paradise. I call it the "book palace of the American people," in which you all have equal rights with me. It is our great national conservatory of books, in which the works of all of you will be welcomed and forever preserved.[121]

Just short of the turn of the century, the Congressional Library was transformed. Spofford's chief achievements, the copyright law and the new building, laid the foundation for developing massive collections and national services. His conviction that a national library was defined by comprehensive collections echoed Jefferson's expansive definition of his own library. Viewing the Library of Congress as both a legislative and a national library, Spofford established what John Cole called its enduring dual role.[122] At the same time, the congressional inquiries indicated that the institution's role would not be merely custodial: the growing Library required an executive experienced in administering a large institution and responsive to the needs of Congress, the federal establishment, other libraries, scholars, and the public.

In retaining its oversight of the Library, Congress rejected both an outside board of trustees and independent national library status. But, as David Mearns wrote, "The building was itself the expression of the Library's national character, . . . the unargued and unarguable recognition of the national responsibility."[123] Spofford moved the Library past its restricted nineteenth-century scope and forecast its future in the twentieth.

CHAPTER 5

Building Collections and Services

ON JUNE 30, 1897, the day before the new law took effect, President McKinley appointed (and the Senate confirmed that same day) the new Librarian of Congress: the fifty-six-year-old journalist and diplomat John Russell Young. At twenty-five, Young had become managing editor of Horace Greeley's *New York Tribune*; resigning because of political differences with Greeley, he next served as the *New York Herald*'s European representative. After President Grant left office, he invited Young, whom he met during the war, to accompany him on his world tour—a journey Young chronicled in *Around the World with General Grant*. President Chester Arthur appointed Young US ambassador to China; serving from 1882 to 1885, he resigned when Arthur left office and resumed his business and political connections in Philadelphia.[1]

With the election of President McKinley, also a friend, Young hoped for a diplomatic or cabinet post. Instead, McKinley nominated him for one of the few offices he had available: Librarian of Congress.[2] "I grieve by day and night that I am not in Peking," Young wrote nostalgically.[3] Nevertheless, according to his friend Henry Watterson, Young "had lived in the old library and loved it. He was both a man of business and a man of books, . . . a man of practical good sense and sympathy."[4]

Young quickly named Spofford Chief Assistant Librarian. And Spofford, then seventy-two, "cheerfully stepped down."[5] But he was no less busy, stationing himself in the midst of activity in the Reading Room. As he told the new Librarian, using the third person, "His life-long habit having been to be constantly and immediately accessible to inquiring readers, he has not deemed it proper to isolate himself, and has spent less than half an hour a day in his own room." Since this left little time for selecting books, he added, "I have been doing much of this work at home and on my way to and from the Library, because the interruptions to it are so constant." Besides perusing sales catalogs and assisting readers, Spofford cited myriad other duties, including answering correspondence, helping assistants find materials, and even checking newly bound books for labeling errors.[6]

With Spofford overseeing operations, Young's business, diplomatic, and political skills served him well as Librarian. He shared Spofford's convictions that the national library should contain a comprehensive collection of the nation's literature and that the purchase of Jefferson's collection established the Library as a research institution. And he stated in his second annual report that "there is no reason why the Library of Congress should not try to rival those noble establishments of the Old World." Viewing the

Library as first among federal libraries,[7] he requested a larger appropriation for 1899 to enhance its stature, but Congress allowed less than half the amount.[8]

As a biographer noted, "One of the most widely traveled men of his generation, Young showed that he was keenly aware of the need to internationalize the Library's collections, to supplement the Americana derived from gifts and copyright deposits." Early in 1898, he requested the State Department's assistance to gather research material abroad, and by the end of the year shipments arrived from eleven legations and seven consulates.[9] After the Spanish-American War, he sought Cuban and Puerto Rican materials, and he unsuccessfully advocated transferring historical manuscripts and presidential papers to the Library from the State Department. Young's 1898 report included appendixes describing the valuable Gardiner Greene Hubbard collection of fine prints and art books, the gift of Mrs. Hubbard; and the Chinese materials purchased from Caleb Cushing, the first US minister to China.[10] The report also chronicled the Library's relationship with the Smithsonian and the history of the purchase of Jefferson's books. Noting that a November 6 explosion in the Capitol had damaged over 1,000 books in the Law Library, with the complete loss of 200 volumes, the Librarian complained that the books were housed in unsafe quarters. He installed in the new building a law collection for the use of law students.[11]

The New Library and Its Staff

Young entered a library that had grown from 70,000 volumes in 1861 to nearly 800,000 in 1897, and from 7 employees to the newly authorized total of 108.[12] His first task was to oversee the move of 800 tons of material across the Capitol's East Plaza, using one-horse wagons hired at $2.50 per day.[13] On November 1, 1897, the building opened to the public, drawing ecstatic praise.[14] The first book requested, the Washington *Evening Star* reported, was *Roger Williams' Year Book*, "of so recent a date that it had not been received;" the second, Martha Lamb's *History of the City of New York*, duly arrived at the Reading Room's imposing circular desk.[15] Young stated that it would be the Library's policy to encourage "the spirit of inquiry"; besides delivering books, the staff would also provide "advice as to reading" and assistance for those who needed specific information. In fact, since much of the collection was not cataloged, assisting readers in the new building was as challenging as it had been in the Capitol.[16]

In addition to the Reading Room, the 1897 law specified separate departments for catalog, copyright, maps, music, manuscripts, periodicals, and art gallery. The Law Library and a congressional reference collection remained in the Capitol. Young directed the staff to acquire books and compile bibliographies on matters of current congressional interest; on November 8, 1897, he opened a reading room for the blind; and on October 1, 1898, he began providing evening service.[17] He also considered a children's service and a circulating department; but perhaps because, in June 1896, Congress had approved establishing a public library in the District of Columbia, neither of these materialized. Along with a request to add printing and binding facilities, the Librarian's 1897 and 1898 reports discussed the problems caused by publishers' use of nondurable paper, but his proposal to establish standards for book paper was not adopted.[18] And Young lost another battle, to the Women's Christian Temperance Union and the Anti-Saloon League, which protested serving wine and beer in the new building.[19]

The greatest challenge was to select new staff. The law directed the Librarian to hire persons with "special aptitude" for library work but did not specify formal training. That stipulation reflected, to some extent, the congressional desire for an excellent staff, and also the 1896 hearings, which featured strong arguments from the library community for a qualified staff. But while the law also specified that employees "shall be appointed solely with reference to their fitness for their particular duties," many congressmen remained eager to secure positions for constituents or friends. Republicans were especially annoyed that President Cleveland had increased civil service coverage from 42,000 to 87,000 positions, sharply decreasing patronage opportunities. Given the political situation, when Young urged the President to place the Library under the Civil Service, McKinley chose to temporize, leaving the Librarian to deal with congressional requests.[20]

Young did name specialists for key posts: Thorvald Solberg, a copyright expert, and James Christian Meinich Hanson (University of Wisconsin Library), for the catalog department. He retained David Hutcheson as Superintendent of the Reading Room and appointed Philip Lee Phillips as Superintendent of the Hall of Maps and Charts. Other specialists included Appleton Prentiss Clark Griffin (Boston Public Library) for the Reading Room, Arthur Kimball (State Librarian of New Hampshire) for the order process, and Dr. Herbert Friedenwald (editor of the *American Jewish Yearbook*) for the manuscripts collection.

While these appointments won praise, many lesser positions remained to be filled.[21] Nearly 3,000 applications arrived, and Hanson observed, "All were brimful of confidence that their great love of books and literary inclinations would enable them to solve all difficulties which might arise in connection with the management of a great library."[22] Although he asked Spofford, Solberg, and Hutcheson to examine the candidates to determine "special aptitude," Young required only modest qualifications—and indeed, at that time few federal positions required more than a secondary education.[23] In the end, he hired only three library school graduates, and only eleven other new staff members had library experience.[24]

There is some evidence that Blacks had reading privileges or joined the Library staff, at least from midcentury onward. George Washington Williams, the author of *History of the Negro Troops in the War of the Rebellion, 1861–1865*, for example, thanked Spofford in the book for making manuscripts available to him. Similarly, Eric Yellin noted that a young, Black government clerk, Swan Marshall Kendrick, habitually "read at the congressional library," and according to Brenda Mitchell-Powell, in the early to mid-twentieth century Blacks from nearby Alexandria, Virginia, used integrated DC Libraries, including the Congressional Library, since the Alexandria Public Library did not serve Blacks.[25]

Spofford continually sought well-qualified employees, although he always received requests from congressmen and other officials to hire their favorites. And he hired some Black employees and, just as significantly, promoted them.[26] The first Black employee recorded as a Library employee, John Francis Nicholas Wilkinson, was hired in 1857, before Spofford became Librarian, and he was assigned custodial duties such as dusting books. However, Spofford discovered that Wilkinson had an excellent memory for both books and people and promoted him to Assistant Librarian in the Law Library. Similarly, Daniel Alexander Payne Murray, who like Wilkinson later became prominent in Washington civic affairs, began work in 1871 and after several years advanced from messenger to Assistant Librarian.[27] Librarian Young also appointed some Black employees, among them the poet Paul Laurence Dunbar and Young's former household employee, Louis Alexander.[28]

With many women entering library work during the late nineteenth century, Spofford had hired the Library's first woman staff member, Bessie A. Dwyer, in 1893 and appointed several other women as well. Young increased the number of women to just over a quarter of the staff—though he later regretted hiring so many because organizing the collections in the new building was physically demanding. His appointments of women and Blacks were generally to the lower-paid positions: Dunbar, for example, worked as a deck attendant.[29] Probably on Spofford's recommendation, Murray was named Chief of the Periodical Division under the new 1896 organization, but Young soon reassigned him to lower-paying, nonsupervisory work, perhaps anticipating (or encountering) opposition to having a Black employee in a key position.[30]

Beset daily by applicants, Young wrote that "there never was a more perplexing problem," and "I cannot put a thousand pegs in a hundred holes." He worried especially about women applicants who had no source of support: while hearing "a hundred sad tales a day," he found that many "have every accomplishment but aptitude for library work."[31] Personnel records revealed that thirty or more of the new staff had filed congressional recommendations.[32] The *New York Evening Post* and *The Nation* criticized the appointments, while *Library Journal* (which had called out Young's appointment as political preferment) declared that the criticisms were probably justified.[33]

A New Librarian

Young was Librarian for just over eighteen months: his diary recorded increasing illness, and he died on January 17, 1899, the cause recorded as Bright's disease. A self-effacing man whose descriptions of events and personalities abound in his writing, his own thoughts usually went unrecorded.[34] He worked diligently to develop the Library and hired able division chiefs, even though he held patronage only partially at bay. "I am trying to build the library far into the future, to make it a true library of research," he wrote.[35] His direction was clear: the development of the collections and the institution on a large scale. "It should be our aim to broaden the Library, safeguard its integrity as a library of reference, and bring it home to the people as belonging to them—a part of their heritage—to make it American in the highest sense. . . . And, while accepting this as the chief end of the Library, it is no less incumbent to seek out and gather in the learning and piety of every age."[36]

Two days after Young's death, Solberg, Hanson, and Hutcheson contacted ALA president William Coolidge Lane (Harvard College Library) and other leaders in the profession. They hoped to secure the nomination of a professional librarian, though many applicants courted support. One was Samuel June Barrows, a lame-duck Republican congressman from Massachusetts endorsed by Navy Secretary John Davis Long and Massachusetts Republican senators George Frisbie Hoar and Henry Cabot Lodge. Another was Thomas G. Alvord, a journalist friend of Young's and the Library's chief clerk, who some at the Library, including Spofford and Solberg, distrusted.[37]

Aware that Melvil Dewey and Herbert Putnam had both refused the appointment in 1896, the librarians were hard pressed for a suitable candidate. When Barrows sought ALA endorsement, Lane told him that the association wanted a trained librarian, but if no professional candidate appeared, it would not oppose Barrows's nomination. Meanwhile, several newspapers and periodicals and also members of Congress, among them Speaker Thomas B. Reed (R-ME), called for a professional.[38]

Unknown to Lane, Dewey—who never hesitated to offer his opinion—had written President McKinley directly to recommend Herbert Putnam. When Richard R. Bowker and Lane met with the President on February 3, 1899, they thought that they might have to concede the nomination to Barrows—only to learn from the President of Dewey's letter. Declaring that he wanted a well-qualified Librarian, McKinley favored Putnam, mentioning that he had known his father, George Palmer Putnam, the founder of the Putnam Publishing House. When Lane named as Putnam's probable conditions a salary increase and a "free hand" in staff appointments and removals, McKinley agreed, authorizing him to offer the nomination to Putnam and to discuss a salary increase with Reed.[39]

Putnam, however, had previously told Barrows that he would refuse the appointment, and now decided he could not accept unless Barrows withdrew. Lane, Bowker, and Putnam's brothers—George Haven, Bishop, and Irving Putnam—pressed hard, but Herbert Putnam was adamant. When McKinley, left with no other choice, nominated Barrows on February 15, Lane appealed to Hoar and Lodge to block confirmation. The Joint Committee on the Library then reported adversely on the nomination; the Senate adjourned without acting; and Barrows, with no hope of confirmation, declined McKinley's offer of a recess appointment. Putnam then accepted and was sworn in on April 5, 1899.[40]

The appointment implied support for an enlarged role for the Library, along the lines of the librarians' 1896 testimony. The selection of the director of the nation's second largest library signaled respect for the profession. And it brought to Washington an experienced administrator who had testified to Congress that their Librarian should combine administrative talent with a bookman's knowledge.[41]

Putnam's Agenda

A graduate of Harvard and the Columbia University Law School, Putnam accepted his first administrative position in 1884 as librarian of the Minneapolis Athenaeum. When the Athenaeum and the Minneapolis Public Library merged in 1888, he became city librarian; but for family reasons, he returned to Boston in 1891 to practice law. In February 1895 he accepted the trustees' offer to become director of the Boston Public Library, one of the library community's most prestigious posts. His success was soon apparent both in Boston and nationally: he was invited to testify at the 1896 hearings, he joined Justin Winsor (Harvard University) and Melvil Dewey as an official delegate to the 1897 International Conference of Librarians in London, and when Winsor died in 1898, Putnam served the remainder of his term as ALA president.[42]

Slight in stature, Putnam was nevertheless an impressive presence, with a gracious but reserved manner. Although only thirty-seven years old, he had never held any but the director's position in each of the institutions he served, and in each one he shaped their future. Centering all decision-making and communications in his office, he closely supervised operations. Some found him aloof and insensitive. But Superintendent of the Reading Room William Warner Bishop observed that Putnam commanded diligence and loyalty: "You felt you were always being held up to the best that was in you." Music Division chief Oscar Sonneck called him "an administrative genius, a diplomat, and a man of culture," who supported "any colleague who had proven his worth." And Charles Harris Hastings, head of the card service, found that while the Librarian would not delegate responsibility except for routine operations, he did request and generally adopted his division chiefs' recommendations.[43] Archibald MacLeish, Putnam's successor, called his administration a "benevolent despotism," while praising his "remarkable creativeness" and declaring that "there have been few institutions of any kind in which the human relationships were warmer than in the Library of Congress under Herbert Putnam."[44]

Putnam established a private dining room in the Library's top floor restaurant, as a means of entertaining and "to enable me to catch the attention of men who may be important to me."[45] Soon dubbed "the Round Table," his luncheons became a Washington institution, drawing congressmen, senior officials, intellectuals, publishers, scientists, celebrities, and Library benefactors.[46] Waldo Gifford Leland, a college student on his first visit to Washington in 1903, recalled, "I was impressed to the point of being awed. From the great windows of the Round Table room, high at the top of the building, I looked across to the Capitol of the United States with the Washington Monument showing its tip over the House wing. Around me were persons of national distinction. Herbert Putnam, whom I still regard as the most perfect host in the United States, or for that matter in Europe, skillfully and imperceptibly guided the conversation to include at one time or another all those at the table, even including myself."[47] After the English writer H. G. Wells visited, he wrote, "I found at last a little group of men who could talk. It was like a small raft upon a limitless empty sea. I lunched with them at their Round Table and afterwards Mr. Putnam showed me the Rotunda, quite the most gracious reading-room the world possesses and explained the wonderful mechanical organization that brings almost every volume in that immense collection within a minute of one's hand. "With all this," I asked him, "why doesn't the place *think*? He seemed, discreetly, to consider it did."[48]

Fostering excellent relations with Congress and the federal establishment was a priority for Putnam, but also essential to his conception of the Library's role was forging links to every constituency that might be important to the Library of Congress. For that task, he enlisted his senior colleagues as well, sending them to professional meetings and to travel, both in the United States and abroad, to establish contacts and purchase materials. The Librarian insisted that "the personality to be considered significant is the personality of the institution itself, of which the personalities of the staff, including myself, are merely components. . . . For though I may attempt definitions of it, and from time to time secure resources for the freer realization of it, the actual development of it rests chiefly with you." While his assertion that the Library staff served "*abreast* of me" certainly was not the staff's perception, it was typical of the modesty he habitually expressed.[49]

Putnam and Congress

Sharing Spofford's and Young's conviction that the Library of Congress was the national library, Putnam parted from them by defining the Library's role as "developing its resources for service to scholarship and . . . extending the benefits of its collections and of its technical processes to the country at large."[50] Like Jewett, he had an ambition to lead the American library community. But while the Library's large Americana collections and the new building were major assets for building a national role, much more was needed. The collections were only partly in order; literally tons of periodicals, maps, manuscripts, music, and prints remained unsorted. The book collection was inadequately cataloged, the building lacked furniture and essential equipment, and much space was still unoccupied.[51]

Putnam began by disclosing the situation both publicly and to Congress—in particular, through his first testimony to the House Appropriations Committee. His tone was temperate, but he "described defects candidly, presented a long list of needs, compared the LC unfavorably with other institutions, and listed only the new building on the 'positive and assuring' side."[52] He requested a 60 percent budget increase overall, and he stated that the entire library needed to be reclassified and the cataloging arrears caught up. He wanted a $50,000 book budget and funds to establish a reading room for current newspapers and periodicals, a purchasing department, departments for exchanges and bibliography, and a reference room for the Smithsonian collection. He also wanted to hire ninety-six additional employees, triple the printing and binding budget, quadruple the allocation for contingent expenses, and purchase an automobile to replace the Library's horse-drawn wagon. He assured the members that his future requests would be modest, compared with the work to be done. "Congress is not to blame for the existing conditions in the Library," he declared. "So far as I know, Congress has never had before a fair statement of what was necessary. That statement is now possible and with that statement in its hands, I fully believe that Congress will do whatever is necessary for this Library." Congress passed the 1901 appropriation bill on April 17, 1900, giving the Librarian much of what he requested, including $50,000 for acquisitions. But Putnam, while pleased, insisted that the members had simply provided reasonable funding to meet important needs, and he intended to request again the items that were rejected.[53] "Knowing precisely what he intended to attain," David Mearns later observed, "he could present an appearance of infinite patience which belied his genius as an opportunist."[54]

A large budget increase for the Library accorded with the nation's expansionist mood, its growing economy, and its increasingly well-educated population. The country had recovered from the 1890s depression, the worst in its history, and, with the Spanish-American War, had become a world power. Tax receipts exceeded expenditures by between $44 million and $77 million during the first four years of the new century, and the federal government grew under the impetus of economic prosperity and increasing scientific, professional, educational, and scholarly activity. By 1900, American publishers had increased their annual output from 2,000 book titles in 1880 to over 6,000, and the number of periodicals and magazines climbed from 600 in 1860 to about 6,000. World's Fairs in Chicago (1893) and Saint Louis (1904) attracted huge crowds, and more than 1,000 public libraries served cities and towns of all sizes. In this climate and with a magnificent building that symbolized the American ambition to equal European cultural institutions, Putnam obtained the essential congressional support. By 1904, he had ninety-one staff in the Catalog Division, and the book budget neared his new target of $100,000.[55]

Putnam also wanted to establish the Library's responsibility for international library relations. His first opportunity came when President McKinley asked Ferdinand Peck, Commissioner General of the US Commission for the 1900 Paris Exposition, to include an exhibit on Blacks' achievements. Peck contacted Putnam, and, as a result, Daniel Murray was assigned to compile a bibliography. His *Preliminary List of Books and Pamphlets by Negro Authors for Paris Exposition and Library of Congress* included 270 titles, and with it Murray began a long quest to collect Black authors (a collection he eventually bequeathed to the Library). Another opportunity came when Putnam was named ALA president for 1903–4 and designated international relations as the theme for the annual conference. As a member of the ALA Council between 1900 and 1905 and chair of the International Relations Committee—a post he held well into the 1920s—the Librarian was well placed to develop foreign library contacts, representing not only the national library but also the profession.[56]

The Professional Staff

Putnam developed a new application form that detailed applicants' qualifications, and like Young, he established a probationary period for new staff. He received requests from senators and representatives for appointments, but taking the advice of several friendly congressmen and federal bureau chiefs, he informed sponsors that positions were available only for those he found capable. Members who called on him were apt to be treated to long explanations of the technical nature of the work before they could present their candidates.

Putnam dealt with the pressure from the members rather than try to place the Library under the Civil Service because Civil Service examinations did not evaluate the technical knowledge or other qualifications that he wanted. He insisted that library schools provided essential technical expertise: he wanted as many graduates as possible for cataloging and classification. For administrative positions, such as Chief Clerk and Register of Copyrights, he sought candidates with a knowledge of business practices; and for specialized work with manuscripts, music, prints, and government documents, he wanted scholars and experts. The salaries he could pay were only just above the average for entering library professionals, but the imposing new building, the rapidly growing collections, and the possibility of eventual promotion proved attractive. Applications always far exceeded the number of openings.[57]

However, like Young, Putnam considered women unsuited for many positions, and he employed fewer women than the proportion of women in the profession. In Putnam's Library of Congress, women rarely served in top leadership positions, and when they did, it was usually only on an "acting" basis.[58]

By 1905, the Librarian could describe "a force somewhat carefully developed, . . . and the division of now 90 positions which deals with the work most technical—that is classification and cataloging—represents, I believe a group as highly expert as is maintained by any library."[59] With Putnam's additions, the staff became a younger group, with more women. What was most important, however, were their credentials. Under Young, most of the staff members had only a primary or secondary education, but Putnam required at least partial secondary school for even junior positions. For those more senior, he required two years of college: among the staff members paid professional-level salaries of $720 and above, most had attended college and some had postgraduate training. Half the staff had knowledge of at least one foreign language, and those hired for the most technical positions included two-thirds library school graduates and one-third experienced librarians. In just a few years, the Library of Congress had a staff that made it a center of professional expertise.[60]

Cataloging, Classification, and Cards

Chief among the Librarian's concerns were the cataloging and classification systems, which were already being transformed when he arrived. Catalog Division chief J. C. M. Hanson and Head Classifier Charles Martel, with Librarian Young's approval, began developing a new classification system. They had completed Class Z (bibliography) and begun Classes E and F (American national and local history) when Putnam became Librarian. Convinced that the Library's cataloging could wield national influence, Putnam considered adopting either the Dewey Decimal Classification or Charles Ammi Cutter's Expansive Classification, two of the most popular systems in American libraries. But Melvil Dewey, while enthusiastic about the Library using his classification, balked at allowing the LC to adapt it. By late 1900, Hanson and Martel (who both opposed using Dewey) had convinced Putnam that their new system would best serve the Library's needs, and reclassification began in January 1901.[61]

Martel established the outline for the Library of Congress Classification, and staff experts developed the detailed schedules for each subject. Its basis was essentially practical: the classification was developed from the collection itself rather than following theories of the organization of knowledge, and it could readily be expanded. Small libraries would not need all the detail of the LC schedules, while more specialized libraries might find them not detailed enough. Nevertheless, by 1906 several federal libraries and one state library had decided to adopt the LC's classification and began requesting advice and copies of the schedules. By 1920, with most schedules completed, the five largest academic libraries—Chicago, Columbia, Cornell, Harvard, and Yale—had adopted the

LC system for all or parts of their collections, and other libraries followed over the years. By the mid-1970s, most of the largest American libraries used the LC system for all or parts of their collections.[62]

In May 1898 Hanson had begun replacing the Library's handwritten catalog with a catalog of printed cards.[63] He reviewed other libraries' cataloging methods, and, "where some general agreement was discernible," he noted, "this naturally influenced decisions. The possible future relations of the Library of Congress to other libraries of America were freely discussed and constantly kept in mind."[64] Rejecting European national libraries' brief-entry tradition, he specified detailed bibliographic descriptions, verification of authors' names, and subject and added entries, which, with the detailed classification, required expert catalogers.[65]

After the 1896 hearings, Putnam had stated his hope that the Library could print its catalog entries on cards and sell them to American libraries.[66] When he became Librarian, he began assessing the prospects for a card service, and at his request the Government Printing Office installed a branch in the Library's basement in the fall of 1900.[67] Putnam traveled during the summer of 1901 to assess librarians' preferences for a card service.[68] Meanwhile, in late 1900 the ALA had appointed the Advisory Committee on Cataloging Rules, chaired by Hanson and charged to formulate a catalog code, drawing in part on Cutter's *Rules for a Dictionary Catalog*, the ALA's *Condensed Rules for an Author and Title Catalog*, and Dewey's *Library School Rules.* Continually besieged by librarians who wanted their favorite practices included, Hanson worked with his committee and the Catalog Division's staff to develop the rules. Joined midway by the Library Association of Great Britain, the seven-year effort produced an Anglo-American code. The new code aligned with the Library's cataloging practices, and it established the LC's leadership in the field.[69]

Putnam addressed the July 1901 ALA conference on "What May Be Done for Libraries by the Nation," declaring, "If there is any way in which our National Library may 'reach out' from Washington it should reach out." He had surveyed librarians' preferences for card style and size and compiled statistics on annual acquisitions. "Having them we are in a position really to estimate the chances," he stated. "Summarily it appears that our cards might effect a great saving to certain libraries and some saving to others."[70] The Library's October 28, 1901, announcement listed a price of 2 cents for the first copy of each card, with additional copies for 0.5 cents. The sale price would cover costs plus 10 percent, a formula developed by the Librarian and the Public Printer. In addition, Richard R. Bowker promised up to $1,000 to cover any first-year deficit and support from his journal, *Publishers Weekly*, for "any feature of the general plan in which I can be of use."[71]

Uniting the nation's largest library with the national professional association to meet the profession's needs was a major innovation. No national library had ever provided such a service, but while Putnam reminded librarians that the cards first had to meet the LC's own requirements, it was also clear that previous efforts to establish centralized cataloging had failed because no other institution or commercial service could fulfill that role. It was soon apparent that Library of Congress cards would influence American libraries' practices; in turn, the card service influenced the LC's acquisitions and cataloging priorities because of the need to include the books most libraries were buying and to ensure timely order fulfillment.[72]

Putnam named Catalog Division Assistant Charles Harris Hastings to head the new Card Section and develop a service for which there was no precedent. Creative and seemingly tireless, Hastings not only sold cards but also sent sample cards on request, answered inquiries, and provided free materials to library schools. The staff also sent large libraries card galley proofs for selection—a service that publishers appreciated as free advertising. New book listings that included card numbers began to appear in book trade publications such as *Publishers Weekly*, enabling librarians to order books and cards at the same time. An ever-growing number of libraries received and filed a depository copy of each card, forming catalogs that allowed users to find information on books not available locally. And federal librarians (and beginning in 1910, other libraries as well) were invited to send the LC their own cataloging copy for printing and receive free cards in return. Nearly as soon as it began, the card service supplied many of librarians' cataloging needs—at a time when Andrew Carnegie's philanthropy was building 2,500 new libraries. Putnam asserted, "The possible utilities are so great; they suggest so obvious, so concrete a return to the people of the United States for the money expended in the maintenance of the Library; and the service which they involve is so obviously an appropriate service for the National Library of the United States that I communicate the project, . . . as the most significant of our undertakings of this first year of the new century."[73]

The National Library

Putnam declared his ambitions for the Library early:

> It is the National Library of the United States. It is thus a bureau of information for the entire country; and as to America for the entire world, for of all American libraries it will sustain the most active and intimate relations with libraries abroad; and through the Smithsonian with all learned societies abroad. It will maintain a corps of highly trained experts who will make known its resources and will aid in research. It will undoubtedly become the most active center of research, for the largest area, of any library in America. It will not merely draw students to Washington; it will by correspondence stimulate research all over the United States.[74]

Putnam would establish the Library of Congress as a provider of services rather than merely a storehouse for books.[75] While his vision would not be fully realized for many years, the 1896 hearings produced many suggestions for developing the Library's role: offering reference and bibliographic services, building a union catalog, distributing public documents, facilitating exchanges, and providing interlibrary loans.[76]

In 1900 the means of locating libraries' holdings were undeveloped, a situation that would only gradually be somewhat remedied by union catalogs and union lists. And interlibrary loan—defined as obtaining a book not held by a reader's local library—was not provided by all libraries; the New York Public Library and the Newberry Library in Chicago, for example, did not participate. European national libraries did not offer interlibrary lending. But Putnam had an interlibrary loan service in Boston, and at least one federal library, the Surgeon General's Library, provided it. A possible stumbling block was that the Joint Committee on the Library had interpreted the statutes as prohibiting LC materials from leaving Washington. But members of Congress themselves sometimes found that judgment inconvenient, and a March 3, 1901, law opened federal "facilities for study and research" to "scientific investigators and duly qualified individuals."[77]

Putnam and his colleagues developed a lending policy: based on the principle that the federal government should provide only those services that local authorities could not, the LC would loan only materials needed for serious research, only materials not otherwise available, and only materials not needed in Washington. Also, since the US Comptroller had ruled that the postal frank could not be used for sending materials, borrowing libraries would need to pay postage costs.[78]

The request for the Library to offer reference and bibliographic assistance was likewise a priority for Putnam, though such services would be provided foremost to Congress. Again, he defined the services by the federal role: the Library would undertake tasks that state and local governments could not. He proposed, for example, that state libraries develop collections of state and local materials: the LC would not extensively collect local materials but would provide bibliographic and location services.[79]

The card and interlibrary loan services promoted interdependence among libraries. Librarians tailored their services and collections to their own clientele, but they also became facilitators, tapping the resources of other libraries, either for individuals who needed materials or information or to support their own institutions. The LC became the central resource for cataloging and cards; for interlibrary loans, the profession developed protocols for borrowing and lending. Cooperative programs in cataloging and resource sharing gained momentum in the American library community throughout the twentieth century and, in the latter decades, increased with the advent of computing and digital communications technologies.

Putnam's Report and the President

In 1901, Putnam issued the *Annual Report of the Librarian of Congress*, a 380-page volume that described the Library's history, organization, facilities, collections, and the technical processes that he and the staff had developed, with high standards set for every area.[80] The report revealed that the book collection surpassed 1 million volumes, the first American library to reach this total. But Putnam was more intent on other goals: "The two reports which I have submitted prior to this have had to deal particularly with the needs to be supplied," he wrote. "It is a satisfaction that the present one can exhibit substantial progress made." With work "far advanced," and with a specialized organization "needing only to be expanded," he declared that the Library "is now in a position to determine what the service shall be—to Congress, to the executive departments and scientific bureaus of the Federal Government, to other libraries, and to scholarship at large." When Congress provided the requested funding on September 14, 1902, he opened the Library on Sundays from 2 to 10 p.m. Soon after, he announced it would be open on every holiday except July 4 and Christmas Day.[81]

Putnam also asked President Theodore Roosevelt to endorse the Library's national role:

> The Library of Congress began as a merely legislative library. While at the Capitol it could be little more than this. The entire force consisted of but 42 persons, including the 24 engaged in the copyright work. The new building, the new provision of space, equipment, and expert service denote a purpose to elevate the Library into one national in scope and service. The Library is already familiarly entitled the "National Library of the United States." If it is not such, there is none other which is.
>
> A national library for the United States should mean in some respects much more than a national library in any other country hitherto meant. The public library in its modern form began in the United States fifty years ago. It is receiving a development here not paralleled elsewhere, in the activity of its service for the general public and also for scholars. There are over 5,000 public libraries in the United States to-day. . . . In the aggregate they represent a great educational interest distinct from the schools; and the movement which has resulted in their creation, development, and enrichment is the most characteristic movement in education during the past half century.
>
> Now as a whole, these libraries in the United States are organizing their work with reference to uniformity in methods, to cooperation in processes, to interchange of service, and in general, to the promotion of efficiency in service. They look to the National Library for standards, for example, for leadership, in all these enterprises. It is now in position to 'standardize' library methods, to promote cooperation, to aid in the elimination of wasteful duplication, to promote interchange of bibliographic service. And not merely by the accumulation and liberal administration of a great collection at Washington, but by the distribution of the results of the bibliographic work which it is putting upon that collection it will be able to perform a service of the greatest utility to the library interests of the United States and to American scholarship. The past two and a half years have been in part a preparation for such a service.
>
> Considering the above: What this Library now already represents in the way of an investment; what it seems to purpose on the part of the federal government towards this great system of education, what its opportunities are as the culminating effort in a library system covering the entire country: considering also the enthusiastic public approval of the building provided for it, the enthusiastic expectation which the library interests of the country cherish for the service which it may do—has not the time come for some reference to it in a statement which includes a summary by the Chief Executive of the notable executive activities of the government?
>
> The Library is now to initiate some of those projects of service for which the past four years have prepared. In these it will make return to the country for the recent great expenditure upon it. A mention now would call notice to the service and promote it; would reassure as to the propriety of the expenditures already made, and would ensure against diminution of it to the injury of the larger service proposed.[82]

Roosevelt, who borrowed books by the hundreds, agreed.[83] In his first annual message (December 3, 1901), he called the public library movement "the most characteristic educational movement of the last fifty years," and cited librarians' efforts "to give greater efficiency to the material they hold, to make it more widely useful, and by avoidance of unnecessary duplication in process to reduce the cost of its administration." The President endorsed national support for libraries and declared that the Library of Congress would become "not merely a center of research but the chief factor in great co-operative efforts for the diffusion of knowledge and the advancement of learning."[84]

Putnam's statement perhaps directed the President's attention also to the so-called Executive Mansion Collection. According to legend, when President and Mrs. Millard Fillmore arrived at the White House in 1850, they found a Bible but little other reading material. Fillmore, who had his own impressive library, appealed to his friend Senator Pearce, as chairman of the Joint Committee on the Library, for funding for books. An appropriation of $2,000 resulted, with another $250 in 1851. While, during the Hayes administration, Spofford exchanged some materials with the White House, the next notable development was Roosevelt's 1903 request to bring the White House collection up to date. That inaugurated what became known as the White House Library Deposit, which eventually grew to several hundred volumes, though it never served all the needs of the chief executives (e.g., Woodrow Wilson personally called Reading Room Superintendent William Warner Bishop to request ten detective stories a week).[85]

Building the Collections

The 1870 copyright law ensured the acquisition of copyrighted works; from the Smithsonian Deposit came a growing collection of learned society, academic, government, and scientific publications; and from the Public Printer came government documents to exchange with foreign governments and institutions. But until the end of the nineteenth century, the Library "did not really enter the field as a purchaser."[86] The collections lacked, for example, state and municipal documents, foreign works, noncopyrighted publications, and other materials that appropriations were too small to cover.[87]

While Putnam, Young, and Spofford all spoke of building comprehensive collections—as Spofford phrased it, "the learning of all lands,"[88] and as Putnam had it, "universal in scope"[89]—the existence of other federal library collections promoted interdependence. The Library usually did not acquire specialized medical titles because the Surgeon General's Library collected those materials. Similarly, the Department of Agriculture Library and the Geological Survey developed significant collections in the sciences.[90] In 1908, Putnam counted twenty-six federal collections that, he observed, had grown up without reference to each other. Quoting William Dawson Johnston (who had left the LC to direct the Bureau of Education's library), Putnam stated that the national library consisted of "that group of libraries maintained by the National Government, of which the Library of Congress is the center," and he suggested that the department libraries limit their collections to their specializations, transfer less relevant materials to the LC, and adopt, insofar as possible, the LC's cataloging rules and classification.[91] While emphasizing the mutual benefits, he clearly intended that the Library of Congress would assume leadership.

Building comprehensive collections was important to American scholars, who usually had to travel to do research. University libraries in 1900 did not and could not match the collections available abroad, despite the ongoing expansion of higher education, the adoption of the continental model of graduate training, and increasing institutional interest in research. Scholars and librarians were well aware of the needs, but they also recognized that no single institution could satisfy their demands. Increasingly, they viewed the nation's library collections, small or large, specialized or general, as interdependent—as resources to be tied together to serve researchers.[92] The Library of Congress's increasing appropriations seemed to present the opportunity to promote American intellectual leadership through federal support. Putnam shared this vision. While attentive to the customary mandate for a national library to assemble the literary and cultural output of the nation, he also concentrated on foreign materials, regardless of time or place. He argued for both comprehensive collecting and for employing experts to systematically build the collections.

Collections and Services

Staff specialists continued both expanding the collections and providing services. The new Division of Bibliography, headed by A. P. C. Griffin, handled the more complicated research inquiries, prepared lists of references, edited LC publications, and entered cooperative ventures. Its staff assisted indexing projects such as *A Union List of Periodicals, Transactions, and Allied Publications Received in the Principal Libraries of the District of Columbia* (1901), while the Catalog Division supported Melvil Dewey's project to produce a new edition of the *ALA Catalog* (1904), a list of books recommended for public libraries (which would include LC card numbers), and a new reference work, the *ALA Portrait Index* (1906).[93]

The Law Library, which already possessed a large collection of American law and British statutes and reports, increased efforts to acquire foreign legislation and historical jurisprudence. The Division of Manuscripts received the Library's first donation of presidential papers when the Francis P. Blair family provided its Andrew Jackson materials in 1903, and the first collection direct from a president, with Theodore Roosevelt's 1917 gift. Other notable additions were J. Pierpont Morgan's collection of letters and documents of the signers of the Declaration of Independence (1912) and the original and second drafts of the Gettysburg Address from the family of Lincoln's private secretary, John Hay (1916).[94] In 1903, after congressional approval of the transfer of historical materials from federal agencies to the Library, President Roosevelt's executive order transferred manuscripts from the State Department—including the records of the Continental Congress; the Federal Convention of 1787; and the papers of Washington, Jefferson, Hamilton, Madison, Monroe, and Franklin.[95]

In considering which materials were appropriate for the collections, Putnam decided against housing federal agencies' records, supporting instead what became a long-term effort to establish the National Archives.[96] But he pursued "the raw material of our colonial history"; in 1906, the LC acquired Benjamin Franklin Stevens's 180-volume *Catalogue-Index of Manuscripts in the Archives of England, France, Holland, and Spain Relating to America, 1763–1783*, with transcriptions of selected documents. Resulting from Stevens's decades-long use of European archives, the compilation provided

American scholars with a means of identifying documentation existing abroad. And after consulting the Carnegie Institution of Washington and the American Historical Association, which were both already active in the field, Putnam employed the Stevens firm to copy manuscripts relating to America, beginning in England with the Public Record Office, the British Museum, and the Bodleian Library at Oxford. The copying project proceeded for many years, extended to French and Spanish archives by 1914, and later to other countries in cooperation with Carnegie's Department of Historical Research, which carried out archival surveys, country by country.[97]

Copyright deposits had built a large music collection, but much of it consisted of popular compositions. Searching for a specialist who appreciated American musical achievement, Putnam had the good fortune to encounter the European-trained Oscar Sonneck, one of the first musicologists in the United States. As Music Division chief, Sonneck concentrated on developing a comprehensive collection of American music, assembling post-1700 European composers' scores in the original or copies and acquiring the entire range of music literature. He declared that

> the ideal should be to place at the disposal of the American student a collection so symmetrical and extensive as to dispense him of the necessity of going abroad whatever his line of investigation may be. This ideal is probably beyond reach, but we may approach it by planfully taking steps in the right direction, . . . [because] no self-respecting-library can afford to be without certain cultural documents, whether they be consulted frequently or seldom. . . . After all, it is not the frequency of use that counts, but the use to which a book is put.

Sonneck's vision of an eventually comprehensive collection accorded with Putnam's—and contributed to establishing musicology as a discipline in the United States.[98]

The Documents Division developed the political science, political economy, and statistics collections as well as broadening the exchange system. Recognizing the need for more active acquisition of government publications, Congress doubled the number of federal documents allocated for exchange to 100, and Putnam hired as Chief Roland Post Falkner, an economist and statistician. With the assistance of State Department representatives abroad, receipts increased, and in 1910 the division began publishing the *Monthly Checklist of State Publications*.[99]

In the Division of Prints, directed by Arthur Jeffrey Parsons, the growing copyright collection of photographs, etchings, engravings, lithographs, and chromolithographs also included the first motion pictures.[100] The division also received important gifts: Mrs. Gardiner Greene Hubbard provided an endowment (1912) for additions to the Hubbard Collection; and in 1917, Mr. and Mrs. Joseph Pennell, the biographers of James McNeill Whistler, presented their collection of Whistleriana; Pennell, himself a noted illustrator, later provided an endowment of over $300,000.[101] Phillip Lee Phillips, chief of the Division of Maps and Charts, built on the growing collection of copyright materials and increased the geography book collection, while Allen B. Slauson directed the Periodicals Division staff to expand the newspaper files and the holdings of periodicals and journals. With significant growth in the book and newspaper collections in particular, space filled rapidly, prompting the construction of new stacks that by 1910 filled the southeast courtyard with forty-four miles of shelving for 946,000 books and 94,000 newspaper volumes.[102]

The staff directed some acquisitions efforts to retrospective collecting: securing important materials that were not acquired when first published. Proceeding volume by volume, they worked to fill gaps, and they occasionally seized opportunities to acquire entire collections through deposits, gifts, or purchases. Gifts were acknowledged, with the permission of the Attorney General (1907), as "to the United States of America, to be placed in the Library of Congress." The valuable John Boyd Thacher Collections came through deposits by Mrs. Thacher: the 840 fifteenth-century imprints and the American exploration and discovery materials after Thacher—an Albany, New York, businessman, politician, and collector—died in 1909; his autograph collection in 1915; and his French Revolution collection in 1921. Reviewers of Frederick W. Ashley's *Catalogue of the John Boyd Thacher Collection of Incunabula* (three volumes, 1915–31) noted the exceptional breadth of examples of early printers and the importance of the catalog for scholarship.[103] Other collections included the 5,000-volume Huitfeldt-Kaas Collection of Scandinavian history (1908), Albert Schatz's opera librettos and music manuscripts (1908 and 1911), and the historian Henry Harrisse's maps, manuscripts, and rare books, centering on the discovery and exploration of America (1915). Putnam perpetually sought potential donors, sent senior colleagues on acquisitions trips, and made at least eight European journeys himself.[104]

Copyright receipts and congressional interest in current foreign and domestic issues broadened the collections. Murray's Colored Author Collection and his subsequent private collecting activities had a counterpart: a concentration on women in public life. In 1903 Spofford acquired the papers of his friend Susan B. Anthony, including also papers of her partner in the women's rights movement, Elizabeth Cady Stanton. It was the beginning of what would become one of the most comprehensive collections relating to women's experiences. Gradually, papers of other suffragists—for example, Carrie Chapman Catt (1947) and the Blackwell family (1960), and of organizations such as the National American Woman Suffrage Association (1961) and its successor, the League of Women Voters (1933)—entered the Manuscripts Division, along with those of women in all walks of life: Margaret Sanger (1942), Clare Booth Luce (1956), Shirley Jackson (1967), Patricia Roberts Harris (1985), and Sandra Day O'Connor (1990).

Nonwestern Collections

While the Library's acquisitions had historically focused on the cultural record of Western civilization, nonwestern materials increasingly entered the collections. The first Chinese materials came through the Emperor's gift of 934 volumes (1869), and subsequently from the Chinese and Manchu collections of Caleb Cushing and the Chinese, Manchu, Mongolian, and Tibetan works acquired by Minister to China William W. Rockhill (1905–9). The Chinese government donated 198 volumes from its Louisiana Purchase Exhibition in 1905, and in 1908 a reprint of the 5,040-volume encyclopedia *Ku Chin Tu Shu Tsi Cheng* of 1728. When Dr. Hing Kwai Fung, a scholar who helped to catalog the Chinese materials, returned to China in 1913, with Putnam's authorization he acquired over 17,000 volumes. From the Department of Agriculture botanist Dr. Walter Tennyson Swingle's travels to the Far East beginning in 1913, the LC received 68,000 more, described in Swingle's contributions to the *Annual Report*. The transfer of 12,819 Chinese, Manchu, Mongolian, and Tibetan volumes from the John Crerar Library in 1928 and Andrew Mellon's 1929 gift of $10,000 to acquire the 22,000-volume private library of Mr. Wang Shu-an of Tientsin augmented the collection. Established in 1928, the Division of Chinese Literature became part of a new Orientalia Division in 1932.[105]

To increase the Middle Eastern and South Asian collections begun with the 1884 gift of Turkish materials from Sultan Abdul Hamid II, in 1904 Putnam purchased the Indologist Albrecht Weber's 3,375-volume collection of Sanskrit and Indica materials. The small Japanese collection increased with the 1905 acquisition of the journalist Crosby Stuart Noyes's Japanese art works and illustrated books and with the 1907 acquisition of 9,000 works selected for the LC by Dr. Kan-Ichi Asakawa of Yale University. With a gift of nearly 10,000 volumes in 1912, collected over many years by the bibliophile Ephraim Deinard, the financier-philanthropist Jacob H. Schiff (at Putnam's behest) inaugurated the collection of Hebraica, Yiddish, and Judaica materials, which further increased with additions from Deinard's later buying trips.[106] With the help of a Russian-born assistant, Alexis V. Babine, the Librarian acquired the University of Prague Professor Martin Hattala's 1,500-volume Slavic philology library in 1904, and in 1906 the 80,000-volume library of the Siberian merchant Gennadii Vasil'evich Yudin, for $40,000.[107]

Especially good fortune attended the Yudin purchase, Putnam later recalled:

> It was the idealism to be counted upon in Congress. Now, I'm not using that term "idealism" loosely. I mean it. During the period of my ministrations, the Library had several instances in which this was tested. In a smaller way it was tested when I reported to an Appropriations Committee that I had spent a half year's appropriation for 80,000 Russian books, and I was asking for an increase of the appropriation for the following year. Some of my colleagues were apprehensive. They said they won't give you any increase, they'll cut it down when it's learned that you've wasted all that money—spent all that money, in their understanding, on 80,000 books that nobody could read, and that Congress does not need in its deliberations. Well, they listened absorbedly. I told them the story of the purchase. They gave the appropriation.[108]

It counted as a purchase, Putnam said, but the amount was only a little over a third of what Yudin paid in over thirty years of collecting, and since the donor intended it as a public benefit, the Librarian called it primarily a gift. Though the immediate use of such specialized collections might be small, he declared that as the one comprehensive library in the country, the LC must acquire foreign materials. The study of some foreign languages and literatures would be mainly in universities, he acknowledged, but the national library would provide for those institutions that could not afford such collections.[109]

The Publication Program

To broaden awareness of the Library's holdings, Putnam inaugurated an ambitious publishing program. It began with important primary sources: the *Journals of the*

Continental Congress (34 volumes, 1904–37) and the *Records of the Virginia Company* (4 volumes, 1904–33). A planned series of library histories, beginning with William Dawson Johnston's *History of the Library of Congress* (1904), proved unsustainable, but book catalogs of the specialized collections steadily appeared: *A Calendar of Washington Manuscripts* (1901); American newspapers (1901); foreign newspapers (1904 and 1929); American eighteenth-century newspapers (1912, revised 1936); maps of America (1901); atlases (9 volumes, 1909–92); American and English genealogies (1910 and 1919); a series of guides to nations' law and legal literature, beginning with Germany, Spain, Argentina, Brazil, and Chile (1912, 1915, and 1917), and continuing well into the 1960s; and a bibliography of international and continental law (1913). There were bibliographies of pre-1800 books on music (1913, 1944), a catalog of opera librettos (1914), and a manuscripts collection handbook (1918, supplemented in 1932 and 1938). In 1912, the Librarian launched an effort to collect American doctoral dissertations and issue an annual bibliography.[110]

A New Copyright Act

By 1899, the 1870 copyright law was generally considered inadequate. When he became Register of Copyrights, Thorvald Solberg urged a comprehensive revision, but Librarian Young did not propose new legislation.[111] Solberg then discussed the law with Putnam, who agreed that efficient copyright administration required changes; in 1903, he included Solberg's "Report on Copyright Legislation" in his annual report.[112] As efforts to amend the statute failed, Solberg suggested that Congress appoint a commission to revise the law, as had been done in England, France, and Germany. However Senator Alfred Kittredge (R-SD), who chaired the Committee on Patents, found that the Republican caucus leader, Senator Thomas Collier Platt (R-NY), opposed the expense of a commission and told Putnam to proceed independently.[113] The Librarian and Solberg organized three meetings, in June and November 1905 and March 1906, inviting representatives from national organizations of publishers, authors, artists, composers, playwrights, photographers, illustrators, printers, and manufacturers, plus the American and New York bar associations. President Roosevelt endorsed copyright revision in his December 5, 1905, annual message.[114]

Inevitably, the meetings exposed the clashing interests of authors, publishers, and printers. They also exposed Putnam to pressures both professional (from librarians) and familial (from his brothers at G. P. Putnam's Sons). The Librarian asked Solberg to draft a bill and assemble supporting materials while also countering complaints and lobbying attempts by strongly asserting the Copyright Office's (and his own) neutrality. "We did not always see eye to eye," Solberg recalled. "But without him we would never have gotten . . . the law through Congress." Insisting that the meetings provided "full discussion and expert criticism," resulting in changes and additions that appeared "sound and safe," Putnam also admitted, "I doubt if there is a single participant whom it satisfies in every particular."[115]

The House and Senate committees on patents held joint hearings in 1906 and 1908, but without result, as disputes, chiefly over the claims of binders and printers and over "canned music" (the recording industry's piano rolls and disks), stalled revision. The

December 1906 hearing was notable for appearances by the composers Victor Herbert and John Philip Sousa—upstaged, however, by Mark Twain, in his eye-catching white serge suit, who argued for extending copyright terms from forty-two years to the life of the author plus fifty years. Afterward, Twain wrote, "When I was down there was the most stupefying jumble of conflicting and apparently irreconcilable interests that was ever seen; and we all said, 'The case is hopeless, absolutely hopeless—out of this chaos nothing can be built.'"[116] But Roosevelt, about to leave office, pressed for action, and Speaker Joseph Cannon (R-IL) suspended House rules to force the bill through on March 3, 1909, just in time for the President to sign it on March 4.

Effective July 1, 1909, the law provided a copyright period of twenty-eight years, renewable for the same term; allowed copyright for unpublished works intended for exhibition or performance; and granted initial recording rights to proprietors of musical compositions. It codified the Copyright Office's responsibilities and authorized the Librarian to dispose of deposits as he saw fit: they could be added to the collections, exchanged, sold, returned to claimants, or transferred to other agencies.[117] This important provision meant that the Library would no longer keep a complete collection of US publications: the staff could select among them while preserving the record of copyright in the *Catalogue of Copyright Entries*.[118] The Library retained the right of unrestricted importation, but other libraries could not import more than one copy of a foreign work, and publishers were irritated (as they always had been) by the only slightly eased mandate that works in English must be manufactured in the United States. The law to some extent balanced competing interests, but it passed only through strong party control and presidential intervention.[119]

The Legislative Reference Service

While responding to congressional requests was always the Library's top priority, in 1911 congressional service remained much the same as in the past: there were the Law Library and a reference collection in the Capitol for the members' use, and private reading rooms for the House and Senate in the Library building. Appropriations for 1907–10 funded a new index to the *Statutes at Large* through 1907. The Bibliography Division compiled lists on subjects of congressional interest, and the Reading Room dispatched materials to members' offices and homes. Staff in the Reading Room, the Documents Division, and the Law Library all responded to members' inquiries, but the number of requests remained small.[120]

However, some members had become interested in the services that state legislative reference bureaus offered, following from the pioneering work of Charles McCarthy in Wisconsin: data collection, bill drafting, translations, and special reports.[121] Aware of the interest in expanded services, Putnam announced on March 4, 1911, that the LC's congressional services would cover "all-night sessions, the morning of holidays and Sunday mornings when Congress is sitting even when eulogies are being delivered." A month later, he produced a lengthy analysis of the existing state legislative reference services. In 1912 Representative John M. Nelson (R-WI) proposed a service that would produce reports on existing law and on legislative proposals, translate foreign legislation, and compile and index materials. Several similar bills were introduced.[122]

Putnam's report listed the services already provided: bibliographies on public issues and pending legislation, material for speeches, reference assistance, and acquiring materials to meet legislative needs. However, "what we do not do, and what a legislative reference division in the Library would do, is to select out of this great collection—now 2,000,000 books and pamphlets—the material that may bear upon one or another of the topics under consideration by Congress or that are likely to be under consideration or that come up under particular discussions." To provide that service, he declared, the Library would need to enlarge the Documents and Bibliography divisions and the Law Library and establish a "Legislative or Congressional Reference Division." Its staff should consist of "a force of scientific experts—whose only aim should be the pursuit of truth, exact and efficient"; the service should never become "distinctly political and partisan." He requested a $25,000 appropriation.[123]

Some congressmen, including Senator Robert La Follette Sr. (R-WI), wanted a more elaborate service, but Nelson continued to consult Putnam about his bill, and the two finally agreed on the provisions, particularly emphasizing that the service must be nonpartisan. In 1913 hearings on the competing bills, the main issues were whether the service should draft bills (which Putnam opposed) and whether the Joint Committee on the Library should appoint or approve the director and staff. Here politics intervened, for the Democrats became the majority party in the House in 1911, and in 1913 with Woodrow Wilson's election as President, they also controlled the Senate. Some members, at least, hoped for appointments to be reserved to the Joint Committee.[124]

The 1915 appropriation act authorized the Librarian to "employ competent persons to prepare such indexes, digests, and compilations of law as may be required for Congress and other official use," and a $25,000 appropriation. The 1916 act broadened the definition to include "translations, indexes, digests, compilations, and bulletins and otherwise data for or bearing on legislation." Putnam assigned Law Librarian James David Thompson to direct the new Legislative Reference Service, and congressional requests increased, from 269 in 1915 to 756 in 1916.[125]

It was the most significant expansion of services since 1901, but the appropriation was essential: while the cost of living and costs of library materials had increased, the federal salary scale had not changed since the mid–nineteenth century, and the Library had steadily lost expert staff.[126] Meanwhile, in 1912 the book collection passed the 2 million–volume mark, with an additional 1 million–plus nonbook items. With an average annual increase of 88,061 books and pamphlets since 1901, the staff had added more books in twelve years than had accumulated during the LC's first century. The Library of Congress had become the third-largest library in the world.[127]

With nearly 2,000 subscribers and forty-one staff members, the card service became the Card Division in 1914. But the two-week timetable for producing cards for copyright books had increased to three, and in the Catalog Division, by 1911 one-third of the staff had less than two years' experience at the Library. With "material from everywhere pouring in and loss of experienced assistants never fully made good the showing is not brilliant," Catalog Division chief Charles Martel confessed.[128] In the Periodicals Division, which had not had a staff increase since 1901, acquisitions had more than doubled by 1912, and in 1915 Putnam refused to assist an ALA project to compile a union list of serials, saying that the Library could not handle the work. He requested salary increments, beginning in 1914 with a proposal to raise the grades of 150 employees, but obtained only small increases. When staff members left, replacements were hired—but fewer of them had full college or postgraduate training or had had professional experience in other libraries.[129]

The Library War Service

American librarians immediately felt the impact of World War I: with increased costs for paper and printing, publishers issued fewer books; foreign exchange channels closed; and shipments of European publications stalled, due variously to government or postal restrictions, a lack of transportation, or tight British import controls.[130] The ALA appointed a committee in November 1916 to cooperate with the LC in negotiations with the State Department and the British Embassy, and Putnam sent Order Division chief Theodore Koch to London to press for the release of shipments. Koch also investigated the activities of the British War Library, and he suggested organizing a similar service to provide reading material for American soldiers. Just after Congress declared war in April 1917, Putnam contacted Frederick P. Keppel, an academician turned War Department adviser, who arranged a meeting with Secretary of War Newton D. Baker.[131]

When Putnam informed ALA president Walter L. Brown (Buffalo Public Library) that the LC might be able to cooperate in providing library services for the armed forces, Brown asked him to chair a committee charged to investigate. Putnam wrote Raymond Fosdick, of the War Department's Commission on Training Camp Activities, to inform him of the ALA's interest, arguing that the American Library Association could provide a "more authoritative service" than any other agency and that the LC could most easily transfer its duplicate materials to a government-sponsored project. At the June 1917 ALA conference, Putnam's committee recommended establishing the War Service Committee (WSC) to raise funds and establish libraries in military camps, and the ALA approved the plan. Immediately following the conference, on June 28, and through Putnam, the ALA received an official invitation from Fosdick. Private funds would be needed for construction and equipment, but the commission would pay utilities, transportation costs, and possibly camp librarians' traveling and living expenses.[132]

The camps would open in September, posing an enormous challenge to organize the work during the summer. The WSC issued publicity, prepared a list of books recommended for camp collections, negotiated publishers' discounts (and in some cases received free books), established twelve book collection centers in large public libraries, and raised over $1.5 million, including a $320,000 Carnegie Corporation grant.[133] With funding assured, on October 4, the committee voted unanimously to name Herbert Putnam general director of the ALA Library War Service. Putnam accepted immediately, later declaring that "the duty to them of the Library of Congress—both as a governmental library and as the national head of our library system—was apparent from the outset."[134] He established War Service headquarters at the LC, where eighty-plus employees occupied cramped quarters, supplemented by LC staff volunteers.

The War Service built thirty-six camp libraries, completing most by early 1918, and by June, the ALA had purchased 300,000 books and gathered gifts of 2 million books and 5 million magazines. Beginning in the spring of 1918, the service sent books abroad as well, ultimately reaching almost 2,000 camps, branches, stations, hospitals, and ships. Overseas dispatch offices opened in Hoboken, Newport News, Boston, Philadelphia, New York, and Brooklyn, and with Navy cooperation and approval from American Expeditionary Force commanding General John J. Pershing, the ALA received permission to ship 50 tons per month with franking privileges. The service established a station in Paris (later the American Library in Paris), but it relied on other organizations to distribute books to military units in the field. War Service operations peaked in mid-1919; and even after the armistice, thousands of soldiers wanted books while awaiting transportation home.[135]

The WSC called for volunteers to staff the libraries, and many library boards of trustees approved several months' leave, often paid leave, for work in the camps. However, Putnam did not consider applications from German Americans, Blacks, and, initially, women. In the segregated military, the YMCA was responsible for camp facilities for Blacks, and Putnam and his colleagues wanted to avoid hiring anyone whose loyalty might be questioned. They also did not hire women as camp library directors, not because of War Department restrictions (as one account mistakenly claimed) but because they were wary of having women in positions of authority in the camps. When several women protested the exclusion at the July 1918 ALA Conference, an annoyed Putnam responded that women were employed in other capacities in the War Service. They were, but mainly as assistants and volunteers.[136]

Book selection was also controlled. The WSC consulted the Army Index, a list of titles that the Military Morale Section banned from the camps, and it also excluded certain types of material, such as light romance. Putnam stated that the service concentrated on providing soldiers with materials that would have "direct value in their military training, and in many cases a possibly lasting value to them as individuals in their subsequent vocations and civic relations." Therefore, he declared, "the question is not of exclusion, but merely one of selection."[137]

A tribute to the War Service's success came from Raymond Fosdick, who wrote upon returning from France, "I found your books everywhere, from the seaport bases to the front line trenches. I found them in dugouts thirty to forty feet below the ground, in cow-barns where the shrapnel had blown part of the roof away, as well as in substantial huts and tents far back from the firing line. And they were well worn books that I saw, showing signs of constant usage. Indeed, the books are in continual demand."[138]

"In continual demand" was also the camp librarians' theme. "When I started this work," commented Burton E. Stevenson (Camp Sherman),

> I had some very plausible theories about the kinds of books the men would want; but I soon discarded them. We have had requests here for every sort of book, from some books by Gene Stratton Porter to Boswell's *Life of Johnson*, and Bergson's *Creative Evolution*. We have had requests for Ibsen's plays, for books on sewage disposal, and so many requests for "A Message to Garcia" that I had a supply mimeographed. In one building there were so many requests for books on religion and ethics that we set up a small reference collection. Broadly speaking, of course, most of the men read fiction; exciting red-blooded

> fiction—detective stories, adventure stories, and so on. But there is also a steady demand for Conrad and Wells and Hardy and Meredith. Poetry is also in demand, and good books of travel go well.[139]

Putnam traveled to France in January 1919 to address administrative and operations issues. He finally asked WSC chairman James I. Wyer (New York State Library) in September to appoint a new director; Wyer named Carl Milam (Birmingham Public Library), who was serving as acting director; and War Service operations moved to New York City. The ALA later transferred its war activities to the military.[140]

The ALA–LC War Service partnership involved both parties in unfamiliar activities: fundraising and publicity campaigns, coordinating federal and private resources; relying on volunteers; and cooperating with the military, the Knights of Columbus, the Red Cross, the YMCA, and the Food Administration. The ALA acknowledged that the service added one more item "to the long list of benefits for which American libraries have to thank the Library and the Librarian of Congress." Putnam returned the compliment by observing that the ALA "had emerged from an organization with aims supposed purely professional, into a Public Service Corporation." "We are none of us quite the same as we were in 1916 or 1917," ALA president William Warner Bishop (University of Michigan) declared in June 1919, and he exhorted the members to build a program for "the greatest possible public service through books and materials." The Executive Board established the Committee on an Enlarged Program for American Library Service.[141] But the postwar optimism, both at ALA and at the LC, would meet disappointments.

CHAPTER 6

War, Prosperity, and Depression

When the United States entered World War I, every part of the Library reported increased demands. Smithsonian Division custodian Paul Brockett wrote, "The military authorities have required everything we could furnish on the subjects of gases, explosives, their constituents and manufacture." Reading Room Superintendent Frederick Ashley noted "great numbers of research workers (many of them new to the task), engaged on tasks new to our Government, are taxing our reference service heavily. . . . The demand for printed material has also shifted in a considerable measure from the well-known book ready in place on the shelf and available in a few minutes to the book still in process of preparation for the shelf and available only after special search, to the book not yet received or the book not published, not available at all, but still more time-consuming." The numbers of evening and Sunday users, Ashley reported, had increased by 10 and 34 percent, respectively.[1]

There were fewer experienced staff to help them. Apparently mostly because salaries had not kept up with living costs, the LC's employees, like other federal employees, in late 1916 organized a local that affiliated with the AFL's National Federation of Federal Employees in 1917.[2] But many simply left: Chief Clerk Allen Boyd calculated personnel losses between January 1917 and June 1918 at 55 percent. Two-fifths of them went into the armed forces. The others mostly obtained positions at higher salaries, and only half of them remained in federal service: living in war-crowded Washington was expensive, and by 1918 the purchasing power of federal and municipal employees had decreased by nearly one-third.[3]

With fifty-two staff changes in two years, Catalog Division senior staff worked overtime, Chief Charles Martel reported, receiving "about half pay for the kind of work they do." In the Card Division, Charles Hastings stated, the experienced staff spent much of their time training newcomers. And Ashley calculated that he had replaced half the Reading Room staff four times between 1915 and 1920. Often, new staff members stayed "a few weeks, perhaps a month or two, but not infrequently only a day or two."[4]

In 1918, Putnam circulated an unusual personal appeal to the staff:

> If you can't live on your salary here, you can't be blamed for taking a higher one elsewhere. But don't for a moment believe that—outside of the fighting ranks themselves—there is any "war work" more necessary or more patriotic than you are doing here. It is our country as a whole which is at war; it is our government *as a whole* which is its agent. And it needs

> to bring to bear in the conflict every one of the elements, every one of the forces, which makes for its efficiency, . . . the Library is one. It has its part to play—an indispensable one. Its efficiency *must* be maintained. And you, who, resisting temptations elsewhere, are aiding to maintain it, can as justly say that you are doing "war work" as any of those who leave it for a bureau with a military title. You can feel also that in "standing by your job" patiently, steadily, at a serious personal sacrifice, you are proving a loyalty as unselfish—as fundamentally patriotic—as any shown in this crisis. To thank you for it would seem to imply that it is a loyalty merely to me or to the Library, whereas it is the higher loyalty to a cause and a principle. But I want you to know how clearly I realize it, how deeply I value it, and how sure I am that in the end, and upon the final reckoning, it will secure the recognition it deserves.[5]

In his 1919 and 1920 reports, Putnam again named salary increases as the Library's top priority. Food costs alone, he noted, had increased 16 percent over the past year, and lower-paid staff members struggled to make ends meet. Congress did pass annual "bonus bills" between 1917 and 1924 to augment federal salaries, but these proved inadequate. Surveys showed that, nationwide, library workers earned less than teachers, social service workers, and business clerks. In 1920, answering a question during appropriation hearings, Putnam told the members that his position was considered the highest-ranking library position in the country, yet public library directors in major cities earned as much as $10,000, while his salary was $6,500.[6]

Congress established the Joint Commission on Reclassification of Salaries in March 1919. It consisted of federal agency representatives, with two from the LC, and its hearings included C. C. Williamson (New York Public Library) representing the ALA, and Putnam and George Bowerman (DC Public Library) testifying for the District of Columbia Library Association. Putnam's recommendations to the commission emphasized compensation differences between the LC staff and professionals in other agencies and the national library's need for specialists.[7]

Congress did not act until 1923, when the Classification Act created the Personnel Classification Board to formulate a new classification plan. That plan defined most library positions as clerical work. In response, the District of Columbia Library Association's Special Committee on Government Librarians—which included Herman Meyer, Frederick Ashley, and Charles Hastings—developed the "Brief and Specifications for Library Service in the Federal Government," arguing that librarians belonged in the Professional and Scientific Service, one of five occupational divisions in the new plan. The board concurred, but Congress did not appropriate funding for salary increases until 1926.[8]

Meanwhile, staff losses continued. While new staff still came mostly from other libraries, from teaching, or as new graduates, the proportions changed: 40 percent were new graduates, as opposed to 20–33 percent before 1914; 30 percent from other libraries, as compared with half to two-thirds before 1914; and 17 percent from teaching, as compared with 10–15 percent previously.[9] Verner Clapp, who got his first LC job in 1922, recalled that among the Reading Room staff no one had a library school degree: they taught each other to assist readers, charge materials, send requests to the stacks, deliver material to and collect it from congressional offices, tend the book carrier, answer the telephone, handle correspondence and interlibrary loans, and compile bibliographies.[10] "As a school for reference work, the Central Desk in the early 1920s is not likely soon to be matched," David Mearns and Clapp recalled. "The Reading Room was at that time very definitely at the center of the Library, and the Library's operations were . . . intimately related to the fulfillment of the Main Reading Room's needs."[11]

With the war economy dismantled and pent-up consumer demand exhausted, by mid-1921 the economy slowed: foreign trade declined by half, farm prices plummeted, and manufacturing output decreased. President Warren G. Harding's administration called for strict economy, aiming to reduce the $26 billion national debt. In the Library, decreased appropriations reduced holiday service and forced the suspension of nearly half the staff of the Legislative Reference Service (LRS). Putnam's 1920 annual report carried a recapitulation of the reasons for establishing the LRS and a discussion of its work. As the appropriation was gradually restored, the Librarian named H. H. B. Meyer as its first permanent Director.[12]

When Congress cut the printing and binding allocation from $250,000 to $212,000, only essential publications continued: catalog cards, the Annual Report, the *Monthly Checklist of State Publications*, and the *Catalogue of Copyright Entries*. Librarians found that they could not obtain some classification schedules, and card orders were delayed. At library association meetings, members called for action, but Putnam advised against letter-writing campaigns. He did concede that individuals could write their congressional delegations and groups could send resolutions of support to the appropriations committees and the Joint Committee on the Library. But when the reclassification bill passed, he declared that further action was unnecessary.[13]

The Library building, in its third decade, was crowded, and cataloging arrears of over 800,000 volumes had accumulated. In 1924, Putnam asked the House Appropriations Committee for twelve additional catalogers, reminding them that the problem had existed over many years, that the Card Division returned a surplus to the Treasury, and that its success depended on good customer service. Saying that he still hoped that receipts would eventually cover cataloging costs, Putnam argued, "All I have claimed has been that the Government was not losing, and that meantime numerous libraries of the country are saving at least five times as much as they pay us." Congress authorized the positions, but until salaries increased, they were hard to fill.[14]

The Shrine

The collections had grown by 1922 to 3 million books and pamphlets, a half million maps, nearly 1 million music items, and 430,000 works of art. Appropriated funds purchased about one-fourth of the materials added, and selected copyright deposits roughly one-eighth. The rest came from gifts, transfers from government agencies, exchanges, copying manuscripts and rare materials, and cataloging the arrears. An astonishing variety of material entered the Library, from the magic and psychic research collection of escape artist Harry Houdini (who was also a bibliophile), to the hundreds of individual donations (e.g., notably, from H. L. Mencken and Mrs. Robert Todd Lincoln), to the

Russian Greek Orthodox Church records of early Alaska. But the Library's resources remained small compared with those of other research libraries: the New York Public Library, for example, had a $21 million endowment, while the LC had only the Hubbard gift of $20,000, which produced $800 annually.[15]

Two acquisitions brought visitors to the Library as no others could. In 1921, Gaillard Hunt, the former chief of the Manuscripts Division who had become librarian and editor in the State Department, suggested to Secretary Charles Evans Hughes transferring the Declaration of Independence and the Constitution from the State Department to the Library, where the public could view them. Hughes took the recommendation to President Harding, who issued an executive order on September 29 transferring the documents to the LC. They arrived the next day, fetched by Herbert Putnam himself, and Congress appropriated $12,000 for an exhibit case. On February 28, 1924, the dedication of the so-called shrine took place on the Library's second floor, attended by President Calvin Coolidge and Mrs. Coolidge, Secretary Hughes, Speaker of the House Frederick Huntington Gillett (R-MA), and Representative Simeon D. Fess (R-OH), chairman of the Joint Committee on the Library. There was no ceremony. But after Putnam placed the documents in the case, the audience, mostly LC staff, sang two stanzas of "America."[16]

The Trust Fund Board

In 1922 Putnam hired Carl Engel (Boston Music Company) as chief of the Music Division. Engel was interested in collecting contemporary works, in particular the manuscript scores belonging to Elizabeth Sprague Coolidge, the founder of an annual music festival held in Pittsfield, Massachusetts. The festivals featured premieres of compositions commissioned by Mrs. Coolidge and those that won her $1,000 Berkshire Prize in an international chamber music competition. Coolidge wanted a permanent home for her collection and concerts, and she welcomed Engel's suggestion that she present the scores to the Library. She also proposed that the Music Division sponsor performances in Washington; however, Putnam objected that such activities were not part of the Library's role and that the LC had no space for concerts. Only when Engel and the composer Mary Carlisle Howe suggested cooperating with the Smithsonian's new Freer Gallery of Art did he consent.[17] The first concerts took place February 7–9, 1924, in the Freer auditorium, limited to a select audience, and the favorable publicity persuaded Putnam. Coolidge decided to transfer all her concerts to the Library, and in October 1924 she offered $60,000 to build an auditorium and an endowment of over $400,000 for concerts, awards for original compositions, and an annual honorarium for the chief of the Music Division.

Mrs. Coolidge supported "the composition and performance of music in ways which might otherwise be considered too unique or too expensive to be ordinarily undertaken, . . . giving precedence to considerations of quality over those of quantity; to artistic rather than to economic values; and to opportunity rather than to expediency." She insisted that the auditorium be equipped for broadcasting because "practically everyone loves chamber music who understands it, . . . and almost everyone understands it who hears it enough." The concerts would reach, Putnam noted, "persons of the requisite understanding, seriousness of purpose and influence in the musical world." He acknowledged that Coolidge's focus on contemporary music might reward "tentative and ephemeral" works but argued that "some will prove of permanent beauty and value." And he described her gifts as "absolutely consistent with the scheme and policy of the Library as the National Library and as an agency of the Federal government, which is, not to duplicate local or ordinary effort, . . . but to do for American scholarship and cultivation what is not likely to be done by other agencies." If he worried about the congressional reception, there was no need: the vote to accept was unanimous.[18]

Since there was no legal provision for federal agencies to accept endowments, Putnam consulted the Joint Committee, and the members accepted the suggestion of James B. Wilbur, a retired Chicago businessman and collector, to create the Library of Congress Trust Fund Board, consisting of the Librarian, the Joint Committee chairman, two presidential appointees, and the Treasury Secretary as chair. The bill proposed a new role for the government as a receiver and administrator of gifts, but Congress did not debate that issue. The members accepted Coolidge's gift on January 23, 1925, and then (also unanimously) voted to establish the board, with presidential approval on March 3, 1925.[19]

Immediately, gifts began to arrive: Richard R. Bowker donated $10,000 for bibliographical services, Wilbur provided a $100,000 endowment to reproduce American history sources held by European archives, and John D. Rockefeller Jr. donated $450,000 over five years for copying primary source materials in American history (1927). The Victor Talking Machine Company presented a Victrola and 412 recordings; the Friends of Music in the Library of Congress was organized in 1928, with Speaker of the House Nicholas Longworth (R-OH) as president; and the following year the Beethoven Association created the Oscar Sonneck Memorial Fund. An appeal to Congress by Justices Louis Brandeis, Harlan Stone, and others increased the Law Library's $3,000 appropriation to $50,000 in 1930, and in 1932, the American Bar Association established the Standing Committee on the Facilities of the Law Library of Congress and the Friends of the Law Library group.[20] Joseph Pennell (d. 1926) left his estate to the Library, including a provision for a committee to select and purchase prints. Assembled in 1937—and including, as Pennell specified, an etcher, a lithographer, and the Fine Arts Division chief—it met annually and encouraged the organization of the National Exhibition of Prints.[21]

Between 1935 and 1937, Mrs. Gertrude Clarke Whittall, widow of a Worcester, Massachusetts, businessman, presented her valuable collection of Antonio Stradivari stringed instruments, François Tourte bows, and music manuscripts, with an endowment to establish the Whittall Foundation.[22] "Like Elizabeth Coolidge," wrote William McGuire, "Gertrude Whittall was a woman of formidable determination and rather unpredictable generosity," who wanted her instruments to be played and enjoyed by the general public. She also provided funding to construct the Whittall Pavilion and courtyard adjacent to the Coolidge Auditorium, opened in 1939. The Coolidge- and Whittall-supported concerts reached beyond a local audience with the first national live broadcast on April 24, 1933.[23]

The Budapest String Quartet, which had a reputation as one of the world's leading ensembles, was invited to the Library to play the Stradivari instruments. Of the initial performances, Music Division chief Harold Spivacke said, "String players always need time to get used to another instrument. . . . They played well, but it was the old story—they didn't like to perform on unfamiliar instruments. So we did a little thinking. Suppose we had a quartet in residence here, and the players had time to make friends with those beautiful instruments?" The result was a contract and a tradition. The Quartet remained at the Library until 1962, when the Juilliard String Quartet succeeded it as resident ensemble.[24]

Establishing the Trust Fund Board was the most important change in the Library's governance since the 1897 act codified the authority of the Librarian. Private funding would supplement, not replace, appropriations, but it would significantly assist development of the collections and support new activities. The staff compiled an 111-page pamphlet, "The Library of Congress: Some Notable Items That It Has, Some Examples of Many Others That It Needs." It was "an unusual frankness in library practice," Putnam admitted, "but we see no reason for secluding from dealers the fact that we lack them and greatly desire them." Another of his long-time wishes was fulfilled when Congress provided funds for a Library of Congress European representative, stationed in Paris.[25]

Putnam also wanted to use private funding for an "interpretive service." "Chairs" would head the divisions, and their federal salaries would be supplemented by gift funds to approximate a university salary. "Consultants" would include subject specialists paid by honoraria. In 1927, the Boston publisher William Evarts Benjamin endowed an American history chair, and a Carnegie Corporation gift established one for the fine arts.[26] In 1933, the Wilbur Fund provided for a chair in geography;[27] and Archer M. Huntington, a scholar and philanthropist, provided $105,000 for contemporary Spanish, Portuguese, and South American materials and $50,000 for a consultant in Hispanic literature (1927–28).[28] The Daniel Guggenheim Fund for the Promotion of Aeronautics supported a chair and acquisitions for the new Division of Aeronautics (1929), augmented in 1930 by the deposit of the Smithsonian's Samuel Pierpont Langley Aeronautical Library and the National Aeronautics Association collection.[29] Huntington established the Chair of Poetry in the English Language in 1936, and the General Education Board supported consultants in English and classical literature, European history, economics, philosophy, and science. Putnam called the ability to attract expertise usually found only in academe "the most significant phase of the evolution of the institution."[30] Nevertheless, the "interpretive service" remained something of a patchwork of short-term consulting tenures.[31]

Popular Culture

By the 1920s, interest in popular cultural forms was increasing, partly fueled by the growth of local radio stations.[32] Some European composers and critics had long appreciated American ethnic and folk expressions, an enthusiasm shared mostly by ethnologists and folklorists rather than musicologists. Universities generally did not include

American folk expression as a subject for teaching and research. But Engel considered folk music important to national musical development (as had Sonneck), and in the mid-1920s he met Robert Winslow Gordon, a folk song collector whose work had been publicized in a monthly column in *Adventure Magazine* and in a *New York Times* series. With Putnam's approval, in 1928 Engel solicited donations to enable Gordon to acquire folk songs for the Library.[33]

Gordon contacted collectors and performers, building a collection of song texts and music and magazines, books, and cylinder recordings. Immersed in collecting and recording, however, he neglected to report regularly to Engel and Putnam. They terminated his services in 1932 but continued to seek support,[34] and in 1933 the American Council of Learned Societies (ACLS) provided funds for equipment and supplies (but no salary) for a consultant: John Lomax, the author of *Cowboy Songs and Other Frontier Ballads* (1910). Putnam named Lomax Honorary Consultant and Curator in American Folk-Song in September 1933, and with his college-age son, Alan, Lomax traveled to gather songs and create recordings, among them those of Lead Belly and other Blacks in southern prisons. Their work—including a book, *American Ballads and Folk Songs* (1934)—attracted further support from the Rockefeller Foundation and the Carnegie Corporation. When Congress provided the first appropriation for the collection in 1937, Alan Lomax became Assistant in Charge, and he spent months on the road meeting folklore scholars, collectors, and performers; participating in festivals; recording; and contacting recording companies that had begun to issue folk music discs. Meanwhile, as an adviser to the Works Progress Administration's Federal Writers Project, John Lomax added collecting former slaves' accounts of their lives to the Project interviewers' agenda, a collection later transferred to the Library.[35]

A pioneer in the field, the Archive of American Folk-Song largely predated academic recognition. It was a new departure for an institution historically devoted to high culture to support the preservation of folk memory as central to American life and to endorse its importance as a field of study. With the support for folksong, Putnam and Engel added a new element to the Library's role as a national cultural institution.[36]

At the same time, V. Valta Parma, the LC's first Curator of Rare Books, culled the collections for items to transfer to the new Rare Book Room. Insisting that popular culture belonged in the Library, he found in copyright storage materials previously not added to the collections: dime novels, popular magazines, comics, children's books, and ephemera. Among them were publications that launched the careers of such writers as Ray Bradbury, Edgar Rice Burroughs, Raymond Chandler, Isaac Asimov, H. P. Lovecraft, and Dashiell Hammett, and brought to readers the stories of Dick Tracy, Flash Gordon, and Tom Mix.[37] With Parma's initiatives, the rare book collections expanded, adding to the valuable items more popular materials that might serve future scholarship and also might need protection against mutilation or theft.[38]

Services to Libraries

By the mid-1920s librarians, particularly in large libraries and universities, reported a growing demand for research materials at a time when the coordination of collections was rudimentary, notable mainly in the publication of the Union List of Serials (ULS, 1927). The ULS listed the library locations of files of journals, periodicals, and serials, but it addressed only part of the need to find materials outside researchers' own libraries. A moving spirit in expanding location services was Ernest Cushing Richardson (Princeton University), who in 1922 became chair of the new ALA Committee on Bibliography.[39]

Citing an increase in interlibrary loan requests, Frederick Ashley suggested at a 1925 ALA conference that the association seek assistance to enhance the Union Catalog. Urged by Richardson, the ALA appealed to John D. Rockefeller Jr., who provided $250,000 (over five years) to improve the LC's bibliographic services. Since 1901 the Card Division had acquired other libraries' printed cards, but Rockefeller's gift provided the opportunity to combine the Library's cards (representing around 975,000 titles) with the other contributions (about 2 million entries). The plans included increasing the number of contributing libraries, adding about 375,000 temporary LC entries, and mounting on cards entries cut from libraries' book catalogs.[40]

When Richardson retired, Putnam invited him to become an Honorary Consultant and, with the Rockefeller gift, named him director of the Union Catalog project with Ernest Kletsch as Curator of the catalog and William Dawson Johnston in charge of a special collections catalog. The staff assembled entries from over 500 US libraries and more than 4,800 special collections, and it organized separate catalogs of Semitic and Slavic materials. By 1932, the Union Catalog had grown from 1.9 million titles to over 8 million—a unique "map" of library resources. In addition to collecting other libraries' cards, the staff invited them to report their holdings represented by earlier LC printed cards, thus enabling librarians to query the Catalog for locations of the books they sought.[41]

By 1927, the Card Division served over 4,000 subscribers, and eighty libraries reported using the LC classification. Library of Congress cataloging dominated library practice nationally and reached abroad: that same year the Carnegie Endowment for International Peace funded a mission headed by William Warner Bishop (University of Michigan) to assist the Vatican in modernizing its library. Bishop recruited several colleagues, including Charles Martel and J. C. M. Hanson (University of Chicago), to assist in formulating a catalog code that reconciled European and American practices.[42]

Dewey Numbers and Cards

One area of cataloging, however, continually begged for help: over 90 percent of American libraries used the Dewey Decimal Classification, and "100s of libraries weep and wail because DC numbers ar not on yur printed cards," Melvil Dewey wrote Putnam (employing, as usual, his simplified spelling system). "I know enuf of practical affairs to realize that it wud cost something to add them, but it wud be an immense help to the 1000s of people who use DC." The ALA Catalog Section proposed in the late 1920s paying catalogers to assign Dewey numbers for LC cards, and since the Library was asked only for work space, Charles Hastings endorsed the plan. After years of hearing pleas for cards with Dewey numbers, he told Putnam, "No matter how pessimistic the rest of us were as to the outcome when the conference started, before it was over we agreed with Mr. Dewey that the numbers must be printed on. At the last conference we were convinced as usual by his logic and wit. His closing words were to this effect: 'When I see the decimal classification numbers appearing on Library of Congress cards, I shall be ready for the nunc dimittis.'"[43]

Hastings proposed asking libraries to pledge funds to cover the first three years' work. The ALA Committee on Cataloging and Classification received Executive Board approval in April 1929 to contact LC card subscribers for contributions, and when the total reached $8,000, Putnam, Dewey, and the ALA provided the resources needed to complete arrangements. The ALA Office for DC Numbers on LC Cards opened on April 1, 1930, and Dewey rejoiced: "This is the greatest step yet taken in rounding out the printed card system which sum of us strugld over so meni years til Dr. Putnam fynali renderd a supreme servis to American libraries by getting it in successful operation. This action puts us agen under great obligations to him & Hastings who hav been so loyal to ALA interests even when it aded to their own personal burdens & all librarians wil be profoundly grateful to them."[44]

The library community had expressed its gratitude earlier—at the ALA's fiftieth anniversary conference in 1926, with a celebration of the Card Division's twenty-fifth anniversary. J. C. M. Hanson represented the LC: Putnam, Martel, and Hastings did not attend.[45] Librarians sympathized with the Library's ongoing cataloging problems: Wilmer Hall (Virginia State Library) commented after a visit that the staff was hard-pressed to cope with the heavy workload. But discontent pervaded the meetings of ALA regional groups, especially because the LC no longer printed cards from copy submitted by other libraries. This meant that librarians could not buy cards for those books, and they were also concerned about the lack of cards for foreign books and about production delays. Research institutions were especially affected: Hanson could obtain cards for only 45 percent of the University of Chicago's new books, and the New York Public Library received cards for only 20 percent of its orders. In 1927 the ALA's Catalog Section appointed a special committee to consider the problems.[46]

Congress and the Budget

Putnam also was concerned: in 1927, he told the House Appropriations Committee that while acquisitions funding remained the same as in 1913, the purchasing power of the $90,000 appropriation had shrunk to about $54,000. He requested a $10,000 increase, asserting that his budget requests were in line with previous expenditures for the Library. Moreover, private donors had provided over $1 million for materials and services that appropriations did not fund, and he had assured them of liberal congressional support. "I do not think there is any question about the desire of Congress to carry through, or the expectation that it will carry through the plans to make that Library what it ought to be," responded Lester Dickinson (R-IA). John Summers (R-WA) then asked Putnam to compare the library with "other great libraries of the world," and while the Librarian noted that the LC's collections could not equal those of major libraries abroad, "the range and sum total of our activities reach far beyond those of any other library anywhere." The next year, he asked again for more catalogers, stating that nearly one-third of the collections needed attention.[47]

Putnam's appeals succeeded. A book stack in the northeast courtyard, completed in 1927, included a dedicated space for rare books: the valuable materials dubbed "the office collection," which had long been locked away. The addition also provided 174 study rooms for "serious researchers," and Putnam established a special study room service.[48] Congress also funded the biennial *State Law Index*; approved raising the Chinese, Semitic, and Slavic collections to division status; and added thirty catalogers. The acquisitions budget finally reached $100,000 per year, and in 1930 it increased to $180,000. The Welch Act (1928) amended the federal salary schedule, increasing the beginning professional salary to $2,000 a year. Also that year, Congress authorized purchasing land for a new building, dubbed "the Annex," and two years later it appropriated funds for construction, including a tunnel to the Main Building, and changes to the East Front, including the new Rare Book Room.[49]

The Annex appropriation had a back story. In January 1928, the *Washington Post* reported on the pending bill to authorize acquiring the land. At the same time, Henry Folger, the Standard Oil executive and Shakespeariana collector, was quietly buying property along East Capitol Street to build a library for his collection. Worried by the report, Folger wrote Putnam, asking if he might have to build elsewhere, but Putnam wrote back "to express of course appreciation of the paramount interest and importance of your plan, and to assure that no governmental project would be allowed to interfere with it."[50] Putnam and Representative Robert Luce (R-MA) modified the bill, which described the publicity-shy Folger's plans only vaguely: half a square of land would be left for a project "cooperative with the larger purposes of the library as an institution." The bill passed, President Coolidge signed it on May 21,[51] and the Librarian predicted that having the Folger nearby would "prove strongly influential with other collectors considering a suitable destination for their collections."[52]

Putnam called it a "new era" for the Library, one in which private funding "has come into cooperation with the Government for the amplification of its resources and service."[53] His 1929 report noted, in addition to the gift of the Harkness collection of colonial Mexican and Peruvian manuscripts, the purchase of the Raymond Toinet sixteenth- and seventeenth-century French literature collection, and the 22,000-volume library of the Wang Family of Tientsin, China.[54] But when colleagues surprised him with a celebration of his thirty years' service in April, he again emphasized,

> My experience is that the projects which make the liveliest appeal to an Appropriation Committee and secure the readiest approval are precisely those which rest on considerations purely ideal, without regard to any direct utility. . . . And the large measures of this sort which have especially characterized the past five years—measures quite hazardous on the theory that Congress took a narrowly exclusive view of our functions—such measures have passed *by unanimous consent* in short sessions when a single obstinate objection would have baffled them.[55]

The Vollbehr Collection

After the October 1929 stock market crash, economic indicators trended down, but amid a general belief that the economy would quickly rebound.[56] Without reference to either, Representative Ross Collins (D-MS) proposed that Congress purchase for $1.5 million the 3,000-volume collection of the German industrial chemist Otto F. Vollbehr and name it the Herbert Putnam Collection of Incunabula. Vollbehr had already given to the LC collections of early printers' devices and wood engravings, and in April 1928 he had exhibited some of his books in the Library's Great Hall.[57]

In a February 7, 1930, floor speech, Collins described Vollbehr's fifteenth-century books as encompassing the period of the discovery of America and "the earliest efforts of culture, thought and printing," and he urged his colleagues to take advantage of the unusual opportunity to enhance the Library's collections.[58] At March 10 hearings, experts testified that the collection would not only quadruple the LC's holdings of early books but also place it among the world's greatest libraries. George Parker Winship (Harvard University) and the private collector A. Edward Newton stated that Vollbehr's Gutenberg Bible, one of only three perfect copies on vellum, alone might cost $3 million, while a single incunabule would go for $1,000; that the collection would complement the Thacher Collection of early printed books; and that the books would be a gift to the nation. The bill failed in the Senate, but Collins and Vollbehr mounted a publicity campaign that captured the popular imagination, drawing an estimated 25,000 expressions of support.[59]

Putnam remained silent, wary of the compliment and worried that the purchase might preclude the Annex appropriation. And House Library Committee chairman Luce refused to make a recommendation, throwing the decision on the House as a whole. But with everyone aware that Vollbehr might sell elsewhere, Putnam formulated a substitute bill that omitted the personal compliment, and on June 9 both the Vollbehr and Annex bills passed the House. At June 16 Senate hearings, Joint Committee chairman Fess requested Putnam's opinion, and the Librarian stated that the purchase would place the Library in the same class as the national libraries of England and France. In 1815, he continued, Congress had paid Thomas Jefferson almost $24,000 for his books, and "in proportion to the resources of the country that sum was not much short of the million and a half" for the Vollbehr. And "what was true of that purchase is certainly true of the one before you. It would form 'a most admirable substratum for a national library,' such as yours is not yet, but should develop into." Given the House's support, he said, he recommended the purchase.[60]

A supplemental appropriations act, signed by President Herbert Hoover on July 3, 1930, provided $1.5 million for the Vollbehr Collection, with presidential praise for "the most important bibliographical event of our time."[61] For 1931, Congress approved a $72,000 increase for acquisitions and $6.5 million for the Annex. And Putnam declared that the members had accepted the Library's "appropriate destiny as not merely a collection of material for purposes merely utilitarian, but an embodiment so far as may now be possible, of influences for the promotion of culture."[62]

The Depression, Library Services, and Books for the Blind

US national income, which in 1929 reached $87.4 billion, decreased to $41.7 billion in 1932; the index of manufacturing production fell from 110 to 57. Four million people were unemployed in 1930; by 1932 12 million were. Prices and incomes fell; hard-hit by budget reductions, libraries cut staff and hours of opening. For the first time, LC card sales decreased in 1932, and the next year dropped again, from 12,419,000 to 10,364,000. The Depression increased demands on libraries generally, and the Library of Congress in particular: interlibrary loan requests increased; congressional queries doubled; and when the Hoover administration called for strict economy and declared a half holiday on Saturday, the busiest day of the week at the LC, Putnam kept the Reading Room open only by requesting staff volunteers. Superintendent Martin Roberts counted four times as many readers as desks: people read standing up.[63]

For 1931 and 1932, Congress increased the Library's funding, but the 1933 appropriation provided less funding for the card service, the Legislative Reference Service, acquisitions, and printing and binding. With 1 million volumes added on average every six years, processing arrears grew: shelves were piled two and three volumes deep, materials were stacked in the cellar, and some staff shared desks or worked in the stacks. On taking office in March 1933, Franklin D. Roosevelt pledged to reduce government costs by 25 percent across the board and balance the budget. Building projects were postponed, including the Annex.[64]

Especially during and after World War I, the Library's services for the blind had increased. Public libraries served blind readers even before Librarian Young established the LC's reading room for the blind; Congress had authorized free postage for loans in 1904; and in 1907 the ALA had formed the Committee on Library Work with the Blind. But Braille print materials were scarce, and eager readers quickly exhausted their local collections. The LC's Reading Room was well attended, and donated funds supported transcriptions to increase the collection, but Putnam had transferred the service to the District of Columbia Public Library in 1910, stating that it was more appropriate for a public library. That library, however, lacked funds for materials for blind readers and served only DC residents. Disappointed users petitioned Congress to intercede, and Putnam reinstated the service in 1912, specifying that it would be national in scope and requesting an appropriation. Congress allowed only a small amount, but a 1913 act directed the American Printing House for the Blind to deposit materials produced with federal funds, and in 1918 the LC began hosting the Red Cross's Braille transcribing service. In 1925 the staff reported that since 1915 borrowers had increased from 200 to 2,000 and circulation from 5,000 to 37,000 volumes.[65]

The ALA committee suggested in 1927 that the American Foundation for the Blind survey libraries that served blind people. The results exposed the scarcity of materials and revealed that more than 90 percent of blind readers' requests came via telephone and mail, often over long distances. The foundation, the Printing House, the Braille Institute of America, and the ALA urged Congress to establish a national program. Among several proposals, the bills introduced by Representative Ruth Pratt (R-NY) and Senator Reed Smoot (R-UT) designated the Library of Congress to provide books for the adult blind and select libraries to circulate them, authorizing an annual appropriation of $100,000.[66] After President Hoover signed the Pratt-Smoot Bill on March 3, 1931, the LC staff selected nineteen regional libraries (including an LC regional service), forming one of the first library networks in the country. The Books for the Adult Blind Project began on July 1, administered first by Legislative Reference Service director Meyer, and later by the Reading Room and the Chief Assistant Librarian. Publishers permitted transcriptions and later (with restrictions to protect copyright), recording their books, and the Free Matter mailing privilege allowed circulating materials without charge.[67]

The project initially included only books in raised type, but a 1934 amendment provided for acquiring the new "talking books" recorded on twelve-inch records at 33 1/3 rpm, played on custom-made machines distributed to the regional libraries.[68] In 1935 the appropriation increased from $100,000 to $175,000; beginning in 1936, President Roosevelt approved the use of relief funds for manufacturing the machines; and in 1937 Congress approved a $275,000 annual appropriation, designating $175,000 for talking books. The first records included only 12 ½ minutes of reading per side and had to be mailed in bulky cartons, twenty-two records per carton. The average book required eight or nine disks, but a reader wanting *Gone with the Wind* received eighty records, and the Bible required 169. Since 1938 statistics showed that just over 75 percent of blind adults could not read raised type, the distribution of talking books greatly expanded the audience. Through the years developments in recording technology would shrink the size of both machines and disks, add tape and cassette machines, and eventually, electronic formats.[69]

The Roosevelt Administration and the Library

When Roosevelt took office, Democrats were eager for patronage after years of Republican administrations and hard times. But civil service regulations controlled about 80 percent of federal jobs: only about 100,000 positions remained outside. In July 1933 the House Democratic Patronage Committee, headed by James McClintic (D-OK), announced that at least half the LC staff had been appointed during the Hoover administration; he charged that Putnam had hired foreigners instead of US citizens and attempted to build a "National University." Putnam immediately sent the committee a list of all employees appointed since March 1913, including information on their salaries, education, training, and experience. Of the 714 staff members, 281 had filed letters from congressional sponsors: 35 percent were sponsored by Republicans, 49 percent by Democrats, and 16 percent had letters from members of both parties. Only twelve employees were noncitizens. Putnam's policy had not changed: he would not hire unqualified individuals, regardless of their sponsors; and if he hired an individual with an influential sponsor, he did so without conceding his prerogative.[70]

Newspapers criticized the Patronage Committee's attack on Putnam, the library community rose to the defense of professionalism, and the *Washington Herald* published articles on experts in the Aeronautics, Card, Fine Arts, Orientalia, and Manuscripts divisions. Nevertheless, Democrats continued to complain. "Congress is laying for us on this particular thing and Putnam seems to be a very hard-headed gentleman," Louis Howe told the President. And after Molly Dewson, head of the Women's Division of the Democratic National Committee, called on Putnam to present candidates, she complained, "We could make no headway even when experts are presented to Dr. Putnam."[71]

When Legislative Reference Service Director Meyer retired in 1935, Kent E. Keller (D-IL, chairman of the House Committee on the Library) and others, including senators Morris Sheppard (D-TX) and Kenneth McKellar (D-TN), supported George

Schulz, a former University of Maryland professor, and the LRS assistant director, as the successor. But Putnam did not appoint Schulz, saying that he wanted to review the LRS organization before deciding on a director.[72] Sheppard then told Putnam that for the LRS congressional preferences should be respected. "If you question this at all," he wrote, "I shall take pleasure in proving it to you at the opening of the next session of Congress, . . . the entire membership of the Senate and House will make a fight to secure it for him." McKellar endorsed Sheppard's threat.[73]

Putnam appointed Schulz on a probationary basis, but it was only the beginning of a struggle: Keller introduced a bill authorizing an annuity for Putnam (who turned seventy in 1931), presenting it as a recognition of many years' service. It did not pass, but Keller persisted in the next Congress, stating that Putnam approved the provisions. The bill drew criticism: some members said the provisions should be applicable to all congressional employees; and some objected that it established an undesirable precedent since Putnam did not contribute to the federal pension fund. At least one, Representative Allen Treadway (R-MA), accused Keller and his supporters of trying to force Putnam out. Finally, Putnam's old friend, Robert Luce, stated that he had discussed the bill with Putnam: "He is not desirous of leaving, but there are certain advantages that make that acceptable. He is still wavering between what would be his own desire and what would be best for the Library." The House vote fell short of the required two-thirds majority.[74]

Resources and Services in the 1930s

In 1934, Putnam informed Congress that the Library of Congress had become the world's largest library, with collections probably larger than the British Museum and the Bibliothèque Nationale. "In some respects," he later stated, "it can never catch up with those two libraries, because many of the books they have collected—and medieval material—we could never get, even if we had the money." Instead, he had focused on obtaining copies: "It may not be the first edition of a book, and only a reproduction of a manuscript, but if the substance is there we may be content," he said, "and so far as equipment and facilities are concerned, we are easily the first in the world. If you will only enable us to perfect the apparatus of catalog and classification, we shall surpass in availability also any library in the world."[75]

Putnam might have raised the issue of national library status then, but he did not. As a legislative branch agency, the LC had direct access to Congress: Putnam did not channel his budget requests through the Budget Bureau, and the Library was not subject to executive branch regulations. He stated,

> The title has not in its effect been limiting. The scope of the collection has from the start been universal and the functions and service as general as the existing physical conditions permitted. The expenditure of $1,500,000 for the acquisition of the Vollbehr Collection (3,000 incunabula of no service to legislation) was the act of Congress itself, upon its own initiative. And no items in my reports have so keenly interested the appropriations committees as our acquisition of the largest Slavic collection outside of Russia and the largest

> Chinese collection outside of China; the expansion of our collections in fields purely cultural; and activities extending the benefits of the institution to the public at large. They deem such extension appropriate because the Library is the National Library; but they have particular relish in them because it is still in *name* the Library of Congress.[76]

The Depression years offered few opportunities for further development. While the collections—cataloged and uncataloged—ceaselessly accumulated, to hire the dozen more consultants Putnam wanted would require an endowment of $750,000 to $1 million. Federal relief programs provided some assistance: Fine Arts Division chief Leicester B. Holland succeeded in having the Historic American Buildings Survey (HABS) records (begun as a Civil Works Administration project and transferred to the National Park Service) deposited at the Library. HABS, the Carnegie Corporation–supported Pictorial Archives of Early American Architecture, and the Carnegie Survey of the Architecture of the South provided core collections in American architecture.[77] The Music Division cooperated with the Federal Music and Federal Writers Projects, producing an index of American composers and an Archive of American Folk-Song catalog. Workers loaned by the Interior Department completed an index of early American architectural illustrations, and Civil Works Administration personnel assisted Smithsonian Division bibliographical projects. The Law Library cooperated on several indexing projects with the District of Columbia Emergency Works Administration and the Works Progress Administration. Relief workers also produced catalogs of Civil War maps and Braille transcriptions.[78]

The Historical Records Survey (HRS), headed by Luther Harris Evans, developed a strong relationship with the Library, transferring bibliographies and archival listings compiled in HRS projects. HRS staff also worked in the Library, calendaring and indexing manuscript collections, translating Russian documents, indexing early congressional documents, and adding entries to the Union Catalog, especially from the HRS's American Imprints Inventory. WPA workers microfilmed the shelflists of federal and other libraries in the District of Columbia, with the data later transcribed onto cards. But in the late 1930s, questioning the need for funding cultural projects, Congress discontinued support.[79]

Library use increased rapidly during the 1930s. Superintendent Martin Roberts recalled that in earlier years, service to Congress and federal offices mostly occupied the staff, plus satisfying the "needs of a recreative reading public." Few researchers engaged lengthy inquiries: "American scholarship had not at that time reached its present development through endowments and other means. And besides, American scholars had not realized that the Library of Congress was rapidly developing into the National Library primarily concerned with the problem of serious research." By 1930, the questions were far more sophisticated: the Library was no longer mostly a place for reading but "a centre of reference work and research."[80]

The increased activity also reflected the rise of institutions such as the Brookings Institution (1916), the National Research Council (1916), the National Bureau of Economic Research (1920), and the Social Science Research Council (1923). In 1930 Reading Room users included 260 faculty members from 93 American universities and

33 from 18 foreign institutions. Forty-two researchers represented 23 different government agencies, while 62 came from research institutions. A flood of students reflected the expansion of the school population during a period when the proportion of seventeen-year-olds completing high school rose to 50 percent and the number of college graduates increased 55 percent. Library use increased nationwide during the Depression, but while most libraries had to reduce acquisitions, copyright deposits ensured the continued growth of the LC's collections.[81]

The staff's attention to readers changed little. Young and Putnam had not limited assistance: Putnam in particular instructed desk attendants to provide information "without limit as to time except so far as governed by the exigencies of the service," and to ensure that each inquiry "reaches the official or division capable of giving him the fullest and most accurate answer."[82] William Warner Bishop, who became Superintendent of the Reading Room in 1907, asked the staff to refer "lengthy inquiries" to the Bibliography Division—though he confessed that did not always happen, "for it is contrary to human nature to give up to another an interesting line of investigation."[83] The Library's 1937 pamphlet, "Information for Readers in the Main Reading Room," stated that assistants would aid readers "so far as is compatible with the needs of others" and might refer questions to other divisions or to consultants.[84]

Cooperative Cataloging and the Union Catalog

The ALA's Catalog Section received a General Education Board grant of $13,500 in 1931 to investigate cataloging issues, and the Executive Board named the Committee on Cooperative Cataloging: Keyes Metcalf (New York Public Library, chair), J. C. M. Hanson (University of Chicago), T. Franklin Currier (Harvard University), Rudolph H. Gjelsness (University of Arizona), and Margaret Mann (University of Michigan). Charles Martel and Catalog Division chief James B. Childs served as consultants. Metcalf sent his assistant, Paul North Rice, on a tour of libraries to assess the situation, and Rice reported concerns about cataloging costs but also willingness to submit copy for foreign books to the LC and to pay higher prices for those cards, and hopes for enlarging the Union Catalog. And when Currier visited Putnam, he found that the Librarian was pleased with the support for the Union Catalog and ready to request funding to maintain it.[85]

The Committee on Cooperative Cataloging's report demonstrated the need to enlarge the card service: LC cards covered only about 62 percent of the titles cataloged by forty-nine large libraries. It also included cost estimates for cataloging foreign titles and books in series; for soliciting, revising, printing, and distributing cataloging contributed by other libraries; and for card sales and income. In October 1932, the ALA received a General Education Board grant of $45,000 for a three-year project. Just as important, Charles Hastings told Metcalf, the report convinced Putnam to consider improving coverage of foreign and series books.[86]

The Committee on Cooperative Cataloging opened an LC office on November 1, aiming to catalog 80 percent of the foreign titles acquired by US libraries: through LC cataloging (40 percent), by other libraries' contributed cataloging (30 percent), and by Union Catalog contributions (10 percent). Thirty-two contributors sent their order slips to Hastings, who decided whether to ask the library to contribute cards to the Union Catalog; and twenty-five libraries agreed to provide cards for series books. Contributors received free cards for each book cataloged plus a small Card Division credit, and the contributed entries sold for 10 percent more than regular LC cards.[87]

The first results were disappointing because some difficult foreign entries required help from specialists both in and outside the Library, and the LC catalogers' practice of revising contributed cataloging brought protests from the contributors—all of which delayed printing. A chief difficulty was that outside catalogers might not be familiar with LC practices.[88] This led to the suggestion that the catalog code needed revision, and the ALA asked for Charles Martel to chair a revision committee. But Martel worked slowly, and three years later Putnam advised Milam that it would be best to name a new chair. The Executive Board appointed Gjelsness, and a 1936 Carnegie Corporation grant funded an LC staff member as an assistant.[89]

Putnam did request an appropriation for the Union Catalog, and he established the Union Catalog Division in 1932, telling the appropriations committees that the Catalog was increasingly useful both within and outside the LC. More and more bibliographic projects drew on it: ALA resources, foundation funding, and learned society support underwrote the second edition of the *Union List of Serials* and also projects to compile union lists of foreign government serials, American newspapers, and international congress and conference proceedings. The Association of Research Libraries (ARL) asked Union Catalog Director Kletsch for a means of locating more books in US libraries, resulting in the *Weekly List of Unlocated Research Books* (1936). Circulating the list to an ever-increasing number of libraries, the staff reported locating more than 60 percent of the titles.[90] Meanwhile, statewide and regional union catalogs began to appear, prompting a Carnegie Corporation–funded invitational conference at the LC in 1936. Representatives of the LC, the ALA, the American Council of Learned Societies, the National Archives, the American Historical Association, the Works Progress Administration, and the Denver Public Library (which hosted a regional catalog) considered issues related to financing and coordinating the work of these catalogs and their relationship to the Union Catalog. Subsequently, some regional catalogs contributed entries to the Union Catalog.[91]

The Library also took over both the Dewey numbers project and cooperative cataloging. Explaining his plan to attach the Dewey work to the Card Division, Putnam told the Appropriations Committee in 1932 that the addition of Dewey numbers was an important improvement to the Library's cards—justified because it would increase sales and, likely, a price increase. In mid-1935, he established the Cooperative Cataloging and Classification Service, an operation that Chief David Haykin discreetly described as "a special problem in administration."[92]

A 1936 cataloging textbook simply assumed that librarians would use LC cards.[93] Yet the Catalog and Card Divisions still struggled, especially when card orders increased by 10 percent in 1936, while reprinting to replenish the stock jumped 20 percent. A printing plant planned for the Annex would double the capacity, but the new building would not open until 1939. Meanwhile, Hastings observed, "Whether the entries to be printed or reprinted were held in the Printing Office, the Catalog Division, or the Card Division made no difference to the subscribers, who were justly aggrieved and made their grievance known in divers ways to the discomfort of the undersigned and some of his associates."[94] In 1936, Putnam requested fourteen new positions, but Congress allowed only a small increase. The June 1937 ALA conference included discussion of a *Library Journal* article on the card service's problems, resulting in the appointment of the Committee on LC Cards to investigate the delays. Armed with survey results from fifty libraries, chairman Nouvart Tashjian (New York University) wrote to Putnam to suggest improvements, and Hastings urged the Librarian to cooperate.[95]

The Association of Research Libraries, founded in 1932, included only the largest libraries. With membership by invitation only, the ARL seemed (at least to its critics) more a private club (initially consisting of male library directors) than an association. The Library was a charter member, but Putnam was not inclined to be closely involved. It was only after repeated urging from ARL executive secretary Donald Gilchrist (University of Rochester) that the Librarian appointed Herman Meyer as the LC's representative.[96]

The ARL proposed a new means of increasing access to LC cataloging. In 1937 a committee of three directors, Harvie Branscomb (Duke), Keyes Metcalf (Harvard), and James Thayer Gerould (Princeton), considered alternatives, and William Warner Bishop consulted Edwards Brothers of Ann Arbor, Michigan, a firm that could reproduce catalog cards in book format. When they broached the idea to Putnam, the Librarian consulted Catalog Division chief Julian Leavitt, who recommended participation. Union Catalog chief George Schwegmann, however, recommended investigating the market before proceeding. To the ARL's chagrin, Putnam rejected the proposal.[97]

National Planning for Libraries

Taking a cue from the Roosevelt administration's 1933 order establishing the National Planning Board, in January 1934 Carl Milam had asked the ALA Executive Board to form the National Library Planning Committee. The committee's ambitious goals included "assumption of responsibility by the state for adequate library service to all inhabitants," including public and school libraries, state libraries, and regional public library systems. It also proposed obtaining federal aid for libraries and establishing the federal library agency that would have the same relationship to libraries that the Bureau of Education had to schools. Supported by ALA president Charles Compton (Saint Louis Public Library) and ALA Federal Relations Committee chair Carleton B. Joeckel (University of Chicago), Milam asked the ALA Council in 1935 to approve lobbying for a federal library agency—at the Library of Congress, in the Bureau of Education, or in another appropriate agency.[98]

With council approval secured, Milam suggested to Putnam placing the federal library bureau in the Library of Congress. The Librarian was not receptive. He pointed out that the Bureau of Education already included some of the proposed activities, such as issuing statistical reports and directories and serving as an information center. It might, he said, be appropriate for the LC to coordinate research libraries' activities to ensure the availability of resources for scholarship—but that task also could be accomplished elsewhere. Questions would be asked and there would be objections to assigning a bureau-like role to the Library. "We should not welcome them," Putnam concluded. "I believe that they would tend to confuse and impede the service to learning which should be the primary duty of our national library."[99] He was probably right in predicting a cool congressional reception for a proposal to place another federal agency in the Library.

Subsequently, the ALA Executive Board worked with Commissioner of Education John W. Studebaker to create an administrative unit, and President Roosevelt signed the bill establishing the Library Service Division on June 23, 1936, providing the library community with a new source of support. At the 1938 ALA conference, Putnam welcomed Ralph M. Dunbar, chief of the new division, saying that "while we at the Library of Congress are always under the temptation to undertake anything within sight that nobody else is paying attention to; . . . from the start I have been convinced [this function] should be annexed to the activities of the Office of Education rather than to the national library."[100]

At the same time, however, Joeckel, as a member of a new ALA Committee on Federal Relations to Libraries, was preparing a memo for President Roosevelt's Advisory Committee on Education. *Library Service,* published in 1938 as one of the committee's monographs, included recommendations for improving and expanding the LC's cataloging services, creating a national center for bibliographic information at the Library, and assessing the need to extend library services on a regional level, perhaps through branches of the national library. Putnam opposed regional libraries as too costly. However, when Representative Collins and Senator McKellar proposed a bill establishing regional libraries, ALA leaders thought that they must have consulted the Librarian. The plan included libraries in New York, Memphis, Chicago, Denver, and San Francisco, initially with deposits of copyrighted materials and government publications. The directors would report to Putnam. But it was unclear whether these would be branches of the LC and whether they would be separate buildings or located in existing libraries. Other concerns included the fear that the regional libraries would usurp public libraries' functions and predictions that publishers would resist providing additional depository copies. The bill never reached the House floor.[101]

The Retirement Controversy

In the fall of 1937, Putnam wrote George Bowerman that he would retire "if that course would serve the interest of the library and I could feel assured as to my successor." He proposed the title of Librarian Emeritus, with an honorarium of one-half his salary.[102] It came in the midst of a crisis: a few days earlier, the Librarian had dismissed George Schulz for insubordination. Senator Sheppard had continued to insist on a permanent appointment, and Putnam had acquiesced in December 1936. But when Schulz submitted his annual report for 1937, Putnam called it "insolent, abusive, and scandalous" and fired the LRS Director. Faced with a congressional investigation, he refused to retire until the matter was settled, and he declined ALA assistance, telling Carl Milam that he would handle the investigation himself.[103]

Sheppard demanded reinstatement, and while newspapers defended Putnam, members of Congress telegraphed protests and some asked the President to intercede. But Roosevelt, having no statutory authority over the LC, referred the matter to the Joint Committee. The syndicated columnist Drew Pearson joined the controversy, alleging that 50,000 books had been stolen, that Putnam hired and fired as he pleased, and that staff in highly paid positions were all Republicans.[104]

Putnam wrote McKellar that he regretted having to dismiss a staff member who was supported by members of Congress. But his decision was not political: "I have no concern with 'politics' in your meaning of that term; nor in my thirty-eight years as Librarian have I to my knowledge made a single appointment, promotion, or dismissal for reasons purely political." His words had no effect, and Schulz's friends on the Hill excoriated Putnam. But then someone leaked Schulz's report. The *Washington Daily News* called it "a torrent of complaint"; Schulz accused several employees of insubordination, complained that Putnam did not allow him to handle staffing matters, and accused the Librarian of "personal censure, ridicule, and contempt of authority." Schulz sent copies of the report to several members of Congress before Putnam saw it, the *News* reported, prompting them to criticize the Librarian.[105]

At the appropriation hearings, Putnam submitted Schulz's report and a written defense of his own actions, and he produced affidavits from LC staff members disclosing that Schulz tried to appoint staff on his own in response to congressional requests and that he pressed subordinates to work on weekends at his Virginia farm. When Sheppard inserted an amendment in an appropriation bill to reserve LRS appointments to Congress, Keller and Joint Committee chair Senator Alben Barkley (D-KY) agreed that it convicted Putnam without formal charges or a hearing. Barkley called the amendment out of order and was sustained by voice vote.[106]

How the controversy would affect the bill to secure Putnam's retirement was not clear. But Bowerman obtained the ALA's endorsement, the committee reported favorably, and it passed—without debate, due to the assurance that the Librarian assented to the provisions. The law designating him Librarian Emeritus became effective July 1, 1938.[107]

Putnam Retires: The 1939 Library

Meanwhile, construction of the Annex went steadily forward as well as several other changes. When the new Supreme Court Building opened in 1935, a $40,000 appropriation for its books severed the long-standing ties between the Court and the Law Library while retaining a small law collection in the Capitol for Congress. In 1936, Archer Huntington provided funding for a reading room for Hispanic materials, and the Library established the Hispanic Foundation (later the Hispanic Division) on July 1, 1939. The new Hispanic Room occupied the space next to the Rare Book Room, displacing the Card Division, which moved to temporary quarters in the southwest courtyard (dubbed "the woodshed" or "the shack"), pending Annex completion.[108]

In *The Saturday Review*, Blair Bolles called the Annex "the 1938 sawed-off skyscraper," a "squarish and squat" building designed as a book stack, a criticism that Chief

Assistant Librarian Martin Roberts countered by referring to "its pure lines, in the modern style," praise echoed more recently as its Art Deco style has been recognized as distinctive among Washington buildings.[109] The five stories provided space for 10,200,000 volumes, with reading and study rooms on the top floor and office and work space on the perimeters of the lower floors. Nevertheless, as Roberts wryly acknowledged, "After the experience of the past two-score years, no one would venture the prediction that the Annex would be ample for the needs of the Library for 'a century and a half to come.'"[110] The building opened on January 3, 1939, housing the science and technology collections; the Copyright Office; the Card, Semitic, Documents, Smithsonian, and Aeronautics divisions; and the new Photoduplication Service, bound newspaper volumes, and printing and binding operations.[111] The reading rooms opened on April 5, Herbert Putnam's fortieth anniversary as Librarian.

When Putnam retired, the Library contained over 5.8 million volumes, more than 1 million maps, 1 million music items, more than 500,000 prints, and "several million" manuscripts. Additions to the collections that year totaled over 236,416 items: 69,126 from copyright deposits, 45,422 by purchase, and the rest through gifts or exchanges. The Library came through the Depression with a larger overall budget and endowments yielding an annual income of over $60,000.[112] In addition to the Law Library's index to state legislation begun in 1928, the weekly *Digest of Public General Bills and Resolutions* appeared in 1936, following on an expanded definition of LRS services in the 1935 appropriations act.[113]

Some of Putnam's colleagues, both in and outside the Library, said privately that he had stayed too long.[114] During his last years, economic and political pressures challenged daily operations, let alone expansion or innovation. But he continued to emphasize the development of comprehensive collections. While balancing other obligations—"public policy, for instance, constitutional limitations, and other expediencies," as he put it—his initiatives built a national cultural institution.[115]

Longtime associates cited his efforts to expand the institution into the Library that he called "universal in scope, national in service."[116] Carnegie Corporation President Frederick P. Keppel called his administration "a fortunate thing for world librarianship and American civilization," and William Warner Bishop wrote, "Now the whole library world—and to a great extent the learned world—leans on the Library of Congress." Representative Lawrence Lewis (D-CO) presented a tribute in the House on February 17, 1939, and the ALA called him "the dean of our profession," who had built the LC into "its present proud position as the world's largest bibliographical institution." Perhaps most gratifying to the Librarian, the American Council of Learned Societies credited him with both addressing scholars' needs and anticipating future research needs, making the Library "an indispensable instrument on the American continent for the promotion of learning and the increase of knowledge."[117] Herbert Putnam, the longest-serving Librarian to date, decisively shaped the Library of Congress's mission and its development.

CHAPTER 7

War and Postwar

PRESIDENT ROOSEVELT had trouble selecting a Librarian. While ignoring the ALA's offer of assistance, he considered several librarians but decided differently.[1] "I do want to put in as Librarian somebody, if possible, who has a distinguished national and international reputation," he wrote Senator McKellar, "an outstanding poet or author or historian whose name would be received by the whole world as a leader in literature or history. . . . I have not found such a paragon yet, but I am still looking."[2]

The President decided on Archibald MacLeish, after consulting with his friend and recent Supreme Court appointee, Justice Felix Frankfurter.[3] Frankfurter was enthusiastic, pointing out that MacLeish's career, as a poet, editor, playwright, teacher, lawyer, and administrator of Harvard's Nieman Foundation (1938–39) demonstrated "qualities seldom found in combination." And he would "bring to the Librarianship intellectual distinction, cultural recognition the world over, a persuasive personality, and a delicate touch in dealing with others, and creative energy in making the Library of Congress the great center of the cultural resources of the Nation in the technological setting of our time."[4]

Born in Glencoe, Illinois, on May 7, 1892, MacLeish graduated from Yale but interrupted his Harvard Law School attendance to enlist. After two years' service in France, he graduated from Harvard in 1919 and entered a Boston law firm. But since practicing law and teaching at night left no time for poetry, in 1923 he moved his family to Paris for five years, where he made many literary acquaintances, among them Ernest Hemingway, John Dos Passos, T. S. Eliot, James Joyce, and Ezra Pound. On returning to the United States, he bought a farm in Conway, Massachusetts, and contributed to Henry Luce's new magazine, *Fortune*, while writing poetry and plays. At the age of forty-seven, he was a well-known writer with liberal political views.[5]

In his own word, "flabbergasted," MacLeish declined because he would have to give up writing. "Either the art or the library would suffer," he told Roosevelt. "One reason why the job of librarian of Congress frightens me is the fact that the job is pretty much a permanent job. A man would hardly be much good at it for three or four years and it would be unfair of him to leave until he had passed his apprenticeship and served for many years thereafter." But Roosevelt "turned on a combination of charm and authority" to convince MacLeish. Biographer Scott Donaldson emphasized his "determination to be of use. . . . He had tried through poetry and drama to make good things happen; now he would try through the more conventional channel of public service." MacLeish finally wrote the President that "it would be a great delight to me to feel that I could be of service to you: a very great delight."[6]

Announced at a June 6, 1939, press conference, the nomination shocked librarians: on the eve of the ALA's San Francisco conference, they were left asking themselves how the profession had fallen short of producing a leader for the national library. *Library Journal* conceded that the President had considered librarians, and some prominent librarians approved the choice. But others complained that MacLeish lacked the professional training or experience to lead a complex organization: ALA president Milton Ferguson (Brooklyn Public Library) said it was like "appointing a man Secretary of Agriculture because he likes cut flowers on his dinner table." On the first day of the conference, the ALA urged Roosevelt to reconsider, stating that "the Congress and the American people should have as a Librarian, . . . one who is not only a gentleman and a scholar but who is also the ablest library administrator available." Fourteen hundred librarians signed the statement. But MacLeish, who had considered asking the President to withdraw the nomination, then decided he would not yield to pressure.[7]

The controversy continued: Representative J. Parnell Thomas (R-NJ and a member of the Special Committee to Investigate Un-American Activities) called MacLeish "a fellow traveler" of the Communist Party.[8] While Henry Seidel Canby editorialized in *The Saturday Review of Literature* that the accusation was a "familiar red herring" and the *New York Times* endorsed MacLeish, the *New York Herald Tribune* and the *New York Sun* called the nominee "completely unequipped." But the *Boston Herald* and the *Boston Daily Globe* favored appointing a nonlibrarian, who might "extend in directions not yet guessed." The journalist John Chamberlain complained that librarians failed to ask "the only relevant questions: what experience as a functioner has he had in the past, and how well has he stood up under the experience?" After a hearing that included both MacLeish and ALA representatives, the Senate Library Committee voted unanimously to confirm. The floor debate again raised discussion on MacLeish's qualifications, but when Majority Leader Barkley called a roll-call vote on June 29, the result was sixty-three to eight in favor, with twenty-five members not voting.[9]

The incoming ALA president, Ralph Munn (Carnegie Library of Pittsburgh), announced that he would ask the Executive Board to approve writing MacLeish to explain that the opposition was solely due to lack of library training and experience. The ALA, he said, should not "sulk like spoiled children." Munn kept that promise, offering "complete and most friendly cooperation." And MacLeish answered that while he regretted some of the opposition's tactics, he hoped that "all those concerned with the present cultural crisis of our civilization and aware of the part libraries must play in that crisis, may work together for the common end."[10] After a midsummer swearing-in officiated by the Conway postmaster, he arrived at the Library on October 2.[11]

MacLeish's Reorganization

Comparing the Library of 1939 to that of 1900, MacLeish commented that "there could be no greater tribute to Mr. Putnam" than his expansion of the collections. Nevertheless, about 1,500,000 items remained unprocessed, and the arrears grew 30,000 volumes annually. The Library had thirty-five divisions: MacLeish called it "not so much an organization in its own right as the lengthened shadow of a man—a man of great force, extraordinary abilities, and a personality which left its fortunate impress upon everything he touched. Only a man of Herbert Putnam's remarkable qualities could have administered an institution the size of the Library by direct and personal supervision of all its operations, and only he if his administration were based on the intimate familiarities of forty years."[12]

MacLeish consulted librarians both in and outside the LC, government officials, academicians, and literary colleagues, and learned quickly. He "plunged boldly ahead at a pace that few if any trained librarians would have attempted," Keyes Metcalf observed.[13] "I did not set out to reorganize the Library of Congress," MacLeish wrote, but "one problem or another would demand action; to take that action it would become necessary to consider the effect of the action on related situations; . . . it would prove simpler to change several things than to change one."[14] He appointed internal committees to examine the acquisitions and processing procedures and called on the General Accounting Office and the Bureau of the Budget to vet financial operations, on the Civil Service Commission to survey position classification, and on the Architect of the Capitol and the DC Fire Department to examine the buildings. He also established the Personnel Office and began discussions with the staff, including union representatives, on developing an employee relations program.[15]

In January 1940 MacLeish requested a supplemental appropriation of $4.2 million and 287 new positions.[16] Perhaps taking a cue from Putnam's long-ago statement, he told the House Appropriations Committee that this was the first time in years "that the needs of the Library have been presented in full to this committee."[17] On March 13, Congress approved the largest-ever annual increase for the LC: $367,591 and 130 new positions, directing that much of the funding be used to catalog the arrears. With the Carnegie Corporation's support, on April 10, MacLeish appointed a Librarian's Committee to examine processing operations: Carleton B. Joeckel (University of Chicago, chair), Paul North Rice (New York Public Library), and Andrew D. Osborn (Harvard University), assisted by consultants Keyes Metcalf (Harvard University), L. Quincy Mumford (New York Public Library), and Francis R. St. John (Enoch Pratt Free Library). Assembled perhaps in part because of MacLeish's inexperience, perhaps in part to mend relations with librarians, and perhaps also to advertise his determination to make major changes, the committee was an innovation: no other Librarian had assembled an outside advisory group.

Its three-hundred-page confidential report, issued in mid-June, provided a thorough critique; for example: "Small wonder that the Library of Congress is often described as a group of libraries within a library. It is in effect a loose federation of principalities, each with strongly developed traditions and with administrative and technical idiosyncrasies." The committee recommended major changes, and MacLeish's statement was likewise straightforward: "the processing operations of the Library of Congress, as they were organized in October 1939, were inadequate to the work to be done and insufficient to the ends to be achieved."[18]

MacLeish followed the recommendations: on July 1, 1940, he established three departments that grouped units by function, subject, or type of material. The Administrative Department, headed by Verner Clapp, included building and grounds, accounting, disbursing, secretarial, and publication functions and added a personnel office and a public information officer. The Reference Department, first headed by Chief Assistant Librarian Luther Evans, with David Mearns as Reference Librarian, provided for the selection of materials and services to users: the Legislative Reference Service, the reading rooms, the Union Catalog, and the Photoduplication Service. A new position, Keeper of the Collections, addressed the physical arrangement and care of the materials. The Processing Department included accessions, descriptive and subject cataloging, cooperative cataloging, catalog preparation and maintenance, and the card service. The Processing reorganization redefined the flow of materials and work assignments, directed by Mumford (loaned by the New York Public Library for one year), with Herman H. Henkle appointed director in January 1942.[19] The Copyright Office and the Law Library remained separate operations.

Experience with this organization led to more changes (with MacLeish's praise for the staff's "admirable patience and consideration"). On July 1, 1943, he established the Acquisitions Department to handle ordering, exchanges, and gifts, with Verner Clapp as director. The Binding and Union Catalog Divisions moved into Processing. The Administrative Department was abolished, and its functions were placed under Evans. Mearns became director of the Reference Department, reorganized in 1944 in three units: the Legislative Reference Service, Public Reference Service, and Circulation Service. A central serial record, a central in-process file, and a central charge file were established.[20]

When a Central and South Asian collection development project funded by the American Council of Learned Societies and the Carnegie Corporation ended on June 30, 1942, Indic materials moved into the Orientalia Division, and the Near East Section was added in 1945.[21] Other units of the Public Reference Service included Aeronautics, the Hispanic Foundation, Manuscripts, Maps, Music, Rare Book, and Slavic, with the Fine Arts Division renamed Prints and Photographs Division in 1944. The Bibliography Division became part of the General Reference and Bibliography Division, and Government Publications and Serials merged into the Serials Division.

The reorganization took much of the five-plus years MacLeish was Librarian. "Mr. MacLeish's greatest triumph is that he 'got away' with the reorganization," Keyes Metcalf later observed. "It seems very doubtful whether anyone else in his position would have done so much in five years."[22]

New Operations

On the General Accounting Office's recommendation, IBM tabulating equipment was installed in 1941, initially used for fiscal and personnel records. The Annex housed the new Photoduplication Service, established through a 1938 grant from the Rockefeller Foundation that included $25,000 for equipment and $10,000 for a revolving fund for supplies and personnel, with expenses covered by receipts. Reporting 4,000 orders in the first year, Chief George Schwegmann noted that many came from scholars and institutions "far from established cultural and library centers" and predicted that inexpensive photographic processes would allow researchers to assemble "the wealth of many libraries."[23]

Among those processes, microfilming was increasingly important. For research libraries, it provided a partial solution to three problems: preservation of endangered materials, the increasing bulk of collections, and acquiring material that could not be purchased—even entire collections, as large libraries and commercial firms began to reproduce rare materials and serials on film, microcards, and microprint.[24] Newspapers issued before 1876 were printed on rag paper, but publishers then turned to wood-pulp stock, which discolored in about fifteen years and became brittle in twenty-five. What librarians called "the preservation problem" was not new; John Russell Young had described it forty years earlier. But it was a problem much in need of a solution, especially at the LC, which by 1940 contained 60,000 newspaper volumes. In response to Putnam's request, Congress had approved funding for 1940 to microfilm the *Washington Post* and the *Evening Star*. From then on, the Photoduplication staff filmed newspapers and produced master copies for reproduction, and the Library acquired current titles on microfilm.[25] The Microfilm Reading Room opened in 1942.[26]

The new Hispanic Foundation room, the Library's first dedicated area studies room, opened on Columbus Day, October 12, 1939, encompassing Spanish, Portuguese, and Hispanic cultures worldwide. Archer Huntington's friend Lewis U. Hanke became the first director, and in 1944, chair of Latin American Studies, bringing with him the annual *Handbook of Latin American Studies* bibliography that he had begun at Harvard in 1935. A 1941 Rockefeller Foundation grant provided initial support, and the LC took over preparation of the *Handbook* in 1945. The Library's first Specialist in Hispanic Culture, the Chilean poet Francisco Aguilera, who arrived in 1942, created the Archive of Hispanic Literature on Tape, a pioneering effort to record prominent authors reading from their works.[27]

Other federal initiatives supported the expansion of Hispanic programming. The State Department had begun negotiating bilateral agreements for exchanging official publications in 1936 and established an Interdepartmental Committee on Scientific and Cultural Cooperation in 1938. Among the LC projects the committee supported were a series of guides to the official publications of Latin American countries and the *United States Quarterly Book List*. Suggested in 1936 by the Inter-American Conference for the Maintenance of Peace, the *Book List* included selected newly published US books, annotated by expert reviewers, with the first issued in 1945. The department's Division of Exchange of Persons brought Latin American librarians to the LC, and the State Department also funded an eight-week conference proposed by Evans, the Assembly of Librarians of the Americas, in 1947.[28]

Canons of Service and Selection

MacLeish's decision to develop a statement of the Library's objectives stemmed partly from the Librarian's Committee recommendations, partly from the work of the staff committee on acquisitions, and partly from Civil Service Commissioner Arthur

Flemming, who recommended it in connection with personnel reclassification. Some of MacLeish's colleagues thought that "the Library of Congress was too big and too old—above all, too old—to ask itself what it was doing and why and for what purpose." But MacLeish was determined to "hammer out working answers which provide a basis for present operations."[29]

The Librarian's 1940 annual report presented the results as two statements. The Canons of Service stated the Library's priorities as, first, serving members of Congress in the conduct of their duties; second, handling research projects for federal agencies where agency staff could not undertake the work; and finally, serving the public, universities, learned societies, and other libraries so long as such services did not interfere with assisting Congress and federal agencies. The Canons of Selection defined the materials the Library would acquire as those needed by Congress and federal agencies, unless other government libraries provided coverage; materials recording "the life and achievements of the people of the United States," except for those kept in the National Archives; materials from those other societies of most concern to the United States; and the documents of all governments.[30]

MacLeish also stated his view of the Library's role:

> By creation and primary responsibility, [it is] the library of the elected representatives of the people of the United States. But Congress long ago extended the use of its library to other officers and offices of the federal government and to the people themselves, placing at the disposition of the users not only the rich collections with which the Library was in time provided, but the skilled services of the scholars, the technicians and the experts in various fields whose first duty was to make the collections serviceable to Congress.

"The Library of Congress thus became what Thomas Jefferson had once called it: 'the Library of the United States'—the library of the people's representatives in Congress, the library of the officers of their government and the library of the people themselves." But it became a people's library not in the usual sense of that term, the sense familiar in the so-called public libraries, but in a very special and significant sense. "As a consequence of the fact that Congress extended to the people the use, not of the collections only, *but of the services of scholarship which had been created to make the collections more usefully available to the Congress*, the Library became a *reference* library to the people—a People's Library of Reference."[31]

The staff Committee on the Acquisitions Policy evaluated collection coverage in forty areas, finding coverage deficient in at least fifteen subjects. Calling these "chasms, not gaps," MacLeish assigned the Reference Department to select material. He obtained Carnegie Corporation funding to recruit Fellows, young scholars from colleges and universities, to survey collections and recommend additions, and he added Associate Fellows selected from the LC staff or loaned by other agencies. His 1940 report rated the collections in American history, bibliography, library science, learned society publications, economics, political science, and related social sciences as "preeminent." He listed as "weak" some areas of European literature and social sciences, non-US history, education, anthropology, and technology. The staff began allotting funds by field to strengthen the collections. Then war intervened.[32]

Advocate for Democracy

Well before MacLeish arrived in Washington, he was an enthusiastic spokesman for democracy and for the important role of libraries: "All of the political things that were happening in the thirties were related. You could follow them down to things that had to do with the life of the individual, the freedom of mind, freedom of speech of individuals, and of course, the library is the mirror of all that."[33]

At Pittsburgh's Carnegie Institute on October 19, 1939, he challenged librarians: "We will either educate the people of this Republic to know, and therefore to value and therefore to preserve their own democratic culture, or we will watch the people of this Republic trade their democratic culture for the nonculture, the obscurantism, the superstition, the brutality, the tyranny, which is overrunning eastern and central and southern Europe." And "it is upon American libraries that the burden of this education must fall," because "they are the only institutions in American life capable of opening to the citizens of the Republic a knowledge of the wealth and richness of the culture which a century and a half of democratic life has produced."[34]

On May 31, 1940, he addressed the ALA, emphasizing librarians' responsibilities as "active and not passive agents of the democratic process," and drawing enthusiastic applause. In an *Atlantic Monthly* article, he described the profession as responsible for keeping "the records of the human spirit" at a time when preservation of such records was "a kind of warfare." He dedicated the Annex's south reading room to Thomas Jefferson on December 15, 1941, commissioning murals by artist Ezra Winter representing Jefferson texts on freedom, labor, the "living generation," education, and democratic government.[35]

MacLeish was closer to the White House than any previous Librarian. "We had a kind of family relationship," he recalled. "We used to go round to meals at the White House quite a bit," and the President sometimes invited Archie and Ada MacLeish to cruise on a Coast Guard cutter or visit Shangri-La.[36] When the Librarian invited the author and critic Alexander Woollcott to serve as an honorary consultant, he assigned him "to maintain for the President in the White House a shelf of the very best mystery, detective, etc., stuff."[37] MacLeish also served as a speechwriter: as Robert Sherwood (another author turned presidential adviser) recalled, the Librarian would arrive after the day's work to join the White House staff.[38] Just after Pearl Harbor, for example, he sent Sherwood a note urging the President to proclaim in his evening broadcast that Americans would "muster all our resources of heart and body for the greatest productive effort ever made by any nation."[39]

Acquisitions

Even before the June 1940 fall of France, libraries' acquisitions suffered, with agents cut off, transportation hazardous or unavailable, exchanges abandoned, paper shortages reducing publishing, and payment procedures unworkable. Librarians revived a World War I strategy, organizing the Joint Committee on Importations in October 1939, which for a time worked through agents in neutral countries, though some libraries stored purchases abroad for the duration rather than risk shipments. Initially, LC acquisitions continued as usual: in September 1939, Chief Assistant Librarian Martin Roberts wrote Miss José Meyer, the Library's Paris representative, urging "we should have all sorts of publications, etc. (other than books) bearing on the war." She reported in September 1940: "In light of recent developments, especially as regards the confiscation and destruction of printed matter by the Gestapo and the rather sinister activities of the Nazi Kulturdirektion in occupied countries, it does seem important that someone on the spot collect diligently and speedily as much of this material as can still be found. Then there is the matter of secret counter-propaganda and also certain types of German propaganda not likely to be distributed abroad by the Germans themselves." Her accounts of Gestapo raids on bookstores and publishing houses, censorship, and life under occupation were so graphic that MacLeish forwarded them to Roosevelt. Meyer left Paris in January 1941, using her German export permit to smuggle materials to the United States.[40]

Using a procedure called the "blanket" order, the Accessions Division sent dealers instructions for selecting recent publications, and to deal with the British embargo on German goods, US officials negotiated for an inspection point in Bermuda, where shipments could be cleared for entry. The Library also relied on staff and Fellows' travel, diplomatic and other federal representatives abroad, and individuals—some not "advisable to mention by name," to collect what they could. LC representative Manuel Sanchez, for example, traveled to Portugal, Spain, North Africa, Italy, and France, beginning in April 1943. Establishing relations with local dealers and collectors and traveling with the military, he acquired an astonishing 38,000 items.[41]

Stateside policies also affected acquisitions: the Post Office began in December 1940 to destroy materials that its inspectors identified as foreign propaganda. Told of the destruction by librarians, booksellers, and scholars, MacLeish appealed to the Justice Department, which ruled in the fall of 1941 that the Library would receive forty-five copies of those publications—with use restricted to government officials and scholars.[42]

War Intelligence

In mid-1940, administration officials asked Colonel William J. Donovan, a distinguished World War I veteran, to assess the economic, military, and political situation, first in England, and later, on a trip to the Mediterranean and the Middle East. On returning to Washington, Donovan discussed his ideas for organized intelligence gathering with MacLeish, among others.[43] Assistant Secretary of State Adolf Berle also contacted the Librarian to suggest establishing a unit to analyze the communications and publications of governments under German occupation. MacLeish discussed the idea with Donovan, telling him that libraries could have an important role in intelligence work.[44]

Donovan urged Roosevelt to create an intelligence operation, and on July 11, the President named him "Coordinator of Information (COI)," with a vague charge to collect and analyze information related to national security. Even before that, in June Donovan had asked MacLeish for help in recruiting a staff, and by the end of July the Librarian had met with colleagues from the American Council of Learned Societies, the

Social Science Research Council, the National Archives, and others to ask for their help in identifying scholars who might join the COI's Research and Analysis unit.[45]

In a July 30 memorandum, Donovan and MacLeish agreed that the LC would establish the Division of Special Information, funded by the COI. Legislative Reference Service Director Ernest S. Griffith organized the division, which the Librarian envisioned as "a reserve corps of intellectuals to support the front-line troops of the Donovan organization."[46] The COI was absorbed into the Office of Strategic Services (OSS) in June 1942. But Research and Analysis staff continued to work in the Annex, and the LC staff gathered materials for them: as MacLeish and Donovan had predicted, "information already existed in the United States which, if gathered together and studied in detail by carefully trained minds, with a knowledge both of the related languages and techniques, would yield valuable and often decisive results."[47]

After the Japanese attack on Pearl Harbor, at Donovan's request, on December 22 the President issued an executive order establishing the Interdepartmental Committee on the Acquisition of Foreign Publications (IDC). Under that order, OSS staff acquired and microfilmed intelligence-related materials abroad, especially in Geneva, Stockholm, Lisbon, Cairo, Istanbul, New Delhi, and Chungking. Learning of similar British operations by the Association of Special Libraries and Information Bureaux (Aslib), Donovan asked the University Microfilms firm, already filming in England, to cooperate with Aslib, and microfilm output reached 5.5 million pages by 1945. The Library organized the IDC publications in a War Agencies collection. Simultaneously, the Office of the Alien Property Custodian (APC) received authorization under the First War Powers Act (1941) to publish foreign copyrighted materials, including scientific and technical books and journals from enemy-controlled countries. The APC established the Advisory Committee on the Periodical Republication Program in October 1942, which included ARL executive secretary Paul North Rice, ALA president Keyes Metcalf, and Luther Evans. They recommended reproducing 116 journals from microfilm by photo-offset, providing over 900 subscribers with scientific literature pertinent to the war effort.[48] Kept secret to protect the dealers and others who supplied the publications, the IDC–Aslib cooperation provided important information about, for example, German efforts to develop atomic weapons.[49]

The day after Pearl Harbor, the Library established a twenty-four-hour telephone reference service for federal agencies, and the Main Reading Room staff handled only war-related work after 6 p.m., transferring public service to the Annex. Circulation of materials to Congress and federal agencies increased two to three times over prewar totals. But at the same time, resignations mounted. By June 30, 1943, 110 staff members had entered military service, and others left for better-paying jobs elsewhere. Turnover peaked at 150 percent that year, while the work week increased on February 2, 1942, from 39 to 44 hours, and a year later to 48.[50]

Air-raid shelters and alarm systems were installed; twenty-one tons of sand, buckets, and shovels were distributed; windows were blacked out; and scrap drives collected rubber, iron, steel, bronze, copper, and even typewriter ribbons. The Legislative Reference Service's War Service Section, with funding from the Office for Emergency Management, produced daily bulletins, and the Geography and Map Division updated campaign maps each day in the Speaker's Lobby. Staff from federal agencies, especially the Army Map Service and the Office of War Information, drew on the special Civilian Defense and War Agencies collections and data from the Census Library Project, a Carnegie Corporation–funded program begun in 1940 in cooperation with the Census Bureau to collect foreign demographic information. A three-year Rockefeller-funded Experimental Division for the Study of Wartime Communication moved into the Library in 1940 to analyze propaganda materials forwarded by the Customs Bureau and the Post Office, and in September 1941 MacLeish established the "Democracy Alcove" in the Main Reading Room, which included the classic texts of the American tradition. By May 1942, 400 employees from 52 federal agencies were conducting war-related research in the Library.[51]

On October 24, 1941, President Roosevelt named MacLeish director of a new agency, the Office of Facts and Figures (OFF). Intended as a public information service on the defense effort, the office produced publications and radio programs, but its vague charge and lack of authority invited trouble—and frustration for MacLeish. "It sounded like a feed trough where you would get prepared information," he said.[52] Noninterventionists suspected the OFF of warmongering, the war agencies' information officers saw it as a competitor, and reporters poked fun at an office that produced little hard news. And while FBI chief J. Edgar Hoover scrutinized the staff's work, members of Congress criticized MacLeish's dual responsibilities.[53] One result was that an appropriations bill amendment from Representatives Everett Dirksen (R-Ill) and John Taber (R-NY) cut the LC acquisitions budget from $173,000 to $55,000. The conference committee restored the funds, but MacLeish was furious, telling the ALA in June 1942 that it was "a fear of letting information reach the people, a fear of scholarship and learning."[54] OFF moved to Foggy Bottom in March 1942, and in July it became part of the new Office of War Information, with MacLeish as assistant director—a position he resigned in June 1943.[55]

Protecting the Collections

Soon after he arrived in Washington, MacLeish had sent a note to the President about protecting the collections: "I cannot help but feel that I should be taking action of some kind, at least to explore the possibilities," he wrote. "You will understand why the question keeps me awake nights and I hope you will forgive me for passing a bit of my insomnia on to you." The media and Roosevelt's advisers warned that being an ocean apart from Europe would not deter attacks, and cultural institutions abroad, including the British Museum and the Bibliothèque Nationale, had begun war planning as early as 1935. In addition to the Declaration of Independence, the Constitution, and other historic documents, the Library housed the Lincoln Cathedral copy of the Magna Carta, which the British had deposited for safekeeping in November 1939.[56]

MacLeish discussed protective measures with colleagues and sought advice from the War Department, the British Embassy, and the Commissioner of Public Buildings. The National Resources Planning Board also considered the problem, and in March 1941 it established the Committee on Conservation of Cultural Resources, which included private organizations, the National Archives, the LC, the National Gallery of

Art, and the National Park Service. When the members agreed to prepare estimates of how much bombproof and fireproof space they needed, MacLeish already had his in hand: in December 1940, he had asked the division chiefs to prepare one list for the most valuable items and another for "items which are rare, costly, of literary and historical importance and should have precedence in being protected." With 704 staff members working 10,000 hours of voluntary overtime, in just over ten weeks the Librarian had the "Report on the Precautionary Measures Regarding Its Collections," compiled by an LC Fellow, Jerrold Orne.[57]

The staff searched for fireproof space outside Washington. While David Mearns, Orne, and Keeper of the Collections Alvin Kremer queried colleges and universities, MacLeish contacted Treasury Secretary Henry Morgenthau to request space at Fort Knox for the most valuable materials.[58] Meanwhile, Secretary of State Cordell Hull called for arming merchant ships, and Washington learned on October 22 that Germany had sunk two US ships, the *Lehigh* and the *Bold Venture*. MacLeish promptly wrote a poem, "Bold Venture," which Senator Claude Pepper (D-FL) took to the floor: "You could have heard a pin drop the attention was so rapt," Pepper said.[59]

When the United States declared war, MacLeish ordered packing to begin. On the night of December 29, 1941, escorted by Secret Service agents and Verner Clapp, cases containing the Declaration of Independence, the Constitution, the Articles of Confederation, the Magna Carta, the original autograph copy of Lincoln's second inaugural address, the first and second autograph drafts of his Gettysburg Address, the Gutenberg Bible, and the Stradivarius instruments left Washington by rail for Fort Knox. "The responsibility had weighed heavily on me for many months," MacLeish wrote, "but never as heavily as on the night when the shipment left the Library of Congress." So secret was the removal that even the British Embassy knew only that the Magna Carta was secure.[60]

Between December 29, 1941, and May 14, 1942, the staff moved more than 4,700 boxes, nearly half of which contained the Manuscripts Division's unique collections, to the University of Virginia, Washington and Lee University, the Virginia Military Institute, and Denison University in Ohio. The institutions provided rent-free space and the guarded premises were undisturbed for the duration, inspected regularly by LC staff. Early in September 1944, MacLeish received Joint Chiefs of Staff approval for the return of material from Fort Knox. On Sunday, October 1, escorted by the US Marine Band and an honor guard, the Declaration, the Constitution, and other stored materials returned to public exhibit, soon joined by a February 1945 gift: an original engrossed copy of the Bill of Rights.[61]

Administration, Staff, and Public Relations

The Civil Service Commission's survey of LC staffing begun in 1941 proceeded only slowly, while MacLeish's annual reports continually dwelled on the LC's low wages. He was finally able to write in 1944 that, with recommendations for upgrading positions, the pay scale "will now enable the Library to recruit and hold professional personnel of the high qualifications and ability which the Library's work requires."[62] He and Evans also developed new staff communication channels. "Tradition held," wrote Verner Clapp, "that there hadn't been a staff meeting in the Library since 1899 when Dr. Putnam had convened one in what is now the Music Division and promptly abandoned the idea in favor of dealing with his associates individually."[63] In 1942, while acting for MacLeish, Evans began meeting with senior administrators, a group that became known as the Librarian's Conference; they also formed the Staff Advisory Committee and continuing interdepartmental committees on acquisitions, processing, bibliography, publications, and defense planning.[64] The first issue of what would become the *Library of Congress Information Bulletin* appeared in January 1942, and the Professional Forum including about one-third of the staff began meeting monthly in April 1943. "Recommendations made in these groups were formally considered and attended to all the way up to the top and the action reported back to the source," Clapp noted.[65]

The appointment of a public information officer and creation of the Exhibits Office signaled a new interest in outreach, beginning with the *Monthly Public Information Bulletin* listing upcoming events. The Library began a juried National Exhibition of Prints supported by the Pennell Fund in 1943, and the White House News Photographers Association brought its annual contest and exhibition to the LC. Luther Evans initiated exhibitions focused on US states and territories: the first, in March 1945, commemorated Florida's admission to the Union. These exhibits—which ended with the 26th, honoring Missouri, in 1972—were popular with both visitors and Congress: Senator Pepper opened the first with an address on Florida history. In 1946, Evans introduced public tours of the Library.[66]

Collecting for the Nation

World War II challenged the collecting practices of American research libraries. As Dan Lacy wrote, much of what most American libraries collected "did not yet venture far beyond the central cultural traditions of Western civilization." But the war effort required up-to-date geographic, economic, industrial, and political information:

> American scholars had been interested in the classical literature of China, but they had not needed to know the precise capacity, line by line, of its railroads. They were concerned with the comparative evolution of the industrial economy in Germany and Great Britain, but not with the exact number, location, internal arrangement and productive capacity of the German ball-bearing plants. They were more familiar with the ideology of Marx than with the views and background of members of the Politburo. . . . For the first time it became necessary—indeed desperately urgent—for the government to know precisely, dependably, and in detail the politics, the economy, the science, and the thought of countries throughout the world.[67]

John Russell Young's and Herbert Putnam's efforts, in particular, had significantly broadened the Library's collections but not necessarily prepared them to meet the wartime demands.

Princeton University Library director Julian Boyd had written in 1940 that "librarians should think now in terms of 'completeness' for the library resources of the whole country; and their whole thought and actions should be addressed to the colossal task of making those resources immediately, flexibly, and freely useful." His words echoed earlier hopes that research libraries might unite in a collecting program.[68] In 1941 MacLeish obtained a Carnegie Corporation grant for the Experimental Division of Library Cooperation, headed by the historian Herbert A. Kellar. Kellar's report, however, did not present specific plans.[69]

Wilmarth Sheldon Lewis was a scholar and collector who focused on the eighteenth-century Whig politician and novelist Horace Walpole. After talking with MacLeish (a fellow Yale alumnus), Lewis volunteered for the job as Coordinator of Information, Donovan's Chief of the Central Information Division of the Research and Analysis Branch. This was not enough for MacLeish, who urged him "to have some connection, any connection" with the Library; and Lewis subsequently proposed forming a group of librarians and collectors who could act as "friendly emissaries throughout the country." MacLeish agreed: his Librarian's Council included Randolph Adams (Clements Library, University of Michigan); Boyd; Belle daCosta Greene (Pierpont Morgan Library); Bernhard Knollenberg (Yale University); Keyes Metcalf (Harvard University); the collectors Lewis, Lessing J. Rosenwald, and Thomas W. Streeter; and Lawrence Wroth (John Carter Brown Library). The council first met on February 27, 1942, and Lewis invited the group's executive committee to his home in Farmington, Connecticut, in October to discuss Boyd's proposal to complete the Union Catalog and create the National Institute of Bibliography.[70]

The council agreed instead on a goal of making accessible in the United States at least one copy of every newly published book in the Latin alphabet likely to be needed for research and to do so by having libraries take responsibility for collecting in assigned subject areas. Written by MacLeish, Boyd, and Metcalf—and approved by the American Council of Learned Societies, the ARL, the ALA, and the Council of National Library Associations—the proposal was submitted to funding agencies in 1943. Funding for the so-called Farmington Plan was not immediately forthcoming, though the Rockefeller Foundation provided support in 1943 to assess Russian holdings in fifteen research libraries, and a 1945 meeting at the Library secured commitments from libraries to acquire Russian materials in assigned fields. A second Rockefeller grant supported cataloging the LC's Russian materials and helped establish the Cyrillic Union Catalog, and in late 1944, the State Department agreed to place Publications Procurement Officers in embassies.[71]

MacLeish also sought opportunities to expand the Library's cultural role. Although the Work Projects Administration (WPA) programs lost funding in August 1939, the Librarian obtained Roosevelt's permission to cooperate with the District of Columbia's WPA to preserve materials produced through WPA work, including materials produced by the state WPA projects. At the request of WPA Commissioner Howard Hunter, on October 8–9, 1941, the Librarian convened WPA officials and prominent writers, artists, and musicians to discuss "the future relationship of the federal government to the practice of the arts." The participants issued a call for federal support, but the declaration of war diverted attention.[72]

The Librarian obtained a $41,520 Carnegie Corporation grant in April 1940 for the Recording Laboratory, which during the war cooperated with the Marine Corps to record battle scenes and soldier interviews. The Laboratory also recorded Music Division concerts and poetry readings, and issued American Folk-Song field recordings. The division was receiving recordings from major companies, including, by the end of the decade, RCA Victor, Capital, Columbia, MGM, Vox, and Decca, and also broadcasts from radio networks.[73]

In 1940 the Rockefeller Foundation provided funding for the two-year Radio Research Project to explore "the usefulness of radio to the work of a library in a democratic state." Alan Lomax, one of the project's leaders, sent researchers and technicians to small towns to record interviews and gather material then edited for distribution to radio stations, libraries, and schools. It was an innovation in documentary production that Director Philip Cohen, engineer Jerome Wiesner, and Lomax described as "letting the people explain themselves and their lives." Other programs included the NBC *Hidden History* series (originally called *America in the Summer of 1941*), which included Lomax's lectures on folk music and programs about responses to Pearl Harbor and the US declaration of war—echoing the "national self-scrutiny" of WPA projects.[74]

In response to a proposal from the Library and the Museum of Modern Art, Rockefeller also provided support (1942–45) for collecting films: the museum staff would select and store films that documented contemporary life, including newsreels, propaganda films, documentaries, and features.[75] At the same time, large numbers of war-related films and broadcasts were being sent to the LC, for example, by the Alien Property Custodian. Concerns about how to store and preserve films prompted President Roosevelt to issue, on July 16, 1943, a directive to the Librarian and the Archivist of the United States to plan a national motion picture archive. It would take many years, however, to approach that goal.[76]

Cultural Programs and Gifts

Celebrations marked the 1943 bicentennial of Thomas Jefferson's birth: President Roosevelt dedicated the Jefferson Memorial on April 13, and the Library hosted a symposium featuring scholars, journalists, and authors discussing "the application of the Jeffersonian experience to our experience."[77] Exhibits included original drafts of the Declaration of Independence loaned by the Adams Manuscript Trust, the New York Public Library, and the Massachusetts Historical Society. The Library's Declaration, returned from Fort Knox for the events, was exhibited at the Memorial, and a book presenting reproductions of the manuscripts included Jefferson scholar Julian Boyd's *The Declaration of Independence: The Evolution of the Text.* There was also a prospectus for a catalog of Jefferson's books, a project planned by the Librarian's Council. The five-volume work was finally completed in 1959 by the bibliographer Millicent Sowerby and was praised by the reviewer Adrienne Koch for including "the comments he made on them, the notes he penned in their margins, the letters he exchanged with a brilliant array of authors and learned friends." More specifically, it "tells us in full detail where Jefferson acquired his books, how much he paid for them, who bound them if binding was required, and Jefferson's textual appraisal of the individual works," Rare Book Division chief Frederick Goff noted.[78]

A spectacular gift came to the Library in 1943 from Lessing J. Rosenwald, the retired chairman of Sears, Roebuck. The collection focused on book illustration, from illuminated manuscripts to incunabula to later rare volumes, and Rosenwald's gifts continued until his death in 1979, ultimately totaling over 2,600 items.[79] Another valuable collection came from Dayton C. Miller, a physicist and acoustics expert, whose 1941 bequest included more than 1,700 instruments (and, notably, flutes owned by Frederick the Great and James Madison), books, prints, photographs, music, correspondence, trade catalogs, and statuary. Bequests from the newspaper world included the 1944 donations of the papers of the journalist William Allen White and the works of the cartoonist Clifford Berryman, who was fondly remembered for his 1902 depiction of Theodore Roosevelt as a teddy bear.[80]

MacLeish wanted to expand beyond collections and programs. The Library, he wrote, "had no relationship whatever with the living culture (music excepted and maybe etchings!) of the country. Most writers thought of it as a museum, and the Library reciprocated in kind. Few living American writers were adequately represented in its collections outside the standard names and the standard works." In sum, "the Library was a very provincial and parochial place for all its vast collections. It touched the American present only through the American past, and not very adequately at that."[81] As a scholar later expressed it, the Librarian became "the conduit between developments in the broader culture and the Library."[82]

MacLeish also emphasized an inclusive cultural vision. In December 1940, the Library opened the exhibition *75 Years of Freedom: Commemoration of the 75th Anniversary of the 13th Amendment to the Constitution of the United States*, encompassing Black endeavors from the performing and graphic arts to literature, inventions, and sports, and with the help of prominent Black advisers such as Alain Locke, W. Grant Still, Carter Woodson, and Sterling Brown.[83] In 1946, another major exhibition celebrated Negro History Week. Seeking "living culture," MacLeish invited intellectuals and writers, among them the German author Thomas Mann, as Fellow in Germanic Literature; the French poet and diplomat Alexis Saint-Léger Léger (pseudonym: Saint-John Perse), as a French literature fellow; and Hu Shih, as a consultant in Chinese literature. Benjamin Botkin began his LC career as Resident Fellow in Folklore, and E. Franklin Frazier, author of the prize-winning *The Negro Family in the United States* and the political scientist and diplomat Ralph Bunche also were Resident Fellows.[84]

The Librarian's attention turned, too, to the Consultant in Poetry, Joseph Auslander, poetry editor of the *North American Review*. Putnam had appointed Auslander in consultation with Archer Huntington, who endowed the position in 1936. But MacLeish, no fan of Auslander's poetry, wanted "a practising poet" in residence to supervise the poetry and literature collections and attract other poets. He proposed making the Poetry Consultant an annual appointment: moving Auslander to a new position as Gift Officer, he appointed Allen Tate as Consultant. Besides developing the literature collections, conferring with scholars, and assisting readers, Tate compiled *Sixty American Poets 1896–1944: A Preliminary Check List* (1945), and the Librarian asked him to launch a new journal, to which the chairs, fellows, and consultants would contribute articles.[85] Specifying that authors should take "a humanistic approach" and write in "to use Defoe's phrase, 'a language understanded of the people,'" Tate produced the first issue of the *Library of Congress Quarterly Journal of Current Acquisitions* in just four months, in November 1943.[86]

In 1944 Tate also organized the Fellows in American Letters, an advisory group that initially included Katherine Anne Porter, Carl Sandburg, Van Wyck Brooks, Katherine Garrison Chapin, Willard Thorp, Paul Green, and Mark Van Doren. Tate and the next Consultant, Louise Bogan, proposed recording poets and novelists reading from their works, but they lacked the necessary funding until Tate put Evans in touch with the Bollingen Foundation. A January 1946 grant of $10,500 provided for the production of twenty-five records of twentieth-century poetry in English, published in 1949, with subsequent grants for more recordings. MacLeish's efforts to attract writers and invigorate the poetry program, Robert Penn Warren later recalled, "brought the Library into a literary relationship with America."[87]

MacLeish, the State Department, and the United Nations

When MacLeish left the Office of War Information in July 1943, he told President Roosevelt that he wanted also to resign as Librarian. The President resisted, but MacLeish persevered. His resignation letter of November 8, 1944, stated that his work was done, with reorganization completed and the evacuated materials returned. "I have tried to administer it as I think you would have wished—as a Library for the people as well as for the people's Government in Washington," he concluded.[88] In December Roosevelt nominated him for the new position of Assistant Secretary of State for Public and Cultural Relations, and he was confirmed, despite congressional questioning on both his politics and his poetry.[89]

MacLeish's move to the State Department came at a critical juncture. After the January 1945 Yalta Conference, as the department rushed to arrange the April United Nations Conference on International Organization in San Francisco, MacLeish suggested that State and the Library organize a library service for the conference.[90] On short notice, the LC staff assembled collections for the trains that carried delegates from the East Coast to the West Coast (for wartime flying restrictions dictated surface travel). For the Conference Library, they formed a 3,000-volume collection focused on international law, politics, and economics: one-third from the LC and the rest loaned by California libraries. Occupying prime space in the conference site, the Veterans' War Memorial Building, Library Director Verner Clapp and a staff assembled from the LC, State, the military, and local libraries fielded inquiries that ranged from requests for a history of the veto from the Congress of Vienna to the present, to the French text of "The Rights of Man" and an English translation of the Russian constitution.[91]

"It was said at the time," David Mearns wrote, "that the President had written him, saying in substance he was glad Mr. MacLeish was not leaving Washington for good but merely exchanging one mausoleum for another, and that Mr. MacLeish had replied with a reminder that 'a rolling stone gathers no Mausoleum.'"[92] MacLeish later called librarianship "a job, a profession, or an art, depending on how it is practiced." For him, it was a job, "in some ways the best job in the federal government," but "I never reached professional rank in anyone's eyes, including my own, and as for art, my commitment was elsewhere." He "learned whatever [I] learned about the librarian's task by doing what had to be done in a situation of almost constant crisis."[93] Contemporaries agreed that he brought much-needed change: Keyes Metcalf called him "the right man at the right time" for the Library of Congress.[94] "Working for Archibald MacLeish was almost never easy," Mearns wrote, "but it was almost always fun."[95] He was "an illuminating and a ventilating engineer," who "instilled a sudden sense of contemporaneity and an awareness of a world beyond the bookstacks. The brush of the comet gave a new dimension to the library." Luther Evans agreed: "The popular identification of a public figure with a public institution" brought recognition of the Library among "persons previously unmindful of its resources and services, . . . men of letters, . . . [and] the scholarly community." Internally, the Library was "invigorated and radically improved, . . . simplified and rationalized." Significantly, Evans concluded, "the outstanding characteristic of that brilliant episode is not the fact that so much was consummated in so short a time, but rather that there is now so little to repent."[96] Like Spofford and Putnam, Archibald MacLeish transformed the Library: through his advocacy of the democratic tradition, through his reorganization of its functions and staff relations, through his initiatives to broaden cultural programs, and as a poet reaching out to fellow authors and the scholarly community.

Truman Appoints Evans

In mid-1944, MacLeish had written the President to suggest Vannevar Bush as his successor. However, Bush was not likely to leave his position as director of the Office of Scientific Research and Development, and Roosevelt responded that he would consider another MacLeish suggestion: "that Princeton fellow." The "fellow" was Julian Boyd, who agonized about "turning my back on an opportunity to serve my country" but ultimately did not leave his work as library director and editor of the Jefferson papers. Roosevelt did not nominate a Librarian before he died.[97]

When the *Washington Star* reported that President Harry Truman was considering nonlibrarians, including Carl Sandburg and Robert Sherwood, ALA president Carl Vitz (Minneapolis Public Library) wrote the President and received an invitation to submit recommendations. After conferring with colleagues, Vitz suggested Keyes Metcalf (Harvard University), Ralph Ulveling (Detroit Public Library), and Acting Librarian Luther Evans. Though there were other candidates, Evans received support from his LC colleagues and from others in the federal establishment, probably including Senator Barkley, chairman of the Joint Committee.[98] Truman's invitation to the ALA and his admiration for the Library (when a congressman, he was a frequent user) helped to mend the Roosevelt administration's sometimes frosty relations with librarians.

Truman nominated Evans on June 18, 1945, and the Senate confirmed him by voice vote eleven days later. Evans was a forty-three-year-old political scientist from Texas whose interest in international relations led first to a teaching career and then, in 1935, to Washington to organize and direct the Work Projects Administration's Historical Records Survey. When the Emergency Relief Administration Act (1939) limited the survey to locally sponsored projects, Evans became director of the Legislative Reference Service, and, less than a year later, Chief Assistant Librarian. As MacLeish's wartime responsibilities became more demanding, Evans handled daily administration.[99]

Sworn in June 30, 1945, between V-E Day on May 8 and V-J Day on September 2, Evans met with President Truman to discuss the President's priorities for the LC: promoting the use of research in federal agencies and extending services to other libraries and to the public. This broad view of the Library's role accorded with Evans's vigorous personality and his ambitions. His appointment was generally popular, and it signaled that he would promote efficient operation as MacLeish had done—in his own way. Verner Clapp called him a "virile political scientist-administrator, professor-politician . . . with a devil-may-care manner and a totally uninhibited laugh," and Evans's bluntness and tendency to "stir up a good fight" enlivened the Librarian's conference. "Time and time again," Clapp reported, "problems which had been all but abandoned as hopeless yielded to one more discussion if protracted and passionate enough. Dr. Evans's staff conference is the best argument I know for the United Nations."[100]

Evans formed ninety-two Staff Discussion Groups. "Attendance at all meetings is a part of the work assignment of employees," he specified, with the hour-long sessions divided between a topic chosen by each group and a topic chosen by the Librarian in consultation with the Staff Advisory Committee. He continued the interdepartmental committees examining policies and approving projects and occasionally rotated senior staff among divisions.[101] Speaking to outside groups on management practices, the Librarian urged wide communication and democratic governance.[102] Two LC staff members later called it "the most complicated lattice of employee suggestion schemes and interunit communications of any Librarian before or since."[103]

A major challenge was recruiting to redress the wartime losses. One solution, the personnel staff suggested, was to offer library school graduates yearlong internships as their first professional experience. The Special Recruitment Program, begun in 1949, paid the beginning professional salary of $3,410, with the prospect of permanent employment. Selected by culling recommendations from library school deans and placement officers, the recruits rotated among divisions, trained by the staff and attending lectures presented by LC specialists. Even if only half remained at the LC, Evans considered the program a success: it drew well-qualified staff and spread knowledge of LC operations.[104]

Mission to Europe

Evans declared that he would not make major changes in an organization that he had helped to reorganize.[105] But where MacLeish's Canons of Selection specified collecting the records of societies and peoples of most concern to the United States, the new Librarian declared that in the postwar world, "no spot on the earth's surface is any longer alien to the interest of the American people," and "however large our collections may now be, they are pitifully and tragically small in comparison with the demands of the nation." The Library's resources should be united with those of other libraries as an "integrated national resource."[106]

An opportunity was at hand. The end of the war brought the opening of acquisitions channels, but some recalled what happened after World War I: "Some of our larger libraries had sent representatives to Europe with sizable sums of money; when the value of the [German] mark declined to practically nothing, they were able to buy subject collections for much less than they were worth from impoverished professors who had built up fine libraries in their fields." Keyes Metcalf called those deals "unfair and improper amid postwar suffering," and he proposed that the ARL ask the Library to sponsor an acquisitions program.[107] He sent a request to Secretary of State Edward Stettinius on behalf of the ARL and ALA, and Evans proposed to the State Department in July 1945 that the government acquire wartime publications and distribute them to research libraries—a request that Assistant Secretary MacLeish supported. The department agreed, MacLeish wrote, that the "national interest is directly affected by the holdings of the many private research libraries," and approved federal assistance, provided that libraries commit to a plan for cooperative purchasing.[108]

At a September 19, 1945, meeting, representatives of the ALA, the ARL, federal libraries, the Army, and the War Department agreed that the Library of Congress would be the central collecting agency for captured publications and for purchases in countries where normal commercial channels were closed. LC representatives also would forward books that libraries had stored abroad for the duration. Robert B. Downs (University of Illinois and ALA Board on Resources chair) directed a survey of 150 large libraries to assess participation, and 113 institutions committed to cover the costs of the Cooperative Acquisitions Project.[109] Thus began the Library of Congress's Mission to Europe.

A rapidly assembled staff, selected "to represent different aspects of the American library system," left Washington on January 4, 1946. They joined others already abroad, including Mission leader Reuben Peiss (formerly of IDC). With the military government providing housing, transit, and warehouse storage, by June 30 the staff had purchased about 17,000 volumes in Germany and more than 7,500 in other countries and had received from the Army 1 million captured or confiscated items, among them Nazi Party archives and books from Adolf Hitler's personal library. However, because the publishing center of Leipzig was in the Russian zone, the military authorities had to negotiate for the removal of war-stored materials. The first shipment was forwarded in July, and three months later Acquisitions Department Director Clapp declared the Mission "substantially completed," having collected an estimated 1.5 million books, maps, pieces of music, phonograph records, and films. Later tallies increased the total to over 2 million.[110]

While examining the mass of material, the LC staff identified items that were mistakenly included and returned them to the owners; the Library also joined the State Department's Interagency Conference on Captured Enemy Documentation, established in 1950 to survey German materials acquired by federal agencies and develop a return policy.[111] The Library again cooperated when President Bill Clinton's Presidential Advisory Commission on Holocaust Assets (PL 105-86, 1998) conducted a two-year investigation that included materials acquired by the National Archives, the LC, and the

Jewish Cultural Reconstruction Commission, an organization that had collected Jewish heirless property in the American Occupation Zone. In the LC's Hebraica Section, the commission staff identified about 2,500 volumes, which the Library agreed to return in response to claims and to unite the remaining items in its online catalog as the Holocaust-Era Judaic Heritage Library.[112]

The Planning Committee

"Of all the circumstances which were present when I assumed the librarianship," Evans wrote, "one was paramount: the knowledge that henceforth we would live and work in a new world. And for me and for my associates it meant that we must revise and rebuild and reconstitute the Library to resolve for its own part and within the terms of its own duties, the problems which this new world would encounter." From September 1945 to March 1946, the Librarian's Conference discussed the need for increased support, resulting in the lengthy "Justification of the Estimates, Library of Congress, Fiscal Year 1947." The request totaled $9,756,852, almost double the 1946 appropriation, including mandated salary increases, eliminating arrearages, increasing acquisitions by 100 percent, and enhancing services to meet federal agencies' postwar needs.[113]

In the spring of 1946, however, Congress was keen to reduce spending: the federal debt was the highest ever, at 106 percent of gross domestic product. The House Appropriations Committee rejected Evans's request, stating that "the kind of Library of Congress proposed by the estimates had not been endorsed in clear policy terms by Congress itself" and asserting "the need for a determination as to what the policy of the Library of Congress is going to be in the way of expansion and service to the public and the Congress." Stating that defining the LC's role was the Joint Committee's responsibility, the Appropriations Committee refused to consider any expansion until there were "officially and specifically sanctioned objectives." "I appealed to the Senate Committee on Appropriations to reject the House view of the matter as far as it concerned the estimates for fiscal year 1947," Evans reported, "and later the House Committee on the Library asked the House Appropriations Committee to reverse its attitude in dealing with the Senate increases in our part of the bill." The final appropriation was $6,069,967, as compared with the 1946 appropriation of $5,104,568, with increases mostly for the Copyright Office and the Legislative Reference Service. A separate act directed consolidating services for the blind in a Division for the Blind, with the appropriation increased from $500,000 to $1,125,000.[114]

Just how surprised Congress was by Evans's request is not clear, but the Librarian took the blame, saying that not enough was done to justify the increases—which he defended as "merely trying to provide adequately for the activities which have been historically approved by Congress."[115] To illustrate that point, David Mearns suggested a chapter on LC history for the 1946 annual report. Couched in appealing prose, his *The Story Up to Now* (1947) presented a strong plea for the Library's national role.[116] And to reinforce his argument that the postwar period brought unprecedented challenges, Evans referenced Vannevar Bush's *Science, the Endless Frontier*, a 1945 report to

President Truman that argued for addressing the research and information needs of "a new era." "Every new discovery depends upon a host of former ones, and every year brings additions to the store of knowledge which must be mastered by the scientist," Bush wrote. "The magnitude of the task of keeping all this knowledge available to the scholar requires that he be provided with every possible aid and convenience. These services may be considered under three headings: (1) interlibrary cooperation, (2) abstracting and translating services, and (3) bibliographic and reference services. At the present time none of these services can be said to be entirely adequate and the rapid expansion of published materials makes it very unlikely that private resources can continue library services even on their present level." He recommended increased funding for the LC and for the Army Medical Library."[117]

In the 1946 report, Evans also announced the formation of the Planning Committee, chaired by Keyes Metcalf, charged to produce "what is believed to be the best judgment of the country, short of the judgment of the Congress itself, as to what role the Library of Congress ought to play in the national life." The committee began by considering the scope of a national library. Concluding that the LC could not perform all national functions satisfactorily, they declared that the Library was at a turning point: it would either fulfill the needs more fully or they would be addressed elsewhere at greater cost and less well.[118]

Submitted to Congress in March 1947, the committee's report also declared that the Library should by law be named "The Library of Congress, The National Library of the United States of America." The report cited the Department of Agriculture Library and the Army Medical Library as comprehensive collections that also should be recognized as national libraries, and suggested that an agency be established to coordinate federal libraries' activities. The group also suggested a National Library Advisory Council to advise the Librarian of Congress.

While the Planning Committee recognized service to Congress and federal agencies as the LC's top priorities, its recommendations also supported services for other libraries and for the public. The Library's acquisitions policy "should be part of a national acquisition policy for all libraries in the United States." It should include at least two copies of all materials related to national security, with one copy stored outside the LC, and one copy of "all currently published material of interest to research in all fields." The Library should have a comprehensive Americana collection and maintain extensive international collections in law, music, documents, prints, maps, rare books, manuscripts, learned society publications, and bibliographic and audiovisual materials. Since there was no comprehensive library for science and technology, the committee recommended increasing the LC's science collections. While such problems as the cataloging arrearage, collection weaknesses, and inadequate services were mentioned, the group did not address administrative and budget matters in detail. The final recommendation was that its report, after review by the Joint Committee on the Library, serve "as a basis for a Charter for the Library of Congress which will provide the legislative authorization required for present and proposed activities of the Library."[119]

Legislative Reorganization and Congressional Scrutiny

Congress did not act on the Planning Committee's report, which perhaps was not surprising considering the challenges of the postwar period.[120] However, the Joint Committee on the Organization of Congress established in 1944 had produced a report that led to the Legislative Reorganization Act of 1946 (PL 79-601). It was the first restructuring since 1789, and a response not only to an increasing workload but also to criticisms of congressional inefficiency.[121] The act provided that the Joint Committee on the Library consist of the chairmen and four members each from the Senate Committee on Rules and Administration and the House Committee on House Administration. These two committees assumed legislative and oversight responsibilities for the LC, while the Joint Committee retained an advisory role.[122] The act also expanded the Legislative Reference Service. Reflecting congressional desire for expertise independent of the executive branch, the service became a separate department, with specialists in nineteen subject areas corresponding to the work of the act's enumerated standing committees. The Service was assigned responsibility for serving as the primary research facility for individual members, supplementing the committees' professional staffs, and acting as consultant on special projects or investigations. A proposal for employing specialists had appeared as early as 1940, when MacLeish and Evans reviewed the LRS, but encountered doubts about whether such a service should be part of LC.[123] The Joint Committee on the Organization of Congress, however, adopted it. As Representative Charles A. Plumley (R-VT) put it, the goal was "to have at the service of Congress research men of the very highest ability in the fields where they are likely to be most useful." With salaries increased to match those of executive branch specialists, the Legislative Reference Service 1947 appropriation nearly doubled.[124]

Still in pursuit of economy, however, Congress scrutinized the Library's organization and staffing. With the federal work week set at 40 hours in 1945, the funding for "Sunday service" provided since 1902 disappeared; to stay open on weekends (when 35 percent of the users came), the LC closed at 6 p.m. on Fridays, Saturdays, and Mondays. In the immediate postwar years, appropriation increases were small, and the 1948 appropriation reduced the staff by 6.5 percent. Yet the reading rooms served 705,898 readers in 1947, a 15 percent increase over the previous year.[125]

Proposing that cataloging costs should be partly supported by card sales, the Appropriations Committee suggested raising prices above the 1901 "cost plus 10 percent" formula. Evans opposed the increase, and when he consulted the ALA and ARL, librarians protested that any increase amounted to a subsidy for LC cataloging when in fact the Library had to catalog its materials anyway. The committee declared that it was "at a complete loss" to understand their opposition "in view of the value and, in fact, the tremendous savings which this service contributes to their operations." But Evans observed, "This change in basic theory leads almost inevitably to the conclusion" that if libraries would be paying more for cards, the LC should be "more responsive to their wishes." Nevertheless, on July 1, 1948, card prices increased from an average of 3 cents per card to 4 cents. Similarly, copyright registration fees increased from $2 to $4 per item, an increase supported by Register of Copyrights Sam Bass Warner, who stated that the new fee was "more commensurate with the costs of services rendered" and did not impose an undue burden on applicants. A year later, Congress approved waiving the fee for foreign authors or publishers who included cataloging information with their deposits; the law also eased the time limits on registration and the limits on the importation of foreign works in English. Warner predicted the law would bring more foreign receipts.[126]

Higher card prices, however, did not produce a subsidy. In the spring of 1949, Evans informed the committee that mandated salary increases, which affected both Card Division and Government Printing Office personnel, had increased costs and sales fell short of recovering cataloging costs. Arguing that the cost-sharing policy was contrary to general federal policy on pricing publications, LC officials were finally successful: as Evans reported, "with a fresh perspective of the problem, the committee withdrew the stipulation." It ended the two-year struggle, and the Librarian called it "an agreeable reversal."[127]

When preparing the appropriation request for fiscal 1949, Evans wrote, "We have decided to make increased estimates only for emergency needs until Congress has taken action of some kind on the policy issues which have recently blocked our progress."[128] Nevertheless, he remained determined to expand the Library's role. Library users' demands had increased, particularly for scientific and technical materials and for information on the Soviet Union, East and South Asia, Africa, and other parts of the world more important to the United States than in the past. Whenever possible, division chiefs and specialists traveled to open acquisitions and exchange channels and developed relationships with colleagues abroad. One such trip in 1947–48, for example, established exchanges with every country of Southeast Asia: Orientalia Division librarian Cecil Hobbs reported that he met with government officials, visited cultural and educational institutions, selected book dealers to fill LC orders, and arranged for microfilming materials. As a result, the division's Indic Studies Section became the South Asia Section. The internal Committee on Area Studies was formed, the European Affairs Division was established in September 1948, and 200 libraries subscribed to the *Monthly List of Russian Accessions* begun that year, funded by the American Council of Learned Societies and the Rockefeller Foundation.[129]

Postwar Acquisitions

The war produced a massive literature. Burton W. Adkinson, acting chief of the Geography and Map Division, reported acquiring both federal agencies' maps and the foreign maps they collected for wartime use. From an average 30,000 acquisitions annually, for three years in a row, the division received over 100,000. With "literally tons" of maps still arriving, in 1950 the staff called for summer help from other institutions, promising to donate duplicates for their map collections. In 1951, volunteers from six universities participated; and supported by the LC, the universities, and the American Geographical Society, the Special Map Processing Project continued over many years.[130]

Aeronautics Division chief Richard Eells reported receiving technical reports from the Department of Commerce's Office of Technical Services and from the Air Matériel

Command; the armed services sent photographs to the Prints and Photographs Division; and the Armed Forces Radio Service began in 1945 to transfer its broadcasts.[131] The newly established Office of Naval Research contracted with the Library in 1947 for assistance with the technical report literature, similar to the service begun in 1946 for the reports of the defunct Office of Scientific Research and Development: the two operations were combined as the Science and Technology Project. The Department of the Air Force requested research services in 1948, and in June 1949 Evans established the Science Division.[132]

Government publishing activity also changed. Wartime restrictions on printing promoted use of the mimeograph and other reproduction methods, resulting in so-called processed publications. Such "near-print" documents by 1948 equaled the number of publications in the Superintendent of Documents' depository system, but bypassed it; the depository program also did not necessarily cover publications issued by federal field offices. In 1946, Evans offered to collect and house these publications under the Library's authority for receiving surplus agency publications. The agencies' response was "cordial, understanding, and altogether reassuring," the Librarian reported, and the ARL, the ALA, the Special Libraries Association, the National Association of State Libraries, and the American Association of Law Libraries sponsored an appeal for funding for a Documents Expediting Project, which by 1952 attracted 75 subscribers, and by 1975, 144. Also collecting the documents of international agencies headquartered in Washington, the project notably acquired material assembled for the International Military Tribunal for the Far East, and the German War Crimes trials in Nuremberg, publications of the American military governments in Germany and Japan, Voice of America scripts, and the *Daily Reports* of the Foreign Broadcast Information Service.[133]

In addition to cataloging, abstracting, and providing service for Defense Department research reports, the Library assisted the Army Map Service, which donated surplus maps to college, university, and public libraries. Evans also worked with the Veterans Administration, undertaking to distribute "about a million" textbooks that had been used in Army and Navy officer training courses. In the postwar period, the Japanese collection grew enormously through the purchase of the Japan Institute library from the Alien Property Custodian, and by transfers from the Reference Library of the Supreme Commander for the Allied Powers, and from the OSS Washington Documents Center.[134]

The Japanese occupation presented another opportunity. The new Japanese constitution, effective May 3, 1947, established the National Diet (legislative assembly) representing the Japanese people, and the Diet petitioned General Douglas MacArthur for assistance in forming a library modeled on the Library of Congress. The representatives of the American library community sent as consultants were Verner Clapp and Charles Harvey Brown, former librarian of Iowa State College and chair of an ALA committee on the Orient. Arriving on December 14, they spent two months conferring with Diet leaders and with the headquarters of the Supreme Commander for the Allied Powers. The National Diet Library Law and the National Diet Library Building Commission Law passed on February 4, 1948. With the appointment of the Diet-named Chief Librarian pending, Clapp and Brown departed on February 11, having also begun planning for a microfilming facility that would fill American libraries' orders for Japanese publications. Housed temporarily in the Akasaka Detached Palace, the Diet Library opened on June 5.[135]

The postwar period also brought important gifts, in particular W. Somerset Maugham's 1945 donation of the manuscript of his novel, *Of Human Bondage*, "in grateful acknowledgement of the kindness and hospitality shown by the people of this country" to British subjects and in recognition of American appreciation of his work.[136] The Woodrow Wilson Room, housing the former President's book collection, was dedicated January 8, 1949. Arts-related gifts included Mary Pickford's motion picture collection (1945), the first major donation to the film collection, and the Sergei Rachmaninoff Archive (1951), the gift of the composer's widow. Just before the Library's sesquicentennial year, the Trust Fund Board announced a $100,000 endowment from the Serge Koussevitzky Foundation to commission new works by distinguished composers.[137]

The most dramatic addition was the opening of Abraham Lincoln's papers. No one had seen them since the President's secretaries, John G. Nicolay and John Hay, perused them for their ten-volume 1890 biography. Approached several times by Herbert Putnam and others, including the Lincoln biographer Ida Tarbell, Robert Todd Lincoln had deposited the papers in May 1919. He deeded them in 1923, to be sealed until twenty-one years after his death, explaining that they "contain many references of a private nature to the ancestors of persons now living which, in my judgment should not be made public." He modified the deed a few months before his death on July 26, 1926, to allow indexing the collection and to permit access subject to his wife's permission, but she allowed only their daughter, Mary Lincoln Isham, and the family attorney to see the collection. Curiosity about the contents increased over time: it was even rumored that the papers might reveal cabinet members' complicity in the assassination. Thirty Lincoln scholars and specialists received invitations to the opening, which took place one minute after midnight on July 26, 1947, with a crowd of about 200 (including staff and reporters) and broadcast by CBS Radio. The collection contained White House records rather than family papers, disappointing some, but the Lincoln scholar James G. Randall commented, "Little of what was basically known has had to be discarded, but in vividness and glowing detail we have much more of his period than before.[138]

Changing Cataloging

The long-awaited revision of the ALA *Cataloging Rules* neared completion in 1939. But when the proposed rules circulated in 1941, swollen from the 88 pages of 1908 to 408, they were not well received. Andrew D. Osborn, in an article that revealed some of the criticisms made by the Librarian's Committee, called it "the crisis in cataloging." Cataloging, he wrote, had become too elaborate and therefore too expensive. His sweeping critique fed the "simmering frustrations of a generation of librarians," Paul Dunkin (Rutgers University) later commented: "Everybody read it, everybody talked or wrote about it, and it gave a name and an atmosphere to a whole era of thinking about cataloging." The "crisis" arrayed advocates of a detailed code against administrators concerned about rising costs and growing arrearages. An ALA committee recommended in 1944 revising the rules for entry and replacing the rules for description.[139]

The ALA's revision proceeded separately from the LC's evaluation of its own cataloging practices, which included meetings in fifteen cities in October and November 1943 to obtain colleagues' advice. Processing Department chief Herman Henkle and Descriptive Cataloging Division chief Lucile Morsch reported that librarians seemed ready to "follow the lead of the Library of Congress if it gives full consideration to the possibilities for simplification." A new staff member, Seymour Lubetzky, worked with them to examine the 1941 rules, and the results appeared as *Studies of Descriptive Cataloging* (1946). Henkle and Morsch recommended that Evans appoint an advisory committee including LC staff and colleagues from other libraries, making the revision, as the Librarian put it, "a mutual intellectual endeavor."[140]

Internal changes accompanied the LC's development of a new code. To eliminate duplication of work, in 1946 the Copyright Office began handling descriptive cataloging for copyright receipts; and to better integrate ordering and cataloging, in 1947 the Acquisitions Department was moved into the Processing Department.[141] Evans defined four cataloging priorities: "rush" (priority one), "hasten" (priority two), regular cataloging (priority three), and "priority four," a brief listing for materials unlikely to be in demand. Nevertheless, altering time-honored cataloging methods came only with great difficulty, amid much debate.[142] The Librarian promised to resist lowering standards, "no matter what arrearage problems we have to face," but insisted on balancing "quality, coverage, and timeliness"[143]

Morsch's revision appeared as the preliminary edition of *Rules for Descriptive Cataloging in the Library of Congress* in June 1947, opening with a statement of principles derived from the *Studies.* It received tentative ALA approval at the June 1948 conference, with publication in 1949. Unlike the 1908 code, the new *Rules* covered some nonbook materials (maps and music); and the staff planned to develop rules for motion pictures, sound recordings, and books for the blind.[144]

Also in 1949, the second edition of the *A.L.A. Cataloging Rules for Author and Title Entries* appeared, but with the character of the rules mostly unchanged. The resulting criticisms prompted the ALA's new Board on Cataloging Policy and Research to ask the Library in 1951 to examine the rules, and Lubetzky was assigned the task. His *Cataloging Rules and Principles* (1953) considered the rules as a system designed to achieve specific objectives (beginning with the question "Is This Rule Necessary?") and called for a thorough revision. The ALA appointed the Catalog Code Revision Committee, which contracted with the LC in 1956 to support Lubetzky's work and to cooperate with similar British and Canadian efforts.[145]

During the rules controversy, the Library issued the fifth edition of *Subject Headings Used in the Dictionary Catalog of the Library of Congress* (1949) and, with the cooperation of the American Association of Law Libraries, a committee began work on a classification for law, Class K, which had never been developed.[146] "It seems now a curious error of judgment," the *Annual Report* noted, citing catalogers' view that "law was merely an aspect of other branches of knowledge" and "the stoutly maintained position of various Law Librarians that no fully developed classification was needed for the management of the legal collection." Werner B. Ellinger, who would spend many years developing Class K, merely observed that most law libraries were small and did not require elaborate classification systems. He began in 1952 to prepare working papers to be critiqued by both librarians and legal scholars.[147]

Herbert Putnam had refused to allow publishing the LC's catalog in book format, but MacLeish readily agreed to the ARL's proposal. *A Catalog of Books Represented by Library of Congress Printed Cards Issued to July 31, 1942* (167 volumes, 1942–46) published by Edwards Brothers had the personal assistance of Card Division chief John Cronin, who examined every card and often traveled to Ann Arbor to advise the publisher. A forty-two-volume supplement covering 1942–47 appeared in 1948. These book catalogs presented the cards alphabetically by author, in reduced format, and MacLeish wrote that they marked "the end of one chapter of American librarianship. It is even truer to say that it marks the beginning of another." Printed inexpensively by the photo-offset process, the book catalogs sold at the old specification of cost plus 10 percent.[148] MacLeish's "beginning" arrived when, starting in January 1947, the Library began issuing monthly, quarterly, and annual supplements under the title *Cumulative Catalog of Library of Congress Printed Cards*: at the June ALA conference, some librarians told the LC's exhibit booth staff that they would copy from the book catalogs instead of ordering cards. In 1950 the Card Division began issuing the *Library of Congress Subject Catalog*, a quarterly publication cumulated annually. With its appearance, the *Cumulative Catalog* became *The Library of Congress Author Catalog*.[149]

When *A Catalog of Books* began to appear, thirty-six libraries agreed to check all or some of their holdings against the volumes as they were published, a number increased to around 100 by 1947.[150] When librarians found titles not included in the catalog, they sent cards for those titles to the Union Catalog, its name changed in 1948 to the National Union Catalog (NUC). In cooperation with the ARL, the Union Catalog Division also collected information on microfilming projects: the first edition of *Newspapers on Microfilm: A Union Checklist* appeared in 1948. The next year, also at the ARL's request, the Library established the Microfilm Clearing House and in 1951 began the *Microfilm Clearing House Bulletin* listing current projects. With the long-awaited Carnegie Corporation–funded inauguration of the Farmington Plan on July 1, 1948, cards representing plan acquisitions also entered the NUC. Begun with publications from French, Swedish, and Swiss dealers, the plan enrolled sixty libraries that selected subject areas to cover, agreeing to acquire all books the dealers sent, to forward cataloging promptly to the NUC, and to make the books available through interlibrary loan. As a plan member, the LC took responsibility for twenty-six subjects.[151]

The Freedom Train and Loyalty Programs

In 1946, Attorney General Thomas C. Clark suggested a traveling exhibition focused on the development of American democratic institutions. Called the Freedom Train and sponsored by the privately funded American Heritage Foundation established for the purpose, its exhibits were chosen by a committee: Julian Boyd (chair); Evans; and Solon Buck, Archivist of the United States. The Library, which had not previously exhibited original documents outside Washington, loaned some of its treasures: among them the so-called Rough Draft of the Declaration of Independence submitted to the Continental Congress, the manuscript of the Gettysburg Address, and President Wilson's draft of the Covenant of the League of Nations. The train visited all the states from 1947 to 1949, drawing over 3.5 million visitors.[152]

Clark suggested the Freedom Train, he later told Congress, as "a means of aiding the country in its internal war against subversive elements" and "reawakening in our people their profound faith in the American historical heritage."[153] He and President Truman, who heartily approved the idea, spoke of the train as a "rededication," but it also reflected the anticommunist sentiment that pervaded postwar politics. In the wake of Republican gains in the 1946 midterm elections, Truman established the President's Temporary Commission on Employee Loyalty, and even as the Freedom Train was planned, he issued Executive Order 9835 (March 21, 1947), which provided for loyalty checks on executive branch employees and job applicants.[154]

After conferring with the Joint Committee, Evans established the Library of Congress Loyalty Review Board on May 16, 1947. As part of the legislative branch, the Library was not covered by the executive order, but counsel for the House Un-American Activities Committee had already alleged that the LC harbored "aliens and foreign-minded Americans."[155] Chief Assistant Librarian Clapp and Associate Register of Copyrights Arthur Fisher expressed concerns, particularly about targeting individuals who had had a "sympathetic association" with organizations on the Attorney General's list of subversive groups. Evans's general order stated that affiliation with such organizations would not be considered proof of disloyalty. Nevertheless, the process vexed Clapp, who Evans placed in charge of the program: he and his fellow Board members, David Mearns and Frederick Wagman, and Fisher and Administrative Department Director John C. L. Andreassen, all were concerned about protecting individuals' rights.[156] But Evans emphasized that the program was intended to safeguard both the government and individuals, and during 1951 appropriations hearings he noted that Clapp had defended the program to the ALA, which had adopted a resolution protesting loyalty programs.[157]

The Bollingen Prize

A loyalty-related issue brought public controversy. In response to a proposal from the Poetry Consultant and the Fellows, in 1948 the Bollingen Foundation provided ten-year funding to establish the annual Bollingen Prize in Poetry: a $1,000 award for the American poet whose book represented the highest achievement during the preceding year. The 1948–49 Consultant, Léonie Adams, and the Fellows would serve as judges: Conrad Aiken, W. H. Auden, Louise Bogan, Katherine Garrison Chapin, T. S. Eliot, Paul Green, Robert Lowell, Katherine Anne Porter, Karl Shapiro, Allen Tate, Willard Thorpe, and Robert Penn Warren. They decided—though not unanimously—to award the 1948 prize to Ezra Pound's *The Pisan Cantos*.

The Fellows acknowledged that the award was controversial: Pound had been indicted for wartime treason; declared unfit to stand trial, he was an inmate of Saint

Elizabeths Hospital in Washington, and his poem included anti-American, anti-Semitic, antidemocratic, and pro-Axis sentiments. But they maintained that "to permit other considerations other than poetic achievement to sway the decision would destroy the significance of the award and would in principle deny the validity of that objective perception of value on which any civilized society must rest." "It was judged as a brilliant, sometimes confused, poetic eruption that expressed a poet's passionate and unrational rationale in a world and a civilization he particularly hated and loved," Roy Basler recalled.[158] Evans called the choice "unfortunate," adding, "from my poetically ignorant point of view Mr. Pound's book is hardly poetry at all," but he refused to intervene, because that would mean "striking a blow against the cause of liberty by overriding scholarly judgment."[159] Archibald MacLeish called the choice "not only misguided but damned close to irresponsible," telling Evans, "It puts you in a position the fellows had no right to put you in." But MacLeish also resented the accusations "of fraud or worse" leveled at the Fellows.[160]

The Fellows formally commended Evans's "directness and courage, and his upholding of their freedom of judgment." But the Librarian and others warned of consequences, ranging from public outrage to congressional intervention. The warnings were, if anything, too mild: *The Saturday Review of Literature*, for example, published poet Robert Hillyer's articles asserting that Pound's work was "a vehicle of contempt for America" and declaring the award "as much an insult to good taste as it was to the basic values of a democratic people."[161] Some other poets, including Louis Untermeyer and Robert Frost, agreed. As predicted, the controversy drew congressional attention, but rather than the investigation demanded by Senator Jacob Javits (R-NY), the Joint Committee on the Library unanimously passed a resolution that the Library not give prizes or awards. Evans immediately announced compliance, thus canceling not only the Bollingen Prize but also the Elizabeth Sprague Coolidge Medal and the Pennell awards for prints. "Whether freedom of scholarship had been sustained or only ignored was unclear," stated the *Annual Report*, but "at least the principle had not been abridged."[162]

CHAPTER 8

Sesquicentennial and Expansion

THE LIBRARY's collections contained over 1 million items by 1900. Herbert Putnam, who ordered the first formal count, in 1902 reported over 1,750,000 items. The collections grew to more than 2 million items by 1910, more than 4 million by 1920, over 7 million by 1930, and approached 10 million in 1940. But the greatest increase was to come: there could hardly be any more dramatic demonstration of the impact of the 1940s than the 1950 total of 28,691,350 items.

The Library's sesquicentennial celebration, launched on April 24, 1950, included special exhibitions: one tracing the LC's history, one focusing on Jefferson's books, and a third commemorating the sesquicentennial of Washington. President Truman spoke at a May 17 Coolidge Auditorium program celebrating the publication of the first volume of *The Papers of Thomas Jefferson*, edited by Julian Boyd and published by Princeton University Press.[1] The ALA devoted a session to the Library at its summer conference, with remarks by Librarian Evans and President Milton E. Lord (Boston Public Library). Historian Ralph Henry Gabriel discussed the Library's relationship with scholarship; Keyes Metcalf, the Library as a bibliographic center; S. R. Ranganathan (University of Delhi), the Library "among national libraries"; and Arthur E. Gropp (Pan American Union), the Library and Hispanic culture. The ALA also hosted a December 12 banquet at Washington's Mayflower Hotel, inviting representatives of learned societies, professional organizations, libraries, institutions, and congressmen. Representative Carl Albert (D-OK), observing that he had sometimes heard references to the "national library," drew enthusiastic applause with his rejoinder: "Why! It would be easier to change the name of Arkansas than to change the name of the Library of Congress." Last words came from eighty-nine-year-old Herbert Putnam, amid a standing ovation.[2] "Very few executives have had the fortune to live with their posterity and to be welcomed with a eulogy instead of an elegy," he responded. "But if you are summoning shades of the past, you must not fail to summon one shade and keep him contemporary—the valiant, persistent . . . Ainsworth Spofford."[3]

International Relations and Copyright

When North Korea invaded South Korea in June 1950, the United Nations voted to send member nations' armed forces to aid South Korea, and President Truman approved

American involvement. At a House Appropriations Committee hearing on July 13, Representative Christopher McGrath (D-NY) noted Librarian Evans's comment—in a Cooperstown, New York, speech—that "the United States might have had a better understanding of Korea if Congress had permitted the Library to employ an expert on that nation." But Evans also had to admit that he had not made that request a priority.[4]

As in World War II, the Korean War exposed gaps in the collections. With increased demands from the military and federal agencies, Evans requested a supplemental appropriation of $178,000, which the House Appropriations Committee denied, instructing him to "redirect personnel and funds to the fullest extent possible to those more urgent projects." The Librarian accordingly increased staffing in the Map, Orientalia, and European Affairs divisions and the Government Publications Reading Room. He also reestablished the Slavic Division (abolished in the 1944 reorganization) as the Slavic and Central European Division (1953).[5]

Citing the "steady upward trend in demands for reference service that has been characteristic over the last five years," the Librarian cautioned that numbers alone provided an incomplete picture of Library use. "We do know that increasingly [requests] require area specialization," he stated, "and we have already pointed out the difficulty of providing that without increased resources . . . and the Library's sustained efforts to build up its foreign collections especially have presented language difficulties as well as problems of mass."[6]

Evans sought opportunities to acquire both historic and contemporary materials through microfilming and international contacts. A 1950 cooperative project with the American Foundation for the Study of Man filmed manuscripts in Saint Catherine's Monastery on Mount Sinai, the world's oldest Christian monastery (c. AD 300). The American Schools of Oriental Research assisted a project to film manuscripts dating from the sixth century AD in the Greek Orthodox Patriarchate Library in Jerusalem and later extended it to the Armenian Patriarchate Library.[7] A project at the Benjamin Franklin Library in Mexico City recorded the official gazettes of Mexican states; selected Japanese Foreign Office files were filmed in 1948; and a state records project in cooperation with the University of North Carolina completed filming in 1950.[8] Other projects proceeded in partnerships with the University of Santiago, Chile; Japan's National Diet Library; and the Instituto de Antropología e Historia in Mexico City.[9]

The Librarian and Register of Copyrights Arthur Fisher led the effort to develop a Universal Copyright Convention, signed at Geneva on September 6, 1952. UNESCO had worked toward the convention since 1946, but it proved difficult to design an accord that acknowledged both existing international agreements and national statutes. When the member nations finally agreed to protect published and unpublished works from other members on the same basis as their own citizens, Congress approved the necessary statutory changes, and President Eisenhower signed the instrument of ratification on November 5, 1954.[10]

Congress also amended the copyright statute in 1952 to extend performing and recording rights to authors and proprietors of nondramatic literary works. The new protections addressed a gap in the law but did not provide the much-needed revision of the 1909 statute. Headed by Fisher, that effort began in 1955 when the LC and the American

Bar Association agreed to conduct studies on parts of the law. Assisted by the Panel of Consultants on General Revision and an ABA committee, the staff produced thirty-four such studies, culminating in the *Report of the Register of Copyrights on the General Revision of the US Copyright Law* (July 1961). The staff drafted a bill in mid-1964, and revised it for hearings in 1965, but at the same time attention turned to addressing new forms of intellectual property: "Two years ago the most significant problems in copyright law revision came from jukebox performances and educational copying," noted the 1967 *Annual Report*." Today they come from community antenna television systems and computers, and two years from now there may well be new interests whose future will be directly affected by the copyright law." The new Register of Copyrights, Abraham L. Kaminstein, called it an old story: the general agreement on the need for revision repeatedly stymied by conflicting interests.[11]

Benefactors and Gifts

Two of the Library's most generous benefactors, Lessing J. Rosenwald and Gertrude Clarke Whittall, continued to add to the collections: notably, Rosenwald's 1952 gift of the fifteenth-century Giant Bible, two volumes in Latin, on vellum, handmade by a master scribe and illustrators in or around Mainz, Germany, between April 4, 1452, and July 9, 1453. It joined the Gutenberg Bible, produced in print at the same time and in the same place, marking the transition from hand-lettering to the printed book.[12] Chicago manufacturer Alfred Whital Stern presented the first of many gifts from his Abraham Lincoln collection in 1952, including Lincoln's own scrapbook of reports of the Lincoln–Douglas debates; and in 1954 the Levin C. Handy Studios collection, including negatives made by Civil War photographer Matthew Brady, was donated by the Handy family.[13] Gifts from Mr. and Mrs. Jean Hersholt included their Hans Christian Andersen collection (1951) and collections of Sir Hugh Walpole and Sinclair Lewis first editions (1954). Materials from the Sigmund Freud Archive began to arrive in 1952, and Walt Kelly presented his "Pogo" cartoon drawings, the Library's first comic strips.[14] Notable music materials included autograph scores of three Victor Herbert operettas, presented by his family; Fritz Kreisler gave the Library his 1733 Guarneri violin, manuscripts, and memorabilia; and other gifts included the collections of Jascha Heifetz, John Philip Sousa, Deems Taylor, George and Ira Gershwin, Geraldine Farrar, Richard Rodgers, William Schuman, and Glenn Miller.[15]

Mrs. Whittall's gifts, which established the Gertrude Clarke Whittall Poetry and Literature Fund (1950–54), raised controversy in the poetry program. Mrs. Whittall favored traditional works, which did not accord with 1950–51 Consultant Conrad Aiken's ideas or with the Fellows' preference for poets reading their own works. Aiken's May 1, 1951, program, selected by Cleanth Brooks, placed him and the Fellows at odds with the Librarian's office, which had promised to consult Mrs. Whittall on the selections: Mrs. Whittall was annoyed, and Aiken and the Fellows protested that their role as consultants was ignored. In September 1952 Evans assigned Roy Basler, chief of the General Reference and Bibliography Division (and also a historian and poet), to supervise literary programs.[16]

Cataloging and Collection Development

Working through postwar acquisitions continued to challenge the staff: between 1947 and 1949, the Library received 7 to 8 million items annually. Nevertheless, work continued on Class K, and cataloging rules for nonbook materials received LC and ALA approval: motion pictures and filmstrips, maps and atlases, music and phonorecords, and books for the blind. In August 1951, the Card Division began producing cards for motion pictures and filmstrips, and two years later for sound recordings.[17]

A much-praised manual of general library practices, David Judson Haykin's *Subject Headings: A Practical Guide* also appeared in 1951 and was followed by the sixth edition of *Subject Headings Used in the Dictionary Catalogs of the Library of Congress* (1953) and *Music Subject Headings* (1952). Librarians welcomed the publication of cataloging tools on a current basis.[18] "I would spend five times the sum that the *Author* and *Subject* catalogs costs us if it were necessary," wrote Lawrence S. Thompson (University of Kentucky). "I won't go over that figure, since you might take us seriously, but, privately, I would guess that we are saving at least one position in Acquisitions and one in Cataloging from the Author catalog." The publication of book catalogs also enabled the Card Division to reduce stock (which grew by 3 million cards annually), freeing 6,200 square feet and 300 catalog cases.[19]

For smaller libraries, the most important development was a change in the publication of the Dewey Decimal Classification. Dewey had willed the copyright to his Lake Placid Club Education Foundation, with publication by Forest Press. But after librarians expressed dissatisfaction with the fifteenth edition (1951), the ALA asked the Library to take over the editorial work. In January 1954, the Washington office moved into the Processing Department, bringing the editors and LC classifiers together to work on a five-year revision effort, advised by the Decimal Classification Editorial Policy Committee.[20]

The Copyright Office issued *Motion Pictures, 1912–1939* (1951), a listing of over 50,000 films registered during the period, and two years later *Motion Pictures, 1894–1912.* After the 1942 discovery of the "paper prints" of early films, a cooperative effort with the American Academy of Motion Picture Arts and Sciences had developed a method for reproducing them on film, notable among them the first films registered, from Thomas Alva Edison's laboratory.[21] Stored in remote vaults, the nitrate films required annual safety inspections, though Mary Pickford's collection of early films was converted to safety (acetate) film. From 1958 through 1964, Congress provided funding for converting the paper print and nitrate films, including the valuable George Kleine collection of early motion pictures.[22]

The Farmington Plan included over fifty members and extended to more than twenty countries by 1953. Critics complained that it brought in some material of little value, but supporters held that practically everything published should be acquired. Modifications "were almost continuous from the outset," wrote Robert B. Downs: subject allocations were changed, for example, to allow area or single-country assignments in places where the book trade was undeveloped. But since the plan covered only new books, other programs emerged, for example, the ACLS-SSRC Joint Committee on Slavic Studies project to obtain Russian publications, for which the Library served as the distributing agency. With State Department assistance for procurement (a continuing problem because Soviet authorities restricted exports), shipments arrived from February 1951 through April 1957 and were allocated among eight US research libraries. When restrictions were relaxed, the program ended, having distributed over 21,000 publications at a cost to the libraries of $42,000.[23]

The Declaration and the Constitution

Even after the National Archives was established in 1934, the Constitution and the Declaration of Independence remained at the Library: Herbert Putnam maintained that moving them required presidential and congressional authorization. President Roosevelt and Archivist R. D. W. Connor did not press for transfer to the Archives, nor did Solon J. Buck, who succeeded Connor in 1941.[24] Luther Evans, however, thought the documents belonged in the Archives. When Wayne Grover (who became Archivist in 1948) attended the LC's September 19, 1951, Constitution Day ceremony that celebrated sealing the Declaration and the Constitution in helium-filled cases, the Librarian told him, "The next ceremony for these documents will be when they're transferred to the National Archives."[25]

Over lunch at the Cosmos Club, Grover and Evans discussed the rationale for the transfer: the Archives building had a specially designed vault for the documents, and the Federal Records Act (1950) required that all permanently valuable noncurrent records be preserved in the Archives. When they approached the White House, President Truman informed congressional leaders of the proposal, and on April 30, 1952, the Joint Committee ordered the transfer. On Saturday, December 13, Armed Forces Special Police placed the documents in a Marine Corps armored personnel carrier, and they traveled to the Archives escorted by tanks, a color guard, the Army Band, and the Air Force Drum and Bugle Corps. The next Monday, Chief Justice Fred Vinson presided over a ceremony that included remarks from the President and Senator Theodore Green (D-RI, chairman of the Joint Committee) and Grover and Evans's presentation of the new exhibit.

Evans acknowledged that the loss of the founding documents was "an emotional wrench": anticipating hard feelings, he had asked the Joint Committee to order rather than request the transfer, and called it "the routine application of the statutes concerning the records of the US Government." David Mearns expressed the staff's regrets in a 1952 *Annual Report* essay, dwelling on the many reverential visits to "the shrine," from heads of state to school children. Afterward, Evans wrote Grover, "I don't know what history will say about our friendly collusion. But I can tell you that I feel darned broad-minded and just a wee bit righteous, something like a fellow who gave up his gal to an ugly clumsy younger brother who wasn't very good at finding gals of his own." Grover, writing back that Evans was justified in feeling righteous, added that he did not mind being an "ugly clumsy little brother."[26]

Loyalty Programs and Intellectual Freedom

Loyalty investigations took a new direction in the spring of 1950, when Senator Clyde R. Hoey (D-NC) launched an inquiry focused on "susceptible individuals." He was understood to mean homosexuals, who some feared were vulnerable to blackmail or other pressures, or perhaps targeted by efforts to undermine the government. While the LC Loyalty Board cases had resulted in only four preinvestigation resignations, two unfavorable determinations, and one case reopened, Hoey's inquiry posed a different challenge: the Librarian's Conference discussed the matter in connection with responding to a Senate Investigations subcommittee questionnaire on LC employees. Between April and November 1950, fifteen LC employees were charged and nine resigned, one was fired, and five cases were pending. In the case of Esther C. Brunauer, dismissed by the State Department in 1952, Evans defended to the Senator's staff his decision to hire her temporarily for nonsensitive work.[27]

Meanwhile, librarians resisted calls to censor their collections. At the ALA's 1952 Conference on Intellectual Freedom, Verner Clapp called the right of free inquiry "a basic premise of research libraries," declaring that calls to deny access to library materials "assaulted a principle too vital to be compromised." With pressure to remove so-called subversive materials increasing across the country and Senator Joe McCarthy's (R-WI) investigation of State Department overseas libraries, the ALA's Intellectual Freedom Committee and the American Book Publishers Council sponsored a conference at the Westchester Country Club in Rye, New York, in May 1953. Twenty-five librarians, publishers, and citizens "representing the public interest" were invited, and Librarian Evans served as chairman. Enthusiastically adopted at the subsequent ALA conference, the Westchester statement, "The Freedom to Read," drew nationwide media coverage. It also drew a well-publicized letter from President Eisenhower to the ALA declaring that American libraries "are and must ever remain the homes of free, inquiring minds."[28]

Loyalty investigations also entered the poetry program. In 1948 Evans had invited William Carlos Williams to serve as Consultant in Poetry, but the appointment was postponed to December 1952 due to Williams's illnesses. In August, however, news reports alleged that he harbored pro-communist sympathies. When in October the Library sent him the usual application form for federal employment, Williams stated that he had not belonged to any communist-related organization. But in December Verner Clapp notified him that the appointment required an FBI investigation, and Williams retained an attorney. Evans revoked the appointment in January—not on loyalty grounds but citing health concerns and "new elements" introduced by the attorney's communications.

The Fellows asked Léonie Adams and Cleanth Brooks to intercede with Evans, and the Librarian subsequently offered Williams an appointment to terminate in September 1953, contingent on a physician's statement and completion of the FBI inquiry. A report on the investigation arrived on June 26, but with Evans's departure early in July, the appointment was never made.[29]

Evans and Congress

Luther Evans had long been interested in international cooperation. Assistant Secretary of State MacLeish sent him as a delegate to the 1945 London conference that established the United Nations Educational, Scientific, and Cultural Organization (UNESCO). Between 1946 and 1952 he was a member, and later chair, of the US National Commission for UNESCO. From 1947 through 1953 he joined the US delegation to UNESCO's General Conferences and in 1949 became a member of its Executive Board.

Evans strengthened the Library's international programming, supporting, for example, the Assembly of Librarians of the Americas in 1947 and, with Vanderbilt University, the International Colloquium on Luso-Brazilian Studies. In 1952 the LC joined the Pan American Union and the Chilean Embassy to host a celebration honoring the Chilean scholar and bibliographer José Toribio Medina. The 1953 Colloquium on Islamic Culture in Its Relation to the Contemporary World, in cooperation with Princeton University, drew scholars from the United States, the Near East, and South Asia. On contract with UNESCO, the staff prepared the report "Bibliographical Services: Their Present State and Possibilities of Improvement" to encourage the production of national bibliographies.[30]

With UNESCO business demanding much time and travel, Evans often used his annual leave to fulfill those obligations. "The broader cultural aims underlying almost all aspects of the UNESCO program correspond to the most humane and enlightened ideals that have guided the policies of the Library of Congress for generations and have persuaded successive Congresses of the United States to support the Library's activities in the field of cultural interchange with other Nations," he wrote. "For those reasons it seemed to me an obligation, which I could not deny, personally to assume quite extensive responsibilities in regard to the development of UNESCO policy and in the conduct of its affairs."[31] As demands on his time increased, he appointed Verner Clapp to the newly created position of Chief Assistant Librarian in 1947. Two years later, he added an Assistant Librarian, David Mearns, then a Deputy Chief Assistant Librarian in 1950, selecting first Dan Lacy and later Frederick H. Wagman (on an interim basis) for the position. When Wagman became director of the Administrative Department, Evans appointed Lucile Morsch—the first woman in LC history to hold such a senior appointment.[32]

Evans's UNESCO commitments and the Library's contracts with federal agencies drew congressional scrutiny: the House Appropriations Committee's report on the 1953 budget request specifically noted activities funded outside appropriations.[33] At the March 1952 hearings, Representatives McGrath and Walter Horan (R-WA) questioned Evans's spending so much time away from the Library. Since the Librarian was abroad at a UNESCO meeting at the time, Clapp testified for the Library. He told the committee that Evans worked eighteen-hour days and weekends and constantly communicated with the Library when absent, but McGrath and Horan complained that Evans was not fulfilling his responsibilities on Capitol Hill. They brought up the Cooperstown speech as well and other criticisms focused on the large arrearage and federal agency contracts. Clapp wrote Evans, "It was obvious that the Committee was waiting for this chance to jump on you, not merely for your present absence, but for previous ones."[34]

The Librarian considered support for other agencies and for scientific research a national priority: even after the hearing, he wrote optimistically, "we had successfully passed the period of readjustment that followed when the Cold War flamed into hostilities in Asia. A pattern for providing materials and information that required area and language specialization had been established. We also had, and knew we had, the know-how as well as the collections for providing large-scale bibliographical services for other Government agencies." He added that rather than imposing charges, such services "should have been done as part of its regular program, had it had the appropriations for it."[35]

Evans was elected Director-General of UNESCO and resigned effective July 5, 1953. Colleagues expressed appreciation for his leadership during the tense postwar period: Foster Mohrhardt (Veterans Administration) and former LC staff member Frederick Wagman (University of Michigan) mentioned his determination to repatriate foreign materials, his success in broadening the acquisitions programs and extending them to other libraries, and his contributions to international library and copyright affairs. Dan Lacy, who had worked with him since HRS days, emphasized his support for freedom of expression but suggested that he had tried too soon to expand the Library's role. He was, Keyes Metcalf declared, "because of his untiring efforts on our behalf, more popular with librarians than any other Librarian had ever been." Noting that appropriations more than doubled, from $4.6 million in 1945 to $9.4 million in 1953, the *Annual Report* stated, "Luther Evans was not one to paint on a small canvas, and to that characteristic much of the expansion of the Library's service in recent years is due." The *Information Bulletin* cited his "system of democratic administration" and "his vision, his drive, and his tremendous capacity for hard work." Daniel Boorstin, a later Librarian, recalled, "His spontaneity and vigor were exemplified in all that he did and particularly in his efforts to broaden the Library's outlook and extend its relationships in the furthering of international culture and the world of books and learning."[36] Though sometimes at odds with Congress, Evans's determination to increase the collections and enhance LC relationships abroad broadened the Library's role, just as his involvement of the LC staff in administration and his outreach to other libraries fostered closer internal and external cooperation.

A New Librarian and Congress

Verner Clapp became Acting Librarian. A longtime staff member, Clapp had no professional training, but he had done much to shape LC programs over the years. MacLeish named him director of the Administrative Department in 1940 and of the new Acquisitions Department in 1943, where he led the European Mission and Cooperative Acquisitions Project, organized the United Nations Conference Library, and joined the US Library Mission to Japan. When Evans named him Chief Assistant Librarian in 1947, the Librarian announced that it was in response to "a wide popular demand." Proving that true, in a tribute to his enduring sense of humor, on Clapp's last day in Acquisitions, the staff all wore black.[37]

Clapp was a respected administrator and ambassador for the Library, but he was not to become Librarian.[38] He resigned in September 1956, moving to the private sector as president of the Council on Library Resources (CLR), a new funding agency established by the Ford Foundation. Colleagues observed that it was a job ideally suited to his "inventive, imaginative, mind," and the advent of CLR proved particularly important for the Library of Congress.[39] Maintaining a close relationship with his LC colleagues, Clapp helped (and, as often, nudged) them to undertake CLR-funded projects to enhance national services. The council's support, in particular for technology- and preservation-related activities, soon made the words "with the aid of a grant from the Council on Library Resources, Inc." ubiquitous in the library community.

The ALA sent the White House a statement of qualifications and an unranked list of six candidates. The association also contacted congressmen and senators, and as rumors arose that nonlibrarians were being considered, it sought support from the National Research Council, the National Academy of Sciences, the American Council on Education, the Social Science Research Council, and the American Council of Learned Societies. In accordance with the White House's request, the candidates' names remained confidential, though it was rumored that Clapp was the ALA's first choice. Eisenhower waited nearly a year, nominating fifty-one-year-old Lawrence Quincy Mumford, director of the Cleveland Public Library, on April 22, 1954.[40]

A native of North Carolina, Mumford received a BA degree from Duke University and an MA from Columbia University's School of Library Science. Keyes Metcalf hired him as a beginning professional for the New York Public Library (NYPL) staff. Between 1929 and 1945, he rose to head both the cataloging and public services operations, winning the respect of such leaders in the profession as Metcalf, Harry M. Lydenberg, and Paul North Rice; and the NYPL loaned him to Librarian MacLeish from September 1940 through August 1941 to organize the LC's new Processing Department. He moved to the Cleveland Public Library in 1945 as assistant director and became director in 1950; he served as president and board member of the Ohio Library Association and had just been elected ALA president for 1954–55. Mumford received the support of the Ohio congressional delegation, the Senate confirmed him "without objection" on July 29, and he was sworn in on September 1, 1954, at a Whittall Pavilion ceremony—the first professional librarian to serve as Librarian of Congress. On arrival, he received Herbert Putnam's greeting: "Welcome, and may good will, good fortune, and good cheer attend you ever."[41] Putnam, presumably, approved of a Librarian who was an experienced administrator.

But while Mumford's election as ALA president acknowledged his leadership in the profession, there was some hesitation, especially within the Association of Research Libraries (ARL). Where MacLeish and Evans had organized national and international acquisitions efforts and provided assistance for research libraries, at least some librarians were not confident that Mumford would support large libraries' needs.

Congress registered its dissatisfaction with the Library. One of the questions at Mumford's July confirmation hearing was, "If you found that the Library of Congress was neglecting its primary duty—that for which it was established—that of service to the Congress and was going into other fields to the detriment of Congress, you would be willing to correct that situation?" In response, Mumford promised to review LC operations.[42] Even before the confirmation hearing, on May 12 he had been summoned by Representative Horan, chair of the House Appropriations Subcommittee, to its hearings. Horan had been so unhappy with the earlier LC presentation that he had abruptly adjourned the hearings, and the subcommittee report admonished, "The new Librarian should be mindful that the Library is the instrument and the creature of Congress. Its duties historically have been to meet the needs of the Members of Congress first and to limit its service to others to that which can be furnished with the funds and staff available." And "the committee has *not* been entirely satisfied with the operation of the Library and with the manner in which its appropriation requests have been presented and justified. It invited the Librarian-designee to attend the hearings as an observer . . . since it expects him to take every action necessary to improve the operations of the Library and place it on a more businesslike basis as soon as possible after he takes office."[43]

Mumford's future LC colleagues had tried to answer the criticisms. Clapp countered, "Mr. Chairman, there is no doubt that the Library of Congress has gone far beyond the purposes for which it was originally created on April 24, 1800." But the statutory basis for extending its scope, he said, began as soon as the first books were acquired and continued down to "so recent a date as 1952." He provided a full list of congressional enactments and the texts of every mention of the Library in the US Code and the *Code of Federal Regulations*. Accompanying those lists was a memorandum titled "National Library" that addressed the historical uses of that term, with comments on issues the members raised: arrearage, card sales, the Law Library, the Loan Division, study room assignments, and work performed for executive branch agencies. It was all reproduced for the confirmation hearing.[44]

The subcommittee's report stated that the Library "operates practically as a free adjunct of the legislative branch" with a chief executive whose conception of his job was left to his judgment "rather than what may be owing to Congress." It noted that LC received little congressional supervision except through appropriation hearings, though the Librarians had generally acknowledged criticisms and suggestions. "It is to be admitted that Congress, in extending the Library's activities by law, has been a factor in making it such a nationwide establishment. Congress justifiably has pride in its Library as the most outstanding library in the world. But it is this same Congress which today stands in second position to the public in use of the Library." And "it is apparent that too often the Library seems to be submerged by its own good intentions. A stopping place—a final line—should be set beyond which its public services and those to the executive agencies cannot go. Indeed, a withdrawal of many of those services or a deemphasis appears to be in order." There were recommendations to "restate its duties, its functions, and its aims," control collection growth, attack the arrearage, limit services to executive agencies and the public, and identify "the propaganda content of new accessions to the Library, although this is a subject which could come under study."[45]

The subcommittee reduced the Library's estimates, adding the familiar comment: "The reductions are due to the committee's feeling that the Library has gone far beyond the functions for which it was originally created." While the Senate committee restored some of the funding, clearly Mumford would have to concentrate on building trust. Nevertheless, he would insist that his funding requests represented genuine needs and that the Library must grow to fulfill its responsibilities for serving Congress, the federal government, and the public. Mumford repeatedly gave Congress credit for responding to LC requests, but he stood his ground.[46]

Mumford's Reorganization

The effects of the decreased 1955 appropriation (including a reduction of forty-one positions) were mostly felt before Mumford arrived. He did make changes: he abolished the vacant position of Assistant Librarian and transferred the Exhibits Office and Information and Publications Office to the Chief Assistant Librarian's office but in 1960 shifted both to a new Assistant Librarian for Public Affairs. He moved the Personnel Office into the Librarian's Office, abolished the European Affairs Division, and changed the variously titled consultant positions to simply "honorary consultant." He continued contracts with other federal agencies and requested reviews of the finances by the Comptroller-General and of the position classification system and loyalty-security program by the Civil Service Commission. Mumford resisted a House Appropriations Committee suggestion that service for the blind be transferred to the Department of Health, Education and Welfare, arguing that it was "essentially a library function" and only the LC had the relationships with the states and private organizations essential to the program. That the committee agreed showed that relations were improving, and in 1956, Congress funded his 1957 request in full, an increase of $377,100; while calling it "a vote of confidence," Mumford continued to assert the Library's responsibilities. The Committee on the Control and Organization of the Collections (1958), for example, produced a statement, "Objectives of the Library of Congress," which was never published but offered "a balance among the several objectives and service goals."[47]

Mumford continued the Librarian's Conference but not the staff discussion groups. He retained interdepartmental committees on Acquisitions, Bibliography and Publications, Processing, Film Cataloging, Manuscript Cataloging, Music Processing, Orientalia Processing, Rules for Cataloging Prints and Photographs, and Rules for Books in Raised Characters, Binding, and later (1968), a Committee on the Motion Picture Program.[48] Deputy Librarian John Lorenz noted that he "has a continuing contact with the major departments of the library" and "each department director does have weekly sessions with the Librarian." But Rutherford D. Rogers, Lorenz's predecessor, mentioned, for example, "status of funds" meetings with only the fiscal staff, perhaps singling out functions that increasingly demanded the Librarian's attention.[49] What was apparently lost, in a growing bureaucracy, was the closer contacts with the staff that MacLeish and Evans had pursued.

Despite its criticisms, Congress steadily increased the Library's activities. One of the most important statutory changes was to eliminate the word "adult" from the Books for the Adult Blind program in July 1952, thus inaugurating service to children.[50] Another was the establishment of the Oliver Wendell Holmes Devise (1955) to administer the Justice's 1931 bequest to the nation. The Librarian became chairman ex officio of an oversight committee appointed by the President, chosen from candidates named by the American Philosophical Society, the Association of American Universities, the American Historical Association, and the Association of American Law Schools. Working from an LC office, the group planned a multivolume history of the Supreme Court. In 1957, legislation provided that the Librarian and the Smithsonian Secretary consult with both the new Lincoln Sesquicentennial Commission and the Civil War Centennial Commission on the deposit of donations to libraries and museums nationwide. That same year, Congress approved funding for the Presidential Papers Program, charged to arrange, index, and microfilm the LC's twenty-three presidential collections.[51]

Federal Aid, Sputnik, and Library Users

The ALA's long efforts to obtain federal aid for libraries finally succeeded when Congress passed the Library Services Act (PL 84-597, 1956), authorizing $7 million annually to be matched by state and local funding for libraries in rural areas, extended to urban areas and to library buildings in the Library Services and Construction Act (PL 88-268, 1964) and extended again to include interlibrary cooperation and services to special groups, including those with physical disabilities (1966). Though the initial funding was small, the legislation signaled increased congressional interest, and in 1958 the ALA joined lobbying efforts for the National Defense Education Act (NDEA, PL 85-864). Heralded by the 1957 launch of the Russian satellite Sputnik, the act provided funding for education, in particular, science, mathematics, and foreign languages programs: a response to the "sense of panic and doom," as Congressman Carl Elliott Sr. (D-AL) put it, that followed the Russian advance.[52]

Calling 1957 the year "when the Nation as a whole gained a new awareness of science," Mumford changed the name of the Science Division to the Science and Technology Division. With National Science Foundation (NSF) support, the division would serve as a depository for materials from the Department of Commerce's Office of Technical Services and the Atomic Energy Commission, with particular attention to Soviet science and technology. The Librarian was an ex officio member of the new Science Information Council, established by the NDEA to advise the NSF, and he also served on the Board of Regents of the new National Library of Medicine (NLM).[53]

Library use seemed to mirror this concentration of attention. The *Information Bulletin* dubbed it the "Holiday Rush," when students and scholars crammed the reading rooms at the end of the year, commenting that their vacations "mean just the opposite for the reference staff." In the Main Reading Room and the Annex's Thomas Jefferson Reading Room, the staff usually served about 280 books per hour, but in the 1958 holidays, the average rose to 695. On December 30, "the day when seats were so scarce in the Main Reading Room that one man settled himself on the floor to read," the Rare Book Room, which usually averaged 25 readers daily, recorded 57, while the Periodicals room served 279, up from 175, all reminiscent of Depression-era crowding.[54]

On September 1, 1958, the Library began restricting service to high school students. For many years, anyone over sixteen could use the reading rooms; but efforts to limit use had not relieved the congestion. Thus, "with regret at limiting in any way its principle and tradition of wide service," the Joint Committee approved requiring students to provide a letter from their school principals certifying their need for materials not available at their school or public libraries. Tours for student groups continued, but the Library maintained that school and public libraries were best equipped to serve students' needs.[55]

Improvements in services to blind readers began with the 1959 adoption of magnetic tape, making it possible, with copyright permission, to have quality recordings made by volunteers at home and allowing the regional libraries to make copies as needed. Robert Bray, chief of the Division for the Blind, called tape recordings "the paperbacks of the talking book field," citing their low cost, compact size, and easy duplication. Two years later, Congress authorized collecting music scores and music instruction materials, and in 1963 the division introduced talking books on ten-inch records with forty-five minutes of playing time on each side. The advent of books on cassette came through a 1968 pilot program, and by 1973 the division had added flexible discs that proved especially appropriate for magazines. Congress extended services to the near-blind and those with physical disabilities through PL 89-522 in 1966: moved in 1967 to Taylor Street NW, the division was renamed the Division for the Blind and Physically Handicapped in 1978.[56]

Expanding Cataloging

For librarians, particularly in research libraries, the most important developments of the 1950s and the 1960s were in acquisitions and cataloging operations. After consultations with the ALA's Board on Resources and the ARL, the Library's survey of book catalog subscribers found that 90 percent favored a Union Catalog. On July 1, 1956, the *Library of Congress Catalog—Books: Authors* became the *National Union Catalog: A Cumulative Author List Representing Library of Congress Printed Cards and Titles Reported by Other American Libraries.* "Other American libraries" meant the 600 libraries reporting their current cataloging to the Union Catalog. The NUC, as it soon became known, enabled librarians and users to find books in many libraries, and it attracted 900 subscribers. In 1959, the ALA's National Union Catalog Subcommittee obtained funding to support the next step—publication of the 1952–55 NUC, which was completed in 1961. The task that still loomed was the publication of the Union Catalog itself, the pre-1952 cards that were available only at the Library of Congress.[57]

With the addition of the Far Eastern Languages Section in the Descriptive Cataloging Division, the card service began printing cards for Chinese, Japanese, and Korean publications in 1958. It was an achievement long in the making, involving not only standardizing cataloging practices for nonwestern materials but also converting calligraphy to print—the work of the Library's Orientalia Processing Committee, in coordination with the ALA's Special Committee on Far Eastern Materials. In 1959, with Rockefeller Foundation funding, the LC produced its first publication on preservation, and with CLR support it began to compile a third edition of the *Union List of Serials* (published 1966).[58]

In 1948 the American Historical Association had recommended to a joint committee of the Society of American Archivists and the American Association for State and Local History that a central register of manuscript collections be established, and in 1951 Evans had agreed to undertake the task. The Manuscripts Division developed cataloging rules, which the ALA approved in 1954, and the staff would compile the *National Union*

Catalog of Manuscript Collections (NUCMC) using the collection descriptions submitted by libraries and archival institutions. Basically a reporting device, the NUCMC (pronounced Nuck-Muck) would not provide the full inventories researchers needed to access collection contents, but it facilitated identifying and locating collections. The first volume appeared in 1962.[59]

Cultural Programs

Mumford asked Archibald MacLeish's advice about the poetry program. Expressing regret that the Fellows had not been as successful as he hoped, MacLeish nevertheless encouraged Mumford to "hold the gains" in literary programming, and the Librarian continued to appoint Consultants in Poetry: first Randall Jarrell, followed by Robert Frost. At Jarrell's suggestion, Mumford formed a new advisory group, the Honorary Consultants in American Letters. But when Representative W. Sterling Cole (R-NY) proposed that the President name a Poet Laureate of the United States, Mumford responded that might be seen as favoring a single literary style. And, evoking the Pound controversy, he reminded Cole that LC had "an unfortunate experience in the making of awards."[60]

Frost, in particular, broadened the Consultant's role: he took every opportunity (beginning with an unprecedented and well-attended press conference) to encourage the government to nurture creativity. He was a popular figure, both in the Library and on the Hill, and after his 1958–59 term ended, Mumford appointed him Honorary Consultant in the Humanities. It was an appointment that he took, he said, "to mean practically everything human that has been brought to book and can be treated in poetry." Invited to read a poem at President John F. Kennedy's inauguration, Frost's appearance underscored the new administration's interest in the arts and cultural institutions.[61] He returned to the LC for a Bollingen Foundation–funded National Poetry Festival in October 1962 that featured eighty American poets. Consultant Louis Untermeyer conceded that the festival brought a few intrafraternity disagreements, but "none of this appeared on the surface. A rapport between the poets and the public was quickly established. . . . It was refutation of the often-repeated charge that the modern poet was writing only for himself and for a few other poets. It was also an affirmation of the hope that poetry was—and is—essentially a communication, a reaching out by the writer and a ready acceptance by the reader."[62]

International Programs and Research Collections

In June 1951 Congress passed PL 82-48 directing the use of interest payments on a loan to India. Five million dollars would be used for exchanges, providing Indian higher education and research institutions with American books and equipment (begun 1955) and bringing Indian materials to the United States (begun 1959). A November 1957 Ford Foundation–funded Conference on American Library Resources on Southern Asia sponsored by the Library and the Association for Asian Studies proposed that money in the Wheat Loan Interest Fund be used to purchase Indian documents for the University of Pennsylvania, the Midwest Interlibrary Center in Chicago, and the University of California. The State Department transferred $84,000 to the LC for the purpose, and Jennings Wood, assistant chief of the Exchange and Gift Division, traveled to India to review the exchange program.[63] Simultaneously, Willam H. Kurth, assistant chief of the Order Division, represented the LC and eleven other libraries in negotiating exchanges in Latin America, and the African Studies Association supported a request to the Carnegie Corporation for $200,000, enabling the Library to establish an African section in 1960.[64]

In September 1958 Congress approved an amendment to the Agricultural Trade Development and Assistance Act of 1954 (PL 83-480) that authorized the Library to use United States–owned foreign currency to acquire materials for US libraries and research centers (under 480, countries purchasing US surplus products paid in local currencies, which had to be spent locally). Prompted by the American Council of Learned Societies and the ARL, Representative John Dingell (D-MI) introduced PL 85-931, an amendment authorizing using the funds to acquire foreign books and journals, deposit them in US institutions, and catalog them or otherwise make the materials accessible. When it passed, Mumford requested foreign currencies for the eight countries in which they were available. Turned down in 1958 and 1959, he reduced the number to three and obtained an appropriation in 1961 to establish offices in New Delhi, Karachi (later Islamabad), and Cairo. The program later expanded to Indonesia, Israel, Yugoslavia, and Ceylon (later Sri Lanka). A 1965 Rockefeller grant initiated a newspaper and gazette microfilming program in New Delhi and, as appropriations continued, more libraries joined the program.[65]

PL 480 (also called "the Special Foreign Acquisitions Program") covered materials from areas that the Farmington Plan did not include and from countries poorly represented in American collections. It also provided broader coverage, including newspapers, serials, and government documents. "Thus for the first time in our history," Robert Vosper (University of California, Los Angeles) wrote, "the Federal government is in the position of enhancing the resources of individual research libraries. Moreover, this development has in fact brought the Federal government directly in the business of the Farmington Plan, at least for a few countries, namely the business of comprehensive current book procurement." Important as that was, the LC's PL 480 director Robert D. Stevens considered the centralized cataloging just as significant: it was the first on the national level, it addressed the stateside problem of finding staff with both language skills and cataloging expertise, and it was paid for by the libraries themselves.[66] PL 480 simultaneously demonstrated the effectiveness of a national program, advertised congressional confidence in Mumford, and launched a new international role for the Library.

Crowding and Cataloging-in-Source

Meanwhile, like Spofford and Putnam, Mumford spent years persuading Congress to provide a new building. His 1956 *Annual Report* observed, "The Main Building presents problems of age and use. Some of its equipment is of the vintage of the building itself and requires increasing attention." In July 1958, with the buildings increasingly crowded and "evidence of encouraging [congressional] interest," Mumford established a planning committee. Two years later, Congress approved leasing space elsewhere, but meanwhile the staff spread into the stacks and study rooms; they reviewed acquisitions policies, replaced volumes with microfilm, and culled the arrears for unwanted items. In mid-1964, the Card Division moved a mile away to the Navy Yard, and the Main Reading Room closed in May for cleaning; replacement of flooring, lighting, and desks; and installation of new HVAC systems and book conveyors. For sixteen months, reader service moved to the Annex; in 1969, the Copyright Office moved to Arlington, Virginia, and the Geography and Map Division moved to Alexandria.[67]

In spite of crowded quarters, services increased. An "All-the-Books" program begun in 1953 asked publishers to send to the LC new titles as soon as bound copies were available so the Library could catalog them and print cards before publication.[68] By June 1959, 2,000 publishers were cooperating; and to increase coverage, the R. R. Bowker Company agreed to loan copies of new books received for listing in *Publishers Weekly* and *Library Journal.* The Library would then send Bowker cataloging information for *Publishers Weekly* and its monthly *American Book Publishing Record.*[69]

Nevertheless, librarians still wanted what they had always wanted: to have cataloging information arrive with their new books. Verner Clapp proposed an experiment to fulfill that wish, called "Cataloging-in-Source." The Library announced in June 1958 a CLR-funded trial: the cataloging staff would receive page proofs of new books, catalog the books, and send the catalog information to the publishers to be printed in the books. A survey of eight libraries would assess how Cataloging-in-Source affected their operations.

C. Sumner Spalding, chief of the Descriptive Cataloging Division, reported success with cataloging rapidly enough to meet publishers' production schedules, though the catalogers worked under tight pressure. Most publishers were pleased with the results, though some were annoyed by delays, added expense, or other problems. Librarians were enthusiastic: with cataloging information printed in books and a camera on every cataloger's desk (a technology not yet developed), it would be possible to produce LC cards locally, instantly, at low cost. The ALA recommended that the Library adopt Cataloging-in-Source permanently.[70]

Nevertheless, Processing Department director John Cronin and Librarian Mumford reported in March 1960 that the program was unfeasible: it was too costly, too disruptive to catalogers' and publishers' schedules, and too unreliable: books in proof were simply not the same as they would emerge from the printer. Amid widespread disappointment, William S. Dix (Princeton University) charged that "the management of the Library of Congress simply does not want to operate such a program." Conceding that it was "a policy decision that the Library had the right to make," Dix continued: "But it is the danger that this conclusion will actually kill for another generation the progress which has brought our profession so close to a major reform that makes me uneasy and that impels me for the first time to write for conscience sake an open letter to the editor of a library journal." Advocating further experiments, Paul Dunkin complained of the "unexpected abdication of leadership by what we had come to look to as the National Library. Is the Library of Congress also the Library of the Nation? This is an administrative decision which must be faced by every Librarian of Congress. The present trend seems to be toward what would be strictly a Library of Congress serving only the Congress." And he asked, "Can the Library of Congress really serve the Congress effectively without serving also every congressman's constituents—i.e., every user or potential user of libraries in the country?"[71]

The Bryant Memorandum

Congress established the National Library of Medicine (NLM) in the Public Health Service in 1956, the successor to the Armed Forces Medical Library. The designation of the NLM as a national library invited discussion about the Library of Congress's status, as did the Secretary of Agriculture's naming the department's library the National Agricultural Library (NAL) on May 23, 1962.[72] Earlier, Senator Claiborne Pell (D-RI), a member of the Joint Committee on the Library, had asked Douglas W. Bryant (Associate Director, Harvard University Library) for a memo on "what the Library of Congress does and ought to do for the Government and the Nation generally."[73] On May 24, Pell inserted Bryant's memo in the *Congressional Record.*

Bryant's analysis went beyond the LC to include "other agencies with closely related functions" and a plea for federal assistance. Research libraries traditionally served scholars, he wrote, but "during recent years, as it has become evident that research is essential to national survival, needs have increased more rapidly than libraries have been able to meet them." And while interlibrary cooperation also had increased, "it is not enough to share resources if their total is inadequate." He called for federal support for library technology, preservation, research libraries, training librarians, and for library-related aid to underdeveloped countries. Bryant advocated congressional recognition of the Library of Congress's national responsibilities ("without necessarily changing its name"), and he proposed creating the National Library Advisory Board that would report to the President. Describing the Library as "anomalous because of the historical accident of its attachment to the Legislative Branch," he stated that it was "desirable," but not "essential," to transfer the LC (excluding the Legislative Reference Service) to the executive branch and to broaden the acquisitions and bibliographic programs, address the arrears, and improve services. Finally, he emphasized that the federal government should lead, not by imposing a program on research libraries "but by encouraging scholars and librarians to formulate their needs and to plan nationally." To that end, he called for "appointment of the best men to the Advisory Board and for a Librarian of Congress who is determined to make the Library all that it ought to be, both within the Government and in its role as the leading library of the nation. The Librarian of Congress must be a man who can administer an extremely diversified and organically complex institution; in addition he must make important decisions on technological innovations in bibliography profoundly affecting the access of scholars to information, supervise the building up of enormous research collections, exercise imaginative leadership nationally, and take advantage of the Library's unique opportunities for contributing to American cultural life. Even an ideal Librarian would require the support and counsel of a strong Advisory Board."

Bryant's critique of Mumford's low-key style was perhaps new to members of Congress, but for advocates of a more aggressive commitment to national services, the memo merely reflected what had been discussed privately for some time. When it was reported early in 1961 that President Kennedy might nominate a new Librarian, the ALA Executive Board had immediately urged the White House to respect the tradition of retaining the Librarian in office. They also contacted the Joint Committee on the Library, and several congressmen opposed a political appointment: for example, Representative Omar Burleson (D-TX) emphasized the importance of nonpartisanship and maintaining "high standards of professional and scholarly excellence," and Representative Fred Schwengel (R-IA) evoked Mumford's successes. The ALA appointed a committee to advise the White House if an opportunity offered, but also pursued contacts close to the administration. The swift reaction, as well as congressional support for Mumford, perhaps discouraged a nomination that might establish a tradition for, in Verner Clapp's estimation, "a rotating political plum."[74]

Invited by the Joint Committee to respond to Bryant, Mumford conferred with colleagues in and outside the Library and produced his response on September 28, which chairman Senator B. Everett Jordan (D-NC) inserted in the *Congressional Record* on October 2, 1962.[75] He expressed "complete agreement" with some of Bryant's observations—such as the need for acquisitions support, for improving the bibliographic apparatus and preservation activities, and for more federal 'participation' in research library programs. Some of the recommendations, he noted, were "neither new nor startling": there had been many proposals to recognize the Library's national role. Asserting that "the Library of Congress today performs more national library functions than any other library in the world," nevertheless, "I have never felt that a change of name was necessary," Mumford wrote. "I would be happy, however, to have the Congress recognize the national responsibilities of the Library of Congress in some formal way." Moreover, congressional "understanding and consistent support" for the Library's national role was evident in "more than doubling our appropriations since I have been in office." Moving the Library into the executive branch would make it subject to administration priorities and oversight, while still dependent on congressional appropriations; thus, "is it not, then, reasonable to believe that rather more advantage than disadvantage attaches to the Library's being in the Legislative Branch?" The Library, he declared, "has not abrogated its leadership in the library world" and "does not find it hard to function as the national library without the name and without a statutory definition of its mission." And, "the officers of the Library are convinced that the institution can accomplish any program suggested by Mr. Bryant or any assigned to it by legislation just as effectively, if not more so, under its present organization as under any of the alternatives suggested."

Mumford promised to consider a Council of Federal Librarians, though he said that some of his colleagues predicted such a group "might be little more than a debating society." With regard to the proposed Advisory Board, he noted Bryant's statement that LC administrators could not serve as advisers to the executive because "they inevitably become identified with their institutions." That statement does not "place a very high estimate on the intellectual integrity of officials of the Library of Congress," he observed, and speculated that "one of the main purposes of the proposed Board is largely to displace the Library as the major instrument through which the Government participates in research library concerns" and to exercise control over the LC. He suggested instead that a temporary commission make recommendations for a national program.

While some considered Bryant's report "an unwarranted attack" on the Library, Mumford commented only that it probably promoted attention to libraries' needs. Neither the LC nor the federal government could be expected to solve all the problems of research libraries, he emphasized, and the LC had been for several years "shoring up its operations." In particular, "the Library's space problem has been worse than frustrating; it has been stifling. There has been a regrettable lack of understanding on this point, which is reflected, I think, in Mr. Bryant's memorandum." Bryant had not mentioned the crowded conditions at all. In response to the call for leadership, Mumford cited accomplishments during his tenure and the need to avoid dictating to other libraries. But "in hewing the fine line between the two positions, perhaps the Library of Congress has of late been too careful to remain in the background rather than pushing to the vanguard."

The Brookings Survey

The Librarian later reported that he had "for some time felt the need to improve communications with the library and scholarly world." Early in 1962 he had begun to assemble three committees: one with representatives from the major library associations and the CLR (it met in time to discuss his response to Bryant), one including scholars in the humanities and social sciences, and one with representatives of the science community.[76]

The new committees had barely met when another report appeared. Luther Evans had returned to Washington in July 1959 as consultant and then director of a CLR-funded Brookings Institution survey of federal libraries. He was assisted by advisory committees of federal librarians (including LC representatives), and the project ended with a June 22, 1963, conference. Evans and his colleagues made two major recommendations. First, the Library of Congress (excluding the Legislative Reference Service), because of its central role in federal library operations, should be transferred to the executive branch, "where it would secure more support and greater financial resources." Second, an advisory federal library council should be established, either by the Bureau of the Budget or jointly by the Bureau and the LC. Conference participants recommended the latter.[77]

Mumford attended the conference and asked to file a response to the parts of the report dealing with the LC, since "many of the comments about it are outdated by a decade or more." He was sharply critical of Evans's argument that transfer to the executive branch would secure more support, noting that transfer would require conformity with executive department requirements that Brookings's survey showed left other federal libraries short of resources and "ensnarled in red tape." And he pointedly described the Library's progress in recovering "ground that was lost in the late 1940s and in the early 1950s." Evans failed to mention, Mumford stated, recent innovations such as the PL 480 program's centralized acquisitions and cataloging. He concluded that the report "presents an inaccurate picture through unwarranted assumptions" and "does a disservice to a great institution and its staff." Evans did not reply.[78]

The House Appropriations Committee's report on the Legislative Branch Appropriations Bill for 1964 supported Mumford, calling the Library "a great cultural and research institution," which

> in the committee's view ought to be brought to a good state of accommodation and efficiency. . . . There have been suggestions over the years, renewed recently, that the Library of Congress ought to be officially designated as the National Library of the United States and its administration shifted to the executive branch. There is considerable reservoir of feeling in the committee against such a proposition of transfer and, very likely the feeling would be shared by many Members of the Congress. The Library is a unique institution. A good many of its services are intimately and peculiarly adapted, in harmony with the original design, for service to the Congress and its committees. Others are national in character and scope. As to the matter of designation, it has been said that custom and tradition are stronger than the law. There would, likely, be considerable opposition to a change of the name, although there would appear to be merit in a formal designation of the Library as the National Library. . . . But even so, it could be said to be a distinction without benefit of the substance of much difference.

The committee recommended an increased appropriation and a third building.[79]

New Services and Tragedy

Mumford continued to emphasize progress. "The windows of the Processing Department open not on Washington alone but on the world," he wrote. "In New Delhi, a small black-haired woman in a bright sari carefully records the information from the book beside her on a Library of Congress data sheet. In Cairo a growing pile of newspapers is stored awaiting microfilming. In Wisbech, near London, negatives of the *Union List of Serials* come in increasing numbers from the unique cameras of Balding & Mansell. In a Midwestern town the staff of a small library unpacks a shipment of new books and finds a complete set of Library of Congress cards tucked in each volume, enabling them to proceed at once with the cataloging process."[80]

A 1963 appropriation established a Children's Book Section, an unusual service for a national library but sought by children's services professionals. The Library had received private funding in 1952 for a consultant, Frances Clarke Sayers (New York Public Library), who recommended establishing a children's literature center, but a search for funding was unsuccessful. Mumford requested an appropriation, and at hearings held March 26, 1962, professional association representatives testified to the need to serve writers, illustrators, publishers, educators, and others who worked with children. The section's annual *Children's Books: A List of Books for Preschool through Junior High School* (retitled *Books for Children* in 1985) first appeared in 1964.[81]

Other new services centered on the sciences. The National Science Foundation provided funding in 1962 for the National Science and Technology Referral Center to gather and disseminate information on organizations and specialists, and the Science

The old Senate Chamber, later the Supreme Court Room, in the Capitol Building, was occupied beginning in 1860 by the Library of Congress's Law Library.

An 1897 drawing of the Library's crowded quarters shows Librarian Spofford (right) and an assistant librarian, David Hutcheson (left, holding a lamp).

The Great Hall of the Thomas Jefferson Building.

The Main Reading Room in the Thomas Jefferson Building, viewed from above.

The Librarian's Ceremonial Office, Thomas Jefferson Building.

The Members' Room in the Thomas Jefferson Building.

In the Catalog and Classification divisions in the Thomas Jefferson Building; staff members are surrounded by card files, reference books, and book trucks, circa 1900.

The Card Division in the Thomas Jefferson Building, crowded to the ceiling with stacks for storing inventory, 1919.

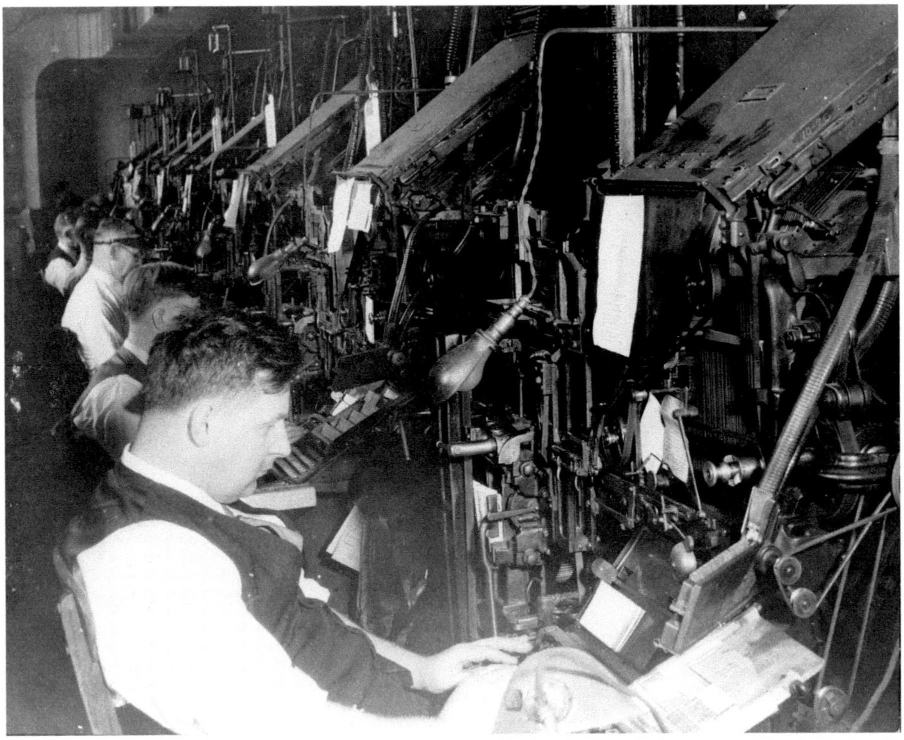

Linotype machines in the Card Division, 1901.

Recording for the Archive of American Folk Song: Doc Reed, John A. Lomax Sr., and Richard Amerson at the home of Mrs. Ruby Pickens Tartt, Livingston, Alabama. Photograph by Ruby Lomax, 1940.

Staff and users at the Main Reading Room's circular desk, circa 1930.

The Rare Book and Special Collections Reading Room in the Thomas Jefferson Building, 1920.

The Thomas Jefferson Reading Room, Library of Congress, John Adams Building, 1940.

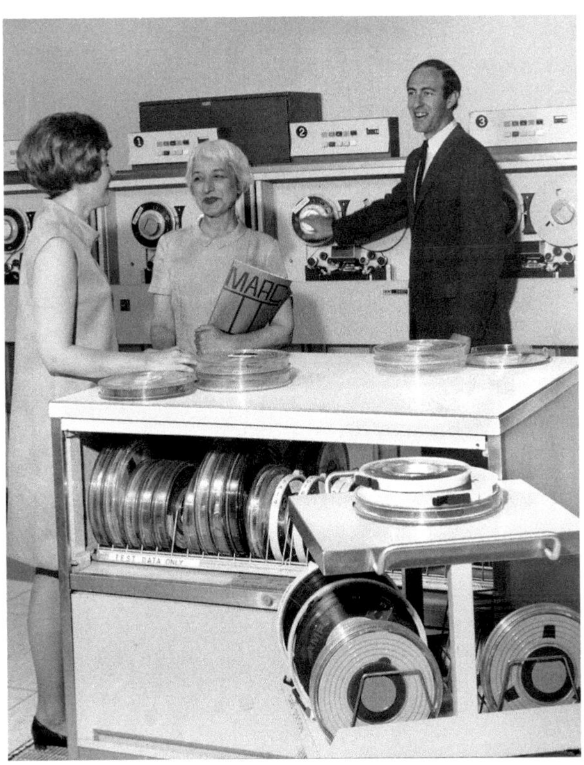

Henriette Avram (center), director of the Machine Readable Cataloging (MARC) pilot project with colleagues in the Information Systems Office computer room, 1968.

James H. Billington taking the oath of office as Librarian of Congress from Supreme Court Chief Justice William Rehnquist. Marjorie Billington holds the Bible, as President Ronald Reagan looks on, 1987.

Opened in 2007, the Library's Packard Campus of the National Audio-Visual Conservation Center, in Culpeper, Virginia, provides a state-of-the-art facility for processing and preserving these collections.

and Technology Division cooperated with the Office of Technical Services to offer research services for a per-hour fee. The Library served as one of twelve Federal Regional Technical Report Centers, developed the Army-supported Cold Regions Bibliography Project, and in 1972 began issuing *LC Science Tracer Bullet* bibliographies, intended to assist readers to locate material on science topics. The Arms Control and Disarmament Agency supported a section in the Reference Department (1964), which began issuing *Arms Control and Disarmament: A Quarterly Bibliography* in 1965.[82]

Mumford began his 1964 *Annual Report* with a review of his ten years' service. On page five, however, a boldface heading intervened: "Death of a President." "Probably no single event in these past 10 years has shown the use and work of a great library more dramatically than the death of President John Fitzgerald Kennedy," he wrote. As Jim Bishop related in *The Day Kennedy Was Shot*, it was Jacqueline Kennedy who, on arriving at Andrews Air Force Base, asked Chief of Protocol Angier Biddle Duke for information on Lincoln's funeral. That involved opening the Library for Arthur Schlesinger Jr. and Richard Goodwin: "In response to a telephone call from the White House, several members of the staff worked until midnight, Friday, November 22, compiling historical information relative to the lying-in-state; again, in the dark hours of Sunday morning, between 1:30 and 5:30, Acting Librarian Rutherford Rogers joined Reference Department staff members, among them Lincoln experts, to compile information on presidential funeral ceremonies." Bishop's reference to "dark hours" was literal: the LC's lighting operated on timing devices, and Schlesinger and Goodwin, who met David Mearns, James O. Sutton, and James I. Robertson Jr. at the LC at about 11 p.m., searched newspapers and periodicals by flashlight.[83]

Public service was suspended from 3 p.m. on November 22nd until the morning of the 26th, but the buildings remained open "to serve as a refuge for the chilled and weary mourners who stood in long lines from Sunday afternoon until Monday morning waiting to pay final homage to the President who lay in state in the Capitol Rotunda." Over 4,000 people entered the Library during that time.[84] Meanwhile, the staff fielded press inquiries and responded to congressional and agency requests for information on such topics as presidential funeral processions and presidential succession. Later, the staff of the Warren Commission requested reference and bibliographical assistance, and inquiries about the Soviet response to the assassination reached the Slavic and Central European Division, while the Secretary's Office archived letters of tribute and condolence. Documentation related to the assassination and funeral was collected, including NBC's entire three-day coverage of the events. *John F. Kennedy, 1917–1963: A Chronological List of References*, appeared in mid-1964.[85]

MARC

When Congress began asking Mumford about using computer technology in 1960, the Librarian had already established the Interdepartmental Committee on Mechanized Information Retrieval (1958).[86] He established the position of Information Systems Specialist in March 1961 and, on the advice of Verner Clapp plus $100,000 from the CLR, contracted with Gilbert W. King (IBM) to produce a feasibility study, *Automation and the Library of Congress*, published in January 1964. While the retrieval of the contents of books was not yet possible, the study team concluded that automation was technically and economically feasible for a large research library's bibliographic system. The report emphasized that one goal of an LC automation program, "because of its central role in the American library world," should be a national system for the interchange of data. Clapp commissioned Lawrence F. Buckland (Inforonics), to examine methods for making bibliographic data machine-readable.[87]

Although some libraries were already experimenting with automation, the forward-looking King study generated "every conceivable emotional reaction," Lucile Morsch wrote. "There are skeptics who think the Council on Library Resources financed a nightmare; it gave some of them the kind of foreboding which they felt when they read *1984*. Others saw the report as a dream of a bright new day that can be ours, given time, the fullest cooperation of librarians and automation experts, and sums of money that are too great for most of us to comprehend." King reported that since equipment manufacturers did not consider libraries a lucrative market, "That is why it is so important that a large-scale project, such as the automation of the Library of Congress, be adequately funded, for the whole library community to be able to bring itself up to the technological well being attendant to other fields."[88]

As the King study proceeded, the LC, the CLR, and the National Science Foundation sponsored a Conference on Libraries and Automation in May 1963 for invited representatives from libraries and the systems development field. The White House sent J. Hillary Kelley from its new Office of Science and Technology, who stated that "having this dichotomy of thought and interest, somewhat like the salesman and the buyer, you bring each other into better focus on problems." Foster Mohrhardt (NAL) observed that it was "a challenge to habit, a little stretching of our minds, an approach that's more visionary possibly than some of us want to take, but it's one that we're going to have to take if we're going to live in the 20th century." Information scientist Robert M. Hayes (University of California, Los Angeles) declared that the LC had taken "the broadest possible view" of an automated future: "oriented toward replacement of the entire Library of Congress card catalog (and ultimately of the National Union Catalog) by a mechanized random-access memory of truly immense capacity." Samuel S. Snyder, director of the LC's Information Systems Office (ISO), explained that the Library planned to develop "a basic bibliographic representation corresponding to what is now on the LC catalog card." To the staff, he was more specific: "long-range plans include the eventual conversion of the National Union Catalog to machine-readable form as the basis for a nationwide automated library network and the distribution of LC catalog cards in both machine-readable and printed form."[89]

In January 1965, the CLR, ARL, and LC met with library directors, technical services librarians, and government and industry representatives to discuss the feasibility of distributing machine-readable cataloging information. Several months later, Henriette Avram and the ISO staff produced "A Proposed Format for a Standardized Machine-Readable Catalog Record," and a second conference in November examined what quickly became known as the MARC format. From the outset, MARC was developed not as an in-house system but as a program for the library community: a

CLR-funded one-year pilot project began weekly distribution of machine-readable catalog records for books to sixteen selected libraries in October 1966. The immediate aim was to provide data and computer programs that librarians could use to produce cards, book catalogs, current awareness listings, or other materials and to report their experiences. Project results and discussions with the NAL, NLM, ALA, and the federal Committee on Scientific and Technical Information guided the design of the MARC II format, broadened to include records for all forms of material.[90]

Avram, a programmer who had to learn cataloging, later called the King report's prediction that a complete LC system could be built by 1972 "a fairy tale": the Library, as an information system, was far more complicated than systems developers realized. She had produced the MARC format in record time: "the money came December 1965 and MARC was operational by October," but as she later recalled, everyone who worked with MARC quickly understood the need for librarians and computer experts to combine forces. What was not well understood, Deputy Librarian William Welsh also recalled, was how much it would cost.[91]

Librarian Mumford, NLM director Martin M. Cummings, and Foster Mohrhardt, NAL director and also ALA president-elect, held a press conference at the ALA's June 1967 meeting in San Francisco to announce an agreement to coordinate their automation programs to develop national databases of cataloging information. They established the National Libraries Task Force on Automation and Other Cooperative Services to guide the effort and, advised by the Joint Committee on the Union List of Serials and with funding from the NSF and CLR, to create a National Serials Data Program. The Task Force recommended that library associations endorse MARC II as the national standard for communicating bibliographic information and urged their members to adopt it.[92]

At an early stage of MARC development, the staff received a visit from representatives of the Bodleian Library, Oxford, and the *British National Bibliography* to discuss a UK/MARC pilot project, which the *British National Bibliography* began in 1968. This and other expressions of interest from librarians abroad helped direct the staff's thinking toward exchanging bibliographic records internationally, a development that took shape in succeeding years.[93]

The MARC Distribution Service launched in March 1969. Magnetic tapes recording the LC's cataloging for new English-language books were sent to about sixty selected libraries, with French and German entries soon added. Moved to the Processing Department from the Information Systems Office, the unit became the MARC Editorial Office. With ALA support, the staff had already designed a two-day institute for MARC tape users and begun presenting it at libraries nationwide by mid-1968. Meanwhile, grants from the CLR and Office of Education (1968–71) funded an LC proposal to design a program to convert older catalog records to MARC and a project called Cooperative MARC to test incorporating other libraries' cataloging into the MARC database. MARC development moved quickly, adding records for motion pictures, films and filmstrips, and maps by April 1973;[94] and the Multiple Use MARC System (MUMS) by 1974 enabled LC staff to access and alter records online. By the end of the 1970s, all roman alphabet languages were included and also romanized records for Cyrillic and South Asian languages. Library users would still need the card catalog to find older materials, but the future was clear: the catalog would be electronic, and librarians would no longer worry about the increasing space their catalogs occupied, about filing errors, or about tardy card orders. To facilitate cooperation, the Library suggested that ALA establish an advisory group: the Committee on Machine-Readable Bibliographic Information (known as MARBI), organized in 1974.[95]

International Acquisitions and Cataloging

At the same time, work began on the 754-volume *National Union Catalog, Pre-1956 Imprints.* In June 1964 the ALA's National Union Catalog Subcommittee had agreed to seek funding to prepare the Union Catalog's 16 million cards for publication. The Subcommittee contracted for photo-offset publication with Mansell Information/Publishing Ltd., and established an office in the Processing Department in 1967. The project employed twenty-five to thirty editors, each examining about 1,400 cards weekly to meet the five volumes per month publishing schedule. "Only rarely was there a cushion of finished work," Deputy Librarian William Welsh said later. "The real race was to make each Friday's Pan American Airways Flight 106 to London." The first volumes appeared in 1968; the catalog was completed in 1981. But while editing proceeded, cards continued to accumulate, producing a seventy-volume supplement. Begun just as the first electronic catalog records were appearing, the *NUC Pre-56* made it possible to locate millions of older volumes.[96]

In 1966–67 three more cataloging milestones appeared: the draft classification for Anglo-American law,[97] the seventh edition of *Subject Headings Used in the Dictionary Catalogs of the Library of Congress*, and the ALA's *Anglo-American Cataloging Rules: North American Text.* Begun by Seymour Lubetzky and completed by C. Sumner Spalding (on leave from the LC) and with CLR support, the new rules replaced the 1940s codes. As Lubetzky and other cataloging specialists communicated with catalogers abroad, increasing interest in cooperation led to the October 1961 International Conference on Cataloging Principles in Paris. The British and Canadian library associations joined the ALA and LC in adopting the conference's *Statement of Principles*, which paralleled Lubetzky's code and was consequently published in 1967 in North American and British editions. Combining the rules for entry and the rules for description, the new code had "broader scope, wider coverage of problems, recognition of principles, and logical organization," according to one reviewer. More than five hundred librarians attending a 1967 colloquium held in Toronto agreed that the new code "is a fine piece of work in general, that we are happy with it for the most part," as Andrew Osborn (University of Pittsburgh) summarized the discussions. A subsequent survey found most libraries adopting the code gradually, through the use of LC cataloging.[98]

Meanwhile, with arrears accumulating and cataloging costing member libraries about 16 percent of their operating budgets annually, the Association of Research Libraries had appointed a Committee on Shared Cataloging in 1964. Its CLR-funded study revealed that cataloging was particularly needed for current Western European monographs and that the LC was the logical agency to centralize cataloging, beginning with Farmington Plan books. But the problem of financing remained. The committee reported "some sentiment for Federal funding, perhaps through the LC," but Mumford stated that though he supported centralized cataloging he could not request an appropriation unless Congress authorized the LC to meet national cataloging needs.[99]

President Lyndon B. Johnson's January 12, 1965, education message to the 89th Congress called for a broad program that included—librarians noted—school library resources and instructional materials and the enhancement of college and university library collections. The administration's Elementary and Secondary Education Act passed in March 1965.[100] Meanwhile, "the idea dawned that the centralized cataloging concept might be added," Dix, chair of the Shared Cataloging Committee, wrote, and the ALA and ARL urged the Office of Education and Congress to add library funding to the Higher Education Act, emphasizing the "full approval and active participation of the LC." The ALA and ARL representatives stated during hearings that college and university libraries lacked the funding and staff to acquire and catalog foreign materials and that centralizing cataloging at the LC would draw efficiently on the Library's experts. The program "will help solve a pressing problem of thousands of other libraries of all types," Dix stated. "It is simply a national plan to improve what is now the most costly and inefficient element in library operations" and "release for productive use in the support of teaching and research millions of dollars now spent unnecessarily in duplicative effort."[101]

Representative Edith Green (R-OR), chair of the House subcommittee, and Senator Wayne Morse (D-OR), chair of the Senate subcommittee, agreed. Morse, Dix recalled, "interrupted me half-way through my prepared statement to say: I think you have proved your case. I want to announce that I am willing to introduce this as an amendment. And he did, that afternoon." As William Welsh recalled, "Politically no time could have been riper to launch the most gigantic and most comprehensive cooperative program ever attempted by the library world. Lyndon Johnson sat in the White House and controlled Congress. Higher education became a popular recipient of federal funds and the 'educational industrial complex,' as Congresswoman Green later dubbed the Washington lobby, had a heyday. Fortunately for research libraries and scholarship, libraries had a piece of the action."

Title II-C of the Higher Education Act (PL 89-329, 1965) authorized the Commissioner of Education to transfer funds to the Library of Congress to acquire all current materials of value to scholarship published worldwide, to catalog them promptly, to distribute catalog information on cards "or by other means," and to use for exchange or other purposes materials not needed for the Library's collections. The *Annual Report* called the new National Program for Acquisitions and Cataloging (NPAC) "a clear mandate to provide new and unparalleled services for the benefit of other libraries," and *Library Resources and Technical Services* editorialized, "In other words, the Federal Government, after more than one hundred years of hoping and planning by librarians, has accepted a responsibility for the cataloging of books for non-Federal libraries, as a part of its support for higher education, and has provided funds to begin meeting this responsibility."[102]

Work began with a January 1966 conference (hosted by the British Museum in response to the LC's request) that included representatives from the national libraries and national bibliographies of Austria, England, France, West Germany, and Norway. All agreed to send to the Library of Congress the prepublication entries prepared for their national bibliographies.[103] Local dealers would supply the books in accordance with the LC's selection criteria, with shipments by air freight. The Library opened a London office in 1966, followed by offices in other European countries, and where possible combined NPAC and PL 480 operations. Following the annual International Federation of Library Associations conference in September, representatives of Eastern European national libraries and bibliographic agencies discussed participation with LC officials, and arrangements were made for NLM and NAL participation. "Eventually," Mumford declared, "the LC hopes to make shared cataloging arrangements with every country where the book trade is organized and a national bibliography is published." An extension of the act (PL 90-575, 1968), proposed by the ARL and other library associations, authorized the Library of Congress to also purchase materials for libraries that provided the funds.[104]

PL 480 and NPAC posed enormous challenges. Jerry R. James became the first director of the Eastern Africa (Nairobi) office in 1966, a region with many newly independent countries. It covered over 1,890,000 square miles, a larger area than any other office. "Somehow," he wrote, "a program had to be organized, housed, and staffed to cover an area of almost two million square miles. Within this region, publications were being issued in three European languages, Arabic, and a host of indigenous tongues. In Somalia, a man had just introduced Osmania, a written form for the Somali tongue; perhaps it was just as well that I did not know this for some time." The only way to acquire local publications, he found, was by personal contact: "There was never an end in sight to the rounds of calls on booksellers, libraries, government offices, and institutions."

Also, "I needed some tangible means to convince governments, publishers, and institutions that they too were beneficiaries of our bibliographic work. This was not altruism but rather the self-interested desire to remind everyone concerned that we were there, that we needed their help, that their publications were received and listed, and that we were really helping one another." The result was the quarterly *Accessions List—East Africa*, which published the catalog records produced locally. With James's experience repeated to a varying extent in other overseas centers, accessions lists appeared from the Cairo, Jakarta, Karachi, New Delhi, Rio de Janeiro, and Tel Aviv offices. By 1969, when James's successor, Alvin Moore Jr., surveyed the LC's overseas operations, there were offices in sixteen countries.[105]

The Processing Department was reorganized in 1968 into three units: Acquisitions and Overseas Operations; Cataloging; and Processing Services (later called Bibliographic Products and Services); each headed by an Assistant Director. The new Shared Cataloging Division would implement NPAC in cooperation with the overseas offices, and the staff mounted a recruitment effort to hire foreign language expertise, expanding in-service training into the Office of Cataloging Instruction. While recruitment remained challenging, the program promised efficiency and economy in both acquisitions and cataloging. Jerrold Orne (University of North Carolina) called NPAC "the greatest opportunity ever known as well as the most compelling reason for using central cataloging copy to a degree never before accepted." It will be "nothing less than ridiculous," he declared, "for any library to continue to change the standardized cataloging information."[106]

NPAC considerably broadened the LC's acquisitions program: some members agreed to notify the LC when placing orders for foreign titles that the LC did not have, and the Library would then order and catalog those titles as well. The program was immediately popular: eighty-two academic and research libraries participated by the end of 1967. Reviewing cataloging statistics, Dix found that the year before NPAC began (1965), the LC cataloged 109,978 new titles; by 1972, the total more than doubled, to 243,753. ARL member libraries, which obtained only around 50 percent of their cataloging from the LC before NPAC, by 1975 reported 75 percent. "In other words," he concluded, "the systematic access of US scholars to research materials from other parts of the world has been enormously increased."[107]

The Federal Library Committee

In cooperation with the Bureau of the Budget, Mumford established the Federal Library Committee (FLC) in 1965. It included as permanent members the LC, NAL, NLM, and the cabinet departments plus six independent agency representatives elected by the permanent members to two-year terms. Others—for example, the Office of Education and the Office of Science and Technology—attended as observers, and the bureau took responsibility for channeling FLC recommendations to executive branch agencies. The Librarian, as chairman, would convene all-agency meetings on occasion and seek collaboration with outside agencies as needed. At the first meeting, the FLC appointed six task forces: acquisition and correlation of resources, automation, interlibrary loan, mission and standards of service, procurement procedures, and personnel recruitment. Reporting the initial accomplishments, Mumford stated, "The committee has demonstrated that the need was real and that a joint approach to common problems is not only feasible but also effective." A three-year CLR grant paid expenses, including a position for a full-time executive secretary; the LC provided office space; and in 1969 Congress began providing annual appropriations. A 1973 reorganization added the Atomic Energy Commission, National Aeronautics and Space Administration, National Science Foundation, Smithsonian Institution, Supreme Court, United States Information Agency, Veterans Administration, and the National Archives Office of Presidential Libraries, plus ten regional members and nonvoting representatives from the Army, Navy, and Air Force. With the growth in membership, the FLC became a government-wide coordinating agency that contracted for services for its members.[108]

The National Advisory Commission on Libraries

President Johnson's Executive Order 11301 (September 2, 1966) established the National Advisory Commission on Libraries, consisting of fourteen educators and librarians, and the President's Committee on Libraries, which included the Secretary of Health, Education, and Welfare as chairman, the Secretary of Agriculture, the director of the Office of Science and Technology, the director of the National Science

Foundation, and Librarian Mumford. Douglas M. Knight, president of Duke University, chaired the commission. Charged to consider the nation's library structure and federal support for the development of national library resources, the commission held regional hearings and requested studies of several topics, including the role of the Library of Congress.[109]

Mumford and other LC officials testified on May 22–23, 1967, and at the commission's request, the Librarian submitted a statement on the "Library's View of Itself as the National Library of the United States." It was intended, he said, "as a statement of commitment to the central role of the Library of Congress in the development of a national library and information network."[110] It was not a "blueprint for action" but "a vision and not necessarily a prediction of the role of the Library of Congress as the National Library." The text sounded some old themes, arguing against a charter "that would quickly become outdated" and against moving the LC out of the legislative branch. It would be "highly beneficial if the Congress gave formal recognition of its dual role as the Library of Congress and the National Library of the United States," but Mumford acknowledged that Congress would have to be convinced to fully fund national library functions. Rather than a Board of Advisers, he recommended establishing the proposed National Commission on Libraries and Information Services (NCLIS) but carefully pointed out that a permanent commission would not supplant, but supplement, the LC's relations with Congress.

The statement listed the "Present Functions as a National Library" and "Opportunities for Expanded Services and Activities," describing ambitious initiatives that ranged from comprehensive national acquisitions, cataloging, bibliographic, interlibrary loan, referral, and preservation programs to research and training programs in library and information science, a technical reports center, a publishing arm, and a cultural activities center. Such an expansion would require, the statement concluded, the support of the National Advisory Commission and NCLIS; "lucid and unequivocal" legislation recognizing the Library of Congress as also the National Library; and support from citizens, scholars, and the library community.

The program Mumford and his colleagues outlined and the Librarian's boast that the LC "performed more national functions than any other national library in the world" conveyed both the optimism of the mid-1960s and a more aggressive attitude. The commission also received three background papers that discussed the Library's status: "Research Libraries and the Federal Government," by Charles Blitzer (Smithsonian Institution) and Reuben Clark (attorney, Wilmer, Cutler, and Pickering); "A Broad Look at the Federal Government and Libraries," by Richard H. Leach (Duke University); and "Observations on Government Library Organization and Policy," by Harold Orlans (Brookings Institution). Favoring both stronger federal support for research libraries and designation of the LC as the national library, the authors agreed that the Library had made significant progress in expanding its national role. However, Blitzer and Clark pointed to the LC's sometime reluctance to seek appropriations to fulfill a national role and suggested that the Library be given statutory authority for all research library–related programs and a board of trustees. Orlans wrote that the LC "responds rather than initiates" and seemed "politically and administratively isolated from other major libraries"; he favored transfer to the executive branch, congressional hearings on the Library's status, and the creation of both a permanent library commission and an LC board of regents. Leach stated that the Library fell short in its national library role because it was only one of three national libraries and lacked congressional authorization for some activities. He recommended a study of "the validity of maintaining three independent national libraries."[111]

The commission submitted its final report to the President's Committee on Libraries on October 3, 1968, recommending "that it be declared national policy, enunciated by the President and enacted into law by Congress, that the American people should be provided with library and informational services adequate to their needs, and that the Federal Government, in collaboration with State and local governments and private agencies, should exercise leadership assuring the provision of such services." The first of five supporting recommendations was to establish a National Commission on Libraries and Information Science as a central planning agency. The second was "recognition and strengthening of the role of the Library of Congress as the National Library of the United States and establishment of a Board of Advisers," suggesting as the formal designation "The Library of Congress: The National Library of the United States." The Board should be appointed by the President of the Senate and the Speaker of the House of Representatives and include members of the public and representatives of "scholarly and research organizations, the scientific community, universities and colleges, and research librarianship." Its role would be to advise the Librarian and Congress on developing the collections and national services because the Library, "which has never had a charter or basic constituent act defining its responsibilities, must be formally recognized for its national role and provided with advisers that can help to steer its future responsiveness." The commission specifically ruled out making the LC responsible for a national library system or for programs of assistance or grants to other libraries.[112] Although the NCLIS was subsequently established, no action was taken on recommendations relating to the Library of Congress.

Cultural Organizations and Collection Development

The 1960s brought unprecedented development of the federal cultural sector. The National Foundation on the Arts and Humanities Act of 1965 (PL 89-209) created the National Endowment for the Humanities and the National Endowment for the Arts; and in 1966 the Historic Preservation Act (PL 89-665) provided for protecting cultural properties. Three years later, a congressional charter established the Woodrow Wilson International Center for Scholars. Librarian Mumford became an ex officio member of the foundation and Wilson Center governing boards and also of the Board of Trustees of the National Cultural Center (later the John F. Kennedy Center for the Performing Arts), established by PL 85-874 (1964).[113] The momentum reached the Library with a 1968 agreement with George Washington University to jointly support a doctoral program in American thought and culture, aimed at educating research library administrators.[114]

The 1960s acquisitions reinforced strong collections and opened new fields. The Library in 1966 received a promise to donate the Bay Psalm Book, from Mrs. Adrian

Van Sinderen, of Washington, Connecticut, who owned the only copy in private hands. Stephen Daye, a locksmith-turned-printer, produced that book in Cambridge, Massachusetts, in 1640, the first book printed in the English colonies: *The Whole Booke of Psalmes Faithfully Translated into English Metre.*[115] Other important additions arrived in the wake of the Civil Rights Movement, including the initial donations of the records of the National Association for the Advancement of Colored People (1964) and the National Urban League (1966). With gift funds, the Library began acquiring from collector Charles E. Feinberg the largest collection of Walt Whitman materials in private hands; and the Feinbergs established the Lenore B. and Charles E. Feinberg Fund to acquire materials relating to American writers.[116]

Groucho Marx famously announced on Johnny Carson's October 5, 1965, *Tonight Show* his astonishment at receiving an invitation from Librarian Mumford to donate his papers. Marx told Carson, "I don't know how they got wind of this, but I've been corresponding with a number of people for about twenty-five years: Bob Benchley, James Thurber, Goody Ace, Fred Allen. . . . I was so pleased when I got this thing. Having not finished public school, to find my letters sitting next to the Gettysburg Address, I thought was quite an incongruity in addition to being extremely thrilling. And I am very proud of this thing."[117]

In 1968 the Library and the new (1967) American Film Institute (AFI) announced an agreement to deposit materials from the RKO Film Library: a collection of 740 feature films and 900 short subjects from the 1930s and 1940s. The AFI also provided funding to make the LC the principal depository for master copies of American motion pictures, for purchases of American films, and for their transfer to safety film, assuring the preservation of such classics as *Citizen Kane*, *The Hunchback of Notre Dame*, and *Top Hat* and the work of such directors as Orson Welles, John Ford, George Stevens, and Alfred Hitchcock. Through the AFI, the Library also received the collections of Hal Roach, producer and collector of silent and sound comedies; Warner Brothers and Paramount Pictures; and Maurice Zouary, an independent producer.[118]

At a banquet commemorating its sixtieth anniversary, the National Press Club presented its collection to the LC. The club began recording speeches at its luncheons and other functions in 1952: "a veritable roll call of contemporary newsmakers," including presidents, politicians, and foreign leaders such as de Gaulle and Khrushchev, and celebrities such as Artur Rubinstein, Arnold Toynbee, and Eddie Arcaro. A similar collection came from Lawrence Spivak on behalf of NBC: Spivak originated the *Meet the Press* radio program in 1945 and transferred it to television two years later. In addition to the 1949–65 films of the television series, he presented his personal papers and radio program recordings, including interviews with national and international figures.[119]

The Madison Building

As the decade ended, there was still no third building: "As all the librarians concerned with new buildings know, neither approval or appropriations for them are obtained quickly or easily," Mumford wrote resignedly. A competing proposal had appeared: on April 8, 1960, Congress had established the James Madison Memorial Commission, chaired by Harold W. Dodds (former president, Princeton University). The commission proposed that because Madison's achievements "were so largely in the realm of the intellect, which led him to be called the Father of the Constitution, a library building to be administered by the Library of Congress naturally appeared to be a most appropriate and significant means for memorializing his contributions to America."[120]

Mumford and the staff cooperated as the commission planned a building that would include exhibit and reader space and house the presidential papers collections, but they also made it known that the building would serve only a fraction of the LC's needs. Neither a new Library of Congress building nor a Madison Memorial received authorization over the next several years, but finally a new proposal appeared for a much larger building that would include a Madison memorial. A 1965 act authorized $75 million for planning and constructing the Library of Congress James Madison Memorial Building. The Architect of the Capitol would be responsible for construction, "under the direction of the House Office Building Commission, the Senate Office Building Commission, the Joint Committee on the Library," and in consultation with the Madison Memorial Commission and an American Institute of Architects committee.[121]

Estimates of space needs substantially exceeded the probable available space and had to be reduced—"as any librarian could have predicted," Mumford noted. The result was the decision to house in the Madison Building units with physical needs "least suited to the design and arrangement of the Main Building and the Annex and to restore these two structures to their original use insofar as the service program of the Library will allow." Most administrative operations would move to the new building, as would the Copyright Office, Law Library, Legislative Reference Service, Processing Department, and the Geography and Map, Manuscript, Music, Prints and Photographs, and Serial and Government Publications divisions. The Madison Building would be "in keeping with the design of the existing Federal buildings on Capitol Hill," Mumford wrote. "It will have none of the Renaissance splendor of its 70-year-old sister across the street, which prompted one enthusiastic viewer of 1897 to write to John Russell Young, then Librarian of Congress: 'Not till I stand before the judgment seat of God do I expect ever to see it transcended.' And were Mr. Young alive today, attempting to fit computers among the cupids and catalogers along the curtains, he might be tempted to say amen." The design had to conform to existing laws, site characteristics, and the unwritten rule that no building on the Hill could rise higher than the Capitol dome. "Architects, librarians, trustees, and citizens' committees will not be surprised to hear that the design of the building has been criticized," said Mumford. "Was there ever a new library that was not?"[122]

The Preservation Office

Plans for the Madison Building included the new Preservation Office, established in 1967 under the leadership of Frazer G. Poole.[123] Mumford told the Appropriations Committee that increasingly complex preservation problems required "a unified approach" and more effective cooperation with other libraries. Pressure for that "approach" had steadily increased: the ARL had established the Committee on Preservation of Research

Library Materials in 1960, and its 1964 report proposed a national preservation collection holding at least one copy of every deteriorating book.[124]

In December 1965, the ARL recommended that the LC establish a national program, and Mumford had agreed, though warning that authorizing legislation was required.[125] Since the staff was examining the collections to determine what needed to be microfilmed, the ARL, urged by Clapp, also proposed a CLR-funded project to identify "brittle books" at the Library: volumes printed on acidic paper. Begun in 1967, the project compared the LC's books with counterparts in other libraries, concluding that it would be feasible to establish a national preservation collection, with preserved titles recorded in the recently begun CLR-funded *National Register of Microform Masters* (1965).[126]

The Preservation Office absorbed Processing Services' Binding Office and the Reference Department's Collections Maintenance and Preservation Office and established restoration and microfilming sections. The CLR provided funding in 1972 for a research and testing unit, and the office began providing advisory services and training programs. The Motion Picture Preservation Laboratory, which was established in 1970, moved to Wright-Patterson Air Force Base in Dayton in 1981 due to concerns about handling flammable material onsite.[127]

The End of the 1960s

The 1960s discussions of the Library's status produced no change: Congress would neither consent to a transfer to the executive branch nor agree to establish an oversight board. But the research library community's criticisms abated with the LC's willingness to seek Title II-C appropriations, its cooperative efforts in automation planning, the invention of MARC, and the beginning of the national preservation program. The race toward an automated future that would affect all libraries and library users had just begun.[128]

CHAPTER 9

The National Library in the Networking Age

IN 1970, THE Library's collections and services were scattered among eleven different locations in Washington, Virginia, Maryland, and Ohio. The collections had grown from nearly 39 million items in 1960 to over 61 million, a 57 percent increase, and congressional inquiries had grown from 81,000 to over 170,000. Subscriptions to the card service had increased from 10,000 to 30,000, and Division for the Blind and Physically Handicapped users had grown from about 68,000 to an estimated 200,000. Still relying on volunteers for transcribing, narrating, and equipment repair, the division began designating "subregional libraries," placing collections in local public libraries.[1] With the expansion of services to federal agencies, Mumford had renamed the Air Research Division the Defense Research Division (1963) and then the Federal Research Division (1970).[2]

Ever more cramped for space, the Library also faced another challenge in 1970. Librarians wanted Cataloging-in-Source revived, and for good reason: the production of printed card titles had increased from 111,000 in 1960 to 244,000 in 1969; and card sales had grown from $35 to $101 million. Joseph L. Wheeler, retired director of the Enoch Pratt Free Library in Baltimore, published a hard-hitting article in 1969 calling it a "costly, delaying, and belittling problem, which concerns every library and is giving all libraries a black eye." Rejecting centralized processing, shared cataloging, and MARC tapes as too expensive for small libraries and commercial services as too slow, Wheeler called the LC's statement that the program was not "desirable," "a whopper," and the earlier experiment "half-hearted." At the ALA's 1970 summer conference, he declared that "95 percent of about 60,000 public, college, school, and special libraries really wanted Cataloging-in-Source then; they want it today." Verner Clapp, who spoke next, credited Wheeler and mid-1969 discussions between the ALA's Resources and Technical Services Division and the American Book Publishers Council with bringing Cataloging-in-Source "alive and kicking out of the womb."[3]

Clapp was kinder than Wheeler; he called CIS "superb" and said "it worked." But "it destroyed itself" by requiring that each book be processed instantly and hand-carried to the next step, causing "insupportable" tension. He reported the results of a May 1970 survey of 391 libraries to assess interest in his proposal for the "Cataloging-in-Publication" (CIP) program, concluding that "it stirs the blood of librarians as much in 1970 as it did in 1959." He predicted that CIP would be "welcomed and used," but its success would depend on funding, the LC's cooperation, and meeting publishers' schedules.[4]

Processing Department director William Welsh then stated that the staff would investigate alternatives, contingent on further surveys of libraries and publishers by Clapp, availability of funding for a pilot project, availability of space, and eliminating the earlier problems. The Library was, Welsh declared, "determined to make it succeed."[5]

With funding from the Council on Library Resources and the National Endowment for the Humanities, and in cooperation with the Association of American Publishers, the CIP pilot began on July 1, 1971. LC catalogers would use publishers' galleys and communications to compile cataloging information to be printed in the books and supplied on the MARC tapes; if necessary, they would update the MARC entries after publication. Tape subscribers would therefore get cataloging information even before the books were published. With the success of the pilot project, beginning in 1974 Congress provided appropriations for CIP, which by that time included over 600 publishers.[6]

From the beginning of the card service through 1971, card sales provided much of the revenue the Library returned to the Treasury. The all-time high came in 1968, when the service sold nearly 79 million cards to 25,000 subscribers and employed nearly one-fifth of the LC's staff. By 1969, the automated CARDS system, which supplied on-demand reproductions, allowed the service to dispense with its inventory.[7] In 1972, sales of book catalogs, MARC tapes, and other publications exceeded card sales for the first time. Renamed the Cataloging Distribution Service (CDS) in 1975, the service continued to produce LC cataloging in different formats and introduced the *Chinese Cooperative Catalog*, a microfiche publication recording the holdings of the twelve largest Chinese collections in the United States. CDS continued to produce and sell printed cards until 1997.[8]

PL 480, NPAC, and China

Meanwhile, the National Program for Acquisitions and Cataloging pursued shared cataloging arrangements with twenty-two countries, and the Public Law 480 program operated through seven centers. Forty-one US libraries were receiving publications from one or more of these countries, and microfilming operations included the official gazettes of India, Pakistan, Nepal, Ceylon, and Indonesia. In 1969, the CLR provided funding to the ARL to assess interest in a national program to improve access to the foreign press, and Norman J. Shaffer, the Photoduplication Service's assistant chief for bibliographic services, conducted the survey. Finding that 43 US institutions expressed interest and recommended 749 newspaper titles from 132 countries for filming, he recommended establishing a national office at the LC, and the Library created the position of coordinator in 1972. The LC's *Newspapers on Microfilm*, retitled *Newspapers in Microform*, split into two volumes: United States and Foreign Countries; and in 1973, the office began publishing the *Foreign Newspaper and Gazette Report* to provide information about current and planned projects.[9]

At the same time, President Richard Nixon's visit to China in February 1972 opened relations that had been closed since 1949. During that time, the Library had been able to acquire materials from the People's Republic of China and Tibet only through the New Delhi field office, from dealers in Hong Kong and Taipei, and through interagency transfers. Nixon's initiative emphasized the "normalization" of relations, including trade and cultural exchanges, and several months after the President's trip, LC staff member Chi Wang traveled to his native country and visited the National Library in Beijing. In September 1973, a Chinese library delegation visited the United States, and after the United States–People's Republic of China Cultural Agreement was signed in January 1979, National Library director Liu Jiping invited a delegation of ALA, ARL, and Association of Asian Studies representatives, led by the LC's Processing Department director, William Welsh. That visit helped to establish exchange agreements with the National Library and others as well as a blanket order placed with a Beijing book dealer. When the National Library invited an LC visit shortly after President Ronald Reagan's trip in early 1984, Welsh, by that time Deputy Librarian, again headed a delegation.[10]

Library Cooperation

The development of MARC, the ability to link computers via telecommunications lines, and increasingly strapped library budgets promoted cooperative efforts. Established in 1967, the Ohio College Library Center (OCLC), a nonprofit organization of fifty-four academic institutions, began providing cataloging services in 1971, using the MARC tapes. It grew rapidly, soon extending to libraries outside Ohio and to non-US libraries in 2002.[11] Member libraries contributed their cataloging to the OCLC database and received printed cards customized according to their specifications. OCLC demonstrated new possibilities for library networking. Its appearance, together with other "bibliographic utilities"—the Research Libraries Group's Research Libraries Information Network (RLIN), the Western Library Network (WLN), and the University of Toronto Library Automation System (UTLAS)—by 1978, seemed initially to divide the library community into joiners and nonjoiners and among rivals that made MARC records the base of their services.[12]

In June 1973, the Federal Library Committee contracted with OCLC to experiment with access to OCLC's system. Seventeen libraries and the Library of Congress joined the two-year project and, with its successful conclusion, by 1978 the system, called FEDLINK, included 157 members; and the FLC also contracted with commercial vendors for database services. With continual growth in membership and services, the FLC was reorganized and renamed the Federal Library and Information Center Committee in 1984; an international expansion in 1986, when the system served over 1,000 libraries, extended services to American military libraries abroad. In 2012 FEDLINK became the Federal Library and Information Network.[13]

The shift to bibliographic utilities and to regional networks that offered services to their members came quickly. "The *kind* of thing going on at OCLC," *American Libraries* editor Arthur Plotnik wrote, "is not simply the building up of someone else's database in little bits and bytes, but perhaps the biggest revolution in access to library collections since books were unchained from the shelves." Joe A. Hewitt, a University of North Carolina librarian, visited the forty-seven original OCLC members to assess their use of the services. He intended his study to assist librarians who were trying to decide whether to join a network. But by the time he completed it, the issue had become not whether to affiliate, but how. Having access to MARC and to other libraries' bibliographic records helped not only catalogers but also acquisitions, interlibrary loan, serials, and reference librarians.[14]

The Library of Congress completed the first phase of the planned National Serials Data Program (NSDP) with the development of a MARC format for serials, and the LC, the NAL, and the NLM began inputting their current serials cataloging in January 1973. Subscribers received the first MARC serials tapes in June.[15] The NSDP also served as the US representative to the International Serials Data System (ISDS), a network created in 1972 by UNESCO and the International Council of Scientific Unions. Each national center was responsible for assigning eight-digit International Standard Serial Numbers (ISSNs) to domestic publications and reporting them to the ISDS.[16] The ISSN soon became the unique identifier for a confusing set of publications that often had similar titles; and notably, responding to the NSDP's and publishers' requests, the US Postal Service agreed in 1977 to use the ISSN as its official registration number for serials mailed at second-class or controlled circulation rates.[17]

Some research libraries were developing their own serials databases, but librarians were concerned that local bibliographic records were not compatible with the slowly developing NSDP database. An Ad Hoc Discussion Group on Serials Data Bases that included US and Canadian librarians and NSDP representatives met at the June 1973 ALA conference and subsequently obtained CLR support to build a large database quickly; in November 1975 the Minnesota Union List of Serials and MARC serials records were combined in an OCLC database.[18] At first called CONSER, for Conversion of Serials, its name was changed to the Cooperative Online Serials Program in 1986. Further contributions to the database came from the United States Newspaper Program, the *National Register of Microform Masters*, and *New Serial Titles*.[19]

The Congressional Research Service

Congress had established the Joint Committee on the Organization of Congress in 1965. It raised some of the same issues that drove the debates over the Library's status: for example, some members advocated removing the Legislative Reference Service from the LC.[20] Ultimately, however, the committee's June 17, 1970, report declared that "the Library serves as a useful mantle for protecting the Service from partisan pressures," and its effectiveness "will be enhanced by its continual instant access to the Library's collections and administrative support services."[21]

Under the Legislative Reorganization Act of 1970 (PL 91-510), the Legislative Reference Service became the Congressional Research Service (CRS), effective January 3, 1971. The act directed its expansion to encompass systematic policy research and analysis and to employ experts in subject fields beyond those specified in the statute.[22] The CRS would provide continuous liaison to congressional committees and members' offices, originate studies in anticipation of requests, pursue working relationships with other agencies, and contract as needed with outside experts or organizations. At the beginning of each Congress, the staff would prepare a list of subjects and policy areas that committees might pursue and a list of federal programs and activities scheduled to expire.[23]

In effect distancing the Library's legislative from its national functions, the act required the Librarian to accord the CRS "complete research independence and the maximum administrative independence consistent with [its] objectives." The Librarian would appoint the CRS director (at a higher salary than other LC administrators), but only after consultation with the Joint Committee on the Library, and the director would submit a separate annual report to the committee. These provisions represented the first formal limitations on the Librarian's authority since 1897 and a significant enhancement of the Library's legislative role. The changes also seemed to produce what some called a "cultural split" within the Library.[24]

The wider role that the act defined meant that the CRS, and the LC as well, would address more congressional needs. For example, during investigations by the Senate Select Committee on Presidential Campaign Activities, chaired by Senator Sam Ervin (D-NC), Chief Counsel Sam Dash and the staff met with the LC's Information Systems Office staff to discuss the committee's needs. Within two weeks, the staff developed and tested sample MARC-II-based programs and had the system running a week before public hearings began. Three times weekly, at midnight, a committee staff member, escorted by police, transferred tape cartridges for entry and merge operations, and at 6 a.m., the tapes were returned to the committee. The committee also made its tapes available to special prosecutors Archibald Cox and Leon Jaworski, to the House Judiciary Committee, to state and local bar associations investigating unethical conduct connected to the Watergate scandal, and to attorneys for Watergate defendants.[25]

Discrimination Allegations

In the fall of 1961, the *Washington Afro-American* reported allegations of racial discrimination in the Library. In response, Mumford stated that it was the LC's policy to prohibit discrimination "for reasons of race, creed, color, sex, national origin, or lawful political affiliation," and he appointed a Fair Employment Practices Officer and a committee to examine employment practices. The first officer, Vincent A. Doyle, compared LC employment with a June 1962 study by the President's Committee on Equal Opportunity, finding that 24.9 percent of LC employees were Black compared with 13 percent in other federal agencies. Half the Blacks in lower-graded positions had advanced beyond salary step four, as compared with 31 percent in other agencies. Blacks in the higher-graded positions (GS 10-13), who overall had almost exactly the same educational qualifications as others in that group, however, had not advanced beyond step four at the same rate as other GS 10-13 staff. An update a year later showed Black employment had increased to 27.5 percent, a gain of 173 positions, with advances in all salary grades.[26]

But dissatisfaction with hiring and promotion policies persisted. A 1971 survey showed that Blacks accounted for 38 percent of all LC employees, but they were 73.9 percent of those in grades 1–4, 48.3 percent in grades 5–8, 16.1 percent in grades 9–11, 5.5 percent in grades 12–13, 1.6 percent in grades 14–15, and 3.9 percent in grades 16–18. Staff members organized the Black Employees of the Library of Congress (1971) and Ethnic Employees of the Library of Congress (1973), both of which would challenge the Library's personnel practices. In June 1971, after a work stoppage by deck attendants, an LC staff member brought complaints of discrimination in recruitment, promotion, and training to the ALA. The ALA Council authorized an inquiry and directed that Librarian Mumford be formally notified of its "grave concern."[27]

The staff members who took part in the June 23–25 work stoppage presented a memo detailing their complaints regarding position classifications, promotion policy, and working conditions. When supervisors asked them to return to work, promising that their complaints would be considered, most of them refused and continued to occupy seats in the Main Reading Room. The Library announced a position classification upgrade on the third day, but the group then held an outdoor rally described as "disruptive." When they resumed the sit-in on Monday, June 28, those who resisted orders to return to work were separated.[28]

Mumford announced the Equal Opportunity [EO] Program to replace the Fair Employment Practices Program, effective September 1971, which provided for stationing EO officers and counselors in all LC buildings. A few weeks later, ALA executive secretary David Clift notified the Librarian that a fact-finding team would visit the LC and requested a list of employees to testify. Such an inquiry was unprecedented, and Mumford referred Clift's letter to the Joint Committee on the Library. Representative Wayne L. Hays (D-OH), a Joint Committee member, declared that the ALA was "infringing on and usurping the oversight responsibilities of Congress," and "under no circumstances can we permit an outside non-governmental agency to make such an inquiry." But he also expressed concern, stating that he had already met with "the individuals who apparently instigated this action by the American Library Association" and invited them to document their charges. When the ALA team visited the LC, because of the Joint Committee's directive, the Library did not provide access to records or meet officially with them, though the staff did discuss personnel policies informally with some of the members. The team interviewed thirty witnesses who were critical of the LC's practices and found evidence of discrimination in promotion but inconclusive evidence regarding recruitment and training.[29]

On reading the report, Mumford telegraphed ALA president Keith Doms (Free Library of Philadelphia) that he was "deeply disturbed" at the conclusions and urged the ALA to ask the witnesses to "present their specific complaints in order that we can eradicate any injustices that exist." A subsequent ALA Council discussion acknowledged that the report did not sufficiently consider congressional constraints on the Library. At the June 1972 ALA convention, Deputy Librarian John Lorenz reported on the LC's revised personnel program, and the ALA Council voted not to censure the Library.[30] Meanwhile, the Equal Employment Act of 1972 (PL 92-261) extended the Civil Rights Act of 1964 to government employees, requiring the Library to establish an Affirmative Action program and mechanisms for hearing and resolving complaints.[31]

The ALA Council voted at its 1973 midwinter meeting to continue its inquiry, and another team visited the Library in June and September 1973. Its report, presented at the midwinter meeting in 1974, made further recommendations for improving upward communication and requested to examine the LC's Equal Employment Opportunity Plan. The Library's new assistant director of Personnel for Equality Programs, Eugene Walton, addressed the council, describing his experience in the recently established position. Noting improvements in LC policies over the two-year period, the ALA team recommended continued monitoring.[32]

Concurrently, Barbara A. Ringer, Assistant Register of Copyrights and a Copyright Office staff member since 1949, had filed suit charging discrimination on September 2, 1971. A well-known copyright expert, Ringer had been a candidate for Register when Mumford instead appointed George D. Cary. She took a leave of absence in May 1972 to direct the Copyright Division of UNESCO's Office of International Standards and Legal Affairs while the lawsuit proceeded. On February 28, 1973, the US District Court for the District of Columbia ruled that the office of Register be vacated, having determined that the Library had violated its personnel regulations in appointing Cary. Cary retired on March 9, and Ringer was appointed Register in September.[33]

Mumford established human relations committees in the divisions and the Library-wide Human Relations Council. Two years' work produced the Affirmative Action Plan, with supplemental appropriations for implementation and for the establishment of the Equal Employment Opportunity Office.[34] The Federal Women's Program Coordinator was appointed in April 1973, and subsequently, coordinators for Hispanic and handicapped affairs (1984) and Library-wide programs were added to assist advancement—for example, incentive awards, employment and career development seminars, details, and job fairs. A contractor recommended changes to LC employment tests and qualification requirements to eliminate bias; and the Training, Appraisal, and Promotion plan provided a channel for advancement through demonstrated competence. A 1974 study of labor-management relations throughout the federal government led to establishing the Library's Labor–Management Relations and Appeals Office (1975). This office conducted the LC's first elections for union representation, recognizing the Congressional Research Employees Association, the Law Library of Congress United Association of Employees, and a chapter of the American Federation of State, County, and Municipal Employees, AFL-CIO, for collective bargaining purposes.[35] Dissatisfied employees filed complaints with the Equal Employment Opportunity Office, but the subsequent five-year investigation resulted in a denial of their claims. A class action lawsuit was filed in February 1982.[36]

American Revolution's Bicentennial

In 1966, Congress created a commission to plan celebrations of the American Revolution's bicentennial. Chaired by Carlisle H. Humelshine, president of Colonial Williamsburg, the group included eight members of Congress; sixteen representatives from the academic, cultural, and business communities; and ex officio federal officials. As a member, Mumford, with congressional approval, established an LC office in 1968 to cooperate with the commission. *The American Revolution: A Selected Reading List* appeared that same year, and in 1970 Mumford appointed an advisory committee of ten historians, which adopted the theme "Liberty and Learning," quoting James Madison's "What spectacle can be more edifying or more seasonable, than that of Liberty & Learning, each leaning on the other for their mutual and surest support?" The Cafritz Foundation supported a symposium series between 1972 and 1976, featuring papers presented by scholars of the Revolutionary period; and an exhibition, *To Set a Country Free*, opened on April 24, 1975. Among the bicentennial office's publications was the Ford Foundation–supported *Letters of Delegates to Congress, 1774–1789* (26 volumes, 1978–2000), which resulted from finding in the manuscript collections material that shed new light on the struggle for independence. But perhaps the most appropriate commemoration was the completion of the index to the Thomas Jefferson Papers, which brought the two-decade Presidential Papers program to a conclusion.[37]

Mumford Retires

The James Madison Memorial Building, whose construction began on May 1, 1971, with the cornerstone laid on March 8, 1974, by that December had a partial roof and some exterior marble in place. L. Quincy Mumford retired on December 31, 1974, before its completion.[38]

The Mumford years saw a major expansion of the Library. Under his administration, the collections more than doubled, rising from 33 million to nearly 74 million items; the staff, from under 1,564 to 4,250; and annual appropriations, from $9,400,000 to $96,696,000. He obtained the funding to automate operations, to launch a preservation program, to add services for people with disabilities, and to develop acquisitions and cataloging operations that by 1974 included forty countries. A House Appropriations Committee's investigation of the National Program for Acquisitions and Cataloging concluded that the savings to the member libraries exceeded the total appropriations for the program.[39]

Former deputy librarian Rutherford D. Rogers wrote that too few people outside the LC recognized Mumford's achievements in extending the Library's role and services. The ARL expressed appreciation at its January 1975 meeting, citing his "astute participation in many levels of governmental relationships, a perception of national, public, and professional needs, and a cordial and mutually productive interaction with many professional and business communities." John Cole, writing more than two decades later, stated that Mumford joined Spofford and Putnam as one of three "expansionist" Librarians of Congress. Like Herbert Putnam, Mumford always insisted that Congress could be depended on "to recognize the national responsibilities of the Library of Congress in a way that matters most—with understanding and consistent support."[40] He gained Congress's confidence early in his tenure, and that confidence brought support not only for foreign acquisitions and cataloging initiatives and for automation and preservation programs but also for a third building. As an experienced library administrator well versed in operational detail, he perhaps was more able to extend the Library's role than a nonlibrarian might have done at that time. However, during the Mumford years, which saw the Library's staff nearly triple, the MacLeish–Evans policy of fostering staff involvement perhaps inevitably diminished, as several divisions moved away from Capitol Hill and an increasingly large bureaucracy distanced the Librarian's Office from much of the staff.

The Boorstin Nomination

The ALA Executive Board sent a statement on the Library's role to the White House, with a list of candidates: Page Ackerman (University of California, Los Angeles), Lillian Bradshaw (Dallas Public Library), Charles Churchwell (Miami University of Ohio), Keith Doms (Free Library of Philadelphia), John G. Lorenz (Deputy Librarian of Congress, and Acting Librarian), and Rutherford Rogers (Yale University).[41] However, on June 20, 1975, President Gerald Ford nominated Daniel J. Boorstin, the senior historian of the Smithsonian Institution.

The association opposed Boorstin as it had MacLeish: he did not have the "demonstrated leadership and administrative qualities which constitute basic and essential characteristics necessary in the Librarian of Congress."[42] Also opposed were the Black Employees of the Library of Congress, the Ethnic Employees of the Library of Congress, the Library of Congress Professional Association, and the Capital Area Council of Federal Employees, AFL-CIO, citing a lack of understanding of minorities in his books and his opposition to affirmative action.[43] Herman Wouk, representing the Authors League of America, and Smithsonian secretary S. Dillon Ripley, however, spoke in favor of the nomination, and major newspapers, including the *Washington Post,* supported confirmation. Boorstin also had bipartisan congressional support, including, for example, senators Mark O. Hatfield (R-OR), Adlai E. Stevenson III (D-IL), and Charles H. Percy (R-IL) and representatives Carl Albert (D-OK, Speaker of the House) and John J. Rhodes (R-AZ, House Minority Leader). The confirmation hearing recalled the MacLeish controversy: as then, some members questioned whether Boorstin, a prolific writer, would devote enough attention to the Library; and some disliked his books and his politics—but others predicted that he would renew the focus on cultural affairs that marked MacLeish's administration.[44]

Born in Atlanta in 1914, Boorstin received a BA summa cum laude from Harvard, a BA in jurisprudence as a Rhodes Scholar at Oxford, and a bachelor of civil laws from Oxford. He passed the English bar examination and became a barrister-at-law in 1937 but returned to the United States as a Sterling Fellow at Yale Law School, earning a doctorate in judicial science. From 1938 to 1942 he taught at Harvard Law School, later joining the faculties of Swarthmore College and the University of Chicago, where he was appointed Preston and Sterling Morton Distinguished Service Professor of History in 1966. He left Chicago in 1969 to become director of the Smithsonian's Museum of History and Technology but stepped down in 1973 to become its Senior Historian. His book *The Americans: The Democratic Experience* had just won the 1974 Pulitzer Prize in History.[45]

At the three-day hearing, Senator Pell asked Boorstin whether he was familiar with the thirteen-year-old Bryant memorandum, saying that the recommendations "had real merit" but Mumford had been "very upset and disturbed" and "had various criticisms." Boorstin replied that he had read the memorandum and noted the recommendation to change the Library's name and move it into the executive branch but also stated, "I would say, Senator, that I have a great attachment to the name of the Library of Congress and would be sorry to see that name changed. I also think that its location in the legislative branch is a piece of good fortune for all of us, as scholars, who have benefited from the generosity of the legislative—and I would also not like to see that changed."[46]

Pell also asked what Boorstin would do "to find out what are the major problems of the Library, and what should be done about them." Boorstin replied that he would try "to discover the extent to which the Library is or is not serving its constituents satisfactorily" by questioning members of Congress and "the professional librarians, professional scholars, the general public, the press and other media and also the staff of the Library, not only to see what could be done to improve morale, but also to have the advice of the staff." Pell then asked whether Boorstin had considered having a task force make recommendations, and Boorstin replied that while he was not willing to make commitments, if such a group was assembled, he would consider it his duty to share the recommendations with Congress.[47]

The Senate Committee on Rules and Administration, chaired by Howard W. Cannon (D-NV), reported favorably, and the Senate confirmed Boorstin without debate on September 26. The new Librarian set a precedent by requesting a Great Hall swearing-in ceremony on November 12, attended also for the first time by both the President (Ford) and the Vice President (Nelson Rockefeller). Speaker Albert administered the oath, with Representative Lucien N. Nedzi (D-MI), chairman of the Joint Committee, presiding. Again the Library's dual role was emphasized, this time by Nedzi when introducing the President: "As its name reveals, the Library is the Library of the Congress—a fact in which the Congress of the United States takes great pride—and, of equal importance, if not more so, it is a national library that serves all of the people of the United States."[48]

NCLIS and National Networking

Boorstin entered a library world in the throes of change and a Library of Congress rapidly developing electronic resources. In April 1975, a terminal was installed in the Science Reading Room, providing public access to the National Referral Center's information resources, MARC, and some Congressional Research Service databases; and a terminal appeared in the Main Reading Room in May 1976. The Information Systems Office was uniting access to the Multiple Use MARC System,[49] and the clumsily titled SCORPIO (Subject Content Oriented Retriever for Processing Information On-Line; developed for the CRS) in the Library of Congress Information System (known as LOCIS). Over the next several years, the Library began providing Senate and House offices with terminals while continuing to add computer services in its own buildings.[50]

PL 91-345 (1970) had created the National Commission on Libraries and Information Science (NCLIS), consisting of the Librarian of Congress (ex officio) and fourteen members confirmed by the Senate. Charged to appraise resources; analyze needs; plan for meeting the needs; coordinate federal, state, and local activities; and promote research, the commission was authorized to contract with public and private agencies, conduct hearings, accept private funding, and disseminate its reports. President Nixon had wanted the commission placed in the Department of Health, Education, and Welfare; and he criticized the provision for private funding but nevertheless signed the bill. Though his statement called the commission's task "a crucial one for the continuing health and enrichment of our nation," Nixon did not nominate members until a year later.[51]

Just after Boorstin's nomination, the NCLIS released its first report in July 1975, stating its intent "to ensure that future development of the nation's information resources will occur in a cohesive manner according to a national plan." One of the objectives was "to plan, develop and implement a nationwide network," and the report cited MARC as "the most powerful force for bibliographic standardization." The commission stated that the Library of Congress should be designated as the national library, with nine areas of responsibility: national lending library of last resort, expansion of the NPAC and MARC, online distribution of bibliographic data, an expanded general reference program, a national serials service, a training center on LC techniques and processes, improved access to state and local publications, and further implementation of a national preservation program. "The participation of the Library is crucial to the development of a National Program and to the operation of the nationwide network," the commission emphasized, but it conceded that new legislation (and implicitly funding) might be required.[52]

Speaking at an October 1975 ARL meeting, Processing Department Director William Welsh committed the LC to "serve as the national center as we move into a new era of bibliographic control made possible by computerized library networks. The Library's role will be to develop and maintain standard bibliographic devices that will promote consistency in decentralized input to a comprehensive national database," because the LC "recognizes that it cannot supply 100% of the cataloging information that is required nationally." Welsh stated that the Library would provide name authority records, subject headings, LC and Dewey classification numbers, and cataloging for roman and nonroman alphabet materials in all physical formats. He emphasized particularly that the Library would not terminate any existing services (including its book catalogs and cards) unless it had "strong assurance that their transfer would not adversely affect the library community. That is a stronger statement than appeared earlier," he said, "and it is changed to reflect many comments that I received on that point." The Library would also assist network development "as secondary distributors of LC bibliographic data online." "When Welsh wants to exert some muscle in the library world," *American Libraries* observed, "he rolls up his sleeves and does it himself, in full view of all." And that was the case despite his disclaimer that it was the view of the Processing Department, not of the Library. To the editors, it was "not a pussyfooting suggestion of what the library role *might* be if this or that legislation were to pass." Welsh's commitment presumably carried Boorstin's assent.

Two other speakers, Henriette Avram and John Rather, echoed Welsh's assurance of a gradual transition. Rather, the Chief of the Technical Processes Research Office described work on the LC's Core Bibliographic System as "proceeding," its slow pace aimed at producing the best possible results. "We always have someone on the outside telling us how we can best do our own work," he commented. "And though we try to be responsive to those needs we still have to ensure the integrity of the internal processing system, which is indeed the core of our national service to libraries in this country." These statements seemed to respond to the NCLIS report as well as to the ARL's concerns.[53]

Boorstin's Task Force

Boorstin moved quickly. On January 16, 1976, he created the eleven-member Task Force on Goals, Organization, and Planning, charged to conduct "a full-scale review of the Library and its activities" within a year. Private funding supported eight outside advisory groups, each representing one of the Library's constituencies. In a communication to the staff, Boorstin promised that "the review will be wide-ranging, free, and imaginative. It will start with our primary duty to serve the Congress. It will take account of those changes in technology, in the nation and the world, which affect our usefulness to the Congress and our effectiveness as a national library." He posed questions to guide the review, which task force chairman John Y. Cole declared "called for nothing less than a redefinition of the role of the Library of Congress in American life."

Boorstin's questions charted his agenda: he wanted the Library especially to "more effectively encourage research and creativity in the interest of Congress and the nation"; to better serve constituencies, such as the blind and the media; to improve "the nation's reading"; to offer guidance to readers and viewers amid the rapid increases in graphic and printed sources; and to "preserve and enrich the tradition of the book."[54]

He was also keen to enhance the Library's visibility and its relationships with scholars, authors, publishers, and cultural leaders. Symbolically, his first acts included opening the bronze exterior doors long closed to the public, furnishing the terrace with tables, and ordering the Neptune Fountain outside the front of the 1897 main building repaired. He often spoke of the Library as "the world's greatest Multi-Media Encyclopedia," the parts represented by the specialized reading rooms, with the Main Reading Room as the index or integrating element.[55]

The task force's advisory groups represented the arts, humanities, law, libraries, media, publishing, science and technology, and social sciences. There were also fourteen subcommittees: area studies, automation and reference services, bibliographic access, the Library's bibliographic role, collections development, the Library's cultural role, government documents, loan and photoduplication services, serials management, services to Congress, services to libraries, services to staff, training and staff development and a user survey. Altogether, several hundred individuals participated, about three-fourths of them LC staff members.

The final report, *The Library of Congress in Perspective*, contained thirty-three major recommendations. The cover letter emphasized two points: "The Library must develop a sense of wholeness that it does not have at present and it must develop a stronger sense of service to all its users." That meant that each administrative unit "must view itself as an integral part of the Library of Congress, not solely as an individual department or division that serves a special clientele." The divisive nature of an organization containing technical, format, and subject or client-oriented units, long recognized, had only increased with the Library's rapid growth.

The report embraced the conception of the Library's role as a national cultural institution with special obligations to the American people. Its first and concluding chapters, focused on the congressional and national roles, urged a new codification of laws relating to the LC and an explicit statement of purposes, privileges, and responsibilities.

But while asserting the intention to provide national and even international library leadership, the task force affirmed that "the Library can fulfill the high hopes we have expressed for it only if it remains in the legislative branch." The report recommended establishing a Board of Advisers, but that board should include members from all the Library's constituencies (including the Joint Committee's chairman and vice chairman); and it would not usurp the congressional oversight function. The emphasis was instead on increasing consultation: the Library should be simultaneously a leader and a partner: "assuming the responsibility for seeing that essential tasks are performed but always remembering that those tasks might be best performed elsewhere."[56]

Other chapters of the report addressed access to collections and services, collection development, bibliographic control, cultural and educational programs, staff development and communication, planning and management, and "unique opportunities for service." The recommendations ranged from the most basic, such as examining the not-on-shelf problem, to reviewing key functions on a Library-wide basis, such as the proposals to establish a collection development office and an interdepartmental cataloging committee. Recommendations for improving leadership and communication included placing the Personnel Office in the Librarian's Office, and the task force endorsed Boorstin's initiative to establish an office of planning and development. The proposals all reflected the "general conclusion that the Library's most pressing organizational problem is not its overall administrative structure, but inadequate coordination and communication between existing administrative units."

Boorstin accepted the report on January 28, 1977, calling it the beginning of "a drama of refreshment and revival" and promising to develop a program of "action, of improvement and of outreach" and also "of inreach in the improvement of opportunities in this Library for people to serve it better and with more excitement."[57]

External reactions were positive but not without criticism. Noël Savage, in *Library Journal*, called it "an unexpectedly terse and well-written document" that "clearly faced up to the severe criticisms that have been leveled at the LC by outsiders for years." The recommendations "in occasionally veiled language point out a lot of flaws in the Library of Congress as a functioning institution, [and] are aimed at pulling into one operating entity a sprawling assemblage of minor fiefdoms and confusing—even conflicting—forces that make little contribution to the proper functioning of the present Library of Congress or to the proposed national and international giant which the library is seen as one day becoming." He named the "forces" as "hostilities" between the cataloging and reference staffs, and "lack of contact" and "parochialism" among specialized collections and offices and the rest of the Library, which the task force proposed to remedy by establishing coordinating committees and a "new line of command positions."

The report made large claims for the Library—as the one organization capable of coordinating the national library network proposed by the NCLIS, as a "major repository of the record of American civilization," as a cultural and educational resource, as a national bibliographic center, and as "a leader of cooperative activities in acquisitions, cataloging, preservation, and reference work." However, Savage wrote, "not everyone wants LC to run the show. . . . The vision that is held out by the report as well as the means by which this vision is to be made flesh, may meet with a lot more opposition outside the Library of Congress than inside it. . . . In some ways, this vision is the first serious proposal for an organization that has been almost conventionally cast aside in recent years as a 'monolithic' system." It proposes a big gamble: the proposed new infrastructure might assist but also might encumber the decision-making process. If the LC envisions itself as "existing in a world in which it is by far the most significant inhabitant," he concluded, that would certainly be challenged.[58]

R. Kathleen Molz, Professor of Library Service at Columbia University, acknowledged that the task force was encouraged to disregard budgetary and statutory limitations but that as a result, some of its recommendations "read like wishful thinking." She suggested that "the buoyant mood of the task force that the Library should make itself not only better, but bigger," seemed to foreclose consideration of some alternatives, especially decentralization of holdings or services. Nevertheless, Molz concluded, the report revealed the dimensions and scope of the Library's problems, shedding light on a complex institution that was not well understood.[59]

Boorstin's Reorganization

Boorstin made some changes ahead of the task force's report, but for the most part reorganization came later.[60] The Office of the Librarian was enlarged, including a Deputy Librarian, an Associate Librarian, an Associate Librarian for National Programs and an Associate Librarian for Management. The office also included the legislative liaison, internal audit, and environment resources offices; the General Counsel's Office; an Equal Employment Opportunity and Special Programs Office; the new Office of Planning and Development; a new Collections Development Office; and a new Center for the Book. The major departments remained the same: the Congressional Research Service, the Law Library, the Copyright Office (with the Register now named Assistant Librarian for Copyright Services), an Assistant Librarian for Research Services, and an Assistant Librarian for Processing Services. As Savage noted, the outcome was a larger bureaucracy.

The Management directorate included a new Automated Systems Office, the Photoduplication Service, Personnel and Labor Relations, and administrative services. National Programs encompassed the National Library Service for the Blind and Physically Handicapped; a new American Folklife Center; the Children's Literature Center; a new Network Development Office; the Federal Library Committee; the information, publishing, and exhibits offices; and a new Educational Liaison Office.

Research Services included three branches: Area Studies, General Reference, and Special Collections, with the Preservation Office and a new Performing Arts Library reporting directly to the Assistant Librarian for Research Services. Area Studies included the European Division (which combined the Slavic and Central European Division with Western Europe), the Asian Division (formerly the Orientalia Division), the Hispanic Division, and a new African and Middle Eastern Division uniting the African, Hebraic, and Near East sections. General Reference included the Reading Rooms and the Serial, Collections Management, Loan, Federal Research, and Science and Technology divisions, with the Serial Division expanded to include government publications. Special Collections included the Music, Prints and Photographs, Manuscript, Geography and

Map, Rare Book and Special Collections divisions, and a new Motion Picture, Broadcasting, and Recorded Sound Division.

Processing Services included Acquisitions and Overseas Operations; Cataloging; and Catalog Maintenance, Production, and Publication. With the later addition of the Network Development Office, the latter branch became the office for Processing Systems, Networks, and Automation Planning. Parts of Processing Services and Research Services that had responsibility for selecting materials moved to the new Collections Development Office in the Librarian's Office.

Boorstin retained interdepartmental committees, and he established an "Executive Session," a twice-monthly meeting of senior staff. He also heeded congressional opinion, for example, with regard to the Law Library. He considered revoking its separate status, an idea that met resistance from both the staff and from many law librarians, who viewed it as a threat to their libraries' traditional autonomy within their institutions. Congress requested an outside assessment, and the Arthur D. Little firm's 1979–80 study produced *Strengthening the Law Library of Congress: Service to the Congress through Helping Meet National Needs for Legal Information.* The report recommended that the Law Library remain a separate organization within the LC; the proposal that it become a separate agency was rejected as too costly and likely to hinder congressional service. Confirming general congressional satisfaction with the existing services but also stating that the Law Library had not provided national leadership, the report also recommended broadening its management, addressing processing needs, developing and implementing Class K, providing additional resources, considering charging for services, and furthering the integration of legal with social science research.[61]

Charged to review and implement the task force's recommendations, the Office of Planning and Development took on a role that included assisting the reorganization, helping to bridge gaps, identifying redundancies, and reporting progress. Some of its initiatives, Director Charles Goodrum pointed out, came from task force recommendations that might be "generalized as lifting *use* of the collections to the levels we have traditionally accorded acquiring the collections and processing them"; for example, establishing the Computer Catalog Center. The office also worked on the "why don't they ever do anything about" issues: for example, the not-on-shelf problem, duplication in cataloging operations, and interrelating automation efforts. Support for its efforts came, he observed, from an "astonishing vector of forces": a new Librarian intent on change, experienced leaders working with new office heads, the opportunities the Madison Building offered for realignment, and new technologies. Two years later, Goodrum's successor, Robert Zich, concluded that "most of the more urgent recommendations have, in fact, been implemented."[62] Those that were not found infeasible—technically, politically, or financially—perhaps reflected the task force's ambitious effort to define an institution that could be all things to all constituencies.

Cultural Programs

The first Smithsonian Festival of American Folklife, held on the National Mall in 1967, demonstrated the growing interest in preserving regional, religious, familial, occupational, and ethnic cultures. In a further demonstration of that interest and with Boorstin's support, the American Folklife Preservation Act (PL 94-201, 1976) established the American Folklife Center at the Library with a Board of Trustees that initially included presidential and congressional appointees and federal cultural agency officials and later added appointees named by the Librarian of Congress and the presidents of the American Folklore Society and the Society for Ethnomusicology. Boorstin appointed Alan Jabbour as Director, effective August 2, 1976, and the Archive of Folk Song, later renamed the Archive of Folk Culture (1981), moved from the Music Division to the center on July 31, 1978. The center's charge was to develop programs "for the preservation, support, revitalization, and dissemination of American folklife," including collecting materials, issuing recordings, and sponsoring performances, exhibitions, workshops, research, and publications. An early initiative echoed the recording journeys of the 1930s: field projects documenting folklife traditions. The center began a noon concert series on the Neptune Plaza in 1976 and issued the quarterly *Folklife Center News* beginning in January 1978.[63]

At his swearing-in ceremony, Boorstin had pledged "to keep alive and flourishing the tradition of the Book," reprising thoughts he had expressed several years earlier.[64] He called the belief that new technologies replaced the old "the Displacive Fallacy," insisting that books and emerging technologies could complement each other.[65] He proposed the Center for the Book, an idea endorsed by the task force, and at his request, Representative Nedzi and Senator Cannon sponsored legislation that became PL 95-129 (1977). On signing the bill, President Jimmy Carter even included a handwritten note, approving the law as part of his own "continuing commitment to scholarly research and the development of public interest in books and reading."[66]

The legislation gave the Librarian authority to raise private funds to support the center's program and publications. John Cole was named founding director, and Cole and Boorstin recruited the National Advisory Board, which included authors, publishers, booksellers, librarians, scholars, media representatives, and members of the public. Three subcommittees were immediately formed: book, reading, and literacy promotion; the international role of the book; and the history of books and printing.

The center's early programs included collaborating with the Book Industry Study Group on *Reading in America 1978*, a study of adults' book-buying and book-reading habits, and "Read More About It," a partnership with CBS Television that drew an enthusiastic public response. Presented by celebrities, the center's lists of books about the subjects of CBS programs sent viewers to their libraries and bookstores. The idea of collaborating with the media had appeared during the center's "planning year" meetings and again in a symposium cosponsored with the Office of Education: "Television, the Book, and the Classroom," which addressed the concern that television was replacing reading. The center subsequently also developed reading promotion projects with ABC (which introduced the animated character Captain O. G. Readmore); NBC; and other network, publishing, and association partners.

In the mid-1980s the center began to establish affiliated centers, which focused on both local and statewide book and reading promotion programs. The first two, Florida (1984) and Illinois (1985), set the pattern for what became a fifty-state network by

2002. On its tenth anniversary, a congressional joint resolution recognized the center's first national reading promotion campaign, "Year of the Reader," with a proclamation by President Ronald Reagan.[67] First Lady Barbara Bush served as honorary chair of the next three: "Year of the Young Reader" (1989), "Year of the Lifetime Reader" (1991), and "Explore New Worlds—READ!" (1992). The center mounted "Books Change Lives" for 1993–94, "Shape Your Future—READ!" in 1995–96, "Building a Nation of Readers" for 1997–2000, and, with First Lady Laura Bush as chair, "Telling America's Stories," 2001–2.

Scholarly Programs

In keeping with his concern for books and reading, Boorstin brought his scholar's perspective to the Library. "One of my jobs as Librarian," he declared, "is to be a catalyst, an avenue between the world of ideas and everything else that goes on here."[68] While relying on the professional staff in technical areas, he was keenly interested in collection development, copyright, reading promotion, and the Library's role in American life. At a February 12, 1976, press conference, he produced a box wrapped in brown paper and tied with faded tape that he had discovered in the Librarian's Office safe. Inside the enclosed leather box was a smaller blue cardboard container identified by a label, perhaps in Robert Lincoln's hand: "Contents of the President's pockets on the night of April 14, 1865." The items Abraham Lincoln carried that night had been given to Herbert Putnam in October 1937 by Lincoln's granddaughter, Mary Lincoln Isham, but never displayed; Boorstin announced that he wanted the public to see them as a way to humanize the "mythologically engulfed" president. They included two pairs of spectacles, one mended with string; an ivory pocket knife; a gold-mounted watch fob; a white linen handkerchief with "A. Lincoln" embroidered in red; a sleeve button with gold initial "L" on dark blue enamel; and a brown leather wallet lined in purple silk, containing a pencil, a five-dollar Confederate note (perhaps acquired on a visit to Richmond and Petersburg earlier in April); and nine newspaper clippings, some from his reelection campaign.[69]

Observing that the Library had not just one but several annexes, the Librarian proposed changing the name of the LC's second building. On September 21, 1976, the Annex became the Library of Congress Thomas Jefferson Building (PL 94-264), in recognition of the importance of Jefferson's library in the LC's history, and the Librarian also took the occasion to congratulate the ALA on its centennial anniversary.[70]

He also declared "a special need" for a Council of Scholars: "Such a group will bring together those who collect, arrange, and preserve the raw materials of scholarship and the literary arts, and those who reinterpret and vivify them anew for each generation." Established in late 1980, the privately funded council had a rotating membership of approximately two dozen, representing a broad spectrum of disciplines. Boorstin wanted these members to provide advice on strengthening connections to the scholarly world, explore the extent to which the Library's collections supported the most ambitious research in all fields, and deliberate "large issues in the world of ideas." Among the first council appointments, notably, was Archibald MacLeish, named honorary chairman.

Creativity: A Continuing Inventory of Knowledge, a book containing the papers from the council's first symposium, appeared in 1982 as the first installment of the planned national inventory of knowledge.[71]

Boorstin's interest in extending the Library's constituencies also led to a new partnership. The Performing Arts Library, a joint venture of the LC and the John F. Kennedy Center for the Performing Arts, opened March 8, 1979. First proposed in 1973 by the Kennedy Center's Advisory Committee on the Arts, the library was conceived as a reference center with access to the LC's music, theater, dance, and film collections. The facility included a 4,000-volume collection, computers linked to the LC, and listening and viewing equipment; and a grant from the National Home Library Foundation supported expansion of the collection, together with recordings from the Recording Industry Association of America. Under a revised agreement effective October 1, 1994, the LC ceased providing staff but maintained the reference collection and supplied materials for exhibit.[72]

Copyright Laws

The 1970s brought long-awaited copyright legislation. PL 92-140 (1971) provided for the registration and deposit of sound recordings produced after February 15, 1972. The so-called Record Privacy Bill was designed to protect against unauthorized duplication and use of copyrighted recordings. As a result of international copyright activities, the United States ratified the International Convention for the Protection of Producers and Phonograms against Unauthorized Duplication of Their Programs on March 10, 1974, and a May 1974 conference in Brussels adopted the Convention Relating to the Distribution of Program-Carrying Signals Transmitted by Satellite, aimed at preventing ground stations from picking up and distributing material unlawfully. The United States also signed the Brussels Convention.[73]

Most important, President Ford approved the Copyright Act of 1976 (PL 94-553), which became effective January 1, 1978. It completely replaced the 1909 act, aiming both to bring American practices closer to those of other nations and to address technological advances. The act protected works copyrighted after the effective date for the author's life plus fifty years; both published and unpublished works would receive protection, and eight categories of "works of authorship" were made eligible for copyright regardless of physical format. Registration was voluntary (though necessary for full protection); but the law mandated the deposit of works carrying a copyright notice, thus assuring the flow of acquisitions for the Library's collections. There were new provisions on complex issues—for example, "fair use," a definition of uses (e.g., photocopying) that would not constitute copyright infringement, and compulsory licensing for cable television retransmissions, jukeboxes, and recording companies. The licensing system, providing for paying fees to copyright holders for the use of their works, would be administered by the Copyright Royalty Tribunal.[74] The law also directed the Register of Copyrights to report to Congress every five years on whether the statute was appropriately balancing creators' rights and users' needs.[75]

A 1974 act had created the National Commission on New Technological Uses of Copyrighted Works (known as CONTU; PL 93-573), a twelve-member group appointed by the President with the Librarian as an ex officio voting member and the Register as an ex-officio nonvoting member. Its study of copyright issues, completed in 1978, resulted in the Computer Software Copyright Act (PL 96-517, 1980), which provided protection for computer programs that embodied an author's original expression. The next year, the Copyright Office registered its first database, and later, the Semiconductor Chip Act (PL 98-620, 1984) designated computer chip designs as intellectual property, with a ten-year protection of the rights to produce, import, and distribute them.[76]

At the same time, Boorstin and the new Register of Copyrights, David Ladd, watched with concern a bill before the 96th Congress, HR 6933, to amend the patent and trademark laws. Section nine directed the Comptroller General to assess the efficiency of the Copyright Office and the Copyright Royalty Tribunal and provide a recommendation on merging them with the Patent and Trademark Office. Asking that section nine be removed, Boorstin emphasized the relationship of the copyright function to the LC's mission to house and service the nation's intellectual resources, saying the merger "would not serve the creators of intellectual property as well as has the Library of Congress in its more than *110* years of stewardship." Ladd cited the office's close connection to Library management, its record-keeping function that also provided cataloging information, and its dependence on the LC's computer systems. The House Committee on Government Operations' subcommittee deleted section nine by unanimous vote.[77]

The 1976 copyright law also included television and radio programming. Legislative efforts dated to 1970, when Senator Howard Baker (R-TN) and Representative Spark Matsunaga (D-HI) began working on what became section 113 of the act, which created an American Television and Radio Archives to collect and preserve programs, allowing their acquisition through purchase, transfer, exchange, gift, deposit, or off-the-air taping.[78] In 1978 the Motion Picture Section in the Prints and Photographs Division and the Music Division's Recorded Sound Section formed the new Motion Picture, Broadcasting, and Recorded Sound Division.[79]

The first deposit of the entire output of a broadcasting organization came in 1976, when National Public Radio divided its recorded programs between the National Archives (news and public affairs) and the Library (cultural programs). NBC's gift included its archives of 1926–70 radio programs and 1948–77 television programs (in 1978 and 1986, respectively), and the Armed Forces Radio and Television Service contributed 32,000 transcriptions. In February 1979, the House of Representatives began to televise its proceedings, and the Senate approved television coverage in 1986, and copies of both were deposited in the Library and the National Archives.[80]

National Initiatives

By 1976, the Preservation Office had a staff of over 140 and comprehensive programs of binding, reformatting, research and testing, conservation, and collections maintenance. As Boorstin became acquainted with preservation issues and librarians' longstanding interest in national leadership, he proposed a planning conference, which was funded by the Council on Library Resources and held in December 1976. It resulted in the formation of the Ad Hoc Advisory Committee for a National Preservation Program and the LC's commitment to develop the program. In July 1977, the Library took the first step by appointing a National Preservation Program Officer.[81]

The National Commission on Libraries and Information Science in 1975 had proposed establishing a national periodicals center, citing researchers' increasing demands for journals at a time when steadily rising subscription costs absorbed an ever-larger share of libraries' budgets. The NCLIS report, *Effective Access to the Periodical Literature: A National Program* (1977), proposed a central collection to provide efficient, economical delivery service; to work with the publishing community; and to help build a national library system. The NCLIS recommended that the LC operate the center after an initial grant-funded period.[82]

The Library asked the Council on Library Resources to develop plans for the center. The August 1978 CLR response proposed a national library board to govern not only the periodicals center but also national bibliographic, communications, and preservation programs. However, the library community was divided on the proposal, and publishers and information industry companies opposed it, viewing the center as a competitor. In March 1979, Deputy Librarian William Welsh recommended that the NCLIS, not the LC, administer the center. The Library, he stated, could operate the center only if no-cost space and initial foundation support were available. Congress ultimately authorized establishing the center, but it never provided funding.[83]

In April 1976, Welsh had invited representatives of bibliographic utilities, networks, and federal partners, including the NCLIS, to the first of several CLR-funded meetings on networking issues. Preliminary results of an LC-commissioned survey of twenty-three libraries and network organizations had reported general agreement that the Library should take a leading role in coordinating network development. The meetings evolved into the Library's Network Advisory Committee (NAC), with the LC Network Development Office headed by Henriette Avram serving as secretariat. The first NAC position paper, "Toward a National Library and Information Service Network: The Library Bibliographic Component," appeared in mid-1977, and a briefing held at the June ALA convention drew a standing-room-only crowd.[84]

In late 1978, the Council on Library Resources obtained $5 million from seven private foundations and from the National Endowment for the Humanities for its Bibliographic Service Development Program. The council proposed to link the OCLC, the RLIN, and the LC's computer systems, citing as long-range goals "the provision of effective bibliographic services for all who need them; the improvement of bibliographic products; and stabilization of costs of many bibliographic processes in individual libraries." The announcement stated that the system "should take full advantage of the nation's capability to produce bibliographic records, it should seek to promote conformity to national standards, and it should make the resulting bibliographic data more readily available to all libraries. The approach to be taken is based upon the belief that if the bibliographic service can satisfy the detailed bibliographic, processing, and support requirements of the largest libraries, then most requirements of all other libraries will also be satisfied." The key to success was "the commitment and performance of the Library of Congress, which is the proper and reasonable keystone of the bibliographic structure of the nation." Without a national program, the council contended, a network might develop anyway, but an ad hoc approach would likely result in redundant or incomplete operations. The Bibliographic Service Development Program would build on the Library of Congress's databases, the OCLC service model, established standards, and existing systems. Its program committee included representatives of the bibliographic utilities, the LC, and the library community, while the LC's Network Advisory Committee continued as a forum, expanded to include both public and private sector information producers.[85] In 1980, the LC's Catalog Maintenance, Production, and Publication unit was renamed; Henriette Avram became director for Processing Systems, Networks, and Automation Planning.

Closing the Card Catalog

In 1977, the Library announced that its card catalog would be closed, well ahead of the actual date that filing in it ceased: December 31, 1980.[86] The decision, not unexpected in the library community, drew widespread comment from the press and from a public that viewed card catalogs as iconic: the physical symbols of all that meant the library. "Part of the joy," wrote Christopher Hitchens in the *Times Literary Supplement*, "is the business of pulling out the smooth drawers and going through the beautifully arranged cards. As any reader knows, the pleasure lies in what you find while you are looking: in the distractions from the main quarry." Citing a common complaint, Stanley Goldberg wrote, "Hundreds of people can use the card catalog at the same time. On a busy day, that is often the case. For hundreds to use the computer catalog, hundreds of terminals are required. I am often discouraged from using the computer for trivial searches because of people waiting for the terminals." But he admitted, "I have no doubt that the computer catalog is here to stay." Library managers, while perhaps regretting the loss of a time-honored tool, had another view: "Many librarians didn't know why we were automating," William Welsh once said. "It was to get rid of card catalog maintenance." His blunt declaration resounded with library administrators who recognized the enormous costs associated with the LC's card files—and their own as well.[87]

The evolution was swift. In less than a decade, MARC had expanded to include all roman-alphabet languages, the system moved from tape to online, and annual production increased from 60,000 to 180,000 records. On May 31, 1978, when the millionth MARC record entered the database, the Automated Systems Office maintained over 1,100 terminals in the Library and legislative branch offices.[88]

MARC included nonroman script records in romanized form, but not Chinese, Japanese, or Korean records. Encouraged by the American Council of Learned Societies, the Association for Asian Studies, the Social Science Research Council, and the ARL, in 1979 the Library signed an agreement with the Research Libraries Information Network to develop a system to automate Chinese, Japanese, and Korean (CJK) bibliographic records. With the introduction of RLIN'S CJK terminals in 1983, catalog records in both roman and nonroman formats could be entered into the RLIN database, making possible the retrieval of East Asian materials as readily as Western-language publications. In 1991 the LC adopted RLIN's new cataloging system, known as JACKPHY (Japanese, Chinese, Korean, Persian, Hebraic and Yiddish).[89]

With the guidance of the Joint Steering Committee for Revision of AACR, another revision of the cataloging rules had begun in 1974. The members included the ALA, the LC, the British Library, the Library Association of Great Britain, and the Canadian Committee on Cataloging representing the National Library of Canada and the Canadian library associations. Soliciting input from many groups—ranging, for example, from the ALA's Social Responsibilities Round Table to its Information Science and Automation Division—code revision aimed at reconciling the American and British versions, incorporating changes to the 1967 text, maintaining conformity with the Paris principles, improving the rules for nonbook materials and electronic records, and standardizing to promote the international interchange of bibliographic data. Paul Winkler (of the Library of Congress) was named editor, with Michael Gorman (British Library) as associate editor. The new code, as the second edition of the *Anglo-American Cataloging Rules*—dubbed AACR2—appeared in late 1978.[90]

The Library announced it would adopt AACR2 at the same time the catalog closed, another decision that raised much discussion. To allay some of the anxieties, particularly over the number of changes AACR2 would require in local catalogs, the ALA and LC sponsored a series of conferences and workshops to help librarians understand what adoption might require, and the Library announced that card printing and card sales would continue as long as demand justified the service. "As tempers cooled," wrote Mary Ellen Soper years later, "recommendations grew for libraries to adopt the new code completely and integrate catalog records prepared according to its rules" with earlier records. A major factor was the bibliographic utilities' ability to change their massive databases to conform to AACR2. Many libraries started new catalogs of electronic records and converted their card catalogs over time. Several years later, after surveying subscribers' preferences, in 1983 the LC began issuing the *National Union Catalog* in microfiche rather than print volumes. Thus, by the mid-1980s, the Library made its cataloging available through tape or online MARC records, by subscription to the microfiche, through the on-demand CARDS system, and through the CIP records in new books. And the Library still sold cards.[91]

The White House Conference

The Nixon and Ford administrations did not make library support a priority, but Congress included funds for the first White House Conference on Library and Information Services in the supplemental appropriations act signed on May 4, 1977 (PL 95-26). President Carter called the conference for November 1979, and state and local preconferences elected the delegates, one-third of them librarians. NCLIS chairman Charles Benton chaired the conference, and Librarian Boorstin addressed the group on the shift from what he called the "Age of Publishing" to the "Age of Broadcasting." "In our time our libraries have two paradoxical & sometimes conflicting roles," he declared. "Of course we must be repositories of information. But somehow we must also remain places of refuge from the tidal waves of information—and misinformation. Our libraries must be conspicuously the treasuries of news that stays news." The delegates produced sixty-four resolutions, concerned broadly with increasing library and information services and maintaining local control.[92] While the conference supported strengthening the LC's role in activities related to literacy, resource sharing, networking, and preservation, the 1979 meeting helped perhaps more to marshal support nationwide—in particular, through partnerships with civic leaders. A small but enduring achievement was the adoption of the sign depicting a person with an open book in hand to mark the location of a library.

The Madison Building

The dedication of the James Madison Memorial Building took place April 24, 1980, the 180th anniversary of the day President John Adams signed the act creating the Library of Congress. The building had a difficult history. In 1970 increased funding was proposed to complete the interior, but Speaker of the House Carl Albert (D-OK) in 1971 recommended postponement until a location was determined for a fourth House office building. A later funding request met opposition from members who petitioned the Speaker in mid-1974 for office space in the building. The delay was finally overcome through "efforts by the press, librarians, influential Senators, and several congressmen." Among them was Boorstin, whose swearing-in speech noted that the Library's crowded condition "diminishes us all" while complimenting Congress's "enlightened and generous understanding of our mission." Additional funding was authorized in 1976 (PL 94-219) and 1978 (PL 95-548), and offices began moving into the building in late 1979. Among the last to arrive, on June 11, 1982, were the Librarian and his staff, whose sixth-floor suite overlooks the Capitol and the House office buildings. The original Librarian's office, Room 108 in the 1897 building, is preserved as a historical space.[93]

For the dedication, the Speaker of the House, the Joint Committee on the Library, other members of Congress, the Architect of the Capitol, Boorstin, and L. Quincy Mumford attended the outdoor celebration, which featured not Washington's usual military ensemble but instead bluegrass, gospel, and country music, courtesy of the American Folklife Center. A special exhibition, *James Madison and the Search for Nationhood*, recognized the Founding Father, and on November 20, 1981, President Reagan presided at the dedication of the first-floor Madison Memorial Hall.

Notwithstanding Boorstin's renaming the Annex, on April 1, 1980, Joint Committee members Pell and Nedzi introduced bills to designate the 1897 building as the Library of Congress Thomas Jefferson Building and the Annex as the Library of Congress John Adams Building. With hearings on May 7, the bill passed the House that day and the Senate on June 3; President Carter approved it on June 13 (PL 96-269). The legislation honored the three presidents associated with the Library's origins: Adams for signing the founding legislation, Jefferson for offering his library to Congress, and Madison for both his early interest in a congressional library and for signing the legislation approving the purchase of Jefferson's collection. The Madison Building opened on May 28. In addition to Madison Memorial Hall, a sixth-floor assembly room was later named the Mumford Room, and a third-floor auditorium for film screenings was dedicated as the Mary Pickford Theater on May 10, 1983, with a symposium celebrating the silent film actress's career. The second-floor room reserved for congressional use became the La

Follette Congressional Reading Room, honoring senators Robert Marion La Follette (R-WI), who introduced legislation establishing the Legislative Reference Service, and his son, Robert Marion La Follette Jr. (R-WI).[94]

As space long occupied by staff and offices cleared, the Jefferson and Adams buildings, though time-worn, returned to their original appearances. Boorstin had suggested the need to restore the older buildings as early as 1977, resulting in a 1984 appropriation of $81.5 million for a restoration and renovation project that was not completed until 1995 (PL 98-396). He also encouraged mounting major exhibitions: the first, *Building a Better Mouse: 50 Years of Animation*, featured an appealing poster with Mickey surrounded by cranes and workmen, and from its debut in November 1978 it drew an enthusiastic audience. Another, the American Folklife Center's appreciation of *The American Cowboy*, began a yearlong series of similarly themed programs. President Reagan, who attended the March 24, 1983, opening reception, commented with his usual genial humor that he had looked in vain for a display on his film *Cattle Queen of Montana* (1954).[95]

New Technologies

By 1985, the Preservation Office had developed elements of the National Preservation Program, including offering advisory services, publication of research results, participating in cooperative projects, providing services to other federal agencies, and developing internships and training programs. The office cooperated with the ALA's Resources and Technical Services Division in 1983–85 outreach conferences on preservation methods and hosted numerous American and foreign visitors interested in its services.[96]

Years of research on the problem of acid paper had seemed to come to fruition in 1976, when the office patented a deacidification process that promised to restore alkaline content and retard deterioration. The process used the chemical diethyl zinc (DEZ), which required tight control due to its pyrophoric properties. After initial testing using a kitchen pressure cooker and in a vacuum chamber at a General Electric Company facility in Valley Forge, Pennsylvania, in 1982 5,000 volumes were treated at the National Aeronautics and Space Administration's Goddard Space Flight center, in a facility formerly used for testing materials for outer space.

Public Law 98-427 (1984) authorized construction of a deacidification facility at Fort Detrick, Maryland. But fires in late 1985 and early 1986 closed the Goddard plant, and a review by NASA's Accident Investigation Board cited procedural errors, design flaws, and equipment failures. Preservation Office director Peter Sparks announced that the office would continue the work with a new contractor, Texas Alkyls Chemical Company. The House Appropriations Committee requested an evaluation by the Office of Technology Assessment, which found "high potential for success" but also cautioned that safety regulation needed constant attention and that evaluation of other processes would be "prudent."[97]

At the same time, staff members from several offices and divisions tested high-density storage technologies. The LC's first computerized system to store images on disk and reproduce them in facsimile was the Cataloging Distribution Service's (CDS's) DEMAND system; developed in partnership with Xerox Electro-Optical Systems, it enabled CDS to reproduce card images in response to subscribers' requests.[98] The Optical Disk Pilot Program began in 1982 to assess using disk storage for both print and nonprint materials. The disks provided much-higher-density storage than microforms, but the costs, copyright implications, reproduction quality, potential for research use, and utility as a preservation medium all required investigation. The first reader station, providing access to images on analog laser videodisks, opened in the Prints and Photographs Reading Room in 1984, followed by a digital optical disk station in the Newspaper and Current Periodicals Reading Room in January 1986. The first digital audio disk, holding 668 early sound recordings, became available in the Performing Arts Reading Room in 1987. CDS began offering products on compact discs (CD-ROMs) in 1986.[99]

Congressional interest in the challenges that new technologies posed took the form of a request for an inquiry into the continuing influence of books. At a press conference on December 7, 1984, Boorstin delivered the report *Books in Our Future* to Joint Committee chairman Senator Charles Mathias Jr. (R-MD), who had requested the study. Conducted by the Center for the Book, the study included interviews with authors, publishers, booksellers, computer experts, librarians, scientists, educators, and scholars; the center's advisory board; and the Advisory Committee on the Book in the Future. Reflecting both agreements and disagreements between the advisers, and also between members of the Council of Scholars, the report concluded that technology was not a threat to books and reading and recommended "cautious enthusiasm" for new technologies. Most of the advisers, however, did agree with Boorstin that illiteracy and "aliteracy" (a term he coined to describe nonreaders) threatened the "culture of the book," and also with his call to establish a national goal of abolishing illiteracy by 1989, the bicentennial of the US Constitution. The report provided recommendations for action by private organizations, Congress, the executive branch, and the Library; and the center subsequently compiled *The Community of the Book: A Directory of Selected Organizations and Programs* (1986), a listing of its "reading promotion partners": organizations supporting books, reading, and literacy projects.[100]

Boorstin and Congress

Senator Spark Matsunaga, a fourteen-year House veteran who was elected to the Senate in 1976, had introduced a bill to establish the Office of Poet Laureate of the United States every year since 1963. Reelected in 1982, he submitted the proposal as an amendment to PL 99-194 (1985), the reauthorization of the Foundation on the Arts, Humanities, and Museums Act. As had Mumford, Boorstin opposed the proposal as potentially overshadowing the Library's Consultant in Poetry and politicizing poetry by making it a presidential appointment. The Senate Committee on Labor and Human Resources endorsed Boorstin's request that the Librarian make the appointment, and the title became Poet Laureate Consultant in Poetry, with a tenure of one or two years, compensated by endowment funds. The act specifically recognized the position "as equivalent to that of Poet Laureate of the United States." Boorstin named Robert Penn Warren, the 1944–45 Consultant, as the first laureate, calling him "a serious, though not a solemn surveyor of our America." Beyond providing for an annual National Endowment for the Arts–sponsored poetry program and encouraging federal agencies to invite the Laureate's participation in "ceremonial and other occasions of celebration," the act specified no duties. Heeding some former Consultants' fears of federal intrusion, the Library has kept the Laureates free to work on their own projects; many of them have pursued initiatives to raise poetry's public profile and broaden its constituencies.[101]

A less auspicious result, however, came when in the regular 1986 appropriations legislation (PL 99-151), and through the Balanced Budget and Emergency Deficit Control Act of 1985 (PL 99-177), the Library lost the largest amount in its history: $18.3 million. Boorstin announced that the cuts would have an impact on every area, including services to Congress. A subsequent reduction-in-force affected 124 positions and abolished 70 jobs.[102]

Boorstin had had good relations with Congress, which he once called "our least appreciated and least understood institution," but he was also a vigorous advocate, and he spoke out at the February 20, 1986, House Appropriations Committee hearings.[103] "I would be failing in my oath of office," he said, "if I did not take this opportunity to sound the alarm, and inform the Committee as clearly and as honestly as I can of what is happening to your great Library, and what will happen if this Committee—the only agency of our government with the power to act—does not act promptly." The Library would have to stop collecting some current material, reduce service hours, leave much material uncataloged, and cease some essential preservation measures. The staff, he said, had spent hours "trying to figure out how to meet the sudden demand for a Procrustes cut in each of our appropriations by an arbitrary percentage." He continued:

> Historians will not fail to note that a people who could spend $300 billion on their defense would not spend $18 million on their knowledge—and could not even keep their libraries open in the evening. Historians will look with amazement and incredulity at a nation that could once afford to build grand structures bearing the names of Thomas Jefferson, John Adams, and James Madison—all lovers and champions of knowledge—yet decided it could no longer afford to acquire as effectively and abundantly as possible, the current sources of knowledge. . . . I beg this Committee to recognize that knowledge is not simply another commodity. On the contrary, knowledge is never used up, it increases by diffusion, and grows by dispersion. Knowledge and Information cannot be quantitatively assessed, as a percentage of GNP. Any willful cut in our resources of knowledge is an act of self-destruction.[104]

Then, Representative Victor Fazio (D-CA) recalled, "Dan got down in the trenches": he reduced the hours of service from 77.5 to 54.5 per week. That brought widespread objections: for example, from a group calling itself the "Books Not Bombs Campaign to Save the Library of Congress." In March its members staged a sit-in in the Main Reading Room, staying well past the new 5:30 p.m. closing time. After three days, police arrested eighteen of the protesters and ten of them appeared before the District of Columbia Superior Court. Eight were sentenced to community service and supervised probation.[105]

The Joint Committee convened a May 7 hearing in response to the "many persons who had voiced concerns." They included representatives of the ALA, the ARL, professional associations, university faculty members and students, and independent researchers. Saying that the reduction in service hours "was one of the most painful decisions I have had to make in my decade as the Librarian of Congress," Boorstin stated, "An institution which has a duty to three constituencies—the illustrious dead, the vocal living, and the voiceless unborn—has no easy problem. The more the Congress cuts our resources—as it has for some inexplicable reason, doubling the cut imposed on most other Federal agencies—the more difficult and more painful and less satisfying are our priorities in service to one or another of our constituencies." Congress restored $867,000 in a July supplemental appropriations act (PL 99-349) that allowed resuming regular Library hours on July 10 and added funding for acquisitions and cataloging. Even so acquisitions, already suffering from the reduced purchasing power of the dollar abroad, decreased 13.3 percent.[106]

In another controversy, the House had voted 216–93 in July 1985 to prevent the National Library Service for the Blind and Physically Handicapped from acquiring a Braille version of *Playboy* magazine (a reduction of $103,000). Boorstin had expressed "profound regret" at the House action "as its way of censoring material made available to the blind community through our Library of Congress service. The next step might be to deny funds to the Library of Congress for purchase of books which the House deemed inappropriate, subversive, or unacceptable to the majority of the House. Censorship has no place in a free society." He appealed unsuccessfully to the Senate to restore funding. In a December press conference, representatives Fazio and Jerry Lewis (R-CA) announced that the American Council for the Blind, the ALA, the Blinded Veterans Association, Playboy Enterprises, and others would challenge the decision as denying blind users their First Amendment rights. In the September 1986 decision on *American Foundation for the Blind, et al. v. Daniel J. Boorstin*, US District Judge Thomas F. Hogan directed the production and distribution of both Braille and talking book editions of *Playboy*.[107]

National and International Networking

Early in 1985, the Library's MARC records became available internationally in UNIMARC, a format developed by the International Federation of Library Associations to enable the exchange and distribution of bibliographic records among institutions and organizations that used differing versions of MARC. As a means of furthering IFLA's program of Universal Bibliographic Control, UNIMARC was the product of long development; first published in 1977, it enabled institutions to use conversion programs to make UNIMARC records compatible with their own systems. The Library began converting UNIMARC records into MARC, thus allowing records from foreign bibliographic agencies to enter its database—an invaluable service for shared cataloging.[108]

Simultaneously, the Council on Library Resources Linked Systems Project continued work to establish computer-to-computer exchanges between the Library, OCLC, and RLIN. In October 1986, the first phase was completed with the distribution of name authority records (i.e., the established forms of names used by catalogers) from the LC to RLIN, followed by distribution to OCLC in January 1987.[109] In June 1987, RLIN member Yale University submitted the first authority record via the Linked Systems Project link, and Indiana University submitted the first OCLC bibliographic record in March 1988.[110] The next step was the interchange of full bibliographic records, and to that end, eight university libraries participated in the National Coordinated Cataloging Program project to contribute catalog records via telecommunication to the Library. Though the Linked Systems Project's link was not yet ready, the CLR-funded pilot began in 1988, limited to current materials in Western European languages and with the goal of providing timely coverage of recent books.[111] Since the contributing libraries also created authority records and assigned LC subject headings and classification numbers, the Library could accept their cataloging as its own. But the results were disappointing: telecommunications costs were high; some participants found the LC's standards too demanding; and some ceased participation, thus decreasing the number of records created.[112]

Boorstin Retires

On December 10, 1986, Daniel Boorstin announced that he would step down on June 15, 1987, "to become a full-time citizen of the Republic of Letters." He wanted to spend time writing and lecturing but also hoped "to continue to serve the Library."[113] The ALA's tribute, one of many from library and scholarly organizations, cited especially the Center for the Book and *Books in Our Future,* his "active continuation of the Library's tradition of pioneering in the use of new technology," his speech to the White House Conference on knowledge and information, and "your pride, your infectious enthusiasm, and your true love of the library, . . . which you have so aptly called 'a multi-media encyclopedia.'"

Boorstin served just short of a dozen years, but he did much to broaden the Library's constituencies and increase public awareness of the Library through his promotion of books and reading, through an expanded exhibitions program, through his Council of Scholars, and through his advocacy of the Library's role in American life. Congress named him Librarian of Congress Emeritus, the title previously given only to Herbert Putnam.[114] And in an article on Boorstin, the first scholar–Librarian of Congress, the *New York Times* described the Librarianship as "perhaps the leading public intellectual position in the nation."[115]

CHAPTER 10

Bicentennial and Beyond

PRESIDENT REAGAN nominated James Hadley Billington, director of the Woodrow Wilson International Center for Scholars, as the thirteenth Librarian of Congress on April 17, 1987. As with previous nominations, there were a number of distinguished candidates, including the political theorist and author Russell Kirk; the historian Gertrude Himmelfarb; Robert Middlekauff, director of the Huntington Library and Art Gallery; and Vartan Gregorian, director of the New York Public Library.[1] The ALA, as in the past, stated that the position should be "filled from the ranks of distinguished librarians" but also expressed a hope for cordial relations. Other library organizations followed suit, and Librarian Boorstin endorsed the nomination.[2] The Library of Congress's unions and employee organizations urged attention to employment equity and affirmative action as top priorities for the new Librarian. Among the candidates, Billington stood out as a scholar who was also an experienced administrator. He also had served the President as an adviser and accompanied congressional delegations on visits to Russia. Responding to senators' questions at the confirmation hearing, Billington said that he had not entered into the Library's "detailed structures and problems" but would "take a fresh look." He was confirmed on July 24.[3]

On September 14, in the Jefferson Building's Great Hall, Chief Justice William Rehnquist administered the oath of office, with members of Congress and President Reagan in attendance. Billington's remarks highlighted his intention to move the Library "out more broadly," to make its resources more widely available, but also "in more deeply," focusing on the talented LC staff and extensive collections.[4] At a press conference later that day, he again emphasized outreach, saying, "We may find new ways to share some of the richness of this repository of national memory with people in place." And he expressed a concern to "sort out and make sense of all this profusion of publication and information that exists in our world, and establish some priorities within it," with the Library "playing a catalytic if not a leadership role, in helping turn information into knowledge and distill it all into some wisdom." He also echoed his predecessors' views of the LC as the instrument of a democratic nation—adding his own characterization to MacLeish's "people's library of reference" and Boorstin's "the world's greatest Multi-Media Encyclopedia," Billington called it "the living encyclopedia of democracy."[5]

Born in Bryn Mawr, Pennsylvania, on June 1, 1929, Billington received a bachelor's degree from Princeton University and a doctorate as a Rhodes Scholar at Balliol College, Oxford University. After military service, he taught history at Harvard and

Princeton universities. He became director of the Wilson Center in 1973, considerably enlarging its programs and inaugurating *The Wilson Quarterly* in 1976. A prolific scholar of Russian history, two of his books—*The Icon and the Axe* (1966) and *Fire in the Minds of Men* (1980)—received National Book Award nominations. He served on the editorial boards of *Foreign Affairs* and *Theology Today,* was a member of Phi Beta Kappa and the American Academy of Arts and Sciences, and held a Guggenheim Fellowship. He also had been the director of the American Association for the Advancement of Slavic Studies and a member of the Board of Foreign Scholarships, which administered academic exchanges under the Fulbright-Hays Act.

Billington's Reorganization

Soon after he arrived, on December 9, the Main Reading Room closed for renovation, part of the Boorstin-initiated restoration of the Jefferson and Adams buildings. Coolidge Auditorium concerts moved in 1989 to the National Academy of Sciences auditorium and in 1995 to the Kennedy Center. Services for readers moved to the Social Science and Local History and Genealogy Reading Rooms and on weekends also to the European, Hispanic, and Manuscript Reading Rooms. When it reopened on June 3, 1991, the Main Reading Room was for the first time carpeted, with walls and iron shelves painted in the original colors. Reader desks surrounded the central desk as before—replicas of the originals but wired for telecommunications. The semicircular card catalog was out of sight; the computer reigned—though in a scrupulously restored nineteenth-century setting. *Roll Call* called the Reading Room "the most beautiful interior space in Washington"; and when the Great Hall reopened in January 1993, the *Washington Post* exclaimed, "What a splendid place this is," praising the "blessedly high standards of quality" of the restoration.[6]

Billington established the Management and Planning Committee (MAP) of more than two dozen staff members and the external National Advisory Committee of academicians; legislators; and business, government, library, and information industry representatives. He contracted with Arthur Young Inc. to examine operations and asked the General Accounting Office to perform an audit. He had the staff schedule forums in ten states, inviting, in particular, members of Congress and their district staffs, and he participated in them as well as hosting informal discussions with LC staff.

The MAP Committee charge included five tasks: (1) analyze ways to increase the efficiency and economy of the administration and improve job satisfaction; (2) increase the direct scholarly use of the collections; (3) improve service to Congress and to other federal agencies; (4) broaden and rationalize national library service to external constituencies; and (5) improve methods for selecting, cataloging, preserving, and maintaining collections. Subsumed under these were familiar questions, such as what should be discontinued and what might be initiated, how to extend use, and how to optimize processing and reduce costs.[7]

By the mid-1980s, the increasing capacities for providing access to information and materials provoked sharp-edged discussions: new technologies offered both the means of reaching a wider audience and possibilities for preservation. As the LC's Stephen

Ostrow put it, "We must establish a continuum of priorities against which the necessity of preserving materials in their original formats or the suitability of substituting surrogates must be measured." The MAP Committee discussed using technology to address pressing collections needs.[8]

Its 300-page November 1988 report contained 108 recommendations outlining a vision for the Library's future. Senior managers considered the recommendations at a December retreat, at which Billington proposed an organization operated by management teams, which he intended as a more collegial, less hierarchical administrative structure. Staff members in each unit developed proposals, and a Transition Team including managers and the labor union presidents began planning the new organization. The reorganization became effective October 1, 1989.[9]

The Management Team, conceived as a policy and planning group, included the Librarian, the Deputy Librarian, and the directors of the CRS, Collections Services, Constituent Services, the Copyright Office, Cultural Affairs, Library Management Services, Special Projects, and the Law Library. Billington established the Development Office, the Office of Communications, the Inspector General's Office, and the Office of Scholarly Programs. The Librarian's Office included the Deputy Librarian, the Legislative Liaison Office (renamed Congressional Relations Office in 1993), and the General Counsel's Office.

The Copyright Office and CRS remained independent units. Library Management Services included Financial Services, Human Resources, Information Technology Services, and Integrated Support Services. The Security Office and the Equal Opportunity Complaints Office reported directly to the Associate Librarian for Management.

Cultural Affairs included units formerly in National Programs: the American Folklife Center, the Exhibits Office (renamed Interpretive Programs), the Information Office (renamed Public Affairs), and the Publishing Office. It also added the Office of Special Events and Public Programs, which had been part of the Educational Liaison Office. Also included were the new Development Office, the Center for the Book, the Council of Scholars, and the Poetry and Literature Center. The Office of Education Services was added in 1991 to conduct, for example, summer institutes and class visits.

Collections Services and Constituent Services included the largest numbers of staff members. To the former Processing Services and Research Services departments were added the Collections Development Office (renamed the Collections Policy Office in 1992), the National Library Service for the Blind and Physically Handicapped, the Children's Literature Center, the Federal Library and Information Center Committee, Visitor Services, and Library Distribution Services (including the Cataloging Distribution Service, the Federal Research Division, the Retail Marketing Unit, and the Photoduplication Service).

Special Project teams, intended to focus on Library-wide issues, addressed unprocessed arrearages; improving the affirmative action program; and planning for an off-site storage facility, a science and technology service, and internal communications. The communications team established a weekly publication for the staff, *The Gazette*, in April 1990, while the *Information Bulletin* continued as a biweekly (by July 1997, monthly) for the external audience. The National Reference Service, established in June

1991, centralized responses to external inquiries. The Science and Technology Information Service team proposed a one-year appointment of an associate librarian to formulate a program.[10]

An early reorganization project, "whole book cataloging," began as an experiment in May 1989. It combined the descriptive and subject cataloging operations, which had been separate since the 1940s. The goals were to reduce processing time and enhance job satisfaction, but the underlying impetus was the growing arrearage. The experiment showed that the whole book approach produced high-quality work at acceptable productivity and cost levels and reduced handling time for high-priority materials. The reorganization created four new divisions: Regional and Cooperative Cataloging, Arts and Sciences, Social Sciences and History, and Literature. Nonbook materials (except music scores) remained in the existing Special Materials Division. Some staff members questioned the plan to simultaneously reorganize and reduce the arrears, and some questioned whether the catalogers would adapt well to handling both descriptive and subject work. Petitions asking Billington to reconsider drew 164 signatures. Nevertheless, the whole book approach was adopted.[11]

Development Opportunities

Billington intimated at his confirmation hearing that he would seek private funding for activities not supported by appropriations. He received congressional approval to establish the Development Office in March 1988, and in response to his proposal to recognize exceptional achievements in "the life of the mind," the Joint Committee on April 15 reversed the 1948 decision prohibiting the Library from giving awards or prizes. Two years later, the family of Rebekah Johnson Bobbitt, President Johnson's sister, proposed the $10,000 Rebekah Johnson Bobbitt Poetry Prize, to be presented biannually to the best poetry book published by a living US citizen during the preceding two years. Publishers would submit nominations to the selection committee, which included the Librarian, the Poet Laureate, a publisher appointed by the Academy of American Poets, and a literary critic appointed by the Bobbitt family.[12] In 1998, the Witter Bynner Foundation began providing awards to two or more emerging poets each year, as designated by the Poet Laureate.

In January 1990, with the Joint Committee's approval, the Librarian established the James Madison Council as a private-sector advisory group. Council members contribute ideas, expertise, and financial support to strengthen the collections and programs. With a steadily increasing membership that reached beyond the original target of 100 by the end of 1996, the council provided major funding for Billington's initiatives, for example, the Junior Fellows Program for college students, the National Digital Library Program, and the Library's Bicentennial celebration.[13]

Also, at the Librarian's request, Congress passed legislation enlarging the Trust Fund Board in February 1992 (PL 102-246), authorizing the Speaker of the House and the Senate majority leader each to appoint four public members of the board, with two named by the President. Ex officio members remained the same: the Librarian, the Treasury Secretary, and the Joint Committee chairman.[14] In March, the 1930s organization, Friends of the Law Library, was revived, and the Philip Lee Phillips Society was organized in 1995 as a friends group supporting the Geography and Map Division.

Appropriations and Strategic Planning

Billington requested the largest appropriation increase since World War II for 1991: a 22 percent jump, from $267 million to $326 million. Since 1984 there had been only small increases, he stated, while the Library had absorbed inflationary costs, budget sequestrations, and most mandated pay increases. The results were the loss of 475 positions and an arrearage of 38 million items. In response to the Appropriations subcommittee's request, the Library had submitted a report on the arrearage that outlined an approach to the problem; and with existing space filled close to capacity, Billington requested a storage facility. He also emphasized, "The constancy of congressional support has been the most important selling point in our recently successful efforts to increase private funding."[15] The conference report prioritized reducing the arrears, approving 163 new positions for that purpose.[16]

Meeting with the ALA Council during the June 1990 conference, the Librarian emphasized the need for grassroots support for the LC's services to libraries and his desire to cooperate with the library community. The council endorsed his appropriation request. But a proposal to charge fees for some LC services, an idea that Billington and Associate Librarian Donald Curran discussed with several groups during the conference, drew criticism. Curran stated that certain services had always carried charges, such as for photoduplication; but the new fees would be for new or enhanced services requested by, for example, businesses, such as expedited document delivery. But librarians remained wary; and publishers and the information industry, as always, generally opposed fee-based services as competition with the private sector.[17]

The 1991 appropriations deliberations stretched into the new fiscal year. But after an October 25 Senate floor debate, the Library was exempted from a 5 percent cut for legislative branch agencies: Senator Timothy Wirth (D-CO) noted that the LC appropriation had increased over six years at only half the rate of inflation while costs had risen "astronomically"; and he called the LC "absolutely crucial to the budget of every library in every city, in every state in this nation." His amendment drew bipartisan support: Congress authorized just over $299 million, a 12 percent increase, and included in the Architect of the Capitol's budget funds to acquire property for an LC child care facility. The 1992 appropriation provided a 5.6 percent increase in response to Billington's requests for systems modernization and new technology.[18]

In late 1992 the Management Team approved the first Library of Congress Strategic Plan, for 1993–2000. It was the first comprehensive plan because, Billington speculated, "the assumption seems to have been that the core resources of the Library—its great collections and staff—were never seriously at risk whatever the vagaries of the annual budget process." Defining the Library's mission as "to celebrate and to preserve for future generations a universal collection of knowledge and creativity," the first phase (1993–96) focused on optimizing congressional service, increasing electronic access, reducing arrearages, securing and preserving the collections, improving financial management, assuring hiring and workforce equity, and acquiring storage space. Phase two (1997–2000) added implementation of the "Electronic Library" through dissemination of collections and services online.[19]

But the Library's 1993 appropriation request was reduced by nearly $12.5 million as Congress grappled with the federal budget deficit.[20] A hiring freeze, first imposed in May 1992, continued; evening and weekend hours were curtailed; the position of Associate Librarian for Management was eliminated in the fall of 1992; and the Special Projects and Science and Technology Information units were abolished in May 1993.[21]

The Second White House Conference

President Reagan called the second White House Conference on Library and Information Services (WHCLIS II) in 1988, but it did not take place until July 1991, preceded by preconference meetings in states and territories and one sponsored by the Federal Library and Information Center Committee for its members. The Network Advisory Committee's preconference, "Networks for Networkers II," also produced recommendations for the Conference. The WHCLIS II report, sent to President George H. W. Bush in November, included ninety-five recommendations in priority order. The Library was the subject of several: increase support for the National Library Service for the Blind and Physically Handicapped and expand assistance for print-handicapped persons; amend the copyright statute "to accommodate the impact of new and emerging technologies"; designate the Law Library as the National Law Library, "charged with assuming a leadership in coordinating access to the literature of the law for the benefit of all library users"; and provide "adequate funding" for organizations with "national information missions," including the LC. As with WHCLIS I, the main result was to publicize the views of the library community and its supporters.[22]

Russian Initiatives

Billington's first years in office coincided with President Mikhail Gorbachev's efforts to restructure the USSR's political and economic systems, an attempted coup by his opponents, his resignation in December 1991, and the breakup of the Soviet Union. It was also a period of rapprochement due to the warming relationship between presidents Reagan and Gorbachev, which continued in the George H. W. Bush administration.[23] Billington placed the Library in the midst of these events. After his nomination, he joined an American Council of Learned Societies–sponsored delegation that negotiated the Agreement of Cooperation in Library Affairs and established the US–USSR Commission on Library Cooperation for 1987–1991.[24] In May 1988 he convened "The Millennium of the Baptism of Rus': The Impact of Christianity on the Culture of the Eastern Slavs," a conference on aspects of Russian, Ukrainian, and Byelorussian (after 1991, Belarusian) cultures that included Soviet scholars previously unable to participate in Western meetings.[25] The LC–Library of the Academy of Sciences of the USSR agreement was signed on June 17, 1988, after a February fire destroyed part of that library's collections. Billington secured Getty Conservation Institute funding for the LC to coordinate international assistance to restore the collections, and the parties agreed to cooperate on activities—for example, the Billington-led delegation to the October 1991 conference: "The National Library in the Life of the Nation: The Library of Congress and the Lenin State Library." An LC acquisitions office opened in Moscow in February 1990, and in May, as Bush and Gorbachev met to discuss a trade agreement that included intellectual property guarantees, the president's wife, Raisa Gorbachev, opened an LC exhibition of Russian manuscripts, mostly loaned by the Academy of Sciences Institute of Russian Literature. The Gorbachevs visited the LC again in May 1992 for a seminar on developments in the former USSR, and in June, the Library opened the "Revelations from the Russian Archives" exhibition, which spanned the 1917 October Revolution to the attempted coup of August 19–21, 1991. It presented (and for the first time, selectively, online) previously secret documents that, Billington said, "might offer serious historians some insights as to how the communist regime remained in power so long and may tell why it fell apart so fast." He had been in Moscow during the attempted coup, calling it "the most exhilarating experience of my life"; and the subsequent LC exhibition, "The Press for Freedom," documented the breakup of the Soviet Union.[26] Another Russian chief executive visited in September 1994, when presidents Boris Yeltsin and Bill Clinton opened "In the Beginning Was the Word: The Russian Church and Native Alaskan Culture," welcomed by Billington in English and Russian. A 1997 "Meta-Exchange Pilot Project" began sending US books to Russian libraries.[27]

Between 1990 and 1996, the Special Task Force on Development of Parliamentary Institutions in Eastern Europe, appointed by Speaker Thomas S. Foley (D-WA) and chaired by Representative Martin Frost (D-TX), led an effort to inform the new governments about the structures of democratic institutions and societies. The CRS was asked to administer the program, with funding from foundations and the Agency for International Development.[28] The CRS also joined the Congressional Commission on Security and Cooperation in Europe to sponsor a conference on parliamentary responsibilities in economic development and provided briefings for Eastern European visitors on such topics as building parliamentary libraries and strengthening constituent relations. In 1999 Congress asked the Library to administer the Russian Leadership Program (PL 106-31; PL 106-113), which brought the Russian Federation's political and civic leaders to visit American cities, enabling them to increase their knowledge of urban political and economic systems.[29]

Paper, Films, and Recordings

The Preservation staff continued to search for a facility that could meet the Library's specifications for a deacidification program. A board headed by a representative from the Congressional Office of Technology Assessment reviewed data from testing laboratories and visited each site but reported that none satisfied the requirement to increase the useful life of paper by at least three times without harming books, readers, or equipment operators. The staff consequently explored alternatives to the DEZ process and, with congressional approval, contracted with Pennsylvania-based Preservation Technologies to test its Bookkeeper process, which exposed paper to acid-neutralizing magnesium oxide particles, leaving a protective alkaline reserve. With some fine-tuning of the process, Bookkeeper met the LC's specifications, resulting in the first of several contracts in 1995. With congressional approval, in 2000 mass deacidification became a permanent part of the Preservation Office's work.[30]

In 1988 Congress approved the Film Preservation Act (PL 100-446), which established the National Film Preservation Board and the National Film Registry.[31] Under its provisions, the Librarian convenes the board annually, representing the motion picture guilds, critics, and the archival and scholarly communities, to help select twenty-five films of cultural, historical, or aesthetic value for preservation. A 1992 reauthorization (PL 102-307) directed the Librarian to report to Congress on the status of preservation activities in major US film archives and establish a comprehensive program in cooperation with film archivists and copyright owners. The first report, *Film Preservation 1993: A Study of the Current State of American Film Preservation*, revealed that fewer than 10 percent of feature films of the 1910s and fewer than 20 percent of those of the 1920s survived in complete form, that safety film could decay, and that color film tended to fade. Billington then appointed a committee to plan a national preservation program. Building on the 1993 study, its report recommended establishing a federally chartered foundation affiliated with the board to raise funds for preserving films and increasing access to them.[32]

The National Film Preservation Act of 1996 (PL 104-285) reauthorized the board and created the National Film Preservation Foundation to provide grants to nonprofit institutions to preserve documentaries, public domain films, silent films, and other noncommercial works that otherwise might not survive. The Librarian was authorized to select the board of directors and to serve as an ex officio member. Operating expenses were initially covered by donations, but beginning in 1999 the foundation became eligible to receive appropriations to match private funding.[33]

The National Recording Preservation Act, modeled on the film preservation legislation (PL 106-474, 2000), charged the Librarian to develop the program in cooperation with sound recording archivists, educators and historians, copyright owners, recording industry representatives, and other interested parties. The act established the National Recording Registry (2003), the National Recording Preservation Board (2002), and the separate National Recording Preservation Foundation to raise gifts to be matched by federal funds. The board's 2005 study found that most recordings created between 1890 and 1964 were inaccessible, mainly because technological changes made playback equipment obsolete and copyright holders had not reissued their recordings for public sale.[34]

The act also mandated a study of preservation practices, resulting in *The State of Recorded Sound Preservation in the United States: A National Legacy at Risk in the Digital* Age (2010). In addition to public hearings, interviews, and written submissions, the board commissioned studies on copyright and other issues that affected preservation and access to commercial and unpublished recordings, including an assessment of the survival rates of recordings dating back to the nineteenth century: *The Library of Congress National Recording Preservation Plan* (2012).[35] It presented thirty-two recommendations from task forces on copyright and public access; digital audio preservation and technical standards; collection management; public–private partnerships; promoting public awareness and fundraising; and education, training, and research. The board then formed the Radio Preservation Task Force to ascertain the status of efforts to collect and preserve broadcasts. In cooperation with Sony Music Entertainment, the Library opened the National Jukebox website in May 2011, enabling users to play historic recordings, many of which had not been available for years.[36]

Copyright Issues

On March 1, 1989, the United States joined the oldest, most extensive multilateral copyright treaty, the 1886 Berne Convention for the Protection of Literary and Artistic Works.[37] As the value of US exports of copyrighted materials increased (especially motion pictures, recorded music, and computer software), Berne membership became more important but required statutory changes. The 1976 Copyright Act specified that protection began with the creation of a work in any physical medium rather than at publication and conformed to Berne's fifty-year term of protection, but it retained the manufacturing clause and required a copyright notice in each work, both incompatible with Berne. However, in 1984, the United States left UNESCO, which meant abandoning the UNESCO-administered Universal Copyright Convention, and Congress allowed the manufacturing clause to expire in 1986. In making the changes to copyright law, Congress retained the provision for the deposit of American works, ensuring the continued growth of the Library of Congress collections.[38]

Several years later, two congressional initiatives threatened the Library's authority over the Copyright Office. Representative William J. Hughes (D-NJ) and Senator Dennis DeConcini (D-AZ) introduced their Copyright Reform Act on February 16, 1993, proposing to make the Register of Copyrights a presidential appointment, remove the Library's authority over the Copyright Office, and decrease or eliminate incentives to register for a copyright. As a cosponsor, Senator Orrin Hatch (R-UT), stated baldly, the bill might be viewed as addressing "the more fundamental policy question of the extent to which it is proper for the Copyright Act to be employed in the service of building and protecting the collections of the Library of Congress." Billington and Register of Copyrights Ralph Oman opposed the bill. It would, Billington stated, inhibit collecting unpublished works such as television programs, architectural drawings, and photographs. The impact on acquiring published materials was harder to gauge but was likely to increase costs: for every 10,000 unregistered items, the Library would spend an estimated $1.1 million to obtain those works. Several weeks later, the Librarian announced that Hughes and DeConcini had asked the LC to examine the registration system. He named former Register Barbara Ringer and Robert Wedgeworth (University of Illinois, and president of the International Federation of Library Associations) to cochair the Advisory Committee on Copyright Registration and Deposit.[39]

The committee recommended retaining mandatory deposit and simplifying the registration process, and Billington stated that he would support the legislation if it included both, if inducements to deposit and register were retained, and if it provided for monitoring the impact and correcting any problems. At the Senate hearing, spokespersons for authors expressed differing views, while librarians and university press representatives supported the LC. Congress took no further action.[40]

However, two years later Senator Hatch introduced the Omnibus Patent Act on July 16, 1996, which proposed making the Copyright Office a self-supporting part of a new Intellectual Property Organization within the Department of Commerce. The organization would also include the Patent and Trademark Office. Billington and Register Marybeth Peters opposed introducing an untested system that, to become self-supporting, would require a substantial fee increase. While the bill retained the deposit requirement, they predicted fewer registrations and, therefore, significant losses of acquisitions. At the hearing, several committee members expressed misgivings since the bill appeared to disproportionately favor the Patent and Trademark Office; Senator Fred Thompson (R-TN) called it "a solution in search of a problem," and Senator Allen Simpson (R-WY) stated that "a problem does not exist." Again, there was no further action.[41]

After refusing to change the status of the Copyright Office, congressional efforts took a more favorable turn. In what the *Annual Report* called "the most significant improvement in the national reading program since the passage of the Pratt-Smoot Act," Congress approved Senator John H. Chafee's (R-RI) appropriations bill amendment to allow nonprofit agencies to reproduce nondramatic literary works in Braille or recorded or digital formats (PL 104-197, 1996). This meant that the NLS could reproduce such materials without seeking permission from copyright holders. The proposal drew bipartisan support and approval from the Copyright Office, the Association of American Publishers, and organizations representing people with physical disabilities. Publishers, Chafee reported, agreed that his amendment would address "the unintended censorship of blind individuals' access to current information" and that it would not compromise their rights and interests.[42]

New developments in copyright legislation continued. In 1998, despite protests that the bill was too favorable to private industry (in particular, it would protect early Walt Disney films, including the 1928 debut Mickey Mouse film *Steamboat Willie*), President Clinton signed the Copyright Term Extension Act (PL 105-298). Conforming to European Union policy, the law increased the copyright term to life of the author plus seventy years and also extended to anonymous and pseudonymous works, works made for hire, and works in their renewal terms. The statute included the Fairness in Music Licensing Act, which broadened exemptions from royalty payments for small restaurants and bars.[43]

The Digital Millennium Copyright Act (PL 105-304), signed at the same time, adhered to treaties passed by the World Intellectual Property Organization in 1996. As with the Term Extension Act, it pitted those seeking to protect digital property against those who wanted to preserve access to copyrighted materials: the law prohibited circumventing technology that barred access to copyrighted works but gave the Librarian of Congress the power to make exemptions. It also affirmed the Copyright Office's historic role as expert adviser to Congress and the administration and charged it with filing liability notices for infringing copyright of digital works and digital performance rights of sound recordings, reporting to Congress on digital distance education, and (with the Commerce Department's National Telecommunications and Information Administration) reporting on the effects of existing legislation on encryption research.[44]

Early Initiatives and American Memory

Some of Billington's initiatives were short-lived. In 1989, the Library took over the John Crerar Library's National Translations Center, a clearinghouse for English translations of foreign scientific and technical publications, but discontinued it in 1993.[45] With funding from Madison Council member Glenn Jones (Jones International), in 1990 the LC began producing programs based on its collections for cablecast through Mind Extension University, a Jones subsidiary that partnered with colleges and universities to offer credit and noncredit courses. Funding for the project ended in 1997.[46] The National Demonstration Laboratory for Interactive Information Technologies (NDL) moved from the Smithsonian Institution to the Madison Building in 1991. With two-year support from information industry companies, the NDL demonstrated new technologies, for example, virtual reality and voice-activated systems. It moved to the Academy for Educational Development in September 1994.[47]

In response to congressional concerns that the United States lacked current information on Japanese science, technology, and business, in 1992 the Library established the Japan Documentation Center in the Asian Division, and its Tokyo acquisitions office opened in 1994. Funded in part by a grant from the Japan Foundation's Center for Global Partnership, the Documentation Center acquired materials from think tanks and research centers and sponsored conferences and workshops. When funding ceased, it closed March 31, 2000, retaining the materials in the Asian Division.[48]

The most successful new outreach program was American Memory, conceived as a means of addressing both the arrearage (much of which was in nonprint formats) and the Librarian's ambition to increase access.[49] Beginning in 1990, a five-year project recorded portions of the Americana collections on CD-ROMs, with user guides for students and teachers. Over 210,000 items were digitized, and a survey of the forty-four test sites found that middle school and high school students and teachers were enthusiastic users. Billington later wrote that the project showed that "primary documents of knowledge and creativity humanize the study of history and culture" and established a new educational role for the Library.[50] His determination to broaden access through technology brought rejoinders: some critics, both within and outside the LC, considered projects such as American Memory more suited to educational institutions or museums. Others argued that they absorbed resources needed to support the Library's core services.[51] Nevertheless, American Memory commenced a long effort to build digital collections.

The Cook Case and Personnel Changes

A decade after the 1982 initial filing, in August 1992, the US District Court of the District of Columbia's partial summary judgment in the *Howard R. L. Cook et al. v. James H. Billington* class action lawsuit determined that the Library's competitive selection process was subjective, allowing for discrimination. The Court instructed the attorneys to produce a settlement. Approved in 1995, their agreement awarded $8.5 million in back pay to the over 2,000 class members, plus payment of legal expenses. Plaintiffs' lawyers were charged to continue consultation and monitor personnel practices, and the Court retained jurisdiction for a four-year period. It was the largest settlement ever of a lawsuit against a federal agency. With negotiations completed in early 2001, the Court's oversight ended on December 1, 2002. An appeal was denied in 2003.[52]

After the summary judgment, in October 1992 Billington established the Office of the Associate Librarian for Human Resources and ordered its staff to develop a more aggressive affirmative action plan. He hired consulting firms to examine personnel policies, with reports due by January 1993. He assembled the Diversity Advisory Council, including representatives from management, employee organizations, and the unions; expanded the Affirmative Action Intern Program; and in 1994 established the Madison Council–funded Leadership Development Program.

Congress held hearings on the Library's personnel issues in 1990 and 1993. One of the consultants Billington hired, James W. Morrison Jr. (Morrison Associates), stated at the March 1993 hearing conducted by Representative William L. Clay (D-MO) that the Management Team had not made a systematic effort to address underrepresentation. He recommended hiring a Deputy Librarian to strengthen the management of daily operations. He and his colleague, Edmund D. Cooke Jr. (Epstein, Becker & Green) also recommended strengthening human resources services, establishing a new staff selection policy, and developing strong Equal Employment Opportunity and affirmative action programs. The plaintiffs requested full commitment to the consultants' recommendations, an implemented affirmative action plan, establishment of training and professional development programs, and continued congressional oversight.[53] A year later, citing the Library's "slow progress," the subcommittee made eight recommendations for achieving diversity and improving training, employee counseling, affirmative action, and Equal Employment Opportunity programs. Its report directed the LC to submit an implementation plan within ninety days.[54]

In response to the recommendations to establish the positions of Deputy Librarian and Senior Adviser for Diversity, in mid-1994 Billington hired Jo Ann Jenkins, a federal official experienced in minority affairs, as diversity adviser, and Hiram Logan Davis, Michigan State University's director of libraries, as Deputy Librarian of Congress. An experienced administrator, Davis held a doctorate in library science and was a member of the ALA's Black Caucus. When he stepped down to establish the Library's Internal University, he was succeeded in 1996 by Donald L. Scott, a retired Army brigadier general and founding director of AmeriCorps' National Civilian Community Corps.[55] The Internal University represented both an effort to enhance staff skills and to replace staff: in appropriations hearings, Billington repeatedly referred to the large number, as high as 40 percent or more in some units, of retirement-eligible employees and, as the Library increasingly digitized materials, the urgent need for technological expertise.[56]

Outreach and the World Wide Web

While focusing on digitization, Billington also pursued more traditional outreach. *Civilization: The Magazine of the Library of Congress* began publication in December 1994, in collaboration with commercial firms. Its origins dated to a plan of Daniel Boorstin's for a publication for a general audience; in anticipation of such a publication, the *Quarterly Journal of the Library of Congress* had ceased publication in 1983. The Joint Committee approved *Civilization*'s licensing agreement, under which the Library received a $250,000 fee and $1 for each subscription sold. The board of directors and the editorial board included LC representatives, and the Library had veto power over contents, promotion, advertising, and proposed investors. However, the magazine proved financially unsustainable and ceased publication in September 2000.[57]

A documentary film, *Memory and Imagination* (1990), focused on the implications of new technologies for the Library's collections, with celebrity guest appearances, and Billington obtained private funding to launch major exhibitions: *1992: An Ongoing Voyage* celebrated the Columbus Quincentenary; *Rome Reborn: The Vatican Library and Renaissance Culture* began a series of exhibitions on great libraries; the *African American Mosaic* presented resources for the study of Black life and culture; and *Scrolls from the Dead Sea* brought to the LC materials seldom seen.[58] In cooperation with the National Institute of Mental Health, the Library celebrated the institute's *Decade of the Brain* with a conference series and presentations for members of Congress and their staffs.[59] The 250th anniversary of Thomas Jefferson's birth brought an April 13, 1993, announcement of the Library's so-called 100-millionth acquisition, a collection of 745 watercolor paintings and pencil drawings by John Rubens Smith, an early-nineteenth-century American artist—the gift of the Madison Council and the owner, Mrs. Joseph Carson.[60]

The most important advance in broadening access came in 1993 when the Joint Committee on the Library approved an LC website on the internet. In April, the Library of Congress Information System became available, followed by the home page, www.loc.gov. At the June 1994 ALA conference, the LC exhibit featured the site, with material from the Dead Sea Scrolls, Vatican Library, Columbian Quincentenary, African American Mosaic, and Russian archives exhibitions; the Library of Congress Information System; the LC News Service; and LC MARVEL, a bulletin board service. Exhibit-goers also could view American Memory and the CD-based Cataloger's Desktop.[61] The ALA approved resolutions supporting the Library's budget request for 1994, and the Association for Library Collections and Technical Services added a congratulatory letter recognizing the efforts to address the arrears, establish a Cooperative Cataloging Council, and introduce whole book cataloging.[62]

The Cooperative Cataloging Council began in April 1993 when, with the Council on Library Resources' support, the Library assembled an advisory group—including OCLC, Columbia University, the University of Texas, RLG, the Stockton–San Joaquin County Public Library, and Harvard University. The group developed the Program for Cooperative Cataloging, which in 1997 consolidated the Library's cataloging programs. Its Policy and Steering Committee included the LC, the British Library, the National Library of Canada, OCLC, and RLG, with the LC as secretariat.[63] *Library Journal* editor

Francine Fialkoff attributed the "new attitude of cooperation" to new management in cataloging and less LC-centered policies.[64] Meanwhile, the Bibliographic Enrichment Advisory Team, which was formed in 1992, began to enhance catalog records by adding tables of contents, publishers' descriptions, and links to electronic resources.[65]

New services appeared everywhere in the Library, including internet-connected public access terminals in six reading rooms. In January 1995 a new website named THOMAS (for Jefferson) responded to a congressional mandate to make federal legislative information publicly available; and 1996 appropriations legislation (PL 104-53, 1995) directed the LC to develop the Legislative Information System for the members and their staffs.[66] The Copyright Office's Electronic Registration, Recordation, and Deposit System (known as CORDS)—which was initiated in 1993 in cooperation with the Corporation for National Research Initiatives and was funded jointly with the Defense Advanced Research Projects Agency—worked toward making registration and eventually actual copyright deposit available via the internet.[67] Electronic Cataloging in Publication, begun as an experiment in 1993, allowed publishers to submit applications and galley proofs online, and by 2013 it had expanded to include e-books.[68] With Madison Council funding and assistance from technology firms, the Geography and Map Division developed the Geographic Information System,[69] and the Law Library's Global Legal Information Network (GLIN) debuted online in 1996. Member nations and international organizations contributed statutes to GLIN, and partnerships with the World Bank, the Inter-American Development Bank, the Center for Economic Analysis of Law, and the National Aeronautics and Space Administration enabled it to hold annual meetings, contribute to members' start-up costs, and add materials such as judicial decisions, legislative records, and regulations.[70]

The National Digital Library

Plans for expansion were briefly threatened when the Joint Committee on the Reorganization of Congress proposed the Legislative Reorganization Act of 1994. Appearing before the Senate Committee on Rules and Administration, Billington and CRS director Daniel Mulhollan opposed the provisions for downsizing since the LC had reduced its staff by 12 percent since 1980; for reauthorizing the Library every eight years; and for eliminating the Joint Committee on the Library.[71] Citing the LC's historically strong relations with Congress, Billington stated, "I respectfully suggest that there is already sufficient oversight of the Library by the Congress." Staff cuts, he said, would result in the loss of 211 more positions, a backlog of congressional requests, reduced service hours, copyright registration delays, and growing arrearage. Much of the Library's electronic service "is—and will be—financed privately," he said. "But the Library will not be able to sustain, let alone expand, its services if we continue to be subjected to forced reductions in staff and services." Senators Pell, Daniel Patrick Moynihan (D-NY), and Robert Packwood (R-OR) also opposed the elimination of the Joint Committee, and Billington's pleas succeeded: Congress increased the appropriation by 5.4 percent (still short of the requested 7.9 percent), retained the Joint Committee, and removed the reauthorization provision.[72]

American Memory provided the foundation for the National Digital Library program launched in late 1994. With Madison Council funding, in July 1993 the Library had convened the "Delivering Electronic Information in a Knowledge-Based Democracy" conference, cochaired by Vice President Al Gore and Billington and including Senator J. Robert Kerrey (D-NE), Representative Ed Markey (D-MA), and Representative Newt Gingrich (R-GA). The group discussed possibilities for making electronic information more widely available, and Markey predicted that Congress would help: "The good news is that almost every member of Congress supported the information superhighway. The bad news is that no one has the vaguest idea of what it is. And in between that gap, there's tremendous opportunity for us to construct something here for the country."[73]

For the NDL, Congress approved $15 million, to be supplemented with $45 million in private donations. Appropriated funds would support the technology infrastructure and predigitization processing and preservation costs. Private gifts would fund digital conversion by contractors. As with American Memory, the NDL aimed both at addressing the arrears and extending access to the collections—but through the internet rather than less efficient, more expensive distribution on disk.

At the October 13, 1994, opening of the Digital Library Visitors' Center in the Madison Building, Billington announced gifts totaling $13 million: from Madison Council chairman John W. Kluge, the David and Lucile Packard Foundation, and the W. K. Kellogg Foundation. He stated that the Library would provide access to its digitized collections to the public and the private sector alike and that the materials could be enhanced for sale as commercial or educational products. The NDL focused on the two-thirds of the Library's collections in nonbook formats and on Americana. Supplemented by the Learning Page (1996) for K-12 teachers, the 1997–2001 American Memory Fellows program for teachers and media specialists, annual Educators Institutes beginning in 2004, and the Teaching with Primary Sources program beginning in 2006, the NDL drew bipartisan support.[74] Often speaking of making the LC's digital resources freely available as "getting the champagne out of the bottle," the Librarian declared that, unlike television, "this new interactive, multimedia world does, after all, engage the active mind in intellectual calisthenics and in creative interplay with useful information." He predicted that the NDL would contain 5 million items by 2000. As it happened, production topped his estimate.[75]

The National Library Service for the Blind and Physically Handicapped began developing digital talking books in the mid-1990s, forming the Digital Talking-Book Standards Committee, which included librarians and organizations representing those with physical disabilities. The American National Standards Institute subsequently approved a new standard intended to ensure uniformity both nationally and internationally, covering output through synthetic speech, Braille display or large print display, and specifications for indexing and retrieving information. An NLS–Industrial Designers Society of America–sponsored competition subsequently challenged students at society-accredited schools to design versatile playback machines—with tactile features for the blind, sound amplification for the hearing impaired, and special controls for those with limited dexterity.[76]

The NLS launched Web-Braille in August 1999, a password-protected website providing free access for US residents and Americans abroad to digitized Braille books and magazines, and extended the content to music materials two years later. A link to the NLS *International Union Catalog* made it possible for individuals, schools, and libraries possessing Braille output devices to search for an item in the catalog and download or read it online. A decade later, the service adopted a digital talking book machine, and in 2013 the Braille and Audio Reading Download (known as BARD) service began enabling users to hear as well as read materials on mobile devices.[77]

Herb Becker, director of the LC's Information Technology Services, explained what seemed, in the mid-1990s, a series of rapid advances: personal computers became much more cost-effective and powerful, scanning technology was also cheaper and better, storage technology improved, the internet promoted widespread access, the development of telecommunication protocols facilitated computer-to-computer communications, increasing standardization made it easier to share information electronically, and the emergence of standard image formats and compression technologies facilitated putting images online. Summing up the technological evolution, Becker emphasized the difference between computerizing bibliographic data in the late 1960s and digitizing content in the 1990s, calling it "a big change in the concept of a Library in the 21st century."[78]

Fort Meade and Collections Security

The efforts to process the arrearage also were linked to the development of a state-of-the-art, high-density storage facility at the Army's Fort George G. Meade in Maryland. After Congress authorized the transfer of 100 acres from the Defense Department (PL 103-110, 1993), the Architect of the Capitol designed thirteen climate-controlled modules to be built over a fifty-year period. When construction began in 1999, about 17 million items were shelved on Capitol Hill and others were stored elsewhere, including rented space in Landover and Suitland, Maryland, and at the Wright-Patterson Air Force Base in Ohio. The first of the new storage modules, which opened in November 2002, housed an estimated 1.2 million books and bound serials, shelved by size in custom-designed, bar-coded containers, retrieved by forklifts. At the opening ceremony, Billington stated that a paper-based item with a life expectancy of perhaps 40 years would extend to 240 years at Fort Meade. Library users may request stored items, with daily deliveries to Capitol Hill.[79]

Fort Meade was also linked to anxieties about collection security. Librarians have always struggled to protect their collections, particularly in libraries where users can access materials themselves. Spofford's 1861 inventory of the Library's 70,000 volumes showed 1,300 missing or borrowed but not returned volumes, and the 1896 theft of volumes from his office was discovered only when a book dealer identified them. Librarians have generally sought to protect valuable materials by placing them in closed stacks or locked spaces accessible only through well-supervised reading rooms. The Library of Congress had its own guard force after moving into the Jefferson Building and opened the Rare Book Room, with separate, secure stacks, in 1934. The Madison Building included an electronic security system, and all three buildings had security controls, including closed-circuit television monitors. While the LC staff discovered losses over the years, such losses were generally not publicized. However, concerns increased after the FBI's 1987 arrest of Charles Merrill Mount, an art historian who stole letters of James McNeill Whistler, Winston Churchill, and Henry James from the LC and the National Archives. In response to the 1990–91 Persian Gulf War, entrance inspections were added to existing exit inspections, and staff identification badges were issued. As the staff continued to discover losses and volumes missing valuable illustrations, Billington appointed the Collections Security Oversight Committee in 1992.[80]

Security measures subsequently implemented required all users to have photo identification badges and to leave personal belongings in lockers or cloakrooms. Public access to the stacks, formerly allowed to some researchers, was abolished and entry points were electronically secured; theft detection and surveillance equipment, barriers, X-ray machines, and metal detectors were installed; and valuable materials were moved into vaults and locked cages.[81] Predictably, the restrictions drew criticism, both from LC staff members who could no longer freely enter the stacks and from scholars who cherished stack access. Others called them essential to protect the collections.[82]

August 1995 press reports of thefts and mutilation in the Jefferson Building prompted Billington to order staff to investigate a US attorney's office complaint that the problems were not reported and to contract with the Computer Sciences Corporation to review security policy. The Library's Inspector General informed Congress in November that since the stacks were closed in March 1992, there had been no evidence of thefts or mutilation. However, senators Mark Hatfield (R-OR) and Connie Mack (R-FL) requested a General Accounting Office (GAO) investigation.[83]

The GAO Reports

The GAO contracted with Booz Allen Hamilton for a management survey and with Price Waterhouse for an audit. Auditors concluded that the Library had made progress in addressing problems identified in the 1991 audit (the first in LC history) but recommended improving financial management, security, facilities management, and internal controls. The Booz Allen report surprisingly suggested that the LC disperse some collections among other institutions and become a "national information/knowledge broker" and "referral agency." It raised several possibilities: (1) that the LC abandon its ad hoc role as a national library and focus its mission on Congress and the federal government, (2) that the LC strengthen its national role and deemphasize its international reach, and (3) that the LC continue to serve constituencies worldwide, which would require increased resources. Or the LC could continue congressional service, and a separate national library could be established. Booz Allen considered separating the Copyright Office and the Congressional Research Service from the Library but concluded that both should remain. The report also recommended that the LC charge publishers for cataloging, fully recover copyright registration costs, and improve information technology management.[84]

At the Joint Committee's hearing on May 7, 1996, Billington emphatically opposed the main Booz Allen proposal: "The Library rejects in the strongest terms this challenge to its historic mission. It seems inconceivable that the world's largest and most varied record of human knowledge—in effect, America's strategic information reserve—should be pulled apart and scattered as America is entering the Information Age." The result would be "there would be literally nothing left of the present Library but a constantly changing information switchboard service and vestigial collections of miscellaneous materials." He emphasized that service to Congress and the federal government must not depend on other libraries, which were subject to their own governing boards and institutional agendas. And he corrected the report's mistaken understanding of "a universal collection" as "collecting everything": the intent historically had been "a collection that covers the most important works in all subject areas" and in many languages and physical formats, providing Congress with "a supply of material that is larger in size and more varied and inclusive than anywhere else in America."

When they learned that Hatfield's and Mack's request to the Comptroller General did not include examining the Library's mission, committee members questioned the recommendations. The GAO and Booz Allen representatives replied that they had raised the issue to stimulate debate. Summarizing committee opinion, Hatfield stated that "we do not want to scale back the Library of Congress" and added that Congress has "a continuing obligation to maintain the Library's mission in light of not only our national interests but in the interests of the world." He asked Billington to submit recommendations for improvements.[85]

Surrounding events highlighted the Library's role in the information revolution. Earlier in 1996, President Clinton had signed (on paper and electronically) the Telecommunications Act (PL 104-104) into law in a Main Reading Room ceremony, the first time such an event was held at the Library. Vice President Al Gore, Speaker Newt Gingrich, and other congressmen attended, as did Secretary of Commerce Ronald H. Brown, chair of the National Information Infrastructure Task Force. Two months later, Gingrich and Representative William M. Thomas (R-CA) attended an LC reception celebrating the Ameritech Corporation's gift of $2 million for three annual competitions among nonfederal libraries, museums, historical societies, and archives to digitize collections for the American Memory website. And after the May 7 hearing, more than 120 senators and representatives attended a privately funded Great Hall celebration of the restoration of the Jefferson and Adams buildings, which also honored retiring Joint Committee members Hatfield and Pell. Billed as a "Salute to Congress," the evening brought further comments on the Booz Allen report: Gingrich, for example, "emphatically disagreed" with the recommendation to shrink "the greatest knowledge asset this country has." And Representative Richard Gephardt (D-MO) remarked, "Let's face it. Any time that Speaker Gingrich and Senator [Trent] Lott (R-MS) and Senator [Tom] Daschle (D-SD) and I can come together to support the very same cause, you can be sure it is a really good cause. . . . The Library of Congress is simply one of the greatest cultural, historical, and educational resources in the entire world."[86]

Reorganization

Appropriations for 1996 included the requested $3 million for the National Digital Library and a $2.4 million increase in retention of receipts. However, the Library had to absorb pay and price level increases—an effective cut of $15.6 million.[87] In September 1995, Billington established the Executive Committee, stating that the team model "has often prevented decisions from being made in a timely way and sometimes rendered the mission and priorities of the institution subservient to the needs of individual service units." He consolidated Collections Services, Constituent Services, and Cultural Affairs in the Library Services unit, headed by an associate librarian. Other members of the Executive Committee were the Deputy Librarian, Chief of Staff, CRS Director, Law Librarian, and Register of Copyrights. The Management Team, renamed the Senior Management Reporting Group, became the Operations Committee in November 1999, and rather than replace retiring Deputy Librarian Scott, Billington named Jenkins Chief Operating Officer in 2007.[88]

The new organization placed all library functions—acquisitions, cataloging, public service, and preservation—together.[89] Offices collectively called the "enabling infrastructure" within the Librarian's Office included Planning, Management, and Evaluation; Financial Services; Human Resources; Internal University; Information Technology Services; Integrated Support Services; and Security.[90]

In connection with the reorganization, Billington issued "The Mission and Strategic Priorities of the Library of Congress" as part of the 1997–2004 Strategic Plan. Reminiscent of MacLeish's Canons and approved by Congress in May 1996, the document expressed the Library's mission as "to make its resources available and useful to the Congress and the American people and to sustain and preserve a universal collection of knowledge and creativity for future generations." The Librarian named as the first priority "to make knowledge and creativity available to the United States Congress," and as the second, "to preserve, secure, and sustain for the present and future use of the Congress and the nation," (1) the record of American history and creativity and (2) "a universal collection of human knowledge." The third priority was to make the collections maximally accessible to Congress, the federal government, and the public; and the fourth was "to add interpretive and educational value." He noted as essentials the "motivation and mobilization of human resources"; the "provision and delivery of electronic services"; allocations of space and equipment for preservation, accessibility, and efficiency; and the operation of "modern financial and information systems to facilitate decision-making and ensure accountability." If cuts became necessary, he stated, they would be made in priority order.[91]

The 1997–2004 plan also linked the priorities to specific tasks and funding needs, including establishing the Security Office, headed by the director of Security. Produced by the end of 1997, the Library's first comprehensive security plan placed the collections in five classes according to risk levels, with different controls for each class. Three other areas were targeted for improvement: human resources, technology, and congressional services. The 2004–8 plan continued the focus on security, integrating physical security with preservation and inventory management.[92]

The Jefferson Building reopened in 1997, its one hundredth anniversary, after twelve years of restoration. After the ribbon cutting on May 1, a celebratory dinner included Madison Council members, President Clinton, members of Congress, and the Supreme Court Justices. The President and others presented readings from the Library's historic documents and viewed the commemorative exhibition *American Treasures of the Library of Congress.* Another exhibition, *The Thomas Jefferson Building: Book Palace of the American People*, opened on the building's official anniversary in November. The African and Middle Eastern, Asian, and European divisions and reading rooms all had new quarters in the building, joining the Hispanic Division to create a symbolic center of world cultures. There were also the new Visitors' Center, an expanded sales shop, and an orientation film narrated by Madison Council member James Earl Jones. In honor of the Music Division's centennial, the Coolidge Auditorium began the concert season on October 30; and in March 1998, the one hundredth anniversary of George Gershwin's birth, the George and Ira Gershwin Room opened.[93] The Jefferson Building also featured the Swann Gallery of Caricature and Cartoons, and in 2011 it added the Herblock Gallery to exhibit cartoonist Herbert L. Block's work.[94]

The Integrated Library System

Congress approved another automation project, the Integrated Library System (ILS), in the 1998 appropriation. Planned to provide, for the first time, comprehensive inventory control, the ILS would unite the separate files of cataloging, serials, circulation, binding, and preservation records. On May 15, 1998, Endeavor Information Systems received the contract for its Voyager ILS. Implementing it before existing systems might balk at distinguishing 1900 from 2000 (the "year 2000 problem"), required installing software on about 3,000 staff and public workstations, loading roughly 12 million bibliographic records and 4 million authority records, and converting the huge shelflist and serials card files. Simultaneously, and in coordination with OCLC and RLG, the staff changed from the Wade-Giles Chinese romanization system to Pinyin romanization, aligning with the use of Pinyin in federal agencies. Implementation of the ILS for the Congressional Research Service and the National Library Service for the Blind and Physically Handicapped, the next set of tasks, followed acceptance of the system in August 2000, and the loan and collection management functions merged in 2002. Several years later, an upgrade included conversion to Unicode, the international standard for character sets.[95]

The ILS provided new capabilities, not only for collections control but also for locating materials. A search by author, title, or subject retrieved catalog records for materials in different physical formats and showed their current locations—for example, on the shelf, in use, being microfilmed or bound, or in storage. A search by classification number provided a virtual tour of the shelves. By 2009, users could submit most requests online, thus eliminating paper call slips.[96]

Bicentennial and Gifts to the Nation

Established in 1996 to plan the Library's two hundredth birthday celebration, the Bicentennial Steering Committee chose "Libraries-Creativity-Liberty" as the theme, encompassing the commitment to sharing recorded knowledge and all libraries' role in connecting knowledge and information to citizenship in a democracy. It also referenced

Jefferson's belief "that self-government depended on the free, unhampered pursuit of truth by an informed and involved citizenry."[97]

In 2000, the collections contained nearly 121 million items: 27.8 million books and printed materials, including 5,700 books printed before 1500; 54 million manuscripts; 13 million microforms; 4.6 million maps; 4.2 million music items; and 13.5 million photographs, posters, moving images, prints, and drawings. More than 10,000 items were added, and the LC website recorded 4 million transactions each day. The total arrearage was just over 19 million items, decreased by 51.6 percent since September 1989.

Honored by a proclamation from President Clinton, a congressional resolution (114 Stat 3138), and other tributes, the celebration took place on and around April 24, with programs, exhibitions, symposia, concerts, and publications designed, as Billington put it, to celebrate "the creative use of knowledge in libraries everywhere."[98] "Gifts to the Nation," a central theme, referenced the Library as Congress's gift to the nation, and the LC's gift of its resources to the public. Gifts included $1 million from Madison Council member Jerry Jones and his wife, Gene, to replace the volumes in Thomas Jefferson's library destroyed in the 1851 fire. There were also choreographer Martha Graham's archive and comedian Bob Hope's donation of his papers and broadcasts (including his 88,000-page Joke File), with funding from the Hope family and the Bob Hope Foundation to create the Bob Hope Gallery of American Entertainment in the Jefferson Building.[99] In cooperation with the Advertising Council, the America's Library website for children and families debuted, the staff constructed the "Bicentennial Time Capsule," and commemorative coins and a postage stamp were issued. The Library's first "Living Legend" awards honored seventy-eight artists, writers, filmmakers, entertainers, athletes, and other public figures who notably contributed to American life. The "Local Legacies" project invited members of Congress to submit local projects' documentation of cultural traditions or events, with those materials added to the collections. In response to a bipartisan congressional mandate, on Veterans Day, the Folklife Center inaugurated the Veterans Oral History Project (PL 106-380) to collect veterans' and civilian participants' accounts of their service, with the American Association of Retired Persons as a founding sponsor and an advisory council that included current and former members.[100] Poet Laureate Robert Pinsky organized nationwide readings of "My Favorite Poem," and the ALA and the Library cosponsored a photography contest: "Beyond Words: Celebrating America's Libraries."[101]

Joint Committee chair Senator Ted Stevens (R-AK) and Billington announced at an October 5 press conference Madison Council chairman Kluge's gift of $60 million to establish the John W. Kluge Center in the Library and the John W. Kluge Prize in the Human Sciences. Kluge spoke of how his council experience showed him that private-sector funding "can help propel an institution like the Library beyond its government-supported role to become a leader in education and scholarship," and hoped the center and the award would "build on these accomplishments and enhance the dialog between scholars and lawmakers to the benefit of our larger democratic society."[102]

At the Kluge Center's dedication in May 2003, Billington sounded a similar note: the gift would help to restore "that wonderful, creative interaction between the world of thought and the world of action, between knowledge and the power of the mind, which is embedded in the very nature of the Library of Congress itself." In addition to the Kluge Prize, the gift endowed chairs in American Law and Governance, Societies and Cultures of the North, Societies and Cultures of the South, Technology and Society, and Modern Culture. In the center's Jefferson Building quarters, these senior scholars are joined by junior fellows chosen through grant competitions and by scholars funded through other organizations. Among the first arrivals was Distinguished Visiting Scholar Robert Remini (University of Illinois, Chicago), whose *The House: The History of the House of Representatives*, requested by Congress and commissioned by the Librarian (PL 106-99, 1999), appeared in 2006. The Scholars Council advises the Librarian on matters relating to the center and on scholarship at the Library.[103]

Just after the Bicentennial, the Library concluded its largest single purchase ever: $10 million for the only known copy of Martin Waldseemüller's 1507 map, owned by Prince Johannes Waldburg-Wolfegg of Baden Württemberg, Germany. The map was the first to clearly depict places unknown to Europeans: the Western Hemisphere and the Pacific as a separate ocean. Titled "A Drawing of the Whole Earth Following the Tradition of Ptolemy and the Travels of Amerigo Vespucci and Others," the map also was the first to name "America," honoring Vespucci's recognition of a new world. A researcher had discovered the map in the Waldburg family's collection in 1901, but it was not until 1992 that the Prince indicated willingness to negotiate the sale. A limited export license from the German government and the Baden-Württemberg state government was procured in 1999, and the purchase concluded in 2003, with a $5 million appropriation and contributions from Discovery Communications, the Madison Council, and other donors. German chancellor Angela Merkel, who officially transferred the map at an April 30, 2007, Great Hall ceremony, acknowledged some opposition in Germany but called it the right decision because "the map is important for the cultural identity of America."[104]

Another important gift came from the Jay I. Kislak Foundation of Miami Lakes, Florida: a 4,000-item collection of rare books, manuscripts, documents, maps, and art of the Americas. While the Kislak Collection centered on the discovery, contact, and colonial periods—especially in Florida, the Caribbean, and Mesoamerica—the materials extended from 1200 BC through the early decades of US history. It included another Waldseemüller map, the Carta Marina (1516), which represented North America but did not name either the Pacific Ocean or America. The foundation also established the Kislak American Studies Program to support scholarship on the culture and history of the Americas.[105]

The National Book Festival, 9/11, and Iraq

Taking reading promotion to a new level, on September 8, 2001, about 30,000 book lovers attended the first National Book Festival, held on the Capitol's East Plaza and at the Library. Sponsored by the LC, suggested and hosted by First Lady (and former librarian) Laura Bush, and supported by the Madison Council and other contributors, the festival featured author readings, book signings, music, storytelling, and storybook characters. The National Basketball Association and the Women's National Basketball

Association sent players to tout their "Read to Achieve" initiative; the Center for the Book and its reading promotion partners and state centers contributed exhibits; and the LC staff presented information on preservation, copyright, and other services. White tents billowed in the breeze, authors mingled, concession stands offered refreshments, and groups presented music from a diversity of traditions.[106] Three days later, the 9/11 terrorist attacks brought an end to the festival's lighthearted mood: one commentator called it "that one last safe and friendly day." Nevertheless, the book festival survived as an annual event, and it thrives as a place to meet favorite authors, illustrators, and other celebrities—in person or via broadcast, podcast, or website. As attendance grew, the festival migrated, first to the National Mall in 2002 and then to the Walter E. Washington Convention Center in 2014.[107]

The attacks brought a flood of requests for information on subjects associated with 9/11 and homeland security. Billington requested five new CRS positions, including specialists in Islamic and Arabic affairs, public health and epidemiology, infrastructure and systems analysis, biochemistry, and comparative religion. The staff discovered in the collections a copy of Osama bin Laden's 1991 book on the anti-Soviet campaign in Afghanistan, an English translation of the laws of Afghanistan, and a Federal Research Division report on terrorism that predicted that al-Qaeda could crash airplanes into the Pentagon, the CIA, and the White House. The Library launched its September 11 web archive, and a year later, an exhibition: *Witness and Response: September 11 Acquisitions at the Library of Congress*. Poet Laureate Billy Collins recited his commemorative poem, *The Names*, at a September 2002 ceremonial session of Congress held in New York City.[108]

In the wake of 9/11 and amid continuing apprehension, the United States, with its coalition partners, invaded Iraq on March 20, 2003. Billington joined US postinvasion planning efforts, announcing that the LC would provide assistance for the damaged National Library of Iraq and the House of Manuscripts. He sent two Arabic speakers and a conservation specialist to accompany a State Department mission to Baghdad, and between October 25 and November 3, the team assessed the damage. Observing that the destruction of the Saddam Hussein regime's documents appeared deliberate, they found most collections in disarray but intact: after April fires destroyed Hussein's records, Iraqi librarians had sealed the stacks and enlisted community leaders' assistance to move material elsewhere for safekeeping. The LC report to the Coalition of Provisional Authority recommended preservation measures for damaged material, moving the Library to another building, and using the old National Library building for the national archives.[109]

The NRC Report and Digital Initiatives

When the five-year National Digital Library Program ended, the American Memory website featured more than seventy multimedia LC collections and materials from thirty-three other institutions.[110] Billington then commissioned a National Research Council (NRC) review of the Library's readiness for the digital age, and he requested funding for a Digital Futures initiative to address materials that were "born digital," to expand to international sources, and to help to guide national and international standards and preservation efforts.[111] It would be, he told the Appropriations Committee, "a new kind of 21st-century library for all Americans—the National Online Library" and the hub of an international network. The 11.1 percent appropriation increase, he explained, would address mandatory pay raises and provide 192 new staff. The Library would still have fewer staff (by 281) than in 1992, but "the tidal wave of internet activity now imposes a level of workload that requires the Library to rebuild a portion of its workforce that has been reduced or funded privately since 1992." The funding would allow retaining NDL staff as well as address anticipated retirements that would affect, in particular, the Congressional Research Service.[112]

At an oversight hearing on June 27, 2000, Billington and Deputy Librarian Scott told the Senate Committee on Rules and Administration that their top priority, requested since the 1980s, was legislation to allow receipts from fee-based services (Dewey Classification work, the Cataloging Distribution Service, FEDLINK, the Federal Research Division, the gift shop, and duplication and delivery services) to be used without fiscal year limitations. Auditors had repeatedly suggested such legislation, and with bills already introduced in both houses, discussion turned to other topics.[113] Chairman Stevens told Billington that it was increasingly difficult to gain congressional support for "all the facets of the modern Library," and "your needs have grown far beyond the needs of Congress." He wondered whether Billington would consider dividing the Library into several smaller organizations, each with a chief executive and its own collections and programs, and whether Congress could help the LC obtain more private support.

Billington replied: "I think there is value and virtue on keeping it together." He noted the symbiotic relationships between the collections and the need to use materials in different formats to address any given topic. Modern librarianship and scholarship, he said, are about "putting things together rather than taking things apart," and capturing information digitally brought the most recent, timely materials directly to Congress. When Senator Thad Cochran (R-MS) asked whether projects such as the America's Library website diverted funding from the CRS, Billington replied that the CRS and Congress remained top priority: "Congress will benefit from the rapid digital conveyance of information," the Librarian concluded. "I do not think the CRS has been getting the short end of the stick. The biggest strain is in the infrastructure."[114]

The NRC report appeared on July 26, produced by its sixteen-member Committee on an Information Strategy for the Library of Congress. It drew praise: for Billington's decision to request an external study; for involving the NRC, which had a history of rigorous assessments; and for its broad view of "how the Library of Congress and the digital world connect up with our society, with the whole system of libraries, and the management of cultural and intellectual heritage in this country." The committee assessed the LC's progress in addressing "born digital" materials as "very slow" and recommended developing an overall plan for acquiring and preserving those materials and also involving other libraries in a coordinated effort to select the materials worth keeping, determine how to access them, and decide how and where to archive them. As the chairman, James J. O'Donnell (University of Pennsylvania), stated, "The walls of the venerable place have not yet sufficiently been penetrated by the thrilling possibilities of the moment, and . . . if this moment is lost, the library risks subsiding into gray irrelevance." Sharply critical of aspects of LC operations, particularly information technology operations and the lack of technological expertise among top management, the committee recommended appointing a deputy librarian for strategic initiatives and establishing both an internal research and planning group and a panel of outside experts. Noting that noncompetitive pay and burdensome regulations made attracting well-qualified staff difficult, they called for investments in continuing education and training.[115]

Billington called the report "one of the most interesting collective challenges in the history of the Library of Congress." Effective October 2, the Librarian named the National Digital Library's director, Laura Campbell, Associate Librarian for Strategic Initiatives, with responsibility for digital initiatives, websites, social media, and content distribution. The new office included the NDL, Information Technology Services, and the Educational Outreach Office. In December, Congress approved a special $99.8 million appropriation for a nationwide effort to collect and preserve digital material, and on May 1, 2001, Campbell convened the National Digital Strategy Advisory Board.[116]

The board developed the National Digital Information Infrastructure and Preservation Program (NDIIPP), issuing *Preserving Our Digital Heritage: Plan for the National Digital Information Infrastructure and Preservation Program* in October 2002. After Congress approved the plan, and released $35 million for the next phase, in 2004 the program selected eight institutions to collaborate in building digital collections. Their projects included developing web archiving tools, preserving digital public television, developing a distributed preservation network, developing preservation and archiving strategies for geospatial data, capturing documents published on the Web, and preserving the records of dot-com companies and digital data such as public opinion polls. The next year, NDIIPP partnered with the National Science Foundation to develop a digital preservation research grants program, and in 2008 the Library began working with other federal agencies to develop common digitization guidelines.[117]

The program also reached state and local governments through the Preserving State Government Information initiative, and another initiative, Preserving Creative America, was launched after the Library brought more than fifty private-sector producers together to discuss preservation standards for graphics, illustrations, motion pictures, sound recordings, still photography, and other media. The Electronic Deposit for Electronic Journals Project addressed designing a repository and developing acquisition and preservation policies.[118]

The Section 108 Study Group examined the copyright statute that allowed libraries and archives exceptions for copying to replace and preserve copyrighted works. Its charge was to update the law for the digital environment, a task that the Digital Millennium Copyright Act of 1998 had only partially addressed. The Library assembled the group—which included experts from the library, publishing, scholarly, and entertainment communities—but the LC had no control over its conclusions. Among the March 2008 recommendations were to add museums to the excepted institutions and to allow the reproduction of publicly available online content for preservation and access needs.[119]

On the tenth anniversary of the NDIIPP, the Library announced formation of the National Digital Stewardship Alliance, a collaboration of institutions and organizations committed to preserving and providing access to digital content. The alliance began with a core set of NDIIPP founding members and project partners. After four years at the LC, it moved to the Council on Library and Information Resources.[120]

The National Research Council report had also called attention to "obsolete workflows," advising that rather than simply automate existing processes, the staff should "examine the processes themselves and rationalize them across unit boundaries." In 2004 Library Services "realigned" its fifty-three units in five directorates: Acquisitions and Bibliographic Access, Collections and Services, Partnerships and Outreach Programs, Preservation, and Technology Policy. Among the goals were to "streamline" acquisitions and cataloging and to recognize electronic resources as an increasingly important part of the collections.[121] Associate Librarian for Library Services Deanna Marcum followed up in 2006 by convening a group to consider access to materials in the online environment and the implications for online catalogs.[122] Its January 2008 report, *On the Record: Report of the Library of Congress Working Group on the Future of Bibliographic Control*, presented 108 technical recommendations, most of which the Library accepted. An important outcome was the further integration of acquisitions and cataloging: no matter how an item was received—by copyright deposit, purchase, gift, or exchange—it was assigned to a geographically based team. A book on German history, for example, would be ordered, cataloged, and processed by the directorate's Germanic and Slavic Division.[123]

The World Digital Library and Outreach

Looking beyond the NDL, Billington formed several partnerships with foreign institutions to build the Global Gateways website highlighting the relationships of the United States with other nations. The first project, "Meeting of Frontiers," united materials from the Library of Congress and Alaskan and Russian libraries in an English–Russian website.[124] A second featured "Parallel Histories: Spain, the United States, and the American Frontier," and subsequent projects included materials from Brazil, the Netherlands, and France.[125]

Building on the Gateway, the Librarian proposed to the US National Commission for UNESCO on June 6, 2005, the creation of the multilingual World Digital Library. His *Washington Post* op-ed declared that "because the internet is by definition international, and because cultural materials have a special human appeal that transcends politics, there is enormous potential for increasing transcultural understanding." In November, he announced a $3 million gift from Google for the digital collection.[126]

Both UNESCO and the International Federation of Library Associations and Institutions supported the project, and a December 2006 meeting hosted by UNESCO and the Library established committees on system architecture, content selection, standardization, and other requirements. Developed by LC staff, the World Digital Library website incorporated Billington's conception that "world history" was not the sum of separate national and regional histories but instead "a subdiscipline in its own right, focused on offering comparative, cross-national and cross-cultural perspectives—at its best helping people ask the big questions about what civilizations share in common and what makes them distinctive." It launched on April 21, 2009, with content in more than forty languages. Digital conversion centers were established at the national libraries of Brazil, Egypt, Uganda, and Iraq, and in 2010 the partners adopted a charter providing for the Executive Council, standing committees, and an annual meeting. By the end of 2013, when Billington announced a project for "virtual repatriation" of Afghan materials in the LC's collections, the site included material from eighty countries.[127]

Postbicentennial activities included other new outreach programs. A project called "The Library of Congress Comes to Your Hometown" launched in 2003 when Billington traveled with Representative Bob Ney (R-OH) and LC staff members to Ohio cities. With the assistance of the Ohio Arts Council, the Cleveland and Columbus public libraries, and other partners, programs, workshops, clinics, and a concert welcomed the public at large.[128] "Songs of America," presented in September 2005 at the National Book Festival, continued with a seven-month concert tour by the baritone Thomas Hampson. Funded by the Madison Council, and attracting participation from congressional offices, cultural organizations, and institutions, the tour included school visits, master classes, teacher institutes, conservation workshops, film showings, cybercasts, lectures, and exhibits. A second tour launched in 2009.[129]

The Library continued the "Living Legend" awards, and it created the Gershwin Prize for Popular Song in 2007. The first Lifetime Achievement Award for the Writing of Fiction, which recognized Herman Wouk in 2008, began a series initially called Creative Achievement Awards for Fiction and, later, the Prize for American Fiction. Presented at the National Book Festival, the award honors writers whose work is distinguished for mastery of the art and for originality.

The Library named Jon Scieszka in 2008 as the Library's first National Ambassador for Young People's Literature. The two-year appointment recognizes authors or illustrators whose works foster awareness of the importance of books, reading, literacy, and education in young lives. The Center for the Book collaborated with the Children's Book Council to administer the program and mounted a Read.gov website for educators and families.[130] In 2009, the Young Readers Center opened in the Jefferson Building as a place for children and their families; the room has a noncirculating collection and features website access, National Book Festival presentations, and special programs. In support of the LC's continuing emphasis on literacy, in 2012 Madison Council member David M. Rubenstein established the annual Library of Congress Literacy Awards program honoring nonprofit organizations nationally and worldwide that contribute significantly to increasing literacy levels and literacy awareness.[131]

National Audio-Visual Conservation Center

Planning had begun in the early 1990s for the Packard Campus of the National Audio-Visual Conservation Center (NAVCC), a facility housing the Motion Picture, Broadcasting, and Recorded Sound Division's collections. While most users access these materials in the Madison Building, the Packard complex provides state-of-the-art storage and preservation. With congressional authorization (PL 105-44, 1997), the David and Lucile Packard Foundation acquired, on behalf of the LC and the Architect of the Capitol, a forty-five-acre site near Culpeper, Virginia; and in May 1998, the foundation granted an additional $10 million. Subsequently the Packard Humanities Institute provided $155 million—one of the largest-ever gifts to the federal government—and Congress appropriated $82.1 million for construction.[132]

When the NAVCC was proposed, digital technologies could not handle the enormous data streams that audio and video produced; systems that could economically and reliably preserve digital audio and video were not commercially available. It was the development of fiber-optic-based network technology in the late 1990s that made larger-scale digitization possible. LC staff collaborated with the private sector to design and develop NAVCC systems, sometimes dubbing the center a "file-making factory."[133]

Opened in July 2007, the Packard campus includes facilities for collection storage, a central plant, nitrate film storage, and preservation operations. A 200-seat theater evokes the early days of cinema, with a custom-made organ to accompany silent films. The staff can mass-transfer materials from deteriorating media to digital files that can be refreshed as needed, migrated to new technologies as they evolve, and maintained as an archive; other systems provide for the recovery and repair of damaged materials. In 2012 the Universal Music Group, owner of the largest number of record labels in the industry, donated over 200,000 master recordings, and the NAVCC formed partnerships with, for example, the Corporation for Public Broadcasting, which in 2013 agreed to support the digitization and transfer of Boston's WGBH television and radio programs and also regional and local programs to the Library as the American Archive of Public Broadcasting.[134]

The Library, Congress, and the Public

The Capitol Visitor Center, a long-planned congressional project, connects to the Jefferson Building's ground floor—a connection for which Billington successfully advocated. Expecting a large increase in visitors, the LC staff developed new programs in cooperation with Microsoft Corporation, with the slogan "Bringing Knowledge into Life." The design included virtual tours and interactive kiosks for four exhibits: "Exploring the Early Americas," with selections from the Kislak Collection, and the Waldseemüller and other early maps; "Creating the United States," exhibiting founding documents; "The Great Hall," on the art and architecture of the Jefferson Building; and "Thomas Jefferson's Library," re-creating the library Jefferson sold to Congress. Visitors could use touch screens to activate curators' descriptions, rotate objects, turn pages, read translations, and zoom in for details. The "Passport to Knowledge" given to exhibition visitors enabled each user to bookmark items for later viewing.[135]

The much-publicized April 12, 2008, opening of the Capitol Visitor Center brought enthusiastic praise for the interactive technology and multimedia presentations. The book festival–like scene included music and poetry performances on the plaza and a History Channel–produced film.[136] On April 23, Billington announced that the Main Reading Room would be opened to readers over age sixteen, saying that the Library was always "looking for ways to create new lifelong learners, to expand access to knowledge, and to spark the creativity of future generations."[137]

Much earlier, in 2003, Representative Ray LaHood (R-IL) had asked what the LC was doing to promote congressional use, suggesting that the members did not use the Library because they did not know enough about it. Billington sent the LC staff to ask him for ideas, which led to an initiative by LaHood and Representative Earl Blumenauer (D-OR) to form the Library of Congress Congressional Caucus. A January 29, 2008, "Dear Colleague" letter got a favorable response from members, and a June dinner at the LC generated suggestions for publicizing the Library to constituents and expanding services—for example, to young visitors.[138] After a celebration marking the Legislative Information System's tenth anniversary, the Library launched the Congressional Caucus. Intended to focus attention on the LC's resources and stimulate discussion of how to better serve and inform the members, the caucus saw some of its suggestions adopted, among them, establishing the Young Readers Center. Increasingly, the Library hosted congressional events, especially swearing-in ceremonies, for which the staff provided, as requested, religious or political texts.[139]

The annual film and recording registry selections, the Book Festival, and the growing number of LC-sponsored awards caught the public's eye. The *Library of Congress Information Bulletin* ceased in 2011 after nearly seventy years, as a bimonthly general-interest *Library of Congress Magazine* debuted in 2012. While *The Gazette* continued as the staff news organ, the *Magazine* introduced more visual content.[140] Major exhibitions had always drawn news coverage, but the scale of attention seemed to broaden. CBS News interviewed the Librarian in 2011, for example—when National Film Registry selections included *The Exorcist*, *The Empire Strikes Back*, *Saturday Night Fever*, *Airplane*, and *All the President's Men*—and the National Recording Registry featured "Take Me Out to the Ball Game," "Stand by Your Man," and *Songs of the Humpback Whale*. Billington, the reporter noted, "pushes the board to find examples from under-represented categories like industrial and abstract films." The Librarian said he liked "getting educated by the list," noting that the process drew nominations ranging from industry moguls to the LC staff.[141]

The staff launched one of the first federal agency blogs in 2007, and in 2008 the Prints and Photographs Division began a pilot project on the photo-sharing site Flickr. It was immediately popular: users commented on features, identified subjects, and related the images to their own collections. From there, the staff moved on to more blogs and established a presence on social media.[142] An outgrowth of Hampson's tours, the Library of Congress Celebrates the Songs of America website documents American music, composers, performers, and scholars, using sheet music, recordings, videos, manuscripts, maps, and print materials.[143]

Mission Challenges

Yet the LC Inspector General's report on efforts to meet the challenges of the *LC21* report stated that much remained to be done. The product of an Inspector General contract with A-Tech Systems, the report was discussed at an April 2009 Committee on

House Administration hearing. Its central criticisms were that the Information Technology Services (ITS) strategic plan did not align with the Library's Strategic Plan; that the placement of ITS within the National Digital Information Infrastructure and Preservation Program diverted attention from infrastructure to programs; and that NDIIPP director Campbell, though carrying the title of Chief Information Officer (CIO) since 2002, had only limited authority to enforce Library-wide information technology (IT) policies.[144] The Library expressed agreement with most of the findings, but to the recommendation that the Library separate IT support functions from programmatic functions, Billington and Campbell replied that such a major change required further consideration.[145] A December 2011 follow-up report noted some progress on the recommendations but again called for separating IT from NDIIPP, establishing the separate Office of Chief Information Officer, consolidating and strengthening IT services, and updating the strategic plan. The Library concurred with these recommendations.[146]

During 2010, managers and staff developed the Library's Strategic Plan for the years 2011–16, updating the Mission Statement to place more emphasis on service to Congress but also acknowledging the broader role: "The Library's Mission is to support the Congress in fulfilling its constitutional duties and to further the progress of knowledge and creativity for the benefit of the American people." The plan included five strategic goals: service to Congress; acquisition and preservation of, and access to, a universal collection of knowledge and the record of creativity; sustaining a national copyright system; leading and working with external communities to advance knowledge and creativity; and managing proactively for demonstrable results.[147]

However, in 2013 the Library operated under continuing resolutions that imposed a 2012 budget level plus a sequester of funds, due to congressional efforts to reduce the federal deficit. The loss of $30.8 million resulted in across-the-board reductions and a three-day Library-wide staff furlough. Billington's appropriation request for 2014 was limited to the mandatory pay increase and the price-level increases needed to sustain acquisitions and the copyright registration system and retain Congressional Research Service experts. Even so, CRS staffing was at the lowest level in more than thirty years, and the staff numbered 1,300 fewer than twenty years ago. The year began with a government shutdown, but appropriations increased by 3.4 percent, with partial restoration of sequestered funds.[148]

Several administrative changes accompanied the budget squeeze. Plans were announced in October 2012 for the "Center for Knowledge": the Local History and Genealogy Reading Room, Computer Catalog Center, Microform Reading Room, and Digital Reference Service merged with the Main Reading Room, reducing service points and therefore staff on duty. At the same time, a new website, Congress.gov, united THOMAS and the Legislative Information System.[149] The new Collection Development Office began in 2012 to review the seventy-plus policies that guided decisions on what to acquire, and to consider web archiving and digital collection management strategies. Catalogers began using the new Resource Description and Access (RDA) cataloging code in 2013, which was designed for the digital environment, and they continued work on the Bibframe system, begun in 2011 to replace the latest version of MARC.[150] Plans were made to explore fixed-location shelving for materials kept on Capitol Hill, and work continued to scan books in the public domain for the Internet Archive, Biodiversity Heritage Library, and HathiTrust.[151]

Billington Retires

Following up on the Inspector General's 2009 and 2011 reports, the House Appropriations Committee's report on the 2015 Legislative Branch Appropriations Bill asked the Government Accountability Office to review the Library's IT management. The review covered strategic planning, governance and investment management, information security and privacy, provision of services, and leadership. The preliminary results, shared with the Library in January 2015, noted that there had been five temporary chief information officers within two years and the Deputy Librarian who oversaw IT policy was recently reassigned. The GAO recommended "expeditiously" hiring a permanent CIO with "clear responsibilities and adequate authority" and aligning the IT strategic plan with the agency strategic plan. Other recommendations specified improvements in tracking costs, security, and responses to complaints. Calling the report "a strong basis for further action," Billington then announced a nationwide search for a permanent CIO.[152]

The IT problem came up again in a different context. Beginning in 2013, the House Judiciary Committee had held a series of hearings on modernizing the copyright statute. Among the topics discussed was a proposal to move the Copyright Office to the executive branch, with the Register of Copyrights appointed by the President but term-limited by Congress. During the hearings, one congressman observed that the office was "ill-equipped financially and structurally to handle certain challenges presented by technological developments and the growing demands of the copyright system." Later, Register of Copyrights Maria Pallante, who testified at the first and last hearings, stated during the April 29, 2015, hearing that budget and technological limitations hindered the office's efficiency.[153]

Soon after, on May 18, 2015, Billington announced a "realignment." He abolished the Office of Strategic Initiatives and established the National and International Outreach unit and the Office of Chief Operating Officer. The latter included the Chief Information Officer, who also would be a member of the Executive Committee. The changes resulted, the Librarian said, from a two-year "Futures Program" that involved staff discussions leading toward the 2016–20 strategic plan. The intent was to strengthen Information Technology Services and other support functions, give outreach more prominence, and increasingly integrate digital and analog collections management. The reorganization would be effective on October 1.[154]

On June 10, Billington announced that he would retire effective January 1, 2016, which he later changed to September 30, 2015.[155] Beyond the announcement, there was no further explanation, although a permanent CIO was hired in September.

The Billington years brought a whirlwind of initiatives, projects, and reorganizations. The collections doubled while the Librarian simultaneously created a digital library. Billington raised millions of dollars in private support—for the National Digital Library, the Kluge Center, the National Audio-Visual Conservation Center and other projects, and for awards and prizes recognizing achievements in all fields of knowledge. While sometimes opposing congressional proposals, he was popular with the members, who gave him full credit for the Library's rapid entry into the online environment; and he made the LC a frequent host for their meetings and special events. He was sometimes less well regarded by the staff, many of whom grew weary of his constant embrace of new projects, and frequent reorganizations.[156] Praised for his ability to attract donors and create partnerships, but criticized for the Library's technological failures, he was an innovator rather than a manager. Yet if he had not, as once projected, led the Library to "turn information into knowledge," he had nonetheless pushed the institution to enter the rapidly expanding world of the internet.

On February 24, 2016, President Barack Obama nominated Carla D. Hayden, chief executive officer of the Enoch Pratt Free Library in Baltimore, as the fourteenth Librarian of Congress. The Senate confirmed her on July 13 for a ten-year term, making the office term-limited for the first time. Hayden was the first woman and the first Black to serve as Librarian. The third Librarian who previously headed a large public library, like Putnam and Mumford, she had previously served (2003–4) as president of the American Library Association.

Conclusion

WHEN OFFERING his books to Congress, Thomas Jefferson asserted, "There is in fact no subject to which a member of Congress may not have occasion to refer."[1] Early Librarians of Congress and the Joint Committee on the Library added only modestly to the collection, but Congress, perhaps in agreement, did not formally restrict its scope. Ainsworth Rand Spofford was the first Librarian of Congress to fully embrace Jefferson's vision: his belief in the power of knowledge and its importance to a democratic society. Spofford sought special appropriations, courted gifts, increased exchanges, and proposed legislation to require copyright registration and, significantly, deposit, which systematically built the collections. His successor, John Russell Young, in a circular letter announcing the completion of the Library's new building, declared, "Its original classification by Thomas Jefferson contemplated a National Library, universal and representative in its character, with all knowledge for its province. The policy of Mr. Jefferson has been followed until what under his inception was a collection of less than 8,000 volumes, has become nearly 800,000, and ranks among the great libraries of the world."[2]

Every Librarian since that time has sought to build not only the collections but also the Library's national role. Like Spofford, Herbert Putnam requested funding for acquisitions, but he also broadened the Library's constituency. He might have cited Jefferson's words to support his proposal to assist other libraries: "I have often thought that nothing would do more extensive good at small expense than the establishment of a small circulating library in every county, to consist of a few well-chosen books to be lent to the people of the county under such regulations as would secure their safe return in due time."[3] When Putnam became Librarian ninety years later, such development was well under way; and with his declaration that the Library would "reach out," the Library of Congress assumed a leadership role in the library community. It also thereby acquired an expanding constituency that would increasingly request senators and representatives to support the Library of Congress's services for libraries.

Spofford and Putnam publicly credited the Library's growth to its unique position in the federal government, and both succeeded in broadening its role by forging close congressional relations. The lack of a constitutional provision or a written charter, Putnam once stated, meant that the LC depended "on grants from Congress in aid of what it proposes to do. But it's always a proposal to do something. The grant isn't a definition of function, nor any evidence that Congress meant to define the function of the Library, or put a limit such as would be in the case of a Constitution for the Library."[4] Congress approved Putnam's expansionist agenda but also asserted its prerogatives, resulting, for example, in the establishment of the Legislative Reference Service and its descendant, the Congressional Research Service.

The members were pleased to accept—and were gratified by—private support for their Library: all the more when it took the form of gifts, bequests, and grants for projects that appropriations would not cover. In particular, Putnam's success in establishing the Trust Fund Board in the mid-1920s, and the subsequent flow of gifts, helped to promote congressional appropriations for both a second building and the purchase of the Vollbehr Collection. The result was to broaden the Library's cultural role and influence, not only through that acquisition but also through concerts, programs, and exhibitions directed to the general public—and through the accumulation of increasingly broad-based national and international collections of materials in all formats. Partnerships with the library community extended the Library's influence through a cooperative cataloging program, the development of the National Union Catalog, and the addition of Dewey numbers to LC catalog cards, which all were later supported by ongoing appropriations.

Just as in World War I, Putnam cooperated with the Army, the ALA, and service agencies to provide books for the troops; and Archibald MacLeish and Luther Evans associated the LC with other federal agencies and the library community during World War II and beyond. MacLeish reorganized the administration and broadened the Library's cultural programs, promoting new relationships with scholars, writers, and poets. Evans proposed building on the Library's postwar Cooperative Acquisitions Project through major expansions of the collections and services to meet the challenges of the postwar world. However, stating that only Congress itself could determine the Library's role, the members rejected his requests, criticized his UNESCO work as a distraction from his official role, and questioned the Library's support for other federal agencies. It was not the first nor the last (but was perhaps the most intense) time that suspicions of lesser attention to congressional wishes entered appropriation debates.

To Evans's successor, L. Quincy Mumford, fell the task of restoring congressional confidence in the Library, and he argued effectively for both the Library's and the library community's interests and needs. Helped by congressional and librarian allies, he seized the opportunity offered by Public Law 480 to establish acquisitions offices abroad and, with Title II-C of the Higher Education Act, again with congressional support and also assistance from the research library community, expanded the foreign centers to include centralized cataloging for the nation's research libraries. Mumford secured grant support for a study of LC automation that resulted in the MARC format, leading to the adoption of online catalogs in both small and large libraries, nationwide and abroad. During a period of strained relations with the ALA and associated congressional pressures, he responded to staff complaints of discrimination by establishing programs to promote equity in employment. He won congressional approval both to construct the Library's third building on Capitol Hill and to organize a national preservation program.

Online catalogs provided the long-sought means of simultaneously accessing the contents of many libraries. As the staff broadened the MARC database to include materials in all formats, the Library began selling its catalog records on magnetic tape. New organizations—such as OCLC, RLG, and regional networks—loaded the MARC tapes into their databases, enabling their member libraries to contribute their own cataloging and to copy the LC's and other libraries' catalog records for local use. The Council on Library Resources' effort to link computer systems—tested by the LC, OCLC, and RLG—ultimately enabled the exchange of catalog records both nationally and internationally. Cooperative efforts with the ARL, the ALA, national libraries, the International Federation of Library Association and Institutions, and the National and International Standards Organizations intensely occupied the Library's staff starting in Mumford's administration—mostly outside public view but sustained through appropriations.

Observing that history rather than administrative logic had driven the Library's development, Douglas W. Bryant's 1962 report to Congress noted that the LC's functions might provide the basis for several federal agencies. The report renewed discussions—in the library community, in Congress, in other constituent groups, and through external management evaluations—about creating an oversight board for the Library or detaching some LC functions, most prominently the Copyright Office and the Congressional Research Service. Such discussions recurred periodically, and Congress also periodically debated these issues, but in the end the members resisted all attempts at change.

Daniel Boorstin and James Billington came to the Librarianship intent on emphasizing public services and outreach, scholarly research, and public programs. Boorstin's Center for the Book and Council of Scholars directed attention to topics of public and congressional interest, such as the endurance of books and reading in the computer age, and to contemporary scholarship. He welcomed legislation to establish the American Folklife Center with its activities focused on the diverse folklore, popular entertainment, and popular culture fields; and his conferences and exhibitions attracted wide attention. At the same time, Boorstin obtained appropriations for restoring and modernizing the Jefferson and Adams buildings, while executing a congressional mandate to broaden services through the Congressional Research Service and supporting longstanding congressional efforts to pass a comprehensive copyright statute.

Billington's ambition to share the collections more widely built on Boorstin's Center for the Book's public–private support model: he organized the Madison Council as the Library's major support group, and he leveraged massive private funding for new projects. From the council came the support to establish the John W. Kluge Center for Scholars, combined private funding and appropriations built the National Audio-Visual Conservation Center, and legislation established new film and recording preservation programs. Billington responded to congressional urging to increase security and decrease the cataloging arrearage, and he expanded personnel programs after a judgment for the plaintiffs in the lawsuit that capped yearslong staff complaints of discrimination. In the face of occasional congressional doubts, he successfully advocated for continued collection building, for constructing a state-of-the-art remote storage facility, and for connecting the Library to the Capitol Visitor Center. Having demonstrated via American Memory the value of the collections for education, he gained congressional consent to establish an LC web presence and enlisted both private support and appropriations for his National Digital Library. Billington extended the reach of the Library's products, services, and programs through both traditional and new technologies, perhaps most excitingly by implementing First Lady Laura Bush's initiative to establish the National Book Festival.

Billington also drew more scrutiny—from Congress, librarians, the LC staff, and the media—of the Library's operations than any previous administration. Nevertheless, congressional relations were critical to his success: he extended CRS services, involved the members as advisers and participants in Library activities, took a leadership role in their initiative to assist new Eastern European governments, and responded to their mandates to record the experiences of Civil Rights Movement participants and veterans.

The Library of Congress is the nation's oldest cultural institution. Its first sixty years, marked by three disastrous fires, passed without significant developments other than to establish the Law Library. The next eight decades saw a remarkable expansion. During that time, several statutes—the Copyright Law of 1870, the laws enabling card sales and interlibrary lending, and the legislation creating the Trust Fund Board—set important precedents for the Library's further development: acquisitions through copyright deposits, partnerships with outside constituencies, and the cultivation of private support. Significantly, these statutes, as Putnam remarked, resulted from the Library's own proposals "to do something"—that is, to take the initiative to persuade Congress to act.

Significant extensions of the Library's activities and acquisitions programs from the 1940s onward heightened the importance of the Library's congressional relations. While Congress generally responded favorably—in particular to Mumford's, Boorstin's, and Billington's proposals—it was never without scrutiny. Attempts to detach one or the other of the Library's functions or to change its mission, whether originating with the members or outside, all failed, leaving the Library free to seize opportunities, in particular heralding with the MARC format libraries' evolution to networking, nationally and internationally. With good reason, Librarians of Congress have long defended the Library's residence in the legislative branch: Congress has supported its services to other libraries, scholars, educators, the federal establishment, and the general public; and members of Congress have generally welcomed new initiatives that have broadened its role.[5]

APPENDIX: LIBRARIANS OF CONGRESS

There are no known illustrations of the first two Librarians: John J. Beckley (1802–1807) and Patrick Magruder (1807–1815).

George Watterston, third Librarian of Congress, 1815–29.

John Silva Meehan, fourth Librarian of Congress, 1829–61.

John Gould Stephenson, fifth Librarian of Congress, 1861–64.

Ainsworth Rand Spofford, sixth Librarian of Congress, 1864–97.

John Russell Young, seventh Librarian of Congress, 1897–99.

Herbert Putnam, eighth Librarian of Congress, 1899–1939, with the Library's recently-acquired (1930) three-volume Gutenberg Bible. One of only three perfect existing vellum copies, the Bible was printed in 1450 by Johannes Gutenberg in Mainz, Germany.

The ninth Librarian of Congress, Archibald MacLeish (1939–44; center), examines the Declaration with Verner Warren Clapp, director of the Acquisitions Department, and David Chambers Mearns, director of the Reference Department. The Declaration of Independence returned to the Library from wartime storage in Fort Knox, Kentucky, in the fall of 1944.

Luther Harris Evans, tenth Librarian of Congress, 1945–53, with Eleanor Roosevelt at a display of UNESCO publications, circa 1946.

Lawrence Quincy Mumford, eleventh Librarian of Congress, 1954–74.

Daniel J. Boorstin (center) is sworn in on November 12, 1975, as the twelfth Librarian of Congress by Carl Albert, Speaker of the House (right), with President Gerald R. Ford on the left.

Thirteenth Librarian of Congress James H. Billington (right) walks with former Soviet president Mikhail Gorbachev (center) on the US Capitol grounds across the street from the Library of Congress, 1992.

NOTES

Preface

1. *ARLC*, 1957, 6.

2. Verner W. Clapp, "Libraries in the Life of the Nation: The National Library," Canadian Library Association, Occasional Paper 2, December 1953; Paul L. Berry, "National Libraries in General and in the United States," 34–46, in *Libraries and the Challenge of Change*, edited by K. E. Ingram and Albertina A. Jefferson (London: Mansell, 1975).

Chapter 1

1. 1 Stat 130; Robert P. Watson, *George Washington's Final Battle: The Epic Struggle to Build a Capital; City and a Nation* (Washington, DC: Georgetown University Press, 2021), 121–63; Gaillard Hunt, "Locating the Capital," *Annual Report of the American Historical Association, 1895* (Washington, DC: GPO, 1896), 289–95; Kenneth R. Bowling, "The Federal Government and the Republican Court Move to Philadelphia, November 1790–March 1791," in *Neither Separate nor Equal: Congress in the 1790s*, edited by Kenneth R. Bowling and Donald R. Kennon, (Athens: Ohio University Press for US Capitol Historical Society, 2000), 3–33.

2. Papers of the Continental Congress, item 186.

3. *Journals of the Continental Congress,* 24: 83–92; 25: 858–59.

4. Robert A. Rutland, "Madison's Bookish Habits," *QJLC* 37 (1980): 176–91, noted Jefferson's influence on Madison's collecting and his list of books for Congress. Robert A. Rutland, *"Well Acquainted with Books": The Founding Framers of 1787* (Washington, DC: LC, 1987), includes the list.

5. *Journals of the Continental Congress,* 25: 858–59.

6. William C. diGiacomantonio, "To Form the Character of the American People: Public Support for the Arts, Sciences and Morality in the First Federal Congress," in *Inventing Congress: Origins and Establishment of the First Federal Congress*, edited by Kenneth R. Bowling and Donald R. Kennon (Athens: Ohio University Press for US Capitol Historical Society, 1999), 227; Tom Glynn and Craig C. Hagensick, "Books for the Use of the United States in Congress Assembled, 1783 and 1800," *L&C* 37 (Spring 2002): 109–22; Fulmer Mood, "The Continental Congress and the Plan for a Library of Congress in 1782–1783: An Episode in American Cultural History," *Pennsylvania Magazine of History and Biography* 72 (1948): 3–24; Carl Ostrowski, *Books, Maps, and Politics: A Cultural History of the Library of Congress, 1783–1861* (Amherst: University of Massachusetts Press, 2004), 8–20.

7. Austin Baxter Keep, *History of the New York Society Library* (Boston: Gregg Press, 1972; orig. pub. 1908), 208, 210.

8. *AC* 1: 705.

9. *AC* 2: 1603; Mearns, *Story*, 1–2.

10. *AC* 2: 1703; Johnston, *History*, 18–19.

11. Ostrowski, *Books, Maps*, 22–37; Mearns, *Story*, 2.

12. diGiacomantonio, "To Form the Character," 227–28; Ostrowski, *Books, Maps*, 20–24.

13. John Y. Cole, *For Congress and the Nation: A Chronological History of the Library of Congress* (Washington, DC: LC, 1979), 3; Rutland, *"Well Acquainted,"* 13.

14. Edwin Wolf II, *"At the Instance of Benjamin Franklin": A Brief History of the Library Company of Philadelphia, 1731–1976* (Philadelphia: Library Company, 1976), 12–13.

15. Rutland, *"Well Acquainted,"* 14–22.

16. Mearns, *Story*, 4–5; Johnston, *History*, 19–20.

17. Mearns, *Story*, 5–6.

18. 2 Stat 55, at 56.

19. Mearns, *Story*, 6–8, stated that Section 5 was in the original House bill; Mood, "Continental Congress," noted that some members—including Madison, Bland, and Elias Boudinot (Pro-administration-NJ)—were also present in 1782–83.

20. Quoted by David McCullough, *John Adams* (New York: Simon & Schuster, 2001), 222–23; Richard Alan Ryerson, *John Adams's Republic: The One, the Few, and the Many* (Baltimore: Johns Hopkins University Press, 2016), 225–26.

21. McCullough, *John Adams*, 536, 618–19.

22. Donald H. Mugridge, "A Shipment of Books," *QJLC* 8 (1950): 5–16. Waln was then a director, and Bingham had been a director, of the Library Company of Philadelphia.

23. Mearns, *Story*, 9; Johnston, *History*, 23–24; Mugridge, "Shipment," 8–11.

24. LC, *The First Booklist of the Library of Congress: A Facsimile* (Washington, DC: LC, 1981); Mugridge, "Shipment," 10–14; Glynn and Hagensick, "Books," 116–20.

25. Letter from Cadell & Davies transmitting an invoice of books, December 11, 1800, Rare Book and Special Collections Division, LC; Mearns, *Story*, 9.

26. Mearns, *Story*, 10; Johnston, *History*, 24–25.

27. McCullough, *John Adams*, 542–43; Constance McLaughlin Green, *Washington: A History of the Capital, 1800–1950* (Princeton, NJ: Princeton University Press, 1962), 1: 3–4, 21; Anne Cary Morris., ed., *The Diary and Letters of Gouverneur Morris* (New York: Charles Scribner's Sons, 1888) 2: 395; William Parker Cutler, *Life, Journals and Correspondence of the Reverend Manasseh Cutler, LLD*, by his grandchildren William Parker Cutler and Julia Perkins Cutler (Athens: Ohio University Press, 1987), 50; Charles F. Adams, ed., *Letters of Mrs. Adams* (Boston, 1848), 383; Catherine Allgor, *A Perfect Union: Dolley Madison and the Creation of the American Nation* (New York: Henry Holt, 2006), 49; Claude G. Bowers, *Jefferson and Hamilton: The Struggle for Democracy in America* (Saint Clair Shores, MI: Scholarly Press, 1972), 487. On the site, see Scott W. Berg, "The Beginning of the Road," *Washington Post Magazine*, August 31, 2008, 13; Kenneth R. Bowling, *The Creation of Washington, DC: The Idea and Location of the American Capital* (Fairfax, VA: George Mason University Press, 1991), 237–45.

28. *AC* 11: 311.

29. Ostrowski, *Books, Maps*, 53; *AC* 12: 1292–94; *ASP Miscellaneous Series*, 1: 253–54.

30. *AC* 11: 349–50, 352–54.

31. *AC* 11: 19.

32. 2 Stat 128; Mearns, *Story*, 10–11; Johnston, *History*, 26–33, 222–23.

33. The appointment came three days after the bill passed, suggesting that Jefferson was aware of the provisions beforehand: John B. Boles, *Jefferson: Architect of American Liberty* (New York: Basic Books, 2017), 347.

34. For the 1800 presidential campaign, Beckley published, anonymously, "Address to the People of the United States with an Epitome and Vindication of the Public Life and Character

of Thomas Jefferson" (Philadelphia, 1800): Gerald Gawalt, ed., *The Political Writings of John James Beckley* (Washington, DC: LC, 1995), 166–89. On Beckley's political activities, see Gloria Jahoda, "John Beckley: Jefferson's Campaign Manager," *Bulletin of the New York Public Library* 64 (May 1960): 257; Joanne Freeman, *Affairs of Honor: National Politics in the New Republic* (New Haven, CT: Yale University Press, 2001), 85; and Edmund Berkeley and Dorothy Smith Berkeley, *John Beckley: Zealous Partisan in a Nation Divided* (Philadelphia: American Philosophical Society, 1973), 239.

35. Ainsworth R. Spofford, "The Library of Congress, or National Library," in *Public Libraries in the United States of America*, edited by US Bureau of Education (Washington, DC: GPO, 1876), 254.

36. Beckley fired a Federalist clerk, Josias Wilson King, in 1805. King then addressed a memorial to the House of Representatives stating that Beckley failed to split the library compensation with him as promised; the House Committee on Accounts ruled against him: Mearns, *Story*, 11; Johnston, *History*, 35; Edmund Berkeley and Dorothy Smith Berkeley, "The First Librarian of Congress: John Beckley," in *Librarians*, 22, 26.

37. *AC* 7: 198, 986.

38. The House had moved to a temporary structure pending South Wing completion: Mearns, *Story*, 10; Johnston, *History*, 34, 41–43; Anne-Imelda Radice, *The Original Library of Congress: The History (1800–1814) of the Library of Congress in the United States Capitol*, Senate Committee Print, 97th Congress, 1st Sess., August 1981 (Washington, DC: GPO, 1981), 6.

39. Green, *Washington*, 1: 37, 43–46. The diplomat Augustus John Foster wrote that houses were small, and "scarce any but public functionaries and foreign envoys are so situated as to be able to give entertainments": Richard Beale Davis, ed., *Jeffersonian America; Notes on the United States of America Collected in the Years 1805–6–7 and 11–12 by Sir Augustus John Foster, Bart.* (San Marino, CA: Huntington Library, 1954), 8. The new federal buildings also served as sites of worship, though Saint Patrick's Catholic Church had opened in 1794. The first schools opened in 1806; bookstores appeared at an early date, but the earliest subscription libraries struggled: Gordon S. Brown, *Incidental Architect: William Thornton and the Cultural Life of Early Washington, 1794–1828* (Athens: Ohio University Press, 2009), 52–53; James Young, *The Washington Community, 1800–1828* (New York: Columbia University Press, 1966), 88–102.

40. Quoted by Herman R. Friis, "Baron Alexander von Humboldt's Visit to Washington, DC, June 1 through June 13, 1804," *RCHS* 1960–62: 1–35. He came to meet President Jefferson, whose *Notes on the State of Virginia* he admired.

41. *William Plumer's Memorandum of Proceedings in the United States Senate: 1803–1807*, edited by Everett Brown (New York: Da Capo Press, 1969), 541.

42. Thomas Jefferson to Abraham Baldwin, April 14, 1802, Founders Online, https://founders.archives.gov/documents/Jefferson.01-37-02-0195-0001; Boles, *Jefferson*, 347. Jefferson also sent Baldwin a Philadelphia bookseller's catalog of Benjamin Franklin's library, asking him to consider purchasing certain items: Coulter E. Merton, *Abraham Baldwin: Patriot, Educator, and Founding* Father (Arlington, VA: Vandamere Press, 1987), 217. Senator George Logan (D-R-PA), also interested in developing the collection, wrote his wife's cousin John Dickinson for recommendations: Frederick B. Tolles, *George Logan of Philadelphia* (New York: Oxford University Press, 1953), 232. The joint committee's budget was exhausted by the time Jefferson's recommendation arrived, and Franklin's library was sold off piecemeal: Kevin J. Hayes, *The Road to Monticello: The Life and Times of Thomas Jefferson* (New York: Oxford University Press, 2008), 550.

43. Mearns, *Story*, 13.

44. Berkeley and Berkeley, "First Librarian," 15–16; Ostrowski, *Books, Maps*, 54–60; Johnston, *History*, 50–53.

45. Johnston, *History*, 38.

46. Ostrowski, *Books, Maps*, 44–47.

47. 2 Stat 308; *AC* 19: 1375; Johnston, *History*, 54–55.

48. "Dr. Mitchill's Letters from Washington," *Harper's New Monthly Magazine* 58 (April 1879): 741.

49. *AC* 15: 54–55, 184; *ASP Miscellaneous Series*, 1: 437; Johnston, *History*, 45.

50. 2 Stat 350.

51. Mearns, *Story*, 14; Johnston, *History*, 47–48; John Quincy Adams, *Memoirs*, edited by Charles Francis Adams (Philadelphia: J. B. Lippincott, 1874), 1: 424.

52. Johnston, *History*, 41–43.

53. *AC* 17: 783–87.

54. Martin K. Gordon, "Patrick Magruder: Citizen, Congressman, Librarian of Congress," in *Librarians*, 42–44.

55. Johnston, *History*, 58–61.

56. Carolyn Hoover Sung, "Catharine Mitchill's Letters from Washington, 1806–1812," *QJLC* 34 (1977): 180.

57. "Report of the Superintendent of the Reading Rooms," 1931, LCA.

58. 2 Stat 612; 2 Stat 786; Johnston, *History*, 55–57.

59. 2 Stat 667; "A History of the Committee on House Administration, 1947–2012," 361. The Joint Committee on the Library is the oldest congressional joint committee. The number of House members increased to five in 1888: these members constituted the House Committee on the Library. In 1902 the Joint Committee was increased to five members from each house: 32 Stat 735.

60. 2 Stat 643.

61. LC, *The 1812 Catalogue of the Library of Congress: A Facsimile* (Washington, DC: LC, 1982). It is not known who changed the arrangement: Leo E. LaMontagne, *American Library Classification with Special Reference to the Library of Congress* (Hamden, CT: Shoe String Press, 1961), 44–45.

62. Ostrowski, *Books, Maps*, 60–70.

63. Cole, *For Congress*, 6–7.

64. Green, *Washington*, 1: 55; Stanley Elkins and Eric McKitrick, *The Age of Federalism* (New York: Oxford University Press, 1993), 171–73; Young, *Washington Community*, 23; Gordon S. Wood, *Empire of Liberty: A History of the Early Republic, 1789–1815* (New York: Oxford University Press, 2009), 301; Robert A. McCaughey, *Josiah Quincy, 1772–1864: The Last Federalist* (Cambridge, MA: Harvard University Press, 1974), 45–47; Adam G. Costanzo, *George Washington's Washington* (Athens: University of Georgia Press, 2018), 105.

65. E.g., William Cabell Bruce, *John Randolph of Roanoke* (New York: Octagon Books, 1970), 1: 554–62.

66. Gaillard Hunt, *As We Were: Life in America 1814* (Stockbridge, MA: Berkshire House, 1993), 64.

Chapter 2

1. Donald R. Hickey, *The War of 1812* (Urbana: University of Illinois Press, 1989), 19.

2. Gauthan Rao, *National Duties: Custom Houses and the Making of the American State* (Chicago: University of Chicago Press, 2016), 139–44.

3. J. C. A. Stagg, "The Coming of the War of 1812: The View from the Presidency," *QJLC* 37 (1980): 223–41; Hickey, *War of 1812*, 5–44; Gordon S. Wood, *Empire of Liberty: A History of the Early Republic, 1789–1815* (New York: Oxford University Press, 2009), 660–70; David S. Heidler and Jeanne T. Heidler, *Henry Clay: The Essential American* (New York: Random House, 2010), 84–99.

4. Irving Brandt, *The Fourth President: A Life of James Madison* (New York: Bobbs Merrill, 1970), 540, and Henry Adams, *History of the United States during the Administrations of James Madison* (New York: Library of America, 1986), 727, disputed that US troops were responsible; but Alan Taylor, *The Civil War of 1812* (New York: Alfred A. Knopf, 2010), 217, blamed officers' failure to control the troops. The British cited the incident to justify destroying Washington: Steve Vogel, *Through the Perilous Fight: Six Weeks That Saved the Nation* (New York: Random House, 2013), 194–96; Steve Vogel, "'Mr. Madison Will Have to Put on His Armor': Cockburn and the Capture of Washington," in *America Under Fire: Mr. Madison's War & The Burning of Washington City* (Washington, DC: David M. Rubenstein Center for White House History, 2014), 137–46; John McCavitt, "Capital Conflagrator? Major General Robert Ross," *Capitol Dome* 51 (Fall 2014): 8.

5. Willard Sterne Randall, *Unshackling America: How the War of 1812 Truly Ended the American Revolution* (New York: St. Martin's Press, 2017), 324–33; Alan Taylor, "'The Most Dangerous Spies & Traitors': Runaway Slaves and the British Campaigns in the Chesapeake, 1813–1814," in *America Under Fire*, 113–36.

6. Constance McLaughlin Green, *Washington: A History of the Capital, 1800–1950* (Princeton, NJ: Princeton University Press, 1962), 1: 56-60; James Scott, *Recollections of a Naval Life* (London: Richard Bentley, 1934), 3: 239–40, 272; Anthony Pitch, *The Burning of Washington: The British Invasion of 1814* (Annapolis: Naval Institute Press, 1998), 19–20; J. C. Stagg, *Mr. Madison's War: Politics, Diplomacy, and Warfare in the Early American Republic, 1783–1830* (Princeton, NJ: Princeton University Press, 1983), 410, 416; Randall, *Unshackling America*, 344, 347.

7. *AC* 26: 787.

8. *ASP Miscellaneous Series* 2: 245–46, 260; Carole L. Herrick, *August 24, 1814: Washington in Flames* (Falls Church, VA: Higher Education Publications, 2005), 35; Fergus Bordewich, *Washington: The Making of the American Capital* (New York: HarperCollins, 2008), 260; Pitch, *Burning*, 44–45.

9. Vogel, *Through the Perilous Fight*, 195. Sir Harry George Wakelyn Smith wrote that if the federal government moved to the northern states, northern opposition to the war would force a settlement: Harry George Wakeln Smith, *The Autobiography of Lieutenant General Sir Harry Smith,* edited by G. C. Moore Smith (London: John Murray, 1902), 201.

10. George Gleig, *A Narrative of the Campaigns of the British Army at Washington and New Orleans under Generals Ross, Pakenham, and Lambert in the Years of 1814 and 1816* (London: John Murray, 1932), 134.

11. James Scott, *Recollections of a Naval Life* (London: Richard Bentley, 1834), 3: 301.

12. Herrick, *August 24, 1814*, 96–97; Vogel, *Through the Perilous Fight*, 173–75; Benjamin Latrobe to Jefferson, undated, in *Thomas Jefferson and the National Capital*, edited by Saul K. Padover (Washington, DC: GPO, 1946), 475.

13. Pitch, *Burning*, 104–10, Vogel, *Through the Perilous Fight,* 172. Jon Latimer, *1812: War with America* (Cambridge, MA: Belknap Press of Harvard University Press, 2007), 317, stated that Admiral Cockburn took a volume—*An Account of the Receipts and Expenditures of the United States for the Year 1810*—which he gave to his brother, Sir James Cockburn, Governor of Bermuda. The volume was returned to the LC in 1940, with Cockburn's inscription authenticated by the rare book dealer A. S. W. Rosenbach: *ARLC*, 1940, 202.

14. Vogel, *Through the Perilous Fight*, 357; William Barlow, "Jonathan Fisk's Attempt to Relocate the Nation's Capital," *New-York Historical Society Quarterly* 53 (January 1969): 64–77; *AC* 28: 216–22, 311–23. The invitation was read September 29 in both houses.

15. Adam G. Costanzo, *George Washington's Washington* (Athens: University of Georgia Press, 2018), 113–19; Herrick, *August 24, 1814*, 200–202; Les Standiford, *Washington Burning: How a Frenchman's Vision of Our Nation's Capital Survived Congress, the Founding Fathers, and the British Army* (New York: Crown, 2008), 289–90; Bordewich, *Washington*, 264–66; James Young, *The Washington Community, 1800–1828* (New York: Columbia University Press, 1966), 51; *AC* 13: 215–22, 394–96; *ASP Miscellaneous Series* 2: 252–53; Green, *Washington,* 1: 65–67; Catherine Allgor, *Parlor Politics: In Which the Ladies of Washington Help Build a City and a Government* (Charlottesville: University of Virginia Press, 2000), 96–97; Catherine Allgor, *A Perfect Union: Dolley Madison and the Creation of the American Nation* (New York: Henry Holt, 2006), 322–27; Hickey, *War of 1812*, 240–41; Stagg, *Mr. Madison's War*, 429–30; Daniel Walker Howe, *What Hath God Wrought: The Transformation of America, 1815–1848* (New York: Oxford University Press, 2007), 66–68; *Report of the Committee Appointed on the Twentieth Ult. to Inquire into the Expedience of Rebuilding or Repairing the Public Buildings in the City of Washington and Whether It Is Expedient to Make Any Change in the Sites of Said Buildings* (Washington, DC: Roger C. Weightman, 1814), Marian S. Carson Collection, LC, box 51.

16. *AC* 28: 305–8.

17. Johnston stated that some books were saved (*History*, 67); but Frederick Goff, "Early Library of Congress Bookplates," *QJLC* 26 (January 1969): 55, found only two volumes that came from the collection.

18. *Report of the Committee to Whom Was Referred the Communication of Patrick Magruder, Clerk of the House of Representatives, Relative to the Destruction of the Library Etc., December 12, 1814* (Washington, DC: A. and G. Way, 1814); *AC* 28: 872–76.

19. *Letter from the Clerk of the House of Representatives, Being an Answer to the Report of the Committee to Whom Was Referred His Letter of the 22d of September Last, Relative to the Loss of His Contingent Account and Vouchers* (Washington, DC: A. and G. Way, 1814); *ASP Miscellaneous Series* 2: 258–59.

20. *ASP Miscellaneous Series*. 2: 263–65; Jane Armstrong Hudiburg, "'Doubt, Confusion, and Dismay': Efforts to Save the House and Senate Records in 1814," *Capitol Dome* 51 (Fall 2014): 15.

21. *AC* 28: 1100–1101.

22. In February 1816, the government sued to recover approximately $18,000 from Magruder, but the case never came to trial: Martin K. Gordon, "Patrick Magruder: Citizen, Congressman, Librarian of Congress," in *Librarians*, 53; Lucy Salamanca, *Fortress of Freedom: The Story of the Library of Congress* (Philadelphia: J. B. Lippincott, 1942), 79–81.

23. *AC* 28: 1107–8; 1113–14; *ASP Miscellaneous Series* 2: 267–68.

24. *Niles' Register* 7: 1, 203, as noted by John K. Mahon, *The War of 1812* (New York: Da Capo Press, 1991; orig. pub. 1972), 301; Johnston, *History*, 68; J. Mackay Hitsman, *The Incredible War of 1812: A Military History* (Toronto: Robin Brass Studio, 1999), 244–45; Troy Bickham, *The Weight of Vengeance: The United States, the British Empire, and the War of 1812* (New York: Oxford University Press, 2013), 167–69.

25. In a January 1814 letter to Thomas Cooper, Jefferson had stated that he would give books to the University of Virginia: Arthur Bestor, "Thomas Jefferson and the Freedom of Books," in *Three Presidents and Their Books* (Urbana: University of Illinois Press, 1955), 109. He wrote the same to Madison on October 9, 1809, adding that his library might also go to a national university if one was established: *The Jefferson Bicentennial, 1743–1943: A Catalogue of the Exhibitions*

in the Library of Congress Opened on April 12th (Washington, DC: GPO, 1943), 39; Johnston, *History*, 69.

26. Jefferson to Smith, September 21, 1814, Founders Online, https://founders.archives.gov/documents/Jefferson/03-07-02-0484-0003. Smith received the letter on October 2.

27. Dumas Malone, *Sage of Monticello* (Boston: Little, Brown, 1981), 172; Milligan to Jefferson, September 24, 1814, quoted by Johnston, *History*, 78–79; *Jefferson Bicentennial*, 39–40.

28. *AC* 28: 120, 378, 412; 3 Stat 246; *ASP Miscellaneous Series* 2: 253; Johnston, *History*, 78, 84–85.

29. Charles J. Ingersoll, *History of the Second War between the United States of America and Great Britain* (Philadelphia: Lippincott, Grambo, 1852), 2: 271–72.

30. Carl Ostrowski, *Books, Maps, and Politics: A Cultural History of the Library of Congress, 1783–1861* (Amherst: University of Massachusetts Press, 2004), 75; *AC* 28: 1105.

31. *AC* 28: 1105–6; Johnston, *History*, 85–89. Callender's anti-Federalist tract was written for the 1800 election. Donald H. Mugridge, "A Shipment of Books," *QJLC* 8 (1950): 14–16, discussed the extent to which Jefferson's library replaced the Cadell and Davies shipment.

32. Quoted by Johnston, *History*, 80, 90.

33. *National Intelligencer*, November 16, 1814; quoted by Johnston, *History*, 91.

34. *National Intelligencer*, January 27, 1815, quoted by Johnston, *History*, 74.

35. Randolph G. Adams, *Three Americanists: Henry Harisse, Bibliographer; George Brinley, Book Collector; Thomas Jefferson, Librarian* (Philadelphia: University of Pennsylvania Press, 1939), 90–91; *AC* 28: 1105–6; 3 Stat 195.

36. News of the Treaty of Ghent, signed on December 24, reached Washington over a month later; General Andrew Jackson's January 8 victory at New Orleans was not known until February 6. Congress ratified the treaty on February 19: Mearns, *Story*, 18–24.

37. Jefferson's later count made the total 6,707, but he asked no additional payment: Douglas L. Wilson, "Jefferson's Library," in *Thomas Jefferson: A Reference Bibliography*, edited by Merrill D. Peterson (New York: Charles Scribner's Sons, 1986), 157–79. Jefferson asked the Secretary of the Treasury to pay his creditors two-thirds of the amount, leaving $8,580 for himself: *Library of Congress Sesquicentennial Exhibit, April 24, 1950: Catalog of the Exhibit Commemorating the 150th Anniversary of Its Establishment* (Washington, DC: GPO, 1950), 9.

38. Jefferson habitually had larger volumes rebound: E. Millicent Sowerby, "Thomas Jefferson's Library," *Papers of the Bibliographical Society of America* 50 (1956): 213–28.

39. Gray and Ticknor made the February 1815 visit as young men, before Gray became a well-known politician and intellectual and Ticknor became an academician and author. Traveling from Boston to Washington, they obtained a letter of introduction from John Adams, who knew Gray through his son John Quincy Adams: Kevin J. Hayes, *The Road to Monticello: The Life and Times of Thomas Jefferson* (New York: Oxford University Press, 2008), 558–60; Francis Calley Gray, *Thomas Jefferson in 1814, Being an Account of a Visit to Monticello, Virginia*, with notes and introduction by Henry S. Rowe and Thomas Jefferson Coolidge Jr. (Boston: Club of Odd Volumes, 1924), 70, 73. Gray called the Americana collection "the most valuable in the world."

40. Douglas L. Wilson, *Jefferson's Books* (Charlottesville, VA, Thomas Jefferson Memorial Foundation, 1996), 22–23; Millicent Sowerby, "Some Presentation Copies in the Library of Thomas Jefferson," *QJLC* 8 (November 1950): 78–87; Frederick R. Goff, "T. I.: Mr. Jefferson's Books in Washington, DC," *RCHS*, 50th volume (1980): 82, 86. Frederick R. Goff, "Jefferson the Book Collector," *QJL C* 29 (January 1972): 32–47, stated that the library was worth much more.

41. 3 Stat 225; Congress moved a mile away to the Brick Capitol at the beginning of the 14th Congress (December 1815).

42. William Matheson, "George Watterston, Advocate of the National Library," in *Librarians*, 58; Johnston, *History*, 111–19.

43. Watterston's notice is in Library in the Capitol, box 51, LCA.

44. Jefferson to Smith, May 8, 1815, Founders Online, https://founders.archives.gov/documents/Jefferson/03-08-02-0378; Johnston, *History*, 97–104.

45. *National Intelligencer*, July 14, 1817.

46. Ostrowski, *Books, Maps*, 219.

47. Wilson, "Jefferson's Library," 170.

48. Jefferson to Watterston, May 7, 1815, Founders Online, https://founders.archives.gov/documents/Jefferson/03-08-02-0376.

49. Leo J. LaMontagne, *American Library Classification: With Special Reference to the Library of Congress* (New York: Shoe String Press, 1961), 27–43; Malone, *Sage of Monticello*, 182–84.

50. Jefferson to Adams, June 10, 1815, Founders Online, https://founders.archives.gov/documents/adams/99-02-92-6479; Wilson, "Jefferson's Library," 175–76, 179. Jefferson's later library, often called the "retirement library," contained about 940 titles when it was auctioned in 1829: Mark Dimunation, "'The Whole of Recorded Knowledge: Jefferson as Collector and Reader,'" in *The Libraries, Leadership & Legacy of John Adams and Thomas Jefferson*, edited by Robert C. Baron and Conrad Wright (Golden, CO: Fulcrum and Massachusetts Historical Society, 2010), 21–40. The LC purchased some items at the 1829 sale and added others as opportunities arose.

51. Jefferson to Watterston, March 2, 1816, George Watterston Papers, LC.

52. Quoted by James Gilreath and Douglas L. Wilson, eds., *Thomas Jefferson's Library: A Catalog with the Entries in His Own Order* (Washington, DC: LC, 1989), 4. This is a reproduction of the 1823 manuscript catalog prepared by Nicholas P. Trist, Jefferson's secretary and eventual grandson-in-law. Jefferson's 1815 handwritten catalog, taken by Watterston when he left the Library in 1829, has never been found.

53. *Catalogue of the Library of the United States* (Washington, DC: Jonathan Elliot, 1815). Supplements to the 1815 *Catalogue* (1820, 1825, 1827, 1828) and all further catalogs called it the Library of Congress. In their criticism, congressmen ignored the 1808 catalog's classified arrangement: LaMontagne, *American Library Classification*, 47.

54. Senate Report 26, 14th Congress, 1st Sess., January 26, 1816.

55. Watterston to Jefferson, January 29, 1816, quoted by Johnston, *History*, 149.

56. Senate Report 26, 14th Congress, 1st Sess., January 26, 1816; *ASP Miscellaneous Series* 2: 279–80; Ostrowski, *Books, Maps*, 85; Johnston, *History*, 150–55.

57. Stat 283. The salary was raised again from $1,000 to $1,500 in 1818: 3 Stat 431.

58. Senate Report 34, 14th Congress, 2nd Sess., January 6, 1817.

59. Johnston, *History*, 156–58.

60. *AC* 30: 131, 144. The Library remained inconveniently located away from the Brick Capitol.

61. 3 Stat 477; Johnston, *History*, 124–25; *National Intelligencer*, March 25, 1817; Mearns, *Story*, 30; Salamanca, *Fortress of Freedom*, 119–21.

62. Elmer D. Johnson, *History of Libraries in the Western World* (Metuchen, NJ: Scarecrow Press, 1970), 166.

63. 3 Stat 477; 3 Stat 555, at 556; 4 Stat 60; Johnston, History, 125–27.

64. Jefferson to Watterston, September 1, 1820, Founders Online, https://founders.archives.gov/documents/Jefferson/03-16-02-0188; Johnston, *History*, 159.

65. *AC* 39: 1742–43.

66. Samuel Eliot Morison, *Harrison Gray Otis, 1765–1848: The Urbane Federalist* (Boston: Houghton Mifflin, 1969), 416; Allgor, *Parlor Politics*, 104, 212–13.

67. Quoted by Allgor, *Perfect Union*, 176.

68. Mearns, *Story*, 20.

69. John Y. Cole, *Jefferson's Legacy: A Brief History of the Library of Congress* (Washington, DC: LC, 1993), 14.

70. Johnston, *History*, 158–60.

Chapter 3

1. Frances Wright, *Views of Society and Manners in America*, edited by Paul R. Baker (Cambridge, MA: Belknap Press of Harvard University Press, 1963), 265.

2. Johnston, *History*, 127–28, 223–24.

3. Mearns, *Story*, 30; William Matheson, "George Watterston, Advocate of the National Library," in *Librarians*, 57–65, was skeptical of Anne Royall's favorable description of Watterston in her 1826 *Sketches of History, Life, and Manners, in the United States* (New York: Johnson Reprint Corp., 1970), 151.

4. George Watterston, *A Wanderer in Washington* (Washington, DC: Washington Press, 1827); *The L... Family at Washington, or, a Winter in the Metropolis* (Washington, DC: Davis and Force, 1822), 35, 37. Watterston was the first writer to set a novel in Washington.

5. *National Intelligencer*, August 28, 1823, quoted by Carl Ostrowski, *Books, Maps, and Politics: A Cultural History of the Library of Congress, 1783–1861* (Amherst: University of Massachusetts Press, 2004), 97.

6. *National Intelligencer*, January 1, 1825; *National Journal*, April 12, 1827.

7. Frances Milton Trollope, *Domestic Manners of the Americans* (London: Printed for Whittaker, Treacher & Co., 1832), 1: 326.

8. Mearns, *Story*, 32.

9. Watterston, *Wanderer*, 218.

10. Helen Nicolay, *Our Capital on the Potomac* (New York: Century Co., 1924), 166–68; William Dawson Johnston, "Early History of the Washington Library Company and Other Local Libraries," *RCHS* 7 (1903–4): 20–38; Gordon S. Brown, *Incidental Architect: William Thornton and the Cultural Life of Early Washington, DC, 1794–1928* (Athens: Ohio University Press for US Capitol Historical Society, 2009), 103. Ostrowski, *Books, Maps*, 133–39, stated that in the 1830s complaints about women using the Library for socializing and skimming picture books increased, reflecting a desire to limit women's "participation in the political realm."

11. House of Representatives Report 69, 18th Congress, 1st Sess.; Johnston, *History*, 160–63; 3 Stat 60; 3 Stat 82.

12. Mearns, *Story*, 34; Johnston, *History*, 215–23.

13. *ARLC*, 1931, 389–90.

14. Mearns, *Story*, 34–35; Johnston, *History*, 132–34, includes Everett's account and that of the *National Intelligencer*, December 24, 1825.

15. Watterston to Edward Everett, January 2, 9, 1826, Watterston Papers, LC.

16. Johnston, *History*, 135–38; House Report 66, 19th Congress, 1st Sess., February 6, 1826, in "Documentary History of the Construction and Development of the United States Capitol Building and Grounds" (GPO, 1904), 270–71.

17. *ARLC*, 1931, 390; Ostrowski, *Books, Maps*, 89, refers to Everett's probable knowledge of Harvard president John T. Kirkland's *North American Review* article (December 1818) on

the need to support scholarly research. Everett later supported establishing the Boston Public Library, the first municipally funded free public library in the United States.

18. Mary B. Ellis, "The Hale Family Papers," *QJLC* 12 (May 1955): 110. As Ambassador to Great Britain, 1841–45, Everett continued to purchase materials for the Library.

19. 3 Stat 628; Johnston, *History*, 165–66.

20. Lucy Salamanca, *Fortress of Freedom: The Story of the Library of Congress* (Philadelphia: J. B. Lippincott, 1942), 143–49; Watterston to William Czar Bradley, July 8, 1826; Watterston to Everett, December 13, 1826, February 3, 1827, February 22, 1827, March 5, 1828, May 23, 1828, Watterston Papers, LC; Matheson, "George Watterston," 70–72; Ostrowski, *Books, Maps*, 90–91; *ARLC*, 1950, 66.

21. Watterston to Bradley, July 8, 1826, Watterston Papers, LC.

22. Frederick Marryat, *A Diary in America*, edited by Jules Zanger (Bloomington: Indiana University Press, 1960), 191.

23. Everett apologized to Watterston for the oversight but admitted it was probably intentional: Everett to Watterston, July 19, 1828, Watterston Papers, LC; 4 Stat 226; 4 Stat 301.

24. Jackson offered to appoint Charles P. Tutt, who instead preferred the position of US Navy agent at Pensacola: John Y. Cole, "LC in the 19th Century: An Informal Account," *JLH* 9 (1974): 225. Jackson replaced around 10 percent of federal officeholders during the first eighteen months of his term, more than any president since Jefferson: Leonard D. White, *The Jacksonians: A Study in Administrative History, 1829–1861* (New York: Macmillan, 1963), 307–9; Jon Meacham, *American Lion: Andrew Jackson in the White House* (New York: Random House, 2009), 60–61, 82–83, 120–21.

25. *United States' Telegraph*, June 12, 1829; *National Journal*, June 9, June 15, 1829; Ostrowski, *Books, Maps*, 109. Johnston, *History*, 190–99, attributes the *Journal's* statements to Watterston himself.

26. Gales & Seaton's *Register of Debates*, 6: 393; Johnston, *History*, 199–201.

27. Henry Clay to Watterston, July 21, 1829, Watterston Papers, LC.

28. *Washington City Chronicle*, July 11, 1829.

29. Matheson, "George Watterston," 71.

30. James D. Richardson, *A Compilation of the Messages and Papers of the Presidents, 1789–1897* (Washington, DC: GPO, 1896), 2: 449.

31. Johnston, *History*, 178, 201–9; Nancy E. Gwinn, "George Watterston," *DALB*, 543–46. After Watterston died in 1854, the Library's records were returned, but not the catalog.

32. 4 Stat 321; Johnston, *History*, 174–75.

33. John McDonough, "John Silva Meehan," in *Librarians*, 83–84.

34. 4 Stat 429.

35. Ostrowski, *Books, Maps*, 110–13; Johnston, *History*, 225–26, 376; John Y. Cole, *America's Greatest Library: An Illustrated History of the Library of Congress* (Washington, DC: LC, in association with D. Giles Limited, London, 2017), 24.

36. Meehan to Edward Everett, November 7, 1832, John Silva Meehan Papers, Manuscript Division, LC.

37. Additional staff was provided in appropriations for 1831, 1841, and 1856: 4 Stat 452, at 453; 5 Stat 421, at 430; 10 Stat 643, at 645.

38. McDonough, "John Silva Meehan," 82; Johnston, *History*, 354–55; Dan Lacy, "The Library of Congress: A Sesquicentenary Review II: The Organization of the Collections," *LQ* 20 (October 1950): 235.

39. 5 Stat 648.

40. 4 Stat 579; Johnston, *History*, 248–51; Ostrowski, *Books, Maps*, 117; *LCIB* 31 (July 28, 1972): 336; *Law Library, 1832–1982* (Washington, DC: LC, 1982).

41. The LC requested an appropriation for books for the Court until 1962; after that, the appropriation was moved to the judicial branch bill: *LCIB* 44 (January 7, 1985): 3–4.

42. 5 Stat 163, at 175; catalogs appeared in 1839, 1849, and 1860: Johnston, *History*, 251.

43. McDonough, "John Silva Meehan," 82–83; Mearns, *Story*, 40–41. Mearns cited borrowing privileges as "a timid step, perhaps, indeed, a step taken in the dark, toward national functions."

44. *National Intelligencer*, January 8, 1834; December 5, 1834.

45. Lewis Cass, *A Discourse Pronounced . . . before the American Historical Society, January 30, 1836* (Washington, DC: P. Thompson, 1836), 17.

46. Senate Report 242, 24th Congress, 1st Sess., March 15, 1836.

47. John Y. Cole, *For Congress and the Nation: A Chronological History of the Library of Congress* (Washington, DC: LC, 1979), 16–17; *North American Review* 45 (1837): 146–47; Charles Bowen, "Public Libraries," in *The American Almanac and Repository of Useful Knowledge for the Year 1837* (Boston: Charles Bowen, 1836), 82; Mearns, *Story*, 43–49.

48. Johnston, *History*, 209, attributed Clay's motion to bitterness over Watterston's dismissal.

49. Mearns, *Story*, 49.

50. Cole, *For Congress*, 18; David Lowenthal, *George Perkins Marsh, Prophet of Conservation* (Seattle: University of Washington Press, 2000), 79; Johnston, *History*, 243–45.

51. 4 Stat 743; 5 Stat 409; Senate Doc. 521, 26th Congress, 1st Sess., 1840; Robert D. Stevens, *The Role of the Library of Congress in the International Exchange of Official Publications: A Brief History* (Washington, DC: LC, 1953), 2–4; Johnston, *History*, 253–54.

52. 9 Stat 240.

53. The French government refused to support Vattemare's program, informing Meehan that it preferred to exchange through diplomatic channels: McDonough, "John Silva Meehan," 94–95; Nancy E. Gwinn, "The Library of Congress, the Smithsonian Institution, and the Global Exchange of Government Documents, 1834–1889," in *The Library of Congress and the Center for the Book: Historical Essays in Honor of John Y. Cole*, edited by Mary Niles Maack (Washington, DC: LC, in association with University of Texas Press, 2011), 139–54.

54. House Report 590, 30th Congress, 1st Sess.; 10 Stat 76, at 77; Johnston, *History*, 254–65; Stevens, *Role*, 5–9.

55. *CG*, February 15, 1839, 185; Senate Report 16, 26th Congress, 1st Sess., *Report of the Librarian of Congress Transmitting . . . a Catalogue of All the Laws and of All the Legislative and Executive Journals and Documents of the Several States and Territories Now in the Library* (Washington, DC: Blair & Rives, 1839); Johnston, *History*, 251–53.

56. Quoted by Cole, *For Congress*, 17.

57. Ostrowski, *Books, Maps*, 121–24, 133–39, 219.

58. Congress had accepted James Smithson's 1829 bequest to establish the Smithsonian Institution in 1836.

59. An amendment passed April 29, 1802, added designs, engravings, and etchings; an act of February 3, 1831 (4 Stat 436), added musical compositions and changed the procedure: district court clerks would receive the deposits and forward them to the Secretary of State. In Wheaton v. Peters (1834), the Supreme Court ruled that deposit was essential to validate copyright.

60. 9 Stat 102, at 106.

61. Ray W. Frantz Jr., "A Reexamination of the Influence of Literary Nationalism on the Public Library," *JLH* 1 (July 1966): 182–86.

62. John Y. Cole, "Of Copyright, Men, & a National Library,'" *QJLC* 28 (1971): 114–36.

63. Carl Ostrowski, "James Alfred Pearce and the Question of a National Library in Antebellum America," *L&C* 35 (Spring 2000): 257; John McDonough, "John Silva Meehan," *DALB*, 356.

64. E.g., when Henry Clay proposed in 1850 to purchase the manuscript of George Washington's Farewell Address, Pearce objected that it was "valuable merely as [a] relic[s]," *CG*, January 28, 1850, 227; Benjamin Perley Poore, *Reminiscences of Sixty Years in the National Metropolis* (Philadelphia: Hubbard Brothers, 1886), 176–77; Johnston, *History*, 268–69, 327–40, 374–75. Congress approved the purchase, but the manuscript was sold at auction that same day.

65. Johnston, *History*, 380; Ostrowski, "James Alfred Pearce," 258; John Y. Cole., ed., *The Library of Congress in Perspective: A Volume Based on the Reports of the 1976 Librarian's Task Force and Advisory Groups* (New York: R. R. Bowker, 1978), 10.

66. McDonough, "John Silva Meehan," 85; *CG*, January 9, 1845, 116; William J. Rhees, ed., *The Smithsonian Institution: Documents Relative to Its Origin and History* (Washington, DC: Smithsonian Institution, 1879), 144–45, 160–61; *Mr. Robbins's Speech on the Subject of an Institution to Be Founded on the Smithsonian Legacy Delivered in the Senate of the United States on the 10th January AD 1839* (Washington, DC: Gales and Seaton, 1839).

67. Ostrowski, *Books, Maps*, 151.

68. Rhees, *Smithsonian*, 419, 268, 313–18; *CG*, January 8, 1845, 105–6.

69. Rhees, *Smithsonian*, 292. Marsh's April 23, 1846, House speech, quoted by Johnston, *History*, 270–71, admitted, "there is no one branch of liberal study, even among those of greatest interest to ourselves, in which it is not miserably deficient."

70. Rhees, *Smithsonian*, 374–77, 415–19; *CG*, January 9, 1845, 115–17; David Lowenthal, *George Perkins Marsh: Versatile Vermonter* (New York: Columbia University Press, 1958), 81–85; William J. Cooper, *The Lost Founding Father: John Quincy Adams and the Transformation of American Politics* (New York: Liveright, 2018), 349–51. Jean V. Matthews, "Libraries, Books, and the Nature of America: The Creation of the Smithsonian Institution," *JLH* 16 (Winter 1981): 152–65.

71. 9 Stat 102; Cyrus Adler, "The Smithsonian Library," in *The Smithsonian Institution, 1846–1896: The History of Its First Half Century*, edited by George Brown Goode (New York: Arno Press, 1970), 270.

72. "Sixth Annual Report of the Board of Regents of the Smithsonian Institution . . . 1851," 32nd Congress, 1st Sess., Senate Misc. Document 108 (1852), 22; Michael H. Harris, ed., *The Age of Jewett: Charles Coffin Jewett and American Librarianship, 1841–1868* (Littleton, CO: Libraries Unlimited, 1975), 25; Gwinn, "Library of Congress," 111–13.

73. Joseph A. Borome, *Charles Coffin Jewett* (Chicago: ALA, 1951), 28–29; Harris, *Age of Jewett*, 25–26. In connection with his plan, Jewett conducted a survey of American libraries: William J. Rhees, *Manual of Public Libraries, Institutions, and Societies in the United States and British Provinces of North America* (Philadelphia: J. B. Lippincott, 1859). He also developed cataloging rules to standardize the entries: Michael H. Harris, "Charles Coffin Jewett," *DALB*, 272–73.

74. *North American Review* 71 (July 1850): 220; *Norton's Literary Gazette* II (February 15, 1852), 23.

75. "Fourth Annual Report of the Board of Regents of the Smithsonian Institution . . . 1849," 31st Congress, 1st Sess., Senate Misc. Document 120 (1850), 35.

76. *Norton's Literary Gazette*, 3: 175; George Burwell Utley, *The Librarians' Conference of 1853: A Chapter in American Library History*, edited by Gilbert H. Doane (Chicago: ALA, 1951). During the last half of the century, private circulating and mercantile libraries dwindled as tax-supported public libraries were built; state libraries were established; historical society

libraries grew; and John Jacob Astor, James Lenox, and George Peabody provided funding for major libraries in New York City and Baltimore.

77. Borome, *Charles Coffin Jewett*, 97–98; Charles Coffin Jewett, "The Smithsonian Institution and Its Plan of Cataloging," in *Age of Jewett*, ed. Harris, 120–30; Utley, *Librarians' Conference*, 69–73; Johnston, *History*, 358–64,455–67.

78. Meehan to Pearce, April 2, 1855, Librarian's Letterbooks, LCA.

79. Borome, *Charles Coffin Jewett*, 75–90.

80. Johnston, *History*, 487–504.

81. Rufus Choate, *The Works of Rufus Choate, with a Memoir of His Life*, edited by Samuel Gilman Brown (New York: AMS Press, 1973), 102–8; "Tenth Annual Report of the Board of Regents of the Smithsonian Institution . . . 1855," Senate Misc. Document 54, 34th Congress, 3rd Sess. (1857), 83–86; Borome, *Charles Coffin Jewett*, 94.

82. Ostrowski, *Books, Maps*, 160–64; the Jewett quotation is from the "Fourth Annual Report of the Board of Regents . . .1849" (1850), 35. See also Bernard Steiner, "James Alfred Pearce," *Maryland Historical Magazine* 17 (September 1922): 269–83; 18 (March 1923): 38–52; Ostrowski, "James Alfred Pearce," 266–72; Poore, *Reminiscences*, 176–77.

83. Constance McLaughlin Green, *Washington: A History of the Capital, 1800–1950* (Princeton, NJ: Princeton University Press, 1962), 1: 178–99.

84. Ostrowski, *Books, Maps*, 164–67; the Marsh quotation is from Richard D. Brown, *Knowledge Is Power: The Diffusion of Information in Early America, 1700–1865* (New York: Oxford University Press, 1989), 243–44; Ostrowski, "James Alfred Pearce," 268–71. Ben Perley Poore recalled hearing that Pearce refused in 1857 to subscribe to *The Atlantic Monthly,* considering it too radical: *Reminiscences*, 176–77. On congressional antagonisms, see Joanne B. Freeman, *The Field of Blood: Violence in Congress and the Road to Civil War* (New York: Farrar, Straus & Giroux, 2018); and Chris M. Asch and George D. Musgrove, *Chocolate City: A History of Race and Democracy in the Nation's Capital* (Chapel Hill: University of North Carolina Press, 2017), 99–105.

85. *Norton's Literary Gazette* 2 (February 15, 1855): 67; Borome, *Charles Coffin Jewett*, 94.

86. Ostrowski, *Books, Maps*, 167–70.

87. Mearns, *Story*, 57–58; Johnston, *History*, 183–86, 310–26; Charles C. Jewett, *Notices of Public Libraries in the United States* (Washington, DC: Printed for the House of Representatives, 1851), 192.

88. *Washington Republic*, December 27, 1851.

89. *National Intelligencer*, December 25, 1851.

90. Diary, December 24, 1851, 292, Meehan Papers, LC; Mearns, *Story*, 63–65, lists the losses.

91. *CG*, December 26, 1851, 153–54; McDonough, "John Silva Meehan," 87; E. Millicent Sowerby, "Catalogue of the Library of Thomas Jefferson," LC, 1952–59, 1: vii; *Washington Republic*, December 27, 1851; Mearns, *Story*, 60–62; Johnston, *History*, 275–84.

92. Benjamin Brown French, *Witness to the Young Republic: A Yankee's Journal, 1828–1870* (Hanover, NH: University Press of New England, 1989), 224–25. Meehan cited a House messenger's report that a flawed chimney flue caused the fire: Diary, December 25, 1851, 293, Meehan Papers, LC.

93. Quoted in Meehan's Diary, January 2, 1852, 304, Meehan Papers, LC.

94. 10 Stat 1; McDonough, "John Silva Meehan," 90; Diary, January 24, 1852, 326–27, Meehan Papers, LC.

95. Senate Report 63, 32nd Congress, 1st Sess. Walter reported in December that the estimate was too low and requested a deficiency appropriation of $20,500: House of Representatives, Executive Doc. 18, 32nd Congress, 2nd Sess.

96. 10 Stat 3.

97. 10 Stat 76, at 77; "Documentary History of the Construction," 341–52.

98. *National Intelligencer*, April 8 and 14, 1852. Johnston, *History*, 302, speculated that Jewett was the author.

99. Johnston, *History*, 301–10; Mearns, *Story*, 64; Ostrowski, *Books, Maps*, 170–73; Ostrowski, "James Alfred Pearce," 258–61; Poore, *Reminiscences*, 386.

100. Diary, July 21, August 6, August 7, August 31, September 28, October 27, 1852, Meehan Papers, LC; Cole, *For Congress*, 24; McDonough, "John Silva Meehan," 89; Johnston, *History*, 298–99.

101. Ostrowski, *Books, Maps*, 205.

102. Quoted by William C. Allen, *History of the United States Capitol: A Chronology of Design, Construction, and Politics* (Washington, DC: GPO, 2001), 222.

103. Johnston, *History*, 351; Cole, *For Congress*, 26.

104. 11 Stat 253.

105. Cole, *For Congress*, 26; 11 Stat 379, at 380; Cole, "Of Copyright," 121.

106. Johnston, *History*, 311–47.

107. *ARLC*, 1931, 391–92.

108. McDonough, "John Silva Meehan," 93–94.

109. McDonough, 97–98.

110. Johnston, *History*, 227. Frederick W. Ashley called the years 1800–1864 a period lacking "continuity of purpose": Ashley, "Three Eras in the Library of Congress," in *Essays*, 58–60. Dan Lacy called it a time of "mediocre direction and planless buying": Dan Lacy, "The Library of Congress: A Sesquicentenary Review. I. The Development of the Collections," *LQ* 20 (July 1950): 157.

111. Robert F. Dalzell Jr., *Daniel Webster and the Trial of American Nationalism, 1843–1852* (Boston: Houghton Mifflin, 1973), 99.

112. 5 Stat 534; 9 Stat 284. The Wilkes expedition circumnavigated the globe from 1838 to 1842, mapping unknown waters and acquiring a specimen collection deposited in the Smithsonian. The expedition's books, manuscripts, and maps were included in the Smithsonian Deposit later transferred to the LC, inaugurating Indonesian and Malaysia collections: LC, *Library of Congress Asian Collections, An Illustrated Guide* (Washington, DC: LC, 2000), 50–51. In *Two Centuries of Federal Information* (Stroudsberg, PA: Dowden, Hutchinson & Ross, 1978), 13, Burton W. Adkinson cited the Wilkes publication as a precedent for the LC's later publications program.

113. Johnston, *History*, 247; 10 Stat 546, at 572; 10 Stat 643, at 645.

Chapter 4

1. Constance Carter, "John Gould Stephenson: Largely Known and Much Liked," in *Librarians*, 106–7.

2. William Pitt Fessenden Papers, LC, reel 1.

3. Carter, "John Gould Stephenson," 108–9.

4. *ARLC*, January 7, 1863.

5. Carter, "John Gould Stephenson, 109–10; Richard G. Wood, "Librarian-in-Arms: The Career of John G. Stephenson," *LQ* 19 (October 1949): 266–67; Senate Misc. Document 8, 37th Congress, 2nd Sess., 3–4.

6. Henry B. Blackwell, "Dr. Spofford in Cincinnati, 1845–1860," in *Ainsworth Rand Spofford, 1825–1908: A Memorial Meeting at the Library of Congress* (New York: Printed for DCLA by Webster Press, 1909), 16–20; John Y. Cole, "Ainsworth Rand Spofford," *DALB*, 499–501.

7. Spofford to Sarah Spofford, August 5, 1861, Ainsworth Rand Spofford Papers, LC.

8. Spofford to Henry B. Blackwell, May 2, 1862, National American Woman Suffrage Association Records, LC.

9. Quoted by John Y. Cole, "Ainsworth Rand Spofford: The Valiant and Persistent Librarian of Congress," in *Librarians*, 138.

10. John Y. Cole, "Ainsworth Spofford and the 'National Library'" (PhD diss., George Washington University, 1971), 72; Ralph Waldo Emerson, *Journals*, edited by Edward Waldo Emerson and Waldo Emerson Forbes (Boston: Houghton, Mifflin, 1913), 9: 395–96.

11. John Y. Cole, ed., *Ainsworth Rand Spofford: Bookman and Librarian* (Littleton, CO: Libraries Unlimited, 1975), 27–29; this also includes "The First Annual Report (1861)," 55–63.

12. *Indianapolis Journal*, November 28, 1863, quoted by Carter, "John Gould Stephenson," 112.

13. *ARLC*, 1931, 392–93; David C. Mearns, "Mr. Lincoln and the Books He Read," in *Three Presidents and Their Books*, edited by Arthur Bestor, David C. Mearns, and Jonathan W. Daniels (Urbana: University of Illinois Press, 1955), 45–88, found more than 125 loans "to Lincoln's account."

14. Cole, "Ainsworth Spofford," 69; Carter, "John Gould Stephenson, 112–15; John Y. Cole, "John Gould Stephenson," *DALB*, 506–8. William Dawson Johnston, "Dr. Spofford and the Library of Congress, 1861–1897," in *Ainsworth Rand Spofford: A Memorial Meeting*, 383, wrote that Stephenson resigned due to "speculations created by the war," citing a June 8, 1872, congressional reference to paying the Library's London agent $1,480 that Stephenson failed to remit in 1862. It is not clear, Cole stated, whether the deficiency was due to speculation or to problems with payments.

15. Cole, "Valiant and Persistent," 131–32; *LCIB* 55 (February 19, 1996): 52.

16. Cole, "Valiant and Persistent," 119. See also Johnston, "Dr. Spofford," 23–24; David C. Mearns, "Ainsworth the Unforgettable," *QJLC* 25 (January 1968): 2–3; Herbert Putnam, "Introductory Remarks," in *Ainsworth Rand Spofford: A Memorial Meeting at the Library of Congress, November 12, 1908, at Four O'clock, the Librarian of Congress Presiding* (New York: Webster Press for District of Columbia Library Association, 1909), 7–15. Frederick Ashley, however, described Spofford as "primarily a collector of books": Frederick W. Ashley, "Three Eras in the Library of Congress," in *Essays*, 60–62.

17. Carl Ostrowski, "'The Choice of Books': Ainsworth Rand Spofford, the Ideology of Reading, and Literary Collections at the Library of Congress in the 1870s," in *The Library of Congress and the Center for the Book: Historical Essays in Honor of John Y. Cole*, edited by Mary Niles Maack (Washington, DC: LC, in association with University of Texas Press, 2011), 102–16.

18. Ainsworth Rand Spofford, *Book for All Readers* (New York: G. P. Putnam's Sons, 1900), 259–60.

19. Mearns, *Story*, 77.

20. John Y. Cole, "The Library of Congress in the Nineteenth Century: An Informal Account," *JLH* 9 (1974): 227–28; Mearns, "Ainsworth the Unforgettable," 2–3.

21. Cole, "Valiant and Persistent," 131–32; *LCIB*, September 21–27, 1948, 9–10.

22. Cole, "Valiant and Persistent," 129.

23. A. R. Spofford, "The Library of Congress, or National Library," in *Public Libraries in the United States of America, Their History, Condition and Management* (Washington, DC: GPO, 1876), 254–62; Cole, "Ainsworth Spofford," 3, 5; Spofford, "The Function of a National Library," 103–9, in *Ainsworth Rand Spofford*, ed. Cole.

24. Dan Lacy, "The Library of Congress: A Sesquicentenary Review, I: The Development of the Collections," *LQ* 20 (July 1950): 158.

25. Spofford to Blackwell, May 2, 1862; Carter, "John Gould Stephenson," 110. Mearns, *Story*, 71, attributed the 1861 report to one of the Assistant Librarians; Cole identified both the 1861 and 1863 reports as written by Spofford: Cole, "Valiant and Persistent," 129; *LCIB* 59 (October 2000): 238.

26. *ARLC*, 1863; Cole, "Valiant and Persistent," 130–31.

27. *Alphabetical Catalogue of the Library of Congress: Authors* (GPO, 1864), 3–4. Spofford published annual supplements until 1876: *ARLC*, 1869, 2–3; 1875, 5; Dan Lacy, "The Library of Congress: A Sesquicentenary Review II: The Organization of the Collections," *LQ* 20 (October 1950): 236.

28. Spofford to Fessenden, October 22, 1864, Librarian's Letterbooks, LCA; Cole, "Ainsworth Spofford," 87–92.

29. 13 Stat 445, at 448; *ARLC*, 1866,1–2; "Documentary History of the Construction and Development of the United States Capitol Building and Grounds" (GPO, 1904), 362–68.

30. Spofford, *Book for All Readers*, 404; Spofford, "The Copyright System of the United States—Its Origin and Its Growth," in *Proceedings and Addresses: Celebration of the Beginning of the Second Century of the American Patent System* (Washington, DC: Press of Gedney and Roberts, 1892), 145–60; 13 Stat 540; 14 Stat 395.

31. Cole, "Ainsworth Spofford," 96–102; *CG*, February 22, 1865, 981. Ashley, "Three Eras," 60–61, cites the acts that trebled the space and established copyright deposit as beginning the second era in the LC's history.

32. "Annual Report of the Board of Regents of the Smithsonian Institution . . . 1864" (GPO, 1865), 58–59; "Annual Report . . . 1865" (GPO, 1866), 70, 116–20; Heather Ewing, *The Lost World of James Smithson: Science, Revolution, and the Birth of the Smithsonian* (New York: Bloomsbury USA, 2007), 332.

33. Smithsonian exchanges then included its "Contributions to Knowledge" (begun 1848), the "Reports" (begun 1850), and the "Miscellaneous Contributions" (begun 1862): Robert D. Stevens, *The Role of the Library of Congress in the International Exchange of Official Publications: A Brief History* (Washington, DC: LC, 1953), 10–11; Nancy E. Gwinn, "The Library of Congress and the Smithsonian Institution: A Legislated Relationship," *Encyclopedia*, 94–95.

34. *ARLC*, 1866, 3; Ainsworth Rand Spofford, "Relations between the Smithsonian Institution and the Library of Congress," in *The Smithsonian Institution, 1846–1896: The History of Its First Half Century*, edited by George Brown Goode (New York: Arno Press, 1970), 823–30.

35. 14 Stat 13 also authorized hiring two assistants. In the mid-1880s, Spofford began loaning books to DC citizens who provided a security deposit, but ceased the loans in 1894 to prepare for moving into the new building: John Y. Cole and Jane Aikin, "America's Library: A Brief History of the Library of Congress," *Encyclopedia*, 6; Mearns, *Story*, 102; Senate Misc. Document 6, 38th Congress, 2nd Sess., December 20, 1866; Cole, "Ainsworth Spofford," 94–95, 103–9; John Y. Cole, ed., *The Library of Congress in Perspective: A Volume Based on the Reports of the 1976 Librarian's Task Force and Advisory Groups* (New York: R. R. Bowker, 1978), 12; John Y. Cole, *Jefferson's Legacy: A Brief History of the Library of Congress* (Washington, DC: LC, 1993), 23. The Smithsonian did develop its own library, leading to occasional disputes over collecting policies: Cyrus Adler, "The Smithsonian Library," in *The Smithsonian Institution, 1846–1896: The History of Its First Half Century*, edited by George Brown Goode (New York: Arno Press, 1970), 203; Gwinn, "Library of Congress," 95–102.

36. 14 Stat 573; 15 Stat 260; *ARLC*, 1867, 5.

37. *ARLC*, 1867, 5; 1885, 6–7; 1887, 5–6; John Y. Cole, *For Congress and the Nation: A Chronological History of the Library of Congress* (Washington, DC: LC, 1979), 33, 36; Mearns, *Story*, 104–6; Stevens, *Role*, 12–14. The Brussels Conventions (1886; effective 1889) named the

Smithsonian as the US agent on behalf of the LC; this responsibility was shifted to the GPO in December 1977: Cole, *For Congress*, 44; Stevens, *Role*, 14–16; Edmond L. Applebaum, "Foreign Acquisitions Programs of the Library of Congress," in *Acquisition of Foreign Materials for US Libraries*, 2nd ed., edited by Theodore Samore (Metuchen, NJ: Scarecrow Press, 1982), 17.

38. Ainsworth Rand Spofford, "The Life and Labors of Peter Force, Mayor of Washington," *RCHS* 2 (1899): 219–34; 14 Stat 457, at 464.

39. Cole, "Ainsworth Spofford," 118–21; Frederick R. Goff, "Peter Force," *Papers of the Bibliographical Society of America* 44 (1950): 1–16.

40. Quoted by Cole, "Ainsworth Spofford," 122.

41. A. R. Spofford, *Special Report of the Librarian of Congress to the Joint Committee on the Library Concerning the Historical Library of Peter Force* (Washington, DC: LC, 1867), 4, 8; Cole, *Ainsworth Rand Spofford*, 64–69.

42. Frederick R. Goff, "The Oldest Library in Washington: The Rare Book Division of the Library of Congress," *RCHS*, 1969–70: 334–38.

43. Lacy, "Sesquicentenary Review: I," 159, cited the copyright, exchange, and Force Library acquisition as the congressional actions that "established the fate of its library." Force's papers and correspondence were acquired later: *ARLC*, 1915, 73–74.

44. *ARLC*, 1875, 6; Mearns, *Story*, 109–11; Neil Harris, "Public Funding for Rarity: Some Debates," *L&C* 31 (Winter 1996): 36–55.

45. *ARLC*, 1867, 2–3; 1869, 3–4; 1874, 8. With the Joint Committee's consent, Spofford did bar children under sixteen and closed access to the shelves. The committee rejected his request for lighting, but an 1888 statute specified that the Law Library be open daily during sessions; 25 Stat 256, at 262.

46. *ARLC*, 1866, 5; 1868, 4; Cole, "Ainsworth Spofford," 131–32; Joint Committee on the Library, *Condition of the Library of Congress*, 54th Congress, 2nd Sess., 1896–97, Senate Report 1573 (Washington, DC: GPO, 1897), 99–100.

47. Spofford to Jenckes, April 9, 1870, Thomas A. Jenckes Papers, LC; Cole, "Ainsworth Spofford," 132–35; *CG*, April 14, 1870, 2683–84; 16 Stat 198, at 212–13; John Y. Cole, "Ainsworth Spofford and the Copyright Law of 1870," *JLH* 6 (1971): 34–40. After Jenckes spoke, Representative John A. Peters (R-ME) moved to raise Spofford's salary from $2,500 to $4,000, citing the increased responsibility: Mearns, *Story*, 94–96.

48. Cole, "Ainsworth Spofford," 135–36; Ainsworth Rand Spofford, "The Library of the United States," *Forum* 14 (1892): 373; John Y. Cole, "Of Copyright, Men, & a National Library,'" *QJLC* 28 (1971): 129; Mearns, *Story*, 92. At Spofford's request, the law was amended in 1874 to shift recording of labels and prints on manufactured items to the Patent Office: 18 Stat 78, at 79; *ARLC*, 1872, 4–5; 1873, 4.

49. *ARLC*, 1870, 4; 1871, 4–6; 1872, 6–11; Cole, "Ainsworth Spofford," 137–41.

50. *ARLC*, 1871, 5; 1875, 10.

51. *ARLC*, 1872, 6; 1874, 7.

52. The Continental Publishing Company of New York published McCabe's book in 1873 under the pseudonym Edwin Winslow Martin. Chapter 19 describes the Library.

53. John Y. Cole, "LC and ALA," *LJ* 98 (October 15, 1973): 2965–70; *LJ* 1: 171. ALA members also proposed at various times that the Library distribute public documents, offer interlibrary loan, and establish a separate copyright department: Jane A. Rosenberg, "Foundation for Service: The 1896 Hearings on the Library of Congress," *JLH* 21 (Winter 1986): 111–12.

54. Cole, *For Congress*, 35, 41; Senate Report 187, 47th Congress, 1st Sess.; 22 Stat 302, at 329, 338; 22 Stat 603, at 632; Senate Misc. Document 84, 48th Congress, 1st Sess.

55. Cole, *For Congress*, 42.

56. Cole, "Valiant and Persistent," 134.

57. Senate Report 578, 47th Congress, 1st Sess.; 22 Stat 382.

58. *ARLC*, 1882, 6.

59. "House Committee on Appropriations, Sundry Civil Appropriations Bill," report to accompany HR 4729, 43rd Congress, 2nd Sess., House Report 149 (GPO, 1875), 24.

60. Quoted in *LCIB*, April 15–21, 1947, 10.

61. Frank G. Carpenter, "Uncle Sam's Book-Case," *Cosmopolitan* 3 (April 1887): 114–17.

62. Quoted by Ron Chernow, *Grant* (New York: Penguin Press, 2017), 645.

63. Constance McLaughlin Green, *Washington: A History of the Capital, 1800–1950* (Princeton, NJ: Princeton University Press, 1962), 2: 92–100; Alan Lessoff, "Washington under Federal Rule, 1871–1945," in *Berlin–Washington, 1800–2000*, edited by Andreas Daum and Christof Mauch (Washington, DC: German Historical Institute and Cambridge University Press, 2005), 246; Kathryn Allamong Jacob, *Capital Elites: High Society in Washington, DC after the Civil War* (Washington, DC: Smithsonian Institution Press, 1995), 164–65. Grant declared moving the federal government from Washington would be unconstitutional, which ended the threats of removal: Kenneth R. Bowling, "From 'Federal Town' to 'National Capital': Ulysses S. Grant and the Reconstruction of Washington, DC," *Washington History* 14, no. 1 (Spring–Summer 2002): 16; Kenneth R. Bowling, "The Compromise of 1790 and the Attempt to Remove the Seat of Federal Government from the Potomac River," in *America under Fire: Mr. Madison's War & the Burning of Washington* (Washington, DC: David M. Rubenstein National Center for White House History, 2014), 13–21; 41 Stat 419.

64. Alan Lessoff, "Gilded Age Washington: Promotional Capital of the Nation, in *Washington DC: Interdisciplinary Approach*, edited by Lothar Hönnighausen and Andreas Falke (Tübingen: A. Francke Verlag, 1992), 35–49; Morton Keller, *Affairs of State: Public Life in Late Nineteenth Century America* (Cambridge, MA: Harvard University Press, 1977), 98–106; A. Hunter Dupree, *Science in the Federal Government* (Cambridge, MA: Belknap Press of Harvard University Press, 1957), 44–90; *CR* 19: 5392–93.

65. 19 Stat 406; 24 Stat 172, at 177.

66. Joint Committee on the Library, *Condition*, 32–33; *ARLC*, 1874, 5–6; S. Branson Marley Jr., "Newspapers and the Library of Congress," *QJLC* 32 (July 1975): 211; Senate, Misc. Document 125, 43rd Congress, 1st Sess.; *ARLC*, 1891, 4–5; 1892, 5. Thereafter, holdings records were kept on 5 x 8-inch manuscript cards available only to the staff: Lacy, "Sesquicentenary Review, II," 236–37.

67. Senate Misc. Document 165, 50th Congress, 1st Sess.; Dorothy S. Eaton and Vincent L. Eaton, "Manuscripts Relating to Early America," *QJLC* 8 (November 1950): 17–18; Cole, *For Congress*, 45.

68. The act protected only works manufactured in the United States and on the condition of reciprocity for US authors: Cole, *For Congress*, 45; 26 Stat 1106; *ARLC*, 1892, 4; Thorvald Solberg, "Copyright and Librarians," *LQ* 4 (April 1934): 189–90; Boyd Rayward, "Manufacture and Copyright: Past History Remaking," *JLH* 3 (January 1968): 12–13; James L. W. West III, "The Chace Act and Anglo-American Literary Relations," *Studies in Bibliography* 45 (1992): 303–11.

69. Quoted by Michael Winship, "The Library of Congress in 1892: Ainsworth Spofford, Houghton Mifflin and Company and *Uncle Tom's Cabin*," in *The Library of Congress and the Center for the Book: Historical Essays in Honor of John Y. Cole*, edited by Mary Niles Maack (Washington, DC: LC, in association with the University of Texas Press, 2011), 117–23.

70. *ARLC*, 1892, 3; Cole, "Of Copyright," 129.

71. Cole, "Of Copyright," 132–34.
72. 27 Stat 395.
73. *ARLC*, 1891, 5; 1893, 193; 28 Stat 582.
74. Joint Committee on the Library, *Condition*, 127, 131–32.
75. Thorvald Solberg, undated memoir, box 8, Thorvald Solberg Papers, LC.
76. Fred Shelley, "Manuscripts in the Library of Congress, 1800–1900," *American Archivist* 11 (January 1948): 11–16; Aaron D. Purcell, "Abstractions of Justice: The Library of Congress's Great Manuscript Robbery, 1896–1897," *American Archivist* 62 (Fall 1999): 325–45.
77. 17 Stat 510, at 513.
78. *ARLC*, 1872, 10. While Spofford habitually spoke of comprehensiveness, he did concede limits: Johnston, "Dr. Spofford," 23–29.
79. LC, "Specifications for the Guidance of Those Who May Submit Designs for a New Building for the Library of Congress" (Washington, DC, 1873); Cole, *For Congress*, 37; John Y. Cole, "A National Monument for a National Library: Ainsworth Rand Spofford and the New Library of Congress, 1871–1897," *RCHS* 48 (1971–72): 477; Cole, "Struggle for a Structure: Ainsworth Rand Spofford and a New Building for the Library of Congress," in *The Library of Congress: The Art and Architecture of the Thomas Jefferson Building*, edited by John Y. Cole and Henry Hope Reed (New York: W. W. Norton, in association with LC, 1997), 31–63.
80. John Y. Cole, "Smithmeyer and Pelz: Embattled Architects of the Library of Congress," *QJLC* 29 (October 1972): 282–307; John L. Smithmeyer, *History of the Construction of the Library of Congress* (Washington, DC: LC, 1906).
81. *ARLC*, 1875, 7; Josephus Nelson and Judith Farley, *Full Circle: Ninety Years of Service in the Main Reading Room* (Washington, DC: LC, 1991), 11; Marley, "Newspapers," 211.
82. Senate Report 387, 44th Congress, 1st Sess.; Cole, "National Monument," 480–81. Morrill made an eloquent plea for a separate building: *CR* 9 (March 31, 1879): 129–32.
83. Hayes, Arthur, and Cleveland all urged Congress to act; Hayes's message specifically supported the Library's national role, as did the ALA's 1881 resolution: *The State of the Union Messages of the Presidents, 1790–1966*, edited by Fred L. Israel (New York: Chelsea House, 1966), 2: 1354–55; 1450; 1553–54; ALA, *Papers and Proceedings of the Fourth General Meeting, 1881*, 73.
84. Cole, "Smithmeyer & Pelz," 285–87; John McDonough, "Justin Smith Morrill and the Library of Congress," *Vermont History* 35 (July 1965): 141–50.
85. 21 Stat 165; Senate Report 1573, 54th Congress, 2nd Sess., 23; Mearns, *Story*, 121–24; William C. Allen, *History of the United States Capitol: A Chronology of Design, Construction, and Politics* (Washington, DC: GPO, 2001), 352–53.
86. Quoted by Cole, "Smithmeyer and Pelz," 289.
87. Cole, *Ainsworth Rand Spofford*, 39; Cole, "Smithmeyer & Pelz," 287–90; John L. Smithmeyer, "The National Library Building: The Proposed Plan," *LJ* 6 (April 1881): 77–81; William F. Poole, "The Construction of Library Buildings," *LJ* 6 (April 1881): 69–77.
88. *Nation* 32 (February 17, 1881), 113; *American Architect and Building News* 15 (January 1, 1884), 1; Samuel Swett Green, *The Public Library Movement in the United States* (Boston: Boston Book Company, 1913), 32.
89. Cole, "Smithmeyer & Pelz"; *LJ* 8 (September–October 1883): 270.
90. *LJ* 9 (November 1884): 188.
91. *Nation* 35 (October 1882): 350–51; *ARLC*, 1869, 4–5. Billings wanted Congress to approve a new building. Internationally known as a public health expert by the 1880s, his congressional support probably matched Spofford's: Wyndham D. Miles, *A History of the National Library of Medicine: The Nation's Treasury of Medical Knowledge* (Washington, DC: GPO, 1981), 141–56;

Carleton B. Chapman, *Order out of Chaos: John Shaw Billings and America's Coming of Age* (Boston: Boston Medical Library, 1994), 166–67, 177; "Annual Report of the Surgeon General, 1882," 16. Approved March 3, 1885 (23 Stat 339), the building opened in 1888.

92. "Documentary History of the Construction," 373–76; Senate Misc. Document 65, 47th Congress, 1st Sess.; Allen, *History of the United States Capitol*, 353. Mearns called the dome proposal "the wackiest" of the ideas for keeping the library in the Capitol: *Story*, 124.

93. *CR* 19: 5573–75, 5593 (June 18–19, 1888).

94. 24 Stat 12.

95. William B. Parker, *The Life and Public Services of Justin Smith Morrill* (Boston, 1924): 321–22.

96. Florence P. Spofford, "Reminiscences of Her Father," *RCHS* 12 (1909): 179–80. The $35,000 was an increase for site acquisition. Spofford referred to Secretary of the Interior Lucius Q. C. Lamar, Samuel James Renwick McMillan (R-MN), James Henderson Blount (D-GA), and John Griffin Carlisle (R-OH).

97. This quotation is from John Y. Cole, "LC in the 19th Century: An Informal Account," *JLH* 9 (1974): 228.

98. House of Representatives Special Committee to Investigate Contracts for the Construction of the Library Building, "Congressional Library Building," House Report 3795, 50th Congress, 2nd Sess.

99. By the 1880s, Congress had made Army Engineers responsible for constructing Washington's public works: Lessoff, "Washington under Federal Rule," 249–50; Cole, "National Monument," 490; on Green and Casey, see Helen-Ann Hilker, "Monument to Civilization: Diary of a Building," *QJLC* 29 (October 1972): 234–66.

100. 25 Stat 505, at 523; 25 Stat 939, at 966; 29 Stat 470; Cole, "National Monument," 491–92; US Army Corps of Engineers, "Letter from the Chief of Engineers of the Army Transmitting a Report Relative to the Construction of the Library," House Misc. Document 12, 50th Congress, 2nd Sess.

101. *ARLC*, 1897: 18–19; Herbert Small, *Handbook of the New Library of Congress in Washington* (Boston: Curtis & Cameron, 1901); Charles H. Baumann, *The Influence of Angus Snead MacDonald and the Snead Bookstack on Library Architecture* (Metuchen, NJ: Scarecrow Press, 1972), 65–75; Kimberly W. Dobbs, "Bernard Richardson Green," *DALB*, 211–12.

102. 28 Stat 764. Smithmeyer and Pelz waged legal battles for compensation for their designs, but lost; the last case ended in 1913: Cole, "Smithmeyer & Pelz," 297–306.

103. Cole, "National Monument," 495–507; "Report of the Superintendent of Construction for the Building of the Library of Congress, December 7, 1896," House Document 20, 54th Congress, 2nd Sess.; Cole, *On These Walls: Inscriptions and Quotations in the Buildings of the Library of Congress* (Washington, DC: LC, 1995); Small, *Handbook*; Cole and Reed, *Library of Congress*. Descriptions by Spofford and William A. Coffin appeared in the *Century Illustrated Monthly Magazine* 53 (March 1897): 682–94.

104. Joint Resolution 35, 54th Congress, 1st Sess., April 2, 1896.

105. 28 Stat 764, at 772.

106. "Special Report of the Librarian of Congress, December 3, 1895," Senate Document 7, 54th Congress, 1st Sess.

107. Cole, *For Congress*, 49.

108. Joint Committee on the Library, *Condition*, 1.

109. *LJ* 21 (1896), 357; Rosenberg, "Foundation," 107–16; Bowker to Quigg, November 18, 1896; Bowker to Rutherford B. Hayes, November 24, 1896, Richard R. Bowker Papers, New

York Public Library. Bowker and Quigg were both New York journalists, and likely were acquainted.

110. Joint Committee on the Library, *Condition*, 139–68, 172–203.

111. Joint Committee on the Library, 228.

112. Joint Committee on the Library, 113.

113. Joint Committee on the Library, 163–64, 206–7, 244.

114. Joint Committee on the Library, 141–50, 220, 254.

115. Rosenberg, "Foundation," 117–19.

116. *CR* 29: 311–19; February 17, 1897: 1945–47; Rosenberg, "Foundation," 122–23. During debate on the appropriations bill, Quigg offered the Joint Committee's proposal as a substitute motion; it was defeated 85–27. Dockery, a supporter of civil service and of increased authority for the Librarian, also introduced a bill in December 1897 providing that the LC "shall be known as and styled as the National Library," with the Librarian designated "Director of the National Library." The Joint Committee approved the bill, but there was no further action: Cole, *Library of Congress in Perspective*, 15–16.

117. *LJ* 22 (1897): 3–4, 7–9. The anonymous author was Edith E. Clarke, Public Documents Library, Washington, DC.

118. 29 Stat 538, at 544. On the Joint Committee's recommendation, in 1922 the office of Superintendent of Building and Grounds was abolished and its responsibilities were transferred to the Architect of the Capitol: 42 Stat 715; *ARLC*, 1922, 7–11.

119. Senate Report 1573, 54th Congress, 2nd Sess.; Rosenberg, "Foundation," 123–26.

120. Mearns, *Story*, 138–39; Hilker, "Monument," 242–43. Cole, *For Congress*, 48, 57, noted that unclassified copyright deposits were moved as early as October 1895.

121. *The Literary Club of Cincinnati, 1849–1903* (Cincinnati: Ebert & Richardson, 1903), 16–17.

122. John Y. Cole, "For Congress and the Nation: The Dual Nature of the Library of Congress," *QJLC* 32 (April 1975): 118–38.

123. Mearns, *Story*, 147.

Chapter 5

1. At the *Tribune*, Young hired Mark Twain to report on his travels, subsequently published as *Innocents Abroad* (1868), *LCIB* 55 (February 5, 1996): 31; John Russell Young, *Around the World with General Grant* (New York: American News Company, 1879); Jean Edward Smith, *Grant* (New York: Simon & Schuster, 2001), 607–12.

2. John Russell Young diary, April 4, 1897, Young Papers, LC; Wayne A. Wiegand, "Herbert Putnam's Appointment as Librarian of Congress," *LQ* 49 (July 1979): 258. Also see educator Nicholas Murray Butler's, *Across the Busy Years: Recollections and Reflections* (New York: Charles Scribner's Sons, 1939), 1: 303–5. Butler tried unsuccessfully to have McKinley appoint an experienced administrator.

3. Young to E. V. Smally, September 20, 1898, Librarian's Letterbooks, LCA.

4. Quoted in *LCIB*, July 26–August 1, 1949, 11.

5. John Y. Cole, "Ainsworth Rand Spofford," *DALB*, 42. John C. Broderick, "John Russell Young: The Internationalist as Librarian," *Librarians*, 153, noted Young's long acquaintance with Spofford.

6. Quoted by Mearns, *Story*, 157. See also Herbert Putnam, "Ainsworth Rand Spofford: A Librarian Past," *Independent* 65 (November 19, 1908): 1149–55.

7. Young's two reports both referred to national library status and what he called the "minor government libraries" that "should not be developed at the expense of the Library of Congress"; *ARLC*, 1898, 45, 47.

8. Young requested $30,000, a large increase over the $4,000 1898 appropriation, plus $5,000 for manuscript purchases, but Congress provided only $15,000: Broderick, "John Russell Young," 167–68.

9. Broderick, "John Russell Young," 168; *ARLC*, 1898, 83–87.

10. *ARLC*, 1898, 16, 52–54. Hubbard was a founder of the National Geographic Society. His widow offered the collection and a $20,000 endowment, requesting that a gallery be named for Hubbard. Congress authorized accepting the gift but refused to name space in a public building for a private citizen and offered instead to administer the collection separately, thereby setting a precedent for the Library's acceptance of collections: 30 Stat 751; 37 Stat 319.

11. *ARLC*, 1898, 39, 67–74, passim; *Law Library, 1832–1982*, 9–11. With three law schools in Washington, students overwhelmed the Law Library's Capitol quarters.

12. 12 Stat 538, at 544.

13. Mearns, *Story*, 139–40.

14. On the building, see Helen-Ann Hilker, *Ten First Street, Southeast: Congress Builds a Library, 1886–1897—An Exhibition in the Great Hall and on the Second Floor of the Thomas Jefferson Building, Library of Congress* (Washington, DC: LC, 1980); Herbert Small, comp., *Handbook of the New Library of Congress in Washington* (Boston: Curtis & Cameron, 1901); John Y. Cole and Henry Hope Reed, *The Library of Congress: The Art and Architecture of the Thomas Jefferson Building* (New York: W. W. Norton, in association with Library of Congress, 1997); John Y. Cole, *On These Walls: Inscriptions & Quotations in the Library of Congress* (Washington, DC: Library of Congress, in association with Scala, London, 2008); *The Library of Congress: An Architectural Alphabet* (San Francisco: Pomegranate, 2000). On reactions to the building, see John Y. Cole, "The Book Palace of the American People: An Introduction and Reflection," *LQ* 80 (October 2010): 304.

15. Quoted by John Y. Cole, *For Congress and the Nation: A Chronological History of the Library of Congress* (Washington, DC: LC, 1979), 59–60; *LCIB*, October 28–November 3, 1947, 2; Martha Lamb, *History of the City of New York*, 3 vols. (New York: A. S. Barnes, 1877–96).

16. *ARLC*, 1898, 11; Josephus Nelson and Judith Farley, *Full Circle: Ninety Years of Service in the Main Reading Room* (Washington, DC: LC, 1991), 15.

17. Cole, *For Congress*, 64; John Y. Cole, "Exhibitions," *Encyclopedia*, 247–50; Charles Goodrum and Helen Dalrymple, *The Library of Congress* (Boulder, CO: Westview Press, 1982), 157–59. Paul Laurence Dunbar read his poetry to an audience in the Reading Room for the Blind, the first of the Library's poetry readings. In 1869, Spofford had suggested evening hours, but the Library's Capitol quarters had no lighting. The 1897 building was the first public building in Washington to fully employ electricity: *ARLC*, 1869, 4; 30 Stat 277, at 284; John Y. Cole, *America's Greatest Library: An Illustrated History of the Library of Congress* (Washington, DC: LC, in association with D. Giles Limited, London, 2017), 72.

18. 29 Stat 244; 30 Stat 1372; *ARLC*, 1897, 49–50; 1898, 45–46, 58–62. Supported by a Carnegie grant, the public library opened in 1903.

19. Members of Congress had long freely brought liquor into the Capitol: John Y. Cole, "LC in the 19th Century: An Informal Account," *JLH* 9 (1974): 233–34; Lewis L. Gould, *The Most Exclusive Club: A History of the Modern United States Senate* (New York: Basic Books, 2005), 19.

20. 29 Stat 538, at 544, 545; Young diary, January 6, 1898; February 14, 1898; Broderick, "John Russell Young," 164–65; H. Wayne Morgan, *William McKinley and His* America, rev. ed. (Kent, OH: Kent State University Press, 2003), 219; Lewis L. Gould, *The Presidency of William*

McKinley (Lawrence: Regents Press of Kansas, 1980), 165–69; Margaret Leech, *In the Days of McKinley* (New York: Harper & Brothers, 1959), 133–35; Jane A. Rosenberg, "Patronage and Professionals: The Transformation of the Library of Congress Staff," *L&C* 26 (Spring 1991): 251–68. A McKinley appointee, Joseph L. Bristow, wrote that senators and representatives "almost wholly controlled the appointments and usually they were willing to follow the recommendation of the President in the matter of legislation"; Joseph L. Bristow, *Fraud and Politics at the Turn of the Century* (New York: Exposition Press, 1952), 64.

21. *LJ* 22 (1897): 379–80.

22. J. C. M. Hanson, "The Library of Congress and Its New Catalogue: Some Unwritten History," in *Essays*, 179–81.

23. Ari Hoogenboom, "The Pendleton Act and the Civil Service," *American Historical Review* 64 (January 1959): 304–5. *ARLC*, 1898, 55–57, includes a list of sample questions for applicants; *ARLC*, 1910, 297–99, notes previous employment practices.

24. Jane Aikin Rosenberg, *The Nation's Great Library: Herbert Putnam and the Library of Congress, 1899–1939* (Urbana: University of Illinois Press, 1993), 20.

25. Personal communications from John Y. Cole, July 4, 2023, and Cheryl Fox, July 7, 2023; George Washington Williams, *History of the Negro Troops in the War of the Rebellion, 1861–1865* (New York: Harper & Brothers 1888), xi; Eric S. Yellin, *Racism in the Nation's Service; Government Workers and the Color Line in Woodrow Wilson's America* (Chapel Hill: University of North Carolina Press, 2013), 11–12; Brenda Mitchell-Powell, *Public in Name Only: The 1939 Alexandria Library Sit-in Demonstration* (Amherst: University of Massachusetts Press, 2022), 23, 37, 46, 51.

26. Congress did hire Black employees, generally as laborers or messengers, but it is not clear whether these employees were assigned to work in the Library. John Silva Meehan mentions one "colored" employee, Albert Cavans, in an undated Diary entry, Meehan Papers, LC, p. 144.

27. Wilkinson had no formal education. He died at his post in 1912 after fifty-five years of service: *ARLC*, 1912, 13; John Y. Cole, "Daniel Murray: A Collector's Legacy," https://loc.gov/collections/african-american-perspectives/rare-books /articles and essays/.

28. John Y. Cole and Jane Aikin, "Employees and Employment," *Encyclopedia*, 225–31; Liah Carvalho, "An Extraordinary Law Librarian," https://blogs.loc.gov/law/2016/02/an-extraordinary-law-librarian/.

29. Dunbar's poem "Sympathy" contains the line "I know why the caged bird sings," referring to his work at LC and/or his previous job as an elevator operator: Linda Keck Wiggins, *Life and Works of Paul Laurence Dunbar* (Washington, DC: Austin-Jenkins, 1907), 73–83; William McGuire, *Poetry's Catbird Seat, the Consultantship in Poetry in the English Language at the Library of Congress, 1937–1987* (Washington, DC: LC, 1988), 26–27, https://blogs.loc.gov/catbird/2013/06/the-caged-bird-sings-paul-laurence-dunbar-at-the-library-of-congress/; *LCM* 8 (January–February 2020): 2.

30. Elizabeth Dowling Taylor, *The Original Black Elite: Daniel Murray and the Story of a Forgotten Era* (New York: HarperCollins, 2017), 149–56; Cole, *America's Greatest Library*, 78–79.

31. Young diary, September 28, 1898; Young to J. W. Babcock, October 18, 1897, Librarians' Letterbooks, LCA; Young to William A. Stone, August 11, 1897; Young to O. N. Denny, August 17, 1897, Young Papers, LC.

32. Hanson, "Library of Congress," 181–91.

33. *LJ* 22 (August 1897): 379; 23 (1898): 47; Thorvald Solberg's unsigned article in *The Nation*, criticized both the administration and the staff: "The Librarianship of the Library of Congress," *Nation* 68, no. 1758 (March 9, 1899): 178–79. Broderick, "John Russell Young," 84–86, nevertheless credited Young with "sturdy independence" in administration.

34. Broderick, "John Russell Young," 170–71.

35. Young diary, June 12, 1898.

36. *ARLC*, 1898, 47.

37. Spofford wrote President McKinley to warn him about Alvord, January 28, 1899, McKinley Papers, LC.

38. David C. Mearns, "Herbert Putnam: Librarian of the United States," *DC Libraries* 26 (January 1955): 377–90; Wayne Wiegand, *The Politics of an Emerging Profession: The American Library Association, 1876–1917* (New York: Greenwood Press, 1986), 108–9; Thorvald Solberg, "A Chapter in the Unwritten History of the Library of Congress from January 17 to April 5, 1899," *LQ* 9 (July 1939): 285–98; William C. Lane, "The Appointment of a Librarian of Congress," *LJ* 24 (1899): 100; Richard R. Bowker, "The Appointment of Herbert Putnam as Librarian of Congress," 15–21, in *Essays*; Hanson, "Library of Congress," 188–91; Reed to McKinley, January 25, 1899; George F. Hoar, Henry Cabot Lodge, William E. Chandler, Jacob H. Gallinger, and Eugene Hale to McKinley, March 3, 1899, McKinley Papers.

39. Rosenberg, *Nation's Great Library*, 20–21; Solberg, "Chapter," 285–91; Bowker, "Appointment of Herbert Putnam," in *Essays*, 15–21. Lane's account is in the Solberg Papers, LC. The $5,000 Librarian's salary, less than Putnam's $6,000 Boston salary, was raised to $6,000 (31 Stat 86, at 93 [1900]) and to $6,500 in 1912 (*ARLC*, 1912, 15).

40. Rosenberg, *Nation's Great Library*, 21–22; Edward McClung Fleming, *R. R. Bowker: Militant Liberal* (Norman: University of Oklahoma Press, 1952), 79–80; George Haven Putnam to Bowker, February 14, 1899, box 92, Richard Rogers Bowker Papers, New York Public Library; Thorvald Solberg to Bowker, February 11, 1899, box 82, Bowker Papers; Lane to Bowker, February 8, 1899, box 35, Bowker Papers; Bowker, "Appointment of Herbert Putnam," 19; Mearns, "Herbert Putnam: Librarian," 380–90; Dennis Thomison, *A History of the American Library Association, 1876–1972* (Chicago: ALA, 1978), 44–46. The Senate confirmed Putnam on December 12.

41. Joint Committee on the Library, *Condition of the Library of Congress*, 54th Congress, 2nd Sess., 1896–97, Senate Report 1573 (Washington, DC: GPO, 1897), 179–203, 216–28.

42. Gratia Countryman, "Mr. Putnam and the Minneapolis Public Library," in *Essays*, 5–9; David C. Mearns, "Herbert Putnam, Librarian of the United States: The Minneapolis Years," *Wilson Library Bulletin* 29 (September 1954): 59–63; Charles F. D. Belden, "The Library Service of Herbert Putnam in Boston," in *Essays*, 10–14; Jane Aikin, "'Referred to the Librarian with Power to Act': Herbert Putnam and the Boston Public Library," 27–37, in *Occasional Paper 212* (Champaign: Graduate School of Library and Information Science at University of Illinois, 2002).

43. Rosenberg, *Nation's Great Library*, 25–27; William Warner Bishop, "The Library of Congress, 1907–15: Fragments of Autobiography," *LQ* 18 (January 1948): 23; Sonneck to Carl Engel, October 21, 1921, in *Oscar Sonneck and American Music*, edited by William Lichtenwanger (Urbana: University of Illinois Press, 1983), 115.

44. Archibald MacLeish, "Herbert Putnam, 1861–1955," *Proceedings of the American Academy of Arts and Letters and the National Institute of Arts and Letters,* 2nd series, no. 7 (New York, 1957), 151–56.

45. Herbert Putnam to Beth Putnam, April 9 and 25, May 7, and November 15, 1899, Herbert Putnam Papers, LC.

46. C. Glenn Sparks, *Doyen of Librarians: A Biography of William Warner Bishop* (Metuchen, NJ: Scarecrow Press, 1993), 69–70. During the MacLeish administration, the room that housed the Round Table became the Poetry Room, the office of the Consultant in Poetry.

47. Waldo Gifford Leland, "Some Early Recollections of an Itinerant Historian," *Proceedings of the American Antiquarian Society* 61, part 2 (October 1951): 269–70. Manuscripts Division chief Worthington C. Ford brought Leland to the Round Table after interviewing him for a position on the Carnegie Institution–funded project that resulted in Claude Van Tyne and Leland's *Guide to the Archives of the Government of the United States in Washington* (Washington, DC: Carnegie Institution, 1904).

48. H. G. Wells, *The Future in America: A Search after Realities* (New York: Harper & Brothers, 1906), 237–38. Wells was quite disappointed in American intellectual life.

49. Quoted by David C. Mearns, "Herbert Putnam and His Responsible Eye," in *Herbert Putnam, 1861–1955: A Memorial Tribute* (Washington, DC, privately published, 1956), 41.

50. Harvard College Class of 1883, *Fiftieth Anniversary* (Cambridge, MA: Printed for the Class, 1933), 276.

51. Rosenberg, *Nation's Great Library*, 24; Frederick W. Ashley, "Three Eras in the Library of Congress," in *Essays*, 63; William Warner Bishop, "Thirty Years of the Library of Congress, 1899 to 1929," in *Essays*, 26; Herbert Putnam, "The Library of Congress," *Atlantic Monthly* 85 (February 1900): 146.

52. Rosenberg, *Nation's Great Library*, 24–25; Putnam, "Library of Congress," 158; Herbert Putnam, "The Library of Congress," *Outlook* 65 (May 12, 1900): 124.

53. *ARLC*, 1899, 27–36; "Legislative, Executive, and Judicial Appropriations Bill, 1901: Hearings Conducted by the Subcommittee of the Committee on Appropriations, House of Representatives" (Washington, DC: GPO, 1900): 4–18; 31 Stat 86; Herbert Putnam to Beth Putnam, April 9, 11, 25, 30, May 27, 1899, January 25, 1900; Putnam to George Bowerman, January 26, 1900, Putnam Papers, LC; Putnam to Helen Haines, April 29, 1900, LCA.

54. David C. Mearns, *The Lincoln Papers: The Story of the Collection* (Garden City, NY: Doubleday, 1948), I, 90.

55. Rosenberg, *Nation's Great Library*, 7–8, 29–30.

56. *ARLC*, 1900, 18; 1926, 17; Taylor, *Original Black Elite*, 223–32; Billie E. Walker, "Daniel Alexander Payne Murray (1852–1925), Forgotten Librarian, Bibliographer, and Historian," *L&C* 40 (Winter 2005): 25–37; Kate McDowell, "A 'Colored Authors Collection' to Exhibit to the World and Educate a Race," in *Education and the Culture of Print in Modern America*, edited by Adam R. Nelson and John L. Rudolph (Madison: University of Wisconsin Press, 2010), 36–56; Rosenberg, *Nation's Great Library*, 64–65; Cole, *America's Greatest Library*, 78–79; John Y. Cole, "Daniel Alexander Payne Murray," *DALB*, 381–82. The LC's Daniel A. P. Murray Association was formed in 1979, honoring Murray's service.

57. Rosenberg, "Patronage and Professionals," 258–60.

58. Herbert Putnam, "What It Means to Be a Librarian," *Ladies' Home Journal*, February 1900, 22; Putnam, "The Prospect," *LJ* 37 (December 1912): 651–58; Putnam, "The Woman in the Library," *LJ* 41 (December 1916): 879–81. E.g., Florence S. Hellman was named Acting Chief of the Division of Bibliography in 1931, but Putnam did not promote her to Chief until 1938. After Archibald MacLeish hired Lucile Morsch as Chief of the new Descriptive Cataloging Division in 1941, women began to assume more top leadership responsibilities.

59. Herbert Putnam, "Library of Congress as a National Library," *LJ* 30 (September 1905): 30.

60. Rosenberg, *Nation's Great Library*, 35–36.

61. Francis Miksa, *The Development of Classification at the Library of Congress*, Occasional Paper 164 (Champaign: Graduate School of Library Science at University of Illinois, 1984), 22; Leo J. LaMontagne, *American Library Classification: With Special Reference to the Library of*

Congress (New York: Shoe String Press, 1961), 225, 230; Hanson, "Library of Congress, and Its New Catalogue," 187.

62. Rosenberg, *Nation's Great Library*, 42–44; J. C. M. Hanson, *What Became of Jens? A Study of Americanization Based on the Reminiscences of J. C. M. Hanson*, edited by Oivind Hovde (Decorah, IA: Luther College Press, 1974), 59; J. C. M. Hanson, "Library of Congress Classification for College Libraries," *LJ* 46 (1921): 151–52; Charles Martel, "The Library of Congress Classification," in *Essays*, 322; Maurice Tauber, "Review of the Use of the Library of Congress Classification," in *The Use of the Library of Congress Classification*, edited by Richard Schimmelpfeng and C. Donald Cook (Chicago: ALA, 1968), 3.

63. Putnam made both the old and the new catalogs accessible to readers: *ARLC*, 1901, 243–44.

64. J. C. M. Hanson, "The Subject Catalogs of the Library of Congress," *BALA* 3 (1909): 386–89; Hanson, "Library of Congress and Its New Catalog," 183–85.

65. After issuing a preliminary list of subject headings (1906), *Subject Headings Used in the Dictionary Catalogues of the Library of Congress* came out in parts, from 1909 to 1914, was revised in 1919, and continued as *Library of Congress Subject Headings* (1975–), with lists of changes issued between editions; Rosenberg, *Nation's Great Library*, 44–45; Alva T. Stone, "The LCSH Century: A Brief History of the *Library of Congress Subject Headings*," in *The LCSH Century: One Hundred Years of the Library of Congress Subject Headings System* (New York: Haworth, 2000), 2; Dan Lacy, "The Library of Congress: A Sesquicentenary Review II: The Organization of the Collections," *LQ* 20 (October 1950): 237–38; *ARLC*, 1909, 52; 1935, 241; *LCIB* 57 (August 1998): 200–201.

66. Joint Committee on the Library, *Condition of the Library of Congress*, 226–27.

67. Hanson, "Library of Congress and Its New Catalog," 184; Charles Harris Hastings, "Reminiscences and Observations on the Card Distribution Work of the Library of Congress," in *Essays*, 195–206.

68. The challenge was to convince librarians to adopt standardized cataloging; most librarians selected the rules they favored from the available codes: William C. Lane, "Cataloging," *LJ* 18 (July 1893): 238–40; and Paul Edlund, "A Monster and a Miracle: The Cataloging Distribution Service of the Library of Congress, 1901–1976," *QJLC* 33 (October 1976): 391–93. John M. Dawson, "A History of Centralized Cataloging," *LRTS* 11 (Winter 1967): 30, stated that by 1900, there was "a climate of opinion favorable to the development of cooperative and centralized cataloging."

69. Rosenberg, *Nation's Great Library*, 45–47; William Warner Bishop, "J. C. M. Hanson and International Cataloging," *LQ* 4 (April 1934): 39–42; Terry M. Heisey, "Early Catalog Code Development in the United States, 1876–1908," *JLH* 11 (July 1976): 225–43; *ARLC*, 1902, 78–81; 1907, 56–57; 1908, 80; American Library Association, *Catalog Rules: Author and Title Entries* (Boston: ALA Publishing Board, 1908).

70. Herbert Putnam, "What May Be Done for Libraries by the Nation," *LJ* 26 (August 1901): 9–15; Edlund, "Monster and a Miracle," 395–97, called it "beautifully appropriate" that Putnam announced his decision at the New York Library Association's September conference at Dewey's Lake Placid Club.

71. Bowker to Putnam, October 14, 1901, quoted in *LCIB*, July 20–26, 1948, 8; 32 Stat 419, at 480; *ARLC*, 1901, 69–74; Rosenberg, *Nation's Great Library*, 48–49. The 1902 legislation was unchanged until the Library of Congress Fiscal Operations Improvement Act (PL 106-481) allowed funds for fee-based services to be used in later fiscal years, subject to appropriations legislation limits: *ARLC*, 2000, 126.

72. Rosenberg, *Nation's Great Library*, 57–59.

73. *ARLC*, 1901, 37; 1910, 72; Hastings, "Reminiscences," 200; William Jerome Wilson, *The Union Catalog of the Library of Congress* (Washington, DC: LC, 1942).

74. Putnam to George Peabody Wetmore, October 20, 1900, Librarian's Letterbook no. 7, LCA.

75. John Y. Cole, "Storehouses and Workshops: American Libraries and the Uses of Knowledge," in *The Organization of Knowledge in Modern America, 1879–1920*, edited by Alexandra Oleson and John Voss (Baltimore: Johns Hopkins University Press, 1979), 364–85.

76. Joint Committee on the Library, *Condition of the Library of Congress*, 145–271.

77. 31 Stat 1010, at 1039; Wyndham D. Miles, *A History of the National Library of Medicine: The Nation's Treasury of Medical Knowledge* (Washington, DC: GPO, 1981), 96–103. John Russell Young had not pressed the issue of lending materials outside Washington; see Mearns, *Story*, 159.

78. Rosenberg, *Nation's Great Library*, 60–62; Bishop, "Library of Congress, 1907–15," 12, 19–20; Putnam, "Library of Congress as a National Library," 30.

79. Herbert Putnam, "Relation of State Libraries and the Library of Congress," *LJ* 25 (December 1900): 729–33; Putnam, "Library of Congress as a National Library," 27; Putnam, "What May Be Done," 9–15.

80. In *On the History of Libraries and Scholarly Communication* (Washington, DC: LC, 1980), 6. I. R. Willison of the British Library called the report "the manifesto that projected the Library of Congress onto the national scene."

81. *ARLC*, 1901, 50; 1903, 47–48. A 1902 count reported 1,114,111 volumes: *ARLC*, 1902, 17, 41. A statement on the Library's services appeared in *ARLC*, 1907, 70–78.

82. Putnam to Theodore Roosevelt, October 15, 1901, Theodore Roosevelt Papers, LC.

83. *LCIB*, October 19–25, 1948, 13. Roosevelt published his own books with G. P. Putnam's Sons.

84. Fred L. Israel, ed., *The State of the Union: Messages of the Presidents, 1790–1966* (New York: Chelsea House, 1966), 2.

85. 9 Stat 523, at 524; *ARLC*, 1952, 9–10; *LCIB*, November 15–21, 1949, 21; Sparks, *Doyen*, 66–67. The Library sent books to the White House as late as the 1940s, but in 1929 the American Booksellers Association began donating 200 selected volumes every four years. In 1962, Jacqueline Kennedy requested a committee of librarians, historians, and publishers to select a new White House library, using private funds and in-kind donations; see Catherine M. Parisian, *The First White House Library: A History and Annotated Catalogue* (University Park: Pennsylvania State University Press, 2010), 1–54.

86. *ARLC*, 1914, 8.

87. Lacy, "Library of Congress: Sesquicentenary Review: I," 159.

88. "Special Report of the Librarian of Congress, December 3, 1895," Senate Document 7, 54th Congress, 1st Sess., 16.

89. Quoted by Mearns, "Herbert Putnam and His Responsible Eye," 41.

90. In 1872, Billings and Spofford agreed to transfer to the Surgeon General's Library one of the two copies of medical books received as copyright deposits. Agriculture Department Librarian William Parker Cutter requested the same transfer in 1893, but it did not begin until Putnam approved it in 1900; see John Y. Cole, "The National Libraries of the United States and Canada," in *Century of Service: Librarianship in the United States and Canada*, edited by Sidney L. Jackson, Eleanor B. Herling, and E. J. Josey (Chicago: ALA, 1976), 245–46.

91. *ARLC*, 1908, 57–66. Putnam did not repeat Spofford's suggestion of uniting federal library collections. Foster E. Mohrhardt, "The Library of the United States Department of

Agriculture," *LQ* 27 (April 1957): 61–82, described its relationship with the LC and other federal libraries.

92. Ralph D. Wagner, *A History of the Farmington Plan* (Lanham, MD: Scarecrow Press, 2002), 7–13.

93. J. Christian Bay, *The Metamorphosis of a Bookworm* (privately printed, 1954), 9–13; Putnam, "What May Be Done"; Rosenberg, *Nation's Great Library,* 54–55.

94. Edwin M. Borchard, "The Law Division of the Library of Congress," in *Essays,* 89–96; Worthington Chauncey Ford, "A Division of Manuscripts," in *Essays,* 156–61; Fred Shelley, "Manuscripts in the Library of Congress, 1800–1900," *American Archivist* 11 (January 1948): 3–19; Herbert Friedenwald, "Manuscripts in the Library of Congress," in *Annual Report of the American Historical Association* (Washington, DC: GPO, 1899), 35–45; *ARLC,* 1923, 3, 50.

95. *ARLC,* 1903, 24–26; Dorothy S. Eaton and Vincent L. Eaton, "Manuscripts Relating to Early America," *QJLC* 8 (November 1950): 17–28. The provision 32 Stat 854, at 865, allowed federal agencies to transfer unneeded materials to the Library; President Taft's 1912 executive order directed the Librarian to review unwanted agency materials to ensure that material of historical interest was preserved: *ARLC,* 1912, 34–35. With the acquisition of the Lincoln Papers (1923), the LC held the papers of eighteen presidents; this was later increased to twenty-three: *ARLC,* 1923, 43.

96. *ARLC,* 1905, 56–58; Lacy, "Library of Congress: Sesquicentenary Review: I," 160–61; *ARLC,* 1923, 52–53; Victor Gondos Jr., *J. Franklin Jameson and the Birth of the National Archives, 1906–1926* (Philadelphia: University of Pennsylvania Press, 1981), 21–22, 85; Cole, *For Congress,* 79–80; *ARLC,* 1911, 26; 1912, 35; 1913, 41–42; 1915, 61–63.

97. *ARLC,* 1905, 56–58; 1906, 27–32; 1921, 177–87; 1922, 58; 1923, 52–53; Charles M. Andrews, "The Story of the Transcripts," in *Essays,* 47–56; Roscoe R. Hill, *American Missions in European Archives* (Mexico City: American Institute of Geography and History, 1951), 65–71. The project first relied on hand transcription, later switching to typed transcriptions and photostats.

98. Quoted by Carol June Bradley, "Oscar G. T. Sonneck: Architect of the 'National Music Collection,'" *JLH* 16 (Spring 1981): 296; see also Carol June Bradley, "Oscar George Theodore Sonneck," *DALB,* 495–99.

99. 31 Stat 1464; Robert D. Stevens, *The Role of the Library of Congress in the International Exchange of Official Publications: A Brief History* (Washington, DC: LC, 1953), 18–22.

100. The first motion pictures were entered for copyright as prints on paper: John Y. Cole, "Of Copyright," 134; 37 Stat 488 (1912), provided for their registration without deposit since the nitrate films were highly flammable: Kemp R. Niver, *Early Motion Pictures: The Paper Print Collection in the Library of Congress* (Washington, DC: LC, 1985). The LC acquired its first phonograph record, a cylinder recording of Kaiser Wilhelm II, in 1904; Cole, *For Congress,* 75, 83.

101. *ARLC,* 1898, 52–54; 1926, 3–5, 150, 335–41; 37 Stat 319. Pennell added to the collection until her death in 1936; *ARLC,* 1931, 254; 1933, 108; 1936, 159–60.

102. Lacy, "Library of Congress: Sesquicentenary Review: I," 161–62; Charles A. Seavey, "Philip Lee Phillips and the Growth of the Library of Congress Map Collection, 1897–1924," *Government Publications Review* 20 (1993): 283–95; 31 Stat 1464; *ARLC,* 1910, 80–81. The LC kept at least two newspaper titles from each state. Foreign newspapers, which were not systematically acquired until after 1900, represented "commercial and political centers throughout the world:" S. Branson Marley Jr., "Newspapers and the Library of Congress," *QJLC* 32 (July 1975): 219.

103. *ARLC*, 1915, 69–70; 1916, 115–19; 1921, 26–28, 41; 1927, 25–29; Peter Van Wingen, "The Incunabula Collections at the Library of Congress," *Rare Books & Manuscripts Librarianship* 5 (Fall 1989): 88–90. Thacher (d. 1927) bequeathed the collections to the LC.

104. John D. Knowlton, ed., *Herbert Putnam: A 1903 Trip to Europe* (Lanham, MD: Scarecrow Press, 2005); *ARLC*, 1908, 17–19; 1909, 21, 38; 1911, 45–48; *LCIB*, December 9–15, 1947, 7.

105. *ARLC*, 1907, 24–31; 1909, 21–23; 1914, 31–34; 1915, 38–42; 1916, 23–35; 1917, 83–92; 1919, 23–30. The Orientalia Division was established as the Division of Semitica and Oriental Literature in 1914. Arthur W. Hummel, "The Growth of the Orientalia Collections," *QJLC* 11 (February 1954): 69–80; *Library of Congress Asian Collections: An Illustrated Guide* (Washington, DC: LC, 2000), 13–18. The 1908 gift acknowledged US partial remission of Chinese reparations from the Boxer Rebellion; *ARLC*, 1938, 459.

106. Myron M. Weinstein, "The First Deinard Collection of the Library of Congress," *Judaica Librarianship* 12 (2006): 31–48; *ARLC*, 1904, 29–31; 1907, 24–29; 1912, 23–25. A Hebraic section was established in 1914 in the Division of Semitica and Oriental Literature.

107. *ARLC*, 1904, 26–27; Edward Kasinec, "Yudin's Books in America: A View from the 21st Century," *Slavic & East European Information Resources* 9, no. 2 (2008): 115–17, suggested that the purchase was politically timely, after President Roosevelt's mediation of the Russo-Japanese War. Roosevelt approved the purchase; Eugene Pivovarov, "Alexis V. Babine in the Library of Congress," *Slavic & East European Information Resources* 3, no. 1 (2002): 59–68.

108. Quoted by David C. Mearns, "The Answers: A Fog-Lade Panorama of LC's Collections," *LJ* 90 (April 15, 1965): 1838–39. Putnam established the Slavic Section, which became the Slavic Division in 1919.

109. Lacy, "Library of Congress: Sesquicentenary Review: I," 162; Hummel, "Growth," 81–85; Sergius Yakobson, "An Autobiography of Gennadiĭ Vasil'evich Yudin," *QJLC* 3 (February 1945): 13–15; *ARLC*, 1904, 31; 1907, 21–24; *LCIB* 24 (September 13, 1965): 502.

110. The dissertation bibliography ceased with the 1938 volume, when it was superseded by an index prepared by the ARL and by *Dissertation Abstracts* published by University Microfilms: *LCIB* 20 (August 26, 1961), 515.

111. Richard Rogers Bowker, *Copyright: Its History and Its Law* (Boston: Houghton Mifflin, 1912), 365–66; Thorvald Solberg, *Copyright Legislation: A Retrospective Summary* (Washington, DC, 1929); Solberg to R. U. Johnson, June 29, 1897, Thorvald Solberg Papers, LC.

112. *ARLC*, 1901, 48–49; 1903, 437–593.

113. George Haven Putnam, *Memories of a Publisher, 1865–1915* (New York: G. P. Putnam's Sons, 1915), 382.

114. Israel, *State of the Union*, 82–83.

115. Putnam to Richard Rogers Bowker, December 9, 1905; Putnam to Frank P. Hill, November 15, 1905; Putnam to Bowker, March 6, 1906, Librarian's Letterbooks, LCA; *ARLC*, 1906, 111–25; *LCIB*, May 3–9, 1949, 13.

116. Quoted by John Muller, *Mark Twain in Washington, DC: The Adventures of a Capital Correspondent* (Charleston, SC: History Press, 2013), 173–77.

117. A later provision allowed transfer or disposal of noncopyright materials: 35 Stat 845, at 858.

118. The 1870 copyright law brought in much material that Spofford considered ephemeral: Carl Ostrowski, "'The Choice of Books': Ainsworth Rand Spofford, the Ideology of Reading, and Literary Collections at the Library of Congress in the 1870s," *L&C* 45 (2010): 73–76. Putnam assigned the superintendent of the Reading Room and the Catalog and Order Division chiefs to select among the copyright deposits: Bishop, "Library of Congress, 1907–1915," 3.

119. 35 Stat 1075; *ARLC*, 1909, 87–90; Richard Rogers Bowker, *Copyright: Its History and Law* (Boston: Houghton Mifflin, 1912), 367–72; Elizabeth Jane Aikin, "High Culture, Low Culture: The Singular Duality of the Library of Congress," *American Studies* 42 (Fall 2001): 45; James L. W. West III, "The Chace Act and Anglo-American Literary Relations," *Studies in Bibliography* 45 (1992): 310.

120. Harold C. Relyea, "Across the Hill: The Congressional Research Service and Providing Research for Congress—A Retrospective on Origins," *Government Information Quarterly* 27 (2010): 416; *ARLC*, 1892, 36. Volumes 1 and 2 of the index were published in 1908 and 1911; *ARLC*, 1908, 31–35; 1911, 34.

121. Marion Casey, *Charles McCarthy: Librarianship and Reform* (Chicago: ALA, 1981), 41; Samuel Rothstein, "The Origins of Legislative Reference Services in the United States," *Legislative Studies Quarterly* 15 (August 1990): 401–11.

122. *CR*, 62nd Congress, 2nd Sess., 1912, 2459–60; *ARLC*, 1911, 183–237; Cole, *For Congress*, 82.

123. *ARLC*, 1911, 78–79, 183–217.

124. "Congressional Reference Bureau: Hearings before the Committee on the Library on Various Bills Proposing the Establishment of a Congressional Reference Bureau," House of Representatives, 62nd Congress, 3rd Sess. (Washington, DC: GPO, 1912); "Legislative Drafting Bureau and Legislative Reference Division of the Library of Congress, Senate Report 1271," 62nd Congress, 3rd Sess., 1913, 30; *ARLC*, 1912, 108–9; 1913, 247–61.

125. *ARLC*, 1914, 10–14; 38 Stat 454, at 463; "Legislative, Executive, and Judicial Appropriation Bill, Hearings before the Subcommittee of the Committee on Appropriations, United States Senate, 63rd Congress, 3rd Sess." (Washington, DC: GPO, 1915), 6–12; Office of the Librarian, Special Order 101, LCA; 38 Stat 997, at 1005; Herbert Putnam, "Legislative Reference for Congress," *American Political Science Review* 9 (August 1915): 542–49. The Legislative Reference Service increasingly took responsibility for American law and public policy research; the Law Library handled foreign and comparative research: *LCIB* 66 (January–February 2007): 23.

126. Daniel Horowitz, *The Morality of Spending: Attitudes toward the Consumer Society in America, 1875–1940* (Chicago: Ivan R. Dee, 1985), 68–73; Rosenberg, *Nation's Great Library*, 83–84.

127. *ARLC*, 1912, 22–23.

128. *ARLC*, 1911, 54; 1914, 15–17; Martel to J. C. M. Hanson, May 29, 1916, J. C. M. Hanson Papers, University of Chicago Library.

129. Rosenberg, *Nation's Great Library*, 72–74, 81–84. Serials include magazines, journals, newspapers, annual reports, and other recurring publications (daily, weekly, monthly, or annually) that are numbered or dated on each issue.

130. *ARLC*, 1918, 21–23; 1920, passim.

131. Frederick P. Keppel, "Herbert Putnam," in *Essays*, 255–56; Arthur Young, *Books for Sammies: The American Library Association and World War I* (Pittsburgh: Beta Phi Mu, 1981), 10. Putnam deflected a proposal from Louis N. Wilson (Clark University) and Ernest Cushing Richardson (Princeton University) to establish a War Library in Washington to be administered by the LC; Lewis C. Branscomb, *Ernest Cushing Richardson* (Metuchen, NJ: Scarecrow Press, 1992), 25–26.

132. George B. Utley, "The Library War Service and Its General Director," in *Essays*, 474–91; Young, *Books for Sammies*, 12–13; Theodore Wesley Koch, *War Service of the American Library Association*, 3rd ed. (Washington, DC: ALA War Service, 1918).

133. Wayne A. Wiegand, *"An Active Instrument for Propaganda": The American Public Library During World War I* (New York: Greenwood Press, 1989), 62–69.

134. *ARLC*, 1919, 10; ALA War Service Committee minutes, October 4, 1917, LCA.

135. Thomison, *History*, 64–65; Young, *Books for Sammies*, 25.

136. Koch, *War Service*, 13; Young, *Books for Sammies*, 33–35; Suzanne M. Stauffer, "Let Us Forget This Cherishing of Women in Library Work: Women in the American Library War Service, 1918–1920," *Libraries, Culture, History, and Society* 3, no. 2 (2019): 155–66.

137. Quoted by Wiegand, *"Active Instrument,"* 100–101; also see Young, *Books for Sammies*, 4–7, 47–55; and Koch, *War Service*, unpaged introduction by Herbert Putnam.

138. Quoted by Young, *Books for Sammies*, 66.

139. Theodore Wesley Koch, *Books in the War: The Romance of Library War Service* (Boston: Houghton Mifflin, 1919), 28.

140. Herbert Putnam, "Statement of the General Director, ALA War Service," *BALA* 13 (1919): 261–63; *ARLC*, 1919, 8–11; *Harvard Class of 1883 Fiftieth Anniversary* (Cambridge, MA: Printed for the Class, 1933), 276–77; Young, *Books for Sammies*, 80–91.

141. *BALA* 12 (1918): 113; Putnam, "Statement," 263; Thomison, *History*, 72–83; Bishop, "American Library Association," 36–38; Arthur P. Young, "Aftermath of a Crusade, World War I and the Enlarged Program of the American Library Association," *LQ* 50 (April 1980): 191–207.

Chapter 6

1. *ARLC*, 1918, 86–88.

2. In 1900, the staff had organized the Library of Congress Beneficiary Association, which provided for a payment to a designated beneficiary on the death of a staff member. It continued to exist after the union was established. Union membership grew during the 1920s but declined during the Depression: Union Activities at the Library of Congress, LCA, box 1.

3. *ARLC*, 1918, 10; Jane Aikin Rosenberg, *The Nation's Great Library: Herbert Putnam and the Library of Congress, 1899–1939* (Urbana: University of Illinois Press, 1993), 91; Constance McLaughlin Green, *Washington: A History of the Capital, 1800–1950* (Princeton, NJ: Princeton University Press, 1962), 2: 244. De facto segregation in Washington increased from the late nineteenth century onward; see Eric S. Yellin, *Racism in the Nation's Service; Government Workers and the Color Line in Woodrow Wilson's America* (Chapel Hill: University of North Carolina Press, 2013), 146 and passim; Chris M. Asch and George D. Musgrove, *Chocolate City: A History of Race and Democracy in the Nation's Capital* (Chapel Hill: University of North Carolina Press, 2017), 219–26. Elizabeth Dowling Taylor, *The Original Black Elite: Daniel Murray and the Story of a Forgotten Era* (New York: HarperCollins, 2017), 155, 336, calculated that Blacks made up 16 percent of the LC's staff in 1895 but decreased to 5.6 percent in 1921 and reported segregation in the LC's cafeteria in 1919; see also *Chicago Whip*, January 31, 1920: I thank Cheryl Fox for this reference.

4. *ARLC*, 1919, 72–73, 85, 90; 1920, 9–10; 1921, 73–74, 82.

5. Herbert Putnam to the Loyal Staff of the Library of Congress, July 25, 1918, LCA.

6. "Legislative, Executive, and Judicial Appropriation Bill, 1921; Hearing before Subcommittee of House Committee on Appropriations, 66th Congress, 2nd Sess." (GPO, 1920), 24–25. Congress raised Putnam's salary to $7,500 and Chief Assistant Librarian Griffin's salary to $4,500 in 1921: Rosenberg, *Nation's Great Library*, 93–94; *ARLC*, 1919, 11; 1920, 7.

7. *ARLC*, 1923, 4–6, 196–210; Mearns, *Story*, 192–94.

8. 42 Stat 1488; *ARLC*, 1925, 143; John Y. Cole, *Capital Libraries and Librarians: A Brief History of the District of Columbia Library Association, 1894–1994* (Washington, DC: LC, 1994), 43–44. The act also mandated annual performance ratings and step increases.

9. Rosenberg, *Nation's Great Library*, 96.

10. Josephus Nelson and Judith Farley, *Full Circle: Ninety Years of Service in the Main Reading Room* (Washington, DC: LC, 1991), 23.

11. *LCIB* 19 (June 6, 1960): 274.

12. *ARLC*, 1920, 102–3, 195–209. Between 1921 and Meyer's retirement in 1935, the LRS staff increased from 5 to 48, congressional inquiries increased from about 1,000 to 25,000, and the appropriation increased from $25,000 to about $92,000: John Y. Cole, "Herman H. B. Meyer," *DALB*, 363.

13. Rosenberg, *Nation's Great Library*, 98–99.

14. Putnam requested new stacks in 1917 and 1923; Congress approved funding in March 1925: *ARLC*, 1917, 213–14; 1923, 112–19; "Legislative Establishment Appropriation Bill, 1925, Hearings before Subcommittee of House Committee on Appropriations, 68th Congress, 1st Sess." (GPO, 1924), 101–4.

15. *ARLC*, 1922, 22, 26; 1925, 29–31; 1928, 27–28; *LCIB*, February 17–23, 1948, 11–12; John T. Dorosh, "The Alaskan Russian Church Archives," *QJLC* 18 (August 1961): 193–203. The number of government documents for exchange increased to 125 (43 Stat 1105, at 1106, 1925) and to 150 (49 Stat 1545, at 1550, 1936); Robert D. Stevens, *The Role of the Library of Congress in the International Exchange of Official Publications: A Brief History* (Washington, DC: LC, 1953), 26–30.

16. Mearns, *Story*, 191–92; David C. Mearns, *The Declaration of Independence: The Story of a Parchment* (Washington, DC: LC, 1950); 42 Stat 434; *LCIB* 56 (August 1997): 269–71, 279. A January 1921 Commerce Department fire that destroyed archives, including the 1890 census, perhaps encouraged the transfer.

17. Mary Howe, *Jottings* (Washington, DC, privately published, 1959), 109–11.

18. Cyrilla Barr, "The 'Faerie Queen' and the 'Archangel': The Correspondence of Elizabeth Sprague Coolidge and Carl Engel," *American Music* 15 (Summer 1997): 162–64; Cyrilla Barr, *The Coolidge Legacy* (Washington, DC: LC, 1997), 34; *ARLC*, 1925, 1–5, 286–90; 1926, 345.

19. 43 Stat 788; 43 Stat 1107; 49 Stat 1205, 1206. The decision was concurrent with a growing relationship between private citizens and institutional collecting, with the establishment between 1919 and 1932, of the Huntington, Clements, Morgan, Clark, and Folger Shakespeare libraries: John Cole, "The Library of Congress and American Scholarship, 1865–1939," in *Libraries and Scholarly Communication in the United States: The Historical Dimension*, edited by Phyllis Dain and John Cole (New York: Greenwood Press, 1990), 54.

20. LC, *Law Library of Congress, 1832–1982* (Washington, DC: LC, 1982), 18–19; *LCIB* 57 (December 1998): 305. The ABA group was later renamed the Standing Committee on the Law Library of Congress.

21. *LCIB* 14 (May 9, 1955): 7–8; Mearns, *Story*, 202–3; *ARLC*, 1926, 3–5; 1937, 5–6.

22. *ARLC*, 1935, 156; 1936, 131–32; 1937, 5.

23. *ARLC*, 1926, 1; 1935, 154; 1938, 156; William McGuire, *Poetry's Catbird Seat: The Consultantship in Poetry in the English Language at the Library of Congress, 1937–1987* (Washington, DC: LC, 1988), 42–43. The first Coolidge Auditorium concerts, held October 28–30, 1925, were later broadcast by the Naval Broadcasting Service and beginning in 1930 by the five-year-old National Broadcasting Company: *LCIB* 67 (January–February 2008): 16.

24. *LCIB* 57 (December 1998): 296–97. On the fortieth anniversary of the Juilliard's residence, the LC ended the residency program: *LCIB* 60 (September 2001): 187, 191; 62 (March 2003): 60–61, 63.

25. *ARLC*, 1926, 3, 7.

26. With that gift, the Division of Prints was renamed the Division of Fine Arts: *ARLC*, 1929, 9.

27. The additional Wilbur funding was provided following a legal settlement: *ARLC*, 1928, 228–37; 1929, 68–73; 1933, 4; Roscoe R. Hill, *American Missions in European Archives* (Mexico City: American Institute of Geography and History, 1951), 71–83.

28. On the Putnam–Huntington friendship, see McGuire, *Poetry's Catbird Seat*, 28–41.

29. *ARLC*, 1929, 8–9; 1930, 3. Langley, the third Smithsonian Secretary, collected materials on aeronautics pioneers.

30. *Harvard Class of 1883 Fiftieth Anniversary* (Cambridge, MA: Printed for the Class, 1933), 278; Herbert Putnam, "Consultants at the National Library," *LQ* 1 (January 1931): 18–21.

31. Samuel Rothstein, *The Development of Reference Services through Academic Traditions, Public Library Practice and Special Librarianship*, ACRL Monograph 14 (Chicago: Association of College and Research Libraries, 1955), 90–91.

32. *ARLC*, 1927, 100; David M. Kennedy, *Freedom from Fear: The American People in Depression and War, 1929–1945* (New York: Oxford University Press, 1999), 228–29.

33. *ARLC*, 1928, 143–45.

34. *ARLC*, 1932, 321–24; Archie Green, "The Archive's Shores," *Folklife Annual* (1985): 61–67; Debora G. Kodish, *Good Friends and Bad Enemies: Robert Winslow Gordon and the Study of American Folksong* (Urbana: University of Illinois Press, 1986).

35. John A. Lomax, *Adventures of a Ballad Hunter* (Austin: University of Texas Press, 2017), 111 and passim; Ronald D. Cohen, *Alan Lomax: Assistant in Charge, the Library of Congress Letters, 1935–1945* (Jackson: University of Mississippi Press, 2011); *LCIB* 58 (August 1999): 196–200; Green, "Archive's Shores," 61–73. The LC acquired Alan Lomax's ethnographic collection in 2004; *LCIB* 63 (May–June 2004): 86–89.

36. Elizabeth Jane Aikin, "High Culture, Low Culture: The Singular Duality of the Library of Congress," *American Studies* 42 (Fall 2001): 52–58. As the Archive began collecting nonmusic materials, the Folklore Section was created in the Music Division in 1946; because it collected outside the United States, it dropped "American" from its name after 1955.

37. Clark Evans, "Librarian in Disguise: V. Valta Parma and the Development of Popular Culture Collections at the Library of Congress," in *Pioneers, Passionate Ladies, and Private Eyes: Dime Novels, Series Books, and Paperbacks*, edited by Larry E. Sullivan and Lydia Cushman Schurman (New York: Haworth, 1996), 24–34; William Matheson, "Seeking the Rare, the Important, the Valuable: The Rare Book Division," *QJLC* 30 (July 1973): 211–14.

38. The policy of sequestering some materials dated at least to Spofford's administration. E.g., the "Delta Collection" included some copyright deposits and items forwarded by postal and customs officials. The collection (except rarities) was integrated into the general collection in 1964: Melissa Adler, "The Keeper of the Collections and the Delta Collection: Regulating Obscenity at the Library of Congress, 1940–1963," *Inter/Actions: UCLA Journal of Education and Information Studies* 12, no. 1 (2016), http://escholarship.org; Melissa Adler, *Cruising the Library: Perversities in the Organization of Knowledge* (New York: Fordham University Press, 2017), 63–82.

39. Lewis C. Branscomb, "Ernest Cushing Richardson," *DALB*, 432–35; *ARLC*, 1939, 341–42.

40. *ARLC*, 1927, 7–9; Lewis C. Branscomb, *Ernest Cushing Richardson* (Metuchen, NJ: Scarecrow Press, 1992), 37–43.

41. The staff also developed a union catalog of manuscripts on the history of chemistry and alchemy (1939). Additional grants supported 1930s special projects: in cooperation with the ACLS, the Library received a General Education Board grant for the three-volume *Census of Medieval and Renaissance Manuscripts in the United States and Canada*, edited by Seymour de Ricci and published 1935–40 by the H. W. Wilson Company, and the ACLS supported the biographical compilation, *Eminent Chinese of the Ch'ing Period* (1943–44), edited by Orientalia Division chief Arthur W. Hummel. A three-year grant from the Carnegie Corporation (1938) funded development of the South and Central Asian collections.

42. William Warner Bishop, "J. C. M. Hanson and International Cataloging," *LQ* 4 (April 1934): 41–42; J. C. M. Hanson, "Organization and Reorganization of Libraries," *LQ* 12 (1942): 529–31; C. Glenn Sparks, *Doyen of Librarians: A Biography of William Warner Bishop* (Metuchen, NJ; Scarecrow Press, 1993), 210–50; *ARLC*, 1928, 11, 173–74, 177–80; Claud Glenn Sparks, "William Warner Bishop," *DALB*, 34; John Phillip Immroth, "James Christian Meinich Hanson," *DALB*, 229; James Bennett Childs and John Y. Cole, "Charles Martel," *DALB*, 344.

43. Dewey to Putnam, January 5, 1925, Verner W. Clapp Papers, LC; Rosenberg, *Nation's Great Library*, 109.

44. Anticipating the DC numbers project, the DC editorial office moved to the LC in 1927: *ARLC*, 1930, 24; Rosenberg, *Nation's Great Library*, 108–11; Julia C. Pressey, "The Decimal Classification Section at the Library of Congress," *Catalogers' and Classifiers' Yearbook* 9 (1940): 38–43; Verner W. Clapp, "DC Numbers on LC Cards," *LRTS* 9 (Fall 1965): 393–96.

45. "A Quarter Century at the National Library," *LJ* 49 (March 15, 1924): 261–64; (April 1, 1924): 321–25; Charles Martel, "Cataloging, 1876–1926," *LJ* 20 (December 1, 1926): 1065–69.

46. Rosenberg, *Nation's Great Library*, 111–13.

47. "Legislative Establishment Appropriations Bill, 1928, Hearings before Subcommittee of House Committee on Appropriations, 69th Congress, 2nd Sess." (GPO, 1927), 117–18; "Legislative Establishment Appropriation Bill, 1929, Hearings before Subcommittee of House Committee on Appropriations, 70th Congress, 1st Sess." (GPO, 1928), 268–69.

48. Marley, "Newspapers," 220; Cole, "Library of Congress and American Scholarship," 35.

49. 44 Stat 1066; 45 Stat 2, at 4, 197, 487, 776; 46 Stat 583; *ARLC*, 1928, 271–72; 1930, 1; Matheson, "Seeking the Rare," 211–12. Putnam had warned in 1926 that the stack would be full in a decade: *LCM* 3 (March–April 2014): 22.

50. Quoted by Stephen H. Grant, *Collecting Shakespeare: The Story of Henry and Emily Folger* (Baltimore: Johns Hopkins University Press, 2016), 143.

51. Andrea E. Mays, *The Millionaire and the Bard: Henry Folger's Obsessive Hunt for Shakespeare's First Folio* (New York: Simon & Schuster, 2015), 226–36; Grant, *Collecting Shakespeare*, 140–44; Senate Report 1175, 70th Congress, 1st Sess.; 45 Stat 622. The Folger Library opened on January 2, 1933. Putnam noted that in the future, the LC would not purchase rare Shakespeariana: *ARLC*, 1932, 21.

52. *ARLC*, 1928, 7, 321–27.

53. Herbert Putnam, "Our National Library," *Review of Reviews* 79 (February 1929): 58–63.

54. *ARLC*, 1929, 5–6, 11–12.

55. Herbert Putnam, "The National Library: Some Recent Developments," *BALA* 22 (1928): 346–55; "Dr. Putnam's Response," *LJ* 54 (May 1, 1929): 386–87. The celebration included a festschrift, a tribute from the ACLS, and unveiling a bust of Putnam by his daughter Brenda, which is still displayed in the Jefferson Building.

56. Lewis L. Gould, *The Most Exclusive Club: A History of the Modern United States Senate* (New York: Basic Books, 2005), 117.

57. *ARLC*, 1928, 159–62, 210–12; *Gazette* 9 (July 31, 1998): 6. Vollbehr hoped a benefactor would present the collection to the LC, but none appeared. Fess and Collins both attended the exhibition.

58. *CR*, 71st Congress, 1st Sess., 3251–57.

59. "Hearing before the Committee on the Library, House of Representatives on H.R. Resolution 6147, a Bill Authorizing $1.5 Million for 3,000 Incunabula" (GPO, 1930); Frederick R. Goff, "Uncle Sam Has a Book," *QJLC* 38 (Summer 1981): 122–33.

60. "Purchase of Vollbehr Collection of Incunabula," Senate Report 965, 71st Congress, 2nd Sess., 1930–31, 2, 5; Elizabeth Snapp, "The Acquisition of the Vollbehr Collection of Incunabula for the Library of Congress," *JLH* 10 (April 1975): 152–61; *ARLC*, 1930, 12–15.

61. Van Wingen, "Incunabula Collections," 91–95; 46 Stat 860, at 861.

62. *ARLC*, 1930, 2.

63. *ARLC*, 1932, 248–49; 1933, 175–76; 1935, 270; Paul Edlund, "A Monster and a Miracle: The Cataloging Distribution Service of the Library of Congress, 1901–1976," *QJLC* 33 (October 1976): 408. The Reading Room had long been open to users age sixteen and above: *ARLC*, 1901, 244.

64. Kennedy, *Freedom from Fear*, 138; 47 Stat 382, at 399, 1489; 48 Stat 8, 274; *ARLC*, 1933, 221–34; 1935, 1–2.

65. *BALA* 1 (July 1907) 44; LC, ed., *That All May Read: Library Services for Blind and Physically Handicapped People* (Washington, DC: LC, 1983), 65–74, 104; 37 Stat 948; *ARLC*, 1912, 106–8; 1925, 140–41, 150; 1933, 187–89. The Red Cross service united with the LC's Books for the Adult Blind project in 1943, which was renamed the Division of Books for the Adult Blind.

66. Among others, Helen Keller and a World War I–blinded soldier, Charles Campbell, testified at the March 27, 1930, hearings: Committee on the Library, "Books for the Adult Blind: Hearing on H.R. 9042, House of Representatives, 71st Congress, 1st Sess., March 27, 1930" (GPO, 1930). "Adult" was subsequently defined as including readers eighteen years of age or older: *ARLC*, 1939, 409–10.

67. 46 Stat 1487; Judith M. Dixon and Alfred D. Hagle, "Free Matter: Nearly a Century of Change," in *That All May Read*, 425–29; Eunice Lovejoy, "History and Standards" in *That All May Read*, 1–8, 75–91; *ARLC*, 1938, 387–91.

68. The use of long-playing records came fourteen years before the LP became an industry standard: *LCIB* 61 (October 2002): 224. Congress approved funding to provide players to readers in 1947: *Gazette* 17 (December 15, 2006): 5.

69. Stephen Prine and George F. Thuronyi, "The National Library Service for the Blind and Physically Handicapped," *Encyclopedia*, 39–45; *That All May Read*, 83–91, 100–103, 128–29; *ARLC*, 1936, 290–93; 1937, 297–98; 1938, 392; *LCIB* 46 (April 13, 1987): 150–51; 48 Stat 678; 50 Stat 72. The books were selected from lists assembled by the staff and outside advisers. Religious, patriotic, and historical titles and literary classics dominated early selections. On selection and copyright issues, see Matthew Rubery, *The Untold Story of the Talking Book* (Cambridge, MA: Harvard University Press, 2016), 66–74; 109–28.

70. *Washington Star*, June 21 and July 6, 1933; Rosenberg, *Nation's Great Library*, 139–40. Gould, *Most Exclusive Club*, 132, noted that Roosevelt withheld patronage from Democratic congressmen until after the "Hundred Days" special session ended on June 16, 1933.

71. Louis M. Howe to the President, December 5, 1933; Mary W. Dewson to Howe, November 28, 29, 1933, Franklin D. Roosevelt Papers, Roosevelt Library, Hyde Park, NY; *Washington Herald*, June 26–30, 1933.

72. Rosenberg, *Nation's Great Library*, 141–42.

73. Sheppard to Putnam, September 4, 1935, LCA.

74. *CR*, 75th Congress, 1st Sess., 1937–38, 9546–47; Rosenberg, *Nation's Great Library*, 142–43.

75. "Legislative Establishment Appropriation Bill for 1935: Hearings before Subcommittee on Appropriations, House of Representatives, 73rd Congress, 2nd Sess." (GPO, 1934), 197–98; "Legislative Establishment Appropriation Bill for 1938: Hearings before the Subcommittee on Appropriations, House of Representatives, 75th Congress, 1st Sess." (GPO, 1937), 98. Putnam also cautioned that "different methods of counting" made comparisons difficult.

76. Emily Miller Danton, *The Library of Tomorrow* (Chicago: ALA, 1939), 184–91; Herbert Putnam, "'Library of Congress' as a Title for the National Library," February 1936, LCA; Putnam to Shirley Putnam O'Hara, March 3, 1929, Putnam Papers, LC.

77. C. Ford Peatross, "Architectural Collections in the Library of Congress," *QJLC* 34 (July 1977): 249–51; LC, *Historic America: Buildings, Structures, and Sites Recorded by the Historic American Buildings Survey and the Historic American Engineering Record* (Washington, DC: LC, 1983); *ARLC*, 1930, 235–36; 1934, 136–37; 1937, 153; 1941, 145; *LCIB* 27 (September 19, 1968): 555–56; LC, "Documenting a Legacy: 40 Years of the Historic American Buildings Survey," *QJLC* 30 (October 1973): 268–94.

78. *ARLC*, 1934, 5, 136–37, 209–10; 1935, 103–4; 129; 1936, 286; 1938, 120, 396; 1940, 133.

79. John Y. Cole, "Amassing American 'Stuff': The Library of Congress and the Federal Arts Projects of the 1930s," *QJLC* 40 (Fall 1983): 356–68; Luther H. Evans, "The Future Program of the Historical Records Survey," in *Archives and Libraries*, edited by A. F. Kuhlman (Chicago: ALA, 1939), 22–27; *ARLC*, 1936, 30; 1937, 50, 122; 1938, 307–9; 1939, 339–41; 1941, 148, 172–80. A "shelflist" is a list of books ordered by classification number.

80. "Annual Report of the Superintendent of the Reading Room, 1929–30," LCA.

81. Elllis Hawley, *The Great War and the Search for a Modern Order: A History of the American People and Their Institutions, 1917–1933*, 2nd ed. (New York: St. Martin's Press, 1992), 43–44, 116; Jane Aikin, "'A Search for Better Ways into the Future': The Library of Congress and Its Users in the Interwar Period," in *Libraries and the Reading Public in Twentieth-Century America*, edited by Christine Pawley and Louise S. Robbins (Madison: University of Wisconsin Press, 2013), 78–93.

82. *ARLC*, 1901, 244.

83. Quoted by Nelson and Farley, *Full Circle*, 20.

84. LC, "Information for Readers in the Main Reading Room" (GPO, 1937), 3.

85. Rosenberg, *Nation's Great Library*, 121–23.

86. *Report of the ALA Cooperative Cataloging Committee to the General Education Board* (New York, privately published, 1932); Keyes Metcalf, *Random Recollections of an Anachronism* (New York: Readex Books, 1980), 349–50.

87. Rosenberg, *Nation's Great Library*, 124–25.

88. *ARLC*, 1933, 159–60; Metcalf, *Random Recollections*, 348–51; Martha M. Yee, "Attempts to Deal with the 'Crisis in Cataloging' at the Library of Congress in the 1940s," *LQ* 57 (January 1987): 14–15.

89. Kathryn Luther Henderson, "Treated with a Degree of Uniformity and Common Sense: Descriptive Cataloging in the United States, 1876–1975," *LT* 25 (Summer 1976): 232–34; Wyllis E. Wright, "The *Anglo-American Cataloging Rules:* A Historical Perspective," *LRTS* 20 (Winter 1976): 36–37.

90. *ARLC*, 1937, 48–49. Subtracting located items resulted in an annual "Select List of Unlocated Research Books," which was circulated to libraries as a buying guide.

91. Committee on Resources of American Libraries, *Report of the Informal Conference on Union Catalogs, Library of Congress, Apr. 17th and 18th, 1936, called by the ALA Committee on Resources of American Libraries and the Carnegie Corporation* (Chicago: ALA, 1936); *ARLC*, 1936, 50–52; 1938, 306–7.

92. "Legislative Establishment Appropriation Bill for 1934: Hearings before Subcommittee of House Committee on Appropriations, 72nd Congress, 2nd Sess." (GPO, 1933), 119; *ARLC*, 1933, 158–59; 1935, 246–47; 1937, 245–46; Clapp, "DC Numbers," 395–96; David Judson Haykin, "Cooperative Cataloging in North America—Problems and Possibilities," *Catalogers and Classifiers' Yearbook* 6 (1937): 26–35; Leonard Ellinwood, "David Judson Haykin," *DALB*, 237–38.

93. Harriet D. MacPherson, *Some Practical Problems of Cataloging* (Chicago: ALA, 1936), 46–51.

94. *ARLC*, 1935, 249–50; 1936, 240–42.

95. "Legislative Establishment Appropriation Bill for 1937: Hearings before Subcommittee of House Committee on Appropriations, 74th Congress, 2nd Sess." (GPO, 1936), 215–22; *ARLC*, 1937, 250–51; Nouvart Tashjian, "Cooperative Cataloging: Another Problem Needs a Solution," *LJ* 62 (April 15, 1937): 329–30; Rosenberg, *Nation's Great Library*, 146–47.

96. Stephen A. McCarthy, "The ARL at Fifty," *Advances in Library Administration and Organization* 3 (1984): 280.

97. According to one report, Putnam feared a decrease in card sales: Paul North Rice, "Has the Association of Research Libraries Proved Worth While?" *C&RL* 8 (July 1947): 352. Other concerns were the editorial workload and the reliability of the technology: Rosenberg, *Nation's Great Library*, 148–49.

98. Redmond Kathleen Molz, *National Planning for Library Service, 1935–1975* (Chicago: ALA, 1984), 31–34; "A National Plan for Libraries," *BALA* 29 (February 1935): 97.

99. Carl Milam to Putnam, January 3, 1935; Putnam to Milam, January 21, 1935, LCA.

100. "Progress in Federal Relations," *BALA* 32 (February 1938): 75; Redmond Kathleen Molz, *Federal Policy and Library Support* (Cambridge, MA: MIT Press, 1976), 15.

101. Rosenberg, *Nation's Great Library*, 149–51; Molz, *National Planning*, 81–83.

102. Putnam to Bowerman, September 25, 1937, LCA.

103. Putnam to Bowerman, September 25, 1937, LCA; Putnam to Schulz, September 17, 1937, LCA; Rosenberg, *Nation's Great Library*, 153–54; Peggy Sullivan, *Carl H. Milam and the American Library Association* (New York: H. W. Wilson, 1976), 168–69.

104. *Washington Herald*, November 16, 20, 1937.

105. Putnam to McKellar, October 16, 1937, LCA; Alfred Friendly, "Schulz Report to Putnam Revealed," *Washington Daily News*, December 23, 1937: *BALA* 32 (January 1939): 47–48.

106. "Legislative Establishment Appropriation Bill for 1939: Hearings before Subcommittee of House Committee on Appropriations, 75th Congress, 3rd Sess." (GPO, 1938), 95–96; *CR*, 75th Congress, 3rd Sess., 1939–40, 6138–48.

107. *ARLC*, 1938, 12–13; 52 Stat 808.

108. *ARLC*, 1935, 104–5; 1937, 4–5; 1953, 83; *LCIB* 9 (January 23, 1950): 20–21; Edlund, "Monster and a Miracle," 411; *Law Library, 1832–1872*, 22. The Law Library moved from the Capitol to the LC in 1950; the requirement for a branch in the Capitol was repealed in 1988 (PL 100-202), and the collection was dismantled January 2, 1998; *ARLC*, 1998, 27.

109. Blair Bolles, "The Library of Congress," *SR* 19 (December 24, 1938): 10–12; *ARLC*, 1937, 356.

110. *ARLC*, 1937, 354, 359. The earlier prediction, of course, came from Spofford.

111. The Manuscripts Division arrived in 1941, housing its collections for the first time in air-conditioned space.

112. *ARLC*, 1939, 15, 430–31.

113. 49 Stat 459, at 471; *ARLC*, 1936, 252.

114. Dennis Thomison, "FDR, the ALA, and Mr. MacLeish: The Selection of the Librarian of Congress, 1939," *LQ* 42 (October 1972): 390; Keyes Metcalf, *My Harvard Library Years, 1937–1955* (Cambridge, MA: Harvard College Library, 1988), 168.

115. "Dr. Putnam's Remarks," *LJ* 63 (March 1, 1938): 196.

116. David C. Mearns, "Herbert Putnam and His Responsible Eye," in *Herbert Putnam, 1861–1955: A Memorial Tribute* (Washington, DC: privately published, 1956), 41.

117. Frederick P. Keppel, "Herbert Putnam," *LJ* 63 (August 1938): 589; William Warner Bishop, "The Library of Congress under Herbert Putnam," *LJ* 63 (August 1938): 588–89; Lawrence Lewis, *A Tribute to Herbert Putnam, Librarian of Congress* (Washington, DC: GPO, 1939); *An Address to Herbert Putnam, Librarian of Congress 1899–1939 by the American Council of Learned Societies Together with His Reply, Washington, January 27, 1939* (Boston: Merrymount Press, 1939).

Chapter 7

1. Dennis Thomison, *A History of the American Library Association, 1876–1972* (Chicago: ALA, 1978), 139–41; Dennis Thomison, "FDR, the ALA, and Mr. MacLeish: The Selection of the Librarian of Congress, 1939," *LQ* 42 (October 1972): 390–91; Betty Schwartz, "The Role of the American Library Association in the Selection of Archibald MacLeish as Librarian of Congress," *JLH* 9 (July 1974): 241–60. The ALA proposed Carl Milam, but Sullivan stated, "A strong endorsement for one person was probably impolitic under the circumstances." Peggy Sullivan, *Carl H. Milam and the American Library Association* (New York: H. W. Wilson, 1976), 170, 172.

2. Roosevelt to McKellar, May 13, 1939, FDR Library, Hyde Park.

3. Roosevelt had met MacLeish: he was among those consulted in December 1938 about establishing the presidential library: Nancy L. Benco, "Archibald MacLeish, The Poet Librarian," in *Librarians*, 204; Waldo G. Leland, "The Creation of the Franklin D. Roosevelt Library: A Personal Narrative," *American Archivist* 18 (January 1955): 11–12.

4. Frankfurter to Roosevelt, May 11, 1939, Felix Frankfurter Papers, LC.

5. Advised by his physician to slow down, in 1938, MacLeish became the curator of Harvard's Nieman Foundation, but it paid only one-third of his *Fortune* earnings; he could not afford to remain: *LCIB* 60 (July–August 2001): 166.

6. Bernard A. Drabeck and Helen E. Ellis, *Archibald MacLeish: Reflections* (Amherst: University of Massachusetts Press, 1986), 129–30; Scott Donaldson, *Archibald MacLeish: An American Life* (Boston: Houghton Mifflin, 1992), 292–94; David C. Mearns, "The Brush of a Comet: Archibald MacLeish at the Library of Congress," *Atlantic Monthly* 215 (May 1965): 90–92; MacLeish to Roosevelt, May 28, 1939, June 1, 1939, in *Letters of Archibald MacLeish, 1907 to 1982*, edited by R. H. Winnick (Boston: Houghton Mifflin, 1983), 301–3; William H. MacLeish, *Uphill with Archie* (New York: Simon & Schuster, 2001), 142–43.

7. Mearns, *Story*, 207–8; Jane Aikin Rosenberg, *The Nation's Great Library: Herbert Putnam and the Library of Congress, 1899–1939* (Urbana: University of Illinois Press, 1993), 157; Scott Donaldson, *Archibald MacLeish: An American Life* (Boston: Houghton Mifflin, 1992), 296–97; Keyes Metcalf, *My Harvard Library Years, 1937–1955: A Sequel to Random Recollections of*

an Anachronism (Cambridge, MA: Harvard University Press, 1988), 164–65; *BALA* 33 (July 1939): 467, 522.

8. Thomison, "FDR," 396.

9. *CR* 84 (June 29, 1939): 8205–12; Donaldson, *Archibald MacLeish*, 297–300; Nancy Benco, "Archibald MacLeish: The Poet Librarian," *Quarterly Journal of the Library of Congress* 33 (July 1976): 233–49, at 207–8; Eva Goldschmidt, "Archibald MacLeish: Librarian of Congress," *C&RL* 30 (January 1969): 12–14; Schwartz, "Role," 247–49; John Chamberlain, "Archibald MacLeish," *SR* 20 (June 24, 1939): 10.

10. Benco, "Archibald MacLeish," 208–9; Goldschmidt, "Archibald MacLeish," 14–15; Ralph Munn and Archibald MacLeish, "Let Us All Cooperate," *LJ* 64 (August 1939): 570; Thomison, *History*, 141–42; *BALA* 33 (1939): 708.

11. Drabeck and Ellis, *Reflections*, 133.

12. *ARLC*, 1940, 3–11, 293; Archibald MacLeish, "The Reorganization of the Library of Congress," *LQ* (1944): 279; Rosenberg, *Nation's Great Library*, 151–53.

13. Keyes Metcalf, "Merits Respect and Gratitude," *LJ* 70 (March 1, 1945): 213.

14. MacLeish, "Reorganization," 279.

15. *ARLC*, 1940, 3, 12; 1941, 332–35; Union Activities, LCA, box 1; Eva M. Goldschmidt, comp., Archibald MacLeish, *Champion of a Cause: Essays and Addresses on Librarianship by Archibald MacLeish* (Chicago: ALA, 1971), 90–94. The two unions were the National Federation of Federal Employees, Local 626, and the United Federal Workers of America, Local 28. New grievance and appeal procedures were invoked in one case: a Black worker, Seth Major, who had been dismissed by his supervisor for performance errors. Supported by the United Federal Workers, Major took his case to the appeals board, which found no grounds for the charges and reinstated him. Library officials appealed to the staff to observe "the amenities of office intercourse"; *Pittsburgh Courier*, August 1, 1942. I thank Cheryl Fox for this reference.

16. *ARLC*, 1940, 11; Martha M. Yee, "Attempts to Deal with the 'Crisis in Cataloging' at the Library of Congress in the 1940s," *LQ* 57 (January 1987): 2–3. The Coordinating Committee of the Processing Divisions had reported in December 1939; its report informed the large budget request, but the GAO report was not submitted until 1942 and the Civil Service Commission report not until 1944: "The New Classification and Pay Plan at the Library of Congress," *LJ* 70 (March 1945): 193–95.

17. "Legislative Branch Appropriation Bill, 1941: Hearings before the Subcommittee of the Committee on Appropriations, House of Representatives, 76th Congress, 3rd Sess." (Washington, DC: GPO, 1940), 2.

18. Paul North Rice, Andrew D. Osborn, and Carleton B. Joeckel, "Report of the Librarian's Committee to the Librarian of Congress on the Processing Operations in the Library of Congress, June 15, 1940," 16, LCA; *ARLC*, 1940, 11–12; John Y. Cole., ed., *The Library of Congress in Perspective: A Volume Based on the Reports of the 1976 Librarian's Task Force and Advisory Groups* (New York: R. R. Bowker, 1978), 27–28.

19. Office of the Librarian, General Order 964, June 29, 1940. LCA; L. Quincy Mumford, "Account of the Reorganization of the Processing Department at the Library of Congress," *Catalogers' and Classifiers' Yearbook* 10 (1941): 45–56; Yee, "Attempts," 14–17.

20. Charles A. Goodrum, "The Administrative Organization of the Library of Congress," 1900–1948 (New York: School of Library Service at Columbia University, 1949), 40–41; *LCIB* 49 (December 17, 1990): 444.

21. *LCIB* 54 (July 10, 1995): 311–15.

22. *ARLC*, 1944, 13–26; Metcalf, "Merits Respect," 213.

23. *ARLC*, 1938, 9; 1940, 193; 1956, 49.

24. Fremont Rider, *The Scholar and the Future of the Research Library* (New York: Hadham Press, 1944), claimed that research libraries doubled in size every sixteen years and suggested microcards (which he invented) as a solution. Some were skeptical—e.g., Keyes Metcalf, "The Promise of Microprint," *C&RL* 6 (March 1945): 170–78—and Robert E. Molyneux later found Rider's claim incorrect: "More Hortatory Than Factual: Fremont Rider's Exponential Growth Hypothesis and the Context of Exponentialism," in *For the Good of the Order: Essays in Honor of Edward G. Holley* (Greenwich, CT: JAI Press, 1994), 85–117.

25. *ARLC*, 1940, 193–94; John Y. Cole, *For Congress and the Nation: A Chronological History of the Library of Congress* (Washington, DC: LC, 1979), 104; Keyes Metcalf, "Some Trends in Research Libraries," in *William Warner Bishop: A Tribute*, edited by Harry Miller Lydenberg and Andrew Keogh (New Haven, CT: Yale University Press, 1941), 145–66; Louis R. Wilson, "The Challenge of the 1930's to the 1940's," *C&RL* 1 (March 1940): 126–27; S. Branson Marley Jr., "Newspapers and the Library of Congress," *QJLC* 32 (July 1975): 207–37; Luther Evans, "Research Libraries in the War Period, 1939–45," *LQ*, October 1947, 252; Dan Lacy, "Microfilming as a Major Acquisitions Tool: Policies, Plans, and Problems," *QJLC* 6 (May 1949): 8–17.

26. *ARLC*, 1942, 96–99; *LCIB* 10 (September 10, 1951): 9.

27. *ARLC*, 1940, 61–78; 1941, 326; 1946, 245; Georgette M. Dorn, "Hispanic Division and Collections," *Encyclopedia*, 271–77; *The Archive of Hispanic Literature on Tape: A Descriptive Guide* (Washington, DC: LC, 1974); *Library of Congress Hispanic and Portuguese Collections: An Illustrated Guide* (Washington, DC: LC, 1996); *LCIB* 58 (October 1999): 235–37, 239.

28. *ARLC*, 1945, 89–90; 1952, 30; *LCIB* 15 (March 19, 1956): 139–40; Robert D. Stevens, *The Role of the Library of Congress in the International Exchange of Official Publications: A Brief History* (Washington, DC: LC, 1953), 32–36; Laurence J. Kipp, *The International Exchange of Publications* (Wakefield, MA: Murray, n.d.); Luther Evans, *Library Cooperation in the Americas* (Washington, DC: LC, 1947). The book list was first supported by the State Department; by Rutgers University Press, 1947–June 1954; and later by Swallow Press with LC support. The title changed (1950) to *United States Quarterly Book Review*; publication ceased in June 1956: *ARLC*, 1956, 34.

29. MacLeish, "Reorganization," 295; Cole, *Library of Congress*, 27.

30. *ARLC*, 1940, 20–29. The Canons of Selection applied to purchased materials, not to gifts or copyright deposits.

31. *ARLC*, 1940, 23–24.

32. *ARLC*, 1940, 3–29; 1941, 44–46, 83–86; "Final Report of the Committee on the Acquisitions Policy of the Library of Congress, December 19, 1939," LCA; Drabeck and Ellis, *Reflections*, 139.

33. Drabeck and Ellis, *Reflections*, 140–41.

34. Archibald MacLeish, *Libraries in the Contemporary Crisis* (Washington, DC: GPO, 1939).

35. Benco, "Archibald MacLeish," 213; Archibald MacLeish, "Of the Librarian's Profession," *Atlantic Monthly* 165 (June 1940): 790; Goldschmidt, *Champion of a Cause*, 21–22; John Y. Cole, *Jefferson's Legacy: A Brief History of the Library of Congress* (Washington, DC: LC, 1992), 36; Cole, *Library of Congress*, 31.

36. Shangri-La, Roosevelt's retreat in Maryland's Catoctin Mountains, was renamed Camp David by President Eisenhower. Drabeck and Ellis, *Reflections*, 143; MacLeish, *Uphill with Archie*, 141–63; Joseph E. Persico, *Roosevelt's Secret War: FDR and World War II Espionage* (New York: Random House, 2001), 204.

37. Jonathan Daniels, "Franklin Delano Roosevelt and Books," in *Three Presidents and Their Books*, edited by Arthur Bestor, David C. Mearns, and Jonathan W. Daniels (Urbana: University of Illinois Press, 1955), 97.

38. Drabeck and Ellis, *Reflections,* 156–57; Donaldson, *Archibald MacLeish,* 310, 343–44, stated that MacLeish had a direct telephone line to the White House. However, David Mearns wrote that rumor "was never verified": "As Alcuin Was Saying," *Pembroke Magazine* 7 (1976): 110–11.

39. MacLeish to Sherwood, December 9, in *Letters,* ed. Winnick, 307–8; Robert E. Sherwood, *Roosevelt and Hopkins* (New York: Harper & Brothers, 1950), 215; Donaldson, *Archibald MacLeish,* 310.

40. Roberts to Meyer, September 7, 1939, LCA; *ARLC,* 1941, 86–87; 1943, 39; Kathy Peiss, *Information Hunters: When Librarians, Soldiers, and Spies Banded Together in World War II Europe* (New York: Oxford University Press, 2019), 29–39.

41. *ARLC,* 1942, 94–95; 1945, 24–26; Peiss, *Information Hunters,* 53–56, 95; Ralph D. Wagner, "Manuel Sanchez: Librarian behind the Lines," *AL* 20 (November 1989): 962–64.

42. Brett Gary, *The Nervous Liberals: Propaganda Anxieties from World War I to the Cold War* (New York: Columbia University Press, 1999), 157–63.

43. Bradley F. Smith, *The Shadow Warriors: OSS and the Origins of the CIA* (New York: Basic Books, 1983), 31–53; Richard Dunlop, *Donovan: America's Master Spy* (Chicago: Rand McNally, 1982), 274–75, 279; Thomas F. Troy, *Wild Bill Donovan, Stephenson, and the Origin of CIA Intrepid* (New Haven, CT: Yale University Press, 1996), 114; Persico, *Roosevelt's Secret War,* 63–79.

44. Gary, *Nervous Liberals,* 163–64. William R. Corson, *Armies of Ignorance: The Rise of the American Intelligence Empire* (New York: Dial Press, 1977), 134–44, stated that Germany's June 22 invasion of Russia influenced the decision to establish an intelligence unit. However, Nicholas Reynolds, *Need to Know: World War II and the Rise of American Intelligence* (New York: Mariner Books, 2022), 1–72, emphasized British intelligence officials' influence.

45. OSS, *War Report of the OSS (Office of Strategic Services)* (New York: Walker, 1976), 48–91; Thomas F. Troy, *Donovan and the CIA: A History of the Establishment of the Central Intelligence Agency* (Frederick, MD: University Publications of America, 1981), 84–85; Barry M. Katz, *Foreign Intelligence: Research and Analysis in the Office of Strategic Services, 1942–1945* (Cambridge, MA: Harvard University Press, 1989), 4; Dunlop, *Donovan,* 300–301; Gary, *Nervous Liberals,* 164–67.

46. Quoted by Peiss, *Information Hunters,* 37.

47. OSS, *War Report,* 52–53; Drabeck and Ellis, *Reflections,* 146; Dunlop, *Donovan,* 296–97; *ARLC,* 1942, 34–35, 152–56; 1943, 18, 24; Luther Evans, "Research Libraries," 242–45; Persico, *Roosevelt's Secret War,* 110–11; William L. Langer, *In and Out of the Ivory Tower* (New York: Neale Watson, 1977), 180–94.

48. PL 77-354; Kathy Peiss, "Cultural Policy in a Time of War: The American Response to Endangered Books in World War II," *LT* 55 (Winter 2007): 370–86; Peiss, *Information Hunters,* 39–67, 95–96; OSS, *War Report,* 60–61; Pamela Spence Richards, "Gathering Enemy Scientific Information in Wartime: The OSS and the Periodical Republication Program," *JLH* 16 (Spring 1981): 253–64; Pamela Spence Richards, "Information Science in Wartime: Pioneer Documentation Activities in World War II," *Journal of the American Society for Information Science* 39 (September 1988): 301–6; *LCIB,* March 23–29, 1946; *QJLC* 3 (August 1946): 35.

49. Pamela Spence Richards, *Scientific Information in Wartime: The Allied-German Rivalry, 1939–1945* (Westport, CT: Greenwood Press, 1994), 73–90; Eugene Power, *Edition of One: The Autobiography of Eugene B. Power, Founder of University Microfilms* (Ann Arbor, MI: University Microfilms, 1990), 134–42; Carol A. Nemeyer, *Scholarly Reprint Publishing in the United States* (New York: R. R. Bowker, 1972), 40–50; Persico, *Roosevelt's Secret War,* 227–28; Peiss, *Information Hunters,* 67.

50. *ARLC*, 1942, 157–58; 1943, 73, 76; Josephus Nelson and Judith Farley, *Full Circle: Ninety Years of Service in the Main Reading Room* (Washington, DC: LC, 1991), 31.

51. *LCIB* 50 (February 11, 1991): 38–40; Luther Evans, "The Library of Congress and the War, May 30, 1942," LCA; Gary, *Nervous Liberals*, 167–73.

52. Executive Order 8922, October 24, 1941; Drabeck and Ellis, *Reflections*, 146–51.

53. John Morton Blum, *V Was for Victory* (New York: Harcourt Brace, 1976), 21–31; Sydney Weinberg, "What to Tell America: The Writers' Quarrel in the Office of War Information," *Journal of American History* 55 (June 1968): 73–77.

54. MacLeish, *Champion of a Cause*, 89; MacLeish to Frankfurter, April 9, 1942, in *Letters*, ed. Winnick, 311–13; "Minutes, Meeting of the Librarian's Council, May 30, 1942," LCA.

55. Donaldson, *Archibald MacLeish*, 349–62.

56. MacLeish to Roosevelt, November 2, 1939, box 342, LCACF; Jane Aikin, "Preparing for a National Emergency: The Committee on Conservation of Cultural Resources, 1939–1944," *LQ* 77 (July 2007): 258–59. Matthew Dallek, *Defenseless under the Night: The Roosevelt Years and the Origins of Homeland Security* (New York: Oxford University Press, 2016), 41–42.

57. MacLeish to the chiefs of the several divisions, December 10, 1940, LCACF; Jerrold Orne, "Library of Congress Prepares for Emergencies," *BALA* 35 (June 1941): 341–48; *ARLC*, 1941, 12–13; 55 Stat 462; Archibald MacLeish, "The Library of Congress Protects Its Collections," *BALA* 36 (February 1942): 74–75.

58. MacLeish to Morgenthau, April 30, 1941, box 733, LCACF; Robert Penn Warren, "The War and the National Muniments," *QJLC* 2 (July–September 1944): 64–73.

59. "'Bold Venture': A Wartime Poem by Archibald MacLeish," *QJLC* 38 (Winter 1981): 2–3.

60. Aikin, "Preparing," 272; MacLeish to Morgenthau, December 30, 1941, box 734, LCACF.

61. David C. Mearns, *The Declaration of Independence: The Story of a Parchment* (Washington, DC: LC, 1950), 13–16; *ARLC*, 1942, 150–52; 1945, 85; *LCIB*, October 1944; Verner Clapp, "The Declaration of Independence: A Case Study in Preservation," *Special Libraries* 62 (December 1971): 503–8; Milton M. Plumb Jr., "The Bill of Rights Comes Home," *QJLC* 2 (January–June 1945): 3044. Barney Balaban, president of Paramount Pictures, presented the copy of the Bill of Rights.

62. *ARLC*, 1941, 332; 1943, 73; 1944, 28; *LCIB*, September 1944; John Y. Cole and Jane Aikin, "Employees and Employment," *Encyclopedia*, 225–31.

63. Verner W. Clapp, "Luther H. Evans," *LJ* 90 (September 1, 1965): 3387. Exasperated at his chiefs' disagreements, Putnam decided that "where two men won't work in harmony I shall have to act directly over the heads of both"; Putnam to Charlotte Putnam, June 15, 17, 18, 1899, Putnam Papers, LC.

64. Donaldson, *Archibald MacLeish*, 378; *ARLC*, 1943, 16, 76–78. The Staff Advisory Committee included union representatives and staff members selected by the Librarian.

65. *ARLC*, 1942, 159; *LCIB*, July–August 1944, 1–2; 59 (August–September 2000): 202–3; Clapp, "Luther H. Evans," 3387.

66. *ARLC*, 1943, 19, 85, 207, 945; Cole, *For Congress*, 125. The exhibits program was transferred to the Prints and Photographs Division in 1944: *ARLC*, 1944, 98. The two *Information Bulletins* merged in July 1943.

67. Lacy, "Sesquicentenary Review: I," 167.

68. Quoted by Ralph D. Wagner, *A History of the Farmington Plan* (Lanham, MD: Scarecrow Press, 2002), 63. Louis Round Wilson, "The Challenge of the 1930's to the 1940's," *C&RL* (March 1940): 131. The ARL charter had called for cooperative development of research collections: William J. Welsh, "ARL/LC: 1932–1982," *Advances in Library Administration and Organization* 3 (1984): 287.

69. *ARLC*, 1941, 15–17; Herbert A. Kellar, *Memoranda on Library Cooperation* (Washington, DC: LC, 1941).

70. *ARLC*, 1942, 19–20; Robin M. Winks, *Cloak & Gown: Scholars in the Secret War, 1939–1961*, 2nd ed. (New Haven, CT: Yale University Press, 1996), 96–102; Wilmarth Sheldon Lewis, *One Man's Education* (New York: Alfred A. Knopf, 1957), 334; 347–51; Peiss, *Information Hunters*, 37–38. The Librarian's Council was later dissolved: Metcalf, *Harvard Library Years*, 170; *LCIB*, January 26–February 1, 1946.

71. *ARLC*, 1943, 41–42; 1945, 35–36; 1950, 113–14; Winks, *Cloak & Gown*, 108; Wagner, *History*, 83–96; Metcalf, *My Harvard Library Years*, 200–203; Keyes D. Metcalf and Edwin E. Williams, "Proposal for a Division of Responsibility among American Libraries in the Acquisition and Recording of Library Materials," *C&RL* 5 (March 1944): 105–9; Evans, "Research Libraries," 261; Edwin E. Williams, "Research Library Acquisitions from Eight Countries," *LQ* 15 (1945): 313–23; Stevens, *Role*, 40; Sergius Yakobson, "The Library of Congress, Its Russian Program and Activities," *American Review on the Soviet Union* 7 (August 1946): 64–66.

72. John Y. Cole, "Amassing American 'Stuff': The Library of Congress and the Federal Arts Projects of the 1930s," *QJLC* 40 (Fall 1983): 371–72; B. A. Botkin, "The Slave as His Own Interpreter," *QJLC* 2 (July–September 1944): 37–63; Jerre Mangione, *The Dream and the Deal: The Federal Writers' Project, 1935–1943* (Syracuse: Syracuse University Press, 1996), 346–47; *ARLC*, 1941, 176–80; 1946, 256; William F. McDonald, *Federal Relief Administration and the Arts* (Columbus: Ohio State University Press, 1969), 316–21.

73. *ARLC*, 1940, 134; B. A. Botkin, "The Archive of American Folk Song: Retrospect and Prospect," *QJLC* 2 (January–June 1945): 61–69; Francisco Aguilera, "An Archive—20 Years Later," *QJLC* 20 (September 1963): 218–22; *LCIB* 15 (January 30, 1956): 52; Donald L. Leavitt, "Recorded Sound in the Library of Congress," *LT* 21 (Summer 1972): 53–59; Motion Pictures, Broadcasting, Recorded Sound, passim.

74. *ARLC*, 1940, 134–35, 149; 1941, 172–76; 1942, 20, 51; *LCIB* 17 (May 5, 1958): 239–40; Alan Gevinson, "What the Neighbors Say: The Radio Research Project of the Library of Congress," in *Performing Arts: Broadcasting* (Washington, DC: LC, 2002), 94–121; John Szwed, *Alan Lomax: The Man Who Recorded the World* (New York: Penguin Books, 2010), 178–80, 187; David M. Kennedy, *Freedom from Fear: The American People in Depression and War, 1929–1945* (New York: Oxford University Press, 1999), 254–57.

75. *ARLC*, 1942, 21; 1943, 213–18; 1945, 34–35; Barbara Deming, "The Library of Congress Film Project: Exposition of a Method," *QJLC* 2 (July–September 1944): 3–36; *LCIB* 51 (April 20, 1992): 42–43. Selection reverted to the LC staff in 1945: *QJLC* 4 (November 1946): 44–45; Evans, "Research Libraries," 246. LC had kept only paper prints of early films and "shooting samples" of films produced after 1913: Kemp R. Niver, "From Film to Paper to Film," *QJLC* 21 (October 1964): 248–64. A 1942 examination of old copyright deposits discovered the paper prints, and MacLeish decided to accept deposits of motion pictures, even though the nitrate film was unstable: *ARLC*, 1942, 21.

76. *ARLC*, 1992, 22; *Motion Pictures, Broadcasting, Recorded Sound*, 42–43.

77. A typescript of the proceedings is in the Rare Book and Special Collections Division.

78. James Gilreath and Douglas L. Wilson later located a copy of Jefferson's catalog prepared by Nicholas P. Trist: *Thomas Jefferson's Library: A Catalog with the Entries in His Own Order* (Clark, NJ: Lawbook Exchange, 2008). On the 1943 celebration, see *ARLC*, 1943, 66–67; Frederick R. Goff, "T. I.: Mr. Jefferson's Books in Washington, DC," *RCHS*, 50th volume (1980): 84; *The Thomas Jefferson Bicentennial, 1743–1943; A Catalogue of the Exhibition at the Library of Congress* (Washington, DC: GPO, 1943); Julian P. Boyd, *The Declaration of Independence: The Evolution of the Text as Shown in Facsimiles of Various Drafts by Its Author*

(Washington, DC: LC, 1943); a revised edition (1999) was edited by Gerard W. Gawalt. The Koch quotation is in *LCIB* 11 (September 8, 1952): 8. See also James Gilreath, "Sowerby Revirescent and Revised," *Papers of the Bibliographical Society of America* 78 (1984): 218–32.

79. *ARLC,* 1943, 173–76; *QJLC* 3 (October 1945); 4 (May 1947): 5–56; 5 (May 1948): 3–51; 6 (May 1949): 18–22, 95–102; 22 (July 1965): 159–206; Van Wingen, "Incunabula Collections," 95–96; Frederick R. Goff., ed., *The Lessing J. Rosenwald Collection: A Catalogue of the Gifts of Lessing J. Rosenwald to the Library of Congress, 1943 to 1975* (Washington, DC: LC, 1977). The books were moved to LC from his Jenkintown, PA, gallery only after his death.

80. Mary Hume Richardson, "The Drawings of Clifford Kennedy Berryman," *QJLC* 3 (February 1946): 6–10; Nelson R. Burr, "The Papers of William Allen White," *QJLC* 4 (November 1946): 10–14; Laura E. Gilliam and William Lichtenwanger, comps., *The Dayton C. Miller Flute Collection: A Checklist of the Instruments* (Washington, DC: LC, 1961).

81. Quoted by Roy Basler, *The Muse and the Librarian* (Westport, CT: Greenwood Press, 1974), 38; *LCIB* 63 (November 2004): 220; John C. Broderick, "American Literature and the Library of Congress: A Personal Perspective," *Encyclopedia,* 109–10.

82. Peggy Ann Kusnerz, "Picturing the Past: Photographs at the Library of Congress" (PhD diss., University of Michigan, 1992), 209.

83. *ARLC,* 1941, 159–61.

84. William McGuire, "The Bollingen Foundation: Mary Mellon's 'Shining Beacon,'" *QJLC* 39 (Fall 1982): 200–211; Kurt S. Maier, "A Fellowship in German Literature: Thomas Mann, Agnes Meyer, and Archibald MacLeish," *QJLC* 36 (Fall 1979): 385–400; Kurt S. Maier, "Immigrants Enrich Library's Culture," *Gazette* 10 (September 10, 1999): 6–8, 10.

85. Donaldson, *Archibald MacLeish,* 326–28; McGuire, *Poetry's Catbird Seat,* 44–62.

86. *QJLC* 1 (July–September 1943): 1; 36 (Winter 1979): 1-3. Tate's successor, Robert Penn Warren, was the next editor, followed by the LC staff. The *QJLC* ceased with the Fall 1983 issue.

87. Drabeck and Ellis, *Reflections,* 136–37; William McGuire, *Poetry's Catbird Seat: The Consultantship in Poetry in the English Language at the Library of Congress, 1937–1987* (Washington, DC: LC, 1988), 92–110; William McGuire, "The Bollingen Foundation: Ezra Pound and the Prize in Poetry," *QJLC* 40 (Winter 1983): 17; *LCIB* 38 (October 26, 1979): 445–47.

88. MacLeish to Roosevelt, November 8, 1944, in *Letters,* ed. Winnick, 324–25.

89. MacLeish told the committee that he had always been "very strongly against Communism": *Nominations—Department of State, Hearings before the Committee on Foreign Relations, United States Senate, 78th Congress, 2nd Session, Dec. 12–13, 1944* (Washington, DC: GPO, 1944), 78–85; McGuire, *Poetry's Catbird Seat,* 86.

90. There was a precedent: the LC had assembled material for the US delegation to the 1919 Paris Peace Conference.

91. MacLeish chaired the US delegation to UNESCO's organizational meeting and first general conference. On leaving the State Department, he returned to Harvard as Boyleston Professor of Rhetoric and Poetry, retiring in 1967.

92. Mearns, *Story,* 215.

93. Archibald MacLeish, *Champion of a Cause* (Chicago: ALA, 1971), ix.

94. Keyes D. Metcalf, "Archibald MacLeish as a Librarian," *Pembroke Magazine* 7 (1976): 118.

95. Mearns, *Story,* 209.

96. John J. Wayne, "The Information Bulletin Turns 50," *LCIB* 51 (January 13, 1992): 6; Mearns, "Brush of a Comet," 92; *ARLC,* 1945, 11–13; *LCIB* 41 (April 30, 1982): 125–27.

97. Boyd to MacLeish, August 18, 1945; MacLeish to Boyd, August 30, 1945, Archibald MacLeish papers, LC; Boyd to MacLeish, January 13, 1945, September 18, 1945, Julian Boyd

Papers, Princeton University Library; Boyd to Harry S. Truman, May 21, 1945, Boyd Papers. Boyd suggested Theodore C. Blegen (University of Minnesota). MacLeish did include Evans among his candidates; Donaldson, *Archibald MacLeish*, 377–78; MacLeish to Roosevelt, February 13, 1945, MacLeish Papers.

98. Also mentioned were David Mearns and Arthur A. Houghton Jr., curator of the Rare Book Division: *Washington Star*, January 21, 1945; Thomison, *History*, 161–62. Truman did not consult MacLeish: Betty Milum, "Choosing MacLeish's Successor: The Recurring Debate," *JLH* 12 (Spring 1977): 92. H. M. Lydenberg to MacLeish, May 8, 1945, MacLeish papers, LC, stated that Vitz named Metcalf as first choice and Evans second but Metcalf refused, and later wrote that he suspected Truman wanted a nominee from west of the Mississippi: Metcalf, *My Harvard Library Years*, 170.

99. William J. Sittig, 'Luther Evans: Man for a New Age," in *Librarians*, 221–24; McDonald, *Federal Relief Administration*, 765–70.

100. Clapp, "Luther H. Evans," 3387.

101. *LCIB* 59 (August–September 2000): 202–3.

102. *LCIB*, March 9–15, 1946; April 12–18, 1949: 9–10; September 27–October 3, 1949: appendix; *ARLC*, 1947, 83–84; Luther Evans, "Staff Participation in Administration," August 12, 1947, LCA; Evans, "The Administration of a Federal Government Agency," *LJ* 75 (August 1950): 1243–49. In 1949, the Staff Advisory Committee consisted of four members appointed by Evans, two union members, and four selected by nonunion staff. The Professional Forum became the Staff Forum in September 1950, including all staff.

103. Charles Goodrum and Helen Dalrymple, *The Library of Congress* (Boulder, CO: Westview Press, 1982), 64; John Y. Cole, "Luther Harris Evans, *DALB-S*, 23. The staff had formed the Library of Congress Recreation Association (1942; renamed Library of Congress Welfare and Recreation Association, 1949), which in 1956 absorbed the Beneficiary Association's assets and included sports and cultural clubs; lunches for foreign language groups began in about 1951. The Library of Congress Professional Association was established in 1969, and the LC Recreation Association in 1992; *Gazette* 7 (September 20, 1996): 5.

104. Charles A. Goodrum, "LC Trains Recruits," *LJ* 77 (March 1, 1952): 393–96; *LCIB* 19 (October 10, 1960): 581–82; Thomison, *History*, 170–74.

105. He reestablished the Administrative Department (1946), combined the Acquisitions and Processing Departments (1947), and the Archive of American Folk Song became part of the Music Division's new Folklore Section: *ARLC*, 1946, 284; 1949, 138.

106. Luther H. Evans, "The Library of Congress Records a New Era of World Progress," *Sunday Star*, Washington, DC, December 2, 1945; Luther Evans, "Problems Facing the Library of Congress," *Special Libraries* 36 (December 1945): 467–70.

107. Metcalf, *My Harvard Library Years*, 203–4.

108. Robert B. Downs, "Wartime Co-operative Acquisitions," *LQ* 19 (July 1949): 157–58; Verner Clapp, "The Purchase of Books in Europe," *C&RL* 7 (April 1946): 127–34. Peiss, *Information Hunters*, 99, 130–45, described private interests' postwar efforts to acquire materials.

109. *ARLC*, 1946, 262–67; Downs, "Wartime Co-operative Acquisitions," 158–59; Peiss, "European Wartime Acquisitions," 863–76; Luther Evans, "More about the German Mission," *LJ* 71 (August 1946): 1014–16.

110. *ARLC*, 1946, 263–65; *LCIB*, March 16–22, 1945; October 8–14, 1945; Downs, "Wartime Co-operative Acquisitions," 165; Reuben Peiss, "Report on Europe," *C&RL* 8 (April 1947): 113–19; Richard S. Hill, "Buying Music in Germany," *QJLC* 4 (November 1946): 15–25; Douewe Stuurman, "The Nazi Collection: A Preliminary Note," *QJLC* 6 (November 1948): 21–22; Paul Vanderbilt, "Prints and Photographs of Nazi Origin," *QJLC* 6 (August 1949): 21–27;

Peiss, *Information Hunters*, 96–121. Reuben Peiss found the book markets poorly stocked and expensive: "European Wartime Acquisitions and the Library of Congress Mission," *LJ* 71 (June 15, 1946): 876, 911. The mission officially ended June 30, 1947.

111. Astrid M. Eckert, *The Struggle for the Files: The Western Allies and the Return of German Archives after the Second World War* (New York: German Historical Institute and Cambridge University Press, 2012), 169–85.

112. *LCIB*, April 20–26, 1946: 4–6; *Washington Post*, January 5, 2000: C1, 8; Robert G. Waite, "Returning Jewish Cultural Property: The Handling of Books Looted by the Nazis in the American Zone of Occupation, 1945 to 1952," *L&C* 37 (Summer 2002): 213–28; Peiss, *Information Hunters*, 211–13; *Plunder and Restitution: The US and Holocaust Victims' Assets: Findings and Recommendations of the Presidential Advisory Commission on Holocaust Assets and Staff Report* (Washington, DC: GPO, 2000), 13–14, 92–201, https://clinton.presidentiallibraries.us/items/show/29349.

113. *ARLC*, 1945, 13; 1946, 230–33, 307–447.

114. *ARLC*, 1946, 11–12, 504–5; *LCIB*, August 13–19, 1946; 60 Stat 386, at 402; 60 Stat 908; LC, *That All May Read: Library Services for Blind and Physically Handicapped People* (Washington, DC: LC, 1983), 108–11.

115. Marlene Morrissey, "The Library's Development, 1945–1953," August 28, 1953, 11, LCA.

116. *ARLC*, 1946, 11–227; *LCIB*, September 24–30, 1946.

117. Quoted in *ARLC*, 1946, 340; G. Pascal Zachary, *Endless Frontier: Vannevar Bush, Engineer of the American Century* (New York: Free Press, 1997), 226–27, 262–65.

118. *ARLC*, 1946, 11, 233–34. The members were Herbert Eugene Bolton (emeritus, University of California); Edward U. Condon (National Bureau of Standards); Douglas S. Freeman (historian and editor); Waldo G. Leland (former director, American Council of Learned Societies); Wilmarth S. Lewis; Carl McFarland (Commission on Federal Administrative Procedure); Kathryn Mier (Missouri State Library Commission); Lessing J. Rosenwald; Ralph R. Shaw (Department of Agriculture Library); and Walter L. Wright Jr. (Princeton University).

119. *ARLC*, 1947, 101–8.

120. James T. Patterson, *Grand Expectations: The United States, 1945–1974* (New York: Oxford University Press, 1996), 114–36; *LCIB*, July 22–28, 1947, 8.

121. 60 Stat 812; David H. Rosenbloom, "'Whose Bureaucracy Is This, Anyway?' Congress' 1946 Answer," *PSOnline* (December 2001): 773–77; Julian E. Zelizer, *On Capitol Hill: The Struggle to Reform Congress and Its Consequences, 1948–2000* (New York: Cambridge University Press, 2004), 20–31; Lewis L. Gould, *The Most Exclusive Club: A History of the Modern United States Senate* (New York: Basic Books, 2009), 178.

122. *History of the Committee on House Administration, 1947–2012*, 366; John Y. Cole, "Joint Committee on the Library," *Encyclopedia*, 285.

123. Cole, *Library of Congress*, 2; *LCIB* 55 (December 30, 1996): 459–60; "Legislative Branch Appropriation Bill for 1941: Hearings before the Subcommittee of the Committee on Appropriations, United States Senate, 76th Congress, 3rd Sess." (Washington, DC: GPO, 1940), 6, 20–21.

124. Ernest S. Griffith and Francis R. Valeo, *Congress: Its Contemporary Role* (New York: New York University Press, 1975), 94; *ARLC*, 1966, 51; Zelizer, *On Capitol Hill*, 31; Roger H. Davidson and Walter J. Oleszek, *Congress against Itself* (Bloomington: Indiana University Press, 1977), 52.

125. *ARLC*, 1947, 32; 1948, 25–26; 1949, 33–34; Nelson and Farley, *Full Circle*, 34–37.

126. *ARLC*, 1948, 95, 111, 119, 188; 1949, 151–52; *LCIB*, January 13–19, 1948, 12–13; January 20–26, 1948, 11; May 4–10, 1948, 13; May 18–24, 1948, 23–24; 63 Stat 153; Marion James,

"The United States and the Movement for Universal Copyright, 1945–53," *LQ* 25 (July 1955): 219–34.

127. *ARLC*, 1949, 127–28. An LC consultant—Ralph Ellsworth of the University of Iowa—recommended in 1948 assessing each library an amount equal to its own cataloging costs; the library community opposed the idea: *LCIB*, November 16–22, 1948, appendix; John M. Dawson, "The Library of Congress: Its Role in Cooperative and Centralized Cataloging," *LT* 16 (July 1967): 89–90; Ralph E. Ellsworth, *Ellsworth on Ellsworth* (Metuchen, NJ: Scarecrow Press, 1980), 84.

128. *LCIB*, September 30–October 6, 1947, 9.

129. Hummel. "Growth," 81–84; *LCIB*, May 25–31, 1948, 9–12; June 8–14, 1948, 12–13, appendix, 5; July 27–August 3, 1948, 8; *ARLC*, 1948, 101; 1949, 66–67; Langer, *In and out of the Ivory Tower*, 230–38.

130. Walter W. Ristow, *The Emergence of Maps in Libraries* (Hamden, CT: Linnet Books, 1980), 289–91.

131. *QJLC* 3 (August 1946): 34, 41; 4 (August 1947): 55; Richard Eells, "Strategic Bombing Photographs," *QJLC* 5 (November 1947): 9–11; Joseph C. Hickerson and James R. Stuart, "All That Is Audible: Recent Recorded Sound Acquisitions in the Music Division," *QJLC* 32 (January 1975): 52–53; Samuel Brylawski, "Armed Forces Radio Service: The Invisible Highway Abroad," *QJLC* 37 (Summer–Fall 1980): 441–57.

132. *ARLC*, 1948, 52, 69–70; 1953, 72–75; 1954, 63–65; Luther Evans, "The Library of Congress as the National Library of Science," *Scientific Monthly* 66 (May 1948): 405–12; Luther Evans, "The Library of Congress and Its Service to Science and Technology," *C&RL* 8 (July 1947): 315–21.

133. *ARLC*, 1949, 116; 1958, 12–13; 1975, 18; *QJLC* 7 (August 1950): 45; *LCIB* 9, no. 50 (August 14, 1950): 14–15; 9 (December 11, 1950): 20; Homer Halvorson, "The Documents Expediting Project in Its First Year," *C&RL* 9 (January 1948): 15–17, 24; *LJ* 74 (November 15, 1949): 1744–46; John L. Andriot, "Documents Expediting Project," *LJ* 77 (April 15, 1952): 693–95.

134. *ARLC*, 1946, 267–70, 280, 296; *LCIB*, April 12–18, 1949, appendix; July 12–18, 1949: 7; November 1–7, 1949: 24; Dan Lacy, "War Measures: Past and Future," *LQ* 23 (July 1953): 90; *LJ* 76 (March 15, 1951): 509. The Library also supported the American Book Center for War-Devastated Libraries, Inc., and later the United States Book Exchange, which Evans conceived as its successor. The Exchange, originally Rockefeller-funded, became a self-supporting organization for the international exchange of materials; the LC housed both organizations for a time: *ARLC*, 1949, 116–17; 1950, 111–14; *LCIB* 11 (October 27, 1952): 11.

135. *LCIB*, February 24–March 1, 1948, 7–9; July 27–August 2: 11–13; *Report of the United States Library Mission to Advise on the Establishment of the National Diet Library of Japan*, Department of State Publication 3200 (Washington, DC: GPO, 1948); Chin Kim, "A New National Library: The National Diet Library of Japan," *JLH* 4 (July 1969): 225–38.

136. W. Somerset Maugham to MacLeish, July 6, 1945, MacLeish papers, LC.

137. Vincent L. Eaton, "Books and Memorabilia of Woodrow Wilson," *QJLC* 4 (November 1946): 2–6; *ARLC*, 1949, 99. The Koussevitzky gift notably prompted others, including Aaron Copland and Leonard Bernstein, to leave collections to the LC: *ARLC*, 1950, 45; *LCIB* 56 (January 27, 1997): 26.

138. *ARLC*, 1948, 14–16, 125; *LCIB* 17 (July 6, 1959): 387–92; 68 (March 2009): 45; Mearns, *Lincoln Papers*, 1: 90–136; Helen D. Bullock, "The Robert Todd Lincoln Collection of the Papers of Abraham Lincoln," *QJLC* 5 (November 1947): 3–8; John Y. Cole, *America's Greatest Library: An Illustrated History of the Library of Congress* (Washington, DC: LC, in association

with D. Giles Limited, London, 2017), 194; John C. Broderick, "David Chambers Mearns," *DALB,* 2: 73. The Lincoln papers joined the Herndon-Weik Collection (acquired in 1941) of Lincoln's law partner, William Henry Herndon. The Nicolay and Hay papers were donated in 1947 and 1952, respectively: Helen D. Bullock, "The Papers of John G. Nicolay, Lincoln's Secretary," *QJLC* 7 (May 1950): 3–8. The Randall quotation is from Merrill D. Peterson, *Lincoln in American Memory* (New York: Oxford University Press, 1994): 327–29.

139. Andrew Osborn, "The Crisis in Cataloging," *LQ* 11 (October 1941): 393–411; H. M. Gallagher, "Dr. Osborn's 1941 'The Crisis in Cataloging': A Shift in Thought toward American Pragmatism," *CCQ* 12, nos. 3–4 (1991): 3–33; Wyllis E. Wright, "The Anglo-American Cataloging Rules: A Historical Perspective," *LRTS* 20 (Winter 1976): 36–37; Paul S. Dunkin, *Cataloging USA* (Chicago: ALA, 1969), 13.

140. *Studies of Descriptive Cataloging: A Report to the Librarian of Congress by the Director of the Processing Department* (Washington, DC: GPO, 1946); *ARLC,* 1947, 70; 1948, 120; Kathryn Luther Henderson, "Treated with a Degree of Uniformity and Common Sense: Descriptive Cataloging in the United States, 1876–1975," *LT* 25 (July 1976): 235–37. The quotation is from Sittig, "Luther Evans," 227. The controversy eventually helped to unite LC and ALA rule-making; Lucile M. Morsch, "'An Incubus and a Hindrance,'" *LRTS* 11, no. 4 (1967): 413.

141. Richard S. Angell, "Copyright Office Speeds Cataloging," *LJ* 74 (June 1, 1949): 862–66, 882; Angell, "Copyright Office Cataloging," *LJ* 74 (June 15, 1949): 926–29, 975. There had been two cataloging operations: in the Catalog Division and in the Copyright Office, for the *Catalogue of Copyright Entries.*

142. *ARLC,* 1947, 17; 1948, 89–91; *LCIB,* February 8–14, 1949, 5–9; October 25–31, 1949, 18–19; Yee, "Attempts," 7–13; Lacy, "Sesquicentenary Review II," 245–49; Andrea L. Stamm, "Minimal Level Cataloging; Past, Present, and Future," in *Technical Services Management, 1965–1990: A Quarter Century of Change and a Look to the Future,* edited by Linda C. Smith and Ruth Carter (New York: Haworth Press, 1996), 192.

143. Quoted by Sittig, "Luther Evans," 231; and by John Y. Cole, "Luther Harris Evans," *DALB-S,* 22–26.

144. *Rules for Descriptive Cataloging in the Library of Congress* (Washington, DC: LC, 1949); *ARLC,* 1947, 73–74; 1948, 21–22, 89–90; 1949, 120–21; Dunkin, *Cataloging USA,* 14–15; Carol June Bradley, "Classifying and Cataloguing Music in American Libraries: A Historical Overview," in *Historical Aspects of Cataloging and Classification,* edited by Martin D. Joachim (New York: Haworth, 2003), 467–81; Raymond C. Swank, "Further Progress in Cataloging," *C&RL* 9 (January 1948): 90–94.

145. *Cataloging Rules and Principles: A Critique of the ALA Rules for Entry and a Proposed Design for Their Revision* (Washington, DC: LC, 1953); Seymour Lubetzky, "The Current Revision of ALA Rules," *LRTS* 4 (Winter 1960): 79–84; Elaine Svenonius and Dorothy McGarry, eds., *Seymour Lubetzky: Writings on the Classical Art of Cataloging* (Englewood, CO: Libraries Unlimited, 2001), xi–xvii; Henderson, "Treated," 237–41; Wright, "Anglo-American Cataloging Rules," 38–40; Michael Carpenter, *Corporate Authorship: Its Role in Library Cataloging* (Westport, CT: Greenwood Press, 1981): 28–29; Marie Louise Prevost, "The Lubetzky Report: Harbinger of Hope," *JCC* 10 (April 1954): 73–76.

146. It was the first time an outside group was formally consulted on LC classification development: Francis L. Miksa, *The Development of Classification at the Library of Congress* (Ann Arbor: University of Michigan Press, 1984), 59.

147. *ARLC,* 1948, 89–90; 1949, 123–24; Leo J. LaMontagne, *American Library Classification: With Special Reference to the Library of Congress* (New York: Shoe String Press, 1961), 334–36; Jolande E. Goldberg, "Development of a Universal Law Classification: A Retrospective on

Library of Congress Class K," in *Historical Aspects,* ed. Joachim, 355–43; Werner B. Ellinger, "Subject Classification of Law," *LQ* 19 (April 1949): 79–104.

148. Archibald MacLeish, "Introduction," in *A Catalog of Books Represented by Library of Congress Printed Cards Issued to July 31, 1942* (Ann Arbor, MI: Edwards Brothers, 1942), 1: vii; Paul Edlund, "A Monster and a Miracle: The Cataloging Distribution Service of the Library of Congress, 1901–1976," *QJLC* 33 (October 1976): 412–13.

149. *LCIB,* August 5–22, 1947, 5; February 8–14, 1948, appendix; *ARLC,* 1950, 125–27. On Cronin's responsibility for LC's book catalogs and introduced prepublication cataloging, see *LRTS* 12 (Fall 1968): passim.

150. *ARLC,* 1948, 95–96; Evans, "Research Libraries," 255.

151. *ARLC,* 1948, 80, 84–85, 98, 101; *LCIB,* January 27–February 2, 1948, 4–5; June 8–14, 1948, 12; 1949, 145–46; John Y. Cole, "Developing a National Foreign Newspaper Microfilming Program," *LRTS* 18 (Winter 1974): 5–7; Keyes Metcalf, "The Farmington Plan," *Harvard Library Bulletin* 2 (Autumn 1948): 206–308; James E. Skipper, "National Planning for Resource Development," *LT* 15 (October 1966): 321–26.

152. *ARLC,* 1948, 12–14, 123–24; William A. Coblenz, "The Freedom Train and the Story of Its Origin: Our Civil Liberties on Wheels," *Manuscripts* 10 (Winter 1950): 3034, 59. Coblenz, a Justice Department employee, made the original suggestion, according to John Kelly's column in the *Washington Post,* May 12, 2019.

153. James Gregory Bradsher, "Taking America's Heritage to the People: The Freedom Train Story," *Prologue* 17 (Winter 1985): 229. In a similar spirit, a $100,000 Rockefeller Foundation grant (December 1948) enabled the LC to sponsor *The Library of Congress Series in American Civilization,* with Ralph Henry Gabriel (Yale University) as general editor: *ARLC,* 1948, 102–3.

154. Richard M. Fried, *Nightmare in Red: The McCarthy Era in Perspective* (New York: Oxford University Press, 1990), 97–99; Patterson, *Grand Expectations,* 179–205.

155. *New Republic* 116 (January 6, 1947): 7; Walter Goodman, *The Committee: The Extraordinary Career of the House Committee on Un-American Activities* (New York: Farrar, Straus & Giroux, 1968), 187–88. A revised version of counsel's report omitted reference to the LC. The LC had a tradition of accepting executive orders on personnel matters if they accorded with congressional intent: Loyalty Program, box 31, Clapp Papers, LC.

156. Wagman noted that Clapp was one of the few officials to speak against the program: *Verner Warren Clapp: A Memorial Tribute, 1901–1972* (Washington, DC: LC, 1973), 10.

157. Louise S. Robbins, "The Library of Congress and Federal Loyalty Programs, 1947–56: No 'Communists or Cocksuckers,'" *LQ* 64 (October 1994): 365–85; *LCIB,* September 7–13, 1948, 4; Verner W. Clapp, "Do You Favor Use or Abuse?" *LJ* 75 (April 15, 1950): 678–81; Clapp to the Librarian, March 28, 1950, box 16, Clapp Papers, LC; Thomison, *History,* 184–87; Louise S. Robbins, *Censorship and the American Library: The American Library Association's Response to Threats to Intellectual Freedom, 1939–1969* (Westport, CT: Greenwood Press, 1996), 40–49.

158. Archibald MacLeish and William Carlos Williams had been appointed fellows but were not involved with the award: *ARLC,* 1948, 103; *LCIB,* February 22–28, 1949, 10–11; Roy Prentice Basler, *The Muse and the Librarian* (London: Bloomsbury, 1974), 10–19; McGuire, "Bollingen Foundation," 17–18.

159. *QJLC* 40 (Winter 1983): 2.

160. MacLeish to Evans, June 7, 1949, MacLeish papers, LC; *LCIB,* August 2–8, 1949, 13–14.

161. Robert Hillyer, "Treason's Strange Fruit: The Case of Ezra Pound and the Bollingen Award," *SR* 32 (June 11, 1949): 9–11, 28; "Ezra Pound and the Bollingen Award," *SR* 32

(June 11, 1949): 20–21; "Poetry's New Priesthood," *SR* 32 (June 18, 1949): 7–9, 38; Evans's response was "A Letter from the Librarian of Congress," *SR* 32 (July 2, 1949): 20–23. See also William Barrett, "A Prize for Pound," *Partisan Review* 16, no. 4 (April 1949): 344–47; "The Question of the Pound Award," *Partisan Review* 16, no. 5 (May 1949): 512–22; Allen Tate and Babette Deutsch, "Further Remarks on the Pound Award," *Partisan Review* 16, no. 6 (June 1949): 666–70; MacLeish to *SR* publisher Harrison Smith, May 27, 1949, in *Letters*, ed. Winnick, 344–46ff; McGuire, "Bollingen Foundation," 25.

162. *ARLC*, 1949, 88–94; William McGuire, *Poetry's Catbird Seat, The Consultantship in Poetry in the English Language at the Library of Congress, 1937–1987* (Washington, DC: LC, 1988), 110–31, https://blogs.loc.gov/catbird/2013/06/the-caged-bird-sings-paul-laurence-dunbar-at-the-library-of-congress/; McGuire, "Bollingen Foundation," 17–25. The Bollingen Prize was later awarded by Yale University Library.

Chapter 8

1. *LCIB* 9, no. 11 (March 12, 1950): 6; no. 16 (April 17, 1950): 1–4; *Library of Congress Sesquicentennial Exhibit, April 24, 1950: Catalog of the Exhibit Commemorating the 150th Anniversary of Its Establishment* (GPO, 1950); *District of Columbia, Sesquicentennial of the Establishment of the Permanent Seat of Government. An Exhibition in the Library of Congress, Washington, DC, April 24, 1950 to April 24, 1951* (GPO, 1951).

2. *BALA* 44 (October 1950); *LCIB* 9, no. 51 (December 18, 1950): 8–11; 58 (April 1999): 70–73.

3. ALA folder, box 18, Putnam Papers, LC.

4. "Hearings before the House Appropriations Subcommittee on the Supplemental Appropriations Bill for 1951, July 13, 1950" (GPO, 1951), 14–16. Evans did hire a Korea specialist, but the Korean Section was not established until December 1989: *ARLC*, 1951, 15; *Library of Congress Asian Collections*, 66–67.

5. *ARLC*, 1951, 14–15, 28; 1953, 8; Marlene Morrissey, "The Library's Development, 1945–1953," 10–14; Arthur W. Hummel, "The Growth of the Orientalia Collections," *QJLC* 11 (February 1954): 8.

6. *ARLC*, 1951, 28–29; 1953, 9.

7. Kenneth W. Clark, "The Microfilming Projects at Mt. Sinai and Jerusalem," *QJLC* 8 (May 1951): 8–12.

8. Edwin G. Beal, "Microfilmed Archives of the Japanese Ministry of Foreign Affairs," *QJLC* 11 (November 1953): 7–11; *LCIB* 18 (January 5, 1959): 8–9; (July 27, 1959): 470–71.

9. *ARLC*, 1950, 101–6; 1953, 16, 20–22; Lester K. Born, "Microfilming Abroad," *C&RL* 11 (July 1950): 256; John Y. Cole, "Developing a National Foreign Newspaper Microfilming Program," *LRTS* 18 (Winter 1974): 5–10; *LCIB* 14 (May 23, 1955): 8–9.

10. *LCIB* 11, no. 45 (November 3, 1952): 5–7; 13, no. 36 (September 7, 1954): 11–14; *ARLC*, 1955, 5; 1961, 62–63; 68 Stat 743; Marion James, "The United States and the Movement for Universal Copyright," *LQ* 25 (July 1955): 219–34.

11. *LCIB* 11, no. 30 (July 21, 1952): 12; 66 Stat 752; *ARLC*, 1959, 72–73, 76–77; 1961, xix; 1964, 76–79; 1965, 84–85; 1967, 99; 1974, 7.

12. Jane Aikin, "Giant Bible of Mainz," *Encyclopedia*, 267–70; Frederick R. Goff, 'The Giant Bible of Mainz," *QJLC* 9 (August 1952): 169–71; *Gazette* 33, no. 40 (October 14, 2022): 3; *The Rosenwald Collection: A Catalogue of Illustrated Books and Manuscripts, of Books from Celebrated Presses, and of Bindings and Maps, 1150–1950* (Washington, DC: privately published, 1954); William Matheson, "Lessing J. Rosenwald: 'A Splendidly Generous Man,'" *QJLC* 37

(Winter 1980): 3–24. In September 1991 for Rosenwald's 100th birthday, the LC dedicated the Rosenwald Memorial Reading Room and published *Vision of a Collector: The Lessing J. Rosenwald Collection in the Library of Congress / Rare Book and Special Collections Division* (Washington, DC: LC, 1991).

13. David C. Mearns, "Alfred Whital Stern and the Hoof Prints," *QJLC* 9 (February 1951): 56–64; Vincent L. Eaton, "Some Highlights of the Alfred Whital Stern Collection," *QJLC* 9 (February 1951): 65–73; David C. Mearns, "Abraham Lincoln Goes to Press: A Documentary Memorandum," *QJLC* 9 (August 1951): 182–91; Frederick R. Goff, "Lincolniana Added to the Stern Collection," *QJLC* 12 (February 1955): 53–56; *LCIB* 13, no. 43 (October 25, 1954): 7; "A Catalog of the Alfred Whital Stern Collection of Lincolniana in the Library of Congress" (LC, 1960); John Sherwood, "Alfred Whital Stern: In Pursuit of the Lincoln Legend," *QJLC* 38 (Spring 1981): 108–16; Hirst D. Milhollen, "The Brady-Handy Collection," *QJLC* 13 (April 1956): 135–42; J. M. Edelstein, "Lincoln Papers in the Stern Bequest," *QJLC* 19 (December 1961): 7–14; *LCIB* 68 (March 2009): 48.

14. Frederick R. Goff, "The Hersholt Collection of Andersoniana, *QJLC* 9 (May 1951): 123–27; Frederick R. Goff, "The Hersholt Gift of Works of Hugh Walpole and Sinclair Lewis," *QJLC* 11 (August 1954): 195–98; Frederick R. Goff, "Catalog of the Jean Hersholt Collection of Hans Christian Andersen" (GPO, 1954); *LCIB* 13, no. 25 (June 21, 1954): 9.

15. *ARLC*, 1951, 42; 1952, 59–60; 1953, 5; Frank C. Campbell, "The Musical Scores of George Gershwin," *QJLC* 11 (May 1954): 127–39. The LC had received its first gift of Gershwin materials in 1939.

16. William McGuire, *Poetry's Catbird Seat, The Consultantship in Poetry in the English Language at the Library of Congress, 1937–1987* (Washington, DC: LC, 1988), 138–48; John C. Broderick, "American Literature and the Library of Congress: A Personal Perspective," *Encyclopedia*, 111; *LCIB* 15 (January 30, 1956): 52; 16 (September 30, 1957): 499–500; 22 (December 9, 1963): 649–52; 35 (May 14, 1976): 271–72, 274, 279–82.

17. *ARLC*, 1951, 74; 1952, 70; 1953, 10.

18. The Library's catalogs were issued in five series: Books: Authors; Books: Subjects; Maps and Atlases; Motion Pictures and Filmstrips; and Music and Phonorecords. The latter three included both author and subject listings. Titles changed in 1973 to Films and Other Materials for Projection and Music; Books on Music; and Sound Recordings—and in 1975 from Books: Subjects to Subject Catalog, expanded to include nonbook materials.

19. *LCIB* 10, no. 19 (May 7, 1951): 1; 12, no. 5 (February 2, 1953): 15.

20. *ARLC*, 1954, 22–23; 1959, 3, 6, 20; LC, *Dewey Decimal Classification and Relative Index*, 16th ed. (New York: H. W. Wilson, 1959); Benjamin A. Custer, 'Dewey Live," *LRTS* 11 (Winter 1967): 51–60; John P. Comaromi, "Knowledge Organized Is Knowledge Kept: The Dewey Decimal Classification, 1873–1976," *QJLC* 33 (October 1976): 311–31; David Judson Haykin, "DDC 16th Edition, Edited by the Library of Congress," *JCC* 10 (April 1954): 92–98; Francis Miksa, *The Development of Classification at the Library of Congress*, Occasional Paper 164 (Champaign: Graduate School of Library Science, University of Illinois, 1984), 64; John P. Comaromi, "The Dewey Decimal Classification: 1965–1990, in *Technical Services Management: 1965–1990*, edited by L. Smith and R. Carter (New York: Routledge, 1996), 223–24; Jane Aikin, "Dewey Decimal Classification," *Encyclopedia*, 221–23. OCLC bought Forest Press in 1988, but the editorial office remained at the LC.

21. *ARLC*, 1954, 9–10; *LCIB* 28 (January 16, 1969): 28–29; *Gazette* 33, no. 40 (October 14, 2022): 1, 7–9.

22. *ARLC*, 1957, 24–31; 1960, 29–30; 72 Stat 864; "Scholar and Screen: Notes on the Motion Picture Collection of the Library of Congress," *QJLC* 21 (October 1964): 265–69. Purchased in

1947, the Kleine Collection helped fill the gap created by not acquiring films from 1912 to 1942: "The George Kleine Collection of Early Motion Pictures in the Library of Congress: A Catalog" (LC, 1980); *LCIB* 40 (April 24, 1981): 133–34. The LC Film technician Kemp R. Niver, who recreated the old films, received an Oscar for his work in 1954: *LCIB* 45 (February 24, 1986): 65–66; *Early Motion Pictures: The Paper Print Collection in the Library of Congress* (Washington, DC: LC, 1986).

23. Keyes Metcalf and Edwin E. Williams, "Notes on the Farmington Plan," *Libri* 1 (1950–51): 13–19; Robert B. Downs, "The Growth of Research Collections," *LT* 25 (July 1976): 63; *ARLC*, 1957, 7, 13.

24. The State Department transferred the Bill of Rights to the Archives in 1938.

25. *LCIB* 10, no. 39 (September 24, 1951): 1–5. The National Bureau of Standards recommended the helium enclosure.

26. *ARLC*, 1952, xiii–xvii; Milton O. Gustafson, "The Empty Shrine: The Transfer of the Declaration of Independence and the Constitution to the National Archives," *American Archivist* 39 (July 1976): 271–85; Donald R. McCoy, *The National Archives: America's Ministry of Documents, 1934–1968* (Chapel Hill: University of North Carolina Press, 1978), 255–56, attributed the first overture to Grover. The 1950 act included presidential papers; however, the LC kept the twenty-three presidential collections it had previously acquired.

27. Verner W. Clapp, "Luther H. Evans," *LJ*, September 1965, 3384–85; Louise S. Robbins, "The Library of Congress and Federal Loyalty Programs, 1947–56: No 'Communists or Cocksuckers,'" *LQ* 64 (October 1994): 376–78. After the President's Executive Order 10450 (April 27, 1953), which included criteria for employee "suitability," the LC's Loyalty Board was replaced by the director of personnel as Personnel Security Officer. Brunauer was on McCarthy's original list of State Department suspects; the department declared her a security risk: Landon R. Storrs, *The Second Red Scare and the Unmaking of the New Deal Left* (Princeton, NJ: Princeton University Press, 2013), 183, 269–70; Richard M. Fried, *Nightmare in Red: The McCarthy Era in Perspective* (New York: Oxford University Press, 1990), 23–29; Larry Tye, *Demagogue: The Life and Long Shadow of Senator Joe McCarthy* (Boston: Houghton Mifflin Harcourt, 2020), 311.

28. American Library Association and American Book Publishers Council, *The Freedom to Read. A Statement Prepared by the Westchester Conference of the American Library Association and the American Book Publishers Council, May 2 and 3, 1953* (Chicago: ALA, 1953); Louise S. Robbins, *Censorship and the American Library: The American Library Association's Response to Threats to Intellectual Freedom, 1939–1969* (Westport, CT: Greenwood Press, 1996), 75–83; Dennis Thomison, *A History of the American Library Association, 1876–1972* (Chicago: ALA, 1978), 188–91.

29. *LCIB* 13 (August 23, 1954): 3; McGuire, *Poetry's Catbird Seat*, 147–64; 402–3; Robbins, "Library of Congress," 376–81; Herbert Leibowitz, *"Something Urgent I Have to Say to You": The Life and World of William Carlos Williams* (New York: Farrar, Straus & Giroux, 2011), 414–19; Reed Whittemore, *William Carlos Williams: Poet from Jersey* (Boston: Houghton Mifflin, 1975), 307–14; Roy Basler, *The Muse and the Librarian* (Westport, CT: Greenwood Press, 1974), 18–22.

30. *LCIB* 11, no. 44 (October 27, 1952): 9–10; 12, no. 38 (September 21, 1953): 13–16; *ARLC*, 1954, 11; *Colloquium on Islamic Culture in Its Relationship to the Contemporary World* (Princeton, NJ: Princeton University Press, 1954); Clapp, "Luther H. Evans," 3389–91; John Y. Cole, "The International Role of the Library of Congress: A Brief History," *LCIB* 49 (January 15, 1990): 17.

31. *ARLC*, 1952, 40.

32. In 1951 Mearns exchanged responsibilities with Solon J. Buck, becoming Chief of the Manuscripts Division and Assistant Librarian for the American Collections, while Buck became Assistant Librarian: John C. Broderick, "David Chambers Mearns," *DALB*, 2: 73; Phyllis A. Richmond, "Lucile M. Morsch," *DALB*, 374–76.

33. *ARLC*, 1953, 9–10; 1954, 62–77; *LCIB* 12 (August 17, 1953): 11; Robert Bray, "Research Projects in the Library of Congress," *Journal of Documentation* 12 (December 1956): 219–26. Federal contracts included an administrative overhead charge, which initially was 10 percent.

34. "House Appropriations Subcommittee Hearings on Legislative Branch Appropriations for 1953, March 26, 1952" (GPO, 1952), 1, 5–6, 198–99; Clapp to Evans, March 26, 1952, box 30, Clapp Papers, LC.

35. *ARLC*, 1952, xvii–xviii.

36. LC, *Luther Harris Evans, 1902–1981: A Memorial Tribute to the Tenth Librarian of Congress* (Washington, DC: LC, 1982); *ARLC*, 1953, 3; *LCIB* 12, no. 27 (July 6, 1953): 1–3; 41 (January 1, 1982): 1–2; (May 14, 1982): 141–43; Keyes D. Metcalf, "Introduction of Mr. Boorstin," in *Libraries and the Life of the Mind in America: Addresses Delivered at the Centennial Celebration of the American Library Association* (Chicago: ALA, 1977), 109–11; Cole, "Luther Harris Evans," 25–26.

37. *LCIB* 15 (September 17, 1956): 502–4.

38. The Eisenhower administration considered Clapp too close to Evans: John Y. Cole, "Lawrence Quincy Mumford," *DALB-S*, 88; and Senator John Marshall Butler (R-MD) opposed his appointment: Deanna B. Marcum, "Reclaiming the Research Library: The Founding of the Council on Library Resources," *L&C 31* (Winter 1996): 113–24; Carl Milam and Frederick Wagman, *Verner Warren Clapp, 1901–1972: A Memorial Tribute* (Washington, DC: LC, 1972), 10–11.

39. Foster E. Mohrhardt, "Verner Warren Clapp," *DALB*, 77–81.

40. Thomison, *History*, 194–95. The ALA's candidates were Clapp; Mumford; Everett McDiarmid, University of Minnesota; Robert Downs, University of Illinois; Ralph Ulveling, Detroit Public Library; and Donald Coney, University of California, Berkeley. All except McDiarmid were librarians. Two political scientists received Republicans' support: Franklin Burdette (University of Maryland) and Warren Reed West (George Washington University): Betty Milum, "Eisenhower, ALA, and the Selection of L. Quincy Mumford," *L&C* 30 (Winter 1995): 26–56. The scholarly organizations named Clapp; Mumford; McDiarmid; Charles Gosnell, New York State Library; Carma Zimmerman, California State Library; Harvie Branscomb, formerly of Vanderbilt University; and Ralph Beals, New York Public Library: *BALA* 48 (April 1954): 188–89.

41. Benjamin E. Powell, "Lawrence Quincy Mumford: Twenty Years of Progress," *Librarians*, 238–45, 255; Rutherford D. Rogers, "LQM of LC," *Bulletin of Bibliography and Magazine Notes* 25 (September–December 1968): 161–65; *LCIB* 13, no. 17 (April 26, 1954): 1–4; *LJ* 79 (September 1, 1954): 1453–54; Cole, "Lawrence Quincy Mumford," 87–91.

42. "Nomination of Lawrence Quincy Mumford to Be Librarian of Congress; Hearing before the Committee on Rules and Administration, United States Senate, 83rd Congress, 2nd Session, July 26, 1954" (GPO, 1954), 9; Powell, "Lawrence Quincy Mumford," 245–47; Rogers, "*LQM*," 164.

43. "Nomination of Lawrence Quincy Mumford," 242; House Report 1614, 83rd Congress, 2nd sess., 4.

44. "Nomination of Lawrence Quincy Mumford," 29–147.

45. Harold H. Velde (R-IL), chair of the House Un-American Activities Committee, had proposed a bill requiring the LC to label books that might be considered subversive; it died in committee: Walter Goodman, *The Committee: The Extraordinary Career of the House Committee on Un-American Activities* (New York: Farrar, Straus & Giroux, 1968), 321. When Senate Rules Committee chair William E. Jenner (R-IN) made the suggestion during the confirmation hearing, Mumford replied that the mass of incoming material made such scrutiny impossible and libraries provided material on all sides of issues: "Nomination of Lawrence Quincy Mumford," 7.

46. "Legislative-Judiciary Appropriations, 1955: Hearings before a Subcommittee of the Committee on Appropriations, United States Senate, 83rd Congress, 2nd Session on H.R. 9203" (GPO, 1954), 37.

47. *ARLC*, 1955, 3–6; *QJLC* 14 (July 11, 1955): 8; *LCIB* 14 (July 11, 1955): 8; John Y. Cole, ed., *The Library of Congress in Perspective: A Volume Based on the Reports of the 1976 Librarian's Task Force and Advisory Groups* (New York: R. R. Bowker, 1978), 47–50.

48. The conference included the Chief Assistant Librarian (retitled Deputy Librarian in 1962), department directors (Administration, Law, Reference, Copyright, Processing, and Legislative Reference), the director of Personnel, and Mumford's executive assistant: "Administering a Giant: An Intimate View," *LJ* 90 (October 1, 1965): 4310.

49. Guy R. Lyle, *The Librarian Speaking: Interviews with University Librarians* (Athens: University of Georgia Press, 1970), 92–93, 122–23.

50. 66 Stat 326; LC, *That All May Read: Library Services for Blind and Physically Handicapped People* (Washington, DC: LC, 1983), 131–56.

51. *ARLC*, 1957, 5, 69; 1959, 5–6, 50; Stat 533; 71 Stat 368; 71 Stat 588; 71 Stat 627; 71 Stat 630; PL 85-147 (1957). The Library has digitized those collections.

52. Thomison, *History*, 192–93, 208; Edmon Low, "Federal Consciousness and Libraries," *AL* 3 (July–August 1972): 717–24; Carl Elliott and Michael D'Orso, *The Cost of Courage: The Journey of an American Congressman* (Tuscaloosa: University of Alabama Press, 1992), 141–71. Rudolph Flesch's bestseller, *Why Johnny Can't Read* (1955), also fostered anxieties about the education system.

53. *ARLC*, 1958, 1–3; 72 Stat 1580; 72 Stat 1598; John Sherrod, "The Technical Report in the Library of Congress," *QJLC* 16 (February 1959): 47–50.

54. *LCIB* 17 (January 13, 1958): 16–17. Six years later, Mumford noted continued heavy use: *ARLC*, 1964, xvii.

55. *LCIB* 17 (August 23, 1958): 474–75; John Y. Cole, *For Congress and the Nation: A Chronological History of the Library of Congress* (Washington, DC: LC, 1979), 143.

56. *LCIB* 19 (August 8, 1960): 469–70; *ARLC*, 1963, xii, 49; 1966, 20; *LCIB* 46 (April 13, 1987): 151; 61 (October 2001): 224; PL 87-765, 1961; PL 89-522, 1966; 76 Stat 763; 80 Stat 330; Marilyn Lundell Majeska, *Talking Books: Pioneering and Beyond* (Washington, DC: LC, 1988), 41ff; LC, *That All May Read*, 147–49, 152–53, 166–70. The division returned to the Library in 2024, with offices in the Adams Building; *Gazette* 35 (March 8, 2024): 1, 8.

57. *ARLC*, 1956, 3; 1960, 8; George A. Schwegmann Jr. and Robert D. Stevens, "The Proposal for a Current Author Catalog of American Library Resources," *C&RL* 17 (January 1956): 28–34; John W. Cronin, "The National Union and Library of Congress Catalogs: Problems and Prospects," *LQ* 34 (January 1964): 77–96. The "Register of Additional Locations," begun in 1962, recorded newly reported holdings.

58. *ARLC*, 1958, 16–17; 1959, 16–18; Cole, *For Congress*, 144; *LCIB* 25 (February 3, 1966): 66–68; A. G. Pickett and M. M. Lemcoe, *Preservation and Storage of Sound Recordings* (Washington, DC: LC, 1959).

59. *ARLC*, 1960, 7; Robert H. Land, "The National Union Catalog of Manuscript Collections," *American Archivist* 17 (July 1954): 195–207; David C. Mearns, "To Be Enduring: The National Union Catalog of Manuscript Collections," *C&RL* 20 (September 1959): 341–46; Broderick, "David Chambers Mearns," 74–75. The name of the Manuscripts Division was changed to the Manuscript Division in 1957.

60. Basler, *Muse and the Librarian*, 37–45. The proposal died in committee: McGuire, *Poetry's Catbird Seat*, 195–201, 229–30.

61. Roy P. Basler, "Robert Frost: Lobbyist for the Arts," *QJLC* 31 (April 1974): 108–15; Roy P. Basler, "Yankee Vergil: Robert Frost in Washington," in *Muse and the Librarian*, 56–77; Arthur M. Schlesinger Jr., *A Thousand Days: John F. Kennedy in the White House* (New York: Crown, 1983), 729–38. The manuscript of Frost's "Dedication" (for which he substituted "The Gift Outright" at the ceremony) was later presented to the LC by his friend Stewart Udall, former Secretary of the Interior: *LCIB* 29 (January 8, 1970): 4, 9.

62. *ARLC*, 1960, 42; 1961, xx; 1963, 44, 47; 1965, 4; LC, *Proceedings of the National Poetry Festival Held in the Library of Congress, October 22–24, 1962* (Washington, DC: LC, 1964); Louis Untermeyer, *Bygones: The Recollections of Louis Untermeyer* (New York: Harcourt, Brace & World, 1965), 218; *LCIB* 29 (April 23, 1970): 185–87; Broderick, "American Literature," 111–12.

63. This program was later absorbed into the PL 480 program: *ARLC*, 1965, 26.

64. *ARLC*, 1959, 8–10; *LCIB* 18 (June 8, 1959): 307–10; (June 15, 1959): 337–38; (October 5, 1959): 608; Julian W. Witherell, "Africana in the Library of Congress: The Role of the African Center," *QJLC* 27 (July 1970): 184–96.

65. *ARLC*, 1960, xiii; 1961, xvi; 1963, 2–5; 1966, 34–37; 72 Stat 1790; James E. Skipper, "National Planning for Resource Development," *LT* 15 (October 1966): 327–31; Robert D. Stevens, "The Library of Congress Public Law 480 Programs," *LRTS* 7 (Spring 1967): 176–88; John G. Lorenz et al., "The Library of Congress Abroad," *LT* 20 (January 1972): 553–54. The Appropriations Committee specified that participating libraries pay a $500 annual fee to the Treasury. The Librarian's PL 480 Advisory Committee included members from NLM, NAL, ACLS, ALA, SLA, ARL, SSRC, AHA, NSF, and the State Department.

66. Stevens, "Library of Congress Public Law 480," 182–87; Robert Vosper, "International Implications of the Shared Cataloging Program: Planning for Resources Development," *Libri* 17 (1967): 285–93. The program reflected some ideas Ralph Ellsworth had proposed in 1948: *LCIB* (November 16–22, 1948): appendix. See also Philip J. McNiff, "The Farmington Plan and the Foreign Acquisitions Programs of American Research Libraries," 145–58; and William S. Dix, "The Public Law 480 Program and the National Program for Acquisitions and Cataloging of the Library of Congress," 159–76, both in *Acquisitions from the 3rd World*, edited by D. A. Clarke (London: Mansell, 1975). The Farmington Plan ceased in 1972. Because the foreign currencies were exhausted, PL 480 was replaced by regular acquisitions channels and NPAC: *ARLC*, 1973, 3, 22. The last PL-480 program ended in 1998.

67. *ARLC*, 1956, 52; 1958, 52; 1959, 3–4, 62, 66–67; 1960, xii–xiii, 27, 50; 1961, xi; 1964, 68; 1965, 11–12; Cole, *For Congress*, 143; 74 Stat 132.

68. *ARLC*, 1953, 27–29; *LCIB* 12 (February 7, 1953): 10–11; John M. Dawson, "The Library of Congress: Its Role in Cooperative and Centralized Cataloging," *LT* 16 (July 1967): 90.

69. *LCIB* 18 (October 5, 1959): 606–7; 20 (February 20, 1961): 109–10; *LJ* 84 (November 15, 1959): 3538.

70. See C. Sumner Spalding, "Cataloging in Source: The Experiment from the Viewpoint of the Library of Congress"; Virginia Drewry, "Consumer Reaction Survey of Cataloging in Source"; and Roy B. Eastin, "Cataloging in Source: The Viewpoint of Publishers"—all in *LRTS*

3 (Fall 1959): 239–56. See also Paul S. Dunkin, ed., "Cataloging in Source: A Symposium," *LRTS* 4 (Fall 1960): 269–84.

71. *ARLC*, 1958, 4; 1959, 18–19; 1960, xiv, 8; *LCIB* 18 (July 6, 1959): 395–96; 19 (August 15, 1960): 483; *LJ* 85 (April 15, 1960): 1535–37; 85 (June 1, 1960): 2064; Dunkin, "Cataloging in Source," 283; LC, *The Cataloging-in-Source Experiment: A Report to the Librarian of Congress by the Director of the Processing Department* (Washington, DC: LC, 1960). As an "improvement in service," the LC began in 1961 to sell wholesalers, jobbers, and publishers cards to enclose in books sold to libraries: *ARLC*, 1961, xviii–xix.

72. *LCIB* 15 (August 13, 1956): 428; 70 Stat 960; Thomison, *History*, 193–93. In 1994, Congress established the National Library of Education within the Department of Education (108 Stat 260).

73. Quoted by Cole, *Library of Congress in Perspective*, 50.

74. Thomison, *History*, 213–14; Dennis Thomison, "Trouble in Camelot: An Early Skirmish of Kennedy's New Frontier," *JLH* 13 (Spring 1978): 148–56; Cole, *Library of Congress in Perspective*, 61; Clapp to Emerson Greenaway, January 19, 1961, box 30, Clapp Papers, LC.

75. When Mumford asked the ARL for suggestions, the ARL Board left it up to individual members to respond: Association of Research Libraries *Minutes,* 60th Meeting, June 16, 1962, 20. "One can surmise," Ed Holley later wrote, "that more was going on here than was ever brought to public attention": Edward G. Holley, "The Influence of ARL on Academic Librarianship, Legislation, and Library Education," *Advances in Library Administration and Organization* 3 (1984): 301.

76. *ARLC*, 1962, xi–xii, 89–111 (which include the memo and Mumford's response); *LCIB* 21 (July 30, 1962): 412–13; 21 (October 8, 1962): 525–26. The librarians' committee agreed that designation as the national library was not important, but there were differing opinions about the LC's role and about an advisory board: Liaison Committee Minutes, July 27, November 15–16, 1962, box 30, Clapp Papers, LC.

77. Harold Orlans, ed., *Federal Departmental Libraries: A Summary Report of a Survey and a Conference by Luther H. Evans and Others* (Washington, DC: Brookings Institution Press, 1963). The idea of coordinating federal libraries appeared at the 1896 hearings and was considered by the ALA's Special Committee on Federal Relations (1937), by the District of Columbia Library Association (leading to informal meetings beginning in August 1941), by MacLeish's Librarian's Committee, and by Evans's Planning Committee: L. Quincy Mumford, J. Lee Westrate, and Paul Howard, "The Establishment of the Federal Library Committee: A Symposium," *DC Libraries* 36 (Summer 1965): 40–43; Marlene Morrisey, "Historical Development and Organization of the Federal Library Committee," *Drexel Library Quarterly* 6 (July–October 1970): 207–31; Cole, *Library of Congress in Perspective*, 27–28.

78. Orlans, *Federal Departmental Libraries*, 144–46.

79. House Report 369, 88th Congress, 1st sess., 16.

80. *ARLC*, 1963, 1.

81. Virginia Haviland, "Serving Those Who Serve Children," *QJLC* 22 (October 1965): 301–16; *QJLC* 70 (April 1973): 166–67. The section was renamed the Children's Literature Center in 1978 and moved to the Rare Book and Special Collections Division in 2006.

82. *ARLC*, 1963, xiii; 1973, 53; *LCIB* 38 (September 7, 1979): 366–67; Marvin W. McFarland, "The National Referral Center," *Special Libraries* 66 (March 1975): 126–32. The center merged with the Science and Technology Division in 1968, but because it added coverage in other areas, it became an independent unit. The Cold Regions Bibliography Project moved to the American Geological Institute at the end of fiscal 2000; *ARLC*, 2000, 86. Funding for the arms control bibliography lapsed in 1973.

83. Jim Bishop, *The Day Kennedy Was Shot* (New York: Funk & Wagnalls, 1968), 32, 418, 487, 548; John Y. Cole, *America's Greatest Library: An Illustrated History of the Library of Congress* (Washington, DC: LC, in association with D. Giles Limited, London, 2017), 164–65; *Gazette* 10 (November 26, 1999): 6–10; *LCM* 2 (July–August 2013): 6; William Manchester, *The Death of a President, November 20–November 25, 1963* (New York: Harper & Row, 1967), 420, 485. Bishop was incorrect; Robert Gooch was Acting Librarian. Mearns was a Lincoln specialist, as was Roy Basler, who received Schlesinger's initial call. Sutton was head of the Newspaper and Periodical Section, Serials Division, and Mearns invited Robertson, director of the US Civil War Centennial Commission and a Lincoln scholar.

84. *LCIB* 22 (December 2, 1963): 637–38.

85. *ARLC*, 1964, xxi–xxiii; *Gazette* 10 (December 3, 1999): 6–10; Mary R. Bucknum, "Motion Picture, Broadcasting, and Recorded Sound Division," *Encyclopedia*, 364.

86. Charles Goodrum and Helen Dalrymple, "Computerization at the Library of Congress: The First Twenty Years," *Wilson Library Bulletin* 57 (October 1982): 115.

87. LC, *Automation and the Library of Congress: A Survey Sponsored by the Council on Library Resources* (Washington, DC: LC, 1964); Lawrence F. Buckland, *Recording of Library of Congress Bibliographical Data in Machine-Readable Form* (Washington, DC: CLR, 1965); *LCIB* 24 (March 8, 1965): 120–21; Peter T. Rohrbach, *FIND: Automation at the Library of Congress—The First Twenty-Five Years and Beyond* (Washington, DC: LC, 1985), 6–11; Cole, *For Congress*, 150.

88. Lucile M. Morsch, "Cataloging at the Library of Congress: A Look into the Future," *Southeastern Librarian* 14 (Winter 1964): 256; Karen M. Spicher, "The Development of the MARC Format," *CCQ* 21, nos. 3–4 (1996): 75–78; Gilbert W. King, 'The Library of Congress Project," *LRTS* 9 (Winter 1965): 91; Suzanne E. Thorin, *Automation at the Library of Congress: Inside Views* (Washington, DC: LC Professional Association, 1986), 2.

89. Barbara Evans Markuson, ed., *Libraries and Automation: Proceedings of the Conference on Libraries and Automation* (Washington, DC: LC, 1964), 248; Robert M. Hayes, Ralph H. Parker, and Gilbert W. King, "Automation and the Library of Congress: Three Views," *LQ* 34 (July 1964): 229; Samuel S. Snyder, "Automation at LC: Philosophy, Plans, Progress," *LJ* 90 (November 1, 1965): 4711; *LCIB* 24 (February 23, 1965): 99–100.

90. Henriette D. Avram, *MARC: Its History and Implications* (Washington, DC: LC 1975), 1–8; "The MARC Pilot Project: Final Report on a Project Sponsored by the Council on Library Resources, Prepared by Henriette D. Avram" (LC, 1968).

91. "An Oral History of MARC," transcription vol. 3, 21, LCA; Arthur Plotnik, William J. Welsh, and Vic Fazio, "Can Bill Welsh Conquer Time and Space for Libraries?" *AL* 15 (December 1984): 768–69; *LCIB* 65 (May 2006): 130, 132.

92. *ARLC*, 1968, 4–6; *LCIB* 26 (June 29, 1967): 407–8; 27 (April 18, 1968): 214–15; (May 16, 1968): 270; 28 (February 27, 1969): 130.

93. *LCIB* 27 (April 25, 1968): 229–30. Avram emphasized standardization: MARC became a national standard in 1971; the International Standards Organization approved US MARC and UK MARC in 1973; Lucia J. Rather and Peter J. de la Garza, "Getting It All Together: International Cataloging Cooperation and Networks," *Journal of Library Automation* 10 (June 1977): 163–69.

94. *ARLC*, 1975, 19; the COMARC effort, however, proved unworkable.

95. *ARLC*, 1965, 15–17; 1966, 18; 1977, 24; 1979, 61; Rohrbach, *FIND*, 14–15; Avram, *MARC*, 9–20; Henriette D. Avram, *RECON Pilot Project: Final* Report (Washington, DC: LC, 1972); Lucia J. Rather, "Exchange of Bibliographic Information in Machine-Readable Form," *LT* 25 (Winter 1977): 625–43. In 1980, LC produced MARC records from the Carrollton

Press's electronic file of LC shelflist records. This so-called PREMARC file was a step toward converting the entire catalog: *LCIB* 42 (February 21, 1983); 43 (June 18, 1984): 211–12; 48 (July 31, 1989): 270–71; 51 (March 9, 1992): 102; Thorin, *Automation,* 6–7.

96. John Y. Cole, ed., *In Celebration: The National Union Catalog, Pre-1956 Imprints* (Washington, DC: LC, 1981). Rowman & Littlefield published the *Slavic Cyrillic Union Catalog of Pre-1956 Imprints* on microfiche in 1980.

97. *LCIB* 26 (March 9, 1967): 182. More schedules followed: *LCIB* 51 (October 5, 1992): 430; 56 (August 1997): 282–83; *ARLC,* 2001, 70–71; 2004, 48.

98. *Statement of Principles Adopted at the International Conference on Cataloging Principles, Paris, October, 1961* (London: IFLA Committee on Cataloging, 1971); *ARLC,* 1967, 43–45; Dunkin, *Cataloging USA,* 16–17; *LCIB* 25 (March 17, 1966): 141–42; (August 4, 1966): 480–81; 26 (March 9, 1967): 183–84; 27 (January 25, 1968): 43; (June 27, 1968): 344; (August 1, 1968): 468; Wyllis E. Wright, "The Anglo-American Cataloging Rules: A Historical Perspective," *LRTS* 20 (Winter 1976): 40–47; Paul S. Dunkin, "Cataloging & Classification—The Big If," *AL* 6 (July–August 1972): 776; Katharine H. Packer and Delores Phillips, eds., *The Code and the Cataloger: Proceedings of the Colloquium on the Anglo-American Cataloging Rules Held at the School of Library Science, University of Toronto, on March 31 and April 1, 1967* (Toronto: University of Toronto Press, 1969), 91; Kathryn Luther Henderson, "Treated with a Degree of Uniformity and Common Sense: Descriptive Cataloging in the United States, 1876–1975, *LT* 25 (July 1976): 242–50. The Paris conference included fifty-four countries and twelve international organizations.

99. *LCIB* 23 (June 29, 1964): 311–13; 24 (February 8, 1965): 73–74; Ralph E. Ellsworth, "Another Chance for Centralized Cataloging," *LJ* 89 (September 1, 1964): 3104–7.

100. "Special Message to the Congress: Toward Full Educational Opportunity, Jan. 12, 1965," *Public Papers of the Presidents of the United States: Lyndon B. Johnson* (Washington, DC: GPO, 1966), 1: 25–33; 79 Stat 27; Robert Dallek, *Flawed Giant: Lyndon Johnson and His Times, 1961–1973* (New York: Oxford University Press, 1998), 189–203; Hugh Davis Graham, *The Uncertain Triumph: Federal Education Policy in the Kennedy and Johnson Years* (Chapel Hill: University of North Carolina Press, 1984), 55–83.

101. "Hearings before the Subcommittee on Education of the Committee on Education and Labor on HR 3220, 89th Congress, 1st Session" (GPO, 1965): 368–84; "Hearings before the Subcommittee on Education of the Committee on Labor and Public Welfare on S. 600, 89th Congress, 1st Session" (GPO, 1965), 597–610; William S. Dix, "Centralized Cataloging and University Libraries–Title II, Part C, of the Higher Education Act of 1965," *LT* 16 (Summer 1967): 97–111; Vosper, "International Implications," 288–89.

102. William S. Dix, "Recent Developments in Centralized Cataloging," *LRTS* 11 (Winter 1967): 32–35; L. Quincy Mumford, "International Breakthrough: An Account of the Operational Beginnings of the Shared Cataloging Program," *LJ* 92 (January 1, 1967): 79–82; John W. Cronin, "Remarks on LC Plans for Implementation of New Centralized Acquisitions and Cataloging Program under Title IIC, Higher Education Act," *LRTS* 11 (Winter 1967): 35–37; *LCIB* 25 (February 10, 1966): 83–86; William J. Welsh, "ARL/LC: 1932–1982," *Advances in Library Administration and Organization* 3 (1984): 290.

103. Dix, "Centralized Cataloging," 109, attributed the idea of using national bibliographies to John Cronin.

104. *ARLC,* 1966, 2–6, 26–34; 1969, 1–2; *LRTS* 11 (Winter 1967): 27; Mumford, "International Breakthrough," 81; John W. Cronin, "Centralized Cataloging at the National and International Level," *LRTS* 11 (Winter 1967): 35–36; Redmond Kathleen Molz, *Federal Policy and Library Support* (Cambridge, MA: MIT Press, 1976), 21–23. The program envisioned electronic

distribution: James E. Skipper, "Future Implications of the Higher Education Act of 1965," *LRTS* 11 (Winter 1967): 46–49; *LCIB* 25 (February 10, 1966): 84–86; (February 17, 1966): 105–6. Starting in fiscal year 1973, funds were appropriated directly to the LC.

105. Jerry R. James, "The Establishment of an Overseas Acquisitions Center: A Personal Reminiscence," *QJLC* 27 (July 1970): 206–12; Alvin Moore Jr., "A Review of the Library of Congress Program in Eastern Africa," in *Conference on the Acquisition of Material from Africa, University of Birmingham, 25th April 1969,* comp. Valerie Bloomfield (Zug, Switzerland: Inter Documentation Company, 1969), 1–6. Printed accession lists ceased as cataloging moved online: *LCIB* 64 (May 2005): 107–15.

106. *ARLC*, 1966, 6; Edmond Applebaum, "Developments at the Library of Congress," *LRTS* 12 (Winter 1968): 18–20.

107. Dix, "Public Law 480," 164–70; John G. Lorenz, "International Implications of the Shared Cataloging Program: Planning for Bibliographical Control," *Libri* 17 (1967): 276–84; *LCIB* 45 (October 27, 1986): 358–59, 363–64; Carol F. Ishimoto, "The National Program for Acquisitions and Cataloging: Its Impact on University Libraries," *C&RL* 34 (March 1973): 127–29. From 1973 on, fiscal constraints forced reductions; by 1987 field offices remained only in Cairo, Islamabad, Jakarta, Nairobi, New Delhi, and Rio de Janeiro: *LCIB* 46 (December 21, 1987): 562–63; James C. Armstrong, "Overseas Operations," *Encyclopedia*, 389–92.

108. *ARLC*, 1965, 20; 1966, 23; Mumford, Westrate, and Howard, "Establishment"; Morrisey, "Historical Development"; Russell Shank and Elaine Sloan, "The Governance of National Libraries and Information Services at the Federal Level," *LT* 26 (Fall 1977): 215. The FLC later invited observers from CLR and library associations: *LCIB* 29 (June 25, 1970): 323–24.

109. The order was drafted before President Kennedy's death: Elizabeth E. Hamer, "Everybody's Library," *LJ* 90 (January 1, 1965): 55; *LCIB* 25 (September 8, 1966): 562–64.

110. *ARLC*, 1969, 2–3.

111. "The Library of Congress as the National Library: Potentialities for Service," in *Libraries at Large: The Resource Book Based on the Materials of the National Advisory Commission on Libraries*, edited by Douglas M. Knight and E. Shepley Nourse (New York: R. R. Bowker, 1969), 435–65; Cole, "Lawrence Quincy Mumford," 90–91; Cole, *Library of Congress in Perspective*, 61–70.

112. National Advisory Commission on Libraries, *Library Services for the Nation's Needs: Toward Fulfillment of a National Policy—Report of the National Advisory Commission on Libraries* (Washington, DC: National Advisory Commission on Libraries, 1968).

113. 79 Stat 845; 82 Stat 1356.

114. *LCIB* 27 (April 4, 1968): 169. The program continued until 1980.

115. Roger J. Trienens, "The Library's Earliest Colonial Imprints," *QJLC* 24 (July 1967): 186–87.

116. John C. Broderick, "The Greatest Whitman Collector and the Greatest Whitman Collection," *QJLC* 27 (April 1970): 2109; *QJLC* 29 (January 15, 1970): 26.

117. Barbara Pruett, "Groucho Marx Runs through the Library of Congress," *Performing Arts: Broadcasting* (Washington, DC: LC, 2002), 186–88; *LCIB* 25 (May 19, 1966): 245–46.

118. *LCIB* 28 (January 16, 1969): 25–27; (September 11, 1969): 455–56; 29 (May 14, 1970): 230–31; (May 21, 1970): 236–37; Lawrence F. Karr, "The American Film Institute and the Library of Congress: A Twenty-Year Perspective," *QJLC* 37 (Summer–Fall 1980): 355–69.

119. *LCIB* 28 (January 16, 1969): 27–28; (June 19, 1969): 309–10.

120. Adrienne Koch, "James Madison and the Library of Congress," *QJLC* 37 (Spring 1980): 159–61; Robert A. Rutland, "Madison's Bookish Habits," *QJLC* 37, no. 2 (Spring 1980): 176–91.

121. *LCIB* 24 (September 13, 1965): 499–500; PL 79-986; "James Madison Memorial Commission, a Summary Account of the Commission's Part in the Planning of the Library of Congress James Madison Memorial Building" (LC, 1973).

122. *ARLC*, 1967, 8–17.

123. The LC's GPO branch handled binding and repair until MacLeish established the Office of the Keeper of the Collections, which in 1963 became the Office of Collections Maintenance and Preservation. Uniting preservation activities followed on the devastating Arno River flood in Florence in November 1966, which drew international attention and influenced the LC's conservation program: Sherelyn Ogden, "The Impact of the Florence Flood on Library Conservation in the United States of America," *Restaurator* 3 (1979): 17–23.

124. Gordon R. Williams, *The Preservation of Deteriorating Books: An Examination of the Problem with Recommendations for a Solution* (Washington, DC: ARL, 1964).

125. "Notes on a Conference Held at LC, 6 Dec. 1965," Association of Research Libraries Papers, LC, box 3.

126. William J. Crowe, "Verner Clapp and Preservation of Library Materials: The Years at the Council on Library Resources," in *Academic Librarianship: Past, Present, and Future*, edited by John Richardson Jr. and Jinnie Y. Davis (Englewood, CO: Libraries Unlimited, 1989), 51–54; Norman J. Shaffer, "Library of Congress Pilot Preservation Project," *C&RL* 30 (January 1969): 5–11; Paul E. Edlund, "The Continuing Quest: Care of LC's Collections," *LJ* 90 (September 1, 1965): 3402; *LCIB* 24 (February 8, 1965): 68–69, 71; 25 (October 20, 1966): 643–44; 26 (January 26, 1967): 67–68; 27 (March 7, 1968): 8–17. NRMM listings were incorporated into *NUC* and *NST* beginning in 1984: *LCIB* 46 (June 1, 1987): 230–31.

127. *LCIB* 26 (March 9, 1967): 178–79; 27 (June 27, 1968): 342–43; 50 (January 14, 1991): 3–6; *ARLC*, 1983, 81; Winston Atkins, "Frazer Glendon Poole," *DALB*-S2: 174–76.

128. Richard H. Leach, "A Broad Look at the Federal Government and Libraries," in *Libraries at Large*, ed. Knight and Nourse, 346–86; Albert P. Marshall, "Review of the *Annual Report of the Librarian of Congress*, 1964," *LQ* 36 (January 1966): 72; Thomas P. Brockway, "Library Problems and the Scholar," *ACLS Newsletter* 17 (March 1966): 6; Harold Orlans, "Observations on Government Library Organization and Policy," in *Libraries at Large*, ed. Knight and Nourse, 387–93.

Chapter 9

1. *LCIB* 30 (August 5, 1971): 446–47; LC, *That All May Read: Library Services for Blind and Physically Handicapped People* (Washington, DC: LC, 1983), 280–82, 312–13. In the mid-1970s, the NLS began contracting for space in four areas of the country (called Multistate Centers) to store books and equipment.

2. *LCIB* 67 (March 2008): 31–36, www.loc.gov/services/federal-research-division/about-this-service/history/.

3. Joseph L. Wheeler, "Top Priority for Cataloging-In-Source," *LJ* 94 (September 15, 1969): 3007–13; Joseph L. Wheeler, "Cataloging In/At Source: Why We Must Have Cataloging in Publication," *LRTS* 15 (Winter 1971): 6–12; Verner W. Clapp, "CIP in Mid-1970," *LRTS* 15 (Winter 1971): 12–23.

4. An ALA–Association of American Publishers committee asked Clapp to help reinstate the program: Verner W. Clapp, "The Greatest Invention since the Title Page? Autobibliography from Incipit to Cataloging-in-Publication," *Wilson Library Bulletin* 46 (December 1971): 355–56.

5. William J. Welsh, "Report on Library of Congress Plans for Cataloging in Publication," *LRTS* 15 (Winter 1971): 23–27; Verner Clapp, "Cataloguing in Publication," *UNESCO Bulletin for Libraries* 27 (January–February 1973): 2–11.

6. *ARLC*, 1974, 4; *LCIB* 30 (June 24, 1971): 372–74; (July 22, 1971): 426–27; (September 23, 1971): 531–34; 33 (January 11, 1974): A-6. In 1984, the NLM began providing CIP data for medical materials: *LCIB* 32 (August 27, 1984): 279–80.

7. Paul Edlund, "A Monster and a Miracle: The Cataloging Distribution Service of the Library of Congress, 1901–1976," *QJLC* 33 (October 1976): 416–19; Stephen R. Salmon, "Development of the Card-Automated Reproduction and Distribution Service (CARDS) at the Library of Congress," in *Proceedings of the 1969 Clinic on Library Applications of Data Processing*, edited by Dewey E. Carroll (Urbana: School of Library Science, University of Illinois, 1969), 98–113. Before CARDS, nearly 600 people worked in two shifts plus overtime; the staff outnumbered every university library staff in the United States except Harvard's, and the CDS occupied 57,600 square feet, larger than the standard football field plus end zones.

8. *Gazette* 8 (May 23, 1997): 1, 10.

9. John Y. Cole, "Developing a National Foreign Newspaper Microfilming Program," *LRTS* 18 (Winter 1974): 10–17; *LCIB* 32 (March 2, 1973): A57–A58.

10. Chi Wang, *Building a Better Chinese Collection for the Library of Congress: Selected Writings* (Lanham, MD: Scarecrow Press, 2012), 1–21, 118; Chris Tudda, *A Cold War Turning Point: Nixon and China, 1969–1972* (Baton Rouge: Louisiana State University Press, 2012), 191–92; *Library of Congress Asian Collections*, 68–69; *LCIB* 38 (August 17, 1979): 317; (November 30, 1979): 487–88; 43 (September 24, 1984): 312–14; *ARLC*, 1982, 73.

11. David H. Brunell, "The Strategic Alliance between OCLC and Networks: Partnerships That Work," in *OCLC 1967–1997: Thirty Years of Furthering Access to the World's Information*, edited by K. Wayne Smith (New York: Haworth, 1998), 19–29; Larry Millsap, "The History of the Online Catalog in North America," in *Technical Services Management: 1965–1990*, edited by L. Smith and R. Carter (New York: Routledge, 1996), 82–84. The name was changed to OCLC, Inc., in 1977; to OCLC Online Computer Library Center, Inc., in 1981; and to OCLC, Inc., in 2017.

12. Henriette D. Avram, *MARC: Its History and Implications* (Washington, DC: LC, 1975), 29–30. Charles Goodrum and Helen Dalrymple, "Computerization at the Library of Congress: The First Twenty Years," *Wilson Library Bulletin* 57 (October 1982): 121, noted that Congress initially refused to let the LC provide computer services to nongovernment facilities, to protect access to congressional data. The so-called bibliographic utilities were "organizations that have hardware, software, and a sizable database of bibliographic records and offer computer-based support for technical and public service operations to a number of libraries"; Henriette Avram, "Production, Dissemination, and Use of Bibliographic Data and Summary of the Conference," *LQ* 47 (July 1977): 355. OCLC and RLG merged between 2006 and 2011.

13. *ARLC*, 1973, 12; 1974, 6; 1975, 10; 1986, 28–29; *LCIB* 43 (December 24, 1984): 425–27; James P. Riley, "Network Topology and the Federal Library Committee," in *The Structure and Governance of Library Networks*, edited by Allen Kent and Thomas J. Galvin (New York: Marcel Dekker, 1978), 99–103; www.loc.gov.flicc/.

14. Arthur Plotnik, "OCLC for You—and Me?!" *AL* 7 (May 1976): 258–67; Joe A. Hewitt, "The Impact of OCLC," *AL* 7 (May 1976): 268–75; Richard De Gennaro, "Library Automation: Changing Patterns," *LJ* 101 (January 1, 1976): 175–83; Susan K. Martin, "The Transformation of Library Networks," *Portal: Libraries and the Academy* 2 (April 2002): vii–x.

15. *LCIB* 29 (March 5, 1970): 111–12; (July 9, 970): 343–44; Josephine S. Pulsifer and Elaine W. Woods, "The MARC Serials Distribution Service," *LCIB* 33 (April 12, 1974): A81–A84.

16. Developed by the International Standards Organization, the ISSN differs from the International Standard Book Number (ISBN) created by the British Library in the 1960s and assigned by publishers: Lucia J. Rather, "Exchange of Bibliographic Information in Machine-Readable Form," *LT* 25 (Winter 1977): 637–38.

17. *LCIB* 33 (June 28, 1974): A122; *ARLC*, 1977, 25.

18. The LC was originally slated to host the database, but the Library could not support it at the time; it remained with OCLC: Suzanne Striedieck, "CONSER and the National Database," *Advances in Serials Management* 3 (1989): 86–92.

19. Lawrence G. Livingston, "A Composite Effort to Build an On-Line National Serials Data Base," *LCIB* 33 (February 1, 1974): A35–A38; Lois Upham, "CONSER: Cooperative Conversion of Serials Project," *LCIB* 33 (November 29, 1974): A245–A48; *ARLC*, 1977, 25; 1978, 55; Lawrence G. Livingston, "The CONSER Project: Current Status and Plans," *LCIB* 34 (February 14, 1975): A38–A42; 38 (August 24, 1979): 333–34; Carol A. Mandel, "Cooperative Cataloging: Models, Issues, Prospects," *Advances in Librarianship* 16 (1992): 47–52; Lori L. Osmus, "The Transformation of Serials Cataloging," in *Technical Services Management*, ed. Smith and Carter, 175–78; Bill Anderson, "History of the CONSER Program (1986–1994)," *Serials Review* 21 (Summer 1995): 1–16.

20. "Organization of Congress: Hearing before the Joint Committee on the Organization of Congress, 89th Congress, 1st Session" (GPO, 1965), part 7, 1109–81; Charles Goodrum and Helen Dalrymple, *The Library of Congress* (Boulder, CO: Westview Press, 1982), 228–29. Advocates cited the separation of state legislative reference libraries from state libraries and from parliamentary libraries—e.g., in Canada and Australia.

21. John Y. Cole, *For Congress and the Nation: A Chronological History of the Library of Congress* (Washington, DC: LC, 1979), 163.

22. The name and elevation in status were proposed in 1958 by CRS director Ernest S. Griffith, *The Legislative Reference Service of the Library of Congress: A Memorandum on Its Achievements, Problems, and Potential, with Recommendations for Its Improvement* (Washington, DC: GPO, 1958), 7–8. From 323 budgeted positions in 1970, the CRS grew to 703 in 1975: John Y. Cole, "The Congressional Research Service," *Encyclopedia, 21.*

23. 84 Stat 1181; Goodrum and Dalrymple, *Library of Congress*, 205–17.

24. Harold C. Relyea, "Across the Hill: The Congressional Research Service and Providing Research for Congress—A Retrospective on Origins," *Government Information Quarterly* 27 (2010): 419; John Y. Cole, "Lawrence Quincy Mumford," *DALB-S*, 90; *ARLC*, 1971, 3; 1979, 28–31; *LCIB* 29 (November 5, 1970): 588–89; Suzanne E. Thorin and Robert Wedgeworth, "Librarians of Congress," *AL* 38 (June–July 2007): 89. A 1985 law required the director to submit budget estimates to the Librarian (PL 99-190): Walter Kravitz, "The Advent of the Modern Congress: The Legislative Reorganization Act of 1970," *Legislative Studies Quarterly* 15 (August 1990): 396.

25. "The Final Report of the Select Committee on Presidential Campaign Activities, United States Senate, Pursuant to S. Res. 60, February 7, 1973, Report No. 93-981, 93rd Congress, 2nd Session" (GPO, 1974), 1087–95; *LCIB* 33 (November 15, 1974): 379–80. The data were transferred to the Library when the committee completed its work, but the Senate Rules Committee retained control of all materials.

26. *LCIB* 21 (January 8, 1962): 15–16; 22 (May 6, 1963): 211–14; 23 (April 27, 1964): 184–86.

27. John Y. Cole and Jane Aikin, "Employees and Employment," *Encyclopedia*, 228–29.

28. *ARLC*, 1971, 9–10; *LCIB* 30 (July 1, 1971): A103–A106; (July 22, 1971): A149–A152; A154; Mumford to Members of the Staff, June 30, 1971 (Special Announcement 416), Union Activities, LCA, box 2.

29. "Three Request[s] for Action Reports: An ALA Report," *AL* 3 (March 1972): 277–79; Cole, *For Congress*, 166.

30. *Gazette* 3 (October 2, 1992): 1, 10–11.

31. The act required federal agencies to develop annual affirmative action plans; the LC was included due to an amendment from senators Allen Cranston (D-CA) and Peter Dominick (R-CO), which Mumford and the Joint Committee supported.

32. *ARLC*, 1972, 7–8; *LCIB* 30 (August 5, 1971): 442–43; 31 (February 3, 1972): 46–47; (February 10, 1972): A21; (July 7, 1972): A107–A108; (July 21, 1972): A117, 118; 32 (February 23, 1973): A42–A43; 33 (March 8, 1974): A70–A71; "Memo: ALA Report: Library of Congress," *AL* 4 (April 1974): 198–204; Cole, *For Congress*, 166.

33. *LCIB* 32 (September 14, 1973): 319, 325; Cole, *For Congress*, 166, 168; *AL* 4 (November 1973): 590.

34. *ARLC*, 1972, 8–9; 1973, 8–9; 1974, 8–9, 70; *LCIB* 31 (June 23, 1972): 279; Cole, *For Congress*, 166.

35. Cole, *For Congress*, 168; *ARLC*, 1975, 10–11; 1976, xxix–xxx; *LCIB* 35 (January 23, 1976).

36. *LCIB* 41 (November 19, 1982): 383–88; 55 (November 18, 1996); *Gazette* 3 (October 9, 1992).

37. *ARLC*, 1976, xxiii–xxiv; PL 89-491; *LCIB* 59 (September 22, 2000): 4–5.

38. Mumford cited making Congress aware of the LC's needs and the approval of a third building as his most gratifying achievements: Arthur Plotnik, "Twenty Years on the Hill: An Anniversary Interview with L. Quincy Mumford," *Wilson Library Bulletin* 48 (January 1974): 395–96. President Nixon's executive order of December 1973 exempted Mumford from mandatory retirement for one year: John Y. Cole, *America's Greatest Library: An Illustrated History of the Library of Congress* (Washington, DC: LC, in association with D. Giles Limited, London, 2017), 179.

39. *ARLC*, 1974, 2, 24; *LCIB* 33 (November 15, 1974): 379, A219–A220.

40. *ARLC*, 1974, 69; *LCIB* 33 (January 3, 1974): 1, 3–5, 34 (February 14, 1975): A35–A37, 41 (August 27, 1982): 257; Rutherford D. Rogers, "LQM of LC," *Bulletin of Bibliography* 25 (September–December 1968); John Y. Cole, "Lawrence Quincy Mumford," *DALB-S*, 90; John Y. Cole, "The National Libraries of the United States and Canada," in *A Century of Service: Librarianship in the United States and Canada*, edited by Sidney L. Jackson, Eleanor B. Herling, and E. J. Josey (Chicago: ALA, 1976), 249–50; John Y. Cole, "The Library of Congress in American Life," *Advances in Librarianship* 8 (1978): 67.

41. *LCIB* 33 (May 24, 1974): 174.

42. Editor Arthur Plotnik, however, predicted acceptance by the library community: *AL* 6 (November 1975): 582.

43. "Underrepresentation of Minorities in Supergrade Positions and above, at the Library of Congress: Hearing Held before the Subcommittee on Libraries and Memorials of the Committee on House Administration . . . April 26, 1990" (GPO, 1990), 71–76.

44. "Nomination of Daniel Boorstin of the District of Columbia to Be Librarian of Congress: Hearings before the Committee on Rules and Administration, US Senate, July 21, 30, and Sept. 10, 1975" (GPO, 1975), 26–29, 34–84, 138–52, 159–206, 328–31, 388–91; Cole, *For Congress*, 175–76; *AL* 6 (November 1975): 582.

45. John Y. Cole, "Daniel J. Boorstin," *Encyclopedia*, 183–85.

46. "Nomination of Daniel Boorstin," 372.

47. Other issues raised in the hearings included Boorstin's late-1930s membership in communist groups, his willing testimony before the House Un-American Activities Committee (1953), his use of federal employees as research assistants at the Smithsonian, and whether, as

an author, he might have conflicts of interest with the Copyright Office; "Nomination of Daniel Boorstin," 62–78, 159–64, 370–72.

48. *LCIB* 34 (November 12, 1975): 458; Kathryn Luther Henderson, "Treated with a Degree of Uniformity and Common Sense: Descriptive Cataloging in the United States, 1876–1975," *LT* 25 (July 1976): 250ff.

49. The Multiple Use MARC System replaced the MARC tapes with an online interactive system; MUMS was retired effective January 11, 2000: *Gazette* 11 (January 21, 2000): 6–8.

50. Avram, *MARC*, 25–30; *ARLC*, 1977, 32–33, 74.

51. *ARLC*, 1970, 6; *LCIB* 29 (July 30, 1970): 374–77; *QJLC* 31 (October 1974): 252–55; 32 (July 1975): 185–88; 84 Stat 440.

52. US National Commission on Libraries and Information Science, *Toward a National Program for Library and Information Services: Goals for Action* (Washington, DC: GPO, 1975), 48–50, 66–70.

53. ARL, *The Library of Congress as the National Bibliographic Center: Report of a Program Sponsored by the Association of Research Libraries, October 16, 1975* (Washington, DC: ARL, 1975), 7–9, 49.

54. John Y. Cole, ed., *The Library of Congress in Perspective: A Volume Based on the Reports of the 1976 Librarian's Task Force and Advisory Groups* (New York: R. R. Bowker, 1978), 75–77; Arthur Plotnik, "Boorstin's Midwinter Briefing to Library Staff Group Highlights His First 100 Days as Librarian," *AL* 7 (March 1976): 7–9, 49.

55. Larry Van Dyne, "Daniel Boorstin Remembers," *Washingtonian*, June 1982, 210–11; *LCIB* 35 (June 11, 1976): 329–30; John Y. Cole, *Jefferson's Legacy: A Brief History of the Library of Congress* (Washington, DC: LC, 1992), 40. Boorstin's concept was embodied by *The Circle of Knowledge: An Exhibition in the Great Hall of the Library of Congress, December 7, 1979–March 16, 1980* (Washington, DC: LC, 1979).

56. The advisory group on libraries, chaired by ALA executive director Robert Wedgeworth, endorsed a national advisory board but expressed skepticism about whether the LC could provide the leadership to form a national bibliographic system: John Cole, "The Library of Congress and American Research Libraries," in *University Library History: An International Review*, edited by James Thompson (London: Clive Bingley, 1980), 202–3. Boorstin did not act on recommendations for codification, a board of advisers, a liaison office to the library community, an academic liaison unit, and an American Studies Division.

57. Cole, *Library of Congress in Perspective*, 133–34.

58. Noël Savage, "Task Force Report: LC Sketches Present Overhaul, Future Leadership," *LJ* 102 (April 1, 1977): 756–59.

59. R. Kathleen Molz, "The Library of Congress: Hydra and Dinosaur," *LJ* 103 (October 15, 1978): 2052–55.

60. Cole, *Library of Congress in Perspective*, 87–88; *ARLC*, 1976, xvii–xviii.

61. *ARLC*, 1977, 1–2; 1980, 92; *LCIB* 37 (March 31, 178): 214–15, 223; (April 14, 1978): 245–52; 38 (July 6, 1979): 256. Goodrum and Dalrymple, *Library of Congress*, 151–55, set Boorstin's proposal in the context of Task Force recommendations and the trend to bring law libraries more closely under the control of their academic institutions.

62. *ARLC*, 1977, 43–44; 1978, 50, 54, 57; 1980, 65–66; *LCIB* 36 (June 3, 1977): 374–76; (June 17, 1977): 428–30; (August 19, 1977): 568A–D; 38 (July 6, 1979): 253–56.

63. "To Establish an American Folklife Foundation in the Library of Congress, Hearings before the Subcommittee on Library and Memorials of the Committee on House Administration, House of Representatives, 93rd Congress, 2nd Sess., May 9–10, 1974" (GPO, 1974); *LCIB*

36 (June 17, 1977): 413–16. The hearings included officials from LC, the Smithsonian, and the NEA, all of which had folklife programs. The LC was willing to host the center; the Smithsonian declined. The 1998 Legislative Branch Appropriations Act (PL 105-275) authorized the center permanently and added several board members, as noted above: *LCIB* 57 (November 1998): 268; Archie Green, "The Archive's Shores," *Folklife Annual* (1985): 61–73; James Hardin and Alan Jabbour, "American Folklife Center and Collections," *Encyclopedia*, 143–49; Peter T. Bartis, "A History of the Archive of Folk Song at the Library of Congress: The First Fifty Years" (PhD diss., University of Pennsylvania, 1982), 250–64. *Folklife Center News* ceased with the summer–fall 2011 issue.

64. Daniel J. Boorstin, "A Design for an Any-Time, Do-It-Yourself, Energy-Free Communication Device," *Harper's* 248 (January 1974): 83–86; *Gazette* 15 (May 7, 2004): 1.

65. John Y. Cole, ed., *The Republic of Letters: Librarian of Congress Daniel J. Boorstin on Books, Reading, and Libraries, 1975–1987* (Washington, DC: LC, 1989), 24–25.

66. John Cole, personal communication, November 9, 2022.

67. John Y. Cole and Carol S. Gold, eds., *Reading in America 1978: Selected Findings of the Book Industry Study Group's 1978 Study of American Book-Reading and Book-Buying Habits and Discussions of Those Findings at the Library of Congress on October 25 and 26, 1978* (Washington, DC: LC, 1978). The center was an early example of a public–private partnership: appropriated funds paid only staff salaries. John Y. Cole, *The Center for the Book in the Library of Congress: The Planning Year* (Washington, DC: LC, 1978); *LCIB* 34 (November 21, 1975): 460; 39 (January 4, 1980): 4–5; 42 (November 14, 1983): 388–90; 43 (December 24, 1984): 428–29; 45 (February 10, 1985): 56–59; 46 (January 26, 1987): 43; 57 (December 1998): 291–92; 62 (January 2003): passim; John Y. Cole, "The Center for the Book in the Library of Congress," *QJLC* 36 (Spring 1979): 178–88; *ARLC*, 1986, 6; John Cole, "A Life at the Library of Congress," in *The Library of Congress and the Center for the Book: Historical Essays in Honor of John Y. Cole*, edited by Mary Niles Maack (Washington, DC: LC, in association with the University of Texas Press, 2011), 11–20.

68. Barbara Gamarekian, "Pondering the Open Doors," *New York Times*, May 2, 1986.

69. *LCIB* 35 (February 27, 1976): 124–25; William Matheson, "Microcosm of the Library: The Rare Book and Special Collections Division," *QJLC* 34 (July 1977): 233. The poetry consultant Stanley Kunitz marked the occasion with a poem, "The Lincoln Relics"; *New Yorker*, February 13, 1978, 32.

70. *ARLC*, 1976, xix–xxi; Senate Report 94-719, March 30, 1976 (GPO, 1976). The 1897 building became known as "the Main Building."

71. *ARLC*, 1980, 4–5. The council included the poetry consultants; William McGuire, *Poetry's Catbird Seat, The Consultantship in Poetry in the English Language at the Library of Congress, 1937–1987* (Washington, DC: LC, 1988), 364–73.

72. *ARLC*, 1978, 74; 1994, 78; *LCIB* 37 (December 15, 1978): 753–54; 38 (March 30, 1979): 105–6.

73. *ARLC*, 1974, 78–80; *LCIB* 30 (November 24, 1971): 660; Cole, *For Congress*, 166; Donald L. Leavitt, "Recorded Sound in the Library of Congress," *LT* 21 (Summer 1972): 56.

74. PL 103-198 (1993) replaced the Tribunal with ad hoc copyright arbitration royalty panels: *ARLC*, 1994, 10. PL 108-419, effective May 31, 2005, replaced panels with an independent Copyright Royalty Board of three judges appointed by the Librarian and paid by the LC: *ARLC*, 2005, 21–22; 2006, 33–35.

75. *ARLC*, 1976, 70–71, 83; 1977, 87–96; 1978, 79–87; 1979, 89–90, 99; 1982, 103–4; *LCIB* 35 (November 19, 1976): 716–18; 40 (March 20, 1981): 95–96. The law allowed using part of the

fees to defray office expenses and recommended the termination of the manufacturing clause in 1982. The office's 1981 report on the economic impact on the printing industry also recommended termination; Congress finally concurred in 1986: *LCIB* 40 (March 13, 1981): 86–87; (August 14, 1981): 267–68; 41 (August 13, 1982): 234. PL 102-307 (1992) changed renewal procedures to exclude the required report on creators/users.

76. *ARLC*, 1975, 7; 1978, 14; *LCIB* 40 (March 4, 1980): 74–75; 44 (January 21, 1985): 9–10; (August 26, 1985): 237–38.

77. *ARLC*, 1980, 105–6. S. 1961 (1996) again proposed merging the Copyright Office and the Patent and Trademark Office within the Commerce Department. The Library again opposed it, the provision was removed, and the bill died in the 104th Congress: *ARLC*, 1996, 90–91.

78. Arlene Balkansky, "Through the Electronic Looking Glass: Television Programs at the Library of Congress," *QJLC* 37 (Summer–Fall 1980); 458–75; PL 94-553, 1976.

79. *LCIB* 36 (January 21, 1977): 297, 299–300; 41 (May 7, 1982): 135–38; *Motion Pictures, Broadcasting, Recorded Sound*, 81.

80. *LCIB* 35 (April 16, 1976): 235–36; *ARLC*, 1985, xix; 1986, 2, 4; *LCIB* 38 (May 18, 1979): 177; 45 (May 5, 1986): 129–30.

81. *A National Preservation Program: Proceedings of the Planning Conference* (Washington, DC: LC, 1980). The conference included preservation specialists, librarians, publishers, and foundation and association representatives; Nancy E. Gwinn, "CLR and Preservation," *C&RL* 42, no. 2 (1981): 117–18; William J. Welsh, "The Preservation Challenge," in *The Library Preservation Program: Models, Priorities, Possibilities*, edited by Jan Merrill-Oldham and Merrily Smith (Chicago: ALA, 1985), 3–4.

82. The foundation-funded National Enquiry into Scholarly Communication also recommended establishing the center: National Enquiry into Scholarly Communication, *Scholarly Communication: The Report of the National Enquiry* (Baltimore: Johns Hopkins University Press, 1979), 18–20, 154–55.

83. *Effective Access to the Periodical Literature: A National Program* prepared by US Task Force on a National Periodicals System (Washington, DC: NCLIS, 1977); *A National Periodicals Center: Technical Development Plan* (Washington, DC: CLR, 1978); *LCIB* 37 (September 15, 1978): 561–62, 570–72; Cole, "Library of Congress and American Research Libraries," 204–5; C. Lee Jones, "The Politics of Consensus," *Journal of Academic Librarianship* 7 (July 1981): 157–58; "Higher Education Amendments of 1979: Hearings before the Subcommittee on Education, Arts and Humanities of the Committee on Labor and Human Resources, United States Senate . . . October 2, 3, 4, 5, 1979" (GPO, 1980), 674–796.

84. LC, *The Role of the Library of Congress in the Evolving National Network: A Study Commissioned by the Library of Congress Network Development Office and Funded by the National Commission on Library and Information Services* (Washington, DC: LC, 1978), 35. Lawrence F. Buckland and William L. Basinski of Inforonoics conducted the survey; "Toward a National Library and Information Service Network: The Library Bibliographic Component," prepared by the Library of Congress Network Advisory Group, edited by Henriette D. Avram and Lenore S. Maruyama, preliminary edition (LC, 1977). Lenore S. Maruyama, *The Library of Congress Network Advisory Committee: Its First Decade* (Washington, DC: LC, 1985), 34, observed that any apprehension about a networking structure imposed from above and about the LC's domination seemed to disappear by the early 1980s as the NAC addressed members' concerns.

85. *LCIB* 38 (April 6, 1979): 132–34; C. Lee Jones, "The National Bibliographic Program," in *Influencing Change in Research Librarianship: A Festschrift for Warren J. Haas*, edited by Martin M. Cummings (Washington, DC: CLR, 1988), 31–34, 38. The NAC's membership by

1979 included the ALA, American Society for Information Science, AMIGOS Bibliographic Council, Association of American Publishers, ARL, Bibliographic Center for Research, California Library Authority for Systems and Services, Chief Officers of State Library Agencies, Council for Computerized Library Networks, CLR, FLC, Information Industry Association, LC, Medical Library Association, Midwest Region Library Network, NAL, NCLIS, National Federation of Abstracting and Indexing Services, NLM, New England Library Information Network, OCLC, RLG, Southeastern Library Network, University of Chicago, and Washington Library Network.

86. At the time, the online catalog included books, serials, and maps. Other materials were accessible only through card catalogs, files, and other listings: *ARLC*, 1981, 59. The main card catalog is still available in space adjacent to the Main Reading Room.

87. Peter T. Rohrbach, *FIND: Automation at the Library of Congress—The First Twenty-Five Years and Beyond* (Washington, DC: LC, 1985), 30–33; *Washington Post*, November 13, 1984; Arthur Plotnik, William J. Welsh, and Vic Fazio, "Can Bill Welsh Conquer Time and Space for Libraries?" *AL* 15 (December 1984): 768; *The Future of Card Catalogs: Report of a Program Sponsored by the Association of Research Libraries, January 18, 1975* (Washington, DC: ARL, 1975). It was assumed that by 1980 (later extended to January 1, 1981) all current cataloging would be electronic, thus allowing a "clean" transition.

88. Rohrbach, *FIND*, 21; *LCIB* 36 (September 2, 1977): 605–6; (November 4, 1977): 743–45; 37 (August 18, 1978): 485–86.

89. *LCIB* 41 (March 26, 1982): 95–100; 42 (October 10, 1983): 347–48; Thomas H. Lee, "The Development of CJK Bibliographic Databases in North America and East Asia," in *National and International Bibliographic Databases: Trends and Prospects,* edited by Michael Carpenter (New York: Haworth, 1988), 11–14. In 2004, JACKPHY transitioned to the web-based system RLIN21, with data stored in Unicode, which supported all languages and scripts: *ARLC*, 2004, 48. The LC adopted Unicode in November 2005 and incorporated JACKPHY into the LC system: *LCIB* 66 (December 2007): 256.

90. *LCIB* 35 (March 5, 1976): 153; 37 (October 20, 1978): 640–52. A revision, AACR2R, appeared in 1988.

91. *LCIB* 41 (October 29, 1982): 357–58; (November 5, 1982): 364; Mary Ellen Soper, "Descriptive Cataloging," in *Technical Services Management*, ed. Smith and Carter, 158–61.

92. "Information for the 1980s: Final Report of the White House Conference on Library and Information Services, 1979" (GPO, 1979); Daniel Boorstin, *"Gresham's Law: Knowledge or Information?" Remarks at the White House Conference on Library and Information Services, November 19, 1979* (Washington, DC: LC, 1980); Virginia H. Mathews, *Libraries, Citizens & Advocacy: The Lasting Effects of Two White House Conferences on Library and Information Services* (Washington, DC: White House Conference on Library and Information Task Force, 2004); *LCIB* 63 (July 2004): 134–35.

93. *ARLC*, 1980, 1–4, 84; Cole, *For Congress*, 162, 165; Cole, *America's Greatest Library*, 186; *LCIB* 39 (May 9, 1980): 154–56; *AL* 6 (December 1975): 629. The 1970 authorization (84 Stat 69, March 16, 1970) specified that the Madison Building would not be a general office building, but Goodrum and Dalrymple, *Library of Congress*, 222, noted that the land originally was designated for congressional offices.

94. *ARLC*, 1980, 6; 1983, 81; *LCIB* 39 (June 27, 1980): 225–26; 42 (January 3,1983): 1–2; (May 9, 1983): 145–46; 44 (March 11,1985): 45–46; Marion Casey, *Charles McCarthy: Librarianship and Reform* (Chicago: ALA, 1981), 41. The Pickford Foundation provided $500,000 over ten years to support programs and other costs: *LCIB* 63 (October 2004): 212–13.

95. "The American Cowboy," funded by United Technologies Corporation, was the first exhibition mounted with private support: *ARLC*, 1983, 20; *LCIB* 67 (October 2008): 171.

96. *ARLC*, 1985, 81–82.

97. *ARLC*, 1984, 1–2; 1986, 9–10, 73; *LCIB* 41 (May 28, 1982): 149–50; (November 12, 1982): 369–70; 45 (March 17, 1986); (September 8, 1986): 310–11; 47 (March 7, 1988): 86; (June 13, 1988): 234–36; US Congress Office of Technology Assessment, *Book Preservation Technologies* (Washington, DC: GPO, 1988). *LJ*'s editorial, "It's Time to Dump DEZ" and Karl Nyren's "The DEZ Process and the Library of Congress," *LJ* 111 (September 15, 1986): 4, 33–35, criticized the LC's failure to share information on DEZ problems; responses included those by William Welsh, "In Defense of DEZ: LC's Perspective," *LJ* 112 (January 1987): 62–63; Harold C. Cannon, *LJ* 112 (January 1987): 12; and Jack C. Thompson, "Mass Deacidification: Thoughts on the Cunha Report," *Restaurator* 9, no. 3 (1988): 147–62.

98. *LCIB* 41 (August 20, 1982): 246; Kenneth E. Harris and Susan E. Schur, *Caring for America's Library: A Brief History of Preservation and Conservation at the Library of Congress* (Washington, DC: LC Preservation Directorate, 2006), 23.

99. *LCIB* 44 (November 11, 1985): 335–39; 45 (February 17, 1986): 51–52, 64; 46 (August 3, 1987): 342–43. Problems relating to costs, copyright, and preservation ultimately mostly precluded using disk storage.

100. Senate Concurrent Resolution 59 (November 1983); LC, *Books in Our Future, A Report from the Librarian of Congress to Congress* (Washington, DC: Joint Committee on the Library, 1984); Maurvene D. Williams, ed., *The Community of the Book*, 3rd ed. (Washington, DC: LC, 1993); the differing views were captured by John Y. Cole, ed., *Books in Our Future: Perspectives and Proposals* (Washington, DC: LC, 1987).

101. *LCIB* 45 (March 10, 1986): 77, 79; McGuire, *Poetry's Catbird Seat*, 424–32; Bibi Marti, "Poetry at the Library of Congress," *LCIB* 64 (November 2004): 221; *Gazette* 19 (July 25, 2008): 7; Craig D'Ooge, "In the Eye of the Library: Poets at the Library of Congress," *AL* 29 (April 1998): 48–52; Prosser Gifford, "Poetry Program and Poets Laureate," *Encyclopedia*, 397–403.

102. The LC's services had recently received top marks in 1984 surveys requested by the House Appropriations Committee: *ARLC*, 1985, xxi, 1–2, 19. On the across-the-boards reductions intended to reduce the federal deficit, see Lewis L. Gould, *The Most Exclusive Club: A History of the Modern United States Senate* (New York: Basic Books, 2005), 283–85; and Robert V. Remini, *The House: The History of the House of Representatives* (New York: HarperCollins, 2006), 459–60.

103. Gamarekian, "Pondering."

104. "Legislative Branch Appropriations: Hearings before a Subcommittee of the Committee on Appropriations, House of Representatives, 99th Congress, 2nd Sess." (GPO, 1986), 197–98; *LCIB* 45 (March 3, 1986): 69, 71–72. Cuts in hours of service included those of the La Follette Congressional Reading Room.

105. *ARLC*, 1986, 3–4, 67–70; *Gazette* 15 (May 7, 2004): 6. The LC closed on Sundays and limited evening service to one night per week.

106. "Impact of Gramm-Rudman-Hollings Budget: Hearing Held before the Joint Committee on the Library . . . May 7, 1986" (GPO, 1986); *LCIB* 45 (May 26, 1986): 191; (July 14, 1986): 261.

107. *LCIB* 45 (January 6, 1986): 3. The *Playboy* controversy dated to 1981, when Representative Chalmers P. Wylie (R-OH) and Senator Mack Mattingly (R-GA) tried to halt funding. Wylie again introduced his amendment in July 1985. The Braille version included only selected printed material: *LCIB* 45 (September 29, 1986): 333–35.

108. *LCIB* 44 (April 29, 1985): 89–90.

109. The Name Authority Cooperative began in 1977 when the GPO and LC agreed to maintain a common-name authority file: *LCIB* 47 (January 25, 1988): 27–28; Mandel, "Cooperative Cataloging," 52–55.

110. *LCIB* 44 (October 29, 1985): 305–6; 46 (June 15, 1987): 254, 278–79; 47 (July 4, 1988): 290; *ARLC*, 1987, 62; *Linked Systems: A Program Sponsored by the Association of Research Libraries, May 5, 1988, Oakland, California* (Washington, DC: ARL, 1988).

111. *LCIB* 46 (October 19, 1987): 449–50; Mandel, "Cooperative Cataloging," 62–69. Participants were Chicago; California, Berkeley; Harvard; Illinois–Urbana-Champaign; Indiana–Bloomington; Michigan–Ann Arbor; Texas–Austin; and Yale. Illinois and Michigan later left the program, but in 1992 the NAL, University of Maryland–College Park, University of Colorado–Boulder, and Saint Louis University School of Law joined.

112. Sarah E. Thomas, "The Core Bibliographic Record and the Program for Cooperative Cataloging," in *Cataloging and Classification Standards and Rules,* edited by John J. Riemer (New York: Haworth, 1996), 93–94.

113. *LCIB* 45 (December 22, 1986): 406–7.

114. PL 100-83, 1987; *LCIB* 46 (April 20, 1987): 158; (August 17, 1987): 357–58; Daniel Boorstin, "Gresham's Law," *New York Times,* January 6, 1987.

115. Boorstin, "Gresham's Law."

Chapter 10

1. *New York Times,* January 6, 1987. Robert M. Warner, former Archivist of the United States, was also suggested but declined to be a candidate.

2. Billington and Boorstin met when Billington became head of the Woodrow Wilson Center: *LCIB* 63 (February–March 2004): 39. The ALA's statement appeared in *LJ* 112 (April 1, 1987): 34.

3. "Nomination of James H. Billington to Be Librarian of Congress; Hearing before the Committee on Rules and Administration, United States Senate," 100th Congress, 1st Sess., July 14, 1987 (Washington, DC: GPO, 1988), 34, 63–89, 103–7; *AL* 18 (July–August 1987): 544–45.

4. John Y. Cole, *America's Greatest Library: An Illustrated History of the Library of Congress* (Washington, DC: LC, in association with D. Giles Limited, London, 2017), 196; *LCIB* 46 (September 21, 1987): 405–8.

5. *LCIB* 46 (October 26, 1987): 459–63; Josephus Nelson and Judith Farley, *Full Circle: Ninety Years of Service in the Main Reading Room* (Washington, DC: LC, 1991), 56.

6. *LCIB* 50 (May 6, 1991): 168; (May 20): 181–89; (July 15, 1991): 264; *Gazette* 8 (April 25, 1997): passim.

7. *LCIB* 47 (January 11, 1988): 9–10; (February 1, 1988): 38–39, 42.

8. John Y. Cole, ed., *Research Collections in the Information Age: The Library of Congress Looks to the Future—Views by Stephen E. Ostrow and Robert Zich* (Washington, DC: LC, 1990), 7.

9. Decisions regarding the Law Library were postponed pending the appointment of a new Law Librarian.

10. *LCIB* 51 (June 15, 1992): 261–65, 273 (November 16, 1992): 487–89. In 1998 the Science and Technology Division merged with the Business/Economics Reference Section to form the Science, Technology, and Business Division: *LCIB* 57 (December 1998): 5. The National Reference Service was renamed the Reference Referral Service on January 1, 1999, and a Collaborative Digital Reference Service project tested offering service via the internet. In 2001, the LC and OCLC developed QuestionPoint, which enabled member libraries to submit inquiries

to a network that linked reference services internationally. The LC began offering assistance to individuals through its Ask a Librarian web page: *ARLC*, 2002, 58; *LCIB* 61 (March–April 2002): 56–59.

11. *LCIB* 49 (October 22, 1990): 356–57; (December 3, 1990): 409; (December 17, 1990): 441; *AL* 20 (September 1989): 716; *Washington Post*, September 27, 1989, noted widespread staff concerns with the reorganization, but a "whole serials" counterpart effort followed: *ARLC*, 1997, 54. A later analysis showed that whole book cataloging did increase productivity, though staff expertise and funding levels also affected the results: *ARLC*, 2003, 65–66.

12. *LCIB* 49 (June 18, 1990): 225. As a graduate student in 1930s Washington, Rebekah Bobbitt was employed at the LC.

13. *LCIB* 49 (February 26, 1990): 88; *ARLC*, 1994, 51. By the council's fifteenth anniversary, members had given 58 percent of the private funds raised since 1990, a total exceeding $153 million: *LCIB* 64 (February 2005): 26. Nevertheless, the council drew criticism for treating its members (and Billington) to elaborate trips abroad and organizing special private events drew criticism: *Washington Post*, August 12, 2015.

14. The Fiscal Operations Improvement Act (PL 106-481, 2000) added the Joint Committee's vice chairman.

15. "Legislative Branch Appropriations for 1991: Hearings before a Subcommittee of the Committee on Appropriations, House of Representatives," 101st Congress, 2nd Sess. (Washington, DC: GPO, 1990), 607, 612, 615; *LCIB* 49 (February 26, 1990): 82, 92–95; (June 18, 1990): 219–20, 227; (July 30, 1990): 278.

16. At its peak on December 31, 1990, the arrearage contained over 40.68 million items; a year later, it had decreased by 3.27 million; and by the end of 1997, it was reduced by 50 percent: *LCIB* 51 (March 9, 1992): 92–95; *Gazette* 8 (December 19, 1997): 1, 9–11.

17. *LCIB* 49 (July 16, 1990): 255–57. One reason for the proposal was the discovery that photoduplication receipts did not cover costs; *Gazette* 1 (October 19, 1990): 1, 3. Several efforts to authorize services on a cost-recovery basis failed: *LCIB* 52 (March 22, 1993): 112–13; 53 (September 5, 1994): 323–24; *Gazette* 4 (March 5, 1993): 1, 11.

18. *LCIB* 49 (November 19, 1990): 400–403; 50 (February 25, 1991): 61, 64–67; (May 6, 1991): 159; *ARLC*, 1990, 19–20. Operated by the LC Child Care Association, the Little Scholars Child Development Center opened in September 1993, the culmination of efforts dating to the early 1970s; *Gazette* 3 (October 16, 1992): 1, 6; 4 (September 24, 1993): 1, 10–11.

19. *LCIB* 51 (November 16, 1992): 479–83; *ARLC*, 1993, 16. The Government Performance and Results Act (PL 103-62, 1993) required executive branch agencies to develop strategic and annual performance plans, and regularly review progress. Congress asked the legislative branch to "abide by the spirit" of this act; *ARLC*, 2006, 159–60.

20. The Omnibus Budget Reconciliation Act (PL 101-508, 1990) required that increased spending be offset by cuts: *LCIB* 52 (June 28, 1993): 255.

21. The *Monthly Checklist of State Publications*, published starting in 1910, ceased in December 1994; *Gazette* 6 (February 19, 1995): 6. Limited foreign interlibrary loan was reinstated in February 1996, but noon concerts on the Neptune Plaza, a twenty-year tradition, were canceled that year for lack of funds.

22. *Information 2000, Library and Information Services for the 21st Century: Final Report of the 1991 White House Conference on Library and Information Services* (Washington, DC: US National Commission on Library and Information Science, 1992); Gordon Flagg and Leonard Kniffel, "Delegates' Skill, Tenacity, Lead WHCLIS to a Promising Conclusion," *AL* 22 (September 1991): 786–804; Virginia H. Mathews, *Libraries, Citizens, & Advocacy: The Lasting*

Effects of Two White House Conferences on Library and Information Services (Washington, DC: White House Conference on Library and Information Taskforce, 2004), 8–13.

23. James T. Patterson, *Restless Giant: The United States from Watergate to Bush v.* Gore (New York: Oxford University Press, 2005), 213–17, 228–29.

24. *LCIB* 46 (August 8, 1987): 341–42; (September 21, 1987): 408–9.

25. *LCIB* 47 (June 20, 1988): 241–43.

26. *LCIB* 48 (January 2, 1989): 3–5; (August 28, 1989): 297–99; (June 18, 1990): 221–22; (July 2, 1990): 241–43; 50 (October 7, 1991): 376–77; 51 (January 27, 1992): 31–32; (June 1, 1992): 227–29; (July 13, 1992): 303–8; 52 (April 19, 1993): 170–73. James H. Billington's *Russia Transformed: Breakthrough to Hope* (New York: Free Press, 1992), appraised the coup in the context of Russian culture and his role as Librarian. He headed a team of scholars to select material for "Revelations," collaborating with the Russian Federation's Committee on Archival Affairs.

27. *LCIB* 53 (October 17, 1994): 390–92; 58 (February 1999): 21, 34–37; John Y. Cole, "The International Role of the Library of Congress: A Brief History," *LCIB* 49 (January 15, 1990): 17–18, 45.

28. *LCIB* 51 (January 27, 1992): 35–38.

29. *LCIB* 49 (September 24, 1990): 321; 50 (April 22, 1991): 139; (October 7, 1991): 367–68; 58 (August 1999): 183–85, 187; 59 (June 2000): 140–41; *ARLC*, 1994, 21n22; 1999, 4, 94; 2000, 142–43; *Washington Post*, July 20, 1999; John Y. Cole, "The Library of Congress and the Democratic Spirit," in *Libraries and Democracy: The Cornerstone of Liberty*, edited by Nancy Kranich (Chicago: ALA, 2001), 180; John Van Oudenaren, "'Great Deeds': Frontiers and Other Adventures at the Library of Congress, 1996–2019," *Slavic & East European Information Resources* 23, no. 3 (2022): 39. Under PL 106-554 (2001), the program became the independent Center for Russian Leadership and later the Open World Leadership Center; Billington chaired its board: *LCIB* 60 (April 2001): 72–73; (May 2001): 106–7; Cole, "International Role," 17–18, 45.

30. *LCIB* 50 (September 23, 1991): 347; 54 (April 17, 1995): 176; 61 (January 2002): 15; *ARLC*, 1994, 37; *LCIB* 56 (April 21, 1997): 148–51; 2000: 108; Kenneth E. Harris and Susan E. Schur, "A Brief History of Preservation and Conservation at the Library of Congress," www.loc.gov/preservation/about /hist/pres-hist.pdf, 23–24. PL 101-423 (1990), directed federal agencies to use acid-free paper; the LC, the National Archives, and the Public Printer were charged to monitor adoption and report to Congress biannually: *LCIB* 51 (April 6, 1992): 135–36.

31. Among the concerns was the effect of computer colorization on historic films; *LCM* 2 (January–February 2013): 16.

32. *LCIB* 52 (July 26, 1993): 297; 53 (February 24, 1994): 63–64. LC, *Film Preservation 1993: A Study of the Current State of American Film Preservation: Report of the Librarian of Congress* (Washington, DC: LC, 1993); LC, *Redefining Film Preservation: A National Plan: Recommendations of the Librarian of Congress in Consultation with the National Film Preservation Board* (Washington, DC: LC, 1994).

33. *Gazette* 7 (November 8, 1996): 9; *LCIB* 56 (July 1997): 246. PL 109-9, the Family Entertainment and Copyright Act (2005) reauthorized the board and foundation, and addressed copyright issues: *ARLC*, 2005, 22–23.

34. *LCIB* 65 (January 2006): 15, 25; (March 2006): 67, 71; Tim Brooks, *Survey of Reissues of US Recordings* (Washington, DC: CLIR and LC, 2005).

35. *The State of Recorded Sound Preservation in the United States: A National Legacy at Risk in the Digital* Age (Washington, DC: CLIR and LC, 2010); *The Library of Congress National*

Recording Preservation Plan, Sponsored by the National Recording Preservation Board of the Library of Congress (Washington, DC: CLIR and LC, 2012).

36. *ARLC*, 2000, 126–27; 2011, 12; *Gazette* 11 (December 15, 2000): 13–14; *LCIB* 61 (March–April 2002): 60; 69 (October 210): 214; 70 (June 2011): 401–5; *LCM* 4 (July–August 2016): 11–13; *Motion Pictures, Broadcasting, Recorded Sound*, 86–87.

37. Thorvald Solberg had unsuccessfully advocated US adherence; William J. Sittig, "Thorvald Solberg," *DALB*, 495.

38. *ARLC*, 1988; The Berne Convention: Hearings before the Subcommittee on Patents, Copyrights and Trademarks of the Committee on the Judiciary, United States Senate, 100th Congress, 2nd Sess. (Washington, DC: GPO, 1988), 137–59; Peter Baldwin, *The Copyright Wars: Three Centuries of Trans-Atlantic Battle* (Princeton, NJ: Princeton University Press, 2015): 235–36; Marshall Leaffer, "American Copyright Law since 1945," in *A History of the Book in America, Volume 5: The Enduring Book*, edited by David Paul Nord, Joan Shelley Rubin, and Michael Schudson (Chapel Hill: University of North Carolina Press, 2009), 158–62. Berne lacked enforcement mechanisms, but the new World Trade Organization (1995) included provisions for enforcement and dispute resolution.

39. *LCIB* 52 (March 22, 1993): 111; (June 14, 1993): 237; (November 15, 1993), 422–24.

40. Library of Congress Advisory Committee on Copyright Registration and Deposit, *ACCORD: Report of the Co-Chairs* (Washington, DC: LC, 1993); *LCIB* 52 (November 15, 1993): 423–24.

41. *ARLC*, 1996, 90–91; *LCIB* 55 (September 16, 1996): 312–13; *Washington Post*, September 19, 1996.

42. *ARLC*, 1996, 81; *Gazette* 7 (September 13, 1996): 5.A29.

43. Baldwin, *Copyright Wars*, 248–52. The law was dubbed the Sonny Bono [R-CA, 1995–98] Act, for the producer and songwriter who sponsored an earlier version but died before enactment.

44. *AL 29* (November 1998): 16; Baldwin, *Copyright Wars*, 283–88; *Report on Copyright and Digital Distance Education* (Washington, DC: US Copyright Office, 1999); Leaffer, "American Copyright Law," 164–65. The Intellectual Property and Communication Omnibus Act of 1999 (PL 106-113) added sound recordings to works made for hire: *LCIB* 59 (January 2000): 17; 69 (October 2010): 215.

45. *ARLC*, 1993, 69.

46. *LCIB* 48 (October 23, 1989): 373–74.

47. *ARLC*, 1992, 6; *Gazette* 5 (September 23, 1994): 10. Senator Gore (D-TN) and Senator Pell presided at the formal opening. A Machine-Readable Collections Reading Room opened in July 1988 to provide access to compact disks, videodisks, and software packages mostly acquired through copyright deposit, closed in 1996, by which time workstations were available in the reading rooms; *Gazette* 7 (February 23, 1996): 1, 8.

48. *ARLC*, 1994, 11; 2000, 84; *LCIB* 59 (April 2000): 95.

49. *LCIB* 48 (May 29, 1989): 193–94; 49 (February 26, 1990): 83–87; 63 (October 2004): 195–201; *Gazette* 6 (April 7, 1995): 10; (April 14, 1995): 1, 10–11.

50. James H. Billington, "The Modern Library and Global Democracy," in *The Meaning of the Library: A Cultural History*, edited by Alice Crawford (Princeton, NJ: Princeton University Press, 2015), 263.

51. Eliza Newlin Carney, "Billington's Book Wars," *National Journal*, March 3, 1992, 695–98.

52. *Gazette* 6 (May 19, 1995): 1, 13–15; (October 6, 1995): 1, 13–15; 7 (November 29, 1996): 1, 10–13; *ARLC*, 2001, 158; 2003, 135. Settlement concluded in early 1997, after decisions on appeals. In 1995 the Congressional Accountability Act (PL 104-1) applied several statutes to

Congress covering the LC under the Family and Medical Leave Act; Employee Polygraph Protection Act; Worker Adjustment and Retraining Notification Act; Veterans' Employment and Reemployment laws; Americans with Disabilities Act; and Occupational Safety and Health Act. Internal tensions continued: for example, when a traveling exhibit, "Back of the Big House: The Cultural Landscape of the Plantation," unexpectedly appeared in the Madison Building, it was quickly removed in response to complaints: *Washington Post*, September 29, 1996; *LCIB* 55 (January 22, 1996): 12. Employees subsequently organized an LC chapter of the national organization Blacks in Government; *Gazette* 7 (November 8, 1996): 8. Samuel Gerald Collins, *Library of Walls: The Library of Congress and the Contradictions of Information Society* (Duluth, MN: Litwin Books, 2008), 118–42, noted employees' continuing concerns.

53. "Underrepresentation of Minorities in Supergrade Positions and above, at the Library of Congress: Hearing Held before the Subcommittee on Libraries and Memorials of the Committee on House Administration" (GPO, 1990); "Library of Congress Personnel Policies and Procedures: Joint Hearings before the Subcommittee on Libraries and Memorials of the Committee on House Administration . . . and the Subcommittee on Oversight and Investigations of the Committee on Post Office and Civil Service" (GPO, 1994), 57, 61, 62, 69–81; *Washington Post*, March 19, 1993; *LCIB* 52 (April 19, 1993): 151–53; *Gazette* 3 (October 9, 1992): 1, 10–11; (October 16, 1992): 1, 7. An *AL* editorial noted that rulings in earlier discrimination cases had generally favored the LC: 23 (October 1992): 728–29.

54. "Slow Progress toward Workforce Diversity at the Library of Congress: Report of the Chairman of the Subcommittee on Libraries and Memorials to the Committee on House Administration. One Hundred Third Congress, Second Session" (GPO, 1994), 3, 13–19; 32–34, 42–46.

55. *LCIB* 53 (June 13, 1994): 235–37; (October 17, 1994): 397; 55 (January 22, 1996): 13; *Gazette* 7 (August 30, 1996): 9; (September 13, 1996): 4–5; "Slow Progress," 71–77.

56. *Gazette* 8 (October 10, 1997): 1, 11; *The Library of Congress Strategic Plan, Fiscal Years 2004–2008* (Washington, DC: LC, 2003); *ARLC*, 2005, 132; in 2005, the Internal University was renamed the Center for Learning and Development.

57. *ARLC*, 1994, 10–11; 2000, 134–35; *LCIB* 53 (May 2, 1994): 167–68; 56 (January 27, 1997): 34.

58. Some Scrolls were exhibited at the LC in 1949, but this exhibition added an online presentation, a conference, and a program on preservation methods: *LCIB* 52 (September 6, 1993): 323–25.

59. Papers from the first three were published in *Neuroscience, Memory, and Language* (Washington, DC: GPO, 1995).

60. *LCIB* 52 (May 17, 1993): 202–5; *Gazette* 7 (May 17, 1996): 1, 12–15.

61. *LCIB* 53 (May 30, 1994): 216. The *Cataloger's Desktop* was followed in 1996 by *Classification Plus* CD, with the *Library of Congress Subject Headings* and *Library of Congress Classification Schedules*, all of which later became web-accessible. Agreements with the ALA, the Society of American Archivists, and OCLC enabled the LC to incorporate their materials; *Gazette* 15 (April 30, 2004): 3, 10; *LCIB* 63 (August 2004): 163.

62. *LCIB* 52 (September 6, 1993): 317–18; (November 1, 1993): 405. LOCIS was superseded by the Integrated Library System; MARVEL was replaced (2003) by web pages: Guy Lamolinara, "The National Digital Library and the Library's Electronic Resources," *Encyclopedia*, 53.

63. David W. Reser, comp., *Towards a New Beginning in Cooperative Cataloging: The History, Progress, and Future of the Cooperative Cataloging Council* (Washington, DC: LC, 1994); *Program for Cooperative Cataloging* brochure (Washington, DC: LC, 2001); *LCIB* 57 (August 1998): 200–201.

64. *LCIB* 53 (February 7, 1994): 49.

65. *ARLC*, 1999, 48; 2000, 86–87; 2003, 70–71; *Gazette* 11 (May 19, 2000): 8.

66. *ARLC*, 1997, 3, 12; *Gazette* 18 (October 19, 2007): 1, 13. THOMAS and the LIS were retired in 2016 and 2020, superseded by Congress.gov.

67. *LCIB* 56 (April 7, 1997): 127, 131; *Gazette* 12 (August 3, 2001): 5. Reengineering the Copyright Office for electronic services required a temporary move (2006) to Arlington, VA: *LCIB* 66 (January–February 2007): 4. The eCO system debuted online registration in 2008.

68. Charles Fenly, *The Cataloging in Publication Program: A Brief History, 1971–2001* (Washington, DC: LC, 2001), 24–27; Jane Aikin, "Cataloging in Publication (CIP)," *Encyclopedia,* 191–92; Beth Davis-Brown and David Williamson, "Cataloging at the Library of Congress in the Digital Age," *CCQ* 22, nos. 3–4 (1996): 171–96; *Gazette* 14 (April 11, 2003): 3.

69. *LCIB* 55 (June 24–July 8, 1996): 251–53, 260; (December 30, 1996): 447.

70. *LCIB* 55 (June 24–July 8, 1996): 254; 66 (October 2007): 212; *ARLC*, 1999, 26–27. When US support ceased in 2012, the GLIN Foundation was created to support these activities.

71. Reauthorization authority, or congressional approval to operate, had mostly applied to executive branch agencies and to statutes.

72. *LCIB* 53 (May 30, 1994): 212, 230–31; *Gazette* 5 (May 20, 1994): 10–11. The legislative branch staff reduction was similar to that for the executive branch suggested by Vice President Gore's National Performance Review.

73. *LCIB* 52 (September 6, 1993); 64 (February 2005): 27; *ARLC*, 1994, 79.

74. *LCIB* 53 (October 31, 1994): 407–13, 416; 54 (June 12, 1995): 251–58, 279; 68 (March 2009): 49; *ARLC*, 1995, 24–27; 2004, 77. The Visitors' Center was renamed the Learning Center in 1999. The Library of Congress Digital Collections and Educational Curricula Act (PL 109-55, 2005) authorized the Teaching with Primary Sources program.

75. *Gazette* 6 (April 7, 1995): 1, 9–11. *LCIB* 59 (November 2000): 262.

76. *ARLC*, 2000, 97–98; 2002, 76; *LCIB* 59 (August–September 2000): 209; 2002: 85–86; 60 (December 2001): 283; 61 (May 2002): 93; (October 2002): 223–25; *Digital Talking Books: Progress to Date* (Washington, DC: NLS, 2002); *Gazette* 17 (December 15, 2006): 5–6. The NLS became the National Library for the Blind and Print Disabled on October 1, 2019.

77. *LCIB* 69 (May 2010): 89; 70 (April 2011): 361; *ARLC*, 2009, 20–21; 2013, 29; *Gazette* 30 (February 8, 2019): 1, 6.

78. *LCIB* 54 (June 12, 1995): 262–63, 279.

79. *Gazette* 10 (November 12, 1999): 1, 4–5; 13; *LCIB* 61 (December 2002): 268–69; 64 (Summer 2005): 136–37; *LCIB* 66 (March 2007): 56–57; 68 (July–August 2009): 140–41; Jeanette Adams, "Fort Meade Is Cool, CALM, and Collected," *Library Services Journal* 1 (Fall 2008): 21–27; *LCM* 5 (May–June 2017): 8–9.

80. *New York Times*, August 19, 1987; *Washington Post,* August 16, 1987; *LCIB* 50 (September 9, 1991): 331; 51 (April 20, 1992): 161n62; *AL* 18 (September 1987): 634; 23 (May 1992): 352–53; Andrea Merrill, "Protecting the Library's Collections," *Encyclopedia*, 433–36.

81. *LCIB* 50 (February 11, 1991): 35; 51 (November 30, 1992): 500–501; 52 (June 28, 1993): 269–75; 54 (October 2, 1995): 413; (December 11, 1995): 480–81, 496–503.

82. "Testimony on LOC Security Proposals and Policies: Hearing before the Joint Committee on the Library, 103rd Congress, 1st Sess., June 15, 1993" (GPO, 1994); *Washington Post*, June 21, August 10, 1992. Congress increased security after two officers were shot in the Capitol on July 24, 1998: *Gazette* 9 (August 7, 1998): 1, 11. The US Capitol Police Board Security Enhancement Plan (February 1999) included the LC; between 2003 and 2009, under PL 110-178, the Library of Congress Police merged with the Capitol Police: *ARLC*, 2000, 143–44; 2010, 6–7; 2011, 5; *Washington Post*, September 6, 2002.

83. *Gazette* 6 (December 1, 1995): 1, 9–15; (December 8, 1995): 1, 11–14; *ARLC*, 1996, 112–17. The allegations came from a staff member, but the LC's Inspector General found them "unsubstantiated and exaggerated": James H. Billington, "Here Today, Here Tomorrow: The Imperative of Collection Security," *AL* 27 (August 1996): 40–41.

84. *ARLC*, 1991, 78; *Management Review of the Library of Congress: Final Report Prepared for the General Accounting Office by Booz Allen & Hamilton* (Washington, DC: GAO, 1996); *Financial Statement Audit for the Library of Congress, Fiscal Year 1995* (Arlington, VA: Price Waterhouse, 1996). The *Washington Post*, December 27, 1995, credited Billington with addressing some of the issues but also highlighted his focus on fundraising and the NDL.

85. *LCIB* 55 (May 13, 1996): 178–79, 193–95; *Gazette* 7 (May 10, 1996): 1, 8–19; (May 17, 1996): 1, 10–11, 15.

86. *ARLC*, 1996, 11–12; *LCIB* 55 (February 19, 1996): 43–45; (April 29, 1996): 155–57; (May 13, 1996): 175–77.

87. *Gazette* 6 (September 29, 1995): 1, 13.

88. *Gazette* 10 (November 19, 1999): 11; *ARLC*, 1996, 118; 2007, vi. There was no Deputy Librarian from 2007 to 2011.

89. *LCIB* 54 (October 2, 1995): 412, 425; *ARLC*, 1996, 68; 1997, vi–ix; 2000, 148–49. The Acquisitions directorate was reorganized in 1997 along geographic lines—Africa/Asian and Overseas, Anglo/American, and European/Latin American: *ARLC*, 1998, 38; *Gazette* 8 (October 17, 1997): 1, 10–11.

90. *LCIB* 55 (May 13, 1996): 178–79, 193–95; *Gazette* 7 (May 10, 1996): 1, 8–19; (May 17, 1996): 1, 10–11, 15; *ARLC*, 1996, 11–12; *LCIB* 55 (February 19, 1996): 43–45; (April 29, 1996): 155–57; (May 13, 1996): 175–77.

91. LC, *Library of Congress Strategic Plan, 1997–2004* (Washington, DC: LC, 1997), 7–9; *Gazette* 6 (October 27, 1995): 7–9.

92. *LCIB* 56 (August 1997): 264–66; 57 (June 1998): 144–45; *ARLC*, 2005, 133–35.

93. *ARLC*, 1997, 1; 1998, 2; *LCIB* 56 (February 10, 1997): 54–57, 60; (May 5–19, 1997): passim; (June 9, 1997): 195–97; *American Treasures in the Library of Congress*, ed. Margaret Wagner (New York: Harry N. Abrams, in association with LC, 1997); *LCIB* 56 (January 27, 1997): 25–27; 57 (September 1998): 232–36.

94. The Caroline and Erwin Swann Collection spans 1780 to 1977, and was donated 1974–77. The Swann Foundation, transferred in 1995, supports research, publications, and fellowships. The Herb Block Foundation donated his cartoons in 2002, with funds for related programming: *LCIB* 70 (April 2011): 362.

95. *ARLC*, 1998, 30; *Gazette* 9 (May 22, 1998): 1, 9–11; 11 (October 6, 2000): 1; 13 (March 8, 2002): 1; *ARLC*, 2000, 3, 73–75, 89–90; *LCIB* 59 (November 2000): 281; 65 (January 2006): 25; Guy Lamolinara, "LC Plans New ILS to Serve Nation's Libraries," *AL* 29 (November 1998): 75.

96. *ARLC*, 2009, 21. Congress had been asking about requesting materials online: *Washington Post*, October 24, 2007.

97. John Y. Cole, "Bicentennial Background: 'Creativity' and the Library of Congress," *LCIB* 58 (September 1999): 210–11; John Y. Cole, *Jefferson's Legacy: A Brief History of the Library of Congress* (Washington, DC: LC, 1992), 7.

98. *Gazette* 8 (October 10, 1998): 1.

99. The LC received over $119.5 million in donations and gifts, including over $37 million from Madison Council members, and over eighty embassies responded to Billington's invitation to donate "something that embodies your nation's achievement of culture." *LCIB* 59 (August–September 2000): 211, 215; *ARLC*, 2001, 1.

100. *LCIB* 61 (July–August 2002): 127–31; 63 (July 2004): 107–18; 69 (January–February 2010): 3–9. The VHP issued *Voices of War: Stories of Service from the Home Front and the Front Lines,* edited by Tom Wiener (Washington, DC: National Geographic Society, 2004) and *Forever a Soldier: Unforgettable Stories of Wartime Service,* edited by Tom Wiener (Washington, DC: National Geographic Society, 2005); acquired and digitized collections; and developed media partnerships. For the congressionally mandated Civil Rights History Project (PL 111-19, 2009), the American Folklife Center and the Smithsonian Institution conducted oral histories and surveyed institutional collections: *ARLC*, 2011, 18; *LCIB* 70 (September–October 2011): 468.

101. *ARLC*, 1999, 78–81; 2000, passim; 2001, 124–27. The Living Legend Award was retired in 2018.

102. *Gazette* 13 (March 29, 2002): 5.

103. *ARLC*, 2000, 136–37; 2002, 609–70; 2006, 91–93; *LCIB* 59 (November 2000): 259, 262; 61 (July–August 2002): 132–33, 136; 62 (June 2003): 130–35; *Gazette* 12 (October 5, 2001): 9. The Library had announced earlier the establishment of the Henry A. Kissinger Chair in Foreign Policy and International Relations and the Kissinger Lecture on Foreign Affairs, the Harissios Papamarkou Chair in Education, and the Ann and Cary Maguire Chair in Ethics and American History: *LCIB* 59 (August–September 2000): 197; October 6, 2000; 60 (October 2001): 234–35. The Staff Fellowship Program supports LC staff members' research.

104. *LCIB* 62 (September 2003): 187–93; 66 (June 2007): 130; 68 (July–August 2009): 153–55; John W. Hessler, *The Naming of America: Martin Waldseemüller's 1507 World Map and the Cosmographiae Introductio* (London: D. Giles, in association with LC, 2008); John W. Hessler and Chet Van Duzer, *Seeing the World Anew: The Radical Vision of Martin Waldseemüller's 1507 & 1516 World Maps* (Delray Beach, FL: Levenger Press, in association with LC, 2012).

105. *Washington Post*, April 7, 2004; *LCM* 4 (September–October 2016): 8–9.

106. As First Lady of Texas, Laura Bush founded the Texas Book Festival in 1996. She continued Barbara Bush's work with the CFB as Honorary Chair of its National Reading Promotion Program: *LCIB* 60 (April 2001): 103; (June–July 2001): 156–58; (October 2001): 218–21; 62 (January 2003): passim. President and Mrs. Barack Obama also served as honorary chairs: *LCIB* 68 (November 2009): 205; *Washington Post*, September 20, 2020.

107. Leonard Kniffel, "Editorial: The Beginning of a Great Festival Suddenly Seems like an Ending," *AL* 32 (October 2001): 43; *ARLC*, 2011, 7; *LCIB* 70 (November–December 2011): 492–93.

108. *ARLC*, 2001, 2–3; 2002, v–vi, 1–3, 61–62, 116–17, 186; *LCIB* 61 (September 2002); 70 (September–October 2011); 452–59. Osama bin Laden, *Battles of the Lion Den of the Arab Partisans in Afghanistan* (translated title; Cairo, 1991); *The Sociology and Psychology of Terrorism: Who Becomes a Terrorist and Why* (Washington, DC: Federal Research Division, 1999). Post-9/11, the discovery of anthrax in the Hart Senate Office Building (and of ricin in early 2004) prompted temporary closures. Supplemental appropriations funded offsite mail and computer facilities and other costs.

109. *LCIB* 62 (December 2003): 298–301, 305. Further extending the LC's ties to the Middle East, Billington visited Iran's National library in November 2004, the highest-level official to travel there since diplomatic relations ceased in 1980: *ARLC*, 2005, 44; *Washington Post*, November 5, 2004.

110. Public interest in the LC's electronic resources surged in the mid-1990s: *Parade* magazine's September 29, 1996, article "resulted in a six-fold jump in loc.gov hits," and *PC Magazine*

cited the LC in a "Best of the Web" listing in February 1997: Lamolinara, "National Digital Library," 199.

111. *ARLC*, 2000, 1–2.

112. *Gazette* 11 (February 4, 2000): 7–13.

113. *Gazette* 11 (December 15, 2000): 1, 11–13; PL 106-481, 2000.

114. *Gazette* 11 (July 14, 2000): 1, 8–9.

115. National Research Council, *LC21: A Digital Strategy for the Library of Congress* (Washington, DC: National Academy Press, 2000), 1–22; *LCIB* 59 (August–September 2000): 195, 218–21.

116. *Gazette* 11 (August 4, 2000): 1, 5–11; (September 29, 2000): 1, 3, 8–10; PL 106-554; *ARLC*, 2001, 4.

117. *ARLC*, 2004, 152; 2005, 154–57; *LCIB* 63 (October 2004): 202–3; *Gazette* 19 (October 24, 2008): 1, 4–5.

118. *LCIB* 64 (Summer 2005): 138, 151; (September 2005): 197, 200, 202; *ARLC*, 2006, 176–83.

119. *LCIB* 67 (April 2008): 59; *Section 108 of Title 17: A Discussion Document of the Register of Copyrights* (Washington, DC: US Copyright Office, 2017), www.copyright.gov/policy/section108/discussion-document.pdf; Deanna Marcum and Roger C. Schonfeld, *Along Came Google: A History of Library Digitization* (Princeton, NJ: Princeton University Press, 2021), 157–59.

120. *LCIB* 69 (October 2010): 226, 228, 230; LC, *Preserving Our Digital Heritage: The National Digital Information Infrastructure and Preservation Program, 2010 Report* (Washington, DC: LC, 2010), 1–7. Marcum and Schonfeld, *Along Came Google,* 162–63, noted that some librarians hoped that the NDIIPP might establish the LC as the national digital library but acknowledged that federal funding constraints made such development unlikely.

121. Partnerships included Business and Retail Marketing, Center for the Book, FLICC, Interpretive Programs, NLS, Kluge Center, Publishing Office, and Visitor Services. The NAVCC and the American Folklife Center reported directly to the Associate Librarian: *ARLC*, 2004, 41; 2005, 42. Planning began in 2006 for the Office of Business Enterprises, established in 2008, for the fee-based services: *ARLC*, 2006, 86; 2009, 13.

122. The effort built on the LC's Bicentennial Conference on Bibliographic Control for the New Millennium: *Confronting the Challenges of Networked Resources and the Web: Proceedings* (Washington, DC: LC, 2001): *ARLC*, 2006, 30.

123. *Gazette* 17 (December 8, 2006): 1, 4; 18 (November 2, 2007): 1, 11; 19 (October 17, 2008): 1, 4–5; *LCIB* 67 (December 2008): 211–15; 68 (December 2009): 229; https/www.loc.gov./bibliographic-future/.

124. Russian cooperation came through the Soros Foundation's Open Society Institute–Russia; *LCIB* 60 (October 2001): 232; *LCIB* 61 (January 2002): 10–11, 15; Van Oudenaren, "'Great Deeds,'" passim.

125. *ARLC*, 2001, 128; 2002, 66, 110, 158–59; 2004, 153; *LCIB* 64 (May 2005): 118–19; http://international.loc.gov/intldl/intldlhome.html.

126. *ARLC*, 2006, 3, 211–12; 2008, 20; *LCIB* 65 (January 2006): 11-12. Billington had already been working with Google president Sergey Brin on digitization of public domain materials: *Washington Post*, November 22, 2005.

127. *LCIB* 66 (December 2007): 251; 67 (January–February 2008): 3–10; (September 2008): 154–55; 68 (May 2009): 87–91; 69 (May 2010): 97; *ARLC*, 2009, 22; 2010, 22; 2013, 31; Van Oudenaren, "'Great Deeds,'" 342–47. The project ended in 2020; WDL remains available on the Library's website.

128. *LCIB* 62 (December 2003): 302–3.

129. *LCIB* 64 (October 2005): 212; (September 2006): 208–14; (October 2006): 227; 68 (July–August 2009): 157; *ARLC*, 2009, 28.

130. *LCIB* 66 (June 2007): 140; 69 (April 2010): 62; *ARLC*, 2012, 43.

131. *LCIB* 68 (November 2009): 208–9.

132. *ARLC*, 1998, 32–33; 2005, 146; *LCIB* 57 (July 1998): 167–68; 65 (July–August 2006): 167–71.

133. Mike Handy, "Innovative Technologies for the NAVCC," *Library Services Journal* 1 (Fall 2008): 2–7.

134. *ARLC*, 2007: 10–11; 2014, 22; *LCIB* 66 (July–August 2007): 147–54; 70 (March 2011): 332; *Gazette* 18 (March 23, 2007): passim; *LCM* 7 (January–February 2019): passim.

135. *LCIB* 66 (July–August 2007): 163; 67 (May 2008): 71–79.

136. *LCIB* 68 (November 2009): 210–11.

137. *ARLC*, 2008, 17; *LCIB* 67 (May 2008): 86–88.

138. *LCIB* 67 (July–August 2008): 132–33.

139. *ARLC*, 2008, 2; 2010, 26; 2011, 5; *LCIB* 70 (January–February 2012): 300–301, 315.

140. *ARLC*, 2012, 21.

141. *LCIB* 70 (January–February 2011): 299; (May 2011): 379–81.

142. *LCM* 2 (March–April 2013): 9; Cole, *America's Greatest Library*, 225.

143. *Gazette* 25 (February 7, 2014): 1, 6.

144. The Clinger-Cohen Act (PL 104-106, 1996) established the office of Chief Information Officer, with designated roles and responsibilities in executive branch agencies. The LC was not bound by this act.

145. "Library of Congress IT Strategic Planning: Hearing before the Committee on House Administration," 111th Congress, 1st Sess., April 29, 2009 (GPO, 2009), 3–10, 21, 84.

146. House Appropriations Committee report 112-148 on the 2012 appropriations bill also asked Billington to "consider" placing IT in the Librarian's Office; see US Government Accountability Office (GAO), "Library of Congress: Strong Leadership Needed to Address Serious Information Technology Management Weaknesses," GAO-15-315, March 2015, 13–16.

147. *ARLC*, 2008, 2; 2010, 5, 26; 2011, 5; LC, *Library of Congress Strategic Plan, Fiscal Years 2011–2016* (Washington, DC: LC, 2010).

148. *ARLC*, 2013, 18. The sequester was imposed for a ten-year period.

149. *ARLC*, 2013, 17, 27–28; *Gazette* 24 (May 31, 2013): 3, 7.

150. This was developed in cooperation with the ALA; RDA replaced AACR2.

151. *ARLC*, 2013, 22–24; 2014, 23; *LCM* 2 (July–August 2013): 5, 23; 3 (July–August 2015): 15.

152. "Strong Leadership," 92–100, 123–26; *Gazette* 26 (January 30, 2015): 3. The *Washington Post*, April 2, 2015, reported congressional reaction to the report as supporting the recommendations but not seeking the Librarian's resignation.

153. GAO, "Register's Perspective on Copyright Review: Hearing before the Committee on the Judiciary, House of Representatives, 114th Congress, 1st Sess.," April 29, 2015 (GPO, 2015), 1–2, 12, 6–16. Pallante's statement followed the GAO's "Information Technology: Copyright Office Needs to Develop Plans That Address Technical and Organizational Challenges Report to the Senate Appropriations Committee" (GAO 15-338, March 2015), 7, 30, citing poor relations between IT management and the Copyright Office and recommending that the office submit plans for improvements to the IT Steering Committee. Follow-up GAO testimony to the Committee on House Administration (GAO 16-197, December 2, 2015) reported some progress but urged implementing all recommendations.

154. *Gazette* 26 (May 22, 2015): 1, 4–5; *ARLC*, 2015, 63.
155. *Gazette* 26 (June 12, 2015): 1, 3; (September 25, 2015): 1–2.
156. *Washington Post*, March 31, June 6, September 3, 2015.

Conclusion

1. Jefferson to Samuel Harrison Smith, September 21, 1814, Founders Online, https://founders.archives.gov/documents/Jefferson/03-07-02-0484-0003.

2. Young circular letter, February 16, 1898, quoted in *LCIB* 11, no. 33 (August 11, 1952): appendix.

3. Jefferson to John Wyche, May 19, 1809, quoted in *LCIB* 11, no. 36 (September 9, 1952): 10.

4. Speech at the ALA's seventy-fifth anniversary banquet, December 1950, box 18, Putnam Papers, LC. Putnam's statement of the relationship with Congress appeared in *ARLC*, 1901, 203–4. Even when Congress ordered the LC to stop awarding prizes in 1949, later congressional action reversed that decision.

5. John Y. Cole, ed., *The Library of Congress in Perspective: A Volume Based on the Reports of the 1976 Librarian's Task Force and Advisory Groups* (New York: R. R. Bowker, 1978), 1–3.

INDEX

ABOUT THE AUTHOR

Jane Aikin—formerly a librarian in academic libraries and a staff member of the Council on Library Resources—retired from the National Endowment for the Humanities in 2016 after serving as director of its Division of Research Programs. She wrote *The Nation's Great Library: Herbert Putnam and the Library of Congress, 1899–1939* (University of Illinois Press, 1993) and was coeditor, with John Y. Cole, of the *Encyclopedia of the Library of Congress: For Congress, the Nation, and the World* (Bernan Press, 2004).